Venice

timeout.com/venice

Time Out Guides Ltd
Universal House
251 Tottenham Court Road
London W1T 7AB
United Kingdom
Tel: +44 (0)20 7813 3000
Fax: +44 (0)20 7813 6001
Email: guides@timeout.com
www.timeout.com

Published by Time Out Guides Ltd, a wholly owned subsidiary of Time Out Group Ltd.
Time Out and the Time Out logo are trademarks of Time Out Group Ltd.

© Time Out Group Ltd 2009
Previous editions 1999, 2001, 2003, 2005, 2007.

10 9 8 7 6 5 4 3 2 1

This edition first published in Great Britain in 2009 by Ebury Publishing.
A Random House Group Company
20 Vauxhall Bridge Road, London SW1V 2SA

Random House Australia Pty Ltd 20 Alfred Street, Milsons Point, Sydney, New South Wales 2061, Australia

Random House New Zealand Ltd 18 Poland Road, Glenfield, Auckland 10, New Zealand

Random House South Africa (Pty) Ltd Isle of Houghton, Corner Boundary Road & Carse O'Gowrie, Houghton 2198, South Africa

Random House UK Limited Reg. No. 954009

For further distribution details, see www.timeout.com.

ISBN: 978-1-84670-107-8

A CIP catalogue record for this book is available from the British Library.

Printed and bound by Firmengruppe APPL, aprinta druck, Wemding, Germany.

The Random House Group Limited supports The Forest Stewardship Council (FSC), the leading international forest certification organisation. All our titles that are printed on Greenpeace approved FSC certified paper carry the FSC logo. Our paper procurement policy can be found at http://www.rbooks.co.uk/environment.

Time Out carbon-offsets its flights with Trees for Cities (www.treesforcities.org).

While every effort has been made to ensure the accuracy of the information contained within this guide, the publishers cannot accept responsibility for any errors it may contain.

Contents

In Context 13

History	14
Venice Today	27
Venetian Painting	32
Architecture	39
The Biennale	47

Sights 51

The Grand Canal	52
San Marco	60
Castello	77
Cannaregio	88
San Polo & Santa Croce	98
Dorsoduro	113
La Giudecca & San Giorgio	127
Lido & Lagoon	131

Consume 143

Hotels	144
Eating Out	164
Cafés, Bars & Gelaterie	182
Shops & Services	193

Arts & Entertainment 213

Calendar	214
Children	218
Film	221
Galleries	224
Gay & Lesbian	229

Music & Nightlife	231
Performing Arts	237
Sport & Fitness	244

The Veneto 249

Getting Started	251
Map: The Veneto	253
Padua	255
Verona	265
Vicenza	275
Treviso & the Northern Veneto	286

Directory 293

Getting Around	295
Resources A-Z	298
Glossary	307
Vocabulary	308
Further Reference	309
Index	310
Advertisers' Index	316

Maps 317

Venice Overview	319
Street Maps	320
Lido	327
La Giudecca	328
Murano	328
Burano	329
Street Index	330
Vaporetto Map	336

Introduction

There's something heart-stopping about leaving the mainland behind you and crossing the Venetian lagoon towards this unlikely jewel in its marshy wilderness, and it doesn't matter whether you're doing it on a boat or in a train, for the first time or on a repeat visit.

Once in Venice, you're faced with an embarrassment of riches. How many other areas of not much more than five square kilometres can boast artistic and architectural marvels in such concentration? You won't know where to begin (though we hope this guide will help).

But as you delve into the Venetian labyrinth, that won't be your only dilemma. The better you get to know the city, the more confidently you venture off the well-beaten trails and into the backstreets (and you should do this as soon as possible, for it's here that many of Venice's most rewarding, lesser-known treasures lie), the more you'll have to cope with famously tetchy *veneziani* who grumble as they push past you on their crowded streets and bridges, and charge you a tourist 'premium' in their already expensive restaurants and bars. However much you love Venice, it isn't always easy to love the Venetians.

Ironically, this is because the locals want you to see their city the same way that they do: these proud citizens want Venice to be marvelled at and appreciated by cultural connoisseurs, not goggled at by raucous day-trippers to an historic theme park; they want to be considered a normal city with a stunning, uplifting difference.

This guide, then, aims to bring visitors and hosts closer by providing an insight into the Venice of the Venetians. We show you the iconic sights, naturally, but also the brand-new openings, the restaurants where locals eat, the bars where they flock to munch *cicheti* and down a *spritz*. We share amusing Venetian anecdotes and enlightening insider knowledge. And we fill you in on brave efforts being made by some Venetians to give *La Serenissima* a *raison d'être* beyond tourism.

Will all this help make the Venetians more indulgent towards you? It's difficult to say. It will certainly round out your Venetian experience, showing you that, far from being merely a magnificent showcase, *La Serenissima* is a living, breathing wonderland.
Anne Hanley, Editor

Venice in Brief

IN CONTEXT

Venice's history is marked by parabolas. From a group of fishing huts to world mercantile leader to washed-up backwater; from mecca for curious travellers to crumbling has-been to major tourist attraction. And if its cultural offerings are on an upwards curve, its social scene seemed to be dipping ever downwards. We ask whether a new breed of dedicated Venetians can help avert creeping Disneyfication.

▶ *For more, see pp14-49.*

SIGHTS

In a relatively tiny area, Venice harbours a wealth of artistic and architectural wonders that even many large nations couldn't lay claim to. Some of Venice's unique and overwhelming sights are displayed in showcase churches and major galleries. Others are harder to find, concealed along warrens of medieval streets. Arm yourself with a map and a sense of adventure.

▶ *For more, see pp52-141.*

CONSUME

Venice is famous for its tourist-trap restaurants and overpriced hotels. But we show you how to avoid them all, by eating where locals go and eating what locals eat, and by choosing your moment to benefit from some extremely tempting accommodation deals. There's shopping advice, too, to steer you away from cheapo glass and made-in-Taiwan masks.

▶ *For more, see pp144-212.*

ARTS & ENTERTAINMENT

Once Europe's party capital, Venice is a quieter city now, and you'll have to look hard to find an after-hours scene. But in its own way, Venice has it. Expect things to be low-key, though… except during the summer months when the nearby beach resorts rock. For a burst of high culture, there's La Fenice; and fans of the seventh art should check out the film festival.

▶ *For more, see pp214-247.*

THE VENETO

Venice spread its control over *terra ferma* for centuries, encouraging a Renaissance building boom and also providing deep-pocketed patronage for church adornment. The cities of the Veneto each have their own character and their own treasures. In between are some beautiful Palladian villas; to the north are the magical winter playgrounds of the Dolomites.

▶ *For more, see pp251-292.*

Venice in 48 Hours

Day 1 The art and culture at Venice's heart

10AM Dedicate your first day to getting some of Venice's major sights under your belt. Start at the heart, with a visit to **St Mark's basilica** (*see p61*), and don't forget to climb up to the loggia to see the famous bronze horses. If you're not culturally overwhelmed already, tour the **Doge's Palace** (*see p67*) next door. Alternatively, take the lift to the top of the **Campanile** (*see p65*) for a bird's-eye view.

NOON Get your breath back by fleeing culture for an hour or so: from the San Zaccaria stop, hop on a vaporetto to the Giudecca and grab a canalside table for lunch at **I Figli delle Stelle** or **Alla Palanca** (for both, *see p180*). Keep an eye out for Palladio's magnificent **San Giorgio Maggiore** (*see p130*) en route.

2PM Sail back to Zattere, and head for the **Gallerie dell'Accademia** (*see p122*), Venice's foremost artistic treasure house. If your preference is for more modern art, choose between the Peggy Guggenheim Collection (*see p121*) and the Punta della Dogana (*see p124*).

4PM Take the route through **campo San Barnaba** to **campo Santa Margherita** (*see p116*) and refresh yourself in one of the many café-bars in this lively square before heading on to the **Frari** (*see p109*) for another art feast.

7PM It's *aperitivo* time, and Venice's cool crowd will be lining up drinks and *cicheti* in the bars at the north-western foot of the Rialto bridge. Stake your claim at a Grand Canal-facing table at **Naranzaria** (*see p176*) or **Bancogiro** (*see p175*). You may get so comfortable, you'll end up eating here too. An after-dinner stroll across the Rialto bridge, to peer down at passing boats, is memorable.

NAVIGATING THE CITY
You'll need a good map and a well-honed sense of direction to navigate Venice's maze of streets, but getting lost is half the fun. When your feet can't take any more pavement pounding or bridge climbing, make for a vaporetto stop.

PACKAGE DEALS
The on-line **Venice Connected** (www.veniceconnected.com) service allows you to pre-book and pre-pay transport passes, tickets for civic museums and public toilets (yes, that's no joke) with variable discounts. You must book at least one week before you arrive; any later, and you pay full price.

Administered by Hellovenezia (*see p296*), the **Venice Card** is a three-day (€73, €66 reductions) or seven-day (€96, €87 reductions) pass covering vaporetto use and free entrance to civic museums and all Chorus churches (*see below*), plus discounts elsewhere. A pricier version also includes the Alilaguna boat service to/from the airport. You can buy your card at tourist offices in Venice, at Treviso airport or by calling 041 2424 and picking it up on arrival. Under-5s travel free with a Venice Card-holder. The transport-only

Day 2 Into the labyrinth for lesser-known gems

10AM Explore further afield today, starting off at the charming **Museo Storico Navale** (*see p85*) for a glimpse of Venice's magnificent maritime past, then head north towards the **Arsenale** (*see p84*). If there are Biennale events on in spaces inside the Arsenale, make sure to take advantage and visit: whether or not you're interested in what's on show, the buildings are worth a look.

NOON There are some great, little-visited churches to explore in the city's north-eastern reaches: make your way past **San Francesco della Vigna** (*see p79*), with its facade by Palladio, and on to **Santi Giovanni e Paolo** (*see p80*). For lunch, try **Algiubagiò** (*see p168*), with its fantastic terrace on the northern lagoon.

3PM Hop on a vaporetto to Orto, and treat yourself to more Tintorettos at the lovely **Madonna dell'Orto** (*see p95*) church. From here it's a pleasant walk through quiet northern Cannaregio to the original Jewish **Ghetto** (*see p93*).

5PM At the Guglie vaporetto stop, take a number 42 boat for a ride past the new **Ponte della Costituzione** (*see p54*), through Venice's industrial wasteland (such as it is), and across to Palanca on the Giudecca. There are few finer places in the world to watch the sun set than the **Skyline Bar** (*see p192*) on the roof of the Molino Stucky Hilton.

7PM From Palanca, the 42 continues back to San Marco. Nearby, the **Osteria San Marco** (*see p165*) is great for bar snacks and gourmet Venetian specialities. An after-dinner stroll through **piazza San Marco** (*see p60*), accompanied by the palm orchestras of the cafés around the square, is a hopelessly romantic end to any day.

Venice Card is not as good a deal as a standard transit pass (*see p296*). There has been talk of fusing the Venice Card with Venice Connected. Hellovenezia also offers the **Rolling Venice** card (€4) which gives hotel, restaurant and transport discounts to 14- to 29-year-olds.

The **Museums of St Mark's Square pass** (€13, €7.50 reductions) covers the Doge's Palace and the Museo Correr trio of museums, plus one other civic museum of your choice (but not St Mark's basilica). Venice's civic museums' **Museum Pass** (www.museicivicivenezia.it) includes the above plus six further attractions, including Ca' Rezzonico. It costs €18 (€12 reductions) and is available at all participating sights. Both are valid for single entry for six months.

The Gallerie dell'Accademia, Ca' d'Oro and Museo Orientale can be visited on the **State Museums ticket** at €11 (€5.50 reductions), available from participating sights.

Sixteen of Venice's churches belong to the **Chorus** scheme (www.chorus.org). A year-long pass, valid for one visit to each, costs €9 (€6 reductions) and can be purchased in churches and at Hellovenezia outlets (*see p296*).

Venice in Profile

THE GRAND CANAL

No other city in the world can boast quite such a magnificent main street as Venice: a graceful backwards-'S' sweep of water, flowing between sumptuous churches and historic *palazzi* of breathtaking beauty. Whether you're doing it for the first time or the 1,000th, making your water-borne way down the Grand Canal is always an extraordinary experience.

▶ *For more, see pp52-59.*

SAN MARCO

The eponymous piazza and basilica are the beating heart of this *sestiere*. In the alleys that wind from this hub towards the Rialto and Accademia bridges are snazzy shops, a great opera house and glowing Madonnas in awe-inspiring churches.

▶ *For more, see pp60-76.*

CASTELLO

A *sestiere* of many parts, Castello stretches from luxury hotels on the lagoon-side riva degli Schiavoni to glorious churches such as Santi Giovanni e Paolo in the west. Further east, beyond the monumental Arsenale, lie the quiet streets of residential workaday Venice.

▶ *For more, see pp77-87.*

CANNAREGIO

Bustling with life along the Cannaregio Canal, quiet and echoing in its alleyways and understated *campi*, this *sestiere* of surprises conceals the original Jewish Ghetto and some great nightlife on the fondamenta della Misericordia.

▶ *For more, see pp88-97.*

SAN POLO & SANTA CROCE

The hectic produce and fish market at the foot of the Rialto Bridge sets the tone for these busy residential *sestieri*, packed with the kind of intimate restaurants and cafés frequented by true Venetians. At the *sestiere*'s heart is the magnificent Frari basilica.

▶ *For more, see pp98-112.*

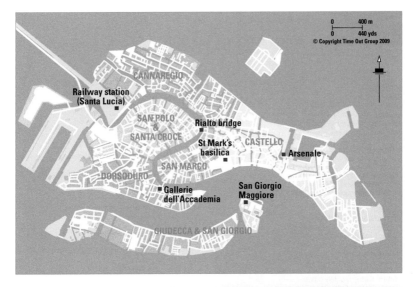

DORSODURO

Artsy Dorsoduro is home to the Peggy Guggenheim Collection and the new Pinault gallery at the Punta della Dogana. But there's lots of nightlife, too, around campo Santa Margherita, plus a vibrant student scene further west in the former industrial zone.
► *For more, see pp113-126.*

LA GIUDECCA & SAN GIORGIO

With a character all of its own, the Giudecca has an industrious past and an alternative future: from boatyards to galleries, this island just gets trendier. Palladio's San Giorgio is a Venetian icon.
► *For more, see pp127-130.*

LIDO & LAGOON

There's a whole other world in the lagoon, from the rather fin-de-siècle beach resort on the long, sandy Lido to misty waterlands dotted with characterful islands.
► *For more, see pp131-141.*

TimeOut Venice

Editorial
Editor Anne Hanley
Deputy Editor John Shandy Watson
Listings Editors Patrizia Lerco
Proofreader Mandy Martinez
Indexer Ismay Atkins

Managing Director Peter Fiennes
Editorial Director Ruth Jarvis
Series Editor Will Fulford-Jones
Business Manager Dan Allen
Editorial Manager Holly Pick
Assistant Management Accountant Ija Krasnikova

Design
Art Director Scott Moore
Art Editor Pinelope Kourmouzoglou
Senior Designer Henry Elphick
Graphic Designers Kei Ishimaru, Nicola Wilson
Advertising Designer Jodi Sher

Picture Desk
Picture Editor Jael Marschner
Deputy Picture Editor Lynn Chambers
Picture Researcher Gemma Walters
Picture Desk Assistant Marzena Zoladz
Picture Librarian Christina Theisen

Advertising
Commercial Director Mark Phillips
International Advertising Manager Kasimir Berger
International Sales Executive Charlie Sokol
Advertising Sales (Venice) Fabio Giannini

Marketing
Marketing Manager Yvonne Poon
**Sales & Marketing Director, North America
& Latin America** Lisa Levinson
Senior Publishing Brand Manager Luthfa Begum
Marketing Designer Anthony Huggins

Production
Group Production Director Mark Lamond
Production Manager Brendan McKeown
Production Controller Damian Bennett
Production Coordinator Kelly Fenlon

Time Out Group
Chairman Tony Elliott
Chief Executive Officer David King
Group General Manager/Director Nichola Coulthard
Time Out Communications Ltd MD David Pepper
Time Out International Ltd MD Cathy Runciman
Time Out Magazine Ltd Publisher/MD Mark Elliott
Group IT Director Simon Chappell
Marketing & Circulation Director Catherine Demajo

Contributors
Introduction Anne Hanley. **History** Anne Hanley. **Venice Today** Anne Hanley. **Venetian Painting** Frederick Ilchman. **Architecture** Anne Hanley. **The Biennale** Lee Marshall. **Sights** Gregory Dowling (*The Whole Punta* Anne Hanley; *Murano Glass* Nicolò Scibilia). **Hotels** Nicky Swallow. **Eating Out** Lee Marshall, Michela Scibilia. **Cafés, Bars & Gelaterie** Jill Weinreich. **Shops & Services** Jo-Ann Titmarsh. **Calendar** Anne Hanley. **Children** Patrizia Lerco. **Film** Jo-Ann Titmarsh. **Galleries** Chiara Barbieri. **Gay & Lesbian** Salvatore Mele. **Music & Nightlife** Kate Davies. **Performing Arts** Kate Davies. **Sport & Fitness** Jo-Ann Titmarsh. **The Veneto: Getting Started** Anne Hanley (*Walk: Chioggia, Not Venice but Trying* Gregory Dowling). **Padua** Charlotte Thomas. **Verona** Kate Davies. **Vicenza** Charlotte Thomas. **Treviso & the Northern Veneto** Jo-Ann Titmarsh. **Directory** Charlotte Thomas (*Glossary, Vocabulary, Further Reference* Anne Hanley).

Maps LS International Cartography, via Decemviri 8, 20138 Milan, Italy. www.geomaker.it

Photography Olivia Rutherford, except: pages 17, 23 AKG-Images/Erich Lessing; page 31 Michela Scibilia; page 37 Bridgeman Art Library; page 42 Daniele Resini; pages 47, 48, 225 Andrew Bannister; page 68 Chandos Records; page 108 Sony Pictures Classics/The Kobal Collection; page 121 Andrea Sarti/CAST1466; page 125 © Michele Crosera; page 178 Rob Greig; page 217 Chris Helgren/Reuters/Corbis; page 223 © EON/DANJAQ/Kobal; pages 237, 240, 241 Michele Crosera; page 238 AKG-Images; page 242 Vito Mastrolonardo. The following images were provided by the featured establishments/artists: pages 34, 105, 165, 214, 224, 227.

The Editor would like to thank Patrizia Lerco, Michela Scibilia, Fulvio Marsigliani, Lee and Clara Marshall, and all contributors to previous editions of *Time Out Venice*, whose work forms the basis for parts of this book.

About the Guide

GETTING AROUND

The back of the book contains street maps of Venice, as well as an overview map of the city and its surroundings. The maps start on page 317; on them are marked the locations of hotels (❶), restaurants (❶), and cafés and bars (❶). The majority of businesses listed in this guide are located in the areas we've mapped; the grid-square references in the listings refer to these maps.

THE ESSENTIALS

For practical information, including visas, disabled access, emergency numbers, lost property, useful websites and local transport, please see the Directory. It begins on page 295.

THE LISTINGS

Addresses, phone numbers, websites, transport information, hours and prices are all included in our listings, as are selected other facilities. All were checked and correct at press time. However, business owners can alter their arrangements at any time, and fluctuating economic conditions can cause prices to change rapidly.

The very best venues in the city, the must-sees and must-dos in every category, have been marked with a red star (★). In the Sights chapters, we've also marked venues with free admission with a FREE symbol.

PHONE NUMBERS

The area code for Venice and its province is 041; for Padua it's 049, for Verona 045 and for Vicenza 0444. You must use the code, whether you're calling from inside or outside the area.

From outside Italy, dial your country's international access code (00 from the UK, 011 from the US), followed by the Italy country code (39), 041 for Venice (without dropping the initial zero) and the rest of the number as listed in the guide. For more on phones, including information on calling abroad from Italy and details of local mobile phone access, *see p304*.

FEEDBACK

We welcome feedback on this guide, both on the venues we've included and on any other locations that you'd like to see featured in future editions. Please email us at guides@timeout.com.

Time Out Guides

Founded in 1968, Time Out has grown from humble beginnings into the leading resource for anyone wanting to know what's happening in the world's greatest cities. Alongside our influential weeklies in London, New York and Chicago, we publish more than 20 magazines in cities as varied as Beijing and Beirut; a range of travel books, with the City Guides now joined by the newer Shortlist series; and an information-packed website. The company remains proudly independent, still owned by Tony Elliott four decades after he launched *Time Out London*.

Written by local experts and illustrated with original photography, our books also retain their independence. No business has been featured because it has advertised, and all restaurants and bars are visited and reviewed anonymously.

ABOUT THE EDITOR

Anne Hanley has lived in Italy since 1984, first in Rome and now in rural Umbria. When she is not editing Italian titles for Time Out Guides – something she has been doing since 1997 – she designs gardens (www.laverzura.com).

A full list of the book's contributors can be found opposite. However, we've also included details of our writers in selected chapters through the guide.

Get the local experience

Over 50 of the world's top destinations available.

In Context

Ex-Junghans housing. *See p46.*

History   **14**
   Profile Veronica Franco   17
   Machinery of State   21
   Population Implosion   24

Venice Today   **27**
   40xVenezia   31

Venetian Painting   **32**
   Deadly Rivals   37

Architecture   **39**
   Mud Houses   42
   Path of Light   45

The Biennale   **47**

History

From a tiny island state to a mighty empire – and back again.

TEXT: ANNE HANLEY

In the fifth century AD, rampaging barbarians forced inhabitants of the towns in the far north east of the Italian peninsula to flee for their lives on to the sandy banks of a desolate lagoon. If this beginning was ignominious, what followed was anything but. From that scared and scattered community – which eked a living by trading in salt and fish – would grow the Most Serene Republic of Venice, one of Europe's most powerful city-states: a republic with a rock-solid system of government that flourished for over a millennium, and a maritime power that wielded almost total control over the shipping routes of the eastern Mediterranean for six centuries. Envied for its luxurious extravagance, hated for its insolent self-assurance, Venice was the exotic odd-piece-out in the patchwork of Europe.

'The keynote of Venetian diplomacy for 1,250 years: staying as far as possible from, and (where possible) profiting by, other people's quarrels.'

LIFE ON THE LAGOON

Until the collapse of the Roman Empire in the fifth century AD, the islands of the Venetian lagoon hosted only transient fishing hamlets. The nearby cities on the mainland, on the other hand, were among the most prosperous in Roman Italy. With the final disintegration of any semblance of security in the late sixth century, their inhabitants fled for their lives into the marshes.

These influxes were meant to be temporary, but as economic life on the mainland collapsed, the lagoon islands came to be thought of as permanent homes. They offered enormous potential in the form of fish and salt – basic necessities. Once settled in the lagoon, the fugitives could also enjoy the relative peace and tranquillity that would be denied to the peoples of mainland Europe for centuries to come.

Enormous public works were necessary almost from the start to shore up and consolidate the islands of the lagoon (*see p42* **Mud Houses**). Huge amounts of timber had to be cut down and transported here. The trunks were sunk deep into the mud as foundations for the mainly wooden buildings of the island villages. And above all, the mainland rivers, which threatened to silt up the lagoon – had to be tamed and diverted.

And yet this battle against nature helped to unite the early lagoon dwellers into a close-knit community and eventually into a republic that was to become one of the strongest and most stable states in European history. The fight against the sea never ended. Even in the 18th century, when the French army was advancing on the lagoon and the Venetian Republic was living its decline and fall, the government invested its last resources in the construction of the *murazzi*, the massive sea walls that run between the Lido, Pellestrina and Chioggia.

EASTERN PROMISE

In 552, Byzantine Emperor Justinian I was determined to reconquer Italy from the barbarians. His first object was the city of Ravenna. But his troops were confronted with an almost insuperable problem: they had made their way overland, via the Dalmatian coast on the eastern side of the Adriatic, but were blocked by the barbarian Goths who controlled the mainland to the north of Venice. The only way they could attack and take Ravenna was to bypass the Goths, crossing the lagoon.

Already by this time, the lagoon communities had adopted a practice that was to be the keynote of Venetian diplomacy for 1,250 years: staying as far as possible from, and (where possible) profiting by, other people's quarrels. Justinian's request presented a dilemma: helping him would be seen as a declaration of war against the Ostrogoths in Ravenna, with whom the lagoon communities had reached a comfortable *modus vivendi*, assuring safety on the mainland for their traders. Yet the Eastern emperor was offering vast monetary and political rewards for transporting his troops.

The communities eventually threw in their lot with Byzantium. Justinian conquered Ravenna and marched on to Rome. From this time on the communities of the lagoon became vassals of the Eastern Empire; Venice would remain technically subject to the Byzantine emperors until considerably later than the Sack of Constantinople – an attack led by Venetians – during the Fourth Crusade in 1204.

It was not until 697, under the growing threat of the barbarian Lombards who then controlled the mainland, that the communities scattered around the lagoon – now officially recognised by Byzantium as a duchy – decided to convert their fragile confederation into a stronger, more centralised state. In this year (or maybe not: some historians have dismissed the story as a Venetian myth), they elected one Paoluccio Anafesto to be their first doge, as the dukes of Venice became known. Yet right from the beginning *il doge* was very different from the other feudal strongmen of Europe.

In the first application of a system that would be honed into shape over the centuries (*see p21* **Machinery of State**), the doge was elected for life by a council chosen by an assembly that represented all the social groups and trades of the island communities. Technically, therefore, the leadership was elected democratically, although the strongest groups soon formed themselves into a dominant oligarchy. Yet democracy of a kind survived in the system of checks and balances employed to ensure that no single section of the ruling elite got its hands on absolute power.

The first ducal power struggle took place in 729. The doge in question, Ipato Orso, achieved the duchy's first outstanding military victory when he dislodged Lombard forces from Ravenna. Success, though, went to Orso's head, and he attempted to transform the doge's office into a hereditary monarchy. Civil war racked the lagoon for two years, ending only when a furious mob forced its way into Orso's house and cut his throat. Troubles continued with the two succeeding doges: both were accused of tyranny, and were not only deposed and exiled but also ceremonially blinded.

CIVIL STRIFE, COMMERCIAL STRENGTH

The lagoon dwellers were becoming a commercial power to be reckoned with in the upper Adriatic, the eastern Mediterranean, the Black Sea and North Africa. Craftsmen were sent abroad to Dalmatia and Istria to study the art of shipbuilding; they learnt so swiftly that by the seventh century the construction and fitting out of seagoing vessels had become a thriving industry. Mercantile expansion and technical advances went hand in hand, as tradesmen brought back materials and techniques from afar – especially the Middle and Far East, where technical and scientific culture was far in advance of the West.

In 781, Pepin, son of the Frankish king Charlemagne, invaded Italy and attacked the Lombards. Wariness of mainland struggles still dominated the duchy's policy and it played for time, unsure whether to sacrifice the alliance with Byzantium to this new and powerful player on the European scene. In the end, however, Pepin's designs on Istria and Dalmatia – part of the Venetian sphere of influence – caused relations to turn frosty. Exasperated by the duchy's fence-sitting, Pepin attacked its ally Grado on the mainland, taking all the mainland positions around Venice, and besieging the lagoon communities from the sea.

In the mid eighth century the confederation had moved its capital from Heraclea in the northern lagoon to Malamocco on the Adriatic coast, where it was at the mercy of Frankish naval forces. In 810, a strong leader emerged in the form of an admiral, Angelo Partecipazio. He abandoned the besieged capital of Malamocco, moving it almost overnight to the island archipelago of Rialto.

Next he ordered his fleet to head out of the lagoon to attack Pepin's ships, then to feign terror and retreat. In hot pursuit, the deep-keeled Frankish ships ran aground on the sandbanks of the lagoon; the locals, with their knowledge of deep-water channels, picked off the crews with ease: thousands were massacred.

After his great victory against the Franks, Partecipazio was elected doge. During his reign, work began on a ducal palace on the site of the current one, and the confederation of islands that made up the lagoon duchy was given the name 'Venetia'. Around the same time, the flourishing city of Torcello began to decline, as the surrounding lagoon waters silted up and malarial mosquitoes took over.

Profile Veronica Franco

La più onorata cortigiana – *the most honoured courtesan.*

It's estimated that at one point in the 16th century, 12,000 of Venice's 100,000 residents were prostitutes. Perhaps it was to be expected, then, that such a significant social grouping should break down into sub-classes. At the very top of the pyramid – living lives which differed from those of other wealthy women only in the small matter of virtue – were *le più honorate cortigiane*: 'most honoured courtesans'.

In a world where wives were part and parcel of mercantile dealings, bringing dowries and/or prestige, and haggled over in the matrimonial marketplace, it was to the honoured courtesans that rich Venetian men turned for cultured company and entertainment, as well as sex.

Veronica Franco made her appearance in the *Catalogo di tutte le principale et più honorate cortigiane di Venezia* in 1565, when she was 20.

Her fees, the catalogue stated, were to be paid to her mother. By that time, she had married, had a child and then left her husband, demanding her dowry back so that she could set up her own household.

A well-read polyglot and skilled player of the spinnet and lute, Veronica published poetry and other writings that rubbished the concept of ideal love for an ideal woman – so popular since Petrarch – in favour of a more down-to-earth assessment of the lot of women, particularly those women who earn their own way with their wits.

So highly esteemed was this meretrix that France's King Henri III sought her company when he visited Venice in 1573. But her most assiduous patron was Domenico Venier, a nobleman whose literary salon was the city's most renowned and illustrious. Venier stood by her when she was driven from Venice during a bout of plague in 1577, when superstitious locals alleged the disease was punishment for the city's vices. (Her absence gave those same locals a chance to ransack her richly appointed home.) And he spoke in her defence in 1580 when the Inquisition charged her with, and acquitted her of, witchcraft.

It's not clear what happened to Veronica between Venier's death in 1582 and her own in 1610. Deprived of her wealth and of her patron, she no doubt discovered the other feature that set the courtesan apart from the 'honest' married woman: security.

THE MAKING OF MYTHS

It was also around this time that Venice set about embroidering a mythology worthy of its ambitions. After Venetian merchants stole the body of St Mark from Alexandria and brought it back with them to their city – traditionally said to be in the year 829 – the city's previous patron, the Byzantine St Theodore, was unceremoniously deposed and the Evangelist – symbolised by a winged lion – set up in his place. A shrine to the saint was erected in the place where St Mark's basilica (*see p61*) would later rise.

Angelo Partecipazio's overwhelming success in both military and civic government led to another tussle for power. Before he died in 827, he made certain that his son Giustiniano would succeed him. When Giustiniano died two years later, his younger brother Giovanni was elected doge, despite dissent and jealousy from rival families. It was a measure of Partecipazio's importance that his surname was to feature repeatedly in the ducal roll of honour over the next century.

BLIND CUNNING

The development of the vast Venetian empire grew out of the mercantile pragmatism that dominated Venetian political thinking. They embarked upon territorial expansion for two main reasons: to secure safe shipping routes and to create permanent trading stations. Harassed by Slav pirates in the upper Adriatic, the Venetians established bases around the area from which to attack the pirate ships: gradually they took over the ports of Grado and Trieste, then expanded along the coastlines of Istria and Dalmatia. In some cases, Venetian protection against pirates was requested; in others, 'help' arrived unbidden.

With the coast well defended, the Venetians rarely bothered to expand their territories into the hinterland. There was, for many centuries, a certain mistrust of *terra ferma*; Venetian citizens were not even allowed to own land outside the lagoon until 1345.

The crusades presented Venice with its greatest opportunity yet for expanding trade routes while reaping a profit. Transporting crusaders to the Holy Land became big business for the city. More importantly, the naïve crusaders were easy prey for

St Mark's basilica.

the professional generals – the *condottieri* – who commanded Venice's army of highly trained mercenaries: the eager defenders of the faith were, as often as not, exploited to extend and consolidate the Venetian empire.

Never was this more true than in the case of the Fourth Crusade, which set off proudly from Venice in 1202 to reconquer Jerusalem. The Venetian war fleet was under the command of Doge Enrico Dandolo, who, though 80 and completely blind, was a supremely cunning leader, outstanding tactician and accomplished diplomat. Other European crusader leaders were persuaded to take time out to conquer the strategic Adriatic port of Zara, thus assuring Venice's control of much of the Dalmatian coast. Even more surprisingly, they let themselves be talked into attacking Constantinople.

Venice's special relationship with the Eastern Empire had always had its ups and downs. In 1081 and 1082, Venice had done the Byzantine emperor a favour when it trounced menacing Normans in the southern Adriatic. But, in 1149, Venice's trading privileges were withdrawn in disgust at Venetian arrogance during a siege of Corfu.

As the Fourth Crusade set out, Dandolo saw that this was an ideal opportunity to remove the Byzantine challenge to Venetian trade hegemony once and for all. He pulled the wool over his fellow crusaders' eyes, with the apparently noble argument that the Eastern emperor must be ousted and replaced by someone willing to reunite the eastern Orthodox and western Roman churches.

They acquiesced, but there was nothing noble about the brutal, bloody, Venetian-led sacking of Constantinople on 13 April 1204, nor about the pillaging that ensued. The Venetians looted the city's greatest treasures, including the celebrated quartet of antique Greek horses that was transported back to Venice and placed above the entrance of St Mark's basilica. Innumerable other artefacts – jewellery, enamels, golden chalices, statuary, columns, precious marbles and much more – were plundered: they are now part of the fabric of Venice's *palazzi* and churches.

But the booty was only a minor consideration for the Venetians and their pragmatic doge: the real prize was the one handed out when the routed Byzantine empire was carved up. The Venetians were not interested in grabbing huge swathes of territory that they knew they couldn't defend. This was left to the French and German knights, who, indeed, lost it within a few decades. Putting their intimate knowledge of eastern trade routes to excellent use, the Venetians hand-picked those islands and ports that could guarantee their merchant ships a safe passage from Venice to the Black Sea and back. These included almost all the main ports on the Dalmatian coast, certain strategic Greek islands, the Sea of Marmara and a number of strategic Black Sea ports.

For many years after the conquest of Constantinople, Venetian ships could sail from Venice to Byzantium without ever leaving waters controlled by their city. Venice marked the turn of events by conferring a new title upon its doge: *Quartae Partis et Dimidiae Totius Imperii Romaniae Dominator* – Lord of a Quarter and Half a Quarter of the Roman Empire.

AGE OF UPRISINGS

In 1297, in what came to be known as the *Serrata del Maggior Consiglio*, the leaders of the Venetian merchant aristocracy decided to limit entry to the Grand Council to those families which had held a seat in the *maggior consiglio* in the previous four years, or to descendants of those who had belonged at any point since 1172. Under these rules, only around 150 extended families were eligible for a place, but the number of council members leapt to some 1,200.

Up-and-coming clans were understandably indignant at the thought of being forever excluded from power and from a coveted place in the *Libro d'oro* – the Golden Book – of the Venetian aristocracy. In 1310, a prosperous merchant, Baiamonte Tiepolo, harnessed the discontent in a rebellion against the aristocratic oligarchy. Had Tiepolo's standard-bearer not been felled by a loose brick knocked out of place by an old lady watching the shenanigans from her window, the uprising may have succeeded.

IN CONTEXT

However, as it was, his troops fled in panic, the uprising was savagely crushed, and the much-feared Council of Ten was granted draconian powers. An extensive network of spies and informers was set up to suppress any future plots.

In 1354, Doge Marino Faliero made a bid to undermine the powers of the Venetian oligarchy while increasing and consolidating his own powers as a permanent hereditary leader. This plot, too, was mercilessly suppressed and Faliero was beheaded.

The Council of Ten – along with the Venetian Inquisition that was also established after the Tiepolo plot of 1310 – wielded its special powers most effectively after the Faliero incident, ensuring that this was the last serious attempt to attack the principle of rule by elite. It was at this time that lion's-head postboxes first appeared at strategic points around the city: Venetians were encouraged to drop written reports of any questionable activity that they noticed through their marble mouths.

LAVISH LOVE AND LUXURY

While Venice's mercantile power was at its zenith from the 13th to the 15th centuries, vast fortunes were amassed and lavished on building and decorating great *palazzi* and churches. It was at this time that the city took on the architectural form still visible today. For sheer luxury, Venice's lifestyle was unequalled anywhere else in Europe.

In the 14th and 15th centuries Venice was one of the largest cities in Europe, with an estimated population of between 150,000 and 200,000 (*see p24* **Population Implosion**). International visitors were generally astounded by *La Serenissima*'s legendary opulence and phenomenal economic dynamism.

When ships set sail from Venice for the Middle East, their holds were crammed with Istrian pine wood, iron ore, cereals, wool, and salted and preserved meats. These were traded for textiles, exotic carpets, perfumes, gold and silverware, spices, precious stones of all kinds, ivory, wax and slaves; with a virtual monopoly on all these much sought-after commodities, Venice was able to sell them on to the rest of Europe's moneyed classes at enormous profit.

The Venetian aristocracy certainly liked to live in domestic comfort. 'The luxury of any ordinary Venetian house,' wrote one traveller in 1492, 'is so extraordinary that in any other city or country it would be sufficient to decorate a royal palace.' The Venetians were also investing huge amounts of money in their summer villas on the mainland, designed and decorated by the leading Veneto architects and painters.

Venetians lavished the same kind of attention on their appearance. Fortunes were spent on the richest textiles and jewellery. Venetian women were famous for the luxury of their clothing, of their furs and of their fabrics woven with gold and silver thread. Their perfumes and cosmetics were the envy of all Europe, as were the beauty and fascination of the courtesans (*see p17* **Profile**) who dominated the social and cultural life of the city.

So dedicated were Venetians to the cult of love and earthly pleasures, that the Patriarch, Venice's cardinal, was compelled to issue orders forbidding the city's nuns from going out on the town at night. Sumptuous festivals of music, theatre and dance were almost daily occurrences during these wild times. The visit of a foreign ruler, a wedding or funeral of a member of the aristocracy, a religious festival, a naval or military victory, or delivery from an epidemic – all these were excuses for public celebrations. The city's foreign communities – Jews, Armenians, Turks, Germans, French and Mongols, many of them permanent residents in this truly cosmopolitan city – would also celebrate their national or religious feast days with enormous pomp.

Despite the wealth of the city and the full employment created by its many trades and industries (at full stretch, the shipyard was capable of launching one fully equipped ship every day), life was not easy for the city's poorest residents, who lived in damp, filthy conditions. Epidemics of disease were also frequent; indeed, more than half the city's population is estimated to have died in the Black Death of 1348-49. Social tension and discontent were rife.

Machinery of State

Navigating the corridors of power.

The longevity of the Venetian republic was due, to a large extent, to a finely honed system of checks and balances that kept the powerful merchant aristocracy closely involved in the machinery of state without allowing any one person or dynasty to lord it over the others. Rules, numbers and duties changed. At the end of the 13th century, what had started out as something close to a democracy became an oligarchy, with only the members of the 200-odd powerful clans included in the *Libro d'oro* (Golden Book) eligible for office. Later, anyone with the necessary funds could buy into the machinery of state.

The main ruling bodies were:

Collegio dei savi

College of Wise Men – a group of experts, elected by the *senato*, who staffed special committees to oversee all aspects of internal, marine and war policy.

Consiglio dei dieci

Council of Ten – appointed by the senato, the council's extensive network of spies brought any would-be subversives to a closed-door trial, in which defence lawyers were forbidden. In time, the increasingly powerful consiglio dei dieci would have the Inquisition to assist it in its task.

Il doge

The Duke – elected for life in a complicated, cheat-proof system of multiple ballots, the sumptuously robed Duke of Venice was glorious to behold. He could not, however, indulge in business of his own, receive foreign ambassadors alone, leave Venice without permission, or accept personal gifts. If his city state tired of him, he could be deposed. With the doge's extended family banned from high office for the term of his reign, many doges hailed from less politically adept clans. Most were very old by the time they donned the *biretta*, the distinctive horned hat – the average age of doges between 1400 and 1570 was 72. However, the doge was the only official privy to all state secrets and eligible to attend all meetings of state organs; he could, if he played his cards right, have a determining effect on Venetian policy.

Maggior consiglio

Great Council – the Republic's parliament – made up of all voting-age males from the clans that were included in the *Libro d'oro* – which elected (and provided the candidates for) most other state offices, including that of the doge.

Minor consiglio

Lesser Council – elected by and from the *maggior consiglio*, this six-man team advised – or kept tabs on – the doge.

Pien collegio

Full College – made up of the *minor consiglio* and the *collegio dei savi*, this became Venice's real government, eventually supplanting the *senato*.

Quarantie

The three supreme courts; the 40 members were chosen by the *senato*.

Senato

Senate – known until the late 14th century as the *pregadi*, the *senato* was the upper house of the Venetian parliament; by the 16th century it had some 300 members.

Serenissima signoria

Most Serene Lordships – the *minor consiglio*, the heads of the three *quarantie* courts and the doge; this body was vested with ultimate executive power.

IN CONTEXT

'Masked nuns were a common sight at the city's gambling houses and theatres.'

GENOESE JEALOUSY

Meanwhile, the enormous wealth of the Venetian Republic and its rapidly expanding empire inevitably provoked jealousy among the other trading nations of the Mediterranean – above all with the powerful city state of Genoa, Venice's main rival for trade with the East.

In 1261, the Genoese had clashed with the Venetians when the former obliged the Byzantine emperor by helping to evict Venice's high-handed merchants from Constantinople. Skirmishes between the two Italian powers continued throughout most of the 14th century, regularly flaring up into periods of open warfare, and often resulting in disastrous defeats for Venice.

By 1379, the situation had become desperate for *La Serenissima*. The Genoese fleet and army had moved into the upper Adriatic and, after a long siege, had taken Chioggia, at the southern end of the lagoon. From here the Genoese attacked and occupied much of the lagoon, including the passage to the open sea. Venice was under siege and began to starve.

Then, in 1380, the city worked another of its miracles of level-headed cunning. Almost the whole of the Genoese fleet was anchored inside the fortified harbour of Chioggia. Vittor Pisani, the admiral of the Venetian fleet, ordered hundreds of small boats to be filled with rocks. Panicked by a surprise Venetian attack on the mouth of the port, the Genoese failed to notice that the small boats were being sunk in the shallow port entrance, preventing any escape. The tables had been well and truly turned, and Venice besieged the trapped Genoese fleet until it was forced to surrender unconditionally. Genoa's days as a great naval power were over, and Venice exulted.

Ironically, however, this victory was to spell the beginning of the end for *La Serenissima*. For though the Republic had reached the climax of its prosperity and had re-acquired its supremacy in the East, concentrating its energies on fighting Genoa was to prove a costly foreign-policy mistake. Venice's leaders badly underestimated the threat posed by the emergence of the Turks as a military power in Asia Minor and the Black Sea area. Convinced – wrongly and ultimately fatally – that diplomacy was the way to deal with the threat from the East, Venice turned its attention to conquering other powers on the Italian mainland.

MAINLAND EXPANSION

For centuries, Venice had followed a conscious policy of steady neutrality towards the various powers that had carved up the Italian mainland. Europe's political upheavals from the end of the 12th century to the end of the 14th century put paid to that neutrality. The bitter rivalry between Venice and the other Italian maritime states, especially Pisa and Genoa, inevitably brought it into conflict with their mainland allies: the Pope, the Scaligera dukes of Verona and a succession of Holy Roman emperors.

The defeat of the vast Scaligera empire (which included much of the Venetian hinterland) by Count Gian Galeazzo Visconti of Milan in 1387 brought the Milanese much too close to the lagoon for comfort. All-important trade routes through north-eastern Italy, across the Alps and into northern Europe beyond were threatened. Venice began a series of wars that led to the conquest of Verona (*see p265*) and its enormous territories in 1405, and also of near neighbours Padua (*see p255*) and Vicenza (*see p275*).

By 1420, Venice had annexed Friuli and Udine; by 1441, *La Serenissima* controlled Brescia, Bergamo, Cremona and Ravenna. The land campaign continued until 1454, when Venice signed a peace treaty with Milan. Though Ravenna soon slipped from Venice's grasp, the rest of the Republic's immense mainland territories were to remain more or less intact for almost 300 years.

PORTUGUESE SPICE THINGS UP

Even as Venice expanded into the mainland, events were conspiring to bring its reign as a political power and trading giant to a close. In 1453, the Ottoman Turks swept into Constantinople, and Venice's crucial trading privileges in the former Byzantine Empire were almost totally lost. In 1487, Vasco da Gama rounded the Cape of Good Hope; in 1489, he became the first European to reach Calcutta by sea, shattering Venice's monopoly on the riches of the East. The arrival of Portuguese ships laden

Battle of Lepanto. See p25.

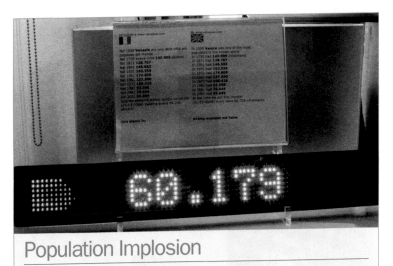

Population Implosion

As tourist numbers rise, the tally of residents keeps on falling.

As the world watches to see whether Venice will sink into the Adriatic, Venetians have their eye on a dramatic drop of another kind. In the window of the Farmacia Morelli in campo San Bartolomeo, a digital clock flashes a constant tally of the residents of *La Serenissima*. And it's going down.

On the cusp of the 14th century, Venice had as many as 200,000 residents, placing it among the largest European cities of the time. It's a moot point how they all squeezed into a city which still today – after massive landfill operations from the late 19th century has a solid surface area of just 5.2 square kilometres.

Through its heyday and its decline, Venice's population ebbed and flowed between this high point, and a low of almost 100,000. By the 1951 census it had bounced back up to 175,000. By 1981, however, that figure had plunged to 93,600. And on 31 December 2008, the population stood at 60,311.

So who is left, and where have the others gone? Locals will complain that Venice is now a ghost town, its residents all elderly and invisible among the tourist hordes. They will tell you that former island dwellers are now in comfortable, dry accommodation on the Venetian mainland. But the average age is not, as many think, well over 65: it's 49 years in the centre, little above the average in Venice as a whole.

The 60,000-odd who remain place island Venice on a demographic par with Margate in Kent or Pine Bluff, Arkansas. Neither of which, clearly, had 2.1 million tourists staying one night or more in 2007, or an average of 34,000 visitors dropping in for a quick look each day. And neither of which has anything to offer that comes close to St Mark's basilica or the Gallerie dell'Accademia.

In 2008, 456 new Venetians were born (and 887 old ones died). In the previous year, the city spawned over 100 new B&Bs, some 50 new registered room-renters and 20 new hotels. All this as locals struggled to afford sky-high rents, exorbitant house prices and crippling maintenance costs in this unique but very difficult city. Perhaps if more people are to be attracted back to stay in the lagoon city, fewer hotels and more help with homes is the secret.

with spices and textiles in Portuguese ports caused a sensation in Europe and despair in Venice. The Venetians hastily drew up plans to open a canal at Suez to beat the Portuguese at their own game, but the project came to nothing.

Instead, cushioned by the spoils and profits of centuries and exhausted by 100 years of almost constant military campaigning, the city sank slowly over the next two centuries into dissipation and decline.

That decline, naturally, was glorious. For most of the 16th century few Venetians behaved as if the writing were on the wall. Such was the enormous wealth of the city that the economic fall-out from the Turks' inexorable progress through the Middle East went almost unnoticed at first. Profits were not as massive as before, but the rich remained very rich and the setbacks in the East were partly counter-balanced by exploitation of the newly acquired *terra ferma* territories.

As revenue gradually declined through the 16th century, spending on life's little pleasures increased, producing an explosion of art, architecture and music. Titian, Tintoretto, Veronese and Giorgione were at work in the city (*see pp35-37*). Meanwhile, Palladio (*see p280* **Profile**), Sanmicheli and Scamozzi were changing the face of architecture (*see pp43-44*) and *litterati* dazzled with their wit and learning. *La Serenissima* rang with music (*see p68* **City of Music**).

On the mainland, however, Venice's arrogant annexation of territory had not been forgotten by the powers that had suffered at her hands. When Venice took advantage of the French invasion of Italy in the final years of the 15th century to extend its territories still further, the Habsburgs, France, Spain and the papacy were so incensed that they clubbed together to form the League of Cambrai, with the sole aim of annihilating Venice.

They came very close to doing so. One Venetian military rout followed another, a number of Venetian-controlled cities defected, and others that did not were laid waste by the hostile forces. Only squabbling within the League of Cambrai stopped Venice itself from being besieged. By 1516, the alliance had fallen to pieces and Venice had regained almost all its territories.

TURKISH DELIGHT

Its coffers almost empty and its mainland dominions left in tatters, Venice was now forced to take stock of the damage that was being done by the Turks.

In 1497, as the Ottomans stormed through the Balkans, *La Serenissima* had been obliged to give up several Aegean islands and the port of Negroponte; two years later, it lost its forts in the Peloponnese, giving the Turks virtually total control of the southern end of the Adriatic. And though Venice was jubilant about securing Cyprus in 1489 – won by pressuring the king's Venetian widow Caterina Cornaro into bequeathing control of the island – the acquisition involved the Republic in almost constant warfare to keep the Turks away from this strategically vital strip of land.

In 1517, Syria and Egypt fell to the Turks; Rhodes followed in 1522; and by 1529 the Ottoman Empire had spread across the southern Mediterranean as far as Morocco. The frightened European powers turned to Venice to help repulse the common foe. But mistrust of the lagoon republic by its new allies was deep and, in their determination to keep Venice from deriving too much financial profit from the war against the Turks, the campaign itself was botched.

In 1538, a Christian fleet was trounced at Preveza in western Greece; in 1571, Venice led a huge European fleet to victory against Turkish warships in the Battle of Lepanto, in what is now the Gulf of Corinth. But despite the self-glorifying propaganda campaign that followed, it became apparent that the Turks were as strong as ever. In a treaty signed after the battle in 1573, Venice was forced ignominiously to hand over Cyprus, its second-last major possession in the eastern Mediterranean. (Crete, the final one, held out until 1669.)

IN CONTEXT

TRADE DEFICIT

By the 17th century, Venice was no longer under any illusion about the gravity of its crisis. The *Savi alla Mercanzia* (state trading commission) noted on 5 July 1610 that 'our commerce and shipping in the West are completely destroyed. In the East only a few businesses are still functioning and they are riddled with debt, without ships and getting weaker by the day. Moreover, and this must be emphasised, only a small quantity of goods is arriving in our city, and it is becoming increasingly difficult to find buyers for them. The nations which used to buy from us now have established their businesses elsewhere. We are facing the almost total annihilation of our commerce.'

Venice was down but not quite out. Between 1681 and 1687, Francesco Morosini, the brilliant strategist then in command of the Venetian fleet, reconquered much of the territory taken by the Turks in the preceding century, including Crete and the Peloponnese. But these moments of glory, celebrated with colossal pomp and ceremony in Venice itself, were invariably short-lived.

Exhausted by debts and the sheer effort of its naval campaigns, the Venetian Republic lacked the resources needed to consolidate its victories. By 1718, it was struggling to keep its head above water as the Austrians and Turks forced it to cede most of its gains in the humiliating Treaty of Passarowitz.

By the time the Venezia Trionfante café (now Caffè Florian; *see p183*) opened for business in piazza San Marco in 1720, the Republic was virtually bankrupt; its governing nobility had grown decadent and politically inert. But decadence was good for the city's growing status as the party capital of Europe. Aristocratic women of all ages and marital states were accompanied in their gadding by handsome young *cisibei* (male escorts), whose professions of chastity fooled nobody. Masked nuns were a common sight at the city's gambling houses and theatres; church officials who tried to confine nuns to the convent by the church of San Zaccaria would be met with a barrage of bricks.

Priests too were not slow to join in the fun: composer-prelate Antonio Vivaldi's supposed affairs with members of his famous female choir were well publicised (*see p81* **Walk**). And though Giacomo Casanova, the embodiment of sexual excess, never actually donned a cassock, he had been a promising student of theology before he realised where his true vocation lay.

THROWING IN THE CAP

Bankrupt, politically and ideologically stagnant and no longer a threat to its former enemies, Venice directed its final heroic efforts not against those erstwhile foes but against the forces of nature. Even as Napoleon prepared to invade Venice in 1797, the city was spending the meagre funds left in its coffers on building the *murazzi*, the vast stone and marble dyke designed to protect the city from the worst ravages of unpredictable Adriatic tides. On 12 May 1797, the last doge, Lodovico Manin, was deposed by the French, who, even before the Republic bowed to the inevitable and voted itself out of existence, had handed control over to Austria. Manin gave his doge's cap to the victors, saying, 'Take this, I don't think I'll be needing it any more.'

In 1805, Napoleon absorbed Venice back into his Kingdom of Italy. Until 1815, when the French emperor's star waned and Venice once again found itself under Austrian control, Napoleon's Venetian plenipotentiaries were given free rein to dismantle churches, dissolve monasteries and redesign bits of the city, including the wide thoroughfare now known as via Garibaldi and its adjoining public gardens.

The last spark of Venice's ancient independent spirit flared up in 1848, when lawyer Daniele Manin (no relation of the last doge) led a popular revolt against the Austrians. An independent republican government was set up, holding out against siege for five heroic months. It was doomed to failure from the outset, however, and the Austrians were soon firmly back in the saddle, keeping their grip on this insignificant backwater until 1866, when a weakened Austria, badly beaten on other fronts by the Prussians, handed the city over to the newly united kingdom of Italy.

IN CONTEXT

Venice Today

Still keeping its head above water.

TEXT: ANNE HANLEY

How do you follow a millennium at the top of the tree – artistically and economically? How do you cope when ignominious decline sets in and you slide into a backwater? Another historical Italian metropolis – Rome – has had time to come to terms with the dilemma, and has expanded and adapted into something approaching a 21st-century city. But Venice, hemmed in by its lagoon and burdened with its unique concentration of riches in a damp, hostile environment, has yet to come to terms with its fate.

Venice today is a place of contradictions, a theme park without the irony and a museum without sufficient true connoisseurs. Its main industry is being gawped at, but it's furiously and famously reticent about accommodating prying outsiders. So what hope is there for the future? The 21st century, with its advanced information technology and footloose workforce, may provide the answer: handled in enlightened fashion, new trends in the way we work could save Venice from irreversible Disneyfication.

'Few such small cities, can lay claim to a population comprising gondoliers, mask-makers, fishermen, monks, nuns, musicians, artists…'

IN CONTEXT

CITY OR THEME PARK?

In June 2006, UK economist John Kay provoked outrage among Venetians and Venice-lovers alike when he wrote in the *Financial Times* that the lagoon city could only be saved by Disney – or some corporation with a solid grasp of organising tourist masses.

'Venice is already a theme park,' Kay argued. 'As a centre of business, politics and culture, it died centuries ago and only the flow of visitors brought it back to life. Today, most people in the city are tourists and most people who work there have come for the day to service the needs of tourists… The economics of the city are the economics of Yosemite and Disneyland, not the economics of Bologna or Los Angeles.'

This is, in part, a gross over-simplification. Most people in Venice at any given moment are Venetian residents. A new generation of young professionals finds this unique city congenial for their IT- or design-oriented purposes (*see p31* **40xVenezia**). And people *do* (occasionally) come to Venice for reasons other than tourism.

But lose yourself in the St Mark's square maelstrom, and you'd never know it. Or wander across the Rialto bridge and you may find yourself asking what *are* these mounds of the tackiest possible souvenirs doing in one of the world's most perfectly preserved artistic and architectural treasure troves?

Is it inertia, or are the city fathers actively encouraging the kind of hit-and-run tourism in which droves of package-tour day-trippers are herded into the most heavily touristed spots in the *centro storico*, never ploughing any more back into the local economy than the price of a plastic gondola? Even those visitors who choose to bed down in *La Serenissima* stay for an average 2.5 nights, against a considerably healthier average in Rome of 3.5 nights.

Souvenir stalls in the **Rialto** area.

Cynics might say that this state of affairs suits Venetians, for whom St Mark's square is a no-go area, and who know alternative routes to just about everywhere: utterly predictable madding crowds confined to easily avoidable areas means that the city's residents can get on with life.

Venice lives on tourism but considers its visitors annoying obstacles; its beauty is unimaginable but quality control is lacking. It's too early to say whether a 2009 attempt by city hall to rectify the hit-and-run situation with an all-encompassing online booking service (you can even pre-reserve your right to use the city's public toilets; *see also p6*) will entice visitors to plan better and appreciate Venice more fully. The initial impression is that it's so complicated, it may put people off.

MEANWHILE, ON TERRA FERMA

Beyond island Venice is another world again, that of the Veneto region. While *La Serenissima* continues to hold the world in her thrall, the *terra ferma* side of the lagoon has come quietly but steadily into its own. Besides being one of Italy's biggest economic success stories, it now has a burgeoning tourist industry as well. In 2007, the Veneto was Italy's most-visited region, with 16 per cent of the national share. Over 14 million people, including 8.7 million non-Italians, checked into a hotel here, spending a total of 61 million nights; admittedly, 55 per cent of these headed for Venice and its province, but Verona clocked up a healthy 21 per cent. And if visitors staying in the Veneto fell by almost one million in 2008, this reflected a national downward trend, largely in response to the global economic climate.

Any success that Venice and the Veneto have experienced has been recent. Venice had slipped far into decline before the city capitulated to Napoleon's troops in 1797. Under Austrian rule (1815-66) it was relegated to the status of a picturesque, inconsequential backwater. But if the city suffered, the fate of its former mainland territories was even worse: with no industry to speak of, and agriculturally backwards, the Veneto ran the semi-feudal south a close race for the title of Italy's own Third World. Between 1876 and 1901, almost 35 per cent of the 5.2 million desperate Italians who sought a better life abroad fled from the crushing poverty of the Veneto and the neighbouring Friuli region.

Massive industrialisation in Venice's mainland Porto Marghera between and after the wars shifted the more impoverished sectors of the population from agricultural to urban areas. But the poverty remained. As recently as 1961, 48 per cent of homes in the north-east had no running water, 72 per cent didn't have a bathroom and 86 per cent had no central heating.

What the people of the Veneto did have, however, was a deep-rooted attachment to their traditional crafts, and a cussedness of character unmatched anywhere in Italy. In the past, both had proved detrimental: when captains of heavy industry sought meek vassals to man the furnaces, many of the natives of the Veneto who protested were forcibly deported to populate Fascist new towns in the malarial swamps south of Rome.

THINGS CAN ONLY GET BETTER

It was not, in fact, until the 1970s that north-eastern determination came into its own. With industrial downscaling all the rage, those family-run workshops that had ridden out the bad times gradually became viable business concerns. Giuliana Benetton's knitting machine gave birth to a global clothing empire centred in Treviso; Leonardo del Vecchio's metalworking lessons in an orphanage spawned Luxottica, the world's biggest spectacle frame maker, based in Belluno; and Ivano Beggio progressed from tinkering with bikes in his father's cycle shop in Noale to running Aprilia, one of Europe's largest manufacturers of motorcycles and scooters. Through the mid to late 1990s a third of the country's huge balance of trade surplus was generated in the north-east. In 1997, local industrialists boasted that the unemployment rate had fallen to zero; in 2007, it stood at 3.3 per cent, well below the national average of 6.1 per cent.

IN CONTEXT

'Much of Venetian life takes place behind closed doors, concealed from the casual observer.'

The 21st century has seen a tarnishing of the Veneto's Midas touch, however. The competitive edge for exports created by a weak lira was lost with the introduction of the euro. Crippling labour costs have forced many businesses to relocate eastwards; a manpower shortfall has been bridged by hiring immigrant workers (at the end of 2007, some 250,000 migrant workers were legally employed in the region, a huge leap from 97,000 in 2000), resulting in an unprecedented ethnic potpourri: learning to live with social and cultural differences is one of the biggest challenges the famously insular Veneto must face today.

The post-war parabola described by island Venice was, if anything, bleaker. As the *terra ferma* became industrialised, workers looked across the water for employment. Realising housing on the mainland was cheaper, drier and easier to park in front of, they moved out in an exodus that brought the population of island Venice plunging from around 175,000 in 1951 to 60,000 or so today (*see p24* **Population Implosion**).

For an area of 5.2 square kilometres (2.0 square miles), however, that's still a respectable figure. Few such small cities, moreover, can lay claim to a population comprising gondoliers, mask-makers, glass-blowers, fishermen, monks, nuns, musicians, artists, writers, architects, historians, academics, restoration experts and many of Italy's rich and famous. Add to that a sizeable student population, a dedicated group of expats and part-time residents and the result is a solid base of 'locals' that gives Venice its distinct flavour.

Because there *is* a 'real' city where dogged residents are prepared to persevere – despite exorbitant prices, grocers turning into mask shops, and the chance that *acqua alta* may cause irreparable damage to their carpets.

And there *are* initiatives under way to keep Venice above water – both literally and figuratively – in the 21st century. For every headline-grabbing problem project – such as Santiago Calatrava's fourth bridge over the Grand Canal (*see p45* **Path of Light**) – others carry on with no fanfare and much success. Take Insula (www.insula.it), for example: a consortium that has worked its way around Venice since 1997, dredging clogged canals, removing hundreds of thousands of cubic metres of mud, and rebuilding footpaths in a quiet but vital maintenance programme. Or 40xVenezia (*see p31*), which is prodding Venetians to take positive action to make their city liveable.

On the mainland, too, things are on the move. In Mestre, the piazza and campanile have been restored. Among the high-tech businesses attracted to the rapidly developing Science and Technology Park at the northern end of Porto Marghera is a nanotechnologies laboratory that makes Venice a world leader in the field.

THE HIDDEN CITY

Dazzled, disorientated and besieged by pigeons, the average visitor to *La Serenissima* may not even realise that a traipse from St Mark's to the Rialto tells them as much about the city as a guided tour of the Tower of London or a lift to the top of the Empire State Building tell about those other metropolises. Much of Venetian life takes place behind closed doors, concealed from the casual observer.

An isolated culture, hedged about by water, one that remained an independent republic for over a millennium, one that once lorded it over the entire Mediterranean, cannot be easily penetrated by an outsider, although everyone and anyone is welcome to try. Otherwise, feel free to sit back and enjoy the show.

40xVenezia

A virtual social network with real-world impact.

All Venetians will tell you that Venice has problems: not sinking problems so much as lifestyle problems, as the population ebbs away (*see p24* **Population Implosion**) and the trek to the baker's gets ever longer with useful traders being pushed out by shops peddling glass animals made abroad. What most Venetians won't do, though, is go much beyond a generic and oft-repeated moan. Solutions have long been thin on the ground. As for direct action: no more than the occasional cry in the wilderness. Until now, that is.

In September 2007, seven friends set up **40xVenezia** (*quaranta per Venezia*, 40 for Venice), a social networking website (www.40xvenezia.it). The idea was to attract thirty- and fortysomething professional Venetian residents to pool concerns and ideas with a view to plugging gaps that successive city councils have failed to address adequately. By the end of 2008, the group had over 1,550 members, making it one of Italy's largest social networks. Copycat 40x networks have since sprung up in places as far as Cagliari in Sardinia and Catania in Sicily.

If the idea seemed outlandish – given the habitual resignation of the city's dwindling population – the effect has been galvanising. The 40x group has gone head-to-head with city hall over proposed new regulations that would have effectively meant any space, just about anywhere, could be transformed into tourist lodging. The group's architect and planner members got drawing to provide an alternative to a new zoning map being drawn up by city planners. In other developments, members intervened en masse to debate and improve the new Venice Connected system (*see p6*). Already, it seems, when 40x raises its voice, the city authorities listen.

The flip side of 40xVenezia is its strictly social(ising) role. Social life in *La Serenissima* was a slow-moving tide until residents discovered **Ning** (www.40xvenezia.ning.com). Now, one post can bring dozens of people to a canal-side bar to discuss pressing issues... or just to enjoy an *ombra* and *cicheto*. With its wired participants in a compact *centro storico*, Venice's social network has a truly (real-world) village feel.

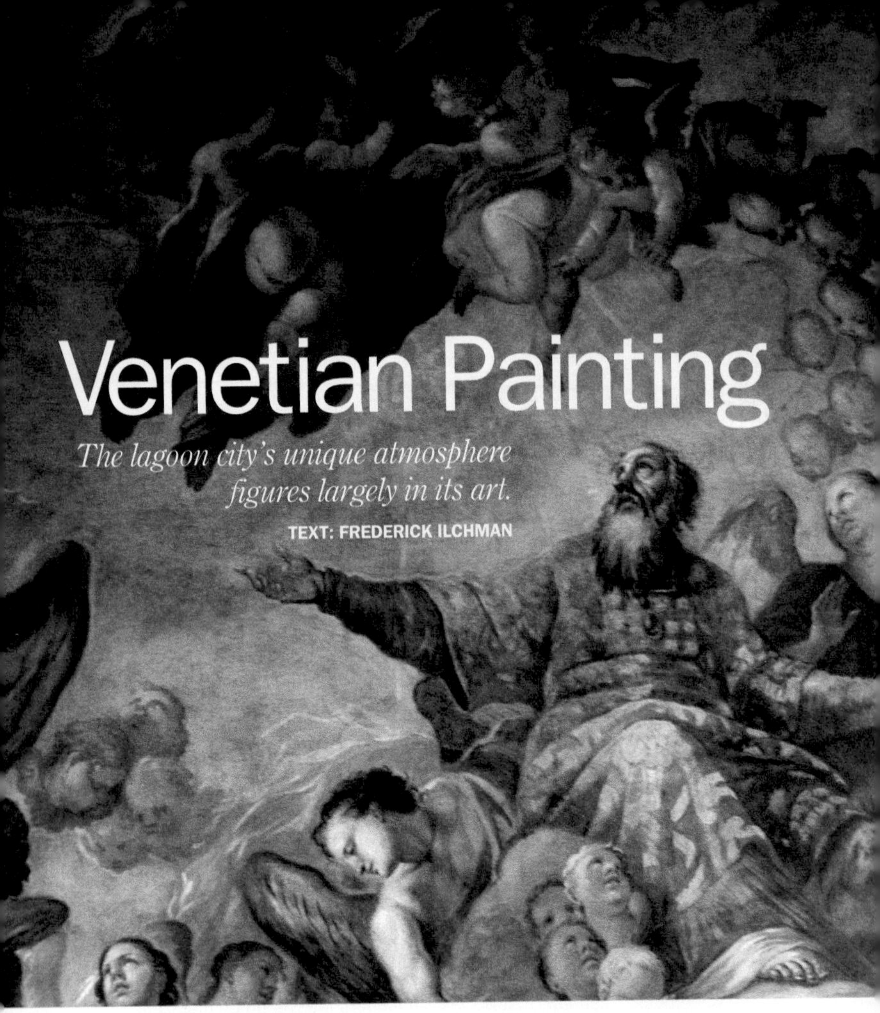

Venetian Painting

*The lagoon city's unique atmosphere
figures largely in its art.*

TEXT: FREDERICK ILCHMAN

*Frederick
Ilchman
spent five
years in Venice
researching
16th-century
painting. He is
now a curator
at the Museum
of Fine Arts
in Boston.*

From the late Middle Ages until the mid 18th century, artists of the highest calibre left their mark all over this unlikely smattering of over-crowded islands in a desolate lagoon. The result today is an anomaly: an extraordinary concentration of artistic treasures, of which the city's dwindling population is still inordinately, possessively proud.

Though little art is made in Venice these days, the city's very particular relationship with the art world continues. The 2009 inauguration of the new contemporary gallery at the Punta della Dogana means Venice's concentration of 20th- and 21st-century art is almost as important as its Renaissance glories. For a damp town buffetted by threatening tides, Venice is truly a unique and precious repository of art.

'The hard contours have softened in Giorgione's work, and for the first time the atmosphere becomes palpable, like damp lagoon air.'

PAINTINGS FOR PLACES

A key element in the effectiveness of Venetian painting is that many great pictures remain in the buildings for which they were painted. Leave the madding crowd at San Marco behind, and you'll soon come across superb pictures in obscure churches: glowing altarpieces and pulsating canvas *laterali* (paintings for side walls of chapels). Seeing these pictures in their original sites reveals how aware painters were of the relation of their works to the surrounding architecture, light and existing artwork.

Yet, exceptionally, the paintings also relate to the physical context of Venice itself. What makes Venetian painting distinctive – the decorated surfaces, asymmetry, shimmering light effects and, above all, warm tonalities – can also be found in the lagoon environment. Renaissance Venice's visual culture encompassed the richness of Islamic art and Byzantine mosaics, the haphazard arrangement of streets and canals with their strong shadows, and light experienced through haze or reflected off moving water.

THE END OF ANONYMITY

Venetian church interiors were once covered with frescoes; the damp climate means that very few of these earliest works survive today. The official history of Venetian painting begins in the 1320s with the first painter to emerge from medieval anonymity, **Paolo Veneziano** (c1290-1362), who worked in egg tempera and gold leaf on wood panel. He championed the composite altarpiece, which would become one of the key formats of Venetian painting. His polyptychs, such as *The Coronation of the Virgin* in the Accademia gallery (*see p122*), were ornately framed, compartmentalised works featuring sumptuous fabrics, a preference for surface decoration and pattern over depth, and a seriousness – or stiffness – derived from Byzantine icons. A love of drapery and textile patterns proved to be a Venetian constant, still visible in Veronese's paintings in the 16th century and even beyond that in Tiepolo's 18th-century works.

Although many painters worked in Venice in the century after Paolo Veneziano, the next major legacy was that of a team, **Giovanni d'Alemagna** (John of Germany) and his brother-in-law **Antonio Vivarini**, active in the mid 15th century. Their three altarpieces in San Zaccaria (dated 1443, *see p82*), one in San Pantalon (*see p111*) and an imposing canvas triptych in the Accademia demonstrate the transition from Gothic to Renaissance.

Although Italian art historians give precedence to Antonio, the sudden decline in the quality of his works after Giovanni's death in 1450 suggests his partner was the brains behind the operation. Antonio's younger brother, **Bartolomeo Vivarini**, who ran the family workshop from the 1470s until about 1491, learned Renaissance style from both painting and sculpture, as seen in the lapidary figures in the altarpiece (1474) in the Cappella Corner of the Frari (*see p109*).

By the next generation, the main players had become more clearly defined. From around 1480 **Giovanni Bellini** directed the dominant workshop in Venice. Most of Bellini's sizeable output, stretching from the late 1450s until his death

IN CONTEXT

in 1516, was painted on wood panel rather than the newer canvas. The important group of early Bellini devotional pictures in the Museo Correr (*see p66*) and the many variations on the Madonna and Child theme in the Accademia show how varied and moving these subjects could be.

Equally impressive is Bellini's magnificent series of altarpieces. In these he perfected the subject of the *Sacra conversazione* (Sacred Conversation), where standing saints flank a seated figure, usually the Virgin Mary, within a setting that evokes the gold mosaics and costly marbles of the Basilica di San Marco (*see p61*). The inner glow afforded by the new medium of oil paint allowed Bellini to model his figures with an astonishing delicacy of light and shadow. One can follow his progress through a series of altarpieces that remain *in situ*: in Santi Giovanni e Paolo (*see p80*), the Frari, San Zaccaria and San Giovanni Crisostomo (*see p91*).

Giovanni's elder brother, **Gentile Bellini**, enjoyed even greater official success: from 1474 until his death in 1507 he directed the decoration of the Palazzo Ducale (*see p67*), replacing crumbling frescoes with huge canvases. He also performed a diplomatic role for the Venetian government, travelling to Constantinople in 1479 to paint for the Ottoman sultan. Although his Palazzo Ducale canvases were destroyed by fire in 1577, his *Procession in Piazza San Marco* (1496), now in the Accademia, shows his ability to depict sumptuous public spectacle with choreographic verve.

Three painters born in the second half of the 15th century, and who were active in the 16th, are worth seeking out. **Cima da Conegliano** (c1459-1517) offers a stiffer style than Bellini, depicting figures standing in dignified repose against crisp landscapes. Cima's best altarpieces, in the Accademia, and at San Giovanni in Bragora (*see p87*), the Madonna dell'Orto (*see p95*) and the Carmini (*see p119*), all demonstrate a mastery of light.

Vittore Carpaccio (c1465-1525) specialised in narrative works for the *scuole* (*see p105* **Back to School**). Two intact cycles from around 1500 are among the treasures of Venetian painting: the grand St Ursula cycle in the Accademia and that of St George and St Jerome in the intimate Scuola di San Giorgio degli Schiavoni (*see p87*).

IN CONTEXT

Crucifixion by Tintoretto.
See p36.

'Titian's handling of paint had become so loose that his forms were not so much defined by contours as caressed into being.'

Lorenzo Lotto (c1480-1556) spent much of his career outside Venice. His best altarpieces in the city, in the Carmini and Santi Giovanni e Paolo, combine an uncanny accuracy – in rendering landscape or cloth, for example – with a deeply felt spirituality. His impressive portraits, such as the *Portrait of a Youth*, in the Accademia, employ an unusual horizontal format.

SECULAR SUBJECTS

At the beginning of the 16th century, Venetian painting took a dramatic turn. Three of Bellini's pupils – Giorgione, Sebastiano del Piombo and Titian – experimented with new secular subject matter and new ways of handling paint. **Giorgione** (c1477-1510) remains one of the great enigmas of art. No other reputation rests on so few surviving pictures. The hard contours and emphasis on surface pattern seen in earlier Venetian painting have softened in his work, and for the first time the atmosphere becomes palpable, like damp lagoon air. Two haunting pictures in the Accademia, *La Tempesta* and *La Vecchia*, may be deliberately enigmatic, more concerned with mood than story. It can be argued that the modern concept of the painting was born in Venice soon after 1500. For the first time, three conditions that we now take for granted were met: these works were all oil on canvas, painted at the artist's initiative, and not intended for a specific location.

Sebastiano del Piombo (c1485-1547) left his mark with a similar emphasis on softened contour and tangible atmosphere. His major altarpiece, which was painted around 1507 and can still be seen in San Giovanni Crisostomo, shows a *Sacra conversazione* in which some of the figures are seen in profile, rather than head on, and hidden in shadow. Even more exciting is a set of standing saints painted as organ shutters, now in the Accademia, which show an unprecedented application of thick paint (*impasto*).

TITIAN AND TINTORETTO

Events conspired to boost the early career of **Titian** (Tiziano Vecellio, c1488-1576) when, in the space of only six years (1510-16), Giorgione fell victim to the plague, Sebastiano del Piombo moved to Rome and Giovanni Bellini passed away. Titian soon staked his claim with a dynamic *Assumption of the Virgin* (1518) for the high altar of the Frari. There he dominated the enormous space by creating the largest panel painting in the world.

The lagoon city is the place to appreciate *in situ* the nearly 70-year span of the master's religious work. These include a second, glorious altarpiece in the Frari (the *Madonna di Ca' Pesaro*), the virile St Christopher fresco in the Palazzo Ducale and the ceiling paintings in the sacristy of the Salute (*see p123*).

For a decade (c1527-39), Titian had a true rival in **Pordenone** (c1483-1539), a painter of muscular figures engaged in violent action. Now, for the first time in decades, Pordenone's work can be appreciated in Venice. The recently restored *Saints Christopher and Martin* in the church of San Rocco (*see p111*) shows an urgent style that had great appeal. Even more interesting is the confrontation in the reopened church of San Giovanni Elemosinario (*see p101*), where Pordenone's bulging figures on the right altar square off against the soft contours of Titian's high altar. Yet, once again, Titian found his road cleared of obstacles when his adversary suddenly died.

By the 1560s, in works such as the extraordinary *Annunciation* in San Salvador (*see p73*), Titian's handling of paint had become so loose that his forms were not so much defined by contours as caressed into being. Line was replaced by quivering patches of warm colouring.

Contemporaries swore that the old artist painted as often with his fingers as with the brush. Nowhere is this tactile quality more apparent than in Titian's final painting, a *Pietà* originally intended for his tomb, and now in the Accademia. Left unfinished at his death during the plague of 1576, this picture summarises the Venetian artistic tradition, with its glittering mosaic dome and forms so dissolved as to challenge the very conventions of painting.

Instead of mourning Titian's death, Jacopo Robusti (c1518-94) – better known as **Tintoretto** – probably breathed a sigh of relief. Though he rose to fame in the late 1540s, he had to wait until he was 58 years old before he could claim the title of Venice's greatest living painter. Yet Tintoretto was canny enough to learn from his rival. He supposedly inscribed the motto 'The drawing of Michelangelo and the colouring of Titian' on the wall of his studio.

Tintoretto's breakthrough work, *The Miracle of the Slave* (1548), now in the Accademia, offered a brash attempt at this synthesis, combining Michelangelo's confident muscular anatomies with Titian's glistening paint surface. Borrowing the figure types and violent compositions of Pordenone, Tintoretto's aggressive and tumultuous canvases marked the end of the decorative narrative painting tradition perfected by Carpaccio.

As Ruskin noted in *The Stones of Venice*, Tintoretto, unlike Titian, is an artist who can only be appreciated in Venice. Among the dozens of works in his home town, the soaring choir paintings in the Madonna dell'Orto (c1560) or the many canvases at the Scuola Grande di San Rocco (*see p112*), executed in 1564-87, amaze in their scale and complexity, notably his wall-sized *Crucifixion* (1565). His many workshop assistants, including two sons and a daughter, allowed him to increase production to unprecedented levels. Tintoretto went even further than Titian in the liberation of the brush stroke. The tradition of bravura handling that goes from Rubens to Delacroix to De Kooning begins with the action painters of 16th-century Venice.

Paolo Veronese (1528-88) made his impact in Venice with a love of rich fabrics and elegant poses that contrasts with Tintoretto's agitated figures. Veronese's savoir faire is best seen in the overpopulated feasts he painted for monastery refectories, such as the *Feast in the House of Levi*, now in the Accademia. Veronese's wit can be seen in one of the few great 16th-century mythological paintings remaining in Venice: *The Rape of Europa*, in the Palazzo Ducale, with its leering, slightly comical bull. His supreme ensemble piece is in San Sebastiano (*see p115*), a church that features altars, ceilings, frescoes and organ shutters all painted by Veronese, as well as the artist's tomb.

Venetian painting was also practised outside Venice: **Jacopo Bassano** (c1510-92) was an artist based in a provincial centre who kept pace with the latest innovations. Alhough his work is best seen in his home town, Bassano del Grappa (*see p288*), a number of canvases in the Accademia and an altarpiece in San Giorgio Maggiore (*see p130*) display characteristic Venetian flickering brush work and dramatic chiaroscuro.

With the following generation, the golden age of Venetian painting drew to a close. The prolific **Palma il Giovane** (c1548-1628) created works loosely in the style of Tintoretto. His finest pictures, such as the *Crucifixion* in the Madonna dell'Orto or those in San Giacomo dell'Orio (*see p104*) or the Oratorio dei Crociferi (*see p97*), all date from the 1580s.

After the deaths of Veronese and Tintoretto, the pressure was gone and the quality of Venetian art took a nosedive, as can be seen at San Giovanni Elemosinario, now open after decades *in restauro*. Outsized canvases by painters active at the end of the 16th century crowd the church's walls but the aforementioned small altarpieces by Titian and Pordenone, executed more than half a century earlier, dominate the space.

The Second Martyrdom of St Sebastian by Veronese.

Deadly Rivals

Competition was cut-throat among Venice's grand masters.

The artistic climate in Renaissance Venice was anything but *serenissimo*. Although a prosperous city throughout the 15th and 16th centuries meant a growing market for art, the competition between artists only grew fiercer. Searching for prestigious commissions, painters both confident and desperate flocked to Venice, crowding the local artists and causing emnity which at times became life-threatening.

A 17th-century biographer tells the story of how **Tintoretto** sought revenge when slandered by the writer Pietro Aretino, a staunch supporter of Titian. Aretino had asked Tintoretto to paint his portrait. At the sitting, Tintoretto pulled out a knife. Aretino thought the worst, but Tintoretto told him to calm down: he was only 'measuring' him. Tintoretto held the blade alongside Aretino's head and then moved toward his feet, concluding: 'You are two and a half daggers tall.' Aretino never disparaged Tintoretto again.

Even when painters didn't draw their swords, they faced off in their art. **Titian** probably accepted a minor altarpiece commission in San Sebastiano (*see p115*) in order to insert himself into a church that **Veronese** was transforming

into a personal monument. Tintoretto outfoxed his rivals and won the competition for a ceiling painting in the Scuola di San Rocco (*see p112*) by installing a finished canvas instead of the requested preparatory sketch.

A fascinating showdown can be seen in San Giovanni Crisostomo (*see p91*), where the elderly **Giovanni Bellini** outshone his former pupil **Sebastiano del Piombo**, some 50 years his junior. Sebastiano struck first, around 1507, with the high altarpiece, boldly setting the central figure of St John Chrysostom in profile and immersed in shadow. He contrasted the saint with a particularly lyrical John the Baptist (note how the scroll winding around his staff mimics the turning of the saint's body and the drapery swirls). Not to be outdone, Bellini's 1513 altarpiece in the right chapel includes similar chessboard paving and a twisting St Christopher, clearly critiquing Sebastiano's Baptist. The central figure is presented as a seated geriatric holding a tome, literally facing off against his rival's prototype. Bellini made sure viewers knew that this was not the work of a young trendy: he signed and dated the painting prominently near Christopher's knee.

BAROQUE AND ROCOCO

In the following years, Baroque in Venice was represented largely by out-of-towners (**Luca Giordano**, whose restored altarpieces adorn the Salute) or by bizarre posturing (**Gian Antonio Fumiani**'s stupefying canvas ceiling in San Pantalon). Exaggerated light effects ruled the day. It was only at the beginning of the 18th century that Venetian painting experienced a resurgence. **Giambattista Piazzetta** (1683-1754) produced a ceiling painting in Santi Giovanni e Paolo and a sequence of altarpieces – particularly those in Santa Maria della Fava (*see p74*), the Gesuati (*see p126*) and San Salvador – all demonstrating restrained elegance and a muted palette.

Giambattista Tiepolo (1696-1770), the greatest painter of the Venetian rococo, adapted the zigzag scheme introduced by Piazzetta for use with warm pastel colours. In his monumental ceilings in the Gesuati, the Pietà (*see p85*) and Ca' Rezzonico (*see p117*), Tiepolo reintroduced frescoes on a large scale after more than two centuries of canvas ceilings. Perhaps the most satisfying place to view his work is the upper room of the Scuola Grande dei Carmini (*see p119*), where the disproportionately low ceiling provides a close-up view of his technique. The dazzling Tiepolo was only one of a number of important artists at work in 18th-century Venice, including his own son, **Giandomenico Tiepolo** (1727-1804).

Though frequently his father's assistant, Giandomenico can be seen at his independent best in an eerie cycle of 14 *Stations of the Cross* in San Polo (*see p101*). **Gaspare Diziani** (1689-1767) deserves credit for three gorgeous ceiling canvases on the life of St Helen in the former meeting room of the Scuola del Vin (wine merchants' confraternity), entered through the church of San Silvestro (*see p101*). Above all, the essence of the Venetian rococo is to be found in the sites where architecture, sculpture and painting were employed to form a unified whole: the Gesuati, Santa Maria della Fava, San Stae (*see p106*) and the furnished rooms of Ca' Rezzonico.

In the 18th century, collectors provided a constant demand for portraits and city views. A female artist, **Rosalba Carriera** (1675-1757), developed a refined portrait style using pastels. **Canaletto** (1697-1768) and **Guardi** (1712-93) offered views of Venice. The popularity of these landscape paintings as Grand Tour souvenirs means that although examples exist in the Accademia and Ca' Rezzonico, both artists are seen at their best in Britain. A different aspect of 18th-century painting, and perhaps Guardi's masterpiece, can be seen in the astonishingly delicate *Stories of Tobias* (1750-53) decorating the organ loft in the church of Angelo Raffaele (*see p113*). **Pietro Longhi** (1702-85) created amusing genre scenes which gently satirised the social life of his day.

PATRONS, NOT PRODUCERS

By the time of Napoleon's conquest in 1797, Venetian painting, like Venetian military power, was a spent force. Over the following 200 years, however, Venice's unique setting and lavish collections have been a magnet for foreign visitors, including artists.

Venice now exhibits painters, rather than producing them. The city's contemporary art scene is increasingly vibrant, with a handful of smaller players and three major institutions: the prestigious Biennale (*see pp47-49*), the Peggy Guggenheim Collection (*see p121* **Profile**), which has expanded and is flourishing, and the extraordinary Palazzo Grassi–Punta della Dogana nexus (*see p75 and p124* **The Whole Punta**).

Although attention is currently focussed on the contemporary, Venice's incomparable artistic heritage will soon get a boost too. Some time in the not-too-distant future, the Grandi Gallerie dell'Accademia will see the light of day. The ground floor of the present Accademia building – used by the city's fine arts school from 1807 to 2003 – is currently being converted into additional galleries so that nearly 650 works (instead of the present 400) can be displayed, many of them specially restored for the opening. Projected amenities include a café, a better bookshop and a less congested entrance. The final result should be worthy of the tremendous collections.

IN CONTEXT

Architecture

Building styles as unique as their watery location.

TEXT: ANNE HANLEY

Venice's history is written in masonry, from its unlikely beginnings on foundations placed upon wooden piles driven into inhospitable marshes – via its heyday when an innate love of extravagant, competitive show led to the construction of superb family *palazzi*, and commerce and conquest furnished the city's lush ornamentation – to its decline and fall when former glories flaked, chipped, peeled and began subsiding into the muddy lagoon.

Through its history, Venice produced few architectural geniuses of its own, preferring to import talent from elsewhere to design its cityscape. Of the four architects who altered the fabric of the city, three are out-of-towners: Tuscan-born Jacopo Sansovino; Vicenza-based Andrea Palladio; and early Renaissance master Mauro Codussi from Bergamo. The only native talent is Baroque wonderboy Baldassare Longhena. All of them contributed to making Venice the unique gem we see today.

Cino Zucchi's **ex-Junghans** housing, Giudecca.

MEDIEVAL AND BYZANTINE

Venetian architecture began in Torcello, where the cathedral of **Santa Maria Assunta** (*see p140*), founded in 639, is the oldest surviving building on the lagoon. It has been remodelled since then – notably in the ninth and 11th centuries – but still retains the simple form of an early Christian basilica. Next door, the 11th-century church of **Santa Fosca** (*see p139*) has a Greek cross plan – also found in **San Giacomo di Rialto** (*see p99*), considered the earliest church in Venice proper. The portico of Santa Fosca exhibits a feature that recurs in the first-floor windows of 12th-century townhouses on the Grand Canal: stilted arches, with horseshoe-shaped arches atop slender columns.

That the history of Venetian architecture can be charted by following the development of the arch is understandable in a city built on mud, where load-bearing capabilities were a prime consideration. In the latter part of the 13th century, the pure, curved Byzantine arch began to sport a point at the top, under the influence of Islamic models. An early example of this can be seen in the heavily restored **Albergo del Selvadego** in calle dell'Ascensione (San Marco). Soon this point developed into a fully fledged ogee arch – a northern Gothic trait.

Meanwhile, the **Basilica di San Marco** (St Mark's basilica; *see p61*) was continuing to evolve. A makeshift chapel for holding St Mark's relics was replaced in 832 by a church modelled on the Church of the Apostles in Constantinople; that burnt down, to be replaced with the one we see today. The main body of the current church, with its Greek cross plan surmounted by five domes, dates from the 11th century; but it was embellished extensively over the next four centuries. Two humbler 12th-century churches, **San Giacomo dell'Orio** (*see p104*) and **San Nicolò dei Mendicoli** (*see p115*), both feature squat, detached bell towers – a key feature of the Veneto-Byzantine style.

GOTHIC AND LATE GOTHIC

In the 14th and 15th centuries, Venetian architecture developed an individual character unmatched before or since. It was at this time that the city's own Arab-tinged version of Gothic came into its own.By the mid 14th century, the ogee arch (two concave-convex curves meeting at the top) had sprouted a point on the inside of its concave edge – producing the cusped arch, which distributes the forces pressing down on it so efficiently that the Victorian art critic John Ruskin decreed that 'all are imperfect except these.'

By the beginning of the 15th century, this basic shape had been hedged around with elaborate tracery and trefoils (clover-shaped openings) and topped with Moorish-looking pinnacles in a peculiarly Venetian take on the flamboyant Gothic style, which reached its apotheosis in the façades of the **Palazzo Ducale** (*see p67*) and the **Ca' d'Oro** (*see p91*) – both completed by 1440.

CHURCHES AND SCUOLE

Outside of St Mark's, church architecture reflected the traditional building styles of the large religious orders that commissioned the work: the cavernous brick monuments of **Santi Giovanni e Paolo** (1430; *see p80*) and the **Frari** (1433; *see p109*) are classic examples of, respectively, the Dominican and Franciscan approaches. Both have a Latin cross plan, a large rose window and a generous sprinkling of pinnacles.

More individual are churches such as **Santo Stefano** (*see p75*), with its wooden ship's-keel roof, and the **Scuola Vecchia della Misericordia** (*see p95*), with its ogee windows and Flemish-style roof gable. Both involved the collaboration of Giovanni and Bartolomeo Bon, who also worked on the Ca' d'Oro.

THE VENETIAN PALAZZO

Majestic Grand Canal palaces (*see also pp52-59*) continued to indulge the yen for elaborate tracery windows, but behind the façade the structure went back centuries. The Venetian palazzo was not only a place of residence; it was also the family business headquarters; the internal division of space reflects this, with loading

Mud Houses

The foundations of a city built on water are not so firm.

If you absolutely must build a city on a squishy base of a hundred-odd marshy islets in an inhospitable lagoon, it's clear you're going to have to think about foundations. Especially if, in time, you want this city to grow into more than a collection of wooden huts on stilts, to become a flourishing trade empire, acquiring some stunning marble-clad churches and *palazzi* in the process.

Beneath the Venetian lagoon is a layer of compacted clay called *caranto*, the remains of the ancient Venetian plain that subsided aeons ago. On top of this firm base are silt deposits that vary in depth – from very shallow by the mainland to many metres deep out by the Adriatic.

As the builders of this most unlikely of cities were soon to realise, nothing of any size would stay vertical unless it was standing firmly on the *caranto*. So great trunks of larch and oak trees were driven down through the mud, to bear the weight of what would then be built above. Lack of oxygen in the clay saved the wood from decomposition, turning the stakes as hard as rock. As you walk through Venice's *calli*, you are, in effect, striding over a petrified forest.

The solution is a good one, but it's certainly not perfect. As the sea level inexorably rises and the *caranto* level subsides – at an estimated one millimetre per year – there's no way that the trunks can be stretched to keep the floor above water.

And occasionally the wood rots, especially if the piles are shaken – with the risk of oxygen sneaking in – by passing motorised water traffic. At which point, those wooden piles will need to be replaced, at a substantial cost – and it's no fun having a forest dragged through your living room floor either.

and storage space below a magnificent first-floor piano nobile. On the roof there was often a raised wooden balcony or *altana*: in a city where space was always at a premium, private courtyards were almost unheard of.

EARLY RENAISSANCE

Venetians were so fond of their own gracefully oriental version of Gothic that they held on to it long after the new classicist orthodoxy had taken over central Italy. For the second half of the 15th century, emergent Renaissance forms existed alongside the Gothic swansong. Sometimes they merged or clashed in the same building, as in the church of **San Zaccaria** (*see p82*), which was begun by Antonio Gambello in 1458 in the pure northern Gothic style but completed by Mauro Codussi in the Renaissance idiom he was then elaborating.

Next to nothing is known about Codussi's background, save that he may have trained under Giovanni Bon. In 1469, he was appointed *protomagister* (works manager) for the church of **San Michele** (*see p133*). Within ten years he had completed the first truly Renaissance building in the city. The austere Istrian marble façade with its classical elements has something Palladian about it, though the curves of the pediment and buttresses are pure Codussi, adapted from a late Gothic model.

LOMBARDESQUE STYLE

Codussi took over a number of projects begun by Pietro Lombardo, who represents the other strand of early Renaissance architecture in northern Italy. This was based on the extensive use of inlaid polychrome marble, Corinthian columns and decorated friezes. Lombardo's masterpiece is **Santa Maria dei Miracoli** (*see p97*), but he also designed – with his sons – the lower part of the façade of the **Scuola Grande di San Marco** (*see p82*), with its trompe l'oeil relief. The Lombardesque style was all the rage for a while, producing such charmers as tiny, lopsided **Ca' Dario** (1487-92) on the Grand Canal.

HIGH RENAISSANCE

Codussi's influence lingered into the 16th century in the work of architects such as Guglielmo dei Grigi and Scarpagnino, both of whom have been credited with the design of the **Palazzo dei Camerlenghi** (1525-28; *see p55*). Around this time, the construction in piazza San Marco of the **Procuratie Vecchie** (*see p60*) and the **Torre dell'Orologio** (*see p71*), both to designs by Codussi, demonstrated that in the centre of civic power, loyalty to the myth of Venice tended to override architectural fashions.

It was not until the late 1520s that something really new turned up, courtesy of Jacopo Sansovino, a Tuscan sculptor. Perhaps it was the influence of his new-found friends Titian and the poet Pietro Aretino that secured him the prestigious position of *protomagister* of St Mark's only two years after his arrival, despite his lack of experience; Sansovino went on to create a series of buildings that changed the face of the city. He began to refine his rational, harmonious Renaissance style in designs for the church of **San Francesco della Vigna** (begun in 1532; *see p79*) and **Palazzo Corner della Ca' Grande** (*see p58*), Venice's first Roman-style palazzo.

But it was in piazza San Marco that Sansovino surpassed himself. **La Zecca** (*see p72*) – the state mint – with its heavy rustication and four-square solidity, is a perfect financial fortress. The **Biblioteca Marciana** (completed in 1554, also known as the Libreria Sansoviniana; *see p67*) is his masterpiece, disguising its classical regularity beneath a typically Venetian wealth of surface detail. The little **Loggetta** at the base of the Campanile (*see p65*) showed that Sansovino was capable of a lightness of touch.

PALLADIAN PRE-EMINENCE

Michele Sanmicheli built the imposing sea defences on the island of Le Vignole, and two hefty Venetian *palazzi*, the **Palazzo Corner Mocenigo** (1559-64) in campo San Polo and the **Palazzo Grimani di San Luca** (1556-75) on the Grand Canal.

IN CONTEXT

'Loyalty to the myth of Venice tended to override architectural fashions.'

But it was another out-of-towner, Andrea Palladio (*see p280* **Profile**), who would set the agenda for what was left of the 16th century. The man who invented the post-Renaissance found it difficult to get a foothold in a city that valued flexibility above critical rigour. But he did design two influential churches: **San Giorgio Maggiore** (begun in 1562; *see p130*) and the **Redentore** (1577-92; *see p129*). The church of **Le Zitelle** (*see p129*) was built to Palladio's plans after the architect's death.

Palladio's disciple, Vincenzo Scamozzi, designed the **Procuratie Nuove** (*see p60*). At the same time, Antonio Da Ponte was commissioned to design a stone bridge at the **Rialto**, in 1588, after designs by Michelangelo and Palladio had been rejected.

BAROQUE

The examples of Sansovino and Palladio continued to be felt well into the 17th century. It wasn't until the arrival of Baldassare Longhena in the 1620s that Venice got twirly bits in any abundance. Longhena was a local boy who first made his mark with the Duomo in Chioggia. But it was with the church of **Santa Maria della Salute** (*see p123*) that he pulled out all the stops. Commissioned in 1632, and 50 years in the making, this highly theatrical church dominates the southern reaches of the Grand Canal.

Longhena was also busy designing a series of impressive *palazzi*, including the huge Grand Canal hulk of **Ca' Pesaro** (1652; *see p103*). He also designed the façade of the **Ospedaletto** (1667-74; *see p82*), with its grotesque telamons. It was a taste of things to come: the overwrought façade continued to develop in the 1670s, extending from the exuberance of the **Scalzi** (*see p92*) and **Santa Maria del Giglio** (*see p76*) – both by Longhena's follower Giuseppe Scalzi – to the bombast of **San Moisè** (*see p76*), a kitsch collaboration between Alessandro Tremignon and sculptor Heinrich Meyring.

NEOCLASSICISM

During the 18th-century decline, limp variations on Palladio and Longhena dominated the scene. Domenico Rossi adorned Palladian orders with swags and statuary in the façades he designed for the churches of **San Stae** (1709-10; *see p106*) and the **Gesuiti** (1715-28; *see p96*). Sumptuous palaces continued to go up along the Grand Canal; one of the last was the solid **Palazzo Grassi** (*see p75*), built between 1748 and 1772. It was designed by Giorgio Massari, who was also responsible for **La Pietà** (*see p85*) – the Vivaldi church – the oval floorplan of which strikes a rare note of originality. The **Palazzo Venier dei Leoni** – now home to the Peggy Guggenheim Collection (*see p121* **Profile**) – also dates from the mid 18th century. Funds ran out after the first storey, giving Venice one of its most bizarrely endearing landmarks.

Giannantonio Selva's **La Fenice** opera house (1790-92; *see p76*) was one of the Serene Republic's last building projects. Napoleon's arrival in 1797 marked the destruction of many churches and convents, but also began a series of clearances that allowed for the creation of the city's first public park, the **Giardini pubblici** (*see p84*), and the nearby thoroughfare now known as **via Garibaldi**. Piazza San Marco took on its present-day appearance at this time too, when the Procuratie Vecchie and Nuove were united by the neoclassical **Ala Napoleonica**.

Under the Austrian occupation (1815-66), restoration replaced construction, and a railway bridge linking Venice to Mestre (1841-42) was built, ending the city's isolation.

In his influential book the *Stones of Venice* (1853), John Ruskin set out to discredit 'the pestilent art of the Renaissance' in favour of 'healthy and beautiful' Gothic. Such was his clout that the city became an architectural sacred cow, untouchable

Path of Light

The controversial fourth bridge across the Grand Canal.

Santiago Calatrava, the Spanish archi-star, promised his bridge over the Grand Canal would be a shining path of light. Instead, the 12-year gestation of the **Ponte della Costituzione** (aka Ponte di Calatrava) was shrouded in dark storm clouds. Now completed, this fourth span is much-used but much-derided.

The 94-metre (308 feet) construction in steel, glass and Istrian marble links the bus terminus at piazzale Roma with the train station, cutting the time it takes to walk between those two hubs, and so easing the pressure on what had always been a most over-subscribed vaporetto hop. Those holding the city purse strings must have wondered, though, whether this shortcut was worth the €20 million or so it eventually cost – a jaw-dropping increase on the original budget of €4.7 million.

Venetians (and visitors) turned out in their thousands in August 2008 to watch the spectacle of the bridge's single span being shipped along the Grand Canal, passing in a bizarre sort of homage below the existing Accademia (1932), Rialto (1592) and Scalzi (1934) bridges. But the cancellation of a fanfare-filled inauguration ceremony that September, and the subsequent inconspicuous removal of barriers to let punters across, showed that city hall was more sensitive than it had been letting on to the bad feeling surrounding the project. (This didn't stop city hall calling in April 2009 for projects for a complete new-look makeover of the Accademia bridge, to howls of derision.)

The chief bugbear from an early stage had been the fact that the disabled had been disregarded. As this guide went to press, the moving capsule Calatrava had unwillingly agreed to tack on to the side of his creation to carry wheelchair users across had yet to materialise.

Though unquestionably elegant, the bridge is not comfortable to use even for the able-bodied, with its shallow steps that change depth as you cross, forcing you to keep your eyes firmly down. And shallow though the steps may be, they are not sufficiently so to pull a trolley-suitcase up them with any ease. An oversight, surely, for a bridge linking two major transport hubs.

by the unclean hand of innovation. Instead, Venice began to recreate its Gothic and Byzantine past, with exercises such as the **Palazzo Franchetti**, a 15th-century edifice by the Ponte dell'Accademia that was redesigned in neo-medieval style (1878-82).

One of the city's most elegant neo-Gothic works is the **cemetery of San Michele** (1872-81). Another landmark from the period is the **Molino Stucky** (1897-1920; *see p127*), a flour mill on the Giudecca designed in Hanseatic Gothic style by Ernest Wullekopf. The turn of the 20th-century was also a boom time for hotels, with the **Excelsior** on the Lido (1898-1908) setting the eclectic, Moorish-Byzantine agenda.

MODERNITY CATCHES UP

Venice's modern architecture is limited. To date, only locally born modernist Carlo Scarpa (1906-78) has created a body of work: the entrance and garden patio of the **Biennale gardens** (1952; *see p84*), the **Olivetti showroom** (1957-58) in piazza San Marco, the entrance lobby of the IUAV architecture faculty near piazzale Roma and the ground-floor reorganisation of the **Museo Querini Stampalia** (1961-63; *see p78*). Scarpa's student, Mario Botta, has recently overhauled the top-floor exhibition rooms of this last establishment.

The 1970s and '80s brought one or two adventurous public housing projects around outlying areas of the city or lagoon, such as Giancarlo De Carlo's low-income housing on the island of Mazzorbo (1979-86). A new high-tech airport terminal by local architect Giampaolo Mar was inaugurated in summer 2002 and the 70-hectare (170 acres) **Parco di San Giuliano**, designed by Boston-based urban planner Antonio Di Mambro, opened on the mainland by Mestre in 2004. Vittorio Gregotti and others worked on the revamp of industrial areas in north-western Cannaregio, including a former slaughterhouse that now houses the university's economics faculty. Milan's Cino Zucchi reworked the Venetian idiom in housing built around the former Junghans factory on the Giudecca. Japanese superstar Tadao Ando refurbished **Palazzo Grassi** (*see p75*) and the **Punta della Dogana** (*see p124* **The Whole Punta**). And Spain's Santiago Calatrava was responsible for the recently installed fourth bridge across the Grand Canal (*see p45* **Path of Light**).

Projects currently in the pipeline include an extension of the **cemetery at San Michele** by London-based architect David Chipperfield, and the **Venice Gateway** hotel and convention complex by Frank Gehry. Despite all this, an air of foot-dragging and lack of commitment hangs over this new-look Venice.

Cino Zucchi's **ex-Junghans** housing, Giudecca.

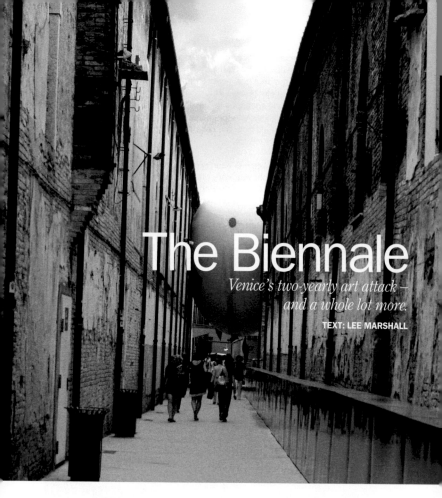

The Biennale

*Venice's two-yearly art attack –
and a whole lot more.*

TEXT: LEE MARSHALL

For many, 'the Biennale' is synonymous with the huge two-yearly contemporary art bonanza hosted in and around the Giardini. In fact, **La Biennale di Venezia** (www.labiennale.org) is a cultural foundation with a far wider mandate, which includes architecture, theatre, music and dance festivals – plus the city's renowned annual film festival.

In terms of visitor numbers and world renown, there's no denying that art and cinema are the Biennale's strongest draws, with architecture trailing a little way behind, and music, theatre and dance bringing up the rear.

Prestigious the Biennale may be, and innovative – for Italy – in attracting financial backing from the private sector, but tough times may place essential state funding under threat. Will keeping the show on the road involve making political compromises?

Attracting over 500,000 annual visitors across its six sections, the Biennale is one of Italy's most influential cultural institutions, though by no means the richest: the film fest, for example, is run on a budget lower than that of the fledgling (and artistically featherweight) Rome film festival. Unusually for Italy, the Biennale has a US-style financial model, mixing sponsorship, public money and income generated from ticket sales and merchandising. Autonomous section directors are not mere political appointees, but are gleaned from the best in their field internationally.

MIXED MEDIA

The *Esposizione Internazionale d'Arte* has been going since 1895, and has attracted healthy controversy pretty much from year one, when an allegorical canvas of cavorting nude women by a certain Giacomo Grosso drew the ire of the Catholic church. It runs each odd year (the next edition is 2011), from June to November. For the international art community, the only days that really count are the three pre-opening days of the vernissage, when Venice becomes a mecca for back-slapping, air-kissing artists, curators, gallery owners, collectors and all the lesser woodland fauna of the art world.

A strange mix of the conceptual and the jingoistic, the **Art Biennale**'s nerve centre is a corner of the *giardini pubblici* (public gardens, often called the Giardini della Biennale; *see p84*) where 30 national pavilions nestle amid shrubberies and flowerbeds. Each country chooses an artist or artists to showcase – though the enormous Italian pavilion has traditionally housed a thematic show as well as the local contingent. Another curated international show takes place in the former ropewalk and munitions store of the Arsenale (*see p84*).

Have-not nations – without pavilions in the Giardini – hire exhibition spaces in historic Venice; there were 47 of these in 2009. As a result, 'doing' the Art Biennale, even in the most superficial fashion, is a two-day task at least. Recent curators of the Biennale's central themed shows include Spanish duo (and the first ever women to hold the job) Maria de Corral and Rosa Martínez (2005); Yale School of Art dean Robert Storr (2007); and Swedish writer, theorist and teacher Daniel Birnbaum (2009).

The **Architecture Biennale**, which has taken place in most even years since 1980 in the same time slot and some of the same venues, is conditioned by the fact that it is rarely the work itself on display. Curators get around this problem in different ways, some more concept-driven, some more in pop-charts mode. There are inevitably a lot of plans, renderings and 3-D models to digest, and the event tends to play to a more specialised audience. Nevertheless, almost 130,000 people visited the 2008 edition.

Watershed by Mike Bouchet at the 2009 Art Biennale.

The **Music, Theatre** and **Dance Biennali** (*see p243*) are not so much unmissable international appointments as a great opportunity for Venetians and lucky visitors to see some quality concerts and performances. Each is annual, spreading out over a month or so – Theatre generally in February/March, Dance in May/June, and Music in September/October – with events taking place in the Teatro Goldoni (*see p239*) and other city venues.

THE SEVENTH ART

The *Mostra Internazionale d'Arte Cinematografica* (aka the **Venice International Film Festival**; *see p222*) is the odd one out among the Biennale's six children, not least because it's held on the Lido, the city's sleepy seaside 'burb. Most of those who attend assume that the festival is an independent entity – and, in a way, they're right. Though it depends for its budget on the Biennale, the film fest is run along the same lines as Cannes or Berlin – by an artistic director advised by a network of selectors and scouts around the globe.

Current director Marco Mueller is a smart, cultured Swiss-Italian cineaste, veteran festival organiser and producer. He has kept Venice in a strong second place in the European Big Three, behind Cannes but a short head in front of Berlin, with an insistence on world premières (among them *Brokeback Mountain* in 2005, *The Queen* in 2006 and *I'm Not There* in 2007), privileged access to some important Asian directors (including anime giants like Hideo Miyazaki) and the luck of his time slot: ten days from late August, perfect for previewing the autumn Oscar contenders and prestige arthouse brigade.

Mueller's initial four-year mandate was renewed in 2008. But the vote of confidence comes at a difficult time for the film festival. The new, €70 million **Palazzo del Cinema**, designed by French architect Rudy Ricciotti and the Italian 5+1AA Studio, should be ready in time for the 2011 edition – which means that the 2009 and 2010 festivals will take place on the edge of a construction site. Both Cannes and Berlin have major film markets, whereas Venice focuses more on critics and film-lovers – making visitor numbers more vulnerable to financial downturns, especially given the price of accommodation on the Lido. And, in recent years, the exponential growth of the Toronto festival – which overlaps with Venice at the beginning of September – has kept many potential North American visitors at home.

THE ART OF POLITICS

Still, Biennale chairman Paolo Baratta, a former banker and government minister, currently in his second stint at the head of the Foundation, is a canny and determined cultural diplomat who knows how to defend his pitch. He has already negotiated important agreements with the Italian navy and Venice city council for the permanent use of the Art Biennale's main venues.

One consequence of this is that after years of discussion, the Art Biennale section of the Giardini – which has always been closed to the public in the 18 months between shows – is to become a year-round exhibition space. This will focus on the renovated **Palazzo delle Esposizioni** (the former Italian Pavilion), with interiors designed by three of the 2009 edition's featured artists: Massimo Bartolini, Tobias Rehberger and Rirkrit Tiravanija.

Art budget cuts by Silvio Berlusconi's proudly lowbrow government have so far spared the Biennale. One hopes that the price isn't increased political interference. The signs are not good: in April 2009, anti-Left Culture Minister Sandro Bondi extracted a promise from Baratta and Mueller to find a slot in the 2009 film festival for Polish director Andre Wajda's *Katyn* – which had already screened at the Berlin festival in 2008 (thus making it a title that Venice wouldn't normally touch). The reason? Because the minister was 'shocked' that a film that portrayed 'one of the most savage massacres ever perpetrated by the Communists' had only been released on seven of Italy's 4,000 screens.

Whatever your carbon footprint, we can reduce it

For over a decade we've been leading the way in carbon offsetting and carbon management.

In that time we've purchased carbon credits from over 200 projects spread across 6 continents. We work with over 300 major commercial clients and thousands of small and medium sized businesses, which rely upon our market-leading quality assurance programme, our experience and absolute commitment to deliver the right solution for each client.

Why not give us a call?

T: London (020) 7833 6000

Sights

Ponte della Costituzione. *See p54.*

The Grand Canal	**52**
San Marco	**60**
City of Music	68
Wet & Dry	72
Castello	**77**
Walk In Vivaldi's Footsteps	81
The Well-heads of Venice	86
Cannaregio	**88**
Sleeping in Turns	93
San Polo & Santa Croce	**98**
Back to School	105
Literary Venice	108

Dorsoduro	**113**
Profile Peggy Guggenheim	
Collection	121
The Whole Punta	124
La Giudecca & San Giorgio	**127**
Bags, Rags & Veg	128
Lido & Lagoon	**131**
Music of the Islands	135
Murano Glass	136

The Grand Canal

Like nothing else on the planet – this is why you came to Venice.

The **Grand Canal** may no longer be teeming with merchandise-laden cargo boats, but it is still the main thoroughfare of Venice, and only a little imagination is needed to understand its historical importance. The three and a half kilometre (two-mile) trip from the railway station to San Marco provides a superb introduction to the city, telling you more about the way Venice works – and has always worked – than any

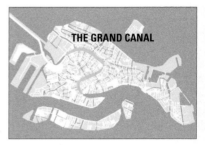

THE GRAND CANAL

historical tome. Every family of note had to have a palazzo here, and this was not just for reasons of social snobbery. The *palazzi* are undeniably splendid but they were first and foremost solid commercial enterprises, and their designs are as practical as they are eye-catching.

SIGHTS

HISTORY & ARCHITECTURE

Most of the notable buildings on the canal were built between the 12th and 18th centuries. When a family decided to rebuild a palazzo, they usually maintained the same basic structure – for the good reason that they could use the same foundations. This resulted in some interesting style hybrids: the Grand Canal offers several examples of *palazzi* in which Veneto-Byzantine or Gothic features are incorporated into the Renaissance or Baroque. Each palazzo typically had a main water-entrance opening on to a large hall with storage space on either side; a *mezzanino* with offices; a piano nobile (main floor – sometimes two in grander buildings) consisting of a spacious reception hall lit by large central windows and flanked on both sides by residential rooms; and a land entrance at the back. Over the centuries, architectural frills and trimmings were added, but the underlying form was stable – and, as always in Venice, it is form that follows function.

In the following description of the most notable *palazzi*, many names recur, for the simple reason that families expanded, younger sons inheriting as well as older ones. Compound

names indicate that the palazzo passed through various hands over time. Originally the term 'palazzo' was reserved for the Doge's Palace. Other *palazzi* were known as *Casa* ('house') or *Ca'* for short: this is still true of some of the older ones, such as Ca' d'Oro (*see p91*).

This chapter deals mainly with canal-side *palazzi*. Churches and museums facing on to the canal are covered elsewhere in the guide (cross references are given). The itinerary on these next pages is best followed from the rear deck of a vaporetto, looking backwards as you make your way from piazzale Roma or the train station (Ferrovia) towards St Mark's square.

INSIDE TRACK
KNOW YOUR VAPORETTI

Though even the locals tend to lump them together, not all Venetian passenger ferries are, strictly speaking, *vaporetti*. A **vaporetto** is a larger, slower and more rounded 230-passenger boat; older models have much sought-after outside seats at the front. It plies routes along the Grand Canal. The 160-passenger **motoscafo** is sleeker, smaller and faster, with outside seats only at the back. It's used on routes encircling the island. **Motonave** are larger (600-1,200 people), double-decker steamers that cross the lagoon regally to the Lido.

About the author

Gregory Dowling teaches American Literature at Venice University and is the author of four thrillers. His most recent publication is a guidebook to Byron's Venice.

RIGHT BANK

From piazzale Roma to the Salute

Vaporetto stop Piazzale Roma

The first notable sight is the new bridge over the Grand Canal, linking the car park to the train station. Officially named the **Ponte della Costituzione**, it is still known to most Venetians as Ponte Calatrava, after its designer, the Spanish architect-superstar Santiago Calatrava (see *p45* **Path of Light**). Its single, elegantly curving arch is constructed of steel, and the pavement is in the traditional Venetian materials of glass and Istrian stone.

Before the Scalzi bridge is the church of **San Simeone Piccolo**, with its high green dome and Corinthian portico. For those arriving in Venice it's a picturesque introduction to the city.

The **Ponte degli Scalzi**, which leads across to the station, was built in stone by Eugenio Miozzi in 1934.

Vaporetto stop Riva di Biasio

Just before the rio del Megio stands the **Fondaco dei Turchi**, a 19th-century reconstruction of the original Veneto-Byzantine building, which was leased to Turkish traders in the 17th century as a residence and warehouse. Some of the original material was used but the effect as a whole is one of pastiche. Once lived in by the poet Torquato Tasso, it's now the **Museo di Storia Naturale** (see *p104*).

The **Depositi del Megio** (state granaries) have a battlemented, plain-brick façade. The sculpted lion is a modern replacement of the original, destroyed at the fall of the Republic.

The church of **San Stae** (see *p106*) has a Baroque façade by Domenico Rossi, with exuberant sculpture.

LEFT BANK

From the railway station to San Marco

Vaporetto stop Ferrovia

At the foot of the Ponte degli Scalzi is the fine Baroque façade of the **Scalzi** church (see *p92*).

Unusually narrow **Palazzo Flangini** is a 17th-century building by Giuseppe Sardi. It owes its shape to the simple fact that the family's money ran out. Just before the wide Cannaregio Canal is the church of **San Geremia**; from the Grand Canal, the apse of the chapel of **Santa Lucia** is visible.

Standing with its main façade on the Cannaregio Canal is **Palazzo Labia**, the 18th-century home of the seriously rich Labia family. The story goes that parties ended with the host throwing his gold dinner plates into the canal to demonstrate his wealth; the servants would then be ordered to fish them out again. The building is now the regional headquarters of the RAI (the Italian state broadcaster). It contains suitably sumptuous frescoes by Tiepolo.

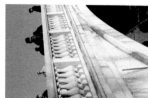

Vaporetto stop San Marcuola

The next building of note is **Palazzo Vendramin Calergi**, an impressive Renaissance palazzo designed by Mauro Codussi in the first decade of the 16th century. It uses his characteristic arched windows incorporating twin smaller arches; porphyry insets decorate the façade. Wagner died here in 1883. It now houses the Venice **Casinò**.

A fairly uneventful stretch ends at the **Ca' d'Oro** (see p91), the most gorgeously ornate Gothic building on the Grand Canal. Yet it is now sober compared with its original appearance, when its decorative features were gilded or painted in ultramarine blue and cinnabar red. It has an open loggia on the piano nobile, like the Doge's Palace, but unlike any other post-Byzantine palazzo.

Vaporetto stop Ca' d'Oro

Just before the rio dei Santi Apostoli is **Palazzo Mangilli Valmarana**, built in 1751 for Joseph Smith, the British consul, who amassed the huge collection of Canaletto paintings that now belongs to the Queen. It now houses the Argentinian Consulate.

Beyond the rio dei Santissimi Apostoli stands the **Ca' da Mosto**, once the site of the Leon Bianco (white lion) Hotel. This is one of the earliest Veneto-Byzantine *palazzi* on the Grand Canal. It still has three of the original five arches of its water-entrance and a long array of Byzantine arches on the first floor.

At the foot of the Rialto bridge is the **Fondaco dei Tedeschi**, a huge residence-cum-warehouse leased to the German community from the 13th century onwards. The present building was designed by Spavento and Scarpagnino in 1505-08 after a fire. The façade once had glorious frescoes by Titian and Giorgione – now in a sad state of repair in the Ca' d'Oro gallery (see p91). The Fondaco – for the time being, still the main post office – was bought by the Benetton group in 2008.

Vaporetto stop San Stae

On the rio di Ca' Pesaro, and with a magnificent side wall curving along the canal in gleaming marble, is **Ca' Pesaro** (see p103), a splendid example of Venetian Baroque by Longhena. After two smaller *palazzi* stands the **Palazzo Corner della Regina**, with a rusticated ground floor featuring grotesque masks, some just above water level. It was built for a branch of the Corner family, who were descended from Caterina Cornaro, Queen of Cyprus; Caterina was born in an earlier house on the site. The present palazzo dates from the 1720s.

The covered fish market, or **Pescaria**, has occupied a site here since the 14th century. The current neo-Gothic construction was built in 1907, replacing an iron one. Beyond this is a building with a parade of arches along the canal; this is the longest façade on the Grand Canal and belongs to Sansovino's **Fabbriche Nuove**, built in 1554-56 for Venice's financial judiciary; it now houses the Court of Assizes. Just beyond this stands the **Fabbriche Vecchie** by Scarpagnino, built after a fire in the early 16th century.

Vaporetto stop Rialto Mercato

Before the Rialto bridge, the **Palazzo dei Camerlenghi** (1523-25) is built around the curve of the canal; the walls lean noticeably. It was the headquarters of the Venetian Exchequer, with a debtors' prison on the ground floor.

RIGHT BANK

The **Ponte di Rialto** was built in 1588-92, to a design by aptly named Antonio Da Ponte. Until the 19th century, it was the only bridge over the Grand Canal. It replaced a wooden one, which can be seen in Carpaccio's painting of *The Miracle of the True Cross* in the Accademia. After the decision was taken to build it, 60 years passed, during the course of which designs by Michelangelo, Vignola, Sansovino and Palladio were rejected. Da Ponte's simple but effective project eventually went ahead, probably because it kept the utilitarian features of the previous structure, with its double row of shops. The bridge thus acts as a continuation of the market at its foot. Palladio's design was more beautiful, but made no provision for the sale of plastic gondolas.

Vaporetto stop San Silvestro

Beyond the San Silvestro vaporetto stop are a few houses with Veneto-Byzantine windows and decorations, including **Ca' Barzizza**, one of the earliest Byzantine houses in Venice. Before the rio San Polo is the 16th-century **Palazzo Cappello Layard**, once the home of Sir Henry Austen Layard, archaeologist and British ambassador to Constantinople.

A little way before the San Tomà stop is the **Palazzo Pisani Moretta**, a large Gothic palazzo of the 15th century, often hired out for parties.

Ponte di Rialto

LEFT BANK

Between the bridge and the Rialto vaporetto stop is **Palazzo Manin Dolfin**, with a portico straddling the *fondamenta*. The façade is by Sansovino (late 1530s); the rest was rebuilt by Ludovico Manin, the forlorn last doge of Venice (*see p26*). It now belongs to the Bank of Italy.

Vaporetto stop Rialto

Palazzetto Dandolo is a Gothic building that appears to have been squeezed tight by its neighbours. Enrico Dandolo, the blind doge who led the ferocious assault on Constantinople in 1204 (*see p19*) was born in an earlier palazzo that stood on this site. **Palazzo Farsetti** and **Palazzo Loredan** are Veneto-Byzantine buildings that now house the city hall and various municipal offices. Though heavily restored, these two adjoining *palazzi* are among the few surviving examples of the 12th-century Venetian house, with its first-floor polyforate window.

Palazzo Grimani is one of the largest *palazzi* on the Grand Canal. Its creator, Michele Sanmicheli, was famous for his military architecture, and this building is characteristically massive and assertive. The Grimani family were nouveaux riches, and wanted each one of their windows to be larger than the front door of the palazzo that used to stand opposite.

Seven *palazzi* further on, before the rio Michiel, stands the pink **Palazzo Benzon**, home of Countess Marina Querini-Benzon, a great society figure at the end of the 18th century. Byron was charmed by her when she was already in her sixties. She inspired a popular song, '*La biondina in gondoleta*', which the gondoliers used to sing before international tourism imposed the Neapolitan '*O' Sole Mio*'.

Before the Sant'Angelo vaporetto stop is the small-scale **Palazzo Corner**, built in the last decade of the 15th century by Mauro Codussi. It is one of the most beautiful early Renaissance buildings in Venice, with a rusticated ground floor, elegant balconies and the characteristic double-arched windows.

Vaporetto stop Sant'Angelo

A little beyond the traghetto (see p296) station for San Tomà stand the four **Palazzi Mocenigo**, with blue and white poles in the water. The central double palazzo (16th century) was where Byron and his menagerie of foxes, monkeys and dogs lived in 1818-19; he wrote to a friend: 'Venice is not an expensive residence… I have my gondola and about 14 servants… and I reside in one of the Mocenigo palaces on the Grand Canal; the rent… is two hundred a year (and I gave more than I need have done)'.

Just before the San Samuele vaporetto stop is heavy, grey-white **Palazzo Grassi** (see p75), designed by Giorgio Massari. This was the last of the great patrician *palazzi*, built in 1748-72 when the city was already in terminal decline. Acquired by Fiat in the 1980s, it was sold again in 2005 to French magnate Francois Pinault and functions as a gallery.

Vaporetto stop San Tomà

Palazzo Balbi (1582-90), whose obelisks are an indication that an admiral lived here, is the seat of the Veneto Regional Council. Looking down the rio Ca' Foscari, you can see the archways of the city's fire station. (Further away, rio Ca' Foscari becomes the rio Novo, a canal dug in the 1930s to provide a short cut to the car park and station; traffic rocked the foundations of the buildings along the canal, so public transport stopped using the rio Novo in the 1980s.) Between the fire station and Palazzo Balbi is a minor building, on a site once scheduled to hold Frank Lloyd Wright's Centre for Foreign Architectural Students. In the end, his designs were judged too radical for so conspicuous a spot.

Just beyond the rio Ca' Foscari come three magnificent mid 15th-century Gothic *palazzi*. The first and largest is **Ca' Foscari**. It was here that Henry III of France was lavishly entertained in 1574 – so lavishly that his reason seems to have been knocked permanently askew. Doge Francesco Foscari died here of a broken heart after being ousted from office. The palazzo is now the headquarters of Venice's Università Ca' Foscari.

The next two buildings are the **Palazzi Giustinian**; Wagner stayed in one of them in the winter of 1858-59, composing part of *Tristan and Isolde*. The horn prelude to the third act was inspired by the mournful cries of the gondoliers.

Ca' Rezzonico (currently being restored; see p117) is a Baroque masterpiece by Longhena, begun in 1667 for the Bon family, then sold to the Rezzonico family. Robert Browning died here, while staying with his profitably married but otherwise talentless son Pen, who bought the palazzo with his wife's money. Later guests included Whistler and Cole Porter. The building now contains the museum of 18th-century Venice.

Vaporetto stop Ca' Rezzonico

Just after the Ca' Rezzonico stop is the 15th-century **Palazzo Loredan**. The **Gallerie dell'Accademia**, once the church and monastery of Santa Maria della Carità, now holds an unrivalled collection of Venetian art (see p122).

Vaporetto stop Accademia

In 1932, the iron **Ponte dell'Accademia** that had been built by the Austrians was replaced by a 'temporary' wooden one. When this was discovered to be on the point of collapse in 1984, the Venetians had grown too fond of it to imagine anything else spanning the canal, so it was rebuilt exactly as before.

After the Accademia four fine Renaissance *palazzi* comes campo San Vio, one of the few *campi* on the Grand Canal. In the corner is the Anglican church of **St George** (*see p303*). To one side of the campo is the 16th-century **Palazzo Barbarigo**, with eye-catching but tacky 19th-century mosaics.

Next is the pretty Gothic **Palazzo da' Mula**.

A little beyond that is the single-storey **Palazzo Venier dei Leoni**. Work ground to a halt in 1749 when the family opposite objected to their light being blocked by such a huge pile. Art collector Peggy Guggenheim lived here from 1949 to 1979: she was the last person in Venice to have her own private gondola. The building now contains the **Peggy Guggenheim Collection** (*see p121* **Profile**).

Next-but-one comes the pure, lopsided charm of the Renaissance **Ca' Dario**, built in the 1470s, perhaps by Pietro Lombardo, with decorative use of coloured marbles and chimney pots. Venetians say the palazzo is cursed: certainly the list of former owners who have met sticky ends is impressive. **Palazzo Salviati** is a 19th-century building with gaudy mosaics advertising the products of the Salviati glass works.

Vaporetto stop San Samuele

A short way beyond the stop, the **Ca' del Duca** incorporates, in one corner, a part of the rusticated base and columns of a palace that Bartolomeo Bon was going to build for the Cornaro family. In 1461, the site was bought by Francesco Sforza, Duke of Milan; Bon's project was never completed.

At the foot of the Accademia bridge is **Palazzo Franchetti**, built in the 15th century but much restored and altered in the 19th; it's now used as a conference centre and for exhibitions.

Immediately beyond this are two **Palazzi Barbaro**, which have literary associations. The first one – 15th-century Gothic, with a fine but battered Renaissance water-entrance – still partly belongs to the Curtis family, who played host to Henry James at intervals between 1870 and 1875. The building was the model for Milly Theale's palazzo in *The Wings of the Dove*.

Just before one of the few Grand Canal gardens comes the bashful **Casetta delle Rose**, set back behind its own small trellised garden. Canova had a studio here; novelist Gabriele D'Annunzio once stayed in the house.

The massive rusticated ground floor of the **Palazzo Corner della Ca' Grande** (now the Prefecture) influenced Longhena's Baroque *palazzi*. The highest of High Renaissance, the imposing pile was commissioned in 1537 from Sansovino for Giacomo Cornaro, and built after 1545. Never one to mince words, Ruskin called it 'one of the worst and coldest buildings of the central Renaissance.'

Ponte dell'
Accademia

The former abbey of **San Gregorio** –now a luxury hotel – is the last building before the Salute stop, with a fine 14th-century relief of St Gregory over a Gothic doorway. (Beyond can be seen the apse of the former church of the same name.)

Vaporetto stop Salute

In a triumphant position, at the opening of the Grand Canal, stands the wonderfully curvy church of **Santa Maria della Salute** (*see p123*), Baldassare Longhena's audacious Baroque creation (1671) took 50 years to build. Every year on 21 November (*see p216*) a procession from the basilica di San Marco makes its way across a specially-erected bridge of boats to the church. Beyond the church is the Patriarchal Seminary.

The left bank ends at Punta della Dogana (Customs Point) with its complex of customs-related buildings: the extensive warehouses, which date from the 19th century and are now a major new contemporary art gallery (*see p124* **The Whole Punta**); and the **Dogana di Mare** (Customs House, 1677), with its tower, gilded ball, weathervane figure of Fortune and spectacular view out across the Bacino di San Marco towards the Lido. Ships wanting to enter Venice would have their cargoes examined here by customs officials.

Vaporetto stop Giglio

After campo Santa Maria del Giglio comes the 15th-century Gothic façade of **Palazzo Gritti**, now one of Venice's poshest hotels (*see p145*). Three *palazzi* further on is the narrow Gothic **Palazzo Contarini Fasan**, traditionally, but quite arbitrarily, known as Desdemona's house. It has beautiful balconies with wheel tracery.

The **Europa & Regina** hotel was once the home of Kay Bronson, an American society hostess whose hospitality was much appreciated by Henry James.

The last notable building is **Ca' Giustinian**, built in the late Gothic style of the 1470s, and once a hotel where Verdi, Gautier, Ruskin and Proust stayed. George Eliot's honeymoon here was ruined when her husband fell (or threw himself) off the balcony into the Grand Canal. Recently restored, it houses the offices of the Biennale (*see pp47-49*).

At the corner of calle Vallaresso is the self-effacing **Harry's Bar** (*see p185*), the near-legendary Venetian watering hole, founded by Arrigo Cipriani senior in the 1930s.

Vaporetto stop San Marco Vallaresso

Just beyond the vaporetto stop lie the pretty **Giardinetti Reali** (*see p61*) and **piazza San Marco** (*see p60*).

San Marco

Explore the corridors leading from the 'drawing room of Europe'.

Napoleon referred to **piazza San Marco** as the 'drawing room of Europe', a description that catches some of its quality: it may not be homely, but it is a supremely civilised meeting place. At times it appears that much of Europe's population is crammed into this great square, at which point the narrow *calli* that wind their way out of it become very enticing.

Three main thoroughfares link the key points of this neighbourhood: one runs from piazza San Marco to the **Rialto bridge**, one from the Rialto to the **Accademia bridge**, and one from the Accademia back to piazza San Marco. For a respite from the jostling crowds, wander off these routes; even in this most tourist-packed *sestiere* you can always find little havens of purely Venetian calm.

SAN MARCO

Map pp323-324	**Restaurants** p165
Hotels p145	**Cafés & Bars** p183

SIGHTS

PIAZZA SAN MARCO & AROUND

Vaporetto San Marco Vallaresso or San Zaccaria.

In magnificent piazza San Marco, Byzantine rubs shoulders with Gothic, late Renaissance and neoclassical. The Venetians have always kept the square clear of monuments (on occasion stooping to mendacity to do so – as with the monument to Bartolomeo Colleoni; *see p78*). This is typical of Venice, where individual glory always plays second fiddle to the common weal.

The north side of the square dates from the early 16th century. Its arches repeat a motif suggested by an earlier Byzantine structure (seen in Gentile Bellini's painting *Translation of the Relics of the Cross* in the Accademia; *see p122*). Here resided the procurators of St Mark's, who were in charge of maintaining the basilica – hence the name of this whole wing, the Procuratie Vecchie. At its eastern end is the **Torre dell'Orologio** (*see p71*).

Construction of the Procuratie Nuove, opposite, went on for most of the first half of the 17th century, to designs by Vincenzo Scamozzi. Napoleon joined the two wings at the far end – not for the sake of symmetry, but in order to create the ballroom that was lacking in the Procuratie Nuove, which had become the imperial residence. So, in 1807, down came Sansovino's church of San Geminiano and up went the Ala Napoleonica, which now houses the **Museo Correr** (*see p66*).

The **Campanile** (*see p65*) and **Basilica di San Marco** (*see p61*) close off the square in all its splendour to the east.

North of the basilica lies the **piazza dei Leoncini**, a small square named after two small marble lions rubbed smooth by generations of children's bottoms. The large palazzo at the far end of the square is the 19th-century residence of the patriarch (cardinal) of Venice.

Between the basilica and the lagoon, the **Piazzetta** is the real entrance to Venice, defined by two free-standing columns of granite. What appears to be a winged lion on top of the eastern column is in fact a chimera from Persia, Syria or maybe China; the wings and book are Venetian additions. St Theodore, who tops the other one, was Venice's first patron saint. Foreign visitors used to disembark here, and were dazzled by the pomp and magnificence. The area directly in front of the **Palazzo Ducale** (Doge's Palace; *see p67*) corresponded to the modern-day parliamentary lobby. Known as the *broglio*, it was the place where councillors conferred and connived (hence the term 'imbroglio'). Opposite the palace stands the **Biblioteca Marciana** (*see p67*), now the main city library.

West of the Piazzetta are the **Giardinetti Reali** (Royal Gardens), created by the French. The dainty neoclassical coffee house by Gustavo Selva is now a tourist information office (*see p305*). By the San Marco Vallaresso vaporetto stop is Harry's Bar (*see p185*), the most famous watering hole in the city, founded in the 1920s and made legendary by Ernest Hemingway, Orson Welles and a round of other famous drinkers.

Heading east from the Piazzetta, you will cross the **ponte della Paglia** (Bridge of Straw). If you can elbow your way to the side of the bridge, there is a photo-op view of the **ponte dei Sospiri** (**Bridge of Sighs**; being restored at the time of writing). From the Bridge of Straw there is also a superb view of the Renaissance façade of the Palazzo Ducale.

TICKETS & PASSES

The museums around piazza San Marco (but not the paying parts of the basilica) can only be visited on a multi-entrance ticket. The full-price Musei di Piazza San Marco ticket costs €12 (€6.50 reductions) and can be bought at the sights themselves. For more information on museum passes, *see p6* **Package Deals**.

★ FREE Basilica di San Marco

San Marco, piazza San Marco (041 522 5205). Vaporetto San Marco Vallaresso or San Zaccaria. **Open** *Basilica, Chancel & Pala d'Oro, Treasury* 9.45am-4.45pm Mon-Sat; 2-5pm Sun. *Loggia & Museo Marciano* 9.45am-4pm daily. **Admission** *Basilica* free. *Chancel & Pala d'Oro* €2; €1 reductions. *Treasury* €3; €1.50 reductions. *Loggia & Museo Marciano* €4; €2 reductions. **No credit cards. Map** p324 J7.

Note: large bags or rucksacks must be deposited (free) in a building in calle San Basso, off the piazzetta dei Leoncini. The basilica is open for mass and private prayer from 7-9.45am, with entrance from the piazzetta dei Leoncini door.

Often seen as the living testimony of Venice's links with Byzantium, St Mark's basilica is also an expression of the city's independence. In the Middle Ages any self-respecting city state had to have a truly important holy relic. So when two Venetian merchants swiped the body of St Mark (though some historians believe they got Alexander the Great's remains by mistake, a theme developed by Steve Berry in his 2007 novel *The Venetian Betrayal*) from Alexandria in 828, concealed from prying Muslim eyes under a protective layer of pork, they were going for the very best – an Evangelist, and an entire body at that. Fortunately, there was a legend (or one was quickly cooked up) that the saint had once been caught in the lagoon in a storm, and so it was fitting that this should be his final resting place.

The Venetians were traders, but they never looked askance at a bit of straightforward looting as well. The basilica – like the city as a whole – is encrusted with trophies brought back from Venice's greatest spoliatory exploit, the Sack of Constantinople in 1204, during the free-for-all that went under the name of the Fourth Crusade.

The present basilica is the third on the site. It was built mainly between 1063 and 1094, although

Piazza San Marco.

SIGHTS

Hellovenezia

OLTRE LA RETE, L'ESPERIENZA.

At the Hellovenezia ticket points, you will find:

TICKETS FOR EVENTS

Purchase tickets for the most important events.

Hellovenezia è un Marchio / Trademark vela

Information
: www.hellovenezia.com
: call center (+39) 041 24 24

the work of decoration continued until the 16th century. The church only became Venice's cathedral in 1807, ten years after the fall of the Republic; until then the bishop exerted his authority from San Pietro in Castello (see p87).

Next door to the Palazzo Ducale, Venice's most important church was associated with political as much as spiritual power. Venetians who came to worship here were very aware that they were guests of the doge, not the pope.

Exterior

The first view of the basilica from the western end of piazza San Marco is an unforgettable experience. It is particularly impressive in the evening, when the mosaics on the façade glow in the light of the setting sun (as they are mostly 17th- and 18th-century replacements, the distance improves them). The façade consists of two orders of five arches, with clusters of columns in the lower order; the upper arches are topped by fantastic Gothic tracery.

The only original mosaic (c1260) is the one over the northernmost door, *The Translation of the Body of St Mark to the Basilica*, which is the earliest known representation of the church. Of curiosity value is the 17th-century mosaic over the southernmost door, which shows the body of St Mark being filched from Alexandria and the Muslims reeling back in disgust from its pork wrapping.

The real treasures on show are the sculptures, particularly the group of three carved arches around the central portal, a Romaneque masterpiece. The inner curve of the outer arch is the liveliest, with its detailed portrayals of Venetian trades, arts, crafts and pastimes. The upper order, with fine 14th-century Gothic sculpture by the Dalle Masegne brothers and later Tuscan and Lombard sculptors, can be seen from the Loggia.

Visible through the doors, the narthex (covered porch) has an opus sectile marble floor; a small lozenge of porphyry by the central door is said to mark the spot where the Emperor Barbarossa paid homage to Pope Alexander III in 1177. The influence of Islamic art comes through in the few remaining grilles that cover the wall niches where early doges were buried. Above, a series of 13th-century mosaics in the Byzantine style shows Old Testament scenes.

The south façade, towards the Palazzo Ducale, was the first side seen by visitors arriving by sea and is thus richly encrusted with trophies proclaiming *La Serenissima*'s might. There was a ceremonial entrance to the basilica here as well, but this was blocked by the construction of the Zen Chapel (see p64) in the 16th century. At the corner by the Doge's Palace stand the Tetrarchs, a fourth-century porphyry group of four conspiratorial-looking kings. These come from Constantinople and are usually accepted as representing Diocletian and his Imperial colleagues. However, popular lore has it that they are four Saracens turned to stone after an attempt to burgle the Treasury.

The two free-standing pillars in front of the Baptistry door, with Syrian carvings from the fifth century, come from Acre, as does the stumpy porphyry column on the corner, known as the Pietra del Bando, where official decrees were read.

The north façade, facing piazzetta dei Leoncini, is also studded with loot, including the carving of 12 sheep on either side of a throne bearing a cross, a seventh-century Byzantine work. Note the beautiful 13th-century Moorish arches of the Porta dei Fiori, which enclose a Nativity scene.

Interior

A lifetime would hardly suffice to see everything contained in this cave of wonders. The lambent interior exudes splendour and mystery, even when bursting with tourists. The basilica is Greek cross in form, surmounted by five great 11th-century domes. The surfaces are totally covered by more than four square kilometres (1.5 square miles) of mosaics, the result of 600 years of labour. The finest pieces, dating from the 12th and 13th centuries, are the work of Venetian craftsmen influenced by Byzantine art but developing their own independent style. The chapels and Baptistry were decorated in the 14th and 15th centuries; a century later, replacements of earlier mosaics were made using cartoons by such artists as Titian and Tintoretto. However, most of these later mosaics are flawed by the attempt to achieve the three-dimensional effects of Renaissance painting.

In the apse, *Christ Pantocrator* is a 16th-century reproduction of a Byzantine original. Beneath, in what may be the oldest mosaics in the church, are four saint-protectors of Venice: Nicholas, Peter, Mark and Hermagoras. The central dome of the Ascension, with its splendidly poised angels and apostles, dates from the early 13th century. The Passion scenes on the west vault (12th century) are a striking blend of Romanesque and Byzantine styles. The Pentecost dome (near the entrance) was probably the first to be decorated; it shows the *Descent of the Holy Spirit*. Four magnificent angels hover in the pendentives.

In the right transept is the *Miraculous Rediscovery of the Body of St Mark*: this refers to an episode that occurred after the second basilica was destroyed by fire, when the secret of the whereabouts of the

SIGHTS

INSIDE TRACK
CURSED COLUMNS

The man who erected the two columns in the **Piazzetta** (see p60) in the 12th century asked for the right to set up gambling tables between them. The authorities agreed, but soon put a damper on the jollity by using the pillars to string up criminals. Superstitious locals still avoid walking between them.

SIGHTS

body was lost. The Evangelist obligingly opened up the pillar where his sarcophagus had been hidden (it's just opposite and is marked by an inlaid marble panel). Notice, too, the gorgeous 12th-century marble, porphyry and glass mosaics on the floor.

Baptistry & Zen Chapel

The Baptistry contains the Gothic tomb of Doge Andrea Dandolo and some interesting mosaics, including an image of Salome dancing. In the adjoining Zen Chapel is the bronze 16th-century tomb of Cardinal Zen (a common Venetian surname). The baptistry and chapel are very rarely open.

Chancel & Pala d'Oro

The Chancel is separated from the body of the church by the iconostasis – a red marble rood screen by the Gothic sculptors Jacobello and Pier Paolo Dalle Masegne, with fine statues of the Madonna, the apostles and St George. Access to the Chancel is via the San Clemente chapel to the right, with a mosaic showing merchants Rustico di Torcello and Buono di Malamocco, apparently about to FedEx the body of St Mark to Venice. St Mark's sarcophagus is visible through the grate underneath the altar. It was moved here from the 11th-century crypt in 1835; the crypt remains a popular venue for society weddings, though it's closed to the rest of us.

The indigestibly opulent *Pala d'Oro* (Gold Altarpiece) is a Byzantine work and, for a change, was acquired honestly. It was made in Constantinople in 976 on the orders of Doge Pietro Orseolo I and further enriched in later years with amethysts, emeralds, pearls, rubies, sapphires and topaz, topped off with a Gothic frame and resetting in 1345. It's a worldly corner of the church, this. Set in the frame of the

Basilica di San Marco. *See p61.*

look to them. They are mostly by Michele Giambono, although some of the figures have been attributed to Jacopo Bellini and to the Florentine Andrea del Castagno, who was in Venice in 1432.

Loggia & Museo Marciano
Of all the pay-to-enter sections of the basilica, this is definitely the most worthwhile – and it's the only part of the church you can visit on Sunday morning. Up a narrow stairway from the narthex are the bronze horses that vie with the lion of St Mark as the city's symbol; here, too, is Paolo Veneziano's exquisite *Pala Feriale*, a painted panel that was used to cover the *Pala d'Oro* on weekdays. The Loggia also provides a marvellous view over the square.

The original bronze horses are now kept indoors. They were among the many treasures brought back from the Sack of Constantinople, where they had stood above the city's Hippodrome. For many years they were attributed to a Greek sculptor of the fourth century BC, but the idea that they may be a Roman work of the second century AD has recently come into favour: the half-moon shape of their eyes is said to have been a Roman character-istic. They were at first placed in front of the Arsenale (*see p84*), but around 1250 were moved to the terrace of the basilica.

In 1797 it was Napoleon's turn to play looter; the horses did not return to Venice from Paris until after his defeat at Waterloo. Apart from the parentheses of the two World Wars, when they were put away in safe storage, they remained on the terrace until 1974, when they were removed for restoration. Since 1982 they have been on display inside the basilica, with exact but soulless copies replacing them outside.

Treasury
This contains a hoard of exquisite Byzantine gold and silver plunder – reliquaries, chalices, cande-labras. If you can stand the glitter, the highlights are a silver perfume censer in the form of a church and two 11th-century icons of the Archangel Michael.

★ Campanile
San Marco, piazza San Marco. Vaporetto San Marco Vallaresso or San Zaccaria. **Open** 9.30am-4.15pm daily (til 9pm in summer). **Admission** €8; €4 reductions. **No credit cards. Map** p324 J7.
At almost 99m (325ft), the Campanile is the city's tallest building, originally built between 888 and 912. Its present appearance, with the stone spire and the gilded angel on top, dates from 1514. In July 1902 it collapsed, imploding in a neat pyramid of rubble; the only victim was the custodian's cat. It was rebuilt exactly 'as it was, where it was', as the town council of the day promised.

The Campanile served both as a watchtower and a bell tower. It provided a site for public humilia-tions: people of 'scandalous behaviour' were hung in a cage from the top. More wholesome fun was provided by the *volo dell'anzolo*, when an *arsenalotto*

curving sacristy door are bronze busts of its maker, Sansovino, and his friends, Titian and Aretino, who helped to get him out of prison in 1545. Aretino was a poet and playwright who moved to Venice in 1527 after scandalising Rome with his *Lewd Sonnets*. A great satirist and hedonist, he is said to have died laughing at a filthy joke about his sister.

The left transept contains the chapel of the Madonna Nicopeia (the Victory Bringer), named after the tenth-century icon on the altar, another Fourth Crusade acquisition. The St Isidore chapel beyond, with its 14th-century mosaics of the life of the saint, is reserved for private prayer and confessions, as is the adjacent Mascoli chapel. The altarpiece in this chapel, featuring Saints Mark and John the Evangelist with the Virgin between them, is a strik-ing piece of Gothic statuary. The chapel's mosaics, dating from 1430-50, have a definite Renaissance

SIGHTS

(shipwright) would slide down a rope strung between the Campanile and the Palazzo Ducale at the end of Carnevale.

Holy Roman Emperor Frederick III rode a horse to the top of the original in 1451; these days visitors take the lift. The view is superb, taking in the Lido, the whole lagoon and (on a clear day) the Dolomites in the distance. Sansovino's little Loggetta at the foot of the tower, which echoes the shape of a Roman triumphal arch, was also rebuilt using bits and pieces found in the rubble.

▶ *For an eye-to-eye view of the Campanile, climb up the Torre dell'Orologio; see p71.*

Museo Correr, Biblioteca Marciana & Museo Archeologico

San Marco 52, piazza San Marco/sottoportego San Geminian (041 240 5211/www.museicivici veneziani.it). Vaporetto San Marco Vallaresso. **Open** 9am-5pm daily. **Admission** by multi-entrance ticket; *see p61.* **Credit** AmEx, MC, V. **Map** p324 H8.

These three adjoining museums are all entered by the same doorway, which is situated beneath the Ala Napoleonica at the western end of piazza San Marco.

Museo Correr

The Museo Correr is Venice's civic museum, dedicated to the history of the Republic. Based on the private collection of Venetian nobleman Teodoro Correr (1750-1830), it is elevated beyond mere curiosity value by the second-floor gallery, which is essential viewing for anyone interested in early Renaissance Venetian painting. The museum is housed in the Ala Napoleonica, the wing that closes off the narrow western end of the piazza, and in the Procuratie Nuove. Napoleon demolished the church of San Geminiano to make way for this exercise in neoclassical regularity, complete with that essential imperial accessory, a ballroom (now often used for temporary exhibitions). The spirit of these years is conserved in the first part of the collection, dedicated to the beautiful if icy sculpture of Antonio

---

INSIDE TRACK
HONOURING NAPOLEON

Napoleon intended to embellish **piazza San Marco** with a statue of himself. In fact, the emperor's likeness spent the brief period of French reign in front of the Doge's palace, then was hastily removed. In 2002, the statue – now in the **Museo Correr** (*see above*) – was donated to the city by the *Comité français pour la Sauvegarde de Venise*. Furious letters were written to the local press suggesting that Venice should respond by donating a statue of Hitler to Paris.

Canova, whose first Venetian commission – the statue of *Daedalus and Icarus*, displayed here – brought him immediate acclaim. Some of the works on display are Canova's plaster models rather than his finished marble statues.

A corridor off to the right leads to a secluded niche containing a heroic statue (1811) of the city's conqueror, Napoleon (*see below* **Inside Track**).

The historical collection, which occupies most of the first floor of the Procuratie Vecchie building, documents Venetian history and social life in the 16th and 17th centuries through displays of globes, lutes, coins and robes. Room 6, devoted to the figure of the doge, features Lazzaro Bastiani's famous portrait of Doge Francesco Foscari (c1460). Room 11 has a collection of Venetian coins, plus Tintoretto's fine *St Justine and the Treasurers*. Beyond are rooms dedicated to the Arsenale (*see p84*): a display of weaponry and some occasionally charming miniature bronzes.

The Quadreria picture gallery upstairs is one of the best places get a grip on the development of Venetian painting between the Byzantine stirrings of Paolo Veneziano and the full-blown Renaissance storytelling of Carpaccio. Rooms 24 to 29 are dedicated to Byzantine and Gothic painters – note Veneziano's fine *St John the Baptist* and the rare allegorical fresco fragments from a 14th-century private house in Room 27. Room 30 fast-forwards abruptly with the macabre, proto-Mannerist *Pietà* (c.1460) of Cosme Turà.

Room 32, the Sala delle Quattro Porte, contains the famous aerial view of Venice by Jacopo de' Barbari, dated 1500. This extraordinary woodcut is so finely detailed that every single church, palazzo and well-head in the city seems to have been diligently portrayed; also on display are the original matrices in pear wood. Beyond here, the Renaissance gets into full swing with Antonello da Messina's *Pietà with Three Angels*, haunting despite the fact that the faces have nearly been erased by cack-handed restoration. The Bellinis get Room 36 to themselves – note the rubicund portrait of Doge Giovanni Mocenigo by Gentile Bellini (1475).

The gallery's most fascinating work, though, must be Vittore Carpaccio's *Two Venetian Noblewomen* – long known erroneously as *The Courtesans* – in Room 38. These two bored women are not angling for trade: they're waiting for their husbands to return from a hunt. This was confirmed when *A Hunt in the Valley* (in the Getty Museum in Los Angeles) was shown to be this painting's other half. Downstairs, the collection continues with rooms dedicated to the Bucintoro (state barge), festivities and trade guilds. The last two rooms have paintings of fairground trials of strength.

Museo Archeologico

This collection of Greek and Roman art and artefacts is interesting not so much for the individual pieces as for the light they cast on the history of collecting. Assembled mainly by Cardinal Domenico Grimani

Palazzo Ducale.

and his nephew Giovanni, the collection is a discerning 16th-century humanist's attempt to surround himself with the classical ideal of beauty. Highlights are the original fifth-century BC Greek statues of goddesses in Room 4, the Grimani Altar in Room 6, and the intricate cameos and intaglios in Room 7 or Room 12 (depending on temporary exhibitions). Room 9 contains a fine head of the Emperor Vespasian.

There are occasional free guided tours in English; call 041 522 5978 for information.

Biblioteca Marciana/Libreria Sansoviniana

In 1468, the great humanist scholar Cardinal Bessarion of Trebizond left his collection of Greek and Latin manuscripts to the state. Venice didn't get round to constructing a proper home for them until 1537. Jacopo Sansovino, a Florentine architect who had settled in Venice after fleeing from the Sack of Rome in 1527, was appointed to create the library, a splendid building right opposite the Palazzo Ducale. With this building, Sansovino brought the ambitious new ideas of the Roman Renaissance to Venice. He also appealed to the Venetian love of surface decoration by endowing his creation with an abundance of statuary. His original plan included a barrel-vault ceiling. This collapsed shortly after construction, however, and the architect was immediately clapped into prison. His rowdy friends Titian and Aretino had to lobby hard to have him released.

The working part of Venice's main library is now housed inside La Zecca (*see p72*) and contains approximately 750,000 volumes and around 13,500 manuscripts, most of them Greek.

The main room has a magnificent ceiling, with seven rows of allegorical medallion paintings, produced by a number of Venetian Mannerist artists as part of a competition. Veronese's *Music* (sixth row from the main entrance) was awarded the gold chain by Titian. Beyond this is the ante-room, in which a partial reconstruction has been made of Cardinal Grimani's collection of classical statues, as arranged by Scamozzi (1596). On the ceiling is *Wisdom*, a late work by Titian. Don't miss Fra Mauro's map of the world (1459), a fascinating testimony to the great precision of Venice's geographical knowledge, with surprisingly accurate depictions of China and India.

There are occasional free guided tours in English; call 041 240 7241 for information.

▶ For information on use of the library, see p301.

★ Palazzo Ducale (Doge's Palace)

San Marco 1, piazzetta San Marco (041 271 5911/bookings 041 520 9070/www.museicivici veneziani.it). Vaporetto San Marco Vallaresso or San Zaccaria. **Open** 9am-5pm daily. *Tours* (book at least two days in advance) 9.55am, 10.45am, 11.35am daily. **Admission** by multi-entrance ticket; *see p61. Tours* €16, €10 reductions. *Audio guide* €5; €8 double. **Credit** AmEx, MC, V. **Map** p324 J8.

An unobtrusive side door halfway down the right wall of the nave in San Marco leads straight into the courtyard of the Palazzo Ducale (Doge's Palace). Today's visitors take a more roundabout route, but that door is a potent symbol of the entwinement of Church and state in the glory days of *La Serenissima*. If the basilica was the Venetian Republic's spiritual nerve centre, the Doge's Palace was its political and judicial hub. The present site was the seat of ducal power from the ninth century onwards, though most of what we see today dates from the mid 15th century. Devastating fires in

City of Music

From organ recitals to opera buffa.

Venice was a late musical developer. There was no organ in the basilica of San Marco until around 1312; a singing school was not founded until around 100 years later. By the end of the 15th century, signs of a musical culture were finally emerging in *La Serenissima* when San Marco's musical activities expanded and the *scuole grandi* (*see p105* **Back to School**) began employing musicians.

Flemish composer **Adrian Willaert** was appointed *maestro di cappella* at San Marco in 1527. This was the most prestigious musical job in the hub of musical life in the city at this time; the *maestro* employed singers, instrumentalists and two organists. The post of organist was highly prestigious; each had charge of a separate instrument, as San Marco had two choir lofts facing each other, a feature that was to play a key part in the development of Venetian compositional style.

In 1568, the musical directorship of San Marco passed to **Andrea Gabrieli** (born c1515). A permanent instrumental ensemble was appointed for the first time; this small nucleus was added to when required, allowing the use of *cori spezzati* (divided choirs), whereby groups of instruments and voices were placed in different galleries. Composers exploited San Marco's peculiar acoustical properties to create dramatic dynamic contrast.

In 1586, Andrea Gabrieli's baton passed to his nephew **Giovanni Gabrieli** (1557-1612) who outshone his uncle by far. In 1613 Cremona-born **Claudio Monteverdi** replaced him. However, the basilica was

beginning to lose its dominance over musical life in Venice. Music was now everywhere: in the streets and on the canals, in private palaces and in brothels. With the opening of the Teatro San Cassiano, in 1637, the focus shifted from San Marco into the opera houses.

Venice was the birthplace of opera as public entertainment, and its many opera houses were widely famous. Monteverdi was the principal opera composer of his day, producing his last operas for Venice, *Il ritorno di Ulisse in patria* (1641) and *L'incoronazione di Poppea* (1642).

Composers churned out new works to satisfy the public's thirst; **Francesco Cavalli** (1602-76) wrote 42, for example. Opera houses were not only music venues, but also social hubs for all walks of life, from the aristocracy and foreign dignitaries to gondoliers, who got in for free. Performances were visually and musically splendid – audiences loved to see gods, angels and spirits, moving ships, live animals, vehicles and trap doors. Solo singing was of the utmost importance; there was virtually no chorus. What the audience wanted above all was to hear beautifully sung arias.

A further challenge to San Marco's hold on musical life emerged in the *ospedali* (charitable institutions founded to care for orphans and illegitimate children), where music was a major part of the curriculum. The Ospedale della Pietà (*see p85*) was well known for its concerts, which drew large audiences not only for its top-notch musical standards but also because the orchestra and choir was made up of teenage girls. **Antonio Vivaldi** (1678-1741)

1574 and 1577 took their toll, but after much heated debate it was decided to restore rather than replace – an enlightened policy for the time.

The palace is the great Gothic building of the city, but is also curiously eastern in style, achieving a marvellous combination of lightness and strength. The ground floor was open to the public; the work of government went on above. This arrangement resulted in a curious reversal of the natural order. The building gets heavier as it rises: the first level has an open

arcade of simple Gothic arches, the second a closed loggia of rich, ornate arcading. The top floor is a solid wall broken by a sequence of Gothic windows. Yet somehow it doesn't seem awkward.

The façade on the Piazzetta side was built in the 15th century as a continuation of the 14th-century waterfront façade. On the corner by the ponte di Paglia (Bridge of Straw) is an exquisite marble relief carving, the *Drunkenness of Noah* from the early 15th century, while on the Piazzetta corner is was employed at the Pietà between 1704 and 1740. The sickly young Antonio had been ordained, but practised music from an early age, becoming a virtuosic violinist and a fine teacher (and, by all accounts, a skilful seducer of young girls).

It was here that Vivaldi composed much of his vast output of instrumental music, including the ubiquitous *Four Seasons*. The fiendishly difficult solo parts were played either by himself or his star pupils. A virtuosic technique was a prerequisite for a soloist and gave rise to a Venetian style of solo concerto of which Vivaldi and **Tomaso Albinoni** were prime exponents.

Vivaldi also wrote some 46 operas, but with his death there was little local talent left, and outsiders took the stage. A new style of opera imported from Naples – the *intermezzo* (a comic interlude) – soon became enormously popular, eventually giving way to *opera buffa* (comic opera) at which Venetian composers excelled, notably **Baldassare Galuppi** (*see p135* **Music of the Islands**).

With the decline of the Venetian Republic in the late 18th century came a fall in fortunes of the city's musical institutions. A chink of light amid the cultural gloom was the inauguration in 1792 of the new **Teatro La Fenice** (*see p76*). Rossini wrote several of his most successful operas for Venice and first performances of Verdi's *Rigoletto* and *La Traviata* premiered at La Fenice in 1851 and 1853. Shortly afterwards, the focus shifted to Rome and Milan.

Few tourists see the great basilica of San Marco in a musical context, but try going in there armed with an iPod loaded with Giovanni Gabrieli's *Sonata pian' e forte*. Look up at the now-empty choir galleries and the vacant organ lofts. Turn up the volume and imagine…

---

a statue of Adam and Eve from the late 14th century. The capitals of the pillars below date from the 14th to the 15th centuries, although many of them are 19th-century copies (some of the originals are on display inside the palace).

The Porta della Carta (Paper Gate – so called because this was where permits were checked), between the palace and the basilica, is a grand piece of florid Gothic architecture and sculpture (1438-42) by Bartolomeo and Giovanni Bon. The statue of Doge

Francesco Foscari and the lion is a copy dating from 1885; French troops smashed the original when they occupied the city in 1797.

Behind the palace's fairy-tale exterior the complex machinery of empire whirred away with assembly-line efficiency. Anyone really interested in the inner workings of the Venetian state should take the 90-minute *Itinerari Segreti* tour. This takes you into those parts of the palace that the official route does not touch: the cramped wooden administrative offices; the stark chambers of the Cancelleria Segreta, where all official documents were written up in triplicate by a team of 24 clerks; the chamber of the three heads of the Council of Ten, connected by a secret door in the wooden panelling to the Sala del Consiglio dei Dieci, and the torture chambers beyond. The tour ends up in the leads – the sweltering prison cells beneath the roof from which Casanova staged his famous escape (probably by bribing the guard, though his own account was far more action hero) – and among the extraordinary beams and rafters above the Sala del Maggior Consiglio (*see p71*).

Following reorganisation, the main visit – for which an audio guide is recommended – now begins at the Porta del Frumento on the lagoon side of the palace. The Museo dell'Opera, just to the left of the ticket barrier, has the best of the 14th-century capitals from the external loggia; the ones you see outside are mostly copies.

In the main courtyard stands the Arco dei Foscari – another fine late-Gothic work, commissioned by Doge Francesco Foscari in 1438, when Venice was at the height of its territorial influence. It was built by Antonio Bregno and Antonio Rizzo. Rizzo also sculpted the figures of Adam and Eve (these too are copies; the originals are in the first-floor *liagò*), which earned him gushing accolades and led to his appointment as official architect in 1483, after one of those disastrous fires. Rizzo had time to oversee the building of the overblown Scala dei Giganti (where doges were crowned) and some of the interior before he was found to have embezzled 12,000 ducats; he promptly fled, and died soon after.

The official route now leads up the ornate Scala d'Oro staircase by Jacopo Sansovino, with stuccoes by Vittoria outlined in 24-carat gold leaf.

First floor: Doge's apartments

The doge's private life was entirely at the service of *La Serenissima* and even his bedroom had to keep up the PR effort. These rooms are occasionally closed or used for temporary exhibitions; when open, the Sala delle Mappe (also known as the Sala dello Scudo) merits scrutiny. Here, in a series of 16th-century maps, is the known world as it radiated from Venice. Just to the right of the entrance is a detailed map of the New World with Bofton (Boston) and Isola Longa (Long Island) clearly marked. Further on, seek out Titian's well-hidden fresco of St Christopher (above a doorway giving on to a staircase): it took the artist a mere three days to complete.

SIGHTS

SIGHTS

Torre dell'Orologio.

Second floor: State rooms

This grandiose series of halls provided steady work for all the great 16th-century Venetian artists. Titian, Tintoretto, Veronese, Palma il Vecchio and Jacopo Bassano all left their mark, though the sheer acreage that had to be covered, and the subjects of the canvases – either allegories or documentary records of the city's pomp and glory – did not always spur them to artistic heights.

The Sala delle Quattro Porte was where the Collegio – the inner cabinet of the Republic – met before the 1574 fire. After substantial renovation it became an ambassadorial waiting room, where humble envoys could gaze enviously at Andrea Vicentino's portrayal of the magnificent reception given to the young King Henry III of France in 1574. The Anticollegio, restored in part by Palladio, has a spectacular gilded stucco ceiling, four Tintorettos and Veronese's blowsy *Rape of Europa*.

Beyond here is the Sala del Collegio, where the inner cabinet convened. The propaganda paintings on the ceiling are by Veronese; note the equal scale of the civic and divine players, and the way both Justice and Peace are mere handmaidens to Venice herself. But for real hubris, stroll into the Sala del Senato, where Tintoretto's ceiling centrepiece shows *The Triumph of Venice*. Here the Senate debated questions of foreign policy, war and commerce, and heard the reports of Venetian ambassadors. Beyond again are the Sala del Consiglio dei Dieci and the Sala della Bussola, where the arcane body set up to act as a check on the doge considered matters of national security. In the former, note Veronese's ceiling panel, *Juno Offering Gifts to Venice*. By the time this was painted in 1553, the classical gods had started to replace St Mark in Venice's self-aggrandising pantheon. The itinerary continues through an armoury.

First floor: State rooms

The Sala dei Censori leads down to a *liagò* (covered, L-shaped loggia), which gives on to the Sala della Quarantia Civil Vecchia (the civil court) and the Sala del Guariento. The latter's faded 14th-century fresco of *The Coronation of the Virgin* by Guariento (for centuries hidden behind Tintoretto's *Paradiso* in the Sala del Maggior Consiglio) looks strangely innocent amid all this worldly propaganda. The shorter arm of the *liagò* has the originals of Antonio Rizzo's stylised marble sculptures of Adam and Eve from the Arco dei Foscari.

Next comes the Sala del Maggior Consiglio – the largest room in the palace. This was in effect the Republic's lower house, though this council of noblemen had fairly limited powers. Before the fire of 1577 the hall had been decorated with paintings by Bellini, Titian, Carpaccio and Veronese. When these works went up in smoke, they were replaced by less exalted ones, with one or two exceptions. Tintoretto's *Paradise*, on the far wall, sketched out by the 70-year-old artist but completed after his death in 1594 by his son Domenico, is liable to induce

vertigo, as much for its theological complexity as its huge scale. In the ceiling panels are works by Veronese and Palma il Giovane; note too the frieze of ducal portraits carried out by Domenico Tintoretto and assistants; the black veil marks where Marin Falier's face would have appeared had he not unwisely conspired against the state in 1356.

On the left side of the hall, a balcony gives a fine view over the southern side of the lagoon. A door leads from the back of the hall into the Sala della Quarantia Civil Nuova and the large Sala dello Scrutinio, where the votes of the *maggior consiglio* were counted; the latter is flanked by vast paintings of victorious naval battles, including a dramatic *Conquest of Zara* by Jacopo Tintoretto and *Battle of Lepanto* by Andrea Vicentino.

Criminal courts & prigioni

Backtracking through the Sala del Maggior Consiglio, a small door on the left leads past the Scala dei Censori to the Sala della Quarantia Criminale – the criminal court. The room next door retains some of the original red and gold leather wall coverings. Beyond this is a small room that has been arranged as a gallery, with Flemish paintings from Cardinal Grimani's collection.

The route now leads over the Bridge of Sighs to the Prigioni Nuove, where petty criminals were kept. Lifers were sent down to the waterlogged *pozzi* (wells) in the basement of the palazzo itself. By the 19th century most visitors were falling for the tour guide legend that, once over the Bridge of Sighs, prisoners would 'descend into the dungeon which none entered and hoped to see the sun again,' as Mark Twain put it. But when this new prison wing was built in 1589, it was acclaimed as a paragon of comfort; in 1608 the English traveller Thomas Coryat remarked, 'I think there is not a fairer prison in all Christendom.'

Some of the cells have their number and capacity painted over the door; one has a trompe l'œil window, drawn in charcoal by a bored inmate. On the lowest level is a small exercise yard, where an unofficial tavern used to operate. Up the stairs beyond is a display of Venetian ceramics found during excavations, and more cells, one with cartoons and caricatures left by 19th-century internees. Back across the Bridge of Sighs, the tour ends on the lower floor in the Avogaria – the offices of the clerks of court. Next to this a bookshop has been set up, with a good selection of works on Venice.

► *For a primer on Venice's convoluted system of government, see p21 Machinery of State.*

Torre dell'Orologio

San Marco 147, piazza San Marco (041 522 4951/www.museiciviciveneziani.it). Vaporetto San Marco Vallaresso or San Zaccaria. **Open** Guided tours in English 10am, 11am, Mon-Wed; 1pm, 2pm, 3pm Thur-Sun. **Admission** €12; €7 reductions. **Credit** AmEx, MC, V. **Map** p324 J7.

Note that there is no lift and the stairs are steep and narrow. Tours can be booked at the Museo Correr (*see p66*), by calling 041 520 9070 or online.

The clock tower, designed by Maurizio Codussi, was built between 1496 and 1506; the wings were an addition, perhaps by Pietro Lombardo. Above the clock face is the Madonna. During Ascension week and at Epiphany, the Magi come out and bow to her every hour, in an angel-led procession. At other times of year the hours and minutes are indicated in Roman and Arabic numerals on either side of the Madonna; this feature dates from 1858 – one of the earliest examples of a digital clock in the world. On the roof, statues of two burly Moors, made of gun-metal and cast in 1497, strike the hour. Another Moore (Roger) sent a villain flying through the clock face in the film *Moonraker*. (That wasn't the only Bond film set in Venice; *see p221* **Inside Track**.)

After lengthy restoration, the tower reopened in 2007. The tour reveals the workings of the clock, which dates from 1753 and was a remake of the original of 1499. Until 1998 the clock was wound manually by a *temporatore* who lived in the tower. Amid controversy the last incumbent was replaced by an electrical mechanism. The tour concludes with the roof of the tower with a fine view over piazza San Marco, the basilica and the palace. *Photos p70*.

FREE La Zecca

San Marco 7, piazzetta San Marco (041 520 8788). Vaporetto San Marco Vallaresso or San Zaccaria. **Open** 8.10am-7pm Mon-Fri; 8.10am-1.30pm Sat. **Admission** free. **Map** p324 J8.

The Mint, designed by Sansovino, was completed by 1547. It coined Venice's gold ducats – later referred to as *zecchini*, whence comes the English word 'sequins'. It is more impregnable in appearance than the neighbouring Biblioteca Marciana (*see p67*), though the façade had to accommodate large windows on the piano nobile (for relief from the heat) and open arches on the ground floor, where the procurators of St Mark's operated a number of cheese shops. It now houses most of the contents of the civic library.

PIAZZA SAN MARCO TO THE RIALTO

Vaporetto Rialto, San Marco Vallaresso or San Zaccaria.

Piazza San Marco is linked to the Rialto by the busiest, richest and narrowest of shopping streets: the Mercerie. The name is plural, since it is divided into five parts: the Merceria

Wet & Dry

Tips for travelling afoot in all weathers.

With their unique transit situation, Venetians have developed a particular etiquette for getting around on foot, with clear rules depending on what the particular weather conditions are.

In general, 'traffic' tends to flow in lanes (keep to the right) with potential for passing. A quick acceleration to the left with a polite '*permesso*' will help part the crowds. Locals take a dim view of anyone obstructing narrow streets as they stand to gawp, or – worse still – spread out their picnics on busy bridges. Slow down and pull off to the side or into a quiet side-street to consult a map or admire a building. Be adventurous and explore remoter districts if you want to avoid the high-season all-day-long traffic jam clogging the main arteries of the city, especially those near San Marco and Rialto.

Acqua alta (high water) presents other problems. Except in truly exceptional cases, all this means is that a couple of inches of water laps into the lowest parts of the city for an hour or two, then recedes. As the water rises, sirens sound five ten-second blasts two hours before the tide's

high point. During the *acqua alta* season (September to April), trestles and wooden planks are stacked up along flood-prone thoroughfares, ready to be transformed into raised walkways where Venetians wait their turn patiently, then proceed slowly but surely. They expect tourists to do the same, or risk an angry telling-off.

Pedestrian etiquette extends beyond the walkways. The streets may be water-logged, but they continue to function as a municipal road network; locals are understandably peeved if tourists doing Gene Kelly impersonations prevent them from reaching their destination dry. Remember, too, that during *acqua alta* you can't see where the pavement stops and the canal begins. Maps posted at vaporetto stops show flood-prone areas; if you don't want to get your feet wet, stick to higher ground or sit out those damp hours in your hotel room or bar. Alternatively, for an atmospheric *acqua alta* experience head to low-lying piazza San Marco.

To see if you'll be facing this challenge, go to www.comune.venezia.it and click on '*previsioni maree*' for tide forecasts.

Campo Santo Stefano. *See p74.*

dell'Orologio; di **San Zulian** (on which stands the church of the same name; *see p74*); del Capitello; di **San Salvador** (with its church of the same name; *see below*) and del 2 Aprile.

Mercerie means 'haberdashers', but we know from John Evelyn's 1645 account of 'one of the most delicious streets in the world' that in among the textile emporia were shops selling perfumes and medicines too. Most of the big-name fashion designers are to be found here now. The ponte dei Baretteri (Hatmakers' Bridge), in the middle of the Mercerie, is a record holder in Venice: six roads lead directly off the bridge.

The Mercerie emerge near campo San Bartolomeo, the square at the foot of the Rialto, with the statue of playwright Carlo Goldoni looking amusedly down at the milling crowds.

Calle dei Stagneri leads out of the campo to the 18th-century church of **Santa Maria della Fava** (in the *sestiere* of Castello, but best approached from here).

★ FREE **San Salvador**

San Marco, campo San Salvador (041 270 2464). Vaporetto Rialto. **Open** 9am-noon, 4-6.15pm Mon-Sat; 4-6pm Sun. **Map** p324 H6.

If you can't make it to Florence on this trip, come to San Salvador instead. Begun by Giorgio Spavento in 1506, it was continued by Tullio Lombardo and completed by Sansovino in 1534. But even though the geometrical sense of space and the use of soft-toned greys and whites exude Tuscan elegance, the key to the church's structure is in fact a combination of three domed Greek crosses, which look back to the Byzantine tradition

of St Mark's. The church contains two great Titians, the *Annunciation* at the end of the right-hand aisle (with the signature '*Tizianus fecit, fecit*' – Titian made this, made this; the repetition was intended either to emphasise the wonder of the artist's creativity, or is a simple mistake) and the *Transfiguration* on the high altar; the latter painting conceals a silver reredos, revealed at Christmas, Easter and 6 August (the feast of San Salvador).

There's also some splendid Veneto-Tuscan sculpture, including Sansovino's monument to Doge Francesco Venier, situated between the second and third altars on the right. At the end of the right transept is the tomb of Cristina Cornaro, the hapless Queen of Cyprus (d.1510), a pawn in a game of Mediterranean strategy that ended with her being forced into abdicating the island to Venetian rule. In the left aisle, the third altar belonged to the school of the Luganagheri (sausage makers), and has vibrant figures of San Rocco and San Sebastiano by Alessandro Vittoria, influenced by Michelangelo's *Slaves*. The sacristy contains delightful 16th-century frescoes of birds and leafage, discovered in the 1920s and restored in 2003.

INSIDE TRACK
ALL AROUND THE CHURCHES

San Giuliano (Zulian to Venetians; *see p74*) is one of only two churches in Venice that you can walk all the way around. The other is the **Angelo Raffaele** in Dorsoduro; *see p113*.

SIGHTS

FREE Santa Maria della Fava

Castello, campo della Fava (041 522 4601).
Vaporetto Rialto. **Open** 8.30-11.30am, 4.30-7pm
Mon-Sat. **Map** p324 H6.

St Mary of the Bean – the name refers to a popular
bean cake produced by a bakery that stood nearby
– is on one of the quieter routes between the Rialto
and San Marco. This 18th-century church is worth
visiting for two paintings by the city's greatest
artists of that period, which neatly illustrate their
contrasting temperaments. Tiepolo's *Education of
the Virgin* (first altar on the right) is an early work,
painted when he was still under the influence of
Giovanni Battista Piazzetta; but the bright colours
and touchingly human relationships of the figures
are nonetheless in contrast with the sombre browns
and reds of the latter's *Virgin and Child with St
Philip Neri* (second altar on the left). In Piazzetta's
more earnest painting, which still bears traces of
Counter-Reformation gravity, the lily, bishop's
mitre and cardinals' hats show the worldly honours
rejected by the saint.

FREE San Zulian

San Marco, mercerie San Zulian (041 523 5383).
Vaporetto San Marco Vallaresso or San Zaccaria.
Open 9am-7pm daily. **Map** p324 J7.

The classical simplicity of Sansovino's façade
(1553-55) for San Zulian is offset by a grand monument to Tommaso Rangone, a wealthy and far
from self-effacing showman-scholar from Ravenna,
whose fortune was made by a treatment for
syphilis, and who wrote a book on how to live to
120 (he only made it to 80). He unilaterally declared
his library to be one of the seven wonders of the
world, and had himself prominently portrayed in
all three of Tintoretto's paintings for the Scuola
Grande di San Marco (now housed in the Gallerie
dell' Accademia; *see p122*).

The interior of San Zulian has a ceiling painting
of *The Apotheosis of St Julian* by Palma il Giovane,
and a Titianesque *Assumption* by the same painter
on the second altar on the right, which also has
good statues of St Catherine of Alexandria and
Daniel by Alessandro Vittoria. The first altar on
the right has a *Pietà* by Veronese.

▶ *Mass is said here in English at 11.30am on
Sundays. Anglicans head across the Grand Canal
to St George's (Dorsoduro 870, campo San Vio)
for sung service at 10.30am on Sundays.*

INSIDE TRACK
LITERARY CRITICISM

The statue of writer **Nicolò Tommaseo**
in campo Santo Stefano is known by
local residents as *Cagalibri* (bookshitter) –
for reasons that become obvious when
the monument is viewed from behind.

FREE Telecom Italia Future Centre

*San Marco 4826, campo San Salvador (041
521 3200/www.futurecentre.telecomitalia.it).*
Vaporetto Rialto. **Open** 10am-6pm Tue-Sun.
Admission free. **Map** p324 H6.

The 16th-century cloisters of the monastery of San
Salvador underwent a thorough restoration in the
1980s, to provide a showcase for the latest offerings of the building's owner, Telecom Italia. The
cloisters are now used to host occasional exhibitions. Be certain not to miss the splendid refectory
with its 16th-century frescoed ceiling.

FROM THE RIALTO TO
THE ACCADEMIA BRIDGE

*Vaporetto Accademia, Rialto, San Samuele
or Sant'Angelo.*

The route from the Rialto to the Accademia
passes through a series of ever-larger squares.
From cosily cramped campo San Bartolomeo,
the well-marked path leads to campo San Luca,
then campo Manin with its 19th-century statue
of Daniele Manin, leader of the 1848 uprising
against the Austrians (*see p26*). An alley to
the left of this campo will lead you to the **Scala
del Bòvolo** (*see p76*), a striking Renaissance
spiral staircase. Back on the main drag, the
calle della Mandola leads to broad campo
Sant'Angelo with its dramatic view of **Santo
Stefano**'s leaning tower (*see p75*); off calle
della Mandola to the right is the Gothic
Palazzo Fortuny (*see below*), once home to
the Spanish fashion designer Mariano Fortuny.

Just before the Accademia bridge (*see p58*),
campo Santo Stefano is second in size only
to piazza San Marco in the *sestiere*. The tables
of several bars scarcely encroach on the space
where children play on their bikes or kick balls
around the statue of Risorgimento ideologue
Nicolò Tommaseo (*see left* **Inside Track**). At
the Accademia bridge end of the square is the
18th-century church of **San Vidal** (*see p75*).

On the Grand Canal to the north-west of
campo Santo Stefano is campo San Samuele,
with a deconsecrated 11th-century church
and the massive **Palazzo Grassi** exhibition
centre (*see p75*). Nearby, in calle Malipiero, the
18th-century love machine, Giacomo Casanova,
was born (though in which house exactly is not
known). The neighbourhood is full of Casanova
associations, including the site of the theatre
where his mother performed (corte Teatro).

Palazzo Fortuny

*San Marco 3780, campo San Benedetto (041
520 0995). Vaporetto Sant'Angelo.* **Open** during
exhibitions 10am-6pm Mon, Wed-Sun (hours
may vary). **Admission** varies, usually €8; €5
reductions. **No credit cards**. **Map** p323 F7.

SIGHTS

This charming 15th-century palazzo, which belonged to Spanish fashion designer Mariano Fortuny (1871-1949), has been undergoing restoration and reorganisation for many years now. However, the piano nobile, where Fortuny had his studio, and the floor above are generally open for temporary exhibitions. These are often photographic, photography being one of Fortuny's interests, alongside theatrical set design, cloth dyes and some elegant silk dresses. Also on display are some of Fortuny's paintings of Middle Eastern views.

Palazzo Grassi

San Marco 3231, campo San Samuele (041 523 1680/www.palazzograssi.it). Vaporetto San Samuele. **Open** *during exhibitions 10am-7pm Mon, Wed-Sun (hours subject to change).* **Admission** *€15 (€20 Palazzo Grassi & Punta della Dogana; see p123); €10 (€14 both) reductions.* **Credit** *MC, V.* **Map** *p323 E7.*

This superbly – though boringly – regular 18th-century palazzo on the Grand Canal was bought in 2005 from the Italian car maker Fiat by French billionaire businessman François-Henri Pinault. Pinault brought in Japanese superstar-architect Tadao Ando for an expensive overhaul, which increased the exhibition space by 2,000sq m (21,000sq ft). The palazzo's past blockbuster shows have varied from contemporary art to exhibitions on ancient civilisations.

▶ *François-Henri Pinault's new mega-gallery in the Punta della Dogana is even more impressive; see p124 The Whole Punta.*

FREE Santo Stefano

San Marco, campo Santo Stefano (041 522 5061/www.chorusvenezia.org). Vaporetto Accademia or San Samuele. **Open** *10am-5pm Mon-Sat.* **Admission** *Church free. Sacristy €3 (or Chorus; see p7).* **Map** *p323 F7.*

Santo Stefano is an Augustinian church, built in the 14th century and altered in the 15th. The façade has a magnificent portal in the florid Gothic style. The large interior, with its splendid ship's-keel roof, is a multicoloured treat, with different marbles used for the columns, capitals, altars and intarsia, and diamond-patterned walls. On the floor is a huge plaque to Doge Morosini (best known for blowing up the Parthenon) and a more modest one to composer Giovanni Gabrieli. On the interior façade to the left of the door is a Renaissance monument by Pietro Lombardo and his sons, decorated with skulls and festoons. In the sacristy are two tenebrous late works by Tintoretto, *The Washing of the Feet* and *The Agony in the Garden* (*The Last Supper* is by the great man's assistants), and three imaginative works by Gaspare Diziani (*Adoration of the Magi, Flight into Egypt, Massacre of the Innocents*).

▶ *Tintoretto's next painting of The Last Supper is in the Scuola di San Rocco; see p112. You'll find the previous one in San Polo; see p101.*

FREE San Vidal

San Marco, campo San Vidal (041 277 0561). Vaporetto Accademia. **Open** *9.30am-6pm daily.* **Map** *p323 E8.*

San Moisè. *See p76.*

SIGHTS

This early 18th-century church, with a façade derived from Palladio, was for years used as an art gallery. It has now been restored and hosts concerts. Over the high altar is a splendid Carpaccio painting (1514) of St Vitalis riding what appears to be one of the bronze horses of San Marco. The third altar on the right has a painting by Piazzetta, *Archangel Raphael and Saints Anthony and Louis*.

► *Classical music concerts by the Interpreti Veneziani are held here most days, beginning at 9pm. For information, see p242.*

Scala Contarini del Bòvolo
San Marco 4299, corte dei Risi (041 532 2920). Vaporetto Rialto. **Closed** for restoration. **Map** p323 G7.

Follow the signs for the Scala del Bòvolo from campo Manin and you will emerge in a narrow courtyard entirely dominated by this elegant Renaissance spiral staircase, built sometime around 1499 by Giovanni Candi. Spiral staircases are called *scale a chiocciola* (snail staircases) in Italian; *bòvolo* is Venetian dialect for snail. It was beautifully restored in 1986 but has been closed again for further restoration – a shame, as the view from the top is charming.

THE ACCADEMIA BRIDGE TO PIAZZA SAN MARCO
Vaporetto Accademia, Giglio or San Marco Vallaresso.

The route from Santo Stefano back to piazza San Marco zigzags at first, passing through small squares, including campo San Maurizio, with its 19th-century church now transformed into the **Museo della Musica** (*see below*), and campo **Santa Maria del Giglio** (aka Santa Maria Zobenigo; *see below*). It winds past banks, hotels and top-dollar antique shops, to end in wide via XXII Marzo, with an intimidating view of the Baroque statuary of **San Moisè** (*see below*). To the left is the opera house, **La Fenice** (*see below*).

Press on and you will be ready for what is arguably the greatest view anywhere in the world: piazza San Marco from the west side.

FREE Museo della Musica
San Marco 2601, campo San Maurizio (041 2411 840). Vaporetto Giglio. **Open** 9.30am-7.30pm daily. **Admission** free. **Map** p323 F8.

This small museum, set up in the ex-church of San Maurizio, is run by the Rivoalto recording company. Serving partly as a sales and promotion outlet, the museum also contains an interesting collection of period instruments. The free visit to the building offers a chance to appreciate the neoclassical interior of the church, designed by Giannantonio Selva, the architect of the Fenice theatre (*see below*).

Santa Maria del Giglio
San Marco, campo Santa Maria Zobenigo (041 275 0462/www.chorusvenezia.org). Vaporetto Giglio. **Open** 10am-5pm Mon-Sat. **Admission** €3 (or Chorus; *see p7*). **No credit cards. Map** p323 G8.

This church's façade totally lacks any Christian symbols (give or take a token angel or two). Built between 1678 and 1683, it's a huge exercise in defiant self-glorification by Admiral Antonio Barbaro, who was dismissed by Doge Francesco Morosini for incompetence in the War of Candia (Crete). On the plinths of the columns are relief plans of towns where he served; his own statue (in the centre) is flanked by representations of Honour, Virtue, Fame and Wisdom.

The interior is more devotional. You may not have heard of the painter Antonio Zanchi (1631-1722), but this is his church. Particularly interesting is *Abraham Teaching the Egyptians Astrology* in the sacristy, while the Cappella Molin has *Ulysses Recognised by his Dog* (an odd subject for a church). The chapel also contains a *Madonna and Child*, which is proudly but erroneously attributed to Rubens. Behind the altar there are two paintings of the Evangelists by Tintoretto, formerly organ doors.

FREE San Moisè
San Marco, campo San Moisè (041 528 5840). Vaporetto San Marco Vallaresso. **Open** 9.30am-12.30pm daily. **Map** p323 H8.

The Baroque façade of San Moisè has been lambasted by just about everybody as one of Venice's truly ugly pieces of architecture. Inside, an extravagant Baroque sculpture occupies the high altar, representing not only Moses receiving the stone tablets but Mount Sinai itself. Near the entrance is the grave of John Law, author of the disastrous Mississippi Bubble scheme that almost sank the French central bank in 1720. *Photo p75.*

★ Teatro La Fenice
San Marco 1983, campo San Fantin (041 2424/041 786 511/www.teatrolafenice.it). Vaporetto Giglio. **Open** times vary. **Admission** €7; €5 reductions. **No credit cards. Map** p323 G8.

Venice's principal opera house – aptly named 'the phoenix' – has a long history of fiery destruction and rebirth. The theatre (1792) designed by Giannantonio Selva replaced the Teatro San Benedetto, which burnt down in 1774. Selva's building was destroyed in 1836, and was rebuilt by the Meduna brothers, recreating the style of Selva. In 1996, a massive blaze broke out, courtesy of two electricians (for the full crime story read John Berendt's *City of Falling Angels*). After years of legal wrangling, the theatre was rebuilt and inaugurated in December 2003. Hidden away from view behind the ornate gilding and faux-Baroque plush are state-of-the-art technological innovations. The tour with audio guide lasts roughly 45 minutes.

► *For further information on performances in La Fenice, see p239.*

Castello

A shipbuilding fortress, the arty Biennale and plenty of fine churches.

Castello is the largest of Venice's six *sestieri* and probably the most varied in character. It takes its name from a defensive fortress that once stood at the eastern end of the city, protecting it from invasion by sea. Still occupying much of the *sestiere*'s north-eastern part is the great expanse of the **Arsenale**, which was once the city's great military powerhouse – now mostly in desolate, if picturesque, abandonment.

But Castello contains a great deal more than just relics of former military splendour. The western end, around **San Zaccaria** and **Santi Giovanni e Paolo**, is second only to piazza San Marco in pomp and grandeur, but head eastwards, beyond the Arsenale, and the tone becomes more homely in the bustling areas around **via Garibaldi** or the leafy calm of **Sant'Elena**.

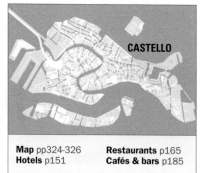

CASTELLO

| Map pp324-326 | Restaurants p165 |
| Hotels p151 | Cafés & bars p185 |

NORTHERN & WESTERN CASTELLO

Vaporetto Celestia, Fondamente Nove, Ospedale, Rialto or San Zaccaria.

The canal dividing the Doge's Palace (*see p67*) from the prison marks the end of the *sestiere* of San Marco. This means that the **Museo Diocesano di Arte Sacra** (*see p78*) and stately **San Zaccaria** (*see p82*), although closely associated with San Marco, actually belong to Castello. But the heart of northern and western Castello lies inland: campo **Santa Maria Formosa** (literally, 'Shapely St Mary'; *see p82*), a large, bustling, irregular-shaped square on the road to just about everywhere.

This square has all you could possibly need: a fine church, a market, a couple of bars and an undertaker. Nearby is the museum-cum-library of the **Fondazione Querini Stampalia** (*see p78*). Buzzing with locals and tourists, the campo is surrounded by *palazzi* that range in style from the very grand to the very homely. It is, in effect, Castello in miniature.

Southward from the campo runs the busy shopping street of **ruga Giuffa**. The first turn to the left off this street leads to the grandiose 16th-century **Palazzo Grimani** (*see p79*).

For more grandeur, head north to campo **Santi Giovanni e Paolo**. The Gothic red brick of the Dominican church (*see p80*) is beautifully set off by the glistening marble on the trompe l'œil façade of the **Scuola Grande di San Marco** (*see p82*) – now a hospital – and the bronze of the equestrian **monument to Bartolomeo Colleoni** (*see p78*) gazing contemptuously down.

It's a short walk through narrow *calli* from Santi Giovanni e Paolo to the fondamenta Nuove, where the northern lagoon comes into view. The cemetery island of San Michele (*see p133*) is always in sight, acting as a grim *memento mori* for patients in the hospital.

Eastwards from Santi Giovanni e Paolo, a road called Barbaria delle Tole (*see p78* **Inside Track**) passes the Baroque church of **Santa**

INSIDE TRACK
A ROUGH STREET?

The busy shopping street of **ruga Giuffa** is named after either a community of Armenian merchants from Julfa, or a band of thugs – *gagiuffos* in 13th-century dialect – who used to terrorise the area.

SIGHTS

Palazzo Grimani.

Maria dei Derelitti (*see p82*) by Baldassare Longhena, with its teetering façade adorned with leering faces. The church now belongs to an old people's home, which contains an exquisite 18th-century music room. Barbaria delle Tole leads into one of the least touristy areas of the city. Here, beyond the old gasworks, is austere **San Francesco della Vigna** (*see p79*).

★ Monument to Bartolomeo Colleoni

Castello, campo Santi Giovanni e Paolo.
Vaporetto Fondamente Nove. **Map** p324 K5.
Bartolomeo Colleoni was a famous *condottiere* (mercenary soldier) who left a legacy to the Republic on the condition that a statue be erected to him in front of St Mark's. Not wishing to clutter up St Mark's square with the statue, but loath to miss out on the money, Venice's wily rulers in 1479 gave him a space in front of the Scuola di San Marco. Geddit? To make up for this flagrant deception, the Republic did Colleoni proud, commissioning the Florentine artist Andrea Verrocchio to create this fine equestrian

statue. On Verrocchio's death it was completed, together with the pedestal, by Alessandro Leopardi (1488-96). It is not a portrait, but a stylised representation of military pride and might. Colleoni's coat of arms (on the pedestal) includes three fig-like objects, a reference to his name, which in Italian sounds very similar to *coglioni* – testicles, of which this soldier was said to possess three.

Museo Diocesano di Arte Sacra

Castello 4312, ponte della Canonica (041 522 9166). Vaporetto San Zaccaria. **Open** 10am-6pm daily. **Admission** *Museum* €4, €2 reductions. *Cloisters only* €1. **No credit cards. Map** p324 J7.
This museum is situated in the ex-monastery of Sant'Apollonia, whose Romanesque cloisters are unique in Venice; even if you don't have time to view the museum itself, it is worth paying the single euro for admission to the cloisters. The museum, which is in the process of being enlarged, contains a number of works of art and clerical artefacts (reliquaries, chalices, missals, crucifixes) from suppressed churches and monasteries. The first room is notable for two energetic paintings by Luca Giordano (*Christ and the Money-Lenders, Massacre of the Innocents*). From the church of San Donato there is a fine altarpiece by Paolo Veneziano, *San Donato e Devoti*, with the saint in relief, in gilded and painted wood.

Museo della Fondazione Querini Stampalia

Castello 5252, campo Santa Maria Formosa (041 271 1411/www.querinistampalia.it). Vaporetto Rialto. **Open** *Museum* 10am-8pm Tue-Sat; 10am-7pm Sun. For library hours, *see p301*. **Admission** *Museum* €8; €6 reductions. *Library* free. **Credit** AmEx, DC, MC, V. **Map** p324 J6.

This Renaissance palazzo and its art collection were bequeathed to Venice by Giovanni Querini, a 19th-century scientist, man of letters and silk producer from one of the city's most ancient families. Querini specified in his will that a library should be created here that would open 'particularly in the evenings for the convenience of scholars,' and that the foundation should promote 'evening assemblies of scholars and scientists.' Today, the Querini Stampalia still exudes something of its founder's spirit: the first-floor library is a great place to study, and the Foundation organises concerts (5pm, 7pm Fri, Sat; included in the admission price).

The ground floor and gardens, redesigned in the 1960s by Carlo Scarpa, offer one of Venice's few successful examples of modern architecture. On the second floor, the gallery contains some important paintings, including Palma il Vecchio's portraits of Francesco and Paola Querini (for whom the palace was built in the 16th century), as well as a marvellous *Presentation in the Temple* by Giovanni Bellini, and a striking *Judith and Holofernes* by Vincenzo Catena. It also has a fascinating series of minor works, such as Gabriele Bella's 67 paintings of Venetian festivals, and a selection of Pietro Longhi's scenes of bourgeois life in 18th-century Venice. On the top floor is a gallery designed by Mario Botta, which hosts exhibitions of contemporary art.

▶ *If you want to see another example of Carlo Scarpa's architecture in Venice, visit the Olivetti showroom in piazza San Marco (San Marco 101).*

★ Palazzo Grimani

Castello 4858, ruga Giuffa (041 520 0345/www. palazzogrimani.org). Vaporetto San Zaccaria. **Open** (guided tours, Italian only; book at least one day in advance) 9.30am, 11.30am, 1.30pm Tue-Sun. **Admission** (plus €1 booking fee) €9; €5 reductions (*see also p6*). **No credit cards.** **Map** p324 K6.

Inaugurated in December 2008 after a restoration process lasting 27 years, this magnificent palazzo is the most significant new museum to open in Venice for many years. The original nucleus of the palace was built by Antonio Grimani, doge of Venice, in the 1520s. However, it is most closely associated with his nephew Giovanni Grimani, cardinal and collector of antiquities. He enlarged and extended the palace, imposing a style of Roman classicism that is especially noticeable in the courtyard, and calling artists from central Italy, including Francesco Salviati and Federico Zuccari, to decorate it. The palazzo was conceived as a grand showcase for his fine collection of antiquities. Its fame was such that it was one of the buildings that Henry III of France insisted on seeing during his visit to Venice in 1574. Film buffs may remember the palace as the setting for the final gory scenes of Nicholas Roeg's film, *Don't Look Now.*

A grand staircase, modelled on the Scala D'Oro of the Doge's palace, leads up to the piano nobile. Highlights of the tour are the Michelangelo-esque Sala della Tribuna, with its multicoloured marbles, where the most important pieces of statuary were once exhibited (a Ganymede being borne off by Jupiter hangs from the ceiling as an example), and the Sala ai Fogliami, the ceiling of which is decorated with foliage and birds painted with scrupulous naturalistic accuracy.

▶ *Cardinal Grimani's collection of antiquities is now mostly in the Museo Archeologico; see p66.*

FREE San Francesco della Vigna

Castello, campo San Francesco della Vigna (041 520 6102). Vaporetto Celestia. **Open** 8am-12.30pm, 3-7pm Mon-Sat; 3-6.30pm Sun. **Map** p325 M6.

San Francesco may be off the beaten track, but the long trek over to the down-at-heel area beyond the gasworks is worth it. In 1534, Jacopo Sansovino was asked by his friend Doge Andrea Gritti to design this church for the Observant Franciscan order. The Tuscan architect opted for a deliberately simple style to match the monastic rule of its inhabitants. The façade (1568-72) was a later addition by Andrea Palladio; it is the first example of his system of superimposed temple fronts.

The dignified, solemn interior consists of a single broad nave with side chapels. The Cappella Giustiniani on the left of the chancel holds a marvellous cycle of bas-reliefs by Pietro Lombardo and school, moved here from an earlier church on the same site. In the nave, the fourth chapel on the right has a *Resurrection* attributed to Paolo Veronese.

Monument to Bartolomeo Colleoni.

SIGHTS

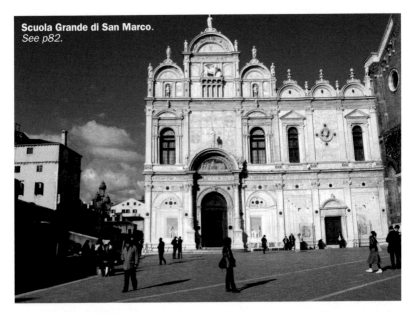

Scuola Grande di San Marco.
See p82.

In the right transept is a fruity, flowery *Madonna and Child Enthroned* (c1450), a signed work by the Greek artist Antonio da Negroponte.

From the left transept, a door leads into the Cappella Santa, which contains a *Madonna and Saints* (1507) by Giovanni Bellini (perhaps assisted by Girolamo da Santacroce). From here, it is possible to make a detour and visit two of the church's peaceful Renaissance cloisters.

Back in the church, the fifth chapel on the left is home to Paolo Veronese's first Venetian commission, the stunning *Holy Family with Saints John the Baptist, Anthony the Abbot and Catherine* (c1551). The third chapel has trompe l'œil frescoes in chiaroscuro by GB Tiepolo (1743, recently restored). The second chapel has three powerful statues of saints Roch, Anthony the Abbot and Sebastian (1565) by Alessandro Vittoria.

▶ *Palladio perfected his system of superimposed temple fronts in the church of San Giorgio Maggiore; see p130.*

★ Santi Giovanni e Paolo (San Zanipolo)

Castello, campo Santi Giovanni e Paolo (041 523 5913). **Vaporetto** *Fondamente Nove.* **Open** 9am-6.30pm Mon-Sat; noon-6.30pm Sun. **Admission** €2.50. **No credit cards. Map** p324 K5.

Santi Giovanni e Paolo was founded by the Dominican order in 1246 but not finished until 1430. Between 1248 and 1778, 25 doges were buried here. The vast interior – 101m (331ft) long – is a single spatial unit; the monks' choir was removed in the

17th century, leaving nothing to impede the view. Santi Giovanni e Paolo is packed with monuments to Venetian heroes as well as doges.

The entrance wall is dedicated to a series of funerary tributes to the Mocenigo family. The grandest – a masterpiece by Pietro, Tullio and Antonio Lombardo – belongs to Pietro Mocenigo, who died in 1476: the doge stands on his own sarcophagus, supported by three warriors representing the three ages of man. The religious reference above – the three Marys at the sepulchre – seems almost an afterthought.

The second altar on the right features an early polyptych by Giovanni Bellini (1465) in its original frame. Continuing down the right side of the church, the huge Baroque mausoleum by Andrea Tirali (1708) has two Valier doges and a *dogaressa* taking a bow before a marble curtain. Tirali also designed the Chapel of St Dominic, notable for its splendid ceiling painting by Giovani Battista Piazzetta of *St Dominic in Glory* (c1727). The right transept has a painting of *St Antonine Distributing Alms* (1542) by Lorenzo Lotto. Above are splendid stained-glass windows, to designs by such Renaissance artists as Bartolomeo Vivarini and Cima da Conegliano (1470-1520).

On the right side of the chancel, with its Baroque high altar, is the Gothic tomb of Michele Morosini; opposite is the tomb of Doge Andrea Vendramin, by the Lombardo family.

The rosary chapel, off the left transept, was gutted by fire in 1867, just after two masterpieces by Titian and Bellini had been placed here for safe keeping. It now contains paintings and furnishings from suppressed churches. The ceiling paintings,

SIGHTS

Walk In Vivaldi's Footsteps

Explore the world of the Four Seasons composer.

Antonio Vivaldi's music disappeared from public sight and hearing for over a century after his death, but there's no getting away from it nowadays in Venice.

The best starting point for a Vivaldi pilgrimage is campo San Giovanni in Bragora (aka campo Bandiera e Moro). The composer was born in this square on 4 March 1678, although the exact house is not known. Two months later he was baptised in the church of **San Giovanni in Bragora** (*see p87*); there's a copy of the baptism certificate next to the font.

Leave the square by calle del Dose and turn right along riva degli Schiavoni. After the first bridge stands the church of **La Pietà** (pictured; *see p85*). The current church was built after Vivaldi's death but it was on this site that he spent most of his working life. He began here as *maestro di violino* in 1703, teaching the orphan girls in the institute attached to the church, and writing music for them. He was to work here until 1740, when he left for Vienna.

To the right of the church is calle della Pietà, which leads to the small **museum** (the Piccolo Museo della Pietà 'Antonio Vivaldi'; *see p85*) dedicated to him. From the museum, continue along the street, which becomes calle dei Greci. At the end turn left towards the ponte dei Greci and proceed along fondamenta dell'Osmarin to campo Santi Filippo e Giacomo. The **Hotel Rio** in this square (no.4358) is where the composer lived in 1705-08 and 1711-22.

Retrace your steps to fondamenta dell'Osmarin and take the first bridge. From here, the ruga Giuffa will lead you to campo Santa Maria Formosa. Make your way around the church to **ponte del Paradiso**, a fine bridge with an archway surmounted by a sculpture of the Madonna. The house at the foot of the bridge (no.4850) is where the composer lived from 1722-30.

At the end of calle del Paradiso, turn right into salizada San Lio, which leads to campo San Bartolomeo. Head towards the Rialto bridge; instead of crossing it, turn left along the fondamenta and cross the first bridge to the **riva del Carbon**. Vivaldi lived in a house on the riva during his final years in Venice, from 1730-40. He then moved from here to Vienna, where he died the following year.

The Annunciation, Assumption and *Adoration of the Shepherds*, are by Paolo Veronese, as is another *Adoration* to the left of the door.

FREE Santa Maria dei Derelitti (Ospedaletto)

Castello 6691, barbarie delle Tole (041 271 9012). Vaporetto Fondamente Nove. **Open** *Church* 3-6pm Sat, Sun. *Hospice* by appointment. **Admission** (incl guided tour) €2. **No credit cards. Map** p324 K5.

The church was built in 1575 within the complex of the Ospedaletto, a hospice for the poor and aged. There is still an old people's home here. Between 1668 and 1674 Baldassare Longhena gave the church its staggering façade, complete with bulging telamons (architectural supports in the shape of male figures) and leering faces. The interior contains interesting 18th-century paintings, including one of Giambattista Tiepolo's earliest works, *The Sacrifice of Isaac* (fourth painting over the arch on the right). The hospice contains an elegant music room with charming frescoes by Jacopo Guarana (1776), depicting girl musicians performing for Apollo; the scene is stolen by a dog in the foreground being tempted with a doughnut. There is also a spiral staircase, apparently unsupported, designed by Sardi and completed by Longhena.

Santa Maria Formosa

Castello, campo Santa Maria Formosa (041 275 0462/www.chorusvenezia.org). Vaporetto San Zaccaria or Rialto. **Open** 10am-5pm Mon-Sat. **Admission** €3 (or Chorus; *see p7*). **No credit cards. Map** p324 J6.

In the pre-Freudian seventh century, St Magnus, Bishop of Oderzo, had a vision in which the Virgin appeared as a buxom (*formosa*) matron, and a church was built in this bustling square to commemorate the fact. The present church was designed by Mauro Codussi in 1492 and has something fittingly bulgy about it. Codussi retained the Greek cross plan of the original in his Renaissance design. It has two façades, one on the canal (1542), the other on the campo (1604). The Baroque campanile has a grotesque mask, now recognised as a portrait of a victim of the disfiguring Von Recklinghausen's disease.

INSIDE TRACK
GIULIA LAMA

Giulia Lama, whose painting in **Santa Maria Formosa** (*see p82*) is one of few by a woman displayed in the city, has been described as a pupil of Giovani Battista Piazzetta. But Piazzetta's only known portrait from life (in the Thyssen-Bornemisza collection in Madrid) is of Giulia Lama: its tenderness suggests she was more than a pupil.

The first chapel in the right aisle has a triptych painted by Bartolomeo Vivarini, *Madonna of the Misericordia* (1473), which includes a realistic *Birth of the Virgin*. The altar in the right transept was the chapel of the Scuola dei Bombardieri, with an altar-piece of St Barbara, patron saint of gunners (a heaven-sent lightning bolt saved Barbara's life when it struck her father as he prepared to kill her) by Palma il Vecchio. Half-hidden by the elaborate high altar is one of the few works on show in Venice by a woman artist: an 18th-century *Allegory of the Foundation of the Church, with Venice, St Magnus and St Maria Formosa* by Giulia Lama.

FREE San Zaccaria

Castello, campo San Zaccaria (041 522 1257). Vaporetto San Zaccaria. **Open** 10am-noon, 4-6pm Mon-Sat; 4-6pm Sun. **Map** p324 K7.

Founded in the ninth century, this church has always had close ties with the Doge's Palace. Eight Venetian rulers were buried in the first church on the site, one was killed outside and another died while seeking sanctuary inside. The body of St Zacharias, the father of John the Baptist, was brought to Venice in the ninth century; it still lies under the second altar on the right.

The current church was begun in 1444 but took decades to complete, making it a curious combination of Gothic and Renaissance. The interior is built on a Gothic plan – the apse, with its ambulatory and radiating cluster of tall-windowed chapels, is unique in Venice – but the architectural decoration is predominantly Renaissance. The façade is a happy mixture of the two styles.

Inside, every inch is covered with paintings, though of varying quality. Giovanni Bellini's magnificent *Madonna and Four Saints* (1505), on the second altar on the left, leaps out of the confusion. In the right aisle is the entrance to the Chapel of St Athanasius (admission €1), which contains carved 15th-century wooden stalls and *The Birth of St John the Baptist*, an early work by Tintoretto, and a striking *Flight into Egypt* by Giandomenico Tiepolo. The adjoining Chapel of St Tarasius was the apse of an earlier church that occupied this site; it has three altarpieces (1443) by Antonio Vivarini and Giovanni d'Alemagna – stiff, iconic works in elaborate Gothic frames.

The frescoed saints in the fan vault are by the Florentine artist Andrea del Castagno. Though painted a year before the altarpieces, they have a realistic vitality that is wholly Renaissance in spirit. In front of the altar are remains of the mosaic floor from the early Romanesque church; the tenth-century crypt below is usually flooded.

FREE Scuola Grande di San Marco (Ospedale Civile)

Castello, campo Santi Giovanni e Paolo (041 529 4111). Vaporetto Fondamente Nove. **Open** 24hrs daily. **Map** p324 K5.

Via Garibaldi. *See p84.*

A Castello calle.

This is one of the six *scuole grandi*, the confraternities of Venice (*see p105* **Back to School**). It's now occupied by the city hospital, which extends all the way back to the lagoon. The façade by Pietro Lombardo and Giovanni Buora (1487-90) was completed by Mauro Codussi (1495). It features magnificent trompe l'œil panels by Tullio and Antonio Lombardo representing two episodes from the life of St Mark and his faithful lion. Over the doorway is a lunette of *St Mark with the Brethren of the School* attributed to Bartolomeo Bon. *Photo p80.*
▶ *Make a game of 'lion-hunting'; see p218.*

SOUTHERN & EASTERN CASTELLO

Vaporetto Arsenale, Giardini, San Pietro, San Zaccaria or Sant'Elena.

The low-rise, clustered buildings of working-class eastern Castello housed the employees of the **Arsenale** (*see p84*) – Venice's docklands. Also here were Venice's foreign communities, as local churches testify: there's **San Giorgio dei Greci** (Greeks; *see p87*), with its adjoining **Museo dell'Istituto Ellenico** (*see p84*) icon museum; and there's also the **Scuola di San Giorgio degli Schiavoni** (Slavs; *see p87*), with its captivating cycle of paintings by Vittorio Carpaccio. The great promenade along the lagoon – the riva degli Schiavoni – was named after the same community.

Inland from the *riva* is the quaint Gothic church of **San Giovanni in Bragora** (*see p87*) and, further back in the warren of streets, the church of **Sant'Antonin** – undoubtedly the only church in Venice in which an elephant has been shot. The unfortunate animal escaped from a circus on the *riva* in 1819 and took refuge in the church, only to be finished off by gunners summoned from the Arsenale.

Back on the riva degli Schiavoni is the church of **La Pietà** (*see p85*), where Vivaldi was choir master. In calle della Pietà, alongside the church, is the **Piccolo Museo della Pietà** (*see p85*), dedicated to the Pietà (a foundling home) and the composer.

Head on eastwards past the **Ca' di Dio**, once a hostel for pilgrims setting out for the Holy Land and now an old people's home, and the *forni pubblici* (public bakeries), where the biscuit (*bis-cotto*, literally 'twice-cooked') – that favourite, scurvy-encouraging staple of ancient mariners – was reputedly invented.

Crossing the bridge over the rio dell'Arsenale, you can see the grand Renaissance entrance to the Arsenale shipyard (*see p84*). Once a hive of empire-building industry, it's now an expanse of empty warehouses and docks, though parts have been beautifully restored and are used for exhibitions.

Just beyond the rio dell'Arsenale, the model-packed **Museo Storico Navale** (*see p85*) lovingly charts Venice's shipbuilding history.

A little further on, the wide and lively via Garibaldi forks off to the left. This road, like the nearby *giardini pubblici* (public gardens), is a legacy of French occupation in the early 19th century. Via Garibaldi leads eventually to the island of **San Pietro**, where the former cathedral (*see p87*) stands among modest, washing-garlanded houses.

Back on the lagoon, the riva degli Schiavoni changes its name after the rio dell'Arsenale to become the riva dei Sette Martiri, named after seven partisans executed here in 1944 (a striking statue – located by the Giardini vaporetto stop and currently being restored – recalls the event). Just beyond here, the shady *giardini pubblici* occupies the place where four suppressed convents once stood. A Renaissance archway from one has been reconstructed in a corner of the gardens. In another corner lies the entrance to the **Biennale** (*see pp47-49*); the international pavilions, ranging in style from the seedy to the pompous, used to remain locked up except for those few weeks every two years when a major contemporary art bonanza would be set up; other more recently created events such as the Biennale dell'Architettura mean the pavilions get more frequent airings.

The riva ends in the sedately residential district of **Sant'Elena**. This, in Venetian terms, is a 'modern' district. In 1872 work began to fill in the *barene* (marshes) that lay between the edge of the city and the ancient island of Sant'Elena, with its charming Gothic church (*see p87*). Also tucked away here is Venice's football stadium (*see p244*).

Arsenale

Castello, campo dell'Arsenale. Vaporetto Arsenale.
Map p325 M7.

The word *arsenale* derives from the Arabic *dar sina'a*, meaning 'house of industry': the industry, and efficiency, of Venice's Arsenale was legendary: the *arsenalotti* could assemble a galley in just a few hours. Shipbuilding activities began here in the 12th century; at the height of the city's power, 16,000 men were employed. Production expanded until the 16th century, when Venice entered its slow but inexorable economic decline.

The imposing land gateway by Antonio Gambello (1460) in campo dell'Arsenale is the first example of Renaissance classical architecture to appear in Venice, although the capitals of the columns are 11th-century Veneto-Byzantine. The winged lion gazing down from above holds a book without the traditional words *Pax tibi Marce* (Peace to you, Mark) – unsuitable in this military context. Outside the gate, four lions keep guard. Those immediately flanking the terrace were looted from Athens in 1687; the larger one stood at the entrance to the port of Piraeus and bears runic inscriptions on its side, hacked there in the 11th century by Norse mercenary soldiers in Byzantine service. The third lion, whose head is clearly less ancient than its body, came from Delos and was placed here to commemorate the recapture of Corfu in 1716.

Shipbuilding activity ceased in 1917, but the Arsenale still remains navy property. Exhibitions and performances are now held in the cavernous spaces within its walls: the *Artiglierie* and the grandiose *Gaggiandre*, dockyards designed by Sansovino. In campo della Tana, on the other side of the rio dell'Arsenale, is the entrance to the *Corderia* (rope factory), an extraordinary building 316m (1,038 ft) long. This vast space is used to house the overflow from the Biennale (*see pp47-49*) and for other temporary shows.

▶ *You can pass through the Arsenale's gates in May during the Mare Maggio festival; see p215.*

Museo dell'Istituto Ellenico

Castello 3412, ponte dei Greci (041 522 6581). Vaporetto San Zaccaria. **Open** 9am-5pm daily. **Admission** €4; €2 reductions. **No credit cards. Map** p324 L7.

The adjacent church of San Giorgio dei Greci was a focal point for the Greek community, which was swollen by refugees after the Turkish capture of Constantinople in 1453. There have been a Greek church, college and school at this location since the end of the 15th century. The oldest piece in the museum's collection is the 14th-century altar cross behind the ticket desk. The icons on display mainly follow the dictates of the Cretan school, with no

Museo Storico Navale.

descent into naturalism, though some of the 17th- and 18th-century pieces make jarring and often kitsch compromises with Western art. The best pieces are those that are resolute in their hieratic (traditional-style Greek) flatness, such as *Christ in Glory among the Apostles* and the Great Deesis from the first half of the 14th century. St George is a popular subject: there is one splendid painting of him dating from the late 15th century. Also on display are priestly robes and other Greek-rite paraphernalia.

▶ *For information on the church itself, see p87.*

Museo Storico Navale

Castello 2148, campo San Biagio (041 520 0276). Vaporetto Arsenale. **Open** 8.45am-1.30pm Mon-Fri; 8.45am-1pm Sat. **Admission** €1.55; 77¢ reductions. **No credit cards. Map** p325 M8.

This museum dedicated to ships and shipbuilding continues an old tradition: under the Republic, the models created for shipbuilders in the final design stages were kept in the Arsenale. Some of the models on display are from that collection.

The ground floor has warships, cannons, explosive speedboats and dodgy-looking manned torpedoes, plus a display of ships through the ages. On the walls are relief models in wood and papier mâché, dating from the 16th to the 18th century, of Venetian fortresses and possessions.

On the first floor are ornamental trimmings and naval instruments, plus a series of impressive models of Venetian ships. Here, too, is a richly gilded model of the Bucintoro, the doges' state barge. The second floor has uniforms, more up-to-date sextants and astrolabes, and models of modern Italian navy vessels. On the third floor there are models of Chinese, Japanese and Korean junks, cruise ships and liners, and a series of fascinating naïve votive paintings, giving thanks for shipwrecks averted or survived.

A room at the back has a display of gondolas, including a 19th-century example with a cabin, and the last privately owned covered gondola in Venice, which belonged to the larger-than-life art collector and bon vivant Peggy Guggenheim.

▶ *For more on the antics of Peggy Guggenheim, and the gallery that bears her name, see p121.*

Piccolo Museo della Pietà
'Antonio Vivaldi'

Castello 3701, calle della Pietà (041 523 9079). Vaporetto Arsenale or San Zaccaria. **Open** 11am-4pm Mon, Wed. **Admission** €3. **No credit cards. Map** p324 L7.

This museum chronicles the activities of the Ospedale della Pietà, the orphanage where Antonio Vivaldi was violin teacher and choir master. Numerous documents recount such details as the rules for admission of children and the rations of food allotted them; the 'Daughters of the Choir' received more generous portions of food and wine. There is also a selection of period instruments.

▶ *For more on Vivaldi, see p66 City of Music.*

🆓 La Pietà
(Santa Maria della Visitazione)

Castello, riva degli Schiavoni (041 523 1096). Vaporetto San Zaccaria. **Open** for services only at 6.30pm Sat. **Map** p324 L8.

By the girls' orphanage of the same name, the church of La Pietà was famous for its music. Antonio Vivaldi, violin and choir master here in the 18th century, wrote some of his finest music for his young charges. The present building, by Giorgio Massari, was begun in 1745, four years after Vivaldi's death. Music inspired its architecture: the interior, reached through a vestibule resembling a foyer, has the oval shape of a concert hall. The ceiling has a *Coronation of the Virgin* (1755) by Giambattista Tiepolo.

▶ *For a Vivaldi-themed itinerary, see p81 Walk.*

Scuola di San Giorgio degli Schiavoni. *See p87.*

SIGHTS

SIGHTS

The Well-heads of Venice

A once-practical architecture that still adds beauty to many a campo.

It's estimated that the number of well-heads in Venice is now around 2,500 – a dramatic drop from the 6,782 counted by city authorities in 1858. The ground level in squares with wells at their centre is often raised, to keep salt water out during high tide. The paving is angled towards drains, where rain water would disappear, sink through filtering systems, and then find its way into cisterns beneath the well-heads. In 1882-84, pipes were laid to bring fresh water to the lagoon city from the mainland. With no practical purpose, monumental well-heads became just one more thing that poor Venetians could sell off to wealthy foreigners.

THE MOST ANCIENT
Corte Correr (between San Zaccaria and Santa Maria Formosa, map p324 K7): a square well-head dating from the ninth or tenth century; the sculpted rosettes are 15th century.

BYZANTINE
Corte del Remer (near San Giovanni Crisostomo, map p321 H5): elegant arches in red Verona marble.

GOTHIC
Corte Veniera (off campo Santi Giovanni e Paolo, map p324 K5): a fine specimen with ogival arches.

Ca' d'Oro (*see p91*): an elaborately carved late-Gothic well in the courtyard.

RENAISSANCE
Campo Santi Giovanni e Paolo (map p324 K5): an elegant well-head with festoon-draped *putti*.

Campo San Zaccaria (map p324 K7), **campo San Giovanni Crisostomo** (map p321 H5), **campo della Maddalena** (map p321 F3): inspired by Corinthian capitals, these have delicate carvings of foliage.

Campo Angelo Raffaele (map p322 B8): cylindrical, with charming carvings of Tobias and the guardian angel.

MANNERIST AND BAROQUE
Campo dei Frari (map p323 E6): a large cylindrical well with a swelling waist.

Campo San Marcuola (map p321 E3): a lavish well with lion heads and scrolled shields amid ornate curlicues.

19TH CENTURY
Campo San Polo (map p321 F6): this octagonal well-head is the largest in the city.

THE MOST MONUMENTAL
Doge's Palace (*see p67*): elaborate Renaissance works in bronze.

I Frari (*see p109*): 18th-century, with pillars, a pediment and statuary in the cloister.

THE MOST SECRET
Calle Bernardo (between campo San Barnaba and Ca' Foscari, map p322 D7): the only well-head in central Venice that still bears the lion of St Mark. In 1797, the French employed a sculptor to remove these symbols of Venetian independence, but he never found this one.

FREE Sant'Elena

Castello 3, Servi di Maria, campo Chiesa Sant'
Elena (041 520 5144). Vaporetto Sant'Elena.
Open 5-7pm Mon-Sat. **Map** off p326 Q11.
The red-brick Gothic church of Sant'Elena contains
no great works of art (the church was deconsecrated
in 1807, turned into an iron foundry, and not opened
again until 1928) but its austere Gothic nakedness
is a relief after all that Venetian ornament. The main
body of the church was being restored at the time
of writing. The only part that could be visited was
the chapel to the right of the entrance containing
the body of St Helen, the irascible mother of the
Emperor Constantine and finder of the True Cross.
(Curiously enough, her body is also to be found in
the Aracoeli church in Rome.) To the left are the
charming cloisters and rose garden tended by the
three monks left in the monastery.

FREE San Giorgio dei Greci

Castello, fondamenta dei Greci (041 523 9569).
Vaporetto San Zaccaria. **Open** 9am-1pm, 3-5pm
Mon, Wed-Sat. **Map** p324 L7.
By the time the church of San Giorgio was begun in
1539, the Greeks were well established in Venice and
held a major stake in the city's scholarly printing
presses. Designed by Sante Lombardo, the church's
interior is fully Orthodox in layout, with its women's
gallery, and high altar behind the iconostasis. A
heady smell of incense lends the church an Eastern
mystique, enhanced by dark-bearded priests in flowing robes. The campanile is decidely lopsided. Next
to the church are the Scuola di San Nicolò (now the
Museo dell'Istituto Ellenico) and the Collegio Flangini
(now seat of the Istituto Ellenico di Studi Bizantini e
post-Bizantini), both by Baldassare Longhena.
▶ *For information about the museum, see p84.*

FREE San Giovanni in Bragora

Castello, campo Bandiera e Moro (041 270 2464).
Vaporetto Arsenale. **Open** 9am-noon, 3.30-5pm
Mon-Sat. **Map** p324 L7.
San Giovanni in Bragora (the meaning of *bragora* is
obscure) is an intimate Gothic structure. The church
where composer Antonio Vivaldi was baptised (a
copy of the entry in the register is on show), San
Giovanni also contains some very fine paintings.
Above the high altar is the recently restored *Baptism*
of Christ (1492-95) by Cima da Conegliano, with a
landscape recalling the countryside around the
painter's home town of Conegliano. A smaller Cima,
on the right of the sacristy door, shows *Constantine*
Holding the Cross and St Helen (1502). On the same
wall, just before the second altar, is a triptych by
Bartolomeo Vivarini, *Madonna and Child and Two*
Saints, dated 1478. The church also contains three
paintings by his nephew Alvise Vivarini, one of
them a splendidly heroic *Resurrection* (1498).
▶ *The figure of Christ in Vivarini's Resurrection*
is based on a statue of Apollo in the Museo
Archeologico; see p66.

San Pietro in Castello

Castello, campo San Pietro (041 275 0462/www.
chorusvenezia.org). Vaporetto San Pietro. **Open**
10am-5pm Mon-Sat. **Admission** €3 (or Chorus;
see p7). **No credit cards. Map** p326 Q8.
Until 1807, San Pietro in Castello was the cathedral
of Venice, and its remote position testifies to the
determination of the Venetian government to keep
the clerical authorities far from the centre of tempo-
ral power. There has probably been a church here
since the seventh century, but the present building
was constructed in 1557 to a design by Palladio.
The body of the first patriarch of Venice, San
Lorenzo Giustiniani, is preserved in an urn elaborately supported by angels above the high altar, a
magnificent piece of Baroque theatricality designed
by Baldassare Longhena (1649). In the right-hand
aisle is the so-called 'St Peter's Throne', a delicately
carved marble work from Antioch containing a
Muslim funerary stele and verses from the Koran.
The Baroque Vendramin Chapel in the left transept
was again designed by Longhena, and contains a
Virgin and Child by the prolific Neapolitan Luca
Giordano. Outside the entrance to the chapel is a
late work by Paolo Veronese, *Saints John the*
Evangelist, Peter and Paul.
▶ *San Pietro's canalside 'church green' of scrappy*
grass under towering trees and a punch-drunk
campanile is a charming place for a picnic.

★ Scuola di San Giorgio degli Schiavoni

Castello 3259A, calle dei Furlani (041 522
8828). Vaporetto Arsenale or San Zaccaria.
Open 2.45-6pm Mon; 9.15am-1pm, 2.45-6pm
Tue-Sat; 9.15am-1pm Sun. **Admission** €3;
€2 reductions. **No credit cards. Map** p324 L7.
The *schiavoni* were Venice's Slav inhabitants, who
had become so numerous and influential by the end
of the 15th century that they could afford to build this
scuola (or meeting house) by the side of their church,
San Giovanni di Malta. The *scuola* houses one of
Vittore Carpaccio's two great Venetian picture cycles.
In 1502, eight years after completing his St Ursula
cycle (now in the Accademia, *see p122*), Carpaccio
was commissioned to paint a series of canvases illustrating the lives of the Dalmatian saints George,
Tryphone and Jerome. In the tradition of the early
Renaissance *istoria* (narrative painting cycle), there
is a wealth of incidental detail, such as the decompos-
ing virgins in *St George and the Dragon*, or the little
dog in the painting of *St Augustine in his Study*
(receiving the news of the death of St Jerome in a
vision) – with its paraphernalia of humanism (astro-
labe, shells, sheet music, archaeological fragments).
   It's worth venturing upstairs to see what the meeting hall of a working *scuola* looks like. San Giorgio
degli Schiavoni still provides scholarships, distributes charity and acts as a focal point for the local
Slav community. The opening hours are notoriously
changeable. *Photo p85.*

SIGHTS

Cannaregio

Escape the hubbub on quiet backstreets and visit the original Ghetto.

Few other cities offer newly arrived tourists such a feast for the eyes as they step out of the railway station. You're greeted not by a dingy carpark or snarling flurry of buses and taxis but by the **Grand Canal** itself. What comes next, if you walk to the centre, is a bit of a let-down: a jostling array of souvenir stalls, grotty bars and downmarket hotels on and around busy **lista di Spagna**, Cannaregio's main thoroughfare.

Concealed beyond, however, is a blissfully calm area of long canalside walks and the occasional, mostly undemanding church. The only big surprise comes in the **Ghetto**, where a thriving Jewish community creates a sudden burst of activity amid the quiet of this second-largest *sestiere*.

CANNAREGIO

Map pp320-321	Hotels p153
& p324	Restaurants p168
	Cafés & Bars p188

Map pp320-321 & p324 Hotels p153 Restaurants p168 Cafés & Bars p188

SIGHTS

THE CANNAREGIO CANAL

Vaporetto Crea, Guglie or Ponte Tre Archi.

Apart from the Grand Canal and the Giudecca there is only one waterway in the city that is dignified by the name of 'canal', and that is the **Cannaregio Canal**. For centuries, this waterway was the main route into Venice from the mainland – and it provides a suitably impressive introduction, with wide *fondamente* on each side and several imposing *palazzi*. It's spanned by two stately bridges, the **ponte delle Guglie** (Bridge of the Obelisks, 1823), and the **ponte dei Tre Archi**, the only three-arch stone bridge in Venice, built by Andrea Tirali in 1688. Heading towards the lagoon from the ponte delle Guglie on the right-hand *fondamenta*, you pass the *sottoportico* leading to the Jewish Ghetto (*see p93*).

Beyond this stands the **Palazzo Nani** (no.1105), a fine Renaissance building dating from the 16th century. Some 200 metres (700 feet) further on is the **Palazzo Surian-Bellotto** (no.968); in the 18th century, this was the French embassy, where Jean-Jacques Rousseau worked – reluctantly – as a secretary. Beyond, **Santa Maria delle Penitenti**, with its unfinished façade, was formerly a home for the city's fallen women.

On the left bank is the **Palazzo Priuli-Manfrin** (nos.342-3), another Tirali creation dating from 1735, in a neoclassical style of such severe plainness that it could almost prefigure 20th-century purist art.

The domineering 17th-century **Palazzo Savorgan** (no.349) – now a school – has huge coats of arms and reliefs of helmets; the owners were descended from Federigo Savorgnan, who, in 1385, became the first non-Venetian to be admitted to Venice's patrician ruling clique. Behind it is the **Parco Savorgnan**, a charming public garden that is one of Venice's better-kept secrets. A little further on, the ponte della Crea spans a canal that was covered over for centuries, only to be re-excavated in 1997.

After passing the ponte dei Tre Archi (with the Renaissance church of **San Giobbe** off to the left; *see p89*), the *fondamenta* continues on to the ex-slaughterhouse, built in the 19th century by the Austrians. It has been taken over and revamped by Venice University's economics faculty.

Two fairly recent housing projects are easily reachable from the canal. From the left bank, calle delle due Corti leads to the Area Saffa, a complex built to designs by Vittorio Gregotti between 1981 and 1994; owing to the enclosed nature of the site and the use of high dividing walls, the overall effect is claustrophobic. More

Il Ghetto. *See p93*.

successful is the housing project of sacca San Gerolamo, at the end of the right bank, to designs by Franco Bortoluzzi (1987-90); the complex makes picturesque use of traditional elements, such as slabs of Istrian marble framing green-shuttered windows and large archways giving on to the lagoon.

FREE San Giobbe

Campo San Giobbe (041 524 1889). Vaporetto Crea or Ponte Tre Archi. **Open** 10am-noon, 3-6pm Mon-Sat; 3.30-6pm Sun. **Map** p320 C2.

Job (Giobbe) has been given saint status by Venice, despite his Old Testament pedigree. The church named after him was built to celebrate the visit in 1463 of St Bernardino of Siena, a high-profile Franciscan evangelist. The first Venetian creation of Pietro Lombardo, it introduced a new classical style, immediately visible in the doorway (three statues by Pietro Lombardo that once adorned it are now in the sacristy).

The interior of what was probably the first single-naved church in Venice is unashamedly Renaissance in style. Members of the Lombardo family are responsible for the carvings in the domed sanctuary, all around the triumphal arch separating the sanctuary from the nave, and on the tombstone of San Giobbe's founder, Cristoforo Moro, in the centre of the sanctuary floor. This doge's name has given rise to associations with Othello, the Moor of Venice; some have seen the mulberry symbol in his tombstone (*moro* means mulberry tree as well as Moor) as the origin of Desdemona's handkerchief, 'spotted with strawberries'.

Most of the church's treasures – altarpieces by Giovanni Bellini and Vittore Carpaccio – are now in the Accademia (*see p122*). An atmospheric *Nativity* by Gerolamo Savoldo remains, as does an *Annunciation with Saints Michael and Anthony* triptych by Antonio Vivarini in the sacristy. The Martini Chapel, the second on the left, is a little bit of Tuscany in Venice. Built for a family of silk-weavers from Lucca, it is attributed to the Florentine Bernardo Rossellino. The terracotta medallions of Christ and the Four Evangelists are by the Della Robbia studio – the only examples of their work in Venice.

▶ *The Lombardo family's masterpiece is Santa Maria dei Miracoli, at the far eastern end of Cannaregio; see p97. For more about Lombardo's other designs, see p43.*

INSIDE TRACK
DEATH IN VENICE

The corte Seconda del Milion (*see p90*) has a splendidly carved horseshoe arch. It was on the well-head in the centre of the *corte* that Dirk Bogarde collapsed in Visconti's *Death in Venice*, his hair dye and mascara trickling down his face in the rain.

Abbazia della Misericordia. *See p95.*

FROM THE STATION
TO THE RIALTO

Vaporetto Ca' d'Oro, Ferrovia, Guglie, Rialto or San Marcuola.

The first parts of Cannaregio to be settled were the islands close to the Rialto area: the parishes of Santi Apostoli and San Giovanni Crisostomo in particular. The zones alongside the Grand Canal were the next to be built up. Urbanisation proceeded northwards, gradually spreading around the convents and monasteries that had been set up earlier in remote areas towards the northern lagoon.

Heading away from the station towards the Rialto, the tourist-tack-filled *lista* leads to the large campo **San Geremia**, overlooked by the church of the same name (containing the shrivelled body of St Lucy) and **Palazzo Labia**, currently occupied by the RAI (Italian state television). The palazzo contains frescoes by Tiepolo, visible by appointment (041 781 111; being restored as this guide went to press).

Once over the Cannaregio Canal (*see p88*) – by way of ponte delle Guglie, a grandiose bridge with obelisks – the route assumes more character, taking in lively street markets with Venetians going about their daily business. Off to the right, in a square giving on to the Grand Canal, is the church of **San Marcuola** (*see p92*), with an unfinished façade. A bit further on, the more picturesque church of **La Maddalena**, inspired by the Pantheon

in Rome, stands in the small campo della Maddalena adorned with a large assortment of fantastic chimney pots.

Beyond this, wide strada Nuova begins. Off to the left is the church of **San Marziale** (*see p92*), with whimsical ceiling paintings; on the strada Nuova itself stands the church of **Santa Fosca**, another mainly 18th-century creation. In front of the church stands a statue of Paolo Sarpi, who helped Venice resist a Papal interdict in the 17th century and faced an assassination attempt as a result. Down a calle to the right is the entrance to the **Ca' d'Oro** (*see p91*), Venice's most splendid Gothic palazzo.

The strada Nuova ends by the church of **Santi Apostoli** (*see p92*); the route to the Rialto soon becomes reassuringly narrow and crooked, passing the church of **San Giovanni Crisostomo** (*see p91*) and the adjacent courtyard of the **corte Seconda del Milion**, where Marco Polo was born in 1256. Some of the Veneto-Byzantine-style houses in the courtyard date from that time. It was to this courtyard that we imagine Marco Polo returning with his father and uncle in 1295, after 24 years travelling the Far East. As the story goes, the three men turned up in the old Polo home dressed in shabby Tartar costume. Nobody recognised them until they threw back their hoods. Then, to general amazement, Marco slit open the lining of their rough clothes and out poured a glittering shower of diamonds and precious stones. The name of the courtyard derives from the title of his own account of his adventures.

There's a plaque commemorating Marco Polo on the rear of the **Teatro Malibran** (*see p239*), formerly the Teatro di San Giovanni Crisostomo, one of Venice's earliest theatres. The theatre was opened once more in 2001, its restoration fast-tracked after the city's opera house, La Fenice, burnt down.

Ca' d'Oro (Galleria Franchetti)
Cannaregio 3932, calle Ca' d'Oro (041 523 8790/ www.artive.arti.beniculturali.it). Vaporetto Ca' d'Oro. **Open** 8.15am-2pm Mon; 8.15am-7.15pm Tue-Sun. **Admission** €5; €2.50 reductions (*see also p6*). **No credit cards. Map** p321 G4.
In its 15th-century heyday, the façade of this pretty townhouse on the Grand Canal must have looked a psychedelic treat: the colour scheme was light blue and burgundy, with 24-carat gold highlights. Though the colour has worn off, the Grand Canal frontage of Ca' d'Oro – built for merchant Marin Contarini between 1421 and 1431 – is still the most elaborate example of the florid Venetian Gothic style besides the Doge's Palace.

Inside, little of the original structure and decor has survived. The pretty courtyard was reconstructed with its original 15th-century staircase and well-head a century ago by Baron Franchetti; the mosaic floor is a 19th-century imitation of the floors in San Marco. The Baron also assembled the collection of paintings, sculptures and coins that is exhibited inside.

The highlight of the collection is Mantegna's *St Sebastian*, a powerful late work; the Palladian frame contrasts oddly with the saint's existential anguish. The rest is good in parts, though not necessarily the

parts you would expect. A small medal of Sultan Mohammed II by Gentile Bellini (a souvenir of his years in Constantinople, being restored as this guide went to press) is more impressive than the worse than faded frescoes by Titian and Giorgione removed from the Fondaco dei Tedeschi (*see p55*). There are some good Renaissance bronzes from deconsecrated churches and small but vigorous plaster models by Bernini for the statues on the fountains in Rome's piazza Navona.

FREE San Giovanni Crisostomo
Cannaregio, campo San Giovanni Crisostomo (041 522 7155). Vaporetto Rialto. **Open** 8.15am-12.15pm, 3-7pm Mon-Sat; 3-7pm Sun. **Map** p321 H5.
This small church by Mauro Codussi is dedicated to St John Chrysostomos, archbishop of Constantinople, and shows a Byzantine influence in its Greek-cross form. It contains two great paintings. On the

SIGHTS

Fondamenta della Misericordia. *See p95.*

SIGHTS

INSIDE TRACK
THE FIRST LAST SUPPER

There are seven paintings of *The Last Supper* by Tintoretto (and his assistants) in Venice, created between 1547 and 1591. Find them all! Get started with his earliest version, in **San Marcuola** (*see below*), and discover how his style developed over the decades.

---

right-hand altar is *Saints Jerome, Christopher and Louis of Toulouse*, signed by Giovanni Bellini and dated 1513. This late work is one of his few Madonna-less altarpieces and shows the Old Master ready to experiment with the atmospheric colouring techniques of such younger artists as Giorgione. On the high altar hangs *Saints John the Baptist, Liberale, Mary Magdalene and Catherine* (c1509) by Sebastiano del Piombo, who trained under Bellini but was also influenced by Giorgione. On the left-hand altar is *Coronation of the Virgin*, a fine relief (1500-02) by Tullio Lombardo.
▶ *For the story of the artistic duel between Bellini and del Piombo, see p37 Deadly Rivals.*

FREE San Marcuola

Cannaregio, campo San Marcuola (041 713 872). Vaporetto San Marcuola. **Open** 10am-noon, 5-6pm Mon-Sat. **Map** p321 E3.
There was no such person as St Marcuola; the name is a local mangling of the over-complicated *santi Ermagora e Fortunato*, two early martyrs. The church, designed by 18th-century architect Giorgio Massari, has been beautifully restored – its gleaming interior comes as a surprise after the unfinished brick façade. It contains some vigorous statues by Gianmaria Morlaiter and, in the chancel, a *Last Supper* (1547) by Tintoretto, his first (but by no means last; *see above*) treatment of the subject; the layout is uncharacteristically symmetrical but indications of the later Tintoretto can be seen in the restless movements of the disciples and the background figures. Opposite is a 17th-century copy of another Tintoretto (*Christ Washing the Feet of His Disciples*).
▶ *Tintoretto's next painting of The Last Supper is in San Trovaso; see p119.*

FREE San Marziale

Cannaregio, campo San Marziale (041 719 933). Vaporetto Ca' d'Oro or San Marcuola. **Open** 4-6.30pm Mon-Sat; 8.30-10am Sun. **Map** p321 G3.
The real joy of this church is its ceiling, with its four luminous paintings (1700-05) by the vivacious colourist Sebastiano Ricci. Two of them depict *God the Father with Angels* and *St Martial in Glory*; the other two recount the miraculous story of the wooden statue of the Madonna and Child that resides on the second altar on the left – apparently,

it made its own way here by boat from Rimini. The high altar has an equally fantastic Baroque extravaganza: a massive marble group of Christ, the world and some angels looms over the altar while St Jerome and companions crouch awkwardly beneath.

FREE Santi Apostoli

Cannaregio, campo Santi Apostoli (041 523 8297). Vaporetto Ca' d'Oro. **Open** 8.30am-noon, 5-7pm Mon-Sat; 4-7pm Sun. **Map** p321 H5.
According to tradition, the 12 apostles appeared to the seventh-century Bishop of Oderzo, St Magnus, telling him to build a church where he saw 12 cranes together – a not uncommon sight when Venice was little more than a series of uninhabited islands poking out of marshes. Magnus followed orders, but the ancient church was rebuilt in the 17th century. Its campanile (1672), crowned by an onion dome added 50 years later, is a Venetian landmark.
The Cappella Corner, off the right side of the nave, is a century older than the rest of the structure. It was built by Mauro Codussi for the dispossessed Queen Caterina Cornaro of Cyprus; she was buried here in 1510 alongside her father and brother but subsequently removed. On the altar is a splendidly theatrical *Communion of St Lucy* by Giambattista Tiepolo; the young saint, whose gouged eyes are in a dish on the floor, is bathed in a heavenly light. The chapel to the right of the high altar has remnants of 14th-century frescoes while the one to the left has a dramatically stormy painting of *The Guardian Angel* by Francesco Maffei.
▶ *Caterina Cornaro's tomb can now be seen in the church of San Salvador; see p73.*

FREE Gli Scalzi

Cannaregio, fondamenta degli Scalzi (041 715 115). Vaporetto Ferrovia. **Open** 7-11.50am, 4-6.45pm Mon-Sat; 4-7pm Sun. **Map** p320 C4.
Officially Santa Maria di Nazareth, this church is better known as Gli Scalzi after the order of *Carmelitani scalzi* (Barefoot Carmelites) to whom it belongs. They bought the plot in 1645 and subsequently commissioned Baldassare Longhena to design the church. The fine façade (1672-80) is the work of Giuseppe Sardi; it was paid for by a newcomer to Venice's ruling patrician class, Gerolamo Cavazza, determined to make his mark on the landscape.
The interior is striking for its coloured marble and massively elaborate baldachin over the high altar. There are many fine Baroque statues, including the *St John of the Cross* by Giovanni Marchiori in the first chapel on the right and the anonymous marble crucifix and wax effigy of Christ in the chapel opposite. An Austrian shell that plummeted through the roof in 1915 destroyed the church's greatest work of art, Tiepolo's fresco, *The Transport of the House of Loreto*, but spared some of the artist's lesser frescoes, *Angels of the Passion* and *Agony in the Garden*, in the first chapel on the left, and *St Theresa in Glory*, which hovers gracefully

above a ham-fisted imitation of Bernini's sculpture, *Ecstasy of St Theresa*, in the second on the right. In the second chapel on the left lie the remains of the last doge of Venice, Lodovico Manin.

▶ *For the story of Manin's capitulation to the French, see p26.*

IL GHETTO

Vaporetto Guglie or San Marcuola.

The word 'ghetto' (like 'arsenal' and 'ciao') is one that Venice has given to the world. It originally meant an iron foundry, a place where iron was *gettato* (cast). Until 1390, when the foundry was transferred to the Arsenale, casting was done on a small island in Cannaregio. In 1516, it was decided to confine the city's Jewish population to this island; here they remained until 1797.

Venetian treatment of the Jews was by no means as harsh as in many European countries, but neither was it a model of open-minded benevolence. The Republic's attitude was governed by practical considerations, and business was done with Jewish merchants at least as early as the tenth century. It was not until 1385, however, that Jewish moneylenders were given permission to reside in the city itself. Twelve years later, permission was revoked amid allegations of irregularities in their banking practices. For a century after that, residence in Venice was limited to two-week stretches. In 1509, when the Venetian mainland territories were overrun by foreign troops, great numbers of Jews took refuge in the city. The clergy seized the opportunity to stir up anti-Jewish feeling and demanded their expulsion. Venice's rulers, however, had begun to see the

Sleeping in Turns

Space was at a premium in the cramped quarters of the historic Ghetto.

Today, pretty **campo del Ghetto Nuovo** (*see above*) gives little idea of the hardships suffered there through the centuries that it hosted the closed community of Jews. Note the houses on the southern and eastern sides of the campo: taller than any others in Venice, they bear witness to how the hopelessly cramped inhabitants, prevented from expanding horizontally, did so vertically. Similar upwards extensions on the other two sides of the square have since been demolished; in times past, however, the open space was hemmed in and towered over on all sides.

During the day, the campo would have buzzed with activity. Christians came to the Ghetto to visit not only the pawnbrokers and money-lenders but also the *strazzerie* (second-hand clothes sellers) and artisans. As successive waves of immigrants arrived, the Ghetto would have resounded with a babble of languages from around the Mediterranean, as well as the northern inflections of Polish and German.

At night, the gates were closed and guarded by armed boats that patrolled the canals circling the small island; the Jews themselves were given the privilege of paying for this guard service.

The ground floors of the buildings around the campo were almost entirely devoted to commercial activities; everything else – residences, synagogues and schools – was located above. Ceilings were low and the staircases were narrow, to save space.

For structural stability, the walls on the ground floor were reinforced and the interior structures made of wood; still, the buildings display some pretty alarming cracks and bulges. There are reports of floors collapsing under the feet of over-enthusiastic wedding parties.

Despite hardship and chronic over-crowding, these outwardly unassuming buildings manage to contain the splendid spaces of the synagogues. The **Scola Canton** and the **Scola Tedesca**, the earliest of the synagogues, are only distinguished on the exterior by the array of five windows and by the small wooden lantern (Scola Canton); inside, however, architects created room for impressive devotional spaces, with rich carvings and decorations (again, all in wood). Clearly, religion played an enormous part in the lives of the inhabitants.

It has been calculated that when the population was at its height (and before the Jews were allowed to spill over into the adjoining areas of the Ghetto Vecchio and Ghetto Novissimo), there were about 5,000 inhabitants, living in an area of 60,000 square metres (650,000 square feet), more than two-fifths of which was given over to commercial and religious uses; this meant an average of about seven square metres (75 square feet) per person. It is even said that, at times, overcrowding was such that the inhabitants had to take it in turns to sleep.

SIGHTS

Campo dei Mori.

SIGHTS

economic advantages of letting them stay, and in 1516 a compromise was reached. In a decision that was to mark the course of Jewish history in Europe, the refugees were given residence permits but confined to the Ghetto.

Restrictions were many and tough. Gates across the bridges to the island were closed an hour after sunset in summer (two hours after winter), reopening at dawn. During the day, Jews had to wear distinctive badges or headgear. Most trades other than money-lending were barred to them. One exception was medicine, for which they were famous: Venetian practicality allowed Jewish doctors to leave the Ghetto at night for professional calls. Another was music: Jewish singers and fiddlers were hired for private parties.

The Ghetto became a stop on the tourist trail. In 1608, traveller Thomas Coryat came to gaze at the Jews – never having seen any in England – and marvelled at the 'sweet-featured persons' and the 'apparel, jewels, chains of gold' of the women.

The original inhabitants were mostly Ashkenazim from Germany; they were joined by Sephardim escaping from persecution in Spain and Portugal and then, increasingly, by Levantine Jews from the Ottoman Empire. These latter proved key figures in trade between Venice and the East, particularly after Venice lost so many of her trading posts in the eastern Mediterranean. By the middle

of the 16th century, the Levantine Jews, the richest community, were given permission to move from the Ghetto Nuovo to the confusingly named Ghetto Vecchio (the 'old Ghetto', the site of an earlier foundry); in 1633, they expanded into the Ghetto Nuovissimo. Nonetheless, the conditions here remained cramped (*see p93* **Sleeping in Turns**). Room was found for five magnificent synagogues, however. The German, Levantine and Spanish synagogues can all be visited as part of the **Museo Ebraico** tour (*see below*).

With the arrival of Napoleon in 1797, Jews gained full citizenship rights; many chose to remain in the Ghetto. In the deportations during the Nazi occupation of Italy in 1943, 202 Venetian Jews were sent to the death camps. The Jewish population of Venice and Mestre now stands at about 500. Only around a dozen Jewish families still live in the Ghetto, but it remains the centre of spiritual, cultural and social life for the Jewish community. Orthodox religious services are held in the Scuola Spagnola in the summer and in the Scuola Levantina in winter.

Museo Ebraico
Cannaregio 2902B, campo del Ghetto Nuovo (041 715 359/www.museoebraico.it). Vaporetto Guglie or San Marcuola. **Open** 10am-5.30pm Mon-Fri, Sun. *Guided tours* (hourly) 10.30am-4.30pm Mon-Thur, Sun; 10.30am-2.30pm Fri. **Admission** *Museum only* €3; €2 reductions. *Museum & synagogues* €8.50; €7 reductions. **Credit** MC, V. **Map** p321 E2.

Venice's Jewish community has been enjoying a renaissance recently, and this well-run museum and cultural centre – founded in 1953 – has been spruced up accordingly, with the addition of a bookshop; a further extension was planned as this guide went to press. In the small museum itself there are ritual objects in silver – Trah finials, Purim and Pesach cases, menorahs – sacred vestments and hangings, and a series of marriage contracts. The museum is best visited as part of a guided tour. This takes in three synagogues – the Scuola Canton (Ashkenazi rite), the Scuola Italiana (Italian rite) and the Scuola Levantina (Sephardic rite).

NORTH-WESTERN CANNAREGIO
Vaporetto Orto, San Marcuola or Sant'Alvise.

If you're tired of the crowds, there's no better place to get away from it all than the north-western areas of Cannaregio. Built around three long parallel canals, it has no large animated squares and (with the exception of the Ghetto; *see p93*) no sudden surprises – just occasional views over the northern lagoon.

However, it does have its landmarks, such as the *vecchia* (old; 14th-century) and *nuova* (new; 16th-century) **Scuole della Misericordia**, the 'new' one being a huge building by Sansovino, its façade never completed. It awaits conversion into a cultural institute. Behind the *scuole*, the picturesque campo dell'Abbazia, overlooked by the Baroque façade of the **Abbazia della Misericordia** and the Gothic façade of the *scuola vecchia*, is one of the most peaceful retreats in Venice; on the façade of the latter you can still see the outlines of sculptures (now in London's Victoria & Albert Museum) by Gothic master Bartolomeo Bon. The building is now used as an art restoration workshop.

On the northernmost canal (the rio della Madonna dell'Orto) are the churches of the **Madonna dell'Orto** (*see below*) and **Sant'Alvise** (*see p96*), as well as many fine *palazzi*. At the eastern end of the *fondamente* along this canal, **Palazzo Contarini dal Zaffo** was built for Gaspare Contarini, a 16th-century scholar, diplomat and cardinal. Behind, a large garden stretches down to the lagoon; in its far corner stands the **Casinò degli Spiriti** (best seen from fondamenta Nuove). It was designed as a meeting place for the 'spirits' (wits) of the day, though the name and the lonely position of the construction have given rise to numerous ghost stories.

The Madonna dell'Orto area may have been the home of an Islamic merchant community in the 12th and 13th centuries, centring on the since-destroyed *Fondaco degli arabi* (a meeting place and storehouse). Opposite the church of Santa Maria dell'Orto is the 15th-century **Palazzo Mastelli**, also known as Palazzo del Camello because of its relief of a turbaned figure with a camel. The Arabic theme carries on across the bridge in **campo dei Mori** ('of the Moors'), named after the three turban-wearing stone figures set into the façade of a building here. The one with the iron nose – dubbed 'Sior Antonio Rioba' – was where disgruntled citizens or local wits would stick their rhyming complaints under cover of darkness; his name was used as a pseudonym for published satires. The three figures are believed to be the Mastelli brothers, owners of the adjacent palazzo, who came to Venice as merchants from the Greek Peloponnese (then known as Morea – which offers another possible explanation of the campo's name).

★ Madonna dell'Orto

Cannaregio, campo Madonna dell'Orto (041 275 0462/www.chorusvenezia.org). Vaporetto Orto. **Open** 10am-5pm Mon-Sat. **Admission** €3 (or Chorus; *see p7*). **No credit cards**. **Map** p321 G2.

Santa Maria dei Miracoli. *See p97.*

SIGHTS

The 'Tintoretto church' was originally dedicated to St Christopher (a magnificent statue of whom stands over the main door), the patron saint of the gondoliers (who ran the ferry service to the islands from a nearby jetty). However, a cult developed around a large, unfinished and supposedly miraculous statue of the Madonna and Child that stood in a nearby garden. In 1377, the sculpture was transferred into the church (it's now in the chapel of San Mauro), and the church's name was changed to the Madonna dell'Orto – of the Garden.

It was rebuilt between 1399 and 1473, and a monastery was constructed alongside. The false gallery at the top of the beautiful Gothic façade is unique in Venice; the sculptures are all fine 15th-century works. But it is the numerous works by Tintoretto that have made the Madonna dell'Orto famous. Tradition has it that the artist began decorating the church as penance for insulting a doge: in fact, it took very little to persuade Tintoretto to get his palette out, and the urgent sincerity of his work here speaks for itself.

Two colossal paintings dominate the side walls of the chancel. On the left is *The Israelites at Mount Sinai*. Opposite is a gruesome *Last Judgment*. Tintoretto had no qualms about mixing religion and myth: note the classical figure of Charon ferrying the souls of the dead. His paintings in the apse include *St Peter's Vision of the Cross* and *The Beheading of St Paul* (or Christopher, according to some), both maelstroms of swirling angelic movement. On the wall of the right aisle is the *Presentation of the Virgin in the Temple*. The Contarini Chapel, off the left aisle, contains the artist's beautiful *St Agnes Reviving the Son of a Roman Prefect*. It is the swooping angels in their dazzling blue vestments that steal the show. Tintoretto, his son Domenico and his artistically gifted daughter Marietta are buried in a chapel off the right aisle.

When the Tintorettos get too much for you, take a look at Cima da Conegliano's masterpiece *Saints John the Baptist, Mark, Jerome and Paul* (1494-95) over the first altar on the right. The saints stand under a ruined portico against a sharp, wintry light. There used to be a small *Madonna and Child* by Giovanni Bellini in the chapel opposite, but it was

---

INSIDE TRACK
PAINTER PORTRAITS?

Local lore says that Tintoretto's *Israelites at Mount Sinai*, in the church of **Madonna dell'Orto** (*see p95*), contains hidden portraits of Venice's artistic top four (Giorgione, Titian, Veronese and Tintoretto himself) in the bearers of the Golden Calf. There's no actual documentary evidence for this, though, nor for the identification of the lady in blue as Mrs Tintoretto.

---

stolen in 1993. The second chapel on the left contains, on the left-hand wall, a painting by Titian of *The Archangel Raphael and Tobias* (and dog) that has been moved here from the church of San Marziale (*see p92*). In a room beneath the bell tower, a small treasury contains reliquaries and other precious objects.
▶ *For an even larger dose of Tintoretto, head for the Scuola di San Rocco; see p112.*

Sant'Alvise

Cannaregio, campo Sant'Alvise (041 275 0462/www.chorusvenezia.org). Vaporetto Sant'Alvise. **Open** 10am-5pm Mon-Sat. **Admission** €3 (or Chorus; *see p7*). **No credit cards. Map** p321 F1.
A pleasingly simple Gothic building of the 14th century, Sant'Alvise's interior was remodelled in the 1600s with extravagant, if not wholly convincing, trompe l'œil effects on the ceiling. On the inner façade is a *barco*, a hanging choir of the 15th century with elegant wrought-iron gratings. Beneath the *barco* are eight charmingly naïve biblical paintings in tempera, attributed to Lazzaro Bastiani. On the right wall of the church are two paintings by Tiepolo, *The Crowning with Thorns* and *The Flagellation*. A larger and livelier work by the same painter, *Road to Calvary*, hangs on the right wall of the chancel, with rather ill-suited circus pageantry.
▶ *Anyone looking for a picnic spot will find a garden nearby, complete with picturesque classical 'ruins'; walk westwards along the fondamenta and take calle del Capitelo to the right.*

EASTERN CANNAREGIO

Vaporetto Fondamente Nove or Rialto.

Behind the straight edge of the Fondamenta Nuove, eastern Cannaregio is more intriguingly closed in, with many narrow alleys (including the Venetian record holder: calle Varisco, which is 52 centimetres (20 inches) wide at its narrowest point, charming courtyards and well-heads, but no major sights, with the exception of the spectacularly ornate church of **I Gesuiti** (*see below*), the **Oratorio dei Crociferi** (*see p97*) and, further east, the miniature marvel of **Santa Maria dei Miracoli** (*see p97*). Titian had a house here, with a garden extending to the lagoon; the courtyard where the house was located is raised to the dignity of a 'campo' and named after the artist.

FREE I Gesuiti

Cannaregio, campo dei Gesuiti (041 528 6579). Vaporetto Fondamente Nove. **Open** 10am-noon, 4-6pm daily. **Map** p324 J3.
The Jesuits were never very popular in Venice, and it wasn't until 1715 that they felt secure enough to build a church here. Even then they chose a comparatively remote plot on the edge of town. But once they made up their mind to go ahead, they went all

Canale delle Fondamenta Nuove.

out: local architect Domenico Rossi was given explicit instructions to dazzle. The result leaves no room for half measures: you love it or you hate it, and most people do the latter.

The exterior, with a façade by Gian Battista Fattoretto, is conventional enough; the interior is anything but. All that tassled, bunched, overpowering drapery is not the work of a rococo set designer gone berserk with luxurious brocades: it's plain old green and white marble. Bernini's altar in St Peter's in Rome was the model for the baldachin over the altar, by Fra Giuseppe Pozzo. The statues above the baldachin are by Giuseppe Torretti, as are the rococo archangels at the corners of the crossing. Titian's *Martyrdom of St Lawrence* (1558-59), over the first altar on the left side, came from an earlier church on this site, and was one of the first successful night scenes ever to be painted.

Oratorio dei Crociferi

Cannaregio 4905, campo dei Gesuiti (041 270 2464). Vaporetto Fondamente Nove. **Open** by appointment; call 041 271 9012. **Map** p324 J3.
Founded in the 13th century by Doge Renier Zeno, the oratory is a sort of primitive *scuola* (*see p105* **Back to School**), with the familiar square central meeting hall but without the quasi-masonic ceremonial trappings. Palma il Giovane's colourful cycle of paintings shows Pope Anacletus instituting the order of the Crociferi (cross-bearers), and dwells on the pious life of Doge Pasquale Cicogna, who was a fervent supporter of the order.

★ Santa Maria dei Miracoli

Cannaregio, campo Santa Maria dei Miracoli (041 275 0462/www.chorusvenezia.org). Vaporetto Fondamente Nove or Rialto. **Open** 10am-5pm Mon-Sat. **Admission** €3 (or Chorus; *see p7*). **No credit cards**. **Map** p324 J5.
Arguably one of the most exquisite churches in the world, Santa Maria dei Miracoli was built in the 1480s to house a miraculous image of the Madonna, reputed to have revived a man who had spent half an hour underwater in the Giudecca Canal, and also to have cancelled all traces of a knife attack on a woman. The building is the work of the Lombardo family, early Renaissance masons who fused architecture, surface detail and sculpture into a unique whole.

Pietro Lombardo may have been a Lombard by birth but he soon got into the Venetian way of doing things, employing Byzantine spoils left over from work on St Mark's to create a work of art displaying an entirely Venetian sensitivity to texture and colour. There is an almost painterly approach to the use of multicoloured marble in the four sides of the church, each of which is of a slightly different shade. The sides have more pilasters than necessary, making the church appear longer than it really is.

Inside, the 50 painted ceiling panels by Pier Maria Pennacchi (1528) are almost impossible to distinguish without binoculars. Instead, turn your attention to the church's true treasures: the delicate carvings by the Lombardos on the columns, steps and balustrade with their exquisite, lifelike details. *Photo p95.*

San Polo
& Santa Croce

From bustling markets to the art treasures of the Frari and scuole.

The *sestieri* of San Polo and Santa Croce nestle in the pear-shaped right-bank bulge created by the loop in the Grand Canal. The eastern portion, tightly clustered around the **Rialto market**, is the city's ancient heart and, despite the invasion of stalls selling trashy tourist-trinkets, you can still feel its steady throb here, particularly in the bustling morning market.

The western part was settled later and has a slightly more spacious feel; its fulcrum is the great religious complex of the **Frari** (*see p109*) and the *scuole* of **San Rocco** (*see p112*) and **San Giovanni Evangelista** (*see p111*). The rio San Polo slices from north to south, changing its name three times en route. As for where one *sestiere* ends and the other begins, it is probably only the local postman who can tell.

SANTA CROCE

SAN POLO

| **Map** pp320-321 | **Restaurants** p173 |
| **Hotels** p157 | **Cafés & Bars** p189 |

SIGHTS

THE RIALTO MARKETS

Vaporetto Rialto or Rialto Mercato.

Rialto, most experts agree, derives from *Rivoaltus* (high bank). It was on this point of higher ground at the mid-point along the Grand Canal that one of the earliest settlements was founded, in the fifth century. The district has been the commercial centre of the city since the market was moved here in 1097.

The present layout of the market zone is the result of a reconstruction project by Scarpagnino undertaken after a devasting fire in 1514. The project made use of the existing foundations, so the present street-plan probably reflects quite faithfully the earliest urban arrangement, with long, narrow parallel blocks running behind the grand *palazzi* along the riva del Vin, and smaller, square blocks further inland for the market workers.

At the foot of the Rialto bridge, where the tourist stalls are thick on the ground, stand (to the south) the **Palazzo dei Dieci Savi**,

which housed the city's tax inspectors but is now used by the ancient but extant lagoon water authority, *Il magistrato alle acque*, and (to the north) the **Palazzo dei Camerlenghi**, which housed the finance department.

Beyond these, the small church of **San Giacomo di Rialto** (known affectionately as San Giacometto; *see p99*) is generally agreed to be the first of the city's churches. All around it stretch the markets – the best place to buy your fruit, veg and seafood. In recent years, this area has taken on a new lease of life as a centre of Venetian night-life (*see p190* **Evening in the Market**), with a number of bars opening under the porticos of the Renaissance *Fabbriche Vecchie* (Scarpagnino, 1520-22), including some opening on to the *Erbaria*.

The name *Erbaria* denotes the fact that vegetables are sold here; there are other examples of such names in the streets and squares nearby (Naranzeria – oranges; Casaria – cheese; Speziali – spices), while the narrower alleys mostly bear the names of ancient inns and taverns – some still in operation –

such as 'The Monkey', 'The Two Swords', 'The Two Moors', 'The Ox', and 'The Bell'. Then, as now, market traders hated to be too far from liquid refreshment.

On the other side of campo San Giacomo from the church, behind the fruit stalls, is a 16th-century statue of a kneeling figure supporting a staircase leading up to a small column of Egyptian granite, from which laws and sentences were pronounced. It was to this figure – the *Gobbo di Rialto* (the Hunchback of the Rialto, although you'll note that he is, in fact, merely crouching; *photo p106*) – that naked malefactors clung in desperate and bloody relief, since the statue marked the end of the gauntlet they were condemned to run from piazza San Marco as an alternative to gaol.

The ruga degli Speziali leads to the **Pescaria** (fishmarket; open Tue-Sat mornings). The present neo-Gothic arcade (1907) replaced an iron structure of the previous century. Beyond the market extends a warren of medieval low-rent housing interspersed with proud *palazzi*. This area is traversed by two main pedestrian routes from the Rialto bridge, one running westward, more or less parallel to the Grand Canal, towards campo San Polo (*see p101*), and the other zigzagging north-westwards via a series of small squares towards campo **San Giacomo dell'Orio** (*see p104*) and the station.

FREE San Giacomo di Rialto
San Polo, campo San Giacomo (041 522 4745). Vaporetto Rialto or Rialto Mercato. **Open** 9.30am-noon, 4-6pm Mon-Sat. **Map** p321 H5.

The traditional foundation date for this church is that of the city itself: 25 March 421. It has undergone several radical reconstructions since then, the last in 1601. Nonetheless, the original Greek-cross plan was always preserved, as were its minuscule dimensions. The interior has columns of ancient marble with 11th-century Corinthian capitals.

In 1177, Pope Alexander III granted plenary indulgence to all those who visited the church on Maundy Thursday; among the eager visitors every year was the doge. The special role of this church in Venetian history was given official recognition after 1532, when Pope Clement VII bestowed the patronage of the church on the doge, effectively annexing it to the Ducal Chapel of St Mark's. The church frequently hosts evening concerts (*see p241*).

▶ *According to Francesco Sansovino (son of the architect and author of the first guide to the city, in 1581), the brick dome may have been a model for the domes of St Mark's; see p61.*

WEST FROM THE RIALTO

Vaporetto Rialto, Rialto Mercato, San Silvestro or San Tomà.

The route to campo San Polo traverses a series of busy shopping streets, passing the church of **San Giovanni Elemosinario** (*see p101*) and the deconsecrated church of **Sant'Aponal**, which has fine Gothic sculpture on its façade. To the south of this route, towards the Grand Canal, stands **San Silvestro** (*see p101*), with a good Tintoretto, while to the north is a fascinating network of quiet, little-visited alleys and courtyards.

SIGHTS

Rialto Market.

HIBISCUS

S.Polo 1060
Ruga Rialto (near Rialto bridge)
041 520 8989

The shop offers an eclectic range of clothing, with different colour ranges and fits, satisfying women's taste in seeking to anticipate the trends with original and exclusive lines both from Italy and abroad.

All garments are chosen with special care, favouring local artisans and using the highest quality fabrics. Hibiscus is always a pleasant surprise, with a wide range of accessories, from costume jewellery, to scarves, hats and more.

Mon - Sat: 09:30 - 19:30   Sun: 11:00 - 19:30

Curiosities worth seeking out (take calle Bianca Cappello from campo Sant'Aponal) include **Palazzo Molin-Cappello**, birthplace of Bianca Cappello, who in 1563 was sentenced to death *in absentia* for eloping with a bank clerk but managed to right things between herself and the Most Serene Republic by later marrying Francesco de' Medici, Grand Duke of Tuscany. North-westwards from here is campiello Albrizzi, overlooked by **Palazzo Albrizzi**, with its sumptuous Baroque interior (unfortunately, it's closed to the public).

After the shadowy closeness of these *calli*, the open expanse of campo **San Polo** – home to the church (*see below*) of the same name – comes as a sudden, sunlit surprise. This is the largest square on this side of the Grand Canal and, in the past, was used for popular occasions such as bull-baiting, religious ceremonies, parades and theatrical spectacles. Venue for an open-air film season (*see p215*) in the summer, its main day-to-day function is that of a vast children's playground.

The curving line of *palazzi* on the east side of the square is explained by the fact that these buildings once gave on to a canal, which was subsequently filled in. The two *palazzi* Soranzo (nos.2169 and 2170-1) are particularly attractive Gothic buildings, with marble facing and good capitals. In the north-west corner is a view of **Palazzo Corner** (the main façade is on rio di San Polo), a 16th-century design by Sanmicheli. Novelist Frederick Rolfe stayed here – until his hosts read the manuscript of his work, *The Desire and Pursuit of the Whole* (1909), which contained vitriolic pen-portraits of their friends. They turned him out of the house, thus earning a place for themselves in this grudge novel.

San Giovanni Elemosinario

San Polo, ruga vecchia San Giovanni (041 275 0462/www.chorusvenezia.org). Vaporetto Rialto, Rialto Mercato or San Silvestro. **Open** 10am-5pm Mon-Sat. **Admission** €3 (or Chorus; *see p7*). **No credit cards**. **Map** p321 G5.

INSIDE TRACK
CASANOVA'S DADDY

It was while playing the violin at an aristocratic wedding feast in one of the Sorani *palazzi* that Casanova first met Senator Bragadin. The aged senator offered Casanova a ride in his gondola, and on the way home suffered a stroke; showing great coolness, Casanova had the gondoliers stop and called a surgeon, saving the man's life. The senator ended up by adopting Casanova.

This small Renaissance church – a Greek cross within a square – was founded in the ninth or tenth century but rebuilt after a fire in 1514, probably by Scarpagnino. On the high altar is a painting by Titian of the titular saint, *St John the Alms Giver*. In the left aisle is a medieval fragment of sculptural relief (12th or 13th century) of the Nativity, which shows an ox and donkey reverently licking the face of the Christ child.

▶ *The body of this St John is preserved in the church of San Giovanni in Bragora; see p87.*

San Polo

San Polo, campo San Polo (041 275 0462/www.chorusvenezia.org). Vaporetto San Silvestro or San Tomà. **Open** 10am-5pm Mon-Sat. **Admission** €3 (or Chorus; *see p7*). **No credit cards**. **Map** p321 F6.

The church of San Polo faces away from the square, towards the canal, although later buildings have deprived it of its façade and water entrance. The campanile (1362) has two 12th-century lions at the base, one brooding over a snake and the other toying with a human head, which Venetians like to think of as that of Count Carmagnola, who was beheaded for treachery in 1402. The Gothic church was extensively altered in the 19th century, when a neo-classical look was imposed on it. Some of this was removed in 1930, but the interior remains a rather awkward hybrid.

Paintings include a *Last Supper* by Tintoretto, to the left of the entrance, and a Tiepolo: *The Virgin Appearing to St John of Nepomuk*. Giambattista Tiepolo's son, Giandomenico, is the author of a brilliant cycle of Stations of the Cross in the Oratory of the Crucifix (entrance is under the organ), freshly restored. He painted these, as well as the ceiling paintings, at the age of 20.

▶ *Tintoretto's next painting of The Last Supper is inside Santo Stefano; see p75. The previous one is in San Simeone Profeta; see p106.*

FREE San Silvestro

San Polo, campo San Silvestro (041 523 8090). Vaporetto San Silvestro. **Open** 7.30-noon, 4-6pm Mon-Sat. Closed some afternoons. **Map** p321 G6.

The church of San Silvestro was rebuilt in the neo-classical style between 1837 and 1843. It contains a *Baptism of Christ* (c1580) by Tintoretto, located over the first altar on the right, with the River Jordan represented as a mountain brook. Opposite this is *St Thomas à Becket Enthroned* (1520) by Girolamo da Santacroce, with the saint in startling white robes against a mountain landscape; the other two saints are 19th-century additions. Off the right aisle (ask the sacristan to let you in) is the former School of the Wine Merchants; on the upper floor there's a chapel with 18th-century frescoes by Gaspare Diziani. Opposite the church is the house (no.1022) where Giorgione died in 1510.

▶ *Who was Giorgione? For a biography, see p35.*

Souvenir stalls near the Rialto.

SIGHTS

NORTH-WEST FROM THE RIALTO

Vaporetto Ferrovia, Rialto Mercato, Riva di Biasio or San Stae.

Yellow signs pointing to 'Ferrovia' mark the zigzagging north-western route from the Rialto, past the fishmarket, and on past campo **San Cassiano**. The uninspiring plain exterior of the church here (*see p104*) gives no clue as to its heavily decorated interior.

Across the bridge is campo **Santa Maria Mater Domini** with its Renaissance church (*see p106*). Before entering the campo, stop on the bridge to admire the view of the curving Grand Canal-facing marble flank of **Ca' Pesaro** (*see p103*), the seat of the **Museo Orientale** and **Galleria d'Arte Moderna**. On the far side of the square, which contains a number of fine Byzantine and Gothic buildings, the yellow road sign indicates that the way to the station is to the left *and* to the right. Take your pick.

The quieter route to the right curls parallel to the Grand Canal. The road towards Ca' Pesaro passes **Palazzo Agnusdio**, a small 14th-century house with an ogival five-light window decorated with bas-reliefs of the Annunciation and symbols of the evangelists; the house used to belong to a family of sausage-makers, who were given patrician status in the 17th century.

Many of the most important sights face on to the Grand Canal, including the 18th-century church of **San Stae** (*see p106*) and the Fondaco dei Turchi (Warehouse of the Turks), home to the **Museo di Storia Naturale** (*see p104*).

On the wide road leading towards San Stae is **Palazzo Mocenigo** (*see p104*), with its collection of textiles and costumes. Nearby is the quiet square of San Zan Degolà (**San Giovanni Decollato**), with a well-preserved 11th-century church (*see p105*). From here, a series of narrow roads leads past the church of **San Simeone Profeta** (*see p106*) to the foot of the Scalzi bridge across the Grand Canal.

Leave campo Santa Maria Mater Domini by the route to the left, on the other hand, and you'll make your way past the near-legendary **Da Fiore** restaurant (*see p175*) to the house (no. 2311) where Aldus Manutius set up the Aldine Press in 1490, and where the humanist Erasmus came to stay in 1508. To the right, by a building with a 14th-century relief of Faith and Justice above its doorway, the rio terà del Parrucchetta (reportedly named after a seller of animal fodder who used to wear a ridiculous wig, or *parrucca*) leads to the large leafy campo

> ### INSIDE TRACK
> ### ACCEPTABLE VICES
>
> Northwest of campo Sant'Aponal is one of Venice's early red-light zones; the district of Ca' Rampana passed on its own name (*carampana* means 'slut') to the Italian language. Just round the corner is the ponte delle Tette (Tits Bridge), where prostitutes were allowed to display their wares with the aim of saving Venetian men from less 'acceptable' vices.

San Giacomo dell'Orio (*see p104*). The campo (which translates as St James of the wolf, the laurel tree, the rio or the Orio family – take your pick) has a pleasantly downbeat feel, with its trees, bars and children. It's dominated by the church with its plump apses and stocky 13th-century campanile. The church has its back and sides to the square; the main entrance was directly from the water.

Ca' Pesaro – Galleria Internazionale d'Arte Moderna
Santa Croce 2076, fondamenta Ca' Pesaro (041 524 0695/www.museiciviciveneziani.it). Vaporetto San Stae. **Open** 10am-5pm Tue-Sun. **Admission** (incl Museo Orientale) €5.50; €3 reductions. **Credit** AmEx, MC, V. **Map** p321 F4.
This grandiose palazzo was built in the second half of the 17th century for the Pesaro family, to a project by Baldassare Longhena. When Longhena died in 1682, the family called in Gian Antonio Gaspari, who concluded it in 1710. The interior of the palazzo still contains some of the original fresco and oil-painted decorations, although the family's great collection of Renaissance paintings was auctioned off in London by the last Pesaro before he died in 1830.

The palazzo passed through many hands until its last owner, Felicita Bevilacqua La Masa, bequeathed it to the city. Into it went the city's collection of modern art, gleaned from the Biennale (*see pp47-49*). The museum now covers a century of mainly Italian art, from the mid 19th century to the 1950s. The stately ground floor is used for temporary shows. At the foot of the staircase stands Giacomo Manzù's tapering bronze statue, *Cardinal.*

The first rooms on the piano nobile contain atmospheric works by 19th-century painters and some striking sculptures by Medardo Rosso. In the central hall are works from the early *Biennali* (up to the 1930s), including pieces by Gustav Klimt and Vassily Kandinsky, alongside more conventional, vast-scale 'salon' paintings. Room 4 holds works by Giorgio Morandi, Joan Mirò and Giorgio De Chirico. After rooms devoted to international art from the 1940s and '50s, the collection finishes up with works by notable post-war Venetian experimentalists such as Armando Pizzinato, Giuseppe Santomaso and Emilio Vedova.
▶ *The Pesaro family is celebrated in Titian's great painting, La Madonna di Ca' Pesaro, in the Frari; see p109.*

Ca' Pesaro – Museo Orientale
Santa Croce 2070, fondamenta Ca' Pesaro (041 524 1173/www.museiciviciveneziani.it). Vaporetto San Stae. **Open** 10am-5pm Tue-Sun. **Admission** (incl Galleria d'Arte Moderna) €5.50; €3 reductions. **Map** p321 F4.
If Japanese art and weaponry of the Edo period (1600-1868) are your thing, you'll love this eclectic collection, put together by Count Enrico di Borbone – a nephew of Louis XVIII – in the course of a round-the-world voyage between 1887 and 1890. After the count's death, the collection was sold off to an Austrian antique merchant; it bounced back to Venice after World War I as reparations.

The collection features parade armour, dolls, decorative saddles and case upon case of curved samurai swords forged by smiths who had to perform a ritual act of purification before putting their irons in the fire. There is also a dwarf-sized lady's

INSIDE TRACK
LUCIFER'S SHADOW

Two paintings in these *sestieri* featured in David Hewson's 2001 novel, *Lucifer's Shadow*: a naïve 18th-century work in **San Giacomo dell'Orio** (*see below-right*) by Gaetano Zompini, showing a Jewish scribe attempting to profane the body of the Virgin; and the *Martyrdom of St Cassian*, in **San Cassiano** (*see right*).

gilded litter, and lacquered picnic cases that prove that the Japanese obsession with compactness indeed pre-dates the Sony Walkman.

FREE Museo di Storia Naturale

Santa Croce 1730, salizada del Fondaco dei Turchi (041 275 0206). Vaporetto San Stae. **Open** 9am-1pm Tue-Fri; 10am-4pm Sat, Sun. **Admission** free. **Map** p321 E4.
This museum has long been undergoing very leisurely restoration. Just two rooms are open to the public. It is housed in the Fondaco dei Turchi, a Venetian-Byzantine building leased to the Turks in the 17th century as a residence and warehouse. The present building is essentially a 19th-century reconstruction of the original. At present, visitors can see the Acquario delle Tegnue, devoted to the aquatic life of the northern Adriatic, and the Sala dei Dinosauri, a state-of-the-art exhibition chronicling the Ligabue expedition to Niger (1973), which unearthed a fossil of the previously unknown *Auronosaurus nigeriensis* and a giant crocodile.

Palazzo Mocenigo

Santa Croce 1992, salizada San Stae (041 721 798/www.museicivicaveneziani.it). Vaporetto San Stae. **Open** 10am-4pm Tue-Sun. **Admission** €4; €2.50 reductions (*see also p6*). **No credit cards**. **Map** p321 F4.
The Palazzo Mocenigo museum serves a double purpose. The interior gives a fine illustration of the sort of furniture and fittings an 18th-century Venetian noble family surrounded itself with. The Mocenigo family provided the Republic with seven doges, and the paintings, friezes and frescoes by late 18th-century artists such as Jacopo Guarana and Gian Battista Canal glorify their achievements.

In the rooms off the main *salone* are the dusty display cases that serve the museum's other function: to chronicle 18th-century Venetian dress. An andrienne dress with bustles so horizontal it could rest a cup and saucer on them, antique lace and silk stockings, a whalebone corset – it's a patchy but charming collection.
▶ *Responsibility for restoring and reproducing the costumes falls to the inmates of Venice's women's prison; see p128 Bags, Rags & Veg.*

FREE San Cassiano

San Polo, campo San Cassiano (041 721 408). Vaporetto Rialto Mercato or San Stae. **Open** 9am-noon, 5-7.30pm Mon-Sat. **Map** p321 F5.
This church has a singularly dull exterior and a heavily decorated interior, with a striking ceiling (which has been freshly restored) by the Tiepolesque painter Constantino Cedini.

The chancel contains three major Tintorettos: *Crucifixion, Resurrection* and *Descent into Limbo*. The *Crucifixion* is particularly interesting for its viewpoint. As Ruskin puts it, 'The horizon is so low, that the spectator must fancy himself lying full length on the grass, or rather among the brambles and luxuriant weeds, of which the foreground is entirely composed.' In the background, the soldiers' spears make a menacing forest against a dramatic stormy sky. Off the left aisle is a small chapel with coloured marbles and inlays of semi-precious stones.

On the wall opposite the altar is a painting by Antonio Balestra, which at first glance looks like a dying saint surrounded by *putti*. On closer inspection it transpires that the chubby children are, in fact, hacking the man to death: the painting represents *The Martyrdom of St Cassian*, a teacher who was murdered by his pupils with their pens. This, of course, makes him the patron saint of schoolteachers.

★ San Giacomo dell'Orio

Santa Croce, campo San Giacomo dell'Orio (041 275 0462/www.chorusvenezia.org). Vaporetto Riva di Biasio. **Open** 10am-5pm Mon-Sat. **Admission** €3 (or Chorus; *see p7*). **No credit cards**. **Map** p321 E5.
The main entrance of San Giacomo dell'Orio faces the canal rather than the campo. The interior is a fascinating mix of architectural and decorative styles. Most of the columns have 12th- or 13th-century Veneto-Byzantine capitals; one has a sixth-century flowered capital and one is a solid piece of smooth verd-antique marble, perhaps from a Roman temple sacked during the Fourth Crusade. Note, too, the fine 14th-century ship's-keel roof. The Sacrestia Nuova, in the right transept, was built in 1903 on the site of the Scuola del Sacramento. This was the original home of the five gilded compartments on the ceiling with paintings by Veronese: an *Allegory of the Faith* surrounded by four Doctors of the Church. Among the paintings in the room is *St John the Baptist Preaching* by Francesco Bassano, which includes a portrait of Titian (in the red hat).

Behind the high altar is a *Madonna and Four Saints* by Lorenzo Lotto, one of his last Venetian paintings. There is a good work by Giovanni Bonconsiglio at the end of the left aisle, *St Lawrence, St Sebastian and St Roch*; St Roch's plague sore has an anatomical precision that is really rather unsettling. St Lawrence also has a chapel all to himself in the left transept, with a central altarpiece by Veronese and two fine early works by Palma il Giovane. As you leave, be sure to have a look at the curious painting to the left of the main door, a naïve 18th-century work by Gaetano Zompini, showing a propaganda miracle involving a Jewish scribe who attempted to profane the body of the Virgin on its way to the sepulchre.

FREE San Giovanni Decollato (San Zan Degolà)
Santa Croce, campo San Giovanni Decollato (041 524 0672). Vaporetto Riva di Biasio. **Open** 10am-noon Mon-Sat. **Map** p321 E4.

The church of Headless Saint John – or San Zan Degolà in Venetian dialect – is a good building to visit if you want a relief from the usual Baroque excesses and ecclesiastic clutter. Restored and reopened in 1994, it preserves much of its original 11th-century appearance. The church's interior has Greek columns with Byzantine capitals supporting ogival arches, and an attractive ship's-keel roof. During the restoration, a splendidly heroic 14th-century fresco of St Michael the Archangel came to light in the right apse. The left apse has some of

Back to School

Part meeting house, part art gallery – Venice's scuole merit some study.

Scuole – a blend of art-treasure house and social institution – are uniquely Venetian establishments. Essentially, they were devotional lay brotherhoods, subject to the state rather than the church. In Venice's complicated system of social checks and balances (*see p21* **Machinery of State**), they gave citizens of wealth – but no hope of ever entering the ruling elite – a place to feel they exerted some influence. The earliest were founded in the 13th century; by the 15th century, there were six *scuole grandi* and as many as 400 minor *scuole*.

The six *scuole grandi* had annually elected officers drawn from the 'citizen' class (sandwiched between the governing patriciate and the unenfranchised *popolani*). While members of the *scuole grandi* – such as the **Scuola Grande**

di San Rocco (pictured; *see p112*), **Scuola Grande di San Marco** (*see p82*) and recently reopened **Scuola Grande di San Giovanni Evangelista** (*see p111*) – were mainly drawn from the wealthier professional classes, the humbler *scuole piccole* were exclusively devotional groups, trade guilds or confraternities of foreign communities (such as the **Scuola di San Giorgio degli Schiavoni**; *see p87*).

The wealthier confraternities devoted a great deal of time and expense to beautifying their meeting houses (the *scuole* themselves), sometimes hiring one major painter to decorate the whole building; this was the case of Tintoretto at San Rocco and Carpaccio at San Giorgio degli Schiavoni. These buildings are essential viewing for anyone interested in the works of these artists.

SIGHTS

Gobbo di Rialto. See p99.

the earliest frescoes in Venice, Veneto-Byzantine works of the early 13th century. The church is used for Russian Orthodox services.

FREE San Simeone Profeta
Santa Croce, campo San Simeone Profeta (041 718 921). Vaporetto Ferrovia. **Open** 8am-noon, 5-6.30pm Mon-Sat. **Map** p320 D4.
More commonly known as San Simeone Grande, this small church of possibly tenth-century foundation underwent numerous alterations in the 18th century. The interior retains its ancient columns with Byzantine capitals. To the left of the entrance is Tintoretto's *Last Supper*, with the priest who commissioned the painting standing to one side, a spectral figure in glowing white robes. The other major work is the stark, powerful statue of a recumbent St Simeon, with an inscription dated 1317 attributing it to an otherwise unknown Marco Romano. The prophet has a 'face full of quietness and majesty, though very ghastly,' as Ruskin puts it. Outside, beneath the portico flanking the church, is a fine 15th-century relief of a bishop praying.
▶ *Tintoretto's next Last Supper is in San Polo; see p101. The previous is in San Trovaso; see p119.*

San Stae
Santa Croce, campo San Stae (041 275 0462/ www.chorusvenezia.org). Vaporetto San Stae. **Open** 10am-5pm Mon-Sat. **Admission** €3 (or Chorus; *see p7*). **No credit cards. Map** p321 F4.
Stae is the Venetian version of Eustachio or Eustace, a martyred saint who was converted to Christianity by the vision of a stag with a crucifix

between his antlers. This church on the Grand Canal has a dramatic late-Baroque façade (1709) by Swiss-born architect Domenico Rossi. The form is essentially Palladian but enlivened by a number of vibrant sculptures, some apparently on the point of leaping straight out of the façade.

Venice's last great blaze of artistic glory came in the 18th century, and the interior is a temple to this swansong. On the side walls of the chancel, all the leading painters operating in Venice in 1722 were asked to pick an apostle. The finest of these are: Tiepolo's *Martyrdom of St Bartholomew* and Sebastiano Ricci's *Liberation of St Peter*, perhaps his best work (both left wall, lower row); Pellegrini's *Martyrdom of St Andrew* and Piazzetta's *Martyrdom of St James*, a disturbingly realistic work showing the saint as a confused old man in the hands of a loutish youth (both right wall, lower row).
▶ *This church is often used for temporary exhibitions; Chorus pass holders (see p7) can see these for free.*

FREE Santa Maria Mater Domini
Santa Croce, calle della Chiesa (041 721 408). Vaporetto San Stae. **Open** 10am-noonTue-Fri. **Map** p321 F5.
This church is set just off the campo of the same name. It was built in the first half of the 16th century to a commission by either Giovanni Buora or Maurizio Codussi. The façade is attributed to Jacopo Sansovino; the harmonious Renaissance interior alternates grey stone with white marble. The *Vision of St Christine*, on the second altar on the right, is by Vincenzo Catena, a spice merchant who painted

in his spare time. St Christine was rescued by angels after being thrown into Lake Bolsena with a millstone tied around her neck; in the painting she adores the Risen Christ, while angels hold up the millstone for her. In the left transept hangs *The Invention of the Cross*, a youthful work by Tintoretto.

FROM THE FRARI TO PIAZZALE ROMA

Vaporetto Piazzale Roma or San Tomà.

At the heart of the western side of the two *sestieri* of San Polo and Santa Croce lies the great gothic bulk of Santa Maria Gloriosa dei Frari (aka **I Frari**; *see p109*), with its 70-metre (230-foot) campanile, matched by the Renaissance magnificence of the *scuola* and church of San Rocco. These buildings contain perhaps the greatest concentration of influential works of art in the city outside piazza San Marco and the Accademia (*see p122*).

Beyond the Frari's convent – which houses Venice's historic archives (*see below* **Inside Track**) – is the **Scuola di San Giovanni Evangelista** (*see p111*), one of the six *scuole grandi* (*see p105* **Back to School**).

North of here runs rio Marin, a canal with *fondamente* on both sides, lined by some fine buildings; these include the late 16th-century **Palazzo Soranzo Capello** (no.770), with a small rear garden that figures in Henry James' *The Aspern Papers*; and the 17th-century **Palazzo Gradenigo**, (no.768) the garden of which was once large enough to host bullfights.

South-west of the Frari is the quiet square of **San Tomà**, with a church on one side and the **Scuola dei Calegheri** ('of the cobblers') opposite; the *scuola* (now a library) has a protective mantle-spreading Madonna over the door. Above it is a relief by Pietro Lombardo of *St Mark Healing the Cobbler Annanius*, who became bishop of Alexandria and subsequently the patron saint of shoemakers.

Directly to the south of here is campo **San Pantalon** (*see p111*), technically in Dorsoduro but best approached from here. Its church has an extraordinary Hollywood-rococo interior. If you walk out of the church towards the canal, an alley to the left will take you into little campiello d'Angaran, where there is a carved roundel of a Byzantine emperor, which possibly dates from the tenth century. Returning to the campo, you'll see a slab in the wall by the canal, which indicates the minimum lengths allowed for the sale of various types of fish.

Just off the square of San Tomà is Palazzo Centani, the birthplace of Carlo Goldoni, the prolific Venetian playwright, which contains a small museum and library: the **Casa di Carlo Goldoni** (*see below*).

Heading west from the Frari, the route leads past the **church** and **scuola** of **San Rocco** (*see p111 and p112*), both treasure troves for Tintoretto-lovers, and ends up in a fairly bland area of 19th-century housing. At the edge of this stands the Baroque church of **San Nicolò dei Tolentini** (*see p111*); the adjoining former monastery houses part of the Venice University Architecture Institute.

The rather forlorn **Giardino Papadopoli**, a small park with Grand Canal views, stands on the site of the church and convent of Santa Croce. The name survives as that of the *sestiere*, but the church is one of many suppressed by the French at the beginning of the 19th century. All that remains of Santa Croce is a crenellated wall next to a hotel on the Grand Canal. The garden was much larger until the rio Novo was cut in 1932-33 to provide faster access from the new car park to the St Mark's area. The canal subsequently had to be closed to regular waterborne traffic, in the early 1990s, owing to subsidence in the adjacent buildings.

Beyond the garden there is little but the carbon-monoxide kingdom of piazzale Roma and the multi-storey car parks. One last curiosity is the complex of bridges across the rio Novo known as Tre Ponti (three bridges); there are, in fact, five interlocking bridges.

Casa di Carlo Goldoni

San Polo 2794, calle dei Nomboli (041 275 9325). Vaporetto San Tomà. **Open** 10am-4pm Mon, Tue, Thur-Sun. **Admission** €2.50; €1.50 reductions (*see also p6*). **No credit cards. Map** p321 E6.

Officially the Casa di Goldoni e Biblioteca di Studi Teatrali (Goldoni's House and Library of Theatre Studies), this museum is really for specialists, though the attractive Gothic courtyard, with its carved wellhead and staircase, is worth seeing. It is the birthplace of Venice's greatest writer, the playwright Carlo Goldoni. Over the course of his career, he transformed

---

INSIDE TRACK
NOTHING THROWN AWAY

The monastery buildings of the **Frari** (*see p109*) contain the State Archives, a monument to Venetian reluctance ever to throw anything away. In 300 rooms, about 15 million volumes and files are conserved, starting from the year 883. Faced with such a daunting wealth of detailed information – from ambassadors' dispatches on foreign courts to spies' reports on noblemen's non-regulation cloaks – grown historians have been reduced to quivering wrecks.

SIGHTS

Literary Venice

Four centuries by the book.

Venice has produced many great painters, sculptors and musicians but few great writers. However, the city was always very pleased to welcome writers from elsewhere, particularly if their output would help to promote the city's image. English writers have always been torn between romantic admiration and puritan disapproval.

The city enters English literature care of **William Shakespeare**. The Bard never actually set foot here, but nonetheless the city of *The Merchant of Venice* and *Othello* is a more fully realised place than, say, the Sicily of *Much Ado About Nothing*. Clearly, Venice was already as powerful an icon as New York is today; the Rialto and gondolas could be mentioned as casually as Wall Street and yellow cabs. Shakespeare's Venice is very much a mercantile city, a place of deals, exchanges and bonds. But it is also a place of licentiousness and scheming, where people aren't always what they seem. Desdemona, according to Iago, is a 'super-subtle Venetian'.

The first detailed description recorded by an English visitor was that of insatiable literary traveller **Thomas Coryat**, who set out on foot from Odcombe in Devon in 1608. *Coryat's Crudities* is one of the first awestruck-tourist descriptions of Venice: 'Such is the rarenesse of the situation of Venice, that it doth even amaze and drive into admiration all strangers that upon their first arrival behold the same.'

In the more cynical 18th century, wariness predominated over bedazzlement. Venice was viewed less as a real place and more as a metaphor – and usually a negative one. **Edward Gibbon** is strikingly dismissive: 'The spectacle of Venice afforded some hours of astonishment and some days of disgust... stinking ditches dignified with the pompous denomination of Canals; a fine bridge spoilt by two rows of houses upon it.'

Then, with the Romantics, decadence was the whole point. **William Beckford**, **Lord Byron** and **Percy Bysshe Shelley** thrilled. They sought shudders by visiting the prisons of the Palazzo Ducale (Doge's Palace; *see p67*), they saw romance in the mix of decay and splendour. Byron's twofold reaction to Venice makes him the most interesting expatriate writer of the period. In his immensely fashionable poem *Childe Harold's Pilgrimage*, he draws Venice as a dream. Its past is melodramatic: dungeons, the Council of Ten, vendettas. It's a purely literary creation, based more on a writerly tradition than on observation. But in *Beppo*, Byron draws a very different picture, describing Venice at Carnevale time: a menacing Turk turns out to be a lost husband; and when this husband finds his wife has taken a lover, all three settle down to live together happily ever after.

Throughout the 19th century, travellers drifted through Venice in their closed gondolas. In their accounts of their visits, they fall into swoons or trances; the city mesmerises them. It's Turner's Venice they describe: a dreamscape where buildings seem less substantial than the dazzling light and shimmering water. In *Pictures From Italy*, **Charles Dickens** recounts the experience of floating through the city, even through St Mark's, described purely in terms of colour and perfumes.

The strongest reaction to all this came from **John Ruskin**. He can be prejudiced, inconsistent and sometimes plain barmy. But the greatest contribution he made to Venetian studies was his continual emphasis on the physical reality of the place. In an age when most visitors saw it through a romantic haze, Ruskin focused

The Merchant of Venice (2004).

his attention on the stones of Venice – the crumbling bricks and marble.

Every major writer on Venice thereafter – **Marcel Proust**, **WD Howells**, **Henry James** – had to break free from Ruskin: it took courage to like the Baroque with Ruskin's fulminations ringing in one's ears. But gradually a new taste arose, in which the ambivalence of Venice played a key role, attracting writers such as **John Addington Symonds** and **Frederick Rolfe**. The mysterious secrecy of the city was perfect for Henry James, who wrote: 'Venice is the refuge of endless strange secrets, broken fortunes and wounded hearts.'

Modernist authors seemed torn between disgust and admiration. **DH Lawrence** and **TS Eliot** saw the city as irredeemably commercial and sordid. Lawrence pictures it as the 'Abhorrent green, slippery city.' Eliot describes a city where 'the rats are underneath the piles.' In **Ezra Pound**'s *Cantos*, on the other hand, the golden age of Venice appears as an image of luminous splendour to set against the corruption of contemporary society based on usury.

Perhaps the finest summation of the two contrasting visions of the city can be found in the narrative poem *The Venetian Vespers* (1979), by the American poet **Anthony Hecht**, whose disturbed protagonist has chosen the city as his place of residence precisely because its internal contrasts so perfectly match his own inner lacerations.

Recent literature and cinema have mostly remained faithful to the *Childe Harold* version of Venice: sex, lies and dirty canals. The city is murky, treacherous and damp in novels by **Ian McEwan**, **Barry Unsworth** and **Lisa St Aubin de Téran**. Romance returns in two more recent novels with Venetian settings: in *An Equal Music*, **Vikram Seth** revives the dream vision, tempering it with Carpaccio-esque humour. The debut bestseller by **Sally Vickers**, *Miss Garnett's Angel,* gives us a refreshingly ungloomy Venice; awe prevails for the protagonist of this novel, who finds her rigid atheism shaken by the almost paradisiacal qualities of what appears to be a city of angels.

Italian theatre, moving it away from the clichés of the *Commedia dell'arte* tradition and introducing a comedy based on realistic observation. On the first floor, there are reproductions of prints based on Goldoni's works and a few 18th-century paintings; however, the best item is a splendid 18th-century miniature theatre complete with puppets of *Commedia dell'arte* figures. The library on the upper floor has theatrical texts and original manuscripts. ▶ *For more information on Venice's playwrights and theatrical history, see pp237.*

★ I Frari

San Polo, campo dei Frari (041 522 2637/ www.chorusvenezia.org). Vaporetto San Tomà. **Open** 9am-6pm Mon-Sat; 1-6pm Sun. **Admission** €3 (or Chorus; *see p7*). **No credit cards**. **Map** p320 D6.

A gloomy Gothic barn, the brick house of God known officially as Santa Maria Gloriosa dei Frari is one of the city's most significant artistic storehouses. The Franciscans were granted the land in about 1250 and completed a first church in 1338. At this point they changed their minds and started work on a larger building, which was finally completed just over a century later. The church is 98m (320ft) long, 48m (158ft) wide at the transept and 28m (92ft) high – just slightly smaller than the Dominicans' Santi Giovanni e Paolo (*see p80*) – and has the second highest campanile in the city. And while the Frari may not have as many dead doges as its Dominican rival, it undoubtedly has the artistic edge. This is one church where the entrance fee is not a recent imposition: tourists have been paying to get into the Frari for over a century. At the entrance you are brought face to face with the long sweep of church with Titian's glorious *Assumption* above the high altar.

Right aisle

In the second bay, on the spot where Titian is believed to be buried (the only victim of the 1575-76 plague who was allowed a city burial), is a loud monument to the artist, commissioned nearly 300 years after his death by the Emperor of Austria. On the third altar is a finer memorial, Alessandro Vittoria's statue of St Jerome, generally believed to be a portrait of his painter friend.

Right transept

To the right of the sacristy door is the tomb of the Blessed Pacifico (a companion of St Francis), attributed to Nanni di Bartolo and Michele da Firenze (1437); the sarcophagus is surrounded by a splendidly carved canopy in the florid Gothic style. The door itself is framed by Lorenzo Bregno's tomb of Benedetto Pesaro, a Venetian general who died in Corfu. To the left of the door is the first equestrian statue in Venice, the monument to Paolo Savelli (d.1405). The third chapel on the right side of this transept has an altarpiece by Bartolomeo Vivarini,

SIGHTS

in its original frame, while the Florentine Chapel, next to the chancel, contains the only work by Donatello in the city: a striking wooden statue of a stark, emaciated St John the Baptist.

Sacristy

Commissioned by the Pesaro family, this contains one of Giovanni Bellini's greatest paintings: the *Madonna and Child with Saints Nicholas, Peter, Benedict and Mark* (1488), still in its original frame. 'It seems painted with molten gems, which have been clarified by time,' wrote Henry James, his eye, as ever, firmly on the prose structure, 'and it is as solemn as it is gorgeous and as simple as it is deep.' Also in the sacristy is a fine Renaissance tabernacle, possibly by Tullio Lombardo, for a reliquary holding Christ's blood.

Chancel

The high altar is dominated by Titian's *Assumption*, a work that seems to open the church up to the heavens. In the golden haze encircling God the Father, there may be a reminiscence of the mosaic tradition of Venice. The upward-soaring movement of the painting may owe something to the Gothic architecture of the building, but the drama and grandeur of the work essentially herald the Baroque.

On the right wall of the chancel is the monument to Francesco Foscari, the saddest doge of all. The story of his forced resignation and death from heartbreak (1547) after the exile of his son Jacopo is recounted in Byron's *The Two Foscari*, which was turned into a particularly gloomy opera by Verdi. The left wall hosts one of the finest Renaissance tombs in Venice, the monument to Doge Niccolò Tron, by Antonio Rizzo (1473). This is the first ducal tomb in which the subject is upright; he sports a magnificent bushy beard grown as a sign of perpetual mourning after the death of his favourite son.

Monks' choir

In the centre of the nave stands the choir, with wooden stalls carved by Marco Cozzi (1468), inlaid with superb intarsia decoration. The choir screen is a mixture of Gothic work by Bartolomeo Bon and Renaissance elements by the Lombardi family.

Left transept

In the third chapel, with an altarpiece by Bartolomeo Vivarini and Marco Basaiti, a slab on the floor marks the grave of composer Claudio Monteverdi. The Corner chapel, at the end, contains a mannered statue of St John the Baptist by Sansovino; this sensitively wistful figure could hardly be more different from Donatello's work of a century earlier.

Left aisle

Another magnificent Titian hangs to the right of the side door: the *Madonna di Ca' Pesaro*. This work was commissioned by Bishop Jacopo Pesaro in 1519

Scuola Grande di San Rocco.
See p112.

and celebrates victory in a naval expedition against the Turks, led by the bellicose cleric in 1502. The bishop is kneeling and waiting for St Peter to introduce him and his family to the Madonna. Behind, an armoured warrior bearing a banner has Turkish prisoners in tow. This work revolutionised altar paintings in Venice. It wasn't just that Titian dared to move the Virgin from the centre of the composition to one side, using the splendid banner as a counterbalance; the real innovation was the rich humanity of the whole work, from the beautifully portrayed family (with the boy turning to stare straight at us) to the Christ child, so naturally active and alive, twisting away from his mother (said to be a portrait of Titian's wife) to gaze curiously at the saints clustered around him. The timeless 'sacred conversation' of Bellini's paintings (*see p34*) here becomes animated, losing some of its sacredness but gaining in drama and realism.

The whole of the next bay, around the side door, is occupied by another piece of Pesaro propaganda – the mastodontic mausoleum of Doge Pesaro (d.1659), attributed to Longhena, with sculptures by Melchior Barthel of Dresden. Supporters of the Baroque have some difficulty defending this one, with its 'blackamoor' caryatids, bronze skeletons and posturing allegories.

The penultimate bay harbours a monument to Canova, carried out by his pupils in 1827, five years after his death, using a design of his own that was intended for the tomb of Titian. His body is buried in his native town of Possagno (see p288), but his heart is conserved in an urn inside the monument. The despondent winged lion has a distinct resemblance to the one in *The Wizard of Oz*.

FREE San Nicolò da Tolentino

Santa Croce, campo dei Tolentini (041 710 806). Vaporetto Piazzale Roma. **Open** 8.30am-noon, 4-7pm Mon-Sat; 4-7pm Sun. **Map** p320 C6.

This church (1591-95), usually known as I Tolentini, was designed by Vincenzo Scamozzi. Its unfinished façade has a massive Corinthian portico (1706-14) added by Andrea Tirali.

The interior is a riot of Baroque decoration, with lavish use of stucco and sprawling frescoes. The most interesting paintings – as so often in the 17th century – are by out-of-towners. On the wall outside the chancel to the left is *St Jerome Succoured by an Angel* by Flemish artist Johann Liss. Outside the chapel in the left transept is *The Charity of St Lawrence* by the Genoese Bernardo Strozzi, in which the magnificently hoary old beggar in the foreground upstages the rather wimpish figure of the saint. In the chancel hangs an *Annunciation* by Neapolitan Luca Giordano; opposite is a splendidly theatrical monument to Francesco Morosini (a 17th-century patriarch of that name, not the doge) by Filippo Parodi (1678), with swirling angels drawing aside a marble curtain to reveal the patriarch lounging at ease on his tomb.

In 1780, the priests of this church handed over all their silverware to a certain 'Romano', who claimed to have a secret new method for cleaning silver and jewellery. He was never seen again.

FREE San Pantalon

Dorsoduro, campo San Pantalon (041 523 5893). Vaporetto San Tomà. **Open** 4-6pm Mon-Sat. **Map** p322 D7.

The dedicatee of this church is St Pantaleon, a court physician to Emperor Galerius, who was arrested, tortured and finally beheaded during Diocletian's persecution of the Christians in the late 3rd century. The saint's story is depicted inside the church in an extraordinary ceiling painting – a huge illusionist work, painted on 40 canvases, by the Cecil B De Mille of the 17th century, Gian Antonio Fumiani. It took him 24 years to complete the task (1680-1704), and at the end of it all he fell with choreographic grace from the scaffolding to his death. Veronese depicts the saint in less melodramatic fashion in the second chapel on the right, in what is possibly his last work, *St Pantaleon Healing a Child*.

To the left of the chancel is the Chapel of the Holy Nail. The nail in question, supposedly from the Crucifixion, is preserved in a small but richly decorated Gothic altar. On the right wall is a fine *Coronation of the Virgin* by Antonio Vivarini and Giovanni d'Alemagna.

FREE San Rocco

San Polo, campo San Rocco (041 523 4864). Vaporetto San Tomà. **Open** 9.30am-5.30pm daily. **Map** p320 D6.

If you have toured the school of San Rocco (see p112) and are in the mood for yet more Tintorettos (perhaps after a stiff drink or a lie down), look no further. Built in Venetian Renaissance style by Bartolomeo Bon from 1489 to 1508, but radically altered by Giovanni Scalfarotto in 1725, the church has paintings by Tintoretto, or his school, on either side of the entrance door, between the first and second altar on the right, and on either side of the chancel. Nearly all are connected with the life of St Roch; the best is probably *St Roch Cures the Plague Victims* (chancel, lower right). The altar paintings are all rather difficult to see; they're high up and not very well lit. Even if you could get a good view, you might not be much the wiser: even Ruskin, Tintoretto's greatest fan, was completely baffled as to their subject matter.

★ Scuola Grande di San Giovanni Evangelista

San Polo 2454, campiello della Scuola (041 718 234/www.scuolasangiovanni.it). Vaporetto San Tomà. **Open** 9.30am-5pm daily. Closed during conferences. **Admission** €5. **No credit cards**. **Map** p320 D5.

Used frequently during the day for conferences and in the evening for concerts, this *scuola* in 2009 began allowing visits at other times. Check the website to confirm open days.

The Scuola Grande di San Giovanni Evangelista is one of the six *scuole grandi* (see p105 **Back to School**); founded in 1261, it is the most ancient of the still existing *scuole*. Originally attached to the church of Sant'Aponal, the *scuola* moved to its present premises in 1340. It grew in size and prestige, especially after the acquisition (1396) of a fragment of the True Cross, an event celebrated in a series of paintings now housed inside the Gallerie dell' Accademia (see p122). The *scuola* was closed at the Fall of the Republic then refounded in 1929 with the blessing of the Pope. Its building and its contents now carefully restored, this is one of Venice's most magnificent structures.

The *scuola* stands in a small courtyard, at the entrance of which is a screen with a superb eagle pediment carved by Pietro Lombardo. The ground-floor, with the large Sala delle Colonne, mostly maintains its medieval aspect, with fragments of medieval carvings on the walls; it was used as a space where members and pilgrims could gather.

The upper floor of the *scuola* is accessed by a magnificent double staircase, a masterpiece by the Renaissance architect Mauro Codussi.

The decoration in the Sala Capitolare is mainly 18th century. The floor is especially fine, with its geometrical patterns of multicoloured marbles that mirror the arrangement of the ceiling paintings. Giambattista Tiepolo was originally commissioned to execute the ceiling-paintings of the Apocalypse but left for Madrid without fulfilling his obligations. His son Giandomenico painted some of the smaller scenes on the ceiling (*The Woman Clothed with the Sun* and *The Four Angels and the Four Evil Winds*); despite their size they easily outshine the larger works at the centre of the sequence. The walls are hung with 17th- and 18th-century paintings recounting the life of St John the Evangelist, by Domenico Tintoretto and others.

Also decorated in the 18th century was the Oratorio della Croce, where a tabernacle holding the precious piece of cross is one of the finest pieces of Venetian goldwork; it is rarely on display. This room originally contained a cycle of paintings by Gentile Bellini and Vittore Carpaccio, now in the Accademia; these days it has to make do with rather less inspired devotional works by Francesco Maggiotto, set within dainty stucco-work. Beyond this room is the Sala dell'Albergo, which contains a series of paintings by Palma il Giovane. The most spirited of these is *St John's Vision of the Four Horsemen*, recently restored.

▶ *The custodian will also open up the church of San Giovanni Evangelista across the courtyard, which has a Gothic apse but is mainly 17th- and 18th-century in its decoration.*

★ Scuola Grande di San Rocco

San Polo 3054, campo San Rocco (041 523 4864/www.scuolagrandesanrocco.it). Vaporetto San Tomà. **Open** 10am-5pm daily. **Admission** €7; €5 reductions. **Credit** AmEx, DC, MC, V. **Map** p320 D6.

The Archbrotherhood of St Roch was the richest of the six *scuole grandi* (*see p105* **Back to School**) in 15th-century Venice. Its members came from the top end of the mercantile and professional classes. It was dedicated to Venice's other patron saint, the French plague protector and dog-lover St Roch (also known as St Rock or San Rocco), whose body was brought here in 1485.

To celebrate the feast day of St Roch (16 August), admission to the *scuola* is free on that day.

The *scuola* operated out of rented accommodation for many years, but at the beginning of the 16th century a permanent base was commissioned. The architecture, designed by Bartolomeo Bon and Scarpagnino, is far less impressive than the interior decoration, which was entrusted to Tintoretto in 1564 after a competition in which he stole a march on his main rivals – Salviati, Zuccari and Veronese – by presenting a finished painting rather than the required sketch.

In three intensive sessions spread out over the following 23 years, Tintoretto went on to make San Rocco his epic masterpiece. Fans and doubters alike should start here; the former will no doubt agree with John Ruskin that paintings such as the *Crucifixion* are 'beyond all analysis and above all praise,' while the latter may well find their prejudices crumbling. True, the devotional intensity of his works can shade a touch too much into kitsch for the 21st-century soul; but his feel for narrative structure remains timeless.

To follow the development of Tintoretto's style, pick up the free explanatory leaflet and the audio guide and begin in the smaller upstairs hall – the Albergo. Here, filling up the whole of the far wall, is the *Crucifixion* (1565). More than anything it is the perfect integration of main plot and sub-plots that strikes the viewer; whereas most paintings are short stories, this is a novel. Note that some restoration work was underway as this guide went to press.

Tintoretto began work on the larger upstairs room in 1575, with Old Testament stories on the ceiling and a Life of Christ cycle around the walls, in which the artist experimented relentlessly with form, lighting and colour. Below the canvases is a characterful series of late 17th-century wooden carvings, including a caricature of Tintoretto himself, just below and to the left of his painting of *The Agony in the Garden*.

Finally, in the ground-floor hall – which the artist decorated between 1583 and 1587, when he was in his sixties – the paintings reach a visionary pitch that has to do with Tintoretto's audacious handling of light and the impressionistic economy of his brush strokes. The *Annunciation*, with its domestic Mary surprised while sewing, and *Flight into Egypt*, with its verdant landscape, are among the painter's masterpieces. *Photos p105 & p110.*

▶ *Tintoretto's next painting of The Last Supper is in San Giorgio Maggiore; see p130. The previous one is in Santo Stefano; see p75.*

Dorsoduro

From workaday Venice to international art treasures.

Stretching from the docklands in the west to the glorious **Salute** church and the **punta della Dogana** in the east, Dorsoduro – literally 'hard back' – is home to a varied social blend. The eastern areas around the Salute, with their quiet *campielli* and well-restored *palazzi*, exude international affluence and culture, while Santa Marta in the west mixes home-grown working class with a busy university population.

In between these geographical and social extremes you'll discover the wholly democratic **campo Santa Margherita**, Dorsoduro's largest square. Here the full range of Venice's shifting population can be seen at all hours: tourists, workers, loafers, tourists, shoppers, students and, of course, tourists.

| **Map** pp322-323 | **Restaurants** p177 |
| **Hotels** p160 | **Cafés & Bars** p191 |

WESTERN DORSODURO

Vaporetto San Basilio or Zattere.

This was one of the first areas in the lagoon to be settled. One seventh-century church here is called **San Nicolò dei Mendicoli** (*see p115*) – 'of the beggars', a hint that the locals have never been in the top income bracket. In the past they were mostly fishermen or salt-pan workers. The area gave its name to one of two factions into which the proletariat was divided: the *nicolotti*. The *nicolotti* enjoyed a certain form of local autonomy under a figure known as the *gastaldo*, who, after his election, would be received with honours by the doge.

The area is still noticeably less sleek than the centre, although fishing was superseded as a source of employment by the port long ago, and subsequently by the Santa Marta cotton mill – now stunningly converted into the **Istituto Universitario di Architettura di Venezia**. Massive redevelopment schemes were talked about for much of this downbeat district, with plans to revitalise it in a vast 'university meets London Docklands' style project, to a design by the late Catalan architect Enric Miralles. The plans included an auditorium, conference hall, restaurant and huge centralised university library, thus providing Venice's universities with something

approaching a genuine campus. After various legal disputes, these ambitious schemes fell through and the two universities of Venice fell back on a more modest development plan, converting some of the ex-warehouses to classrooms and lecture halls; these constitute the Polo didattica di San Basilio, which was inaugurated in March 2008.

Moving eastwards, the atmosphere remains unpretentious around the churches of **Angelo Raffaele** (*see p113*) and **San Sebastiano** (*see p115*), with its splendid decoration by Paolo Veronese. Northwards from here, on the rio di Santa Margherita, are some grander *palazzi*, including **Palazzo Ariani**, with Gothic tracery that is almost oriental in its intricacy, and, further up, the grand **Palazzo Zenobio** (*see p115*), now an Armenian school and institute, containing Tiepolesque frescoes and giving on to an elaborate garden where plays are sometimes performed in the summer.

FREE Angelo Raffaele

Dorsoduro, campo Angelo Raffaele (041 522 8548). Vaporetto San Basilio. **Open** 9am-5.30pm daily. **Map** p322 B8.

Tradition has it that this church was founded by St Magnus in the eighth century, but the present free-standing building – one of only two churches in the city that you can walk around – dates from the 17th century. The ceiling has a lively fresco by

FONDAZIONE
EMILIO E ANNABIANCA
VEDOVA

MAGAZZINI DEL SALE
ZATTERE 266
VENICE ITALY

Architectural project
Renzo Piano

Art consultant
Germano Celant
Chief Curator of the Foundation

President of the Foundation
Alfredo Bianchini

Director of the Foundation
Fabrizio Gazzarri

www.fondazionevedova.org

Gaspare Diziani of *St Michael Driving out Lucifer*, with Lucifer apparently tumbling out of the heavy stucco frame into the church. There are matching *Last Supper*s on either side of the organ (by Bonifacio de' Pitati on the left, and a follower of Titian on the right).

But the real jewels of the church are on the organ loft, where five compartments, painted by Giovanni Antonio Guardi (or perhaps his brother Francesco), recount the story of *Tobias and the Angel* (1750-53). They are works of dazzling luminosity, quite unlike anything else done in Venice at the time. The paintings and the story they recount play a significant role in Sally Vickers' novel *Miss Garnet's Angel* (2000).

Palazzo Zenobio

Dorsoduro 2598, fondamenta del Soccorso (041 241 2397). Vaporetto San Basilio. **Open** 10am-4pm daily. **Admission** €4. **Credit** AmEx, DC, MC, V. **Map** p322 B7.

Built towards the end of the 17th century to a design by Antonio Gaspari, Palazzo Zenobio's broad façade and two wings extending backwards, making it unusual in Venice; the central window crowned by a curved tympanum owes more to the works of the Roman architect Borromini than to local examples. In 1850, the palace was acquired by the Armenian Mechitarist monks of San Servolo and served as a college for Armenian students until 1997. Since then, it has been used as a guesthouse and hired out for special events.

Entrance is via the Atelier 'Il Palazzo', to the left of the main entrance. The interior is sumptuously decorated with 18th-century frescoes and stuccowork. The showpiece of the palace is the Sala degli Specchi, the ballroom frescoed by the French artist Louis Dorigny. He created an elaborate ceiling with mythological figures cavorting amid trompe l'œil pillars and columns. The side rooms are frescoed in a more delicate Tiepolesque style. The formal garden, with its weatherbeaten statues and peaceful avenues, can also be visited.

FREE San Nicolò dei Mendicoli

Dorsoduro, campo San Nicolò (041 275 0382). Vaporetto San Basilio or Santa Marta. **Open** 10am-noon, 3-5.30pm Mon-Sat; 10am-noon Sun. **Map** p322 A8.

San Nicolò is one of the few Venetian churches to have maintained its 13th-century Veneto-Byzantine structure, despite numerous refurbishments over the years. When the church underwent a thorough restoration in the 1970s, traces of the original foundations were uncovered, confirming the church's seventh-century origins. The 15th-century loggia at the front is one of only two extant examples of a once-common architectural feature; it originally served as a shelter for the homeless.

The interior contains a marvellous mishmash of architectural and decorative styles that creates an effect of cluttered charm. The structure is that of a

12th-century basilica, with two colonnades of stocky columns topped by 14th-century capitals. Above are gilded 16th-century statues of the Apostles. The paintings are mainly 17th century. There are also some fine wooden sculptures, including a large statue of San Nicolò made in the 15th century in the workshop of sculptor Bartolomeo Bon. In the small campo outside the church is a column with a diminutive winged lion.

▶ *The only other Venetian church with a loggia out front is the equally ancient San Giacomo di Rialto; see p99.*

★ San Sebastiano

Dorsoduro, fondamenta di San Sebastiano (041 275 0642/www.chorusvenezia.org). Vaporetto San Basilio. **Open** 10am-5pm Mon-Sat. **Admission** €3 (or Chorus; *see p7*). **No credit cards. Map** p322 B8.

This contains perhaps the most brilliantly colourful church interior in Venice, and it's all the work of one man: Paolo Veronese. His first commission was for the sacristy (*see below*). From then on, there was no stopping him: between 1556 and 1565 he completed three large ceiling paintings for the nave of the church, frescoes along the upper parts of the walls, organ shutters, huge narrative canvases for the chancel, and the painting on the high altar.

In July 2008, restoration work began on the ceiling paintings, which had been removed as this guide went to press. They depict scenes from the life of Esther (*Esther Taken to Ahasuerus, Esther Crowned Queen by Ahasuerus* and *The Triumph of Mordecai*). Esther was considered a forerunner of the Virgin, interceding for Jews in the same way that the Virgin interceded for Christians – or (more pertinently) for Venice. These works are full of sumptuous pageantry: no painter gets more splendidly shimmering effects out of clothing, which is probably why Veronese's nude St Sebastians are the least striking figures in the compositions.

The enormous canvases on the side walls of the chancel depict, on the right, *The Martyrdom of St Sebastian* and, on the left, *St Sebastian Encouraging St Mark and St Marcellan*. Other paintings in the church include *St Nicholas*, a late painting by Titian, in the first altar on the right. Paolo Veronese and his brother Benedetto are buried here.

The sacristy (10am-5pm Sat, 1-5pm Sun) contains ceiling paintings of the *Coronation of the Virgin* and the four panels of *The Evangelists*, which are among Veronese's earliest works in Venice (1555). Around the walls are works by Bonifacio de' Pitati and others. Restoration work on the frescoes and structure of the church will continue for some years.

CAMPO SANTA MARGHERITA TO THE ACCADEMIA

Vaporetto Accademia, Ca' Rezzonico, San Basilio or Zattere.

A long, irregular-shaped campo with churches at both ends, **campo Santa Margherita** buzzes day and night, from shoppers at the morning market (Mon-Sat) to hurrying students and scavenging pigeons during the day, and hordes of Venice's under-30s thronging bars at night, much to the irritation of local residents.

There are several ancient *palazzi* around the square, with Byzantine and Gothic features. Isolated in the middle is the **Scuola dei Varoteri**, the School of the Tanners. At the north end is the former church of **Santa Margherita**, long used as a cinema and now beautifully restored as a conference hall for the university; the interior (sneak in the back for a quick gawp if there's a meeting going on) is so theatrical, it's difficult to imagine how it was

ever used for religious purposes. St Margaret's dragon features on the campanile, and the sculpted saint also stands triumphant on the beast between the windows of a house at the north end of the square. A miraculous escape from the dragon's guts for some reason makes her the patron saint of pregnant women. At the other end of the square are the **scuola** and **church of the Carmini** (*see p119*).

Leaving the campo by the southern end, you reach the picturesque rio di San Barnaba. At the eastern end of the *fondamenta* is the entrance to **Ca' Rezzonico** (*see p117*), designed by Longhena and now the museum of 18th-century Venice.

The middle of the three bridges across the canal is ponte dei Pugni, with white marble footprints indicating that this was one of the bridges where punch-ups were held between the rival factions of the *nicolotti*, from the western quarters of the city, and the *castellani*, from the east. These violent brawls were tolerated by the authorities, who saw them as a chance for the working classes to let off steam in a way that was not disruptive to the state. They were banned, however, in 1705, after a particularly bloody fray.

Across the bridge is campo San Barnaba. The church of **San Barnaba** (often used for contemporary art shows) has a picturesque 14th-century campanile; the campo is a fine

Campo Santa Margherita.

SIGHTS

INSIDE TRACK
BY ANY OTHER NAME...

Paolo Veronese's vast *Christ in the House of Levi* in the **Accademia** gallery (*see p122*) was painted as a *Last Supper*. In 1573, the Inquisition took offence at a *Last Supper* in which figures of 'buffoons, drunkards, Germans, dwarves' supposedly insulted church decorum, and threatened Veronese with heresy charges. The artist – with admirable chutzpah – simply changed its name.

place for sitting outside a bar and watching the world go by. Katharine Hepburn fell into the canal flanking the campo in the film *Summertime*, causing permanent damage to her eyesight. In *Indiana Jones and the Last Crusade*, on the other hand, Harrison Ford entered the church (a library in the film) and, after contending with most of Venice's rat population, emerged from a manhole on to the pavement outside.

From the campo, the busy route towards the Accademia (*see p122*) passes alongside the rio della Toletta (where a small plank or *tola* – *tavola* in Italian – once served as a bridge) towards rio San Trovaso. This handsome canal

has twin *fondamente* lined by fine Gothic and Renaissance palaces housing secondary schools and university buildings. Off to the right is the church of **San Trovaso** (*see p119*), with two identical façades, one on to the canal and one on to its own campo. Backing on to the campo is a picturesque *squero*, one of the few remaining yards where gondolas are made.

The Accademia, Venice's most important picture gallery, is just a short walk further. Beyond it is the reconstructed wooden bridge of the same name over the Grand Canal.

Ca' Rezzonico
(Museo del Settecento Veneziano)
Dorsoduro 3136, fondamenta Rezzonico (041 2410 100/www.museiciviciveneziani.it). Vaporetto Ca' Rezzonico. **Open** 10am-5pm Mon, Wed-Sun. **Admission** €6.50; €4.50 reductions (*see also p6*). **Credit** AmEx, DC, MC, V. **Map** p322 D7.
The Museum of 18th-century Venice is a gleaming (if somewhat chilly) showcase for the art of the Republic's twilight years. For most visitors, the paintings on display here will appear less impressive than the palazzo itself, an imposing Grand Canal affair designed by Baldassare Longhena for the Bon family in 1667. Bon ambitions exceeded Bon means, and the unfinished palace was sold on to the Rezzonico family – rich Genoese bankers who bought their way into Venice's nobility. The Rezzonicos' bid for stardom was crowned in 1758 by two events: the

SIGHTS

Campo San Vio.

SIGHTS

election of Carlo Rezzonico as Pope Clement XIII, and the marriage of Ludovico Rezzonico into one of Venice's oldest noble families, the Savorgnan.

Giambattista Tiepolo was called upon to celebrate the marriage on the ceiling of the Sala del Trono; he replied with a composition so playful it's easy to forget that this is all about purchasing rank and power. Giovanni Battista Crosato's over-the-top ceiling frescoes in the ballroom have aged less well but, together with the Murano chandeliers and intricately carved furniture by Andrea Brustolon, they provide an accurate record of the lifestyles of the rich and famous.

There are historical canvases by Giovanni Battista Piazzetta and Antonio Diziani, plus other gems. Detached frescoes of *pulcinellas* by Giandomenico Tiepolo capture the leisured melancholy of the moneyed classes as *La Serenissima* went into terminal decline. Originally painted for the Tiepolo family villa they were moved here in 1936 and recently restored. There are some good genre paintings by Pietro Longhi, and a series of pastel portraits by Rosalba Carriera, a female 'prodigy' who was kept busy by English travellers eager to bring back a souvenir of their Grand Tour. On the third floor is the Egidio Martini gallery, a collection of mainly Venetian works, and a reconstruction of an 18th-century pharmacy, with fine majolica vases.

A staircase at the far end of the entrance hall leads to the 'Mezzanino Browning', where the poet Robert Browning died in 1889. This contains the Mestrovich Collection of Veneto paintings, donated to the city by Ferruccio Mestrovich as a sign of gratitude for the hospitality afforded to his family after they had been expelled from Dalmatia in 1945.

FREE Santa Maria dei Carmini

Dorsoduro, campo dei Carmini (041 522 6553). Vaporetto Ca' Rezzonico or San Basilio. **Open** 8am-noon, 2.30-5.30pm Mon-Sat; 4-6.30pm Sun. **Map** p322 C7.

The church officially called Santa Maria del Carmelo has a tall campanile topped by a statue of the Virgin. It is richly decorated inside, with 17th-century gilt wooden statues over the arcades of the nave and,

---

INSIDE TRACK
BARNABOTTI

In the final years of the Venetian Republic, penniless patricians used to end up in **San Barnaba** (*see p116*), where apartments were provided by the state for their use. The *barnabotti*, as they were known, could make a few *zecchini* by peddling their votes in the *maggior consiglio*; otherwise they hung around in their tattered silk, muttering (after 1789) subversive comments about Liberty, Fraternity and Equality.

---

above, a series of Baroque paintings illustrating the history of the Carmelite order. The best paintings in the church are a *Nativity* by Cima da Conegliano, on the second altar on the right, and *St Nicholas of Bari* by Lorenzo Lotto, opposite; the latter has a dreamy landscape containing tiny figures of St George and the dragon. To the right of the Lotto painting is a Veronese *Holy Family*, moved here from the church of San Barnaba. In the chapel to the right of the high altar is a graceful bronze relief of *The Lamentation over the Dead Christ*, including portraits of Federico da Montefeltro and Battista Sforza, by the Sienese sculptor, painter, inventor, military architect and all-round Renaissance man Francesco di Giorgio.

FREE San Trovaso

Dorsoduro, campo San Trovaso (041 522 2133). Vaporetto Zattere. **Open** 8-11am, 2.30-5.30pm Mon-Sat. **Map** p322 D9.

This church overlooking a quiet campo has two almost identical façades, both modelled on the sub-Palladian church of Le Zitelle (*see p129*) on the Giudecca. The story goes that San Trovaso was built on the very border of the two areas of the city belonging to the rival factions of the *nicolotti* and *castellani*; in the event of a wedding between members of the two factions, each party could make its own sweeping entrance and exit. There was no saint called Trovaso: the name is a Venetian telescoping of martyrs San Protasio and San Gervasio.

There are five works by the Tintoretto family in the church; three are probably by the son, Domenico, including the two on either side of the high altar, which are rich in detail but poor in focus. In the left transept is a smaller-than-usual version of one of Tintoretto's favourite subjects, *The Last Supper*; the tavern setting is strikingly realistic.

In the chapel to the left of the high altar is *The Temptations of St Anthony the Abbot*, featuring enough vices to tempt a saint – note the harlot with 'flames playing around her loins,' as John Ruskin so coyly put it. On the side wall is a charming painting in the international Gothic style by Michele Giambono, *St Chrisogonus on Horseback* (c1450); the saint is a boyish figure on a gold background, with a shyly hesitant expression and a gorgeously fluttering cloak and banner. In the Clary chapel (right transept) is a set of Renaissance marble reliefs (c1470) showing angels playing musical instruments or holding instruments of the Passion. The only attribution scholars will risk is to the conveniently named 'Master of San Trovaso'. *Photo p120.*

▶ *Tintoretto's next Last Supper is in San Simeone Profeta; see p106. His earliest can be found in San Marcuola; see p92.*

Scuola dei Carmini

Dorsoduro 2617, campo dei Carmini (041 528 9420). Vaporetto Ca' Rezzonico or San Basilio. **Open** 11am-4pm daily. **Admission** €5; €2-€4 reductions. **No credit cards. Map** p322 C7.

San Trovaso. *See p119.*

Begun in 1670 to plans by Baldassare Longhena, the building housing this *scuola* run by the Carmelite order was spared the Napoleonic lootings that dispersed the fittings of most of the other *scuole*. So we have a good idea of what an early 18th-century Venetian confraternity HQ must have looked like, from the elaborate Sante Piatti altarpiece downstairs to the staircase with its excrescence of gilded cherubs.

In the main hall of the first floor is one of the most impressive of Giambattista Tiepolo's Venetian ceilings: the airy panels were painted from 1740 to 1743. Don't even try to unravel the story – a celestial donation that supposedly took place in Cambridge, when Simon Stock received the scapular (the badge of the Carmelite order) from the Virgin. What counts, as always with Tiepolo, is the audacity of his off-centre composition. If the atmosphere were not so ultra-refined, there would be something disturbing in the Virgin's sneer of cold contempt and those swirling clouds. The central painting fell from the woodworm-ridden ceiling in August 2000 but has been beautifully restored. In the two adjoining rooms are wooden sculptures by Giacomo Piazzetta and a dramatic *Judith and Holofernes* by his more gifted son Giovanni Battista Piazzetta.

▶ *For the story behind Venice's scuole, see p105 Back to School.*

EASTERN DORSODURO

Vaporetto Accademia, Salute or Zattere.

The eastern reaches of Dorsoduro, between the **Accademia** (*see p122*) and the **Salute** (*see p123*), is an area of elegant, artsy prosperity,

home to artists, writers and wealthy foreigners. Ezra Pound spent his last years in a small house near the Zattere; Peggy Guggenheim hosted her collection of modern artists in her truncated palazzo on the Grand Canal (now the **Peggy Guggenheim Collection**; *see right* **Profile** *and p123*); artists use the vast spaces of the old warehouses on the Zattere as studios. On Sunday mornings, campo San Vio is some corner of a foreign land, as British expats home in on the Anglican church of **St George**. Overlooking the campo, the **Galleria Cini** (*see p123*) has a collection of Ferrarese and Tuscan art.

It is a district of quiet canals and cosy *campielli*, perhaps the most picturesque being campiello Barbaro, behind pretty, lopsided **Ca' Dario** (rumoured, due to sudden deaths of owners over the centuries, to be cursed). But all that money has certainly driven out the locals: nowhere in Venice are you further from a simple *alimentari* (grocery store).

The colossal magnificence of Longhena's church of Santa Maria della Salute brings the residential area to an end. Beyond is the old Dogana di Mare (Customs House). Debate about redeploying this empty space raged for years. For a while it seemed likely that the Peggy Guggenheim Collection would take it over. In the end, the contract for redevelopment went to French magnate Francois Pinault (*see p124* **The Whole Punta**). With the **Punta Della Dogana** gallery open and building work over, it is once again possible to stroll around the *punta*, with its spectacular view across the water towards St Mark's.

Profile Peggy Guggenheim Collection

A startlingly modern collection amassed by an American eccentric.

This remarkable establishment (*see p123*), tucked behind a high wall off a quiet street, is the third most visited museum in the city. It was founded by one of Venice's most colourful expat residents, Peggy Guggenheim, whose father went down in the Titanic, leaving her a fortune.

The money came in useful as she set out to satisfy her ravenous appetite for men and art. Peggy may have hated her bulbous nose – the result of a botched job by a plastic surgeon – but that didn't stop her running up a list of lovers that reads like a who's who of contemporary culture, including Yves Tanguy, Samuel Beckett, Roland Penrose and Max Ernst, to whom she was briefly married. When asked how many husbands she had had, she replied: 'Do you mean mine, or other people's?' Ms Guggenheim took the same voracious approach to art as to men.

She turned up in the lagoon city in 1949 looking for a home for her already sizable collection. A short-sighted curator at the Tate Gallery in London had described her growing pile of surrealist and modernist works as 'non-art'. Venice, still struggling to win back the tourists after World War II, was less finicky, and Peggy found a perfect, eccentric base in Palazzo Venier dei Leoni, a truncated 18th-century Grand Canal palazzo.

There are big European names in her art collection, including Picasso, Duchamp, Brancusi,

Giacometti and Max Ernst, plus a few Americans such as Calder and Jackson Pollock. Highlights include the beautifully enigmatic *Empire of Light* by Magritte and Giacometti's disturbing *Woman with Her Throat Cut*. The flamboyant *Attirement of the Bride*, by Peggy's husband, Max Ernst, often turns up as a Carnevale costume. But perhaps the most startling exhibit of all is the rider of Marino Marini's *Angel of the City* out on the Grand Canal terrace, who thrusts his manhood towards passing *vaporetti*. Never the shrinking wallflower, Peggy took delight in unscrewing the member and pressing it on young men she fancied.

Another wing has been given over to Futurist works on long-term loan from the collection of Gianni Mattioli.

SIGHTS

TAKE A BREAK
The gallery is home to a charming garden, best surveyed from the terrace of the café-restaurant.

★ Gallerie dell'Accademia

*Dorsoduro 1050, campo Carità (041 522 2247/
www.artive.arti.beniculturali.it). Vaporetto
Accademia.* **Open** 8.15am-2pm Mon; 8.15am-
7.15pm Tue-Sun. **Admission** €6.50; €3.25
reductions (*see also p6*). *Audio guide* €5;
€7 double. *Video guide* €6. **No credit cards.**
Map p323 E8.

The Accademia is the essential one-stop shop for
Venetian painting, and one of the world's greatest art
treasure houses. At the time of writing – and possibly for another year or two – it is also a hive of construction and restoration work; though the gallery
will remain open throughout its grand makeover,
visitors should be prepared to find hanging arrangements changed and some rooms closed completely.

The gallery is located inside three former religious
buildings: the Scuola Grande di Santa Maria della
Carità (the oldest of the Venetian *scuole*, founded in
the 13th century), the adjacent church of the Carità,
and the Monastery of the Lateran Canons, a 12th-
century structure remodelled by Andrea Palladio.

It was Napoleon who made the collection possible:
first, by suppressing hundreds of churches, convents
and religious guilds, confiscating their artworks for
the greater good of the state; and second, by moving
the city's Accademia di Belle Arti art school here,
with the mandate both to train students and to act
as a gallery and storeroom for all the evicted artworks, which were originally displayed as models
for pupils to aspire to. The art school moved to a new
site on the nearby Zattere in 2004; the freed-up space
is now being restored and will eventually provide new
exhibition space, with the number of works on show
expected to rise from the current 400 to around 650.

In its current layout, the collection is arranged
chronologically, with the exception of the 15th- and
16th-century works in rooms 19-24 at the end. It opens
with 14th- and 15th-century devotional works by
Paolo Veneziano and others – stiff figures against
gold backdrops in the Byzantine tradition. This
room was the main hall of the *scuola grande*: note
the original ceiling of gilded cherubim. Rooms 2 and
3 have devotional paintings and altarpieces by
Carpaccio, Cima da Conegliano and Giovanni Bellini
(a fine *Enthroned Madonna with Six Saints*).

Rooms 4 and 5 bring us to the Renaissance heart
of the collection: here are Mantegna's *St George*
and Giorgione's mysterious *Tempest*, which has
had art historians reaching for symbolic interpretations for centuries. In Room 6, the three greats of
16th-century Venetian painting – Titian, Tintoretto
and Veronese – are first encountered. But the battle
of the giants gets under way in earnest in Room 10,
where Tintoretto's ghostly chiaroscuro *Transport
of the Body of St Mark* vies for attention with
Titian's moving *Pietà* – his last painting – and
Veronese's huge *Christ in the House of Levi*.

Room 11 covers two centuries, with canvases by
Tintoretto (the exquisite *Madonna dei Camerlenghi*),
Bernardo Strozzi and Tiepolo. The series of rooms
beyond brings the plot up to the 18th century, with
all the old favourites: Canaletto, Guardi, Longhi
and soft-focus, bewigged portraits by female superstar Rosalba Carriera.

Rooms 19 and 20 take us back to the 15th century;
the latter has the rich *Miracle of the Relic of the Cross*
cycle, a collaborative effort by Gentile Bellini,
Carpaccio and others, which is packed with telling
social details; there's even a black gondolier in
Carpaccio's *Miracle of the Cross at the Rialto*.

An even more satisfying cycle has Room 21 to
itself. Carpaccio's *Life of St Ursula* (1490-95) tells the
story of the legendary Breton princess who embarked
on a pilgrimage to Rome with her betrothed so that
he could be baptised into the true faith. All went

SIGHTS

Santa Maria della Salute.

swimmingly until Ursula and all the 11,000 virgins accompanying her were massacred by the Huns in Cologne (the initial 'M' – for martyr – used in one account of the affair caused the multiplication of the number of accompanying maidens from 11 to 11,000, M being the Roman numeral for 1,000). More than the ropey legend, it's the architecture, the ships and the pageantry in these meticulous paintings that grab the attention. Perhaps most striking, amid all the closely thronged, action-packed scenes, is the rapt stillness and solitude of *The Dream of St Ursula*.

Room 23 is the former church of Santa Maria della Carità: here are devotional works by Vivarini, the Bellinis and others. Room 24 – the Albergo room (or secretariat) of the former *scuola* – contains the only work in the whole gallery that is in its original site: Titian's magnificent *Presentation of the Virgin*.

▶ *Don't know your Tintoretto from your Tiepolo? Brush up on Venice's art history; see pp32-38.*

Galleria Cini

Dorsoduro 864, piscina del Forner (041 271 0111/www.cini.it). Vaporetto Accademia. **Open** during exhibitions only. **Admission** varies. **No credit cards. Map** p323 F9.

This collection of Ferrarese and Tuscan art was put together by industrialist Vittorio Cini, who created the Fondazione Cini on the island of San Giorgio Maggiore (*see p129*). It's small but there are one or two gems, such as the unfinished Pontormo double *Portrait of Two Friends* (on the first floor), and Dosso Dossi's *Allegorical Scene* (on the second), a vivacious character study from the D'Este Palace in Ferrara. There are also some delicate, late-medieval ivories and a rare, 14th-century wedding chest decorated with chivalric scenes.

★ Peggy Guggenheim Collection

Dorsoduro 701, fondamenta Venier dei Leoni (041 520 6288/www.guggenheim-venice.it). Vaporetto Accademia or Salute. **Open** 10am-6pm Mon, Wed-Sun. **Admission** €12; €7-€10 reductions. **Credit** AmEx, MC, V. **Map** p323 F9. *See p121* **Profile**.

★ Punta della Dogana

Dorsoduro 2, campo della Salute (041 523 1680/ www.palazzograssi.it). Vaporetto Salute. **Open** 10am-7pm Mon, Wed-Sun. **Admission** €15 (€20 Punta & Palazzo Grassi; *see p75*); €10 (€14 both) reductions. **Credit** MC, V. **Map** p323 G9. *See p124* **The Whole Punta**.

★ FREE Santa Maria della Salute

Dorsoduro, campo della Salute (041 522 5558). Vaporetto Salute. **Open** 9am-noon, 3-5.30pm daily. **Admission** *Church* free. *Sacristy* €2. **No credit cards. Map** p323 G9.

This magnificent Baroque church, queening it over the entrance of the Grand Canal, is almost as recognisable an image of Venice as St Mark's or the Rialto

bridge. It was built between 1631 and 1681 in thanksgiving for the end of Venice's last bout of plague, which had wiped out at least a third of the population in 1630. The church is dedicated to the Madonna, as protector of the city.

The terms of the competition won by 26-year-old architect Baldassare Longhena presented a serious challenge, which beat some of the best architects of the day. The church was to be colossal but inexpensive; the whole structure was to be visually clear on entrance, with an unimpeded view of the high altar, the ambulatory and side altars coming into sight only as one approached the chancel; the light was to be evenly distributed; and the whole building should *creare una bella figura* – show itself off to good effect.

Longhena succeeded brilliantly in satisfying all of these requisites – particularly the last and most Venetian of them. The church takes superb advantage of its dominant position and pays homage to both the Byzantine form of San Marco across the Grand Canal and the classical form of Palladio's Redentore, across the Giudecca Canal.

The architect said he chose the circular shape with the reverent aim of offering a crown to the Madonna. She stands on the lantern above the cupola as described in the Book of Revelations: 'Clothed in the sun, and the moon under her feet, and upon her head a crown of twelve stars.' Beneath her, on the great scroll-brackets around the cupola, stand statues of the apostles – the 12 stars in her crown. This Marian symbolism continues inside the church, where in the centre of the mosaic floor, amid a circle of roses, is an inscription, *Unde origo inde salus* (from the origin comes salvation) – a reference to the legendary birth of Venice under the Virgin's protection.

Longhena's intention was for the visitor to approach the high altar ceremoniously through the main door, with the six side altars only coming into view upon reaching the very centre of the church, where they appear framed theatrically in their separate archways. However, the main door is rarely open and often the central area of the church is roped off, so you have no choice but to walk round the ambulatory and visit the chapels separately.

SIGHTS

The Whole Punta

The Punta della Dogana confirms Venice as a contemporary art hub.

The first days of June 2009 saw a contemporary art logjam in Venice, with the inauguration of the **Fondazione Vedova** (*see p126*), the opening of the biggest ever contemporary art Biennale (*see pp47-49*) and the presentation of the grand new **Punta della Dogana** gallery (*see p123*).

This last had been touted for months as the most significant of the three. In the event, one of the most exciting *Biennali* in years stole the limelight, but there's no denying that the return of the huge *dogana* (customs) building after decades of neglect, wrangling and big-bucks restoration works was an important moment. It's a pity, therefore, that the new gallery contains – as one critic commented wearily – 'endless floors of blue-chip masterpieces. None of this makes any sense.'

In April 2007, a 33-year lease on the huge 17th-century bonded warehouses at the Punta was won by French fashion magnate François Pinault – ranked 39th richest man in the world – to house his collection of 20th- and 21st-century art, reputedly one of the largest anywhere, with over 2,500 pieces. Pinault gave the job of restoring the almost 5,000 square metre space to Japanese architect-superstar Tadao Ando, and wrote out a cheque for €20 million to cover the costs.

Tadao Ando was no stranger to Venetian restoration, having been behind the 2005 makeover of the **Palazzo Grassi** (*see p75*), Pinault's other gallery. There (seven months) as here (14 months), the rapidity with which he gets things done left Italians bewildered, but not bowed. In his notes for the catalogue of the inaugural show, *Mapping the Studio*, Ando expressed his 'great respect for this emblematic building' but also let slip some pique that furious protests from residents had stymied his plans to erect two towering concrete columns symbolizing 'dialogue between the history and the future' by the campo della Salute entrance.

It wasn't the only thing that irked the Venetians. For years, the nearby **Peggy Guggenheim Collection** (*see p121*) had been trying to expand into this space, and many felt that this key city icon deserved a helping hand. Yet the wording of the 2006 competition made it almost impossible for anyone but Pinault to win, critics said.

The Pinault Foundation now intends to use Palazzo Grassi for one-off shows, and the Punta to display pieces from the Frenchman's collection. Whatever you make of those pieces – which range from Dan Flavin to Jeff Koons, from Jean Tinguely to Rachel Whiteread – there's no doubt that the new gallery makes this narrow wedge of land dividing the Grand and Giudecca canals into one of the world's greatest concentrations of modern and contemporary art.

Fondazione Vedova. *See p126.*

The three on the right have paintings by Luca Giordano, a prolific Neapolitan painter who brought a little southern brio into the art of the city at a time (the mid 17th century) when most painting had become limply derivative.

On the opposite side is a clumsily restored *Pentecost*, by Titian, transferred here from the island monastery of Santo Spirito (demolished in 1656). The high altar has a splendidly dynamic sculptural group by Giusto Le Corte, the artist responsible (with assistants) for most of the statues inside and outside the church. This group represents *Venice Kneeling before the Virgin and Child*, while the plague, in the shape of a hideous old hag, scurries off to the right, prodded by a tough-looking *putto*. In the midst of all this marble hubbub is a serene Byzantine icon of the *Madonna and Child*, brought from Crete in 1669 by Francesco Morosini, the Venetian commander responsible for blowing up the Parthenon.

Sacristy

The best paintings are in the sacristy (opens at 10am). Tintoretto's *Marriage at Cana* (1551) was described by Ruskin as 'perhaps the most perfect example which human art has produced of the utmost possible force and sharpness of shadow united with richness of local colour'. He also points out how difficult it is to spot the bride and groom in the painting.

On the altar is a very early Titian of *Saints Mark, Sebastian, Roch, Cosmas and Damian*, saints who were all invoked for protection against the plague; the painting was done during the outbreak of 1509-14. Three later works by Titian (c1540-49) hang on the ceiling, violent Old Testament scenes also brought here from the church of Santo Spirito: *The Sacrifice of Abraham, David Killing Goliath* and *Cain and Abel*. These works established the conventions for all subsequent ceiling paintings in Venice: Titian decided not to go for the worm's-eye view adopted by Mantegna and Correggio, which sacrificed clarity for surprise, and instead chose an oblique viewpoint, as if observing the action from the bottom of a hill. More Old Testament turbulence can be seen in Salviati's *Saul Hurling a Spear at David* and Palma il Giovane's *Samson and Jonah*, in which the whale is represented mainly by a vast lolling rubbery tongue.

LE ZATTERE

Vaporetto Accademia, Salute or Zattere.

From punta della Dogana (*see p120*), the mile-long stretch of **Le Zattere**, Venice's finest promenade after the riva degli Schiavoni, leads westwards past the churches of **I Gesuati** and **Santa Maria della Visitazione** (for both, *see p126*) to the San Nicolò zone.

This long promenade bordering the Giudecca Canal is named after the *zattere* (rafts) that used to moor here, bringing wood and other materials across from the mainland. The paved quayside was created by decree in 1519. It now provides a favourite strolling ground, punctuated by some spectacularly situated (if somewhat shadeless) benches for a picnic.

The eastern end is usually quiet, with the occasional flurry of activity around the rowing clubs now occupying the 14th-century salt warehouses, one of which now hosts the new **Fondazione Vedova** gallery (*see p126*).

Westward from these are the new premises of the **Accademia di Belle Arti** (the school of fine arts that was recently evicted from the Accademia), the church of **Spirito Santo** and the long 16th-century façade of the grimly named **Ospedale degli Incurabili** (the main incurable disease of the time was syphilis). In Ben Jonson's play *Volpone*, the title character's property is confiscated and he himself sent to this hospital at the end of the play.

The liveliest part of the Zattere is around the church of I Gesuati. Venetians flock here at weekends and on warm evenings to savour ice-cream or sip drinks at canalside tables.

The final and widest stretch of the Zattere passes several notable *palazzi*. Towards the end is the 17th-century façade of the **Scuola dei Luganegheri** (sausage-makers' school), with a statue of the sausage-makers' protector, St Anthony Abbot, whose symbol was a hog.

Fondazione Vedova

Dorsoduro 46, calle dello Squero (041 522 6626/ www.fondazionevedova.org). Vaporetto Salute or Zattere. **Open** 11.30am-6.30pm Tue-Sun. **Admission** to be confirmed. **Map** p323 G9.

A selection of works by Venetian artist Emilio Vedova (1919-2006) is now housed in a stunning new gallery, designed by Renzo Piano, in the Magazzini del Sale (salt warehouses). Immense canvasses by this leading member of the European avant-garde are suspended from moving brackets in what curators describe as a 'dynamic' exhibition. *Photo p125.*

Le Zattere. *See p125.*

I Gesuati

Dorsoduro, fondamenta Zattere ai Gesuati (041 275 0642/www.chorusvenezia.org). Vaporetto Zattere. **Open** 10am-5pm Mon-Sat. **Admission** €3 (or Chorus; *see p7*). **No credit cards.** **Map** p323 E9.

This church is officially Santa Maria del Rosario, but it is always known as the Gesuati, after the minor religious order that owned the previous church here. The order merged with the Dominicans – the present owners – in 1668. I Gesuati is a great piece of teamwork by a trio of remarkable rococo artists: architect Giorgio Massari, painter Giambattista Tiepolo and sculptor Giovanni Morlaiter.

The façade deliberately reflects the Palladian church of the Redentore opposite, but the splendidly posturing statues give it that typically 18th-century touch of histrionic flamboyance. Plenty more theatrical sculpture is to be found inside the church, all by Morlaiter. Above is a magnificent ceiling by Tiepolo, with three frescoes on obscure Dominican themes. These works reintroduced frescoes to Venetian art after two centuries of canvas ceiling paintings. The central panel shows St Dominic passing on to a crowd of supplicants the rosary he has just received from the cloud-enthroned Madonna. Tiepolo also painted the surrounding grisailles, which, at first sight, look like stucco reliefs.

There is another brightly coloured Tiepolo on the first altar on the right, *The Virgin and Child with Saints Rosa, Catherine and Agnes*. Tiepolo here plays with optical effects, allowing St Rosa's habit to tumble out of the frame. In his painting of three Dominican saints on the third altar on the right, Giovanni Battista Piazzetta makes use of a narrower and more sober range of colours, going for a more sculptural effect.

FREE Santa Maria della Visitazione

Dorsoduro, fondamenta Zattere ai Gesuati (041 522 4077). Vaporetto Zattere. **Closed** for restoration. **Map** p322 D9.

Confusingly, this has the same name as the Vivaldi church on the riva degli Schiavoni – though the latter is usually known as La Pietà (*see p85*). Santa Maria della Visitazione is now the chapel of the Istituto Don Orione, which has taken over the vast complex of the monastery of the Gesuati next door.

Designed by Tullio Lombardo or Mauro Codussi and built in 1423, the church has an attractive early Renaissance façade. It was suppressed (that rascal Napoleon again) at the beginning of the 19th century and stripped of all its works of art with the exception of the original coffered ceiling, an unexpected delight containing 58 compartments with portraits of saints and prophets by an Umbrian painter of Luca Signorelli's school, one of the few examples of central Italian art in Venice. To the right of the façade is a lion's mouth for secret denunciations: the ones posted here went to the *Magistrati della sanità*, who dealt with matters of public health.

SIGHTS

La Giudecca
& San Giorgio

Prisons, monasteries, posh hotels… and some Palladian glories.

The **Giudecca** lies south of Venice proper, a gondola-shaped strand of islands. Once a place of flourishing monasteries with lush gardens, its nature changed in the 19th century when city authorities began to make use of the abandoned religious houses, converting them into factories and prisons. The factories have almost all closed down, while the prisons remain in use. Giudecca has a reputation as one of the poorer areas in the city, but it manages to attract more than its fair share of celebrities.

LA GIUDECCA

SAN GIORGIO

Map pp322-323	Hotels p162
& pp328-329	Restaurants p180
	Cafés & Bars p192

With its splendid Palladian church facing the Doge's palace across the lagoon, **San Giorgio** is an immediately recognisable Venetian icon.

SIGHTS

LA GIUDECCA

Vaporetto Palanca, Redentore or Zitelle.

The Giudecca was once known as 'Spinalonga', from an imagined resemblance to a fish-skeleton (*spina* means fish bone). Some claim that the present name derives from an early community of Jews, and others to the fact that the island was a place of exile for troublesome nobles, who had been *giudicati*, 'judged'. But the exile was sometimes self-chosen, as people used the islands as a place of rural retreat. Michelangelo, when exiled from Florence in 1529, chose it as a place to mope; three centuries later, during his steamy and highly public love affair with George Sand, Alfred de Musset wrote in praise of the flowery meadows of 'la Zuecca'.

The Giudecca's industrial heritage is in the process of being shaken up: some of the factories remain abandoned, contributing to the run-down appearance of the south side of the Giudecca, but a few have been converted into new residential complexes. The greatest transformation has been that of the **Molino Stucky**, the vast turreted and crenellated

Teutonic mass at the western end of the Giudecca. The largest building in the lagoon, it was built as a flour mill in 1896 and continued to function until 1955. It stood in rat-ridden abandonment until the Acqua Marcia company was finally granted permission to restore and restructure it. It now hosts the Hilton Hotel with its conference centre, roof-top **Skyline Bar** (*see p192*) and swimming pool, and 138 private flats.

The *palazzi* along the northern *fondamenta* enjoy a splendid view of Venice and attract well-heeled outsiders (Elton John and Giorgio

INSIDE TRACK
A SECRET LOOKOUT

Head to the southern side of Giudecca for a lagoon view most tourists never see. To get there, take calle San Giacomo, west of the Redentore; just before the end, turn left along calle degli Orti, and then right. At the end is a small public garden with benches looking out over the quiet southern lagoon and its lonely islands (*see p141*).

Bags, Rags & Veg

Giudecca's women's prison produces some amazing goods.

The island of Giudecca has an industrious history, with the giant Molino Stucky flour mill (now a Hilton hotel; *see p144*) and the Junghans bomb-part factory (now home to a theatre; *see p237*) setting the tone. Some lean decades brought those industrial behemoths to their knees, but in one secluded corner of this little-visited island, a group of women are reversing the downwards trend of industry in a very exclusive hive of activity.

Behind the high walls of a 13th-century former convent on the fondamenta delle Convertite, the 80-odd inmates of the **Casa di Reclusione Femminile** (women's prison) not only run an industrial laundry, washing and ironing for the Molino Stucky Hilton and the Bauer Palladio hotels (*see p145*), but also produce beauty products, clothes and furnishings, and grow organic vegetables in a 6,400-square-metre (1.6-acre) plot that recalls the Giudecca's other traditional vocation – as an island of *orti* (vegetable gardens).

The prison's tailors' workshop hit the headlines some years ago when it came up with faithful reproductions of splendid 18th-century costumes for Palazzo Mocenigo (*see p104*). The workshop continues to produce period costumes – for purchase, and to hire at Carnevale time – but also does a healthy business in contemporary clothes, sequin-encrusted bags, jewellery, a variety of accessories and cushions in plush brocades, all of which are on sale at **Banco No.10** (Castello 3478, salizada Sant'Antonin), near the church of San Giovanni in Bragora.

The inmates' cosmetic products, which are sold in local *profumerie* under the labels *Veneziana Coloniali e Spezie* and *Rio Terà dei Pensieri*, are made in the prison lab under the guidance of a chemist using herbs and medicinal plants grown in the prison garden. Several of Venice's hotels provide these gorgeously perfumed goodies in their rooms.

To sample the edible produce of the *Orto delle Meraviglie* – the 'Garden of Marvels', as the vegetable plot is known – you will have to turn up outside the prison walls on a Thursday morning. Throughout the year, whatever this lovingly tended, chemical-free oasis yields goes on sale to the public.

Banco No.10.

Casa di Reclusione Femminile.

Armani, for example) in search of picturesque holiday homes. Apart from the Hilton, there are a number of other major hotels, including Venice's most expensive, the **Cipriani** (*see p163*), at the eastern end. The island's disused warehouses are popular as studios for artists.

The main sights of the Giudecca are all on this *fondamenta*: **Santa Eufemia** (*see below*), the Palladian churches of **Le Zitelle** ('the spinsters': the convent ran a hospice for poor girls who were trained as lace-makers), which is nearly always closed, and **Il Redentore** (*see below*), as well as several fine *palazzi*.

Near Le Zitelle is the neo-Gothic **Casa De Maria**, with its three large inverted-shield windows. The Bolognese painter Mario De Maria built it for himself from 1910 to 1913. It is the only private palazzo to have the same patterned brickwork as the Doge's Palace.

On the fondamenta Rio della Croce (no.149, close to the Redentore) stands the **Palazzo Munster**, a former infirmary for English sailors. The vitriolic Anglo-Catholic writer Frederick Rolfe received the last sacraments here in 1910, after slagging the hospital off in his novel *The Desire and Pursuit of the Whole*. (He then live for two more vituperative years.)

Opposite is another expat landmark, the '**Garden of Eden**', pleasure ground of Frederic Eden, a disabled Englishman who, like Byron, discovered that Venice was the perfect city for those with disabilities – particularly if they could afford their own gondola and steam launch. After a period in which it belonged to the ex-Queen of Yugoslavia, the garden passed into the hands of the Austrian artist Fritz Hundertwasser. Since his death in 2000, it has belonged to a foundation in his name, which has, reportedly, allowed the garden to remain verdant but totally unkempt.

Il Redentore

Giudecca, campo del Redentore (041 275 0462/ www.chorusvenezia.org). Vaporetto Redentore. **Open** 10am-5pm Mon-Sat. **Admission** €3 (or Chorus; *see p7*). **No credit cards. Map** p328 F11.
Venice's first great plague church was commissioned to celebrate deliverance from the bout of 1575-77. An especially conspicuous site was chosen, one that could be approached in ceremonial fashion. The ceremony continues today, on every third Sunday of July, when a bridge of boats is built across the canal. Palladio designed an eye-catching building whose prominent dome appears to rise directly behind the Greek-temple façade, giving the illusion that the church is centrally planned, as was traditional with sanctuaries and votive temples outside Venice. A broad flight of steps leads to the entrance.

Its solemn, harmonious interior, with a single nave lit by large 'thermal' windows, testifies to Palladio's study of Roman baths. But the Capuchin monks, the

austere order to whom the building was entrusted, were not pleased by its grandeur; Palladio attempted to mollify them by designing their choir stalls in a plain style. The best paintings are in the sacristy, which is rarely open; they include a *Virgin and Child* by Alvise Vivarini and a *Baptism* by Veronese.
► *For more on Palladio and his architectural masterpieces, see p280 Profile.*

FREE Santa Eufemia
Giudecca, fondamenta Santa Eufemia (041 522 5848). Vaporetto Palanca. **Open** 8am-noon, 3-5pm Mon-Sat; 3-7pm Sun. **Map** p328 C10.
This church has a 16th-century Doric portico along its flank. The interior owes its charm to its mix of styles. The nave and aisles are mostly 11th century, with Veneto-Byzantine columns and capitals, while the decoration consists mainly of 18th-century stucco and paintings. Over the first altar on the right is *St Roch and an Angel* by Bartolomeo Vivarini (1480).

ISOLA DI SAN GIORGIO

Vaporetto San Giorgio.

The island of **San Giorgio**, which sits in such a strategic position opposite the Piazzetta, realised its true potential under set designer extraordinaire Andrea Palladio, whose church of **San Giorgio Maggiore** (*see p130*) is one of Venice's most recognisable landmarks. Known originally as the *Isola dei Cipressi* (Cypress Island), it soon became an important Benedictine monastery and centre of learning – a tradition that is carried on today by the **Fondazione Giorgio Cini** (*see below*), which operates a research centre and craft school on the island.

Fondazione Giorgio Cini & Benedictine Monastery
(041 524 0119/www.cini.it). Vaporetto San Giorgio. **Open** *Monastery* (guided tours every hour) 10am-4.30pm Sat, Sun. Mon-Fri by appointment only. **Admission** €12; €10 reductions. **No credit cards. Map** p329 K11.
There has been a Benedictine monastery here since 982, when Doge Tribuno Memmo donated the island to the order. The monastery continued to benefit from ducal donations, acquiring large tracts of land both in and around Venice and abroad. After the church acquired the remains of St Stephen (1109), it was visited yearly by the doge on 26 December, the feast day of the saint. The city authorities often used the island as a luxury hotel for particularly prestigious visitors, such as Cosimo de' Medici in 1433. Cosimo had a magnificent library built here; it was destroyed in 1614, to make way for a more elaborate affair by Longhena.

In 1800, the island hosted the conclave of cardinals that elected Pope Pius VII, after they had been expelled from Rome by Napoleon. In 1806, the French got their own back, supressing the monastery and

SIGHTS

sending its chief artistic treasure – Veronese's *Marriage Feast at Cana* – off to the Louvre, where it still hangs. For the rest of the century, the monastery did ignominious service as a barracks and ammunition store. In 1951, industrialist Vittorio Cini bought the island to set up a foundation in memory of his son, Giorgio, killed in a plane crash in 1949.

The Fondazione Giorgio Cini uses the monastery buildings for its activities, including artistic and musical research (it holds a collection of Vivaldi manuscripts, plus illuminated manuscripts), and a naval college. A portion of the complex was given back to the Benedictines; there are currently eight monks in the monastery. The foundation is now open to the public at weekends for guided tours (in Italian, English, French and German). There are two beautiful cloisters – one by Giovanni Buora (1516-40), the other by Palladio (1579) – an elegant library and staircase by Longhena (1641-53), and a magnificent refectory (where Veronese's painting hung) by Palladio (1561). The tour also includes the splendid garden behind the monastery.

★ FREE San Giorgio Maggiore

(041 522 7827). Vaporetto San Giorgio. **Open** 9.30am-12.30pm, 2.30-5pm Mon-Sat; 2.30-5pm Sun. **Admission** *Church* free. *Campanile* €3. **No credit cards. Map** p329 K10.

This unique spot cried out for a masterpiece. Palladio provided it. This was his first complete solo church (*see also p280* **Profile**); it demonstrates how confident he was in his techniques and objectives. With no hint of influence from the city's Byzantine tradition, Palladio here develops the system of superimposed temple fronts with which he had experimented in the façade of San Francesco della Vigna (*see p79*). The interior maintains the same relations between the orders as the outside, with composite half-columns supporting the gallery and lower Corinthian pilasters supporting the arches.

The effect is of luminosity and harmony, decoration being confined to the altars. Palladio believed that white was the colour most pleasing to God, a credo that happily matched the demand from the Council of Trent for greater lucidity in church services.

There are several good works of art. Over the first altar is an *Adoration of the Shepherds* by Jacopo Bassano, with startling lighting effects. The altar to the right of the high altar has a *Madonna and Child with Nine Saints* by Sebastiano Ricci.

On the side walls of the chancel hang two vast compositions by Tintoretto, a *Last Supper* and the *Gathering of Manna*, painted in the last years of his life. The perspective of each work makes it clear that they were intended to be viewed from the altar rails. Tintoretto combines almost surreal visionary effects (angels swirling out from a lamp's eddying smoke) with touches of superb domestic realism (a cat prying into a basket, a woman stooping over her laundry). Tintoretto's last painting, a moving *Entombment*, hangs in the Cappella dei Morti (open for 11am Mass on Sundays in winter only). It's possible that Tintoretto included himself among the mourners: he has been identified as the bearded man gazing intensely at Christ's face.

In the left transept is a painting by Jacopo and Domenico Tintoretto of the *Martyrdom of St Stephen*, placed above the altar containing the saint's remains (brought from Constantinople in 1109).

From the left transept, follow the signs to the campanile. Just in front of the ticket-office stands the huge statue of an angel that crowned the bell tower until it was struck by lightning in 1993. To the left of the statue, a corridor gives access to the lift that takes you up to the bell tower. The view from the top of the tower is extraordinary: the best possible panorama across Venice itself and the lagoon.

▶ *San Giorgio is home to Tintoretto's seventh and final Last Supper. To see them in the order he painted them, begin at San Marcuola; see p92.*

Isola di San Giorgio. *See p129.*

Lido & Lagoon

Head out across the water for a little tranquility.

Venice's situation is, to say the least, improbable. It lies more or less in the middle of a saltwater lagoon, protected from the open sea by the two slender barriers of the **Lido** and **Pellestrina**. Venice is by no means the only island in the lagoon. If the jostling crowds in piazza San Marco get too much for you, a day out to one or more of these other islands may prove the ideal antidote.

Such destinations as **Murano** and **Burano** can, in high season, seem only marginally less crowded, but the views from the vaporetto of the lagoon's empty reaches are enough to soothe even the most frayed of nerves. Other islands, such as **Sant'Erasmo**, are always bucolically tranquil and almost entirely tourist-free.

| Map p319 &
pp327-329 | Hotels p163
Restaurants p181 |

THE FIGHT WITH THE SEA

For Venetians, the greatest threat has always been the open sea, and their efforts have been devoted over the centuries to strengthening the natural defences offered by Pellestrina and the Lido. In the 18th century, the *murazzi* were created: an impressive barrier of stone and marble blocks all the way down both islands.

Nowadays, the threat is seen as coming from the three *bocche di porto* (the lagoon's openings to the sea) between the Lido and Cavallino, between the Lido and Pellestrina and between Pellestrina and Chioggia. Work has started on creating the highly controversial mobile dyke system known as MoSE.

There are 34 islands on the saltwater lagoon, most of them uninhabited, containing only crumbling masonry, and home to seagulls and lazy lizards. The lagoon itself covers some 520 square kilometres (200 square miles) – the world's biggest wetland. This wild, fragile environment is where Venetians take refuge from the tourist hordes, escaping by boat for picnics on deserted islands, or fishing for bass and bream. Others set off to dig up clams at low tide (most without the requisite licence), or organise hunting expeditions for duck, using the makeshift hides known as *botte* ('barrels', which is what they were originally, sunk into the floor of the lagoon). Many just head out after work, at sunset, to row.

EXPLORING THE LAGOON

To learn more about the lagoon's ecosystem and bird life, catch the blue bus for Chioggia or Sottomarina from piazzale Roma and ask to get off at the WWF's **Oasi Valle Averto** (041 518 5068, open for guided tours only, Apr-Oct 9.30am & 4pm Sat & Sun, Nov-Mar 9.30am & 2.30pm Sat & Sun, admission €8, €5 reductions, free under-6s, minimum ten people). Or contact **Limosa** (041 932 003, www.limosa.it), a group of dedicated environmentalists who organise day trips (or entire holidays) by boat or bike.

For boat hire, fishing and tours, *see p245*.

The Lido

Vaporetto Lido–Santa Maria Elisabetta.

The **Lido** is the northernmost of the two strips of land that separate the lagoon from the open sea. It is no longer the 'bare strand / Of hillocks heaped from ever-shifting sand' that Shelley described in *Julian and Maddalo*, nor is it the playground for wealthy aesthetes that fans of *Death in Venice* might come in fruitless search of. These days, Venice-by-the-sea is a placidly residential suburb, where pale young boys in sailor-suits are in very short supply – an escape from the strangeness of Venice to a normality of supermarkets and cars.

Burano. *See p134.*

SIGHTS

Things perk up in summer when buses are full of city sunbathers and tourists staying in the Lido's overspill hotels. However, the days of all-night partying and gambling are long gone. In 2001, the Lido Casinò closed. Now the only moment when the place stirs to anything like its former vivacity is at the beginning of September when the film festival (*see p222*) rolls into town for two weeks, with its bandwagon of stars, directors, PR people and sleep-deprived, caffeine-driven journalists.

The Lido has few tourist sights as such. Only the church of **San Nicolò** on the riviera San Nicolò – founded in 1044 – can claim any great antiquity. It was here that the doge would come on Ascension Day after marrying Venice to the sea in the ceremony known as *lo sposalizio del mare* (*see p215* **Festa della Sensa**). Inside is the tomb of Nicola Giustiniani, a Benedictine monk who was forced to leave holy orders in 1172 to assure the future of his illustrious family, of which he was the sole heir. He married the doge's daughter, had lots of kids, then went back to being a monk. After his death he was beatified for his spirit of self-sacrifice.

Fans of art nouveau and deco have plenty to look at on the Lido. On the Gran Viale there are two gems: the tiled façade of the **Hungaria Hotel** (no.28), formerly the Ausonia Palace, with its Beardsley-esque nymphs; and **Villa Monplaisir** at no.14, an art deco design from 1906. There are other smaller-scale examples in and around via Lepanto. For full-blown turn-of-the-century exotica, though, it's hard to beat the **Hotel Excelsior** (*see p162* **Inside Track**) on lungomare Marconi, a neo-Moorish party-piece, complete with minaret.

The bus ride south along the lagoon-side promenade of the Lido is uneventful but passes some submerged history. The old town of **Malamocco**, near the south end of the island, was engulfed by a tidal wave in 1107; it had been a flourishing port controlled by Padua. The new town, built further inland, never really amounted to much; today, its sights consist of a few picturesque streets and a pretty bridge.

Offshore from Malamocco is the tiny island of **Poveglia**, once inhabited by 200 families, descendants of the servants of Pietro Tradonico, a ninth-century doge murdered by his rivals. His servants barricaded themselves inside the Palazzo Ducale and only agreed to leave when safe conduct to this new home was promised.

GETTING THERE & AROUND

The main Lido–Santa Maria Elisabetta **vaporetto** stop (often just called 'Lido') is served by frequent boats from Venice and the mainland. The San Nicolò stop, to the north, is served by the no.17 car ferry from Tronchetto.

Bus routes here are confusing. The A (*arancione*, orange) and the B (*blu*) each have two routes, one going south and one north from the main vaporetto stop. The southward route of both (marked 'Alberoni') is the same, along the lagoon to Alberoni at the southern tip of the island, via Malamocco. The northward route of each (marked 'San Nicolò' or 'Ospedale') is circular: the A travels clockwise along the lagoon-front and then turns right towards the sea and the Ospedale al Mare and makes its way back to Santa Maria Elisabetta; the B does more or less the same route anticlockwise. In the summer the routes are extended to include popular beaches. The V (*verde*, green) does a shorter route, travelling to the Palazzo del Cinema on the seafront and ending up at via Parri. In summer there's another circular line, the C (*celeste*, light blue), which also travels to the Palazzo del Cinema and back again.

Finally, bus 11, which departs from the Gran Viale opposite the main vaporetto stop, also heads down to Alberoni but then continues on to the car ferry across to Pellestrina island. **Cycling** is a good way of getting around the pancake-flat Lido; for bike hire, *see p297*.

TOURIST INFORMATION

From June to September, there's a tourist information office at Gran Viale 6A, Lido (041 526 5721, www.turismovenezia.it, open 9.30am-1pm, 3-6.30pm daily, map p327 BB3).

The Northern Lagoon

SAN MICHELE

Vaporetto Cimitero (41 or 42).

Halfway between Venice and Murano, this is the island where tourists begin their lagoon visit. For many Venetians, it's the last stop: San Michele is the city's cemetery (open Apr-Sept 7.30am-6pm daily, Oct-Mar 7.30am-4.30pm daily). Early in the morning, *vaporetti* are packed with Venetians coming over to lay flowers. This is not a morbid spot, though: it is an elegant city of the dead, with more than one famous resident.

An orderly red-brick wall runs around the whole of the island, with a line of tall cypress trees rising high behind it – the inspiration for Böcklin's famously lugubrious painting *Island of the Dead*. The island was originally just a Franciscan monastery, but during the Napoleonic period the grounds that used to extend behind the church were seconded for burials in an effort to stop unhygienic Venetians from digging graves in the *campi* around parish churches.

Before visiting the cemetery, take a look at the church of **San Michele in Isola** (open 7.30am-12.15pm, 3-4pm daily; being restored as this guide went to press); turn left after entering the cemetery and pass through the fine cloisters. The view of the façade is particularly

striking. Designed by Mauro Codussi in the 1460s, this white building of Istrian stone was Venice's first Renaissance church.

In a booth to the left of the entrance by the vaporetto stop, staff hand out maps, which are indispensable for celebrity hunts. In the Greek and Russian Orthodox section of the cemetery are the elaborate tomb of Sergei Pavlovich Diaghilev, who introduced the Ballets Russes to Europe, and a simpler monument to the composer Igor Stravinsky and his wife. The Protestant (*Evangelico*) section has a selection of ships' captains and passengers who ended their days in *La Serenissima*, plus the simple graves of Ezra Pound and Joseph Brodsky.

There's a rather sad children's section and a corner dedicated to the city's gondoliers, their tombs decorated with carvings and statues of gondolas. Visit the cemetery on the *Festa dei morti* – All Souls' Day, 2 November – and the vaporetto is free, but seriously packed.

MURANO

Vaporetto Colonna, Da Mula, Faro, Museo, Navagero or Venier (multiple lines).

After San Michele, the vaporetto continues to **Murano**, one of the larger and more populous islands. In the 16th and 17th centuries, when it was a world centre of glass production and a decadent resort for pleasure-seeking Venetians, Murano had a population of more than 30,000. These days only around 5,000 people live here, many workers commuting from the mainland.

Murano owes its fame to the decision taken in 1291 to transfer all of Venice's glass furnaces to the island because of a fear of fire in the main city. Their products were soon sold all over Europe. The secrets of glass were jealously guarded within the island: any glass-maker leaving Murano was proclaimed a traitor. Even today, there is no official glass school: the delicate skills of blowing and flamework are only learned by apprenticeship to one of

SIGHTS

INSIDE TRACK
ISLAND OF THE DEAD

Most Venetians still want to make that last journey to **San Michele** (*see left*), though these days it's more a temporary parking lot than a final resting place: the island reached saturation point long ago, and even after paying through the nose for a plot, families know that after a suitable period – generally around ten years – the bones of their loved ones will be dug up and transferred to an ossuary elsewhere.

---

the glass masters. At first sight, Murano looks close to being ruined by glass tourism. Dozens of 'guides' swoop on visitors as they pile off the ferry, to whisk them off on tours of furnaces. Even if you head off on your own, you'll find yourself on fondamenta dei Vetrai, a snipers' alley of shops selling glass knick-knacks, most of which are made far from Murano. But there *are* some serious glass-makers on the island and even the tackiest showroom usually has one or two gems. For a guide to the industry and where to buy, *see p136* **Murano Glass**.

There's more to Murano, however, than glass. At the far end of fondamenta dei Vetrai is the nondescript façade of the 14th-century parish church of **San Pietro Martire** (*see below*), which holds important works of art including Bellini's impressive altarpiece triptych. On the other side of the rio dei Vetrai, a striking glass comet made by Simone Cenedese as a decoration for Christmas 2007 seems to have become a permanent feature.

Beyond the church, Murano's Canal Grande is spanned by Ponte Vivarini, an unattractive, 19th-century iron bridge. Before crossing, it is worth looking at the Gothic **Palazzo Da Mula**, just to the left of the bridge; this splendid, 15th-century building has been recently restored and transformed into council offices. In the morning you can stroll through its courtyard, which contains a monumental carved Byzantine arch from an earlier (12th- or 13th-century) building.

On the other side of the bridge, a right turn takes you along fondamenta Cavour; 200 metres further along, it veers sharply to the left, becoming fondamenta Giustinian. The 17th-century Palazzo Giustinian, situated far from the tacky chandeliers and fluorescent clowns, is the **Museo dell'Arte Vetrario** (*see below*), the best place to learn about the history of glass. Just beyond this is Murano's greatest architectural treasure: the 12th-century basilica of **Santi Maria e Donato** (*see below*), with its apse towards the canal.

Return to Ponte Vivarini and walk to the end of fondamenta Sebastiano Venier. The church of **Santa Maria degli Angeli** (open 11am Sun; being restored as this guide went to press) backs on to the convent where Casanova conducted one of his most torrid affairs, with a libertine nun named Maria Morosoni.

Museo dell'Arte Vetrario

Fondamenta Giustinian 8 (041 739 586). *Vaporetto Museo.* **Open** 10am-4pm Mon, Tue, Thur-Sun. **Admission** €5.50; €3 reductions (*see also p6*). **Credit** AmEx, DC, MC, V. **Map** p328 U2.

Housed in beautiful Palazzo Giustinian, built in the late 17th century for the bishop of Torcello, the museum has a huge collection of Murano glass. As

well as the famed chandeliers, which only made their appearance in the 18th century, there are ruby-red beakers, opaque lamps and delicate Venetian *perle* – glass beads that were used in trade and commerce all over the world from the time of Marco Polo. One of the earliest pieces is the 15th-century Barovier marriage cup, decorated with portraits of the bride and groom. In one room is a collection of 17th-century oil lamps in the shapes of animals, some of which are uncannily Disney-like. On the ground floor is a good collection of Roman glassware from near Zara on the Istrian peninsula.

★ FREE San Pietro Martire

Fondamenta dei Vetrai (041 739 704). Vaporetto Colonna or Faro. **Open** 9am-6pm Mon-Fri; 1-6pm Sat; 8am-5pm Sun. **Map** p328 T2.

Behind its unspectacular façade, the church of San Pietro Martire conceals an important work by Giovanni Bellini, backed by a marvellous landscape: *The Virgin and Child Enthroned with St Mark, St Augustine and Doge Agostino Barbarigo.* There is also a Tintoretto *Baptism*, two works by Veronese and his assistants (mainly the latter) and an ornate altarpiece (*Deposition*) by Salviati, which is lit up by the early morning sun. The sacristy (offering of €1.50) contains remarkable woodcarvings from the 17th century and a small museum of reliquaries and other ornaments.

FREE Santi Maria e Donato

Campo San Donato (041 739 056). Vaporetto Museo. **Open** 8am-7pm daily. **Map** p328 V2.

Although altered by over-enthusiastic 19th-century restorers, the exterior of this church is a classic of the Veneto-Byzantine style, with an ornate blind portico on the rear of the apse. Inside is a richly coloured mosaic floor, laid down in 1140 (at the same time as the floor of the basilica di San Marco), with floral and animal motifs. Above, a Byzantine apse mosaic of the Virgin looms out of the darkness surrounded by a field of gold.

BURANO & MAZZORBO

Vaporetto Burano or Mazzorbo (LN, N).

Mazzorbo, the long island before Burano, is a haven of peace, rarely visited by tourists. It is worth getting off here just for the sake of the quiet walk along the canal and then across the long wooden bridge that connects Mazzorbo to Burano. The view from the bridge across the lagoon to Venice is stunning, and there's always a chance you'll have it to yourself.

Mazzorbo was settled around the tenth century. When it became clear that Venice itself had got the upper hand, most of the population simply dismantled their houses brick by brick, transported them by boat to Venice, and rebuilt them there. Today

SIGHTS

Music of the Islands

Murano's and Burano's famous musical sons: Galuppi and Piave.

The islands of the Venice's northern lagoon have contributed both a composer and a librettist to the city's musical hall of fame. The former, **Baldassarre Galuppi** (1706-85; pictured), has a square named after him on his native Burano; the latter, **Francesco Maria Piave** (1810-76), is commemorated with a fondamenta that's located near to Murano's Faro vaporetto stop.

Galuppi began his musical career early, though not gloriously, producing his first disastrous opera flop at the tender age of 16. Undaunted, he persisted until 1729, when his *Dorinda* was a hit. Throughout an 11-year stint as musical director at the Ospedale dei Mendicanti, and a term in the prestigious office of *maestro di cappella* at St Mark's, Galuppi never stopped producing works: over 100 operas, numerous masses, cantatas, oratorios, a good deal of chamber music and some 125 keyboard works.

Piave never achieved the renown of Galuppi in his own time. He wrote 38 librettos in all, for a number of composers, including Saverio Mercadante, Giovanni Pacini and the Irish composer Michael Balfe. But it was the ten librettos he wrote for **Giuseppe Verdi** that made his name.

Piave went to Rome to enter the priesthood but found himself irresistably drawn to writing. He tried his hand at journalism before returning to Venice, where he was bitten by the opera bug. With Verdi, Piave attempted to transform Walter Scott's novel *Woodstock* into an opera with the title *Cromwell*; when this enterprise got nowhere they turned to Victor Hugo's controversial work *Hernani*. The opera opened in Venice in 1844 and was a roaring success – a success that the seasoned Verdi attributed to his being able to make the inexperienced Piave write what he wanted.

Piave became resident poet and stage-manager at La Fenice (*see p239*) that same year and remained there until 1860, when Verdi fixed it for him to take up the same position at La Scala in Milan. The collaboration between the two men would go on to produce such classics as *Rigoletto*, *La Traviata* and *La Forza del Destino*.

For more musicians who have made their mark on Venice, *see p68* **City of Music**.

Baldassare Galuppi
« della Buranello »
Burano   Venezia
18 10 1706   3 1 1785

Mazzorbo is a lazy place of small farms with a pleasant walk to the 14th-century Gothic church of **Santa Caterina** (opening times vary), whose wonky tower still has its original bell dating from 1318 – one of the oldest in Europe. Winston Churchill, a keen amateur painter, set up his easel here more than once after World War II. Facing Burano is an area of attractive, modern, low-cost housing, in shades of lilac, grey and green, designed by the architect Giancarlo De Carlo.

One could almost believe that they invented the adjective picturesque to describe **Burano**. Together with its lace, its multicoloured houses make it a magnet for tourists armed with cameras. The locals are traditionally either fishermen or lace-makers, though there are fewer and fewer of the latter, despite the best efforts of the island's **Scuola di Merletti** (Lace School; *see p138*).

The street leading from the main quay throbs with souvenir shops selling lace, lace and more lace – much of it machine-made in Taiwan. (For suggestions on where to purchase lace, *see p212*.) But Burano is big enough for the visitor to meander through its quiet backstreets and avoid a lace overload. It was in Burano that Carnevale (*see p217* **Profile**) was revived in

Murano Glass

How it's made – and where to buy it.

Murano has been the capital of glass since 1291. In that year, Venice's rulers banished all glass furnaces to this island to avert the kind of conflagrations that would regularly devastate swathes of what was then a largely wooden city. Over the following centuries, the island refined its particular craft. Its vases, chandeliers, mirrors and drinking vessels were shipped over the world by Venice's great merchant fleet.

Nowadays, the assault of glass-blowing hustlers coupled with shop windows packed with glass *objets* of dubious taste and even more dubious origin make it hard to see the island's speciality as a noble art. But behind the tack, Murano remains a special place where centuries of glass-making techniques are still jealously preserved.

Murano glass is divided into medium to large furnace-made pieces (blown glass, sculpture and lamps) and smaller pieces (beads and animals) fashioned from sticks of coloured glass in the heat of a gas jet. Once made, these objects may be engraved or patterned with silver; multi-piece objects need assembling… all of which keeps much of Murano's population employed.

But unless you have your wits about you, you may never get beyond shops and warehouses packed with glass shipped from the Far East. Most hotel porters and concierges in Venice have agreements of some kind with these emporia: don't expect disinterested advice on where to go. Tourist-trade Murano outlets with 'authentic' furnaces being used by 'authentic' glass-blowers rarely sell the articles you'll see produced, whatever the salesmen tell you. Glass shops range from the excellent to the downright rip-off: labels proclaiming '*vetro di Murano*' mean very little ('*vetro artistico di Murano*' is meant to offer a firmer guarantee, though some top producers refuse to bow to this, believing that their reputation is all the guarantee needed).

So, how do you go about making sure you get the real thing? Real Murano glass is fiendishly expensive. There's no such thing as a real €30 vase, or a genuine €5 wine glass… at those prices you can be sure you're taking home something 'authentically' Chinese. If you want genuine without paying much for it, you'll have to resort to the odd glass bead. Moreover, the best workplaces don't allow tourists

in to gawp, though in some cases you will be able to peer through an open front gate. And, occasionally, they'll invite you in if you really intend to purchase. If you're after a true Murano glass experience, just be brave: ring that doorbell and see if they'll humour you and allow you a peek.

Berengo Fine Arts
Fondamenta dei Vetrai 109A (041 739 453/ www.berengo.com). Vaporetto Colonna or Faro. **Open** 10am-5.50pm daily. **Credit** AmEx, MC, V. **Map** p328 T3.
Adriano Berengo commissions various international artists to design brilliantly coloured sculptures – in glass, of course.

Cesare Toffolo
Fondamenta Vetrai 67A (041 736 460/ www.toffolo.com). Vaporetto Colonna. **Open** 10am-6pm daily. Closed Jan. **Credit** AmEx, DC, MC, V. **Map** p328 T3.
In this shop along thronging fondamenta Vetrai, Cesare Toffolo uses glass sticks and a gas flame to create intricate miniatures of Venetian classic designs: cups, vases and even chandeliers.

Davide Penso
Shop & workshop: riva Longa 48. Gallery: riva Longa 4 (041 527 4634/www. artstudiomurano.com). Vaporetto Museo. **Open** 9.30am-1.30pm, 2.30-5.30pm daily. **Credit** AmEx, DC, MC, V. **Map** p328 U2.
Davide Penso makes and shows exquisite glass jewellery. His own creations are all one-off or limited edition pieces with designs drawn from nature: zebra-striped, mother-of-pearl or crocodile-skinned.

Fratelli Barbini
Calle Bertolini 31 (041 739 777). Vaporetto Colonna. **Open** 8am-6pm Mon-Fri; 8am-noon Sat. **Credit** AmEx, DC, MC, V. **Map** p328 T3.
There's only one *fratello* (brother), Guido, left to carry on his family craft: mirror-making. In this workshop he silvers, engraves and mounts them according to long-running traditions.

Galliano Ferro
Fondamenta Colleoni 6 (041 739 477/ www.gallianoferro.it). Vaporetto Faro. **Open** by appointment. **No credit cards**. **Map** p328 U2.

Inspired by 18th-century classics, Ferro's rich, vibrant and intricate works are some of Murano's most sought-after models. There are early 20th-century designs too.

Luigi Camozzo
Fondamenta Venier 3 (041 736 875). Vaporetto Venier. **Open** 10am-6pm Mon-Fri; by appointment Sat, Sun. **Credit** MC, V. **Map** p328 T2.
It'd be over-simplifying things to describe Luigi Camozzo as a glass-engraver. Using a variety of different tools, he carves, sculpts and inscribes wonderfully soft, natural bas-reliefs into glass. Drop by and you may even catch him in action.

Manin 56
Fondamenta Manin 56 (041 527 5392). Vaporetto Faro. **Open** 10am-6pm daily. Closed Jan. **Credit** AmEx, DC, MC, V. **Map** p328 T3.
Sells modern (though slightly staid) lines in glassware and vases from prestigious houses such as Salviati and Vivarini.

Marina e Susanna Sent
Fondamenta Serenella 20 (041 527 4665/ www.marinaesusannasent.com). Vaporetto Colonna. **Open** 10am-5pm Mon-Fri. **Credit** AmEx, DC, MC, V. **Map** p328 S3.
In the Sent sisters' Murano workshop, you'll find clean, modern jewellery in glass, in interesting counterpoise to innovative jewellery in other materials, including wood, coral, paper and rubber. It's always best to call ahead and make an appointment.

Murano Collezioni
Fondamenta Manin 1C (041 736 272). Vaporetto Colonna. **Open** 10.30am-5.30pm Mon-Sat. Closed 2wks Jan. **Credit** AmEx, DC, MC, V. **Map** p328 T3.
This shop sells pieces by some of the lagoon's most respected producers, including Carlo Moretti, Barovier e Toso, and Venini. Room to move about and good lighting will help you make your choice.

Rossana e Rossana
Riva Longa 11 (041 527 4076/www.ro-e-ro. com). Vaporetto Museo. **Open** 10am-6pm daily. **Credit** AmEx, MC, V. **Map** p328 U2.
The place to come for traditional Venetian glass, from filigree pieces to Veronese

vases and elegant goblets that are based on models that were popular in the early years of the last century – all produced by master glass-maker Davide Fuin.

Seguso Viro
Fondamenta Venier 29 (041 527 4255/ www.segusoviro.com). Vaporetto Museo or Venier. **Open** 11am-4pm Mon-Sat. **Credit** AmEx, MC, V. **Map** p328 T2.
Giampaolo Seguso comes from a long line of Venetian glass-makers. His modern blown glass is enhanced by experiments working around Murano traditions. His son Gian Andrea exhibits artistic glass works in his new studio, Roscano (fondamenta dei Vetrai 94, 041 099 0079, www.roscano.com).

Venini
Fondamenta Vetrai 47-50 (041 273 7204/ www.venini.com). Vaporetto Colonna. **Open** 9.30am-5.30pm Mon-Sat. Closed 2wks Aug. **Credit** AmEx, MC, V. **Map** p328 T3.
Venini was the biggest name in Murano glass for much of the 20th century, and remains in the forefront. Classic designs are joined by more innovative pieces, including a selection designed by major international glass artists.

SIGHTS

SIGHTS

Santa Fosca, Torcello.

the 1970s; the modest celebrations here are still far more authentically joyful than the antics of masked tourists cramming piazza San Marco.

Fishermen have lived on Burano since the seventh century. According to local lore they painted their houses different colours so that they could recognise them when fishing out on the lagoon – though in fact only a tiny proportion of the island's houses can actually be seen from the lagoon. Whatever the reason, the *buranelli* still go to great efforts to decorate their houses, and social life centres on the *fondamente* where the men repair nets or tend to their boats moored in the canal below, while their wives – at least in theory – make lace.

Lace was first produced in Burano in the 15th century, originally by nuns, but the trade was quickly picked up by fishermen's wives and daughters. So skilful were the local lace-makers that in the 17th century many were paid handsomely to work in the Alengon lace ateliers in Normandy. Today, most work is done on commission, though interested parties will have to get to know one of the lace-makers in person, as the co-operative that used to represent the old ladies closed down in 1995.

The busy main square of Burano is named after the island's most famous son, Baldassare Galuppi (*see p135* **Music of the Islands**),

a 17th-century composer who collaborated with Carlo Goldoni on a number of operas and who was the subject of a poem by Robert Browning. The square is a good place for sipping a glass of prosecco. Across from the lace museum is the church of **San Martino** (open 8am-noon, 3-7pm daily), containing an early Tiepolo *Crucifixion* and, in the chapel to the right of the chancel, three small paintings by the 15th-century painter Giovanni Mansueti; the *Flight into Egypt* presents the Holy Family amid an imaginative menagerie of beasts and birds. There's a lively morning fish market (Tue-Sat) on the fondamenta della Pescheria.

Scuola di Merletti

Piazza B Galuppi 187 (041 730 034).
Vaporetto LN. **Closed** for restoration until 2010.
Map p329 Y2.

Currently undergoing a major revamp, the Lace School's rooms with painted wooden beams have cases full of elaborate examples of lace-work from the 17th century onwards. There are fans, collars and parasols, and some of the paper pattern-sheets that lace-makers use. The school that gives the museum its name is now virtually defunct, but museum authorities have promised that when the museum reopens, lace-makers will be regularly at work, displaying their handicraft to visitors.

San Francesco del Deserto

From behind the church of San Martino, on Burano, there is a view across the lagoon to the idyllic monastery island of **San Franceso del Deserto**. The island, with its 4,000 cypress trees, is inhabited by a small community of Franciscan monks. Getting there can be quite a challenge. If you take the water taxi from Burano, expect to pay at least €50 for the return ride. A better, and perhaps cheaper, option is to ask one of the local fishermen to give you a lift. They are usually willing to do so for a smallish fee – perhaps €25 for the return trip.

The other-worldly monk who shepherds visitors around will tell the story (only in Italian) of how the island was St Francis's first stop in Europe on his journey back from the Holy Land in 1220. He planted his stick, it grew into a pine and birds flew in to sing for him; there are certainly plenty of them in evidence in the cypress-packed gardens today. The medieval monastery – all warm stone and cloistered calm – is about as far as you can get from the worldly bustle of the Rialto.

★ Convento di San Francesco del Deserto

041 528 6863/www.isola-sanfrancesco deldeserto.it. **Open** 9-11am, 3-5pm Tue-Sat; 3-5pm Sun. **Admission** by donation.

TORCELLO

Vaporetto Torcello (N, T).

This sprawling, marshy island is where the history of Venice began. **Torcello** today is a rural backwater: at the beginning of 2009, its resident population was 20 (and many times that many mosquitoes). It's difficult to believe that in the 14th century more than 20,000 people lived here. It was the first settlement in the lagoon, founded in the fifth century by the citizens of the Roman town of Altino on the mainland. Successive waves of emigration from Altino were sparked off by barbarian invasions, first by Attila and his Huns, and, in the seventh century, by the Lombards. But Torcello's dominance of the lagoon did not last: Venice itself was found to be more salubrious (malaria was rife on Torcello) and more easily defendable. Even the bishop of Torcello chose to live on Murano, in the palace that now houses the glass museum (*see p134*). But past decline is present charm, and rural Torcello is a great antidote to the pedestrian traffic jams around San Marco.

From the ferry jetty, the **campanile** (*see below*) can already be made out; to get there, simply follow the main canal through the island.

Halfway down the canal is the ponte del Diavolo (one of only two ancient bridges in the lagoon without a parapet), where there is a simple *osteria* called **Al Ponte del Diavolo** (041 730 401, closed dinner Tue-Thur & Sun, all Mon and Dec-Jan, average €40) that is known for its reliable cooking; however, most days its only open for lunch and the prices are higher than the rustic simplicity of the *osteria* might suggest.

Torcello's main square has some desultory souvenir stalls, the small but interesting **Museo di Torcello** (*see below*) with archaeological finds from around the lagoon, a battered stone seat known arbitrarily as Attila's throne, and two extraordinary churches.

The 11th-century church of **Santa Fosca** (open Apr-Oct 10.30am-5.30pm daily, Nov-Mar 10am-5pm daily, free) looks somewhat like a miniature version of Istanbul's Santa Sophia, more Byzantine than European with its Greek-cross plan and external colonnade; its bare interior allows the perfect geometry of the space to come to the fore. Next door is the imposing cathedral of **Santa Maria Assunta** (*see p140*). By the churches, the **Locanda Cipriani** (*see p181*) is rated as one of Venice's top restaurants – with prices to match.

Campanile

041 730 119. **Open** 10am-4.15pm daily. **Admission** €4. **No credit cards**.
The view of the lagoon from the top of the campanile was memorably described by Ruskin: 'Far as the eye can reach, a waste of wild sea moor, of a lurid ashen grey.' And he concluded with the elegiac words: 'Mother and daughter, you behold them both in their widowhood, Torcello and Venice.' There is no lift, just a stiff walk up steep ramps.

Museo di Torcello

Palazzo del Consiglio (041 730 761).
Open 10am-5pm Tue-Sun. **Admission** €3.
No credit cards.
The Museum of Torcello has a small but worth-while collection of sculptures and archaeological finds from the cathedral and elsewhere in Torcello. Among the exhibits on the ground floor are late 12th-century fragments of mosaic from the apse of Santa Maria dell'Assunta, and two of the *bocche di*

> ### INSIDE TRACK
> ### TORCELLO TICKETS
>
> A cumulative ticket for Torcello's basilica, campanile and museum is available at the sights themselves and costs €10. A ticket for just the basilica and museum costs €7. Prices include an audio guide for the basilica. No credit cards are accepted.

leone (lions' mouths) where citizens with grudges could post their denunciations. Upstairs are Greco-Byzantine icons, painted panels, bronze seals and pottery fragments, and an exquisite carved ivory statuette of an embracing couple dating from the beginning of the 15th century.

★ Santa Maria Assunta

041 270 2464. **Open** 10am-4.30pm daily.
Admission €4. *Audio guide* €1.
No credit cards.

Dating from 638, the basilica of Santa Maria Assunta is the oldest building on the lagoon. The interior has an elaborate 11th-century mosaic floor, but the main draws are the vivid mosaics on the ceiling vault and walls, which range in date from the ninth century to the end of the 12th. The apse has a simple but stunning mosaic of a *Madonna and Child* on a plain gold background, while the other end of the cathedral is dominated by a huge mosaic of the *Last Judgement.* The theological rigour and narrative complexity of this huge composition suggest comparisons with the *Divine Comedy,* which Dante was writing at about the same time, however the anonymous mosaicists of Torcello were even more concerned than him with striking fear into the hearts of their audience.

LA CERTOSA

Vaporetto Certosa (41 or 42, request stop).

Situated between Sant'Elena and Le Vignole, **La Certosa** was the seat of a monastery, which from 1422 was run by the Certosini monks of Florence. Napoleon suppressed the monastery and the army moved in, staying until 1968, when the island fell into decay and, later, was earmarked to become a park. In 2004, the remaining warehouses and huts became the home of a sailing club (www.vento divenezia.it), which runs a sailing school and a hotel. The rest of the island is open to the public, and makes for a pleasant walk, though views are limited by perimeter walls. If you are lucky, you'll meet the island's goats scrabbling through the thick vegetation.

INSIDE TRACK
HARRY'S OFFSHOOTS

The three big Cipriani concerns in Venice – the **Hotel Cipriani** (*see p162*), **Harry's Bar** (run by Arrigo Cipriani, son of the founder; *see p185*) and the **Locanda Cipriani** (run by Arrigo's sister Carla; *see p181*) on Torcello have no business links; in fact, all have been involved in a long-running legal battle for the right to use the name 'Cipriani'.

SANT'ERASMO

Vaporetto Capannone, Chiesa, or Punta Vela (13, N); Forte Massimiliano (18).

Sant'Erasmo is the best-kept secret of the lagoon: larger than Venice, but with a tiny population that contents itself with growing most of the vegetables eaten in *La Serenissima* (on Rialto market stalls, the sign '*San Rasmo*' is a mark of quality). Venetians refer to the islanders of Sant'Erasmo as *i matti* ('the crazies') because of their shallow gene pool – everybody seems to be called Vignotto or Zanella. There are cars on this island, but as they are only used to drive the few miles from house to boat and back, few are in top-notch condition, a state of affairs favoured by the fact that the island does not have a single policeman. It also lacks a doctor, pharmacy and high school, but there is a supermarket and a tiny primary school. There are also two restaurants: **Ca' Vignotto** (via Forti 71, 041 528 5329, average €25-€30, closed Mon), where bookings are essential, and a fishermen's bar-trattoria – **Ai Tedeschi** (041 521 0738, open 9am-11pm daily) – hidden away on a small sandy beach by the **Forte Massimiliano**. This latter is a moat-surrounded Austrian fort that has been restored. Before restoration, it was used by a local farmer to store his tools; it now has a metal gate barring access and is only open for occasional exhibitions by local painters. In the summer months, there is also a snack bar by the Capannone vaporetto stop.

The main attraction of the island lies in the beautiful country landscapes and lovely walks past traditional Veneto farmhouses, through vineyards and fields of artichokes and asparagus – a breath of fresh air after all the urban crowding of Venice. For those wanting to get around more swiftly, bicycles can be hired from the guesthouse **Lato Azzurro** (041 523 0642), a ten-minute walk southwards from the vaporetto stop Capannone. Rates are €4 for 90 minutes, €8 for half a day; no credit cards.

By the main vaporetto stop (**Chiesa**) is the 20th-century church (on the site of an earlier one founded before 1000; opening hours vary); it's technically named Santi Erme and Erasmo, but it's widely known as simply 'Chiesa'. Over the entrance door is a gruesome painting, attributed to Domenico Tintoretto, of the martyrdom of St Erasmus, who had his intestines wound out of his body on a windlass. The resemblance of a windlass to a capstan resulted in St Erasmus becoming the patron saint of sailors.

If you're around on the first Sunday in October, don't miss the *Festa del mosto,* held to inaugurate the first pressing of new wine. This is perhaps the only chance you'll ever get to witness – or even participate in – a *gara del bisato*: a game in which an eel is dropped into a tub of water blackened by squid ink. Contestants have to plunge their heads into the tub and attempt to catch the eel with their teeth.

Lazzaretto Nuovo & Vignole

Opposite Sant'Erasmo's Capannone vaporetto stop is the tiny island of **Lazzaretto Nuovo**. In the 15th century, the island was fortified as a customs depot and military prison; during the 1576 plague outbreak it became a quarantine centre. The island is now home to a research centre for the archaeologists of the Archeo Club di Venezia, who are excavating its ancient remains, including a church that may date back to the sixth century. Guided tours (041 244 4011, www.lazzarettonuovo.com) are available at 9.45am and 4.45pm on Saturday and Sunday from April to October. A donation is expected. The number 13 vaporetto stops here on request.

The number 13 also stops at the smaller island of **Vignole**, where there is a medieval chapel dedicated to St Erosia.

The Southern Lagoon

The southern part of the lagoon – between Venice, the Lido and the mainland – has 14 small islands, a few of which are still inhabited, though most are out of bounds to tourists. **La Grazia** was for years a quarantine hospital but the structure has now been closed. The huge **San Clemente**, originally a lunatic asylum and later a home for abandoned cats, has been turned into one of the lagoon's plushest hotels.

The islands of **San Servolo** and **San Lazzaro** (for both, *see below*) are served by vaporetto 20, and both are well worth visiting.

San Servolo

From the 18th century until 1978, San Servolo was Venice's mental hospital (in his poem *Julian and Maddalo*, Shelley describes a visit that he paid there with Byron); it is now home to Venice International University (*see p304*). In 2006, the **Museo del Manicomio di San Servolo** (San Servolo Asylum Museum; 041 524 0119) was inaugurated. The museum is open for guided visits only (€3; minimum 5 people); booking is essential. It reveals the different ways in which mental diseases have been treated over the years; there are not only examples of the more or less brutal methods of restraint (chains, straitjackets, handcuffs) but early examples of such treatments as hydro-massage and electrotherapy. The tour ends in the reconstructed 18th-century pharmacy,

which relied partly on medicines obtained from some of the exotic plants grown on the island. After the tour, it is possible to visit the extensive and charming gardens of the island.

San Lazzaro degli Armeni

A further five minutes on the number 20 will take you to the island of **San Lazzaro degli Armeni**. Guided tours (041 526 0104) of this island are given every afternoon for visitors arriving on the mid-afternoon boat (times vary seasonally) from San Zaccaria. The cost is €6 (€3 reductions; no credit cards).

A black-cloaked Armenian priest meets the boat and takes visitors on a detailed tour of the **Monastero Mechitarista**. The tiny island is a global point of reference for Armenia's Catholic minority, visited and supported by Armenians from Italy and abroad. Near the entrance stand the printing presses that helped to distribute Armenian literature all over the world for 200 years. They are now silent, with the monastery's retro line in dictionaries and liturgical texts farmed out to a modern press.

Originally a leper colony, in 1717 the island was presented by the doge to an Armenian abbot called Mekhitar, who was on the run from the Turkish invasion of the Peloponnese. There had been an Armenian community in Venice since the 11th century, centring on the tiny Santa Croce degli Armeni church, just around the corner from piazza San Marco, but the construction of this church and monastery made Venice a world centre of Armenian culture. The monastery was the only one in the whole of Venice to be spared the Napoleonic axe that did away with so many convents and monasteries: the emperor had a soft spot for Armenians and claimed this was an academic rather than a religious institute.

The tour takes in both the cloisters and the church, rebuilt after a fire in 1883. The museum and the modern library contain 40,000 priceless books and manuscripts, and a bizarre collection of gifts donated over the years by visiting Armenians that range from Burmese prayer books to an Egyptian mummy.

The island's most famous student was Lord Byron, who used to take a break from his more earthly pleasures in Venice and row over three times a week to learn Armenian (as he found that his 'mind wanted something craggy to break upon') with the monks. He helped the monks to publish an Armenian-English grammar, although by his own confession he never got beyond the basics of the language. You can buy a completed version of this, plus a number of period maps and an illustrated children's Armenian grammar, in the shop just inside the monastery gate.

SIGHTS

timeout.com/travel
Get the local experience

Dream deli counter at Franchi, in the Prati district, **Rome**

© Gianluca Moggi

Consume

I Figli delle Stelle. *See p180.*

Hotels	**144**
Home and Away	149
The Best Home from Home	151
The Best Hotels with Gardens	155
The Best Utter Luxury	159
Too Many Rooms at the Inn	160

Eating Out	**164**
The Best Blow-outs	167
The Menu	169
The Best Cheap(ish) Eats	171
The Best Vegetarian Bets	173
The Best Child-pleasers	175
Profile Venetian Vino	178
The Best True Venetian	181

Cafés, Bars & Gelaterie	**182**
The Best Grand Cafés	185
The Best Waterside Bars	187
Evening in the Market	190
The Best Aperitivo Haunts	191

Shops & Services	**193**
The Best Serenissima Souvenirs	193
Beads by Attombri	194
The Best Carnevale Suppliers	199
The Best Palate-provokers	201
Cioccolato	202
Profile Ottico Fabbricatore	206
Ye Olde Shoppers	211

Hotels

There are some deals – but you'll have to pay for a Grand Canal view.

You have to stay in Venice, if only for a night – daytrippers miss the lagoon city's after-hours magic. Don't be put off by prices; the financial crisis has turned Venice into a buyers' market (*see p160* **Too Many Rooms at the Inn**), with rooms even in the more luxurious hotels going at fire-sale rates in the off season.

Of course, peak times still pull in visitors in their thronging millions. As well as summer, try to steer away from Carnevale, regattas, Biennale events and important religious festivities including Christmas and Easter. Outside of these times, you'll find that the Lagoon City is refreshingly quiet and cheaper than it has been for a long time – to sleep in, at least.

CONSUME

THE SCENE

Despite the economic downturn, Venice's accommodation sector continues to change and expand. Some of this is retrenching: at the super-luxurious **Danieli** (*see p151*), a massive revamp will reduce the number of rooms, providing more gorgeous suites for demanding top-end travellers. Across on the Lido, the historic **Excelsior** (*see p162* **Inside Track**) and **Des Bains** (*see p163*) have been taken over by the Four Seasons group. They will begin a lengthy refurbishment programme in autumn 2009 to emerge some time later as a 160-room hotel (the former) and sumptuous serviced apartments (the latter).

On the Giudecca, the new **Molino Stucky Hilton** (Giudecca 810, campo San Biagio, 041 272 3311, www.molinostuckyhilton.com), in a vast former flour mill, offers 380 rooms in a smart but ultimately corporate-feeling ambience; its true vocation is obvious in its huge conference facilities. Altogether more elegant is **Ca' Sagredo** (*see p153*) with its art collection worthy of a major gallery. **iQs** (*see p151*), on the other hand, continues the Charming House group's experiments with pared-back style. And the march of the chic B&B shows no signs of slowing, with **Corte 1321** (*see p149* **Home and Away**) and **Locanda Avogaria** (*see p177*) among the new arrivals.

PRICES AND INFORMATION

If you're travelling off-peak, be sure to look at the hotels in the price brackets above the one that you'd usually go for: the range between high and low season can be immense. We have given prices for double rooms only. Check hotel websites for prices of singles and suites.

Facilities for the disabled are scarce in Venetian hotels, partly due to the nature of the buildings. Many establishments do not even have lifts; always check first. We have indicated where disabled rooms are available.

Breakfast is usually included in the price of the room; we have indicated where this is *not* the case.

If you have turned up in Venice without a booking, make for an **AVA** (Venetian Hoteliers' Association) bureau at the Santa Lucia railway station, piazzale Roma or the airport; staff will help you track down a room, charging a small commission that you can claim back on the price of your first night. For last-minute bookings from home, try

---

About the author
Nicky Swallow edits the Charming Small Hotel Guides: Tuscany & Umbria and is the author of a travel guide to Naples. She has lived in Italy since 1981.

➊ Red numbers given in this chapter correspond to the location of each hotel on the street maps. See pp320-329.

AVA's detailed online information and booking service: www.veniceinfo.it. Also worth a look is the www.venicehotel.com site's directory of hotels, B&Bs and campsites.

Some hotels, such as **La Calcina** (*see p161*) and **Messner** (*see p162*), have apartments for longer stays; these are true money-saving options, especially for groups or families. The websites www.viewsonvenice.com and www.veniceapartment.com are also good resources for finding an apartment.

SAN MARCO

Deluxe

Bauer Hotels

San Marco 1459, campo San Moisè (041 520 7022/www.bauerhotels.com). Vaporetto San Marco Vallaresso. **Rooms** 210. **Rates** €280-€770 double. Breakfast €50. **Credit** AmEx, DC, MC, V. **Map** p323 H8 **❶**

This is a hotel of many parts. The main Bauer Hotel occupies an ugly 1940s extension of the original 18th-century hotel building; inside, the vast hall with its marble, gold and black looks like a grand old ocean liner. Luxurious, antique Il Palazzo is housed in the older building and has Grand Canal frontage. Adjacent to the Bauer, Casa Nova is a series of comfortable, sunny serviced apartments. The latest arrival is Bauer Palladio Hotel & Spa, a former convent on the Giudecca with a pretty garden

INSIDE TRACK
FINDING YOUR HOTEL

Even old Venice hands get lost in the city. Make sure you obtain detailed directions before you arrive: ask your hotel for the nearest vaporetto stop, easily identifiable campo (square) and/or landmark (such as a church). Alternatively, you'll need an excellent map and a fiendishly good sense of direction.

but rooms that still have a whiff of the nunnery about them. If you can afford it, Il Palazzo's discreet opulence is perhaps the best bet.
Bars. Business centre. Concierge. Disabled-adapted rooms. Gym. Internet. Restaurant. Room service. Spa. TV.

Gritti Palace

San Marco 2467, campo Santa Maria del Giglio (041 794 611/www.starwoodhotels.com/grittipalace). Vaporetto Giglio. **Rooms** 91. **Rates** €400-€913 double. Breakfast €50. **Credit** AmEx, DC, MC, V. **Map** p323 G8 **❷**

There's a studied air of old-world charm and nobility about this 15th-century palazzo. Refined and opulent, adorned with antiques and fresh flowers, each room is uniquely decorated; one is lined with antique floor-to-ceiling mirrors. If you want a canal or campo

Ca' del Nobile. *See p147.*

CONSUME

Ca' Sagredo. *See p153.*

view, specify when booking: some rooms overlook a dingy courtyard. An aperitivo on the vast canal terrace is an experience in itself.

Bar. Business centre. Concierge. Disabled-adapted rooms. Internet. Restaurant. Room service. TV.
▶ *It's a quick hop across the Grand Canal on a traghetto to the Guggenheim Collection; see p121.*

Hotel Monaco & Grand Canal

San Marco 1332, calle Vallaresso (041 520 0211/www.hotelmonaco.it). Vaporetto San Marco Vallaresso. **Rooms** 99. **Rates** €170-€590 double. **Credit** AmEx, DC, MC, V. **Map** p323 H8 ❸

This Grand Canal classic is a curious hybrid. The lobby and bar area is a fussy mix of classic and modern, the rooms in the main building are untouched by the design revolution, while those on the Grand Canal are ultra-traditional Venetian. More *charmant* is the Palazzo Selvadego residence: no lagoon views, but its rooms are done out in a modern Mediterranean style. Even if you are not staying here, pop in for a look at the extraordinary Teatro Ridotto, a 17th-century jewel that was Venice's first gambling hall.

Bar. Business centre. Concierge. Disabled-adapted rooms. Internet. Restaurant. Room service. TV.
▶ *Even if you can't afford to stay here, it's worth checking out the views from the bar.*

Luna Hotel Baglioni

San Marco 1243, calle larga dell'Ascensione (041 528 9840/www.baglionihotels.com). Vaporetto San Marco Vallaresso. **Rooms** 104. **Rates** €350-€880 double. Breakfast €40. **Credit** AmEx, DC, MC, V. **Map** p323 H8 ❹

In a 15th-century palazzo, this hotel has little remaining period decor, with the exception of the original frescoes and stucco decorations in the conference room. Elsewhere, kilometres of shiny marble, swathes of rich fabric and lots of Murano glass provide the backdrop for luxurious bedrooms and communal areas. Views from the rooms are of the Giardinetti Reali, the lagoon and San Giorgio Maggiore.

Bar. Business centre. Concierge. Disabled-adapted rooms. Internet. Restaurant. Room service. TV.
▶ *Sip a Bellini at nearby Harry's Bar; see p185.*

Palazzo Sant'Angelo sul Canal Grande

San Marco 3878B, fondamenta del Teatro a Sant'Angelo (041 241 1452/www.palazzo santangelo.com). Vaporetto Sant'Angelo. **Rooms** 26. **Rates** €220-€528 double. **Credit** AmEx, DC, MC, V. **Map** p323 F7 ❺

While it enjoys a superb location on the Grand Canal and luxurious facilities, Palazzo Sant'Angelo is rather lacking in soul. The red and gold bedrooms are traditional in style; all have whirlpool baths, fine bed linen, fluffy robes and slippers. Rooms overlooking the Grand Canal cost a lot extra; instead, watch the gondolas drift by from the sitting room and bar area.

Bar. Disabled-adapted rooms. Internet. Room service. TV.

Expensive

Saturnia & International

San Marco 2398, via XXII Marzo (041 520 8377/www.hotelsaturnia.it). Vaporetto San Marco Vallaresso. **Rooms** 93. **Rates** €190-€492 double. **Credit** AmEx, DC, MC, V. **Map** p323 G8 ❻

An old-fashioned, friendly atmosphere pervades this bustling hotel, which celebrated its 100th birthday in 2008. The 14th-century building's interior has been done up in a faux-Renaissance style. The bedrooms vary considerably: the majority are in traditional Venetian style, but five have been given a more contemporary makeover in the retro style of sister hotel Ca' Pisani (*see p161*). The roof terrace has a view across to Santa Maria della Salute.

Bar. Business centre. Concierge. Disabled-adapted room. Internet. Restaurant. Room service. TV.

Moderate

★ Ca' del Nobile

San Marco 987, rio terà delle Colonne (041 528 3473/www.cadelnobile.com). Vaporetto Rialto. **Rooms** 6. **Rates** €110-€260 double. **Credit** AmEx, DC, MC, V. **Map** p323 H7 ❼

The last five years have seen a rash of six-room locandas with near-identical websites opening in Venice (*see p160* **Too Many Rooms at the Inn**), but this compact charmer has an edge on the competition. It's two minutes' walk from piazza San Marco, service is spot-on, there's free Wi-Fi and the warm classic-contemporary decor is a cut above the usual cookie-cutter Casanova look. *Photo p145.*
Internet. TV.

Do Pozzi

San Marco 2373, via XXII Marzo (041 520 7855/www.hoteldopozzi.it). Vaporetto Giglio. **Rooms** 29. **Rates** €98-€280 double. **Credit** AmEx, DC, MC, V. **Map** p323 G8 ❽

This hotel has a homely, friendly feeling and is very appealing in spite of some rather cramped rooms and tiny bathrooms. Although it's situated very near piazza San Marco, it's down a little alleyway

---

INSIDE TRACK
LOCATION, LOCATION

Plush hotels and tourist action centre around St Mark's square and the riva degli Schiavoni, but the crowds thronging outside the front door can tarnish that pampered feel. On the other side of the Grand Canal, in the *sestieri* of Dorsoduro, Santa Croce and San Polo, there are chic little hideaways for those who seek style without the glam trappings.

CONSUME

Discover the city from your back pocket

Essential for your weekend break, 25 top cities available.

and off the main tourist track. In front of the hotel is a lovely courtyard with an ancient well in the middle where guests can eat breakfast or relax. *TV.*

Flora

San Marco 2283A, calle Bergamaschi (041 520 5844/www.hotelflora.it). Vaporetto San Marco Vallaresso. **Rooms** 43. **Rates** €140-€320 double. **Credit** AmEx, DC, MC, V. **Map** p323 G8 **❾**
Book well in advance if you want to stay at the perennially popular Flora. Situated at the bottom of a cul-de-sac near piazza San Marco, it offers a dreamy, tranquil stay in the palazzo adjacent to what's known as Desdemona's house. The decor in the bedrooms is classic Venetian, varying significantly from quite opulent to relatively spartan; some are tiny. There's a cosy bar and a delightful garden with wrought-iron tables and a fountain.
Bar. Internet. TV.

Locanda Art Deco

San Marco 2966, calle delle Botteghe (041 277 0558/www.locandaartdeco.com). Vaporetto San Samuele or Sant'Angelo. **Rooms** 10. **Rates** €80-€170 double. **Credit** AmEx, DC, MC, V. **Map** p323 F7 **❿**
This friendly little hotel is situated off relaxed campo Santo Stefano. The welcoming entrance hall and the simple but stylish bedrooms are dotted with original pieces of 1930s and '40s furniture, and other deco details. There's a tiny breakfast area tucked away on a mezzanine floor.
Internet. TV.
▶ *Calle delle Botteghe is famous for its antique shops. Try Antiquus (p208) and Gaggio (p209), which sells exquisite printed fabrics.*

★ Locanda Novecento

San Marco 2683-4, calle del Dose (041 241 3765/www.novecento.biz). Vaporetto Giglio. **Rooms** 9. **Rates** €150-€260 double. **Credit** AmEx, DC, MC, V. **Map** p323 F8 **⓫**
This home-from-home is a real pleasure to come back to after a hard day's sightseeing, especially when it's warm enough to relax in the delightful little garden. With its friendly, helpful staff, and reading and sitting rooms, Novecento is a very special place to stay. Wooden floors, ethnic textiles, oriental rugs, Indonesian furniture and individually decorated rooms make a refreshing change from the ubiquitous pan-Venetian style. Art shows are regularly mounted in the public rooms.
Internet. TV.

★ Locanda Orseolo

San Marco 1083, corte Zorzi (041 520 4827/ www.locandaorseolo.com). Vaporetto Rialto or San Marco Vallaresso. **Rooms** 15. **Rates** €80-€300 double. **Credit** AmEx, DC, MC, V. **Map** p323 H7 **⓬**
This *locanda* has beamed ceilings, painted wood panelling, leaded windows and rich colours; there's even a tiny water entrance. The immaculate bedrooms are ranged over three floors (there's no lift) and are furnished in a fairly restrained Venetian style. Choose between a canal view (which can be noisy) or quieter rooms overlooking the square. Breakfast is exceptionally generous. The team who run the place bend over backwards to ensure their guests are happy. To find this delightful hotel, go through the iron gate almost opposite the church in campo San Gallo; bear left into a smaller campo and you'll see the sign.
Internet. Room service. TV.

CONSUME

Home and Away

Venice's B&Bs provide some colourful and homely stays.

The plethora of B&Bs in Venice varies from spartan accommodation to rooms in glorious antique-filled palazzi, with an equally wide range of prices reflecting location and facilities. We have listed a few B&Bs here; for more, check the handy www.bed-and-breakfast.it website.

In addition to the cosy **B&B San Marco** (*see p153*) and the B&B rooms just opened up by the restaurant **L'Avogaria** (*see p177*), a few other places are definitely worth considering. **Ca' Miani** (San Marco 2865, calle del Frutarol, 041 241 1868), was one of Venice's first B&Bs and surely the only such place where you can get an in-house hair-do (Pascal, the French owner, is a hairdresser). Three-bedroom **Palazzo**

dal Carlo (Dorsoduro 1163, fondamenta di Borgo, 041 522 6863, www.palazzodal carlo.com) is filled with heirloom antiques, but in spite of the grandeur this is a thoroughly laid-back place to stay thanks to Roberta dal Carlo's warm welcome.

A pretty plant-filled courtyard with a well is the main calling card of **Corte 1321** (San Polo 1321, campiello Ca' Bernardi, 041 522 4923, www.corte 1321.com), a three-room ethno-chic B&B. But the prize for the most unusual B&B experience goes to **Boat & Breakfast**, a lovely 1930s yawl with three cabins, which is moored out on the Giudecca (Giudecca 212A, 335 666 6241 mobile, www.realvenice.it/shaula).

Bags packed, milk cancelled, house raised on stilts.

You've packed the suntan lotion, the snorkel set, the stay-pressed shirts. Just one more thing left to do – your bit for climate change. In some of the world's poorest countries, changing weather patterns are destroying lives.

You can help people to deal with the extreme effects of climate change. Raising houses in flood-prone regions is just one life-saving solution.

**Climate change costs lives.
Give £5 and let's sort it *Here & Now***

www.oxfam.org.uk/climate-change

Be Humankind Ⓧ Oxfam

Budget

San Samuele

San Marco 3358, salizada San Samuele (041 522 8045/www.albergosansamuele.it). Vaporetto San Samuele or Sant'Angelo. **Rooms** 10. **Rates** €46-€120 double. Breakfast €5. **Credit** AmEx, MC, V. **Map** p323 E7 ⓭

Flowers cascade from the window boxes of this delightful, friendly little hotel in an excellent location. The spotlessly clean rooms have a simple, sunny aspect and the welcome is always warm. The San Samuele is several notches above most of its fellow one-star establishments, although both the single rooms and one of the doubles have bathrooms in the corridor. Breakfast (extra) is served in the nearby Locanda Art Deco (*see p149*). San Samuele is very popular: book well in advance.

CASTELLO

Deluxe

★ Danieli

Castello 4196, riva degli Schiavoni (041 522 6480/www.starwoodhotels.com/danieli). Vaporetto San Zaccaria. **Rooms** 223. **Rates** €300-€1170 double. Breakfast €30-€52. **Credit** AmEx, DC, MC, V. **Map** p324 K8 ⓮

Whether or not you're staying at this Venetian classic, twirl through the revolving door to gawp at the magnificent reception hall. The Danieli is split between an unprepossessing 1940s building and the 14th-century Palazzo Dandolo: the former, however, was the first part to benefit from a gorgeous makeover by designer Jacques Garcia. Ten rooms have terraces with lagoon views; all are sumptuously decorated with Rubelli and Fortuny fabrics, antiques and marble bathrooms. Views from the newly revamped roof-top restaurant – where chef Giannicola Colussi, formerly of London's Four Seasons, now presides – are spectacular.

Bar. Business centre. Concierge. Internet. Restaurant. Room service. TV.

THE BEST HOME FROM HOME

For aristocratic but welcoming
Palazzo dal Carlo. *See p149 Home and Away.*

For ethno-chic with a homely touch
Corte 1321. *See p149 Home and Away.*

For patter from a pet parrot
Casa Peron. *See p159.*

For retro and refreshing
Locanda Novecento. *See p149.*

Londra Palace

Castello 4171, riva degli Schiavoni (041 520 0533/www.hotelondra.it). Vaporetto San Zaccaria. **Rooms** 53. **Rates** €265-€625 double. **Credit** AmEx, DC, MC, V. **Map** p324 K7 ⓯

It's no wonder that Tchaikovsky found this hotel – with no fewer than 100 of its bedroom windows facing San Giorgio Maggiore across the lagoon – a congenial spot in which to write his fourth symphony in 1877. Today, the Londra Palace is elegant but restrained, offering traditional-style rooms furnished with antiques and paintings. You can sunbathe on the roof terrace or enjoy a romantic dinner at the restaurant where, in good weather, tables are laid out on the *riva*.

Bar. Concierge. Internet. Restaurant. Room service. TV.

Metropole

Castello 4149, riva degli Schiavoni (041 520 5044/www.hotelmetropole.com). Vaporetto San Zaccaria. **Rooms** 67. **Rates** €210-€580 double. **Credit** AmEx, DC, MC, V. **Map** p324 L8 ⓰

Of all the grand hotels that crowd this part of the *riva*, the Metropole is arguably the most characterful. Owner-manager Pierluigi Beggiato is a passionate collector, and his antiques and curios are dotted in the elegant and varied bedrooms and the sumptuous, spacious public rooms. In winter, tea and cakes are served in the velvet-draped *salone*; in summer, guests relax in the gorgeous garden by the sound of water trickling in the fountain. There are views over the lagoon (for a hefty supplement), the canal, or on to the garden.

Bar. Concierge. Internet. Restaurant. Room service. TV.

► *The Metropole's restaurant, Met (see p168), holds one of Venice's two Michelin stars.*

Expensive

Ca' dei Conti

Castello 4429, fondamenta del Remedio (041 277 0500/www.cadeiconti.com). Vaporetto San Zaccaria. **Rooms** 34. **Rates** €200-€413 double. **Credit** AmEx, DC, MC, V. **Map** p324 J7 ⓱

In a historic palazzo situated on a quiet canal between Santa Maria Formosa and San Marco, this elegant hotel has all the usual four-star comforts. The rooms are tastefully decorated in Venetian style with particular attention paid to fabrics. There's a wonderful little terrace from which to survey the surrounding rooftops too.

Internet. Room service. TV.

Charming House iQs

Castello 4425, campiello Querini Stampalia (041 241 0062/www.thecharminghouse.com). Vaporetto San Zaccaria. **Rooms** 4. **Rates** €220-€780 double. **Credit** AmEx, DC, MC, V. **Map** p324 J6 ⓲

CONSUME

Ca' Nigra Lagoon Resort. See p158.

The latest addition to the Charming House boutique hotel group is as radical a design statement as you'll find in play-safe Venice. If it weren't for the charming, chandeliered *porta d'acqua* gondola entrance and the overhead beams, iQs' four suites could almost be in Milan or New York – though architect Mauro Mazzolini's warm but serious minimalism works well as an antidote to the city's frills and frippery. Be warned that the dark hues can make for a gloomy ambience; but in summer, this is a classy, cool refuge.
Internet. Room service. TV.
▶ *If iQs is full, try the Charming House group's original design hotel, DD 724; see p161.*

Locanda Vivaldi

Castello 4150-2, riva degli Schiavoni (041 277 0477/www.locandavivaldi.it). Vaporetto San Zaccaria. **Rooms** 27. **Rates** €160-€525 double. **Credit** AmEx, DC, MC, V. **Map** p324 L8 ⑲
This luxurious hotel offers tasteful rooms with lashings of modern comforts. Located partly in the house where composer Antonio Vivaldi lived, and next to the church where he taught music (La Pietà; *see p85*), the Vivaldi offers views of the island of San Giorgio from the magnificent roof terrace – where breakfast is served in summer – and from the front bedrooms.
Bar. Business centre. Internet. Room service. TV.
▶ *This hotel makes a good base for our Vivaldi-themed tour; see p81 Walk.*

Savoia & Jolanda

Castello 4187, riva degli Schiavoni (041 520 6644/ 041 522 4130/www.hotelsavoiajolanda.com). Vaporetto San Zaccaria. **Rooms** 51. **Rates** €208-€422 double. **Credit** AmEx, DC, MC, V. **Map** p324 K7 ⑳
A hotel of two different but lovely halves, the Savoia offers rooms with balconies and views across the Bacino di San Marco to San Giorgio Maggiore in one direction, or facing back over Castello towards the glorious façade of San Zaccaria. The decor manages to be pleasantly luxurious without going over the top, and breakfast is a sumptuous spread.
Bar. Concierge. Internet. Restaurant. Room service. TV.

Moderate

Casa Querini

Castello 4388, campo San Giovanni Novo (041 241 1294/www.locandaquerini.com). Vaporetto San Zaccaria. **Closed** Jan. **Rooms** 6. **Rates** €93-€197 double. **Credit** DC, MC, V. **Map** p324 J7 ㉑
This friendly hotel has a pretty little terrace area shaded by big umbrellas on a quiet square between bustling campo Santa Maria Formosa and St Mark's. From a tiny reception area, stairs lead up to bedrooms pleasantly decorated in sober Venetian style; all are spacious, but try to secure one with a view of the square rather than the side alley.
Internet. Room service. TV.

CONSUME

Casa Verardo

Castello 4765, calle della Sacrestia (041 528 6138/www.casaverardo.it). Vaporetto San Zaccaria. **Rooms** 25. **Rates** €90-€360 double. **Credit** AmEx, DC, MC, V. **Map** p324 K7 ❷

Tucked away as it is at the end of a narrow calle, and across its own little bridge only a few minutes from piazza San Marco, the first impression of Casa Verardo is of cool and calm. Walls in the public areas are white and pale lemon while bedrooms are decorated in elegant, tasteful fabrics. There's a pretty courtyard at the back of the building and a terrace off the elegant salon where tables are laid for breakfast. The level of comfort and facilities is above what one would expect at these prices.

Bar. Internet. Room service. TV.

Locanda La Corte

Castello 6317, calle Bressana (041 241 1300/ www.locandalacorte.it). Vaporetto Fondamente Nove. **Rooms** 16. **Rates** €99-€210 double. **Credit** AmEx, DC, MC, V. **Map** p324 K5 ❷

Housed by a narrow canal in a small 16th-century palazzo down the side of the church of Santi Giovanni e Paolo, La Corte is far from the noisy tourist trails. Bedrooms are decorated in restful greens and there is a lovely little courtyard where breakfast is served in summer. There's a bar, too, so you can wind down after a hard day's sightseeing with an *alfresco aperitivo*.

Bar. Disabled-adapted room. Internet. TV.

La Residenza

Castello 3608, campo Bandiera e Moro (041 528 5315/www.venicelaresidenza.com). Vaporetto Arsenale. **Rooms** 14. **Rates** €80-€180 double. **Credit** MC, V. **Map** p324 L7 ❷

Occupying the first and second floors of a grand if rather faded Gothic palazzo, La Residenza possesses a genteel old-fashioned air and offers great value for money. The interior has been spruced up and the splendid stucco work in the vast salon is gleaming. Bedrooms have all been pleasantly refurbished; numbers 221 and 228 overlook the pretty campo. The hotel has the feeling of being far from the crowds, but it is actually within easy walking distance of San Marco.

TV.

Budget

B&B San Marco

Castello 3385L, fondamenta San Giorgio degli Schiavoni (041 522 7589/335 756 6555/www. realvenice.it/smarco). Vaporetto San Zaccaria. **Closed** Jan; 2wks Aug. **Rooms** 3. **Rates** €70-€120 double. **Credit** MC, V. **Map** p324 L7 ❷

One of the few Venetian B&Bs that come close to the British concept of the genre, Marco Scurati's homely apartment lies just behind San Giorgio degli Schiavoni. Three cosy, antique-filled bedrooms share

a bathroom; there's also an apartment that sleeps four (€100-€160). Breakfast is served in Marco's own kitchen and guests are treated as part of the family.

Internet.

► *For more B&Bs, see p149 Home and Away.*

Ca' del Dose

Castello 3801, calle del Dose (041 520 9887/ www.cadeldose.com). Vaporetto Arsenale or San Zaccaria. **Rooms** 5. **Rates** €70-€130 double. **Credit** AmEx, DC, MC, V. **Map** p324 L7 ❷

This friendly guesthouse, on a quiet calle off the busy riva degli Schiavoni, has simple, stylish rooms on three floors. If you book well ahead, you may be able to secure the one at the top with a fabulous little roof terrace; there is no extra charge. In the morning, the means for a simple breakfast are supplied in the rooms and you can order fresh croissants.

TV.

Casa per Ferie

Castello 3701, calle della Pietà (041 244 3639/ www.pietavenezia.org). Vaporetto San Zaccaria. **Rooms** 15. **Rates** €98 double; €38 dorm bed. **No credit cards. Map** p324 L7 ❷

The building which houses this clean, bright hostel is part of the sprawling Pietà complex, which once housed the part of the girls' school where Vivaldi taught. It's spacious, sunny and spotlessly clean, with around 40 beds; there are a couple of singles and six doubles, while the rest are dorm rooms. None have private baths. The rooms occupy the top two floors of the building, so there are some great views, especially from the terrace at the top.

Disabled-adapted rooms.

► *For more about Vivaldi's time at the Pietà, see p68 City of Music.*

Hotel Rio

Castello 4358, campo Santi Filippo e Giacomo (041 523 4810/www.aciugheta-hotelrio.it). Vaporetto San Zaccaria. **Rooms** 7. **Rates** €60-€180 double. **Credit** MC, V. **Map** p324 K7 ❷

This hotel offers pleasant, modern rooms done out with a touch of originality; about half of them have private bathrooms. If you want to pay a bit less, the hotel has simpler rooms in various adjacent buildings. Breakfast is served in the bar in the campo.

TV.

► *The management also runs the Aciugheta and Il Ridotto (see p168) restaurants on this campo.*

CANNAREGIO

Deluxe

Ca' Sagredo

Cannaregio 4198, campo Santa Sofia (041 241 3111/www.casagredohotel.com). Vaporetto Ca' d'Oro. **Rooms** 42. **Rates** €300-€650 double. **Credit** AmEx, DC, MC, V. **Map** p321 G4 ❷

CONSUME

Open since 2007, this Grand Canal palazzo dating back to the 15th century is as much a museum as a hotel, with a magnificent double staircase, a huge rococo ballroom and frescoes by Giambattista Tiepolo among its many treasures. However, aside from six stunning historic suites (one inside a library where Galileo once worked), the room decor is standard luxe-Venetian, and the service can be a little cold and corporate. *Photo p146.*
Bar. Disabled-adapted rooms. Internet. Restaurant. Room service. TV.
▶ *Tiepolo was the greatest painter of the Venetian rococo; for more on his works, see p38.*

Expensive

★ Al Ponte Antico
Cannaregio 5768, calle dell'Aseo (041 241 1944/www.alponteantico.com). Vaporetto Rialto. **Rooms** 7. **Rates** €200-€420 double. **Credit** AmEx, DC, MC, V. **Map** p324 H5 ③⓪
With its padded reception desk, festooned curtains and lashings of brocade in public spaces and most of the bedrooms, the family-run Al Ponte Antico takes the traditional Venetian hotel decor idiom and turns it into something over-the-top and faintly decadent: a pleasant change from the prudish norm. In a 16th-century palazzo on the Grand Canal, with views over the Rialto bridge, Al Ponte Antico's exquisite little balcony overlooks the water, as do some doubles and suites.
Bar. Concierge. Internet. Room service. TV.
▶ *The ornate padded banquettes in the breakfast room might get you musing about Venice's famous courtesans; see p17 Profile.*

Giorgione
Cannaregio 4587, calle larga dei Proverbi (041 522 5810/www.hotelgiorgione.com). Vaporetto Ca' d'Oro. **Rooms** 76. **Rates** €100-€265 double. **Credit** AmEx, DC, MC, V. **Map** p321 H4 ③①
Just off the busy campo Santi Apostoli, the Giorgione exudes warmth. A 15th-century palazzo joins the newer extension around a flower-filled courtyard with a lily pond. Some split-level rooms have terraces overlooking the rooftops.
Bar. Concierge. Disabled-adapted room. Internet. Room service. TV.

Locanda ai Santi Apostoli
Cannaregio 4391A, strada Nuova (041 521 2612/www.locandasantiapostoli.com). Vaporetto Ca' d'Oro. **Closed** Jan-Carnevale. **Rooms** 11. **Rates** €100-€300 double. **Credit** AmEx, DC, MC, V. **Map** p321 H5 ③②
A pair of handsome dark green doors on the busy strada Nuova lead through the courtyard of this palazzo facing on to the Grand Canal, where a lift sweeps you up to the third floor. The hotel feels like an elegant private apartment and the bedrooms are each individually decorated. The two best rooms

---

> ## THE BEST
> ## HOTELS WITH GARDENS
>
> For Grand Canal frontage
> **Ca' Nigra Lagoon Resort**. *See p158.*
>
> For the height of luxuriant
> **Metropole**. *See p151.*
>
> For a well-hidden delight
> **Oltre il Giardino**. *See p159.*

overlook the canal; book well in advance for these and be prepared to pay extra. A comfortable sitting room, filled with antiques, books and magazines, overlooks the water.
Bar. Internet. Room service. TV.

★ Palazzo Abadessa
Cannaregio 4011, calle Priuli (041 241 3784/ www.abadessa.com). Vaporetto Ca' d'Oro. **Rooms** 15. **Rates** €150-€295 double. **Credit** AmEx, DC, MC, V. **Map** p321 H4 ③③
A beautiful shady walled garden is laid out in front of this privately owned 16th-century palazzo, which is filled with family antiques, paintings and silver and where the prevailing atmosphere is that of an aristocratic private home (which it is), restored and opened to guests. A magnificent double stone staircase leads to the dozen impressive bedrooms, some of which are truly vast. Beware, however: the three low-ceilinged doubles on the mezzanine floor are rather cramped.
Internet. Room service. TV.

Moderate

Ca' Dogaressa
Cannaregio 1018, calle del Sotoportego Scuro (041 275 9441/www.cadogaressa.com). Vaporetto Guglie or Tre Archi. **Rooms** 9. **Rates** €85-€170 double. **Credit** AmEx, DC, MC, V. **Map** p320 C2 ③④
This family-run hotel overlooking the Cannaregio canal offers a modern take on 'traditional' Venetian accommodation decor: the Murano glass light fittings and brocade-covered walls are there, but so are neat marble bathrooms, very comfortable beds and air-con. Breakfast is served at tables along the canalside on fine days. There's also a roof terrace with wonderful views.
Internet. Room service. TV.

Locanda del Ghetto
Cannaregio 2892-3, campo del Ghetto Nuovo (041 275 9292/www.locandadelghetto.net). Vaporetto Guglie or San Marcuola. **Rooms** 6. **Rates** €90-€185 double. **Credit** AmEx, DC, MC, V. **Map** p321 E2 ③⑤

The building that houses this stylish guesthouse dates from the 15th century, and several rooms still retain the original decorated wooden ceilings. Upstairs, the light and airy bedrooms are all done out with pale cream walls, honey-coloured parquet floors and pale gold bedcovers; two of them have small terraces on the campo side. Kosher croissants are served in the ground-floor breakfast room, which overlooks a canal.
Internet. Room service. TV.
▶ *For a history of life in the Ghetto, see p93.*

Budget

Ostello Santa Fosca
Cannaregio 2372, fondamenta Daniele Canal (041 715 775/www.santafosca.it). Vaporetto San Marcuola. **Beds** *June-Sept* 100; *Oct-May* 20. **Rates** €25 per person in double; €20 dorm bed. **Credit** AmEx, MC, V. **Map** p321 F3 ❸
This is a student hostel, so during the academic year there are only 20 beds (including one double room) available. During the summer holidays, however, all 100 beds are vacated and students take over the running of the place (not always very efficiently, so make sure you confirm before arriving at midnight). There are a handful of doubles; the remaining rooms are dorms sleeping a maximum of six. None have private bathrooms. During the summer there is a kitchen for guests' use.
▶ *There's a larger youth hostel on Giudecca, the Ostello di Venezia; see p162.*

Rossi
Cannaregio 262, calle delle Procuratie (041 715 164/www.hotelrossi.ve.it). Vaporetto Ferrovia. **Closed** Jan-Carnevale. **Rooms** 14. **Rates** €70-€95 double. **Credit** MC, V. **Map** p320 D3 ❸
Located at the end of a quiet alley, this cheap one-star hotel is quite a find for the area around the railway station (which, as a rule, is best avoided). The basic rooms are acceptably clean and all have air con. New bathrooms have been added recently, but five rooms are still without.

SAN POLO & SANTA CROCE

Deluxe

Papadopoli – Sofitel
Santa Croce 245, Giardini Papadopoli (041 710 4004/www.sofitel-venezia.com). Vaporetto Piazzale Roma. **Rooms** 97. **Rates** €225-€490 double. **Credit** AmEx, DC, MC, V. **Map** p320 C5 ❸
Well placed for piazzale Roma and the railway station, this hotel somehow avoids the total anonymity that chains such as owners Accor-Sofitel often serve up. Rooms at the front of the modern building overlook a canal and bustling campo Tolentini; those on the top floors have stunning views. There is an elegant cocktail bar, and a restaurant housed in a plant-lined winter garden where breakfast is also served.
Bar. Concierge. Internet. Parking. Restaurant. Room service. TV.

CONSUME

Al Ponte Mocenigo. See p158.

La Villeggiatura.

Expensive

Ca' Nigra Lagoon Resort

*Santa Croce 927, campo San Simeon Grande
(041 275 0047/www.hotelcanigra.com).* **Rooms**
22. **Rates** €150-€750 double. **Credit** AmEx,
DC, MC, V. **Map** p320 D4 ❸❾

Ca' Nigra is a classy little hotel with a fantastic
position on the Grand Canal, in a 17th-century villa
painted deep red and set in a beautiful waterside garden. Public spaces and the spacious junior suites are
done out with interesting antique oriental pieces; the
reception area is all glass, chrome and down lighting, while the piano nobile has partially retained the
period decor. Ultra-contemporary bathrooms are
particularly impressive. Pick of the bedrooms is the
Loggia Suite with its private terrace. Guests arriving by water disembark at the hotel's private dock.
Photo p152.
Bar. Disabled-adapted rooms. Internet. TV.

San Cassiano – Ca' Favretto

*Santa Croce 2232, calle de la Rosa (041 524
1768/www.sancassiano.it). Vaporetto San Stae.*
Rooms 35. **Rates** €91-€700 double. **Credit**
AmEx, MC, V. **Map** p321 G4 ❹⓿

In a 14th-century Gothic building standing on the
Grand Canal, the San Cassiano has its own private
jetty, but if you'll be arriving on foot, get good
directions as the hotel is difficult to find. Rooms
are, on the whole, quite elegant. The airy breakfast
room has huge windows overlooking the canal and

there is a tiny but charming veranda right on the
water – a great spot for an early evening *spritz*.
Bar. Disabled-adapted room. Room service. TV.

Moderate

Ai Due Fanali

*Santa Croce 946, campo San Simeon Grande
(041 718 490/www.aiduefanali.com). Vaporetto
Riva di Biasio or Ferrovia.* **Rooms** 16. **Rates**
€95-€230 double. **Credit** AmEx, DC, MC, V.
Map p320 D4 ❹❶

Housed in what was once the annexe of the church
of San Simeon Grande, this neat little hotel faces the
Grand Canal across a pretty, quiet campo. On a terrace at the front, tables are set out under big white
umbrellas; there's also a rooftop breakfast room and
altana (roof terrace). The reception area has antiques,
oriental rugs and fresh flowers, and the 16 smallish
bedrooms have painted bedheads, a refreshing lack
of brocade and good, modern bathrooms.
Room service. TV.

★ Al Ponte Mocenigo

*Santa Croce 2063, fondamenta Rimpetto
Mocenigo (041 524 4797/www.alpontemocenigo.
com). Vaporetto San Stae.* **Rooms** 10. **Rates**
€90-€185 double. **Credit** AmEx, DC, MC, V.
Map p321 F4 ❹❷

A delightful hotel across its own little bridge on a
quiet canal near campo San Stae, this has to be one
of Venice's best value accommodation options. It has

tastefully decorated mod-Venetian rooms – some in a luscious shade of deep red, others in rich gold – and well-appointed bathrooms, not to mention Wi-Fi access throughout, a bar, a Turkish bath, a pretty courtyard garden and genuinely charming owners – Walter and Sandro – who manage to be warm and laid-back in just the right proportions. *Photo p157. Bar. Internet. Room service. TV.*
▶ *If you'd like to compare your digs with those of an 18th-century Venetian noble, visit the nearby Palazzo Mocenigo; see p104.*

Falier

Santa Croce 130, salizada San Pantalon (041 710 882/www.hotelfalier.com). Vaporetto Piazzale Roma or San Tomà. **Rooms** 19. **Rates** €80-€190 double. **Credit** AmEx, MC, V. **Map** p320 C6 ❹❸
This smart little two-star place is well located on busy salizada San Pantalon, ten minutes' walk from the station. Rooms are done out in fairly restrained Venetian style and are surprisingly upmarket considering the reasonable price; those on the second floor are newer. There is a comfy sitting area in the reception hall and a cosy beamed breakfast room. *Internet. Room service. TV.*

Locanda Marinella

Santa Croce 345, rio terà dei Pensieri (041 275 9457/www.locandamarinella.com). Vaporetto Piazzale Roma. **Rooms** 6. **Rates** €85-€135 double. **Credit** MC, V. **Map** p320 B6 ❹❹
On a tree-lined street near piazzale Roma, the Locanda Marinella offers stylish, comfortable rooms done out in pale yellow and blue. A tiny garden at the back is shaded by white umbrellas. This is a good choice for those with late arrivals or early departures. There are two smart little apartments available for rent (€110-€285). *Internet. TV.*

Locanda Sturion

San Polo 679, calle dello Sturion (041 523 6243/ www.locandasturion.com). Vaporetto Rialto Mercato or San Silvestro. **Rooms** 11. **Rates** €120-€350 double. **Credit** AmEx, MC, V. **Map** p321 G6 ❹❺
Established in the late 13th century by the doge as an inn for visiting merchants, this hotel is still thriving – not surprising, given its Grand Canal location. Only two of the rooms overlook the canal (the others give on to a quiet calle), but even if you decide you can't afford the view, you can enjoy it from the breakfast room. It's a long haul up steep stairs, and there's no lift. Staff can be terse. *Internet. Room service. TV.*

★ Oltre il Giardino

San Polo 2542, fondamenta Contarini (041 275 0015/www.oltreilgiardino-venezia.com). Vaporetto San Tomà. **Rooms** 6. **Rates** €150-€250 double. **Credit** AmEx, DC, MC, V. **Map** p321 E6 ❹❻

Tucked away at the end of a narrow fondamenta and accessed through a *giardino* (garden), this attractive villa was once owned by Alma Mahler, widow of the composer Gustav. Today, mother and son Alessandra Zambelli and Lorenzo Muner welcome guests to their stylish yet homely hotel. Here, neutral shades and wood floors provide the backdrop for a mix of antique furniture, contemporary objets and unexpected splashes. Subtly colour-themed bedrooms vary considerably in size. All are equipped with LCD TVs, robes, slippers and Bulgari bath goodies. *Internet. Room service. TV.*

★ La Villeggiatura

San Polo 1569, calle dei Botteri (338 853 1264 mobile/041 524 4673/www.lavilleggiatura.it). Vaporetto Rialto Mercato or San Silvestro. **Rooms** 6. **Rates** €110-€260 double. **Credit** MC, V. **Map** p321 G5 ❹❼
A scruffy entranceway and a steep climb (there's no lift) lead to Francesca Adilardi's charming third-floor apartment, which has six tastefully decorated bedrooms, each with its own character and all spacious and bright. Thai silks are draped over the generous-sized beds and at the windows of the subtly themed rooms, two of which have lovely old parquet floors. There are electric kettles with tea and infusions in the rooms. Breakfast is served around a big table in the sunny dining area. *Internet. TV.*
▶ *Bathroom goodies at La Villeggiatura are made by inmates of Venice's women's prison; see p128 Bags, Rags & Veg.*

Budget

★ Casa Peron

Santa Croce 84, salizada San Pantalon (041 710 021/www.casaperon.com). Vaporetto San Tomà. **Closed** Jan. **Rooms** 11. **Rates** €50-€100 double. **Credit** MC, V. **Map** p320 D6 ❹❸
Casa Peron is an excellent budget choice. The friendly Scarpa family and their parrot Pierino preside over the simple, clean hotel. It's located in the bustling university area, with the shops, restaurants and bars of campo Santa Margherita nearby. Two rooms at the top of the house have private terraces; all have showers, though four are without toilets.

THE BEST UTTER LUXURY

For asking, is Venice out there at all?
Locanda Cipriani. *See p163.*

For reliving the Belle Epoque
Gritti Palace. *See p145.*

For Arts & Crafts meets Moorish
Danieli. *See p151.*

CONSUME

Salieri

Santa Croce 160, fondamenta Minotto (041 710 035/www.hotelsalieri.com). Vaporetto Ferrovia or Piazzale Roma. **Rooms** 10. **Rates** €60-€160 double. **Credit** AmEx, MC, V. **Map** p320 C6 ⓯

This simple one-star located between the railway station and piazzale Roma offers ten bedrooms on three floors that have been recently smartened up. Unusually for a hotel of this category, all have bathrooms, air-con, TV and free Wi-Fi. Some rooms look over a canal; others have garden or rooftop views.

DORSODURO

Expensive

Accademia – Villa Maravege

Dorsoduro 1058, fondamenta Bollani (041 521 0188/www.pensioneaccademia.it). Vaporetto Accademia. **Rooms** 29. **Rates** €140-€279 double. **Credit** AmEx, DC, MC, V. **Map** p322 D8 ⓴

This wonderful secluded 17th-century villa used to be the Russian embassy; in spite of the not always friendly staff, it's perennially popular with visitors seeking comfortable pensione-style accommodation.

Located at the junction of the Toletta and Trovaso canals with the Canal Grande, it has a wonderful waterside patio where breakfast is served, as well as a grassy rear garden. The rooms are stylish, if fairly traditional, with antiques and marble or wood floors. *Bar. Concierge. Internet. Room service. TV.*

American

Dorsoduro 628, fondamenta Bragadin (041 520 4733/www.hotelamerican.com). Vaporetto Accademia. **Rooms** 30. **Rates** €70-€370 double. **Credit** AmEx, MC, V. **Map** p323 E9 ⓾

The pleasant American is a well-run and popular hotel with friendly service. Set on the delightful rio di San Vio, its generally spacious rooms are decorated in antique Venetian style; some have verandas with bright geraniums and look over the canal. Try to secure one of the corner rooms where multiple French windows make for wonderful light. There's a tiny terrace where breakfast is served under a pergola. *Bar. Concierge. Internet. Room service. TV.*

Ca' Maria Adele

Dorsoduro 111, rio terà dei Catecumeni (041 520 3078/www.camariaadele.it). Vaporetto

Too Many Rooms at the Inn

Over-supply is leading to some good deals on accommodation.

For many decades, Venice was a sellers' market, a place where too many visitors fought over too few rooms, with the result that hoteliers could charge more or less what they wanted for accommodation – which ranged, in many cases, from plain shabby to unsalubrious in the extreme. Even the luxe end of the market wasn't exactly forced to put on a particularly good show, and a trend was set for Venice charging much more for much less – a trend that extended well beyond hotels and, in these other fields, continues to this day. Nowadays, however, Venice's accommodation scene is looking like a victim of its own success.

A desperate shortage of beds coupled with a desperate desire to cash in on mass tourism meant that the B&B revolution at the turn of the millennium was hailed as the only way forward. Until then, the lagoon city's non-hotel accommodation had consisted mainly of early-curfewed cells in religious institutions. Between 2000 and 2007, the number of non-hotels with beds available for hire rose an astonishing 890 per cent, though the small dimensions of most establishments (an average across this

sector of 6.4 beds each) meant that pillows on which to rest your head had increased by a relatively 'modest' 251 per cent.

Not to be outdone, hotels were increasing and expanding too, with 20 per cent more hotels offering 26.5 per cent more beds over the same period. At the same time, many were revamping and upgrading, alarmed at the sudden surge in visitor interest for the cute and chic, the homely and welcoming, the touches of style and idiosyncracy – not to mention the lower rates – which made the new B&Bs so attractive.

The statistical result of these shifts was a fall-off in room occupancy in hotels from 72 per cent in 2000 to well below 65 per cent in 2008 (the national average in 2007 was 63.7 per cent) – and this, bear in mind, was before the credit crunch hit – while non-hotels nudged up from 43 per cent in 2000 to just below 50 per cent in 2008. The result for the visitor has been more choice, higher standards and a very noticeable drop in room prices: book on-line for non-peak, non-event times and Venice begins to look like a very good deal indeed. Why city hall and hoteliers should be striving to increase the number of rooms still further is baffling.

Salute. **Rooms** 12. **Rates** €341-€715 double.
Credit AmEx, DC, MC, V. **Map** p323 G9 **62**
Situated in the shadow of the basilica of Santa Maria della Salute, Ca' Maria Adele marries 18th-century Venetian to modern design with some ethnic elements and a host of quirky tongue-in-cheek details thrown in. Brothers Alessio and Nicola Campa preside attentively over 12 luxurious bedrooms, five of which are themed; the red and gold Doge's Room is sumptuous, the Sala Noire ultra-sexy. There's an intimate sitting room on the ground floor with chocolate brown faux-fur on the walls and black pony-skin sofas, plus a Moroccan-style roof terrace for sultry evenings.
Internet. Room service. TV.
▶ *For the story of the Salute's design, see p123.*

Ca' Pisani

Dorsoduro 979A, rio Terà Foscarini (041 277 1478/www.capisanihotel.it). Vaporetto Accademia. **Rooms** 29. **Rates** €210-€345 double.
Credit AmEx, DC, MC, V. **Map** p323 E9 **63**
Ca' Pisani's luxurious, designer-chic rooms done out in art deco style make a refreshing change from the usual fare of brocade, gilt and Murano glass; this was the first hotel to throw off the yawn-making pan-Venetian style, and though it's no longer the only one, it's still one of the most effective. Bedrooms are all generously sized and there's a restaurant with tables outside in the summer, a sauna and a roof terrace.
Bar. Concierge. Disabled-adapted rooms. Internet. Room service. TV.
▶ *The Ca' Pisani is conveniently located behind the Gallerie dell'Accademia; see p122.*

DD 724

Dorsoduro 724, ramo da Mula (041 277 0262/ www.dd724.com). Vaporetto Accademia. **Rooms** 7. **Rates** €200-€520 double. **Credit** AmEx, DC, MC, V. **Map** p323 F9 **64**
Off a gated cul-de-sac (there is a sign, but it's so high there's every chance you'll miss it), DD 724 is a design hotel in miniature. The bedrooms are stylishly understated in pale shades and dark wood, with contemporary artworks from the owner's collection dotted around; one has a little terrace. Bathrooms in pale travertine are tiny but super-modern with walk-in showers. Public spaces (and some bedrooms) are cramped, though, and the atmosphere isn't exactly warm. A recent annexe, DD 694, is located two minutes' walk away at Dorsoduro 694 and has three similarly stylish rooms.
Internet. TV.
▶ *The latest addition to the family is the chic locanda iQs, in Castello; see p151.*

Palazzo Stern

Dorsoduro 2792, calle del Traghetto (041 277 0869/www.palazzostern.com). Vaporetto Ca' Rezzonico. **Rooms** 24. **Rates** €160-€525 double.
Credit AmEx, DC, MC, V. **Map** p322 D8 **65**

Built in the early 20th century in eclectic pastiche style, Palazzo Stern is now home to this elegant hotel. A magnificent wooden staircase leads up to rooms done out in classic Venetian style in pale shades. More expensive rooms have views over the Grand Canal but the standard doubles at the back overlook a lovely garden. On the rooftop terrace is a jacuzzi, which can be booked for €70 an hour. A wonderful breakfast terrace overlooks the canal.
Bar. Disabled-adapted rooms. Internet. Room service. TV.
▶ *You can nip straight across the Grand Canal on a traghetto stationed out in front of the hotel.*

Moderate

Agli Alboretti

Dorsoduro 884, rio terà Foscarini (041 523 0058/www.aglialboretti.com). Vaporetto Accademia. **Closed** 3wks Jan. **Rooms** 23.
Rates €150-€200 double. **Credit** AmEx, MC, V. **Map** p323 E9 **66**
The model ship in the window of the tiny, wood-panelled reception area of this friendly hotel lends a nautical air to the place. The simply decorated rooms are comfortable and well equipped, though some are truly tiny. Each has an electric kettle for tea and coffee. There is a pretty, pergola-covered terrace at the back of the hotel where meals are served in summer. The staff are exceptionally helpful. A fully equipped three-bed apartment is also available (€1,000 per week).
Bar. Concierge. Internet. Restaurant. Room service. TV.

La Calcina

Dorsoduro 780, fondamenta delle Zattere (041 520 6466/www.lacalcina.com). Vaporetto Accademia or Zattere. **Rooms** 29. **Rates** €110-€250 double. **Credit** AmEx, DC, MC, V. **Map** p323 E9 **67**
The open vistas of the Giudecca canal provide the backdrop for meals taken on the terrace of this hotel, a view shared by the bedrooms at the front of the building. With an air of civilised calm, La Calcina is one of the best value hotels in its category. Rooms have parquet floors, 19th-century furniture and a refreshingly uncluttered feel; one single is without private bath. There is an *altana* (suspended roof terrace), and a number of suites and self-catering apartments are available in adjacent buildings. *Photo p163.*
Bar. Internet. Restaurant. Room service. TV.

★ Ca' Zose

Dorsoduro 193B, calle del Bastion (041 522 6635/www.hotelcazose.com). Vaporetto Salute. **Rooms** 12. **Rates** €60-€260 double. **Credit** MC, V. **Map** p323 F9 **68**
The enthusiastic Campanati sisters run this immaculate little guesthouse. There's a tiny, neat breakfast room off the cool white reception area; upstairs,

CONSUME

the dozen bedrooms are done out in a fairly restrained traditional Venetian style with painted furniture. *Internet. TV.*

▶ *Ca' Zose is perfectly located for a visit to the Peggy Guggenheim Collection; see p121 Profile.*

Locanda San Barnaba

Dorsoduro 2785-6, calle del Traghetto (041 241 1233/www.locanda-sanbarnaba.com). Vaporetto Ca' Rezzonico. **Rooms** 13. **Rates** €120-€210 double. **Credit** AmEx, MC, V. **Map** p322 D8 ❺❾

Situated at the end of a quiet alleyway and possessing a welcoming atmosphere, the San Barnaba is one of the better hotels in this price range and area. Its 13 comfortable, individually decorated rooms feature a mix of antique furniture and elegant fabrics. There's a small courtyard and roof terrace, and no bridges to cross to get to the nearest vaporetto. However, there's no lift.
Bar. Internet. TV.

Messner

Dorsoduro 216, fondamenta Ca' Balà (041 522 7443/www.hotelmessner.it). Vaporetto Salute. **Closed** 3wks Dec. **Rooms** 40. **Rates** €65-€160 double. **Credit** AmEx, DC, MC, V. **Map** p323 F9 ❻⓪

The Messner's rather dull, modern rooms may not be very inspiring, but the location, the shady garden and the warm staff more than compensate. Between the main building and two annexes, there is a choice of rooms from fairly basic standards to 'de luxe junior suites'. The hotel also manages some apartments in the area.
Bar. Disabled-adapted rooms. Internet. Restaurant. TV (in some rooms).

Budget

Antica Locanda Montin

Dorsoduro 1147, fondamenta di Borgo (041 522 7151/www.locandamontin.com). Vaporetto Accademia or Zattere. **Rooms** 12. **Rates** €75-€160 double. **Credit** MC, V. **Map** p322 D8 ❻❶

**INSIDE TRACK
THE NEW EXCELSIOR**

The first Venice film festival (*see p222*) was held on the terrace of the **Grand Hotel Excelsior**, a plush early-1900s pseudo-Moorish affair on the Lido. After the 2009 Fest, the place shut down for a two-year makeover that will see it emerge in time for the 2011 event as a 160-room **Four Seasons** hotel (www.fourseasons. com), complete with spa and luxury huts on its private beach.

It's difficult to get a booking in this charming *locanda*, which overlooks a delightful canal. It owes its popularity to the fact that it is also home to one of Venice's most famous – though very overrated – restaurants. Rooms house an eccentric mix of old and new furniture, but the overall feeling is homely and cosy. Only half have private bathrooms.
Bar. Restaurant.

★ Ca' Foscari

Dorsoduro 3887B, calle della Frescada (041 710 401/www.locandacafoscari.com). Vaporetto San Tomà. **Rooms** 11. **Rates** €77-€105 double. **Credit** MC, V. **Map** p322 D7 ❻❷

The Scarpa family has been offering a friendly welcome to guests at this wonderful *locanda* since the 1960s. The simple but cosy and homely rooms are on the second and third floors of the building (no lift); they are done out in cheerful colours and are spotlessly clean. The quietest of them have views over neighbouring gardens while others face the street; not all have private bathrooms.

LA GIUDECCA

See also p145 **Bauer Hotels**.

Deluxe

Cipriani

Giudecca 10, fondamenta San Giovanni (041 520 7744/www.hotelcipriani.com). Hotel launch from San Marco Vallaresso vaporetto stop. **Closed** end Oct-mid Mar. **Rooms** 95. **Rates** €957-€1,452 double. **Credit** AmEx, DC, MC, V. **Map** p329 J11 ❻❸

Set amidst verdant gardens, the Cipriani has great facilities as well as a private harbour for your yacht and a good chance of rubbing shoulders with a film star. Rooms are luxurious and well-appointed – though those not reached by an ongoing revamp can be a little worn at the edges. If this seems too humdrum, take an apartment in the neighbouring 15th-century Palazzo Vendramin, with butler service and private garden. Facilities include tennis courts, a pool, a sauna, a spa and a gym. There's a motorboat to San Marco, but many guests never even leave the premises.
Bars (3). Concierge. Gym. Internet. Pool (outdoor). Restaurants (4). Room service. Spa. TV.

Budget

Ostello di Venezia (Youth Hostel)

Giudecca 86, fondamenta delle Zitelle (041 523 8211/www.ostellovenezia.it). Vaporetto Zitelle. **Closed** 2wks Dec. **Beds** 260. **Rates** €20-€22 per person. **Credit** MC, V. **Map** p329 H11 ❻❹

This large youth hostel (there are 260 beds) offers million-dollar views across the lagoon towards the church of Santa Maria della Salute and San Marco.

La Calcina. *See p161.*

You should book your bed in advance on the hostel's website, especially during the summer months. Unadventurous but very cheap meals are served.

LIDO & LAGOON

Deluxe

Des Bains

Lungomare Marconi 17, Lido (041 526 5921/ www.desbainsvenezia.com). Vaporetto Lido. **Closed** early Nov-mid Mar. **Rooms** 191. **Rates** €230-€820 double. **Credit** AmEx, DC, MC, V. **Map** p327 CC3 ⑥⑤

Thomas Mann wrote, and Luchino Visconti filmed, *Death in Venice* in this glorious art deco hotel set in its own park with private beach and tennis courts. If you wish to experience the Des Bains in its current state, hurry: in autumn 2011 the place will shut down for a massive revamp, to eventually reopen as luxury serviced residences run by the Four Seasons group. *Bar. Concierge. Gym. Internet. Parking (free). Pool (outdoor). Restaurant. Room service. TV.*

San Clemente Palace

Isola di San Clemente (041 244 5001/www. sanclemente.thi-hotels.com). Hotel launch from jetty at piazza San Marco. **Rooms** 200. **Rates** €270-€550 double. **Credit** AmEx, DC, MC, V.

Over time, the island of San Clemente has hosted a hospice for pilgrims, a powder store, an ecclesiastical prison for unruly priests and, more recently, a mental hospital. Today, the restored buildings house this luxurious hotel set in extensive, landscaped grounds with rooms done out in traditional Venetian style, restaurants, a business centre, a beauty farm and all the attendant facilities; there's even a three-hole practice golf course. *Bars (2). Concierge. Business centre. Disabled-adapted rooms. Gym. Internet. Pool (outdoor). Restaurants (4). Room service. Spa. TV.* ▶ *Once you've practiced your golf swing, head to the Lido for a full 18 holes; see p246.*

Expensive

Locanda Cipriani

Torcello, piazza Santa Fosca (041 730 150/www. locandacipriani.com). Vaporetto Torcello. **Rooms** 6. **Rates** €200-€260 double. Half board €50 extra per person. **Credit** AmEx, DC, MC, V.

Some people might argue that there's no point in going to Venice and staying on the island of Torcello, but this famous green-shuttered inn is special enough to justify the remoteness of the setting, at least for a couple of nights. Some of the six rooms (done out in understated, elegant country style) look over the hotel's gorgeous garden; you might end up in the one where Ernest Hemingway wrote *Across the River and into the Trees*, apparently standing up because of haemorrhoids. *Bar. Internet. Restaurant. Room service.* ▶ *The Locanda Cipriani's (expensive) restaurant enjoys a blissful setting under a vine-clad terrace; see p181. Hotel guests can sample it for just €50 extra (on a half-board basis).*

CONSUME

Eating Out

If seafood's your thing, the lagoon city's the place.

An average 34,000 trippers rush through Venice each day, and the majority of the city's restaurants operate with these diners in mind: clearly, there's little real incentive to shoot for culinary excellence when you can be certain that 95 per cent of your guests will drop in once and once only.

But a discerning, faithful clientele of residents keeps standards high in a selection of mainly well-hidden establishments. Seek these out, and you'll eat very well indeed. In most cases it will cost you more than elsewhere in Italy – Venice simply isn't cheap – but you'll have the satisfaction of eating in the local tradition and rubbing shoulders with voluble Venetians rather than frazzled tourists.

THE DINING SCENE

Venice has all the usual panoply of *ristoranti*, *trattorie* and *osterie*, but it is the humble neighbourhood *bacaro* (a sort of wine-oriented trattoria) that is the salvation of the Venetian dining scene. With their blackened beams and rickety wooden tables, *bacari* (accent on the first syllable) are often hidden down backstreets or in quiet *campielli*.

Here, locals crowd the bar, swiftly downing a glass of wine (*un'ombra*) between work and home, and taking the edge off their appetites with one of the *cicheti* (snacks) that line the counter. The etiquette of *cicheti* is fairly straightforward. Once you've taken up your position at the bar and ordered a glass, just reach for the snacks and start eating. Keep tabs on how many you've consumed – though the barman should keep an accurate count. If you sit down at a table and order from the menu – which will include more abundant portions of those *cicheti*, plus a few hot dishes as well – expect prices to be more in line with the norm.

About the authors

Lee Marshall is a contributing editor to Condé Nast Traveller UK *and* Departures, *and writes on cinema for* Screen International. *He has lived in Italy since 1984.* Michela Scibilia *is a graphic designer (www.teodolinda.it) and author of* Venice Osterie *and* Venice Botteghe. *She has lived in Venice since 1986.*

Bacari that are mainly drinking dens are listed in the Cafés, Bars & Pasticcerie chapter (*see pp182-192*). Where food is as much the point as wine, they are listed below.

READING THE LISTINGS

Average restaurant prices are based on a three-course meal for one person, with cover charge and house wine; these may seem high, but remember that it is perfectly OK just to order a pasta course, a salad and a coffee – which may halve the quoted price. For *pizzerie*, average prices are for one pizza, a medium beer and cover charge. In the case of *bacari* that offer both bar snacks and full meals with waiter service, averages are for full sit-down meals. We've used the € symbol to indicate operations offering particularly good value on a budget.

Times given in the listings below refer to the kitchen's opening hours – that is, when it's possible to order food; establishments may keep their doors open well after this.

Unless otherwise indicated (in **blue**), all of the restaurants and *bacari* that we have reviewed in this chapter serve Italian – and, indeed, predominantly Venetian – cuisine.

> ❶ Blue numbers given in this chapter correspond to the location of each restaurant on the street maps.
> *See pp320-329.*

SAN MARCO

Cavatappi

San Marco 525, campo della Guerra (041 296 0252). Vaporetto San Marco Vallaresso. **Meals served** 11am-4pm Tue-Thur, Sun; 11am-4pm, 7-10pm Fri, Sat. Closed Jan. **Average** €35. **Credit** DC, MC, V. **Map** p324 J7 ❶

Clean-cut, modern Cavatappi ('corkscrew') has more than 30 high-quality wines available by the glass from 8.30am to 9pm. Gourmet bar snacks, creative salads and sandwiches are available throughout the day, but owners Marco and Francesca also offer a small lunch and early dinner menu. The *spritz* served here is one of the best in Venice.

Osteria San Marco

San Marco 1610, Frezzeria (041 528 5242). Vaporetto San Marco Vallaresso. **Meals served** 12.30-11pm Mon-Sat. Closed 2wks Jan & 2wks Aug. **Average** €55. **Credit** MC, V. **Map** p323 H8 ❷

This smart, modern *osteria* on a busy shopping street is a breath of fresh air in this touristy area. The four guys behind the operation are serious about food and wine, and their attention to detail shows through both in the selection of bar snacks and wines by the glass, and in the sit-down menu, based on the freshest of local produce. Prices are high, but you're paying for the area as well as the quality. This is one of the few places in Venice where you can eat a proper meal throughout the day.

CASTELLO

Al Covo

Castello 3968, campiello della Pescaria (041 522 3812/www.ristorantealcovo.com). Vaporetto Arsenale. **Meals served** 12.45-2pm, 7.30-10pm

---

INSIDE TRACK
EARLY BIRDS

Bear in mind that there are two time-scales for eating in Venice. The more upmarket restaurants follow standard Italian practice, serving lunch from around 1pm to 3pm and dinner from 7.30pm until at least 10pm. But *bacari* and neighbourhood *trattorie* tend to follow Venetian workers' rhythms, with lunch running from noon to 2pm and dinner from 6.30pm to 9pm. In other words, if you want to eat cheaply, eat early.

Mon, Tue, Fri-Sun. Closed mid Dec-mid Jan & 2wks Aug. **Average** €50. **Credit** MC, V. **Map** p325 M8 ❸

Though Al Covo is hidden in an alley behind the riva degli Schiavoni, it's very much on the international gourmet map. Its reputation is based on a dedication to serving the best seafood, including a sashimi of Adriatic fish and crustaceans, and *paccheri* pasta with pistacchio pesto, mussels and aubergines. The restaurant's decor should make it ideal for a romantic dinner, but in fact it's more for foodies than lovers, and service can be prickly. Chef/owner Cesare Benelli's American wife Diane talks English-speakers through the menu. Desserts are delicious, and there's a two-course taster menu at €44.

€ Al Diporto

Sant'Elena 25, calle Cengio (041 528 5978). Vaporetto Sant'Elena. **Meals served** noon-2pm, 7.30-10pm Tue-Sun. **Average** €30. **Credit** MC, V. **Map** p326 Q10 ❹

Met. *See p168.*

The out-of-the-way location of this authentic Venetian trat helps to limit the tourist hordes: best advice is to get off the boat at Sant'Elena and ask for directions. Once there, grab an outside table or dive into the basic but cheerful interior and order the spaghetti al Diporto (with seafood), *schie* (grey shrimps) with polenta, and their *pièce de resistance*, a magnificent *fritto misto* (mixed seafood fry-up).

★ Alle Testiere

Castello 5801, calle del Mondo Novo
(041 522 7220/www.veneziaristoranti.it).
Vaporetto Rialto. **Meals served** noon-2pm,
7-10.30pm Tue-Sat. Closed late Dec-mid Jan
& late July-Aug. **Average** €55. **Credit** MC, V.
Map p324 J6 ❺
This tiny restaurant is today one of the hottest culinary tickets in Venice. There are so few seats that they do two sittings each evening; booking for the later one (at 9pm) will ensure a more relaxed meal. Bruno, the chef, offers creative variations on Venetian seafood; the *caparossoli* (local clams) sautéed in ginger, and the John Dory fillet sprinkled with aromatic herbs in citrus sauce, are two mouth-watering examples. Sommelier Luca guides diners around a small but well-chosen wine list. The desserts, too, are spectacular.
▶ *If you're not up for a sit-down meal, you can take away creations by the same chef at Pronto Pesce Pronto; see p203.*

Algiubagiò. *See p168.*

THE BEST BLOW-OUTS

For Michelin-starred tradition
Da Fiore. *See p175.*

For virtuoso combos
Met. *See p168.*

For seafood to remember
Osteria di Santa Marina. *See p168.*

Al Portego

Castello 6015, calle Malvasia (041 522 9038/
www.alportego.it). Vaporetto Rialto. **Meals
served** noon-2.30pm, 6.30-9.30pm Mon-Sat;
6.30-9.30pm Sun. Closed 2wks June. **Average**
€25. **No credit cards. Map** p324 J6 ❻
With its wooden decor, this rustic *osteria* smacks of the mountain chalet. Alongside a big barrel of wine, the bar is loaded down with a selection of *cicheti*, from meatballs and tuna balls to *nervetti* stewed with onions. There are also simple pasta dishes, risottos and *secondi*, such as *fegato alla veneziana*, served up for early lunch and dinner.

Corte Sconta

Castello 3886, calle del Pestrin (041 522 7024/
www.veneziaristoranti.it). Vaporetto Arsenale.
Meals served 12.30-2.30pm, 7-10pm Tue-Sat.
Closed Jan & mid July-mid Aug. **Average** €60.
Credit MC, V. **Map** p325 M7 ❼
This trailblazing seafood restaurant is such a firm favourite on the well-informed tourist circuit that it is a good idea to book well in advance. The main act is a procession of seafood *antipasti*. The pasta is home-made and the warm *zabaione* dessert is a delight. Decor is of the modern Bohemian trattoria variety, the ambience loud and friendly. In summer, try to secure one of the tables in the pretty, vine-covered courtyard.

€ Dai Tosi

Castello 738, secco Marina (041 523 7102).
Vaporetto Giardini. **Meals served** noon-2pm
Mon, Tue, Thur; noon-2pm, 7-9.30pm Fri-Sun.
Closed 2wks Aug. **Average** *Pizzeria* €15.
Full meal €30. **Credit** MC, V. **Map** p326 P9 ❽
Pizzeria
In one of Venice's most working-class areas, this pizzeria is a big hit with local families. Beware of another restaurant of the same name on the street: this place (at no.738) is the better of the two. The cuisine is humble but filling, the pizzas are tasty, and you can round the meal off nicely with a killer *sgropin* (a post-prandial refresher made with lemon sorbet, vodka and prosecco). In summer, angle for one of the garden tables.
▶ *This is a welcome retreat to normality for visitors to the nearby Biennale dell'Arte; see p47.*

CONSUME

CONSUME

Met

*Castello 4149, riva degli Schiavoni (041 524
0034/www.hotelmetropole.com). Vaporetto
San Zaccaria.* **Meals served** 7.30-10pm Tue-
Sun. **Average** €90. **Credit** AmEx, DC, MC, V.
Map p324 L7 **⑨**
Dark, red and plush, the Metropole hotel's (*see
p151*) Met restaurant holds one of Venice's two
Michelin stars. No one could describe the creations
of chef Corrado Fasolato as simple – if a virtuoso
performance is what you're after, this is the place.
Prawns and lobster in carrot consommé with
savoury mushroom plumcake; courgette soup with
little venison sandwiches, bacon rolls and garlic
ice cream; and variations on suckling pig may all
feature on the changing menu. The service is both
professional and charming. *Photo p165.*
▶ *Da Fiore holds the other Michelin star; see p175.*

Osteria di Santa Marina

*Castello 5911, campo Santa Marina (041 528
5239). Vaporetto Rialto.* **Meals served** 12.30-
2.30pm, 7.30-9.30pm Tue-Sat. Closed 2wks Jan
& 2wks Aug. **Average** €60. **Credit** DC, MC, V.
Map p324 J6 **⑩**
This upmarket *osteria* in pretty campo Santa Marina
has the kind of professional service and standards
that are too often lacking in Venice, and the ambience
and the high level of the seafood-oriented cuisine justify the price tag. Raw fish feature strongly among
the *antipasti*; *primi* give local tradition a creative
twist in dishes such as the turbot- and mussel-filled
ravioli in celery sauce. The joy of this place is in
the detail: the bread is all home-made, a taster
course turns up just when you were about to ask
what happened to the *branzino*. Book ahead.

Il Ridotto

*Castello 4509, campo Santi Filippo e Giacomo
(041 520 8280/www.ilridotto.com). Vaporetto
San Zaccaria.* **Meals served** noon-2pm, 7-11pm
Mon, Tue, Fri-Sun; 7-10pm Thur. **Average** €60.
Credit AmEx, DC, MC, V. **Map** p324 K7 **⑪**

This tiny up-market restaurant is always an experience, with engaging chef Gianni Bonaccorsi
involving his customers in all his creative angst. He'll
talk you through just how he made those delicious
moscardini (baby octopus), pan-stewed in their own
juices, or tell you exactly where that tasty sea bass,
now resting on a bed of mashed potato and accompanied by a pastry-less tart of fresh vegetables,
was hauled out of the sea.
▶ *Across the campo (no.4357), Gianni's trattoria
L'Aciugheta serves decent pizzas and great cicheto
snacks, and has an interesting selection of wines.*

CANNAREGIO

Al Fontego dei Pescaori

*Cannaregio 3711, sottoportego del Tagliapietra
(041 520 0538/www.alfontego.com). Vaporetto
Ca' d'Oro.* **Meals served** 12.30-2.30pm, 7.30-
10.30pm Tue-Sun. **Average** €45. **Credit** AmEx,
DC, MC, V. **Map** p321 G4 **⑫**
This soberly elegant restaurant, housed in a former
fontego (a Venetian merchants' warehouse), is spacious and welcoming. The seafood menu insists on
fish and fresh veg or herb combos – as in the salad
of shrimps and artichokes, or the spider crab with
asparagus tips. There are also quite a few meaty *secondi*. The excellent wine list has several by-the-glass
options, and there's a pretty garden courtyard.

Algiubagiò

*Cannaregio 5039, Fondamenta Nuove
(041 523 6084/www.algiubagio.net). Vaporetto
Fondamente Nove.* **Open** 6.30am-11.30pm Mon,
Wed-Sun. Closed Jan. **Meals served** noon-3pm,
7-10.30pm Mon, Wed-Sun. **Average** €45.
Credit MC, V. **Map** p324 J3 **⑬**
This busy spot has morphed from bar to full-on
restaurant, now with a vast waterside terrace. The
menu ranges from seafood, meat, salad and cheese
antipasti, through pasta dishes such as tagliolini with
duck and autumn greens, to Angus steak (the house
speciality), prepared every which way. Vegetarians
are well served with a dozen or so options; and there's
a small but well-chosen wine list. A decent spread of
comfort-desserts like tiramisù round off the restaurant's something-for-everyone selection. *Photo p167.*
▶ *Right by the Fondamente Nove vaporetto stop,
this is the perfect place for a quick bite before
heading out to the islands of the northern lagoon.*

Alla Fontana

*Cannaregio 1102, fondamenta Cannaregio
(041 715 077). Vaporetto Guglie.* **Meals served**
Apr-Oct 6.30-10pm Mon, Wed-Sun. *Nov-Mar*
7-10pm Mon-Sat. Closed 3wks Jan-Feb. **Average**
€40. **Credit** AmEx, MC, V. **Map** p320 D2 **⑭**
This traditional *osteria*, just five minutes from the
station, has recently completed its move from
wine-and-snack *bacaro* to bona fide, evening-only
restaurant. 'The Fountain' offers a range of filling

trattoria dishes with a creative twist: tagliatelle with eel, gnocchi with turbot and courgettes, *spezzatino* (braised strips of veal) with polenta. In summer, tables line the busy canal pavement outside.

Alla Frasca
Cannaregio 5176, campiello della Carità (041 528 5433/www.osteriaviniallafrasca.com). Vaporetto Fondamente Nove. **Meals served** *July-Sept* noon-2.15pm, 6.30-11pm Mon-Sat. *Oct-June* noon-2.30pm, 6.30-10pm Tue-Sun. Closed Jan-Carnevale. **Average** €30. **Credit** DC, MC, V. **Map** p324 J4 ⓯
Under new management, La Frasca shows all signs of remaining a pleasant trattoria with a good seafood menu: the *zuppa di pesce* (fish soup) and spaghetti with lobster are particularly good. With outside

tables on a tiny square just south of fondamenta Nuove, it is almost ridiculously picturesque.

Anice Stellato
Cannaregio 3272, fondamenta della Sensa (041 720 744). Vaporetto Guglie or Sant'Alvise. **Meals served** 12.30-2pm, 7.30-10pm Wed-Sun. Closed 3wks Aug. **Average** €38. **Credit** MC, V. **Map** p321 E2 ⓰
The walk-around bar in this friendly *bacaro* fills up with *cichetari* (snacking locals) in the hour before lunch and evening meals. Tables take up two simply decorated rooms, and spill out on to the canalside walk in summer. The name means 'star anise', and spices do play a role in the kitchen, but there are also Venetian classics such as *bigoli in salsa*.

The Menu

Find out how to order boiled veal cartilage – or learn how to avoid it.

ANTIPASTI (STARTERS)
The dozens of *cicheti* – tapas-style snacks – that are served from the counters of the city's traditional *bacaro* (see p164) are essentially *antipasti*; the choice may include: **baccalà mantecato** stockfish beaten into a cream with oil and milk, often served on grilled polenta; **bovoleti** tiny snails cooked in olive oil, parsley and garlic; **carciofi** artichokes, even better if they are **castrauri** – baby artichokes; **canoce** (or **cicale di mare**) mantis shrimps; **folpi/folpeti** baby octopus; **garusoli** sea snails; **moleche** soft-shelled crabs, usually deep-fried; **museto** a boiled pork brawn sausage, generally served on a slice of bread with mustard; **nervetti** boiled veal cartilage; **polpetta** deep-fried spicy meatball; **polenta** yellow or white cornmeal mush, served either runny or in firm sliceable slabs; **sarde in saor** sardines marinated in onion, vinegar, pine nuts and raisins: **schie** tiny grey shrimps, usually served on a bed of soft white polenta; **seppie in nero** cuttlefish in its own ink; **spienza** veal spleen, usually served on a skewer; **trippa e rissa** tripe cooked in broth.

PRIMI (FIRST COURSES)
Bigoli in salsa fat spaghetti in an anchovy and onion sauce; **gnocchi... con granseola** potato gnocchi in spider-crab sauce; **pasta... e ceci** pasta and chickpea soup;

...e fagioli pasta and borlotti bean soup; **spaghetti... alla busara** in anchovy sauce; **...al nero di seppia** in squid-ink sauce; **...con caparossoli/vongole veraci** with clams; **risotto... di zucca** pumpkin risotto.

SECONDI (MAIN COURSES)
In addition to the *antipasti* mentioned above, you may find: **anguilla** eel; **aragosta/astice** spiny lobster/lobster; **branzino** sea bass; **cape longhe** razor clams; **cape sante** scallops; **cernia** grouper; **coda di rospo** anglerfish; **cozze** mussels; **granchio** crab; **granseola** spider crab; **orata** gilt-headed bream; **rombo** turbot; **pesce San Pietro** John Dory; **pesce spada** swordfish; **sogliola** sole; **tonno** tuna; **vongole/caparossoli** clams.
Meat eaters are less well catered for in Venice; local specialities include: **fegato alla veneziana** veal liver cooked in onions; **castradina** a lamb and cabbage broth.

DOLCI
Venice's restaurants are not the best place to feed a sweet habit – with a few exceptions, there are far more tempting pastries to be found on the shelves of the city's *pasticcerie* (see pp182-192). The classic end to a meal here is a plate of **buranei** – sweet egg biscuits – served with a dessert wine such as Fragolino. Then it's quickly on to the more important matter of which grappa to order.

CONSUME

Make the most of London life

Antica Adelaide

Cannaregio 3728, calle larga Doge Priuli (041 523 2629). Vaporetto Ca d'Oro. **Open** 7am-midnight daily. **Meals served** noon-2.30pm, 7.30-10.30pm daily. **Average** €35. **Credit** DC, MC, V. **Map** p321 G4

This historic bar-*osteria* behind tack-filled Strada Nuova reopened in 2006, after painstaking restoration, with dynamic restaurateur and wine buff Alvise Ceccato at the helm. Popular around *aperitivo* time, it has also made a splash on the culinary front, with its unusual menu of revisited traditional dishes from the Veneto – like *oca in onto* (goose in its own fat) or freshwater lagoon fish done *in saor*. There is a large selection of cheeses and cured meats, a good pan-Italian wine list and an admirable programme of charity events.

Bea Vita

Cannaregio 3082, fondamenta delle Cappuccine (041 275 9347/www.osteriabeavita.com). Vaporetto Santa Marta or Tre Archi. **Meals served** noon-2.30pm, 7.30-10.30pm Mon-Sat. **Average** €35. **Credit** DC, MC, V. **Map** p320 D2

On the long canalside promenade just north of the Ghetto, Bea Vita attracts locals with its ample portions and decent prices. After a single *antipasto* you're likely to feel full – but it's worth pushing on through the creative menu. Desserts are mouth-watering. The small wine list includes a decent by-the-glass selection. There's a good €28 seafood taster menu.

Boccadoro

Cannaregio 5405A, campiello Widman (041 521 1021/www.boccadorovenezia.it). Vaporetto Fondamente Nove. **Meals served** 12.30-2.30pm,

---

THE BEST CHEAP(ISH) EATS

For water-side simplicity
Alla Palanca. *See p180.*

For neighbourhood flavour
Al Diporto. *See p165.*

For something exotic
Frary's. *See p176.*

7.30-10.30pm Tue-Sun. **Average** €60. **Credit** AmEx, DC, MC, V. **Map** p324 J5

The cuisine in this restaurant with pleasantly modern decor is excellent, with a focus on fresh fish – such as tuna tartare or *cozze pepate* (peppery mussels). *Secondi* range from simple grilled fish to more adventurous seafood and vegetable pairings. In summer, there are tables outside on a small neighbourhood campo – a great playspace for bored kids.

La Bottega ai Promessi Sposi

Cannaregio 4367, calle dell'Oca (041 241 2747). Vaporetto Ca' d'Oro. **Meals served** 12.30-2.30pm, 8-11pm Mon, Tue, Thur-Sun. **Average** €35. **No credit cards. Map** p321 H4

Taken over recently by former cooks at Ca' D'Oro (Alla Vedova; *see p172*), this pared-back local has a long wooden counter groaning with excellent *cicheti*, a good selection of wines by the glass, and a few tables where diners can sample simple dishes – mainly but not exclusively seafood – with some twists on local stalwarts, such as fried *schie* (tiny grey prawns) on rocket with balsamic vinegar. *Photo p172.*

CONSUME

Boccadoro.

La Bottega ai Promessi Sposi.
See p171.

Signora Marisa is a culinary legend in Venice, with locals calling up days in advance to ask her to pre-pare ancient recipes such as *risotto con le secoe* (risotto made with a cut of beef from around the spine). Pasta dishes include the excellent *tagli-atelle con sugo di masaro* (in duck sauce), while *sec-ondi* range from tripe to roast stuffed pheasant. In summer, tables spill out from the tiny interior on to the *fondamenta*. Book well ahead – and remember, serving times are rigid: turn up late and you'll go hungry. There's a €15 lunch menu.

Da Rioba

Cannaregio 2553, fondamenta della Misericordia (041 524 4379/www.rioba.it). Vaporetto Orto. **Meals served** 12.30-2.30pm, 7.30-10.30pm Tue-Sun. Closed 3wks Jan & 3wks Aug. **Average** €35. **Credit** AmEx, DC, MC, V. **Map** p321 F3 ㉔
Taking its name from the iron-nosed stone figure of a turbaned merchant – known as Sior Rioba – set into a wall in nearby campo dei Mori, Da Rioba is a pleasant place for lunch on warm days, when tables are laid out along the canal. This nouveau-rustic *bacaro* attracts a predominantly Venetian clientele – always a good sign. The menu ranges from local standards like *schie con polenta* to for-ays like red mullet fillets on a bed of artichokes with balsamic sauce.

Fiaschetteria Toscana

Cannaregio 5719, salizada San Giovanni Crisostomo (041 528 5281/www.fiaschetteria toscana.it). Vaporetto Rialto. **Meals served** 7.30-10.30pm Wed; 12.30-2.30pm, 7.30-10.30pm Mon, Thur-Sun. Closed late July-mid Aug. **Average** €50. **Credit** DC, MC, V. **Map** p321 H5 ㉕
Once a depot for Tuscan wine and olive oil, today only a selection of steaks and big Tuscan reds betrays its origins. Otherwise, the cuisine is Venetian, with favourites such as *fegato alla veneziana*. Pasta is not a strong point: leap from the fine *antipasti* to delicious *secondi* like grilled John Dory, or a renowned *fritto misto* (mixed seafood fry-up). Service can be brusque. Take the sting out of the bill with one of the fabulous desserts, and a bottle from one of the biggest wine lists in town.

Mirai

Cannaregio 227, lista di Spagna (041 220 6517/ www.miraivenice.com). Vaporetto Ferrovia. **Meals served** 7.30-11.30pm Tue-Sun. Closed 3wks Jan. **Average** €60. **Credit** AmEx, DC, MC, V. **Map** p320 D3 ㉖ **Japanese**
One of the few interesting international options in Venice, this Japanese restaurant has already built up a steady local following. It does all the classics – sushi, sashimi of salmon, tuna and bream, tempura – and it does them well. The classy modern decor makes for a cool refuge from the tacky lista di Spagna; they've recently opened a garden out back.

Ca' D'Oro (Alla Vedova)

Cannaregio 3912, ramo Ca' d'Oro (041 528 5324). Vaporetto Ca' d'Oro. **Meals served** 11.30am-2.30pm, 6.30-10.30pm Mon-Wed, Fri, Sat; 6.30-11pm Sun. Closed Aug. **Average** €35. **No credit cards. Map** p321 G4 ㉑
Officially Ca' d'Oro, this place is known by locals as Alla Vedova – the Widow's Place. The widow has joined her *marito*, but her family still runs the show. And the traditional brass-pan and wooden-table decor and the warm, intimate atmosphere remain. Tourists head for the tables (it's best to book), where tasty pasta dishes (like spaghetti in cuttlefish ink) and *secondi* are served, while locals stay at the bar snacking on classic *cicheti*, including the best *polpette* (meatballs) in Venice.

Da Alberto

Cannaregio 5401, calle Giacinto Gallina (041 523 8153). Vaporetto Rialto. **Meals served** noon-3pm, 6.30-9.30pm Mon-Sat. Closed mid July-early Aug. **Average** €35. **Credit** MC, V. **Map** p324 J5 ㉒
This *bacaro* with trad decor, not far from campo Santi Giovanni e Paolo, has a well-stocked bar counter. The wide-ranging, sit-down menu is rigidly Venetian, offering utterly traditional *granseola* and *seppie in umido* (stewed cuttlefish), plus seafood pastas and risottos. Book ahead if you want a table.

Dalla Marisa

Cannaregio 652B, fondamenta San Giobbe (041 720 211). Vaporetto Crea or Tre Archi. **Meals served** noon-2.30pm Mon, Wed, Sun; noon-2.30pm, 8-9.15pm Tue, Thur-Sat. Closed Aug. **Average** €35. **No credit cards. Map** p320 C2 ㉓

CONSUME

Naranzaria. *See p176.*

Vini da Gigio

*Cannaregio 3628, fondamenta San Felice
(041 528 5140/www.vinidagigio.com).
Vaporetto Ca' d'Oro.* **Meals served** noon-
2.30pm, 7-10.30pm Wed-Sun. Closed 3wks
Jan-Feb & 3wks Aug-Sept. **Average** €50.
Credit MC, V. **Map** p321 G4 **㉗**

Vini da Gigio is strong on Venetian *antipasti*, including raw sea food; there are also a number of good
meat and game options, like seared cuts of breaded
lamb or tuna in a crust of sesame seeds. As the name
suggests, wine is another forte, with good international and by-the-glass selections. The only draw-
back in this highly recommended restaurant is the
unhurried service. Book well ahead.

SAN POLO & SANTA CROCE

See also p189 **Muro Vino e Cucina**.

★ € Al Garanghelo

*San Polo 1570, Calle dei Botteri (041 721 721/
www.algaranghelo.it). Vaporetto Rialto Mercato
or San Stae.* **Meals served** noon-2.30pm, 6-9pm
Mon, Tue, Thur-Sat; noon-2.30pm Sun. **Average**
€30. **Credit** AmEx, MC, V. **Map** p321 G5 **㉘**

This *osteria-bacaro* offers good, cheap food and
friendly service. All day, the long wooden counter
has a cornucopia of *cicheti* that range from the obvious (meatballs and tunaballs) to more refined treats,
such as halibut in spicy tomato sauce. At mealtimes,
you can sit at tables crammed into the tiny space
and order from a small range of *primi* and *secondi*
that might include a great seafood risotto, or *fegato
alla veneziana*; don't miss the *budino del doge*, a
creamy almond liqueur-flavoured dessert.

Alla Madonna

*San Polo 594, calle della Madonna (041 522 3824/
www.ristoranteallamadonna.com). Vaporetto
Rialto or San Silvestro.* **Meals served** noon-
3pm, 7-10pm Mon, Tue, Thur-Sun. Closed
Christmas-Jan. **Average** €45. **Credit** AmEx,
MC, V. **Map** p321 G6 **㉙**

A sort of high-class canteen, this big, bustling fish
trattoria with its friendly (though brisk) service and
fair-ish prices has been piling in locals and clued-up
tourists for generations. While the cooking will win
no prizes, it offers decent versions of such Venetian
favourites as *granseola* and *anguilla fritta* (fried eel).

★ € Alla Zucca

*Santa Croce 1762, ponte del Megio (041 524
1570/www.lazucca.it). Vaporetto San Stae.*
Meals served 12.30-2.30pm, 7-10.30pm Mon-
Sat. **Average** €30. **Credit** AmEx, DC, MC, V.
Map p321 E4 **㉚**

One of Venice's first 'alternative' trattorias and still
one of the best – not to mention one of the best-value.
By a pretty bridge, the vegetarian-friendly, (mainly)

THE BEST VEGETARIAN BETS

For salads with northern lagoon views
Algiubagiò. *See p168.*

For wholesome on a budget
Alla Zucca. *See above.*

For sharp design
L'Avogaria. *See p177.*

WHEREVER CRIMES AGAINST HUMANITY ARE PERPETRATED.

Across borders and above politics.
Against the most heinous abuses
and the most dangerous oppressors.
From conduct in wartime
to economic, social, and cultural rights.
Everywhere we go,
we build an unimpeachable case
for change and advocate action
at the highest levels.

HUMAN RIGHTS WATCH TYRANNY HAS A WITNESS

WWW.HRW.ORG

HUMA
RIGHT
WATC

THE BEST CHILD-PLEASERS

For tasty pizza and outside space
Birraria La Corte. *See right.*

For a quiet street to run along
Dai Tosi. *See p167.*

female-staffed Pumpkin offers a break from all that seafood. The menu is equally divided between meat (ginger pork with pilau rice) and vegetables (pumpkin and seasoned ricotta quiche). In summer, book ahead for one of the few outside tables.

€ Al Nono Risorto

Santa Croce 2338, sottoportico di Siora Bettina (041 524 1169). Vaporetto San Stae. **Meals served** noon-2.30pm, 7-11pm Mon, Tue, Fri-Sun; 7-11pm Thur. Closed 2wks Jan. **Average** *Pizzeria* €14. *Full meal* €30. **No credit cards**. **Map** p321 F5 ❸❶ **Pizzeria**
There's plenty of attitude in this lively spot. If you want to hang out over a tasty pizza margherita in a shady garden courtyard with Venice's bright young things, this is the place to come. It also does traditional Venetian trattoria fare, at traditional Venetian trattoria prices.

Antiche Carampane

San Polo 1911, rio terà delle Carampane (041 524 0165/www.antichecarampane.com). Vaporetto San Silvestro. **Meals served** 12.30-2.30pm, 7.30-10.30pm Tue-Sat. Closed Aug. **Average** €55. **Credit** AmEx, DC, MC, V. **Map** p321 F5 ❸❷
Fiendishly difficult to find, Antiche Carampane lays its tourist-unfriendly cards on the table with its sign 'no pizza, no lasagne, no *menù turistico*'. But if you manage to break the ice, you'll enjoy a fine (though not cheap) seafood meal that goes beyond the ubiquitous standards to offer recherché local specialities like *spaghetti in cassopipa* (a spicy sauce of shellfish and crustaceans). Leave room for an unbeatable *fritto misto* (mixed seafood fry-up) and their delicious desserts. Inside is cosy; outside is better.

Bancogiro

San Polo 122, campo San Giacomo di Rialto (041 523 2061). Vaporetto Rialto Mercato. **Meals served** noon-11pm Tue-Sun. **Average** €40. **No credit cards**. **Map** p321 H5 ❸❸
The location of this updated *bacaro* is splendid: the main entrance gives on to the busy Rialto square of San Giacomo, while the back door leads to a prime bit of Grand Canal frontage, with tables from which to soak in the view. Bancogiro dispenses excellent wines and *cicheti* to an appreciative crowd dowstairs; upstairs, the restaurant has creative seafood dishes.
▶ *Bancogiro is now under the same management as Osteria San Marco; see p165.*

Birraria La Corte

San Polo 2168, campo San Polo (041 275 0570/ www.birrarialacorte.it). Vaporetto San Silvestro or San Tomà. **Meals served** noon-2.30pm, 7-10.30pm daily. Closed 2wks Nov. **Average** *Pizzeria* €15. *Full meal* €30. **Credit** AmEx, DC, MC, V. **Map** p321 F6 ❸❹ **Pizzeria**
The outside tables of this huge, no-nonsenze pizzeria are a great place to observe life in the campo – and a boon for parents with small children, who can chase pigeons while mum and dad tuck into a decent pizza. The restaurant occupies a former brewery, and beer still takes pride of place over wine. There's also a regular menu with decent pasta options and some good grilled-meat *secondi*.

★ Da Fiore

San Polo 2202, calle del Scaleter (041 721 308/ www.dafiore.net). Vaporetto San Stae or San Tomà. **Meals served** 7.30-10.30pm Tue; 12.30-2.30pm, 7.30-10.30pm Wed-Sun. Closed 3wks Jan & all Aug. **Average** €100. *Set lunch* €50. **Credit** AmEx, DC, MC, V. **Map** p321 E5 ❸❺
Michelin-starred Da Fiore is considered by many to be Venice's best restaurant. Host Maurizio Martin treats his guests with egalitarian courtesy, while his wife Mara concentrates on getting the food right. Raw fish and seafood is a key feature of the *antipasti*; *primi* are equally divided between pasta dishes and a series of faultless risottos. *Secondi* are all about bringing out the flavour of the fish without smothering it in sauce. It's a good, rather than a superlative, dining experience; but that's Venice for you.
▶ *Da Fiore's closest competitor is Met; see p168.*

Da Ignazio

San Polo 2749, calle dei Saoneri (041 523 4852). Vaporetto San Tomà. **Meals served** noon-3pm, 7-10pm Mon-Fri, Sun. Closed 2wks Dec & 3wks July-Aug. **Average** €48. **Credit** AmEx, DC, MC, V. **Map** p321 E6 ❸❻
The big attraction of this tranquil, no-frills, neighbourhood restaurant is its pretty, pergola-shaded courtyard. The cooking is safe, traditional Venetian: mixed seafood *antipasti* might be followed by a good rendition of *spaghetti con caparossoli* or *risi e bisi* (risotto with peas), and grilled fish *secondi*.

INSIDE TRACK
WAYS WITH MEAT

The once-strong local tradition of creative ways with meat is kept alive in a handful of restaurants (among them **Ai Gondolieri**; *see p177*) and one marvellous trattoria, **Dalla Marisa** (*see p172*). It can also be found in bar-counter *cicheti* like *nervetti* (veal cartilage) and *cotechino* (spicy pig's intestine parcels filled with cuts of pork).

CONSUME

Vecio Fritolin.

€ Frary's
San Polo 2559, fondamenta dei Frari (041 720 050). Vaporetto San Tomà. **Meals served** noon-3.30pm, 6-10.30pm Mon, Wed-Sun. **Average** €28. **Credit** AmEx, DC, MC, V. **Map** p321 E6 ③ **Middle Eastern**

A friendly, reasonably-priced spot specialising in Arab cuisine, though there are some Greek and Kurdish dishes too. Couscous comes with a variety of sauces: vegetarian, mutton, chicken or seafood. The *mansaf* (rice with chicken, almonds and yoghurt) is good. At lunch there's a great value two-course menu for just €12.

Naranzaria
San Polo 130, Erbaria (041 724 1035/www. naranzaria.it). **Vaporetto** Rialto or Rialto Mercato. **Open** *Apr-mid Nov* noon-2am Tue-Sun; *mid Nov-Mar* noon-3pm, 6pm-2am Tue-Sun. Closed 10 days Jan. **Meals served** noon-3pm, 7.30-10pm Tue-Sun. **Average** €35. **Credit** MC, V. **Map** p321 H5 ③

This nouveau-*bacaro* offers a selection of fine wines – many of them produced by co-owner Brandino Brandolini – plus a small but interesting menu that ranges from local specialities to couscous and sushi prepared by the restaurant's Japanese chef. There are a few tables upstairs beneath the brick-arched ceiling, but it's the handful of tables outside with a Grand Canal view that make this place truly special. *Photo p173.*
► *See also p190 Evening in the Market.*

Il Refolo
Santa Croce 1459, campiello del Piovan (041 524 0016/www.dafiore.net). **Vaporetto** Riva di Biasio or San Stae. **Meals served** 7-11pm Tue; noon-2.30pm, 7-11pm Wed-Sun. Closed Dec-Jan. **Average** *Pizzeria* €20. *Full meal* €35. **Credit** MC, V. **Map** p321 E4 ③ **Pizzeria**

Il Refolo (the 'Sea Breeze') has tables outside – and only outside – in one of Venice's prettiest squares. Set up by a scion of the Da Fiore dynasty (*see p175*), it is Venice's most luxurious pizzeria – a status that is of course reflected in the prices. There's also a small international-style restaurant menu featuring high-class deli fare; the house white is an above-average Tocai. Be sure to book ahead, even for lunch.

Vecio Fritolin
Santa Croce 2262, calle della Regina (041 522 2881/www.veciofritolin.it). **Vaporetto** San Stae. **Meals served** noon-2.30pm, 7-10.30pm Tue-Sun. **Average** €50. **Credit** AmEx, DC, MC, V. **Map** p321 F5 ④

Wooden beams, sturdy tables and the long bar at the back of the main dining room set the mood in this old-style *bacaro*. But the seasonally-changing menu is more creative than the decor might lead you to expect, with dishes such as cocoa tagliatelle with squid, or a main course of turbot in a crust of black rice with sautéed baby artichokes.
► *You can also sample chef Irina Fregua's lighter creations at lunch time at the café at Palazzo Grassi (10am-6.30pm Mon, Wed-Sun); see p75.*

CONSUME

prawns, tomato and grappa, and fresh tuna baked with sesame, plus a number of vegetarian options.

▶ *L'Avogaria has opened a new three-room B&B (€150-€350 double) with bold print bedheads and minimal design to please style-conscious travellers.*

La Bitta

Dorsoduro 2753A, calle lunga San Barnaba (041 523 0531). Vaporetto Ca' Rezzonico. **Meals served** 6.30-11pm Mon-Sat. Closed July. **Average** €40. **No credit cards. Map** p322 D8

La Bitta, a warm and rustic *osteria* with a small court-yard, stands out by having virtually no fish on the menu. Dishes like *straccetti di pollo ai finferli* (chicken strips with chanterelle mushrooms) or *oca in umido* (stewed goose) make a welcome change. They also have a good selection of cheeses, served with honey or chutney, and intelligent by-the-glass wine options.

Casin dei Nobili

Dorsoduro 2765, sottoportego del Casin dei Nobili (041 241 1841). Vaporetto Ca' Rezzonico. **Meals served** noon-11pm Tue-Sun. **Average** *Pizzeria* €15. *Full meal* €35. **Credit** DC, MC, V. **Map** p322 D8 **Pizzeria**

This large pizzeria-restaurant with artsy-rustic decor serves up tasty pizzas to a mainly student clientele. The usual range of Venetian *primi* and *secondi* is on offer as well, but you'll eat better, and more cheaply, if you stick to pizza. There's a garden out the back.

▶ *The same fare is served at the new, scenic Ristorante Terrazza del Casin dei Nobili, on the Giudecca-facing Zattere (Dorsoduro 924-5, 041 520 6895, closed Thur).*

Oniga

Dorsoduro 2852, campo San Barnaba (041 522 4410/www.oniga.it). Vaporetto Ca' Rezzonico. **Meals served** noon-2.30pm, 7-10.30pm Mon, Wed-Sun. Closed 3wks Jan. **Average** €30. **Credit** AmEx, DC, MC, V. **Map** p322 D8

DORSODURO

Ai Gondolieri

Dorsoduro 366, fondamenta Ospedaletto (041 528 6396/www.aigondolieri.com). Vaporetto Accademia or Salute. **Meals served** noon-3pm, 7-10pm Mon, Wed-Sun. **Average** €65. **Credit** AmEx, MC, V. **Map** p323 F9

If you're looking to splash out, Ai Gondolieri offers a creative menu that belies its ultra-traditional decor and service. It's also, unusually for Venice, fish-free. Rooted in the culinary traditions of north-east Italy, dishes include a warm salad of venison with blueberries, *panzerotti* (pasta parcels) filled with Jerusalem artichokes in Montasio cheese sauce, and pork fillet in pear sauce with wild fennel. Enquire about the price before tasting truffle delights in autumn. The Gondoliers are surprisingly strong on vegetarian dishes.

L'Avogaria

Dorsoduro 1629, calle dell'Avogaria (041 296 0491/www.avogaria.com). Vaporetto San Basilio. **Meals served** 12.30-3pm, 7.30pm-midnight Mon, Wed-Sun. Closed 2wks Jan & 2wks Aug. **Average** €40. **Credit** AmEx, DC, MC, V. **Map** p322 B8

One of the first sharp design eateries to open on the lagoon, L'Avogaria is neither as pretentious nor as expensive as it looks. At lunch, a light two-course meal with wine costs around €15 a head; the pricier dinner menu is more elaborate. The cuisine is from the southern Puglia region and includes pasta with

CONSUME

**INSIDE TRACK
SEAFOOD YOU'VE NEVER SEEN**

The lagoon city has a long and glorious culinary tradition based on fresh seafood. A writhing, glistening variety of sea creatures swims from the stalls of the Rialto and Chioggia markets into local kitchens. Going with the flow of *la cucina veneta* requires a certain spirit of open-minded experimentation. Not everybody has eaten *granseola* (spider crab) before, or *garusoli* (sea snails) or *canoce* (mantis shrimps), but Venice is definitely the place to try these marine curios. To make sense of the bewildering variety of sea creatures, *see p169* **The Menu.**

Profile Venetian Vino

Tasting notes for north-eastern Italian wines.

The wine-growing area that stretches from the Veneto north-east to Friuli is, after Tuscany and Piedmont, one of Italy's strongest, with good whites like tocai and soave backed up by solid reds like valpolicella and cabernet franc. This means that, even in Venice's humbler establishments, you'll find that the house wine is often surprisingly refined.

The grape-growing area is divided into two regions, the **Veneto** and **Friuli-Venezia Giulia**. The latter has the strongest reputation, mostly centred on the Collio and Colli Orientali appellations. This pair of appellations can be confusing. The names Collio and Colli Orientali don't tell you what you're getting in the glass: they are umbrella affairs, each hosting an impressive roster of wines. You might order a Colli Orientali tocai friuliano, or refosco; or a Collio merlot, or sauvignon.

The Veneto region is coming on too. Long considered good only for full-bodied red Amarone and Valpolicella, the region is undergoing an image makeover, thanks to an energetic cluster of winemakers who use local grape varieties like corvina and garganega to turn out some fine and complex red wines. Even Soave, that white two-litre party standby, has come good in the hands of producers like Pieropan or Inama. The Veneto is also home to Italy's favourite fizz, prosecco.

The following are the wines you are most likely to come across in the wine bars and *bacari* reviewed in the Eating Out and Cafés, Bars & Gelaterie chapters of this guide.

RED

Cabernet: When Venetians ask for a glass of cabernet, they generally mean cabernet franc.

A staple of the Veneto's upland wine enclaves, the grape yields an honest, more-ish red with an unmistakeable grassy aroma. For Veneto area cabernets, look out for Mattiello, Costozza and Cavazza. In Friuli, both cabernet sauvignon and cabernet franc have a foothold. Russiz Superiore and La Boatina make some of the best.

Raboso: The classic Venetian winter-warming red, raboso is rough, acidic, tannic and entirely lacking in pretension. The best kind is the stuff served from a huge demijohn in your local *bacaro*.

Refosco: A ruby-red wine with hints of grass and cherries, refosco is one of those varieties that locals like to keep to themselves. Check out the meaty version produced by Dorigo.

Valpolicella, Recioto della Valpolicella & Amarone: Often disappointing, standard Valpolicella suffers from overstretched DOC boundaries and overgenerous yields. But the best, bottled as Valpolicella classico or Valpolicella superiore, can be very good. Amarone and Recioto, the area's two famous *passito* wines, are made from partially dried Valpolicella grapes. Recioto is the sweet version, Amarone the dry. The best producers include Allegrini (Recioto), Bussola, Cantina Sociale Valpolicella, Corte Sant'Alda, Dal Forno, Masi (Amarone), Quintarelli (Amarone), Viviani and Zenato.

ONE FOR THE ROAD

For touring details of the wine-growing area – and notably where to sip grappa and prosecco close to the source – *see pp286-292.*

WHITE & SPARKLING

Soave & Recioto di Soave:
In the Soave classico area, a handful of dynamic winemakers is showing that this blend of garganega and trebbiano is capable of great things: look out in particular for Pieropan's La Rocca or Calvarino selections. In the 1980s, a few producers revived the tradition of Recioto di Soave, a delicious dessert wine made from raisinised garganega grapes. The best producers include Anselmi, Ca' Rugate, Gini, Inama, Pieropan and Suavia.

Friulian whites: The Collio and Colli Orientali appellations turn out some of Italy's most graceful white wines. Four varietals dominate: sauvignon (the Ronco delle Mele cru produced by Venica & Venica is to die for); pinot bianco; pinot grigio; and tocai friuliano (a dry summery white). Producers who do great things with two or more of these varietals include Ascevi, Castello di Spessa, Collavini, Dorigo, Gravner, Humar, Jermann, Kante, Keber, Le Vigne di Zamò, Livio Felluga, Marco Felluga, Miani, Pecorari, Polencic, Primosic, Princic, Puiatti, Rodaro, Ronco dei Tassi, Ronco del Gelso, Ronco del Gnemiz, Russiz Superiore, Schioppetto, Scubla, Toros, Venica & Venica, Villa Russiz and Volpe Pasini. Other white varieties grown in these areas include chardonnay and ribolla gialla, a local grape that makes for fresh and lemony wines. Finally, there is Picolit, the hugely expensive Italian take on Sauternes, made from partially-dried grapes.

Prosecco di Conegliano & Valdobbiadene: The classic Veneto dry white fizz, prosecco comes from vineyards around Valdobbiadene and Conegliano, in the rolling hills north of Treviso. The most highly prized (and expensive) version of prosecco is known as Cartizze. A more rustic, unfizzy version – known as *prosecco spento* or simply *spento* – is served by the glass in *bacari*. The best producers include Bisol, Bortolomiol, Col Vetoraz, Le Colture, Nino Franco and Ruggeri & Co.

CONSUME

With tables outside on campo San Barnaba, Oniga has a friendly, local feel. The menu is adventurous Venetian, though Hungarian chef Annika occasionally does a great goulash. The menu changes frequently but the pasta is consistently excellent. Fish and meat figure among the *secondi*: the pork chop with potatoes and figs is good. Annika's husband Marino is a wine expert, and will guide you through the select list. At lunchtime a meat or fish two-course menu (including side salad and coffee) costs €18 a head.

Pane, Vino e San Daniele
Dorsoduro 1722, campo dell'Angelo Raffaele (041 523 7456). Vaporetto San Basilio. **Open** 9am-11pm Mon, Tue, Thur-Sun. Closed 2wks Jan. **Meals served** noon-2.30pm, 7-10.15pm Mon, Tue, Thur-Sun. **Average** €35. **Credit** MC, V. **Map** p322 B8 **46**
This nouvelle-*osteria* belongs to a chain specialising in the wine and ham of the Friuli region, but the place has a character of its own, determined partly by its high proportion of university patrons, and partly by the fact that the Friulian imprint is varied by dishes reflecting the chef's Sardinian roots, including *coniglio al mirto* (rabbit baked with myrtle). It functions as a bar all day – handy if you just want a drink in the pretty square.

GIUDECCA

★ € Alla Palanca
Giudecca 448, fondamenta del Ponte Piccolo (041 528 7719). Vaporetto Palanca. **Open** 7am-8.30pm Mon-Sat. **Meals served** noon-2.30pm Mon-Sat. **Average** €30. **No credit cards.** **Map** p328 D11 **47**

One of the cheapest meals-with-a-view in Venice is on offer at this humble bar-trattoria on the Giudecca quay. It's a lunch-only place: the rest of the day it operates as a bar. Sit at a quayside table and order from a good-value menu that includes some surprisingly gourmet options: tagliatelle with *funghi porcini*, or swordfish in orange and lemon marinade. Finish up with a delicious chocolate mousse with candied fruit.

★ I Figli delle Stelle
Giudecca 70-71, fondamenta delle Zitelle (041 523 0004/www.ifiglidellestelle.it). Vaporetto Zitelle. **Meals served** noon-2.30pm, 7.30pm-midnight Wed-Sun. **Average** €40. **Credit** AmEx, DC, MC, V. **Map** p329 H11 **49**
Opened in 2008, this comfortable space with a dove-grey wood-clad interior also has outside tables with heart-stopping views across to St Mark's. Helmed by three friends – from Venice, Rome and Bari – the cuisine is pan-Italian, with broad bean purée and seasonal vegetables among the *antipasti*, *orecchiette* pasta with tomato and baked ricotta, and lamb baked with sun-dried tomatoes. There's occasional live music, and huge sofas to relax in with an *aperitivo*.

Harry's Dolci
Giudecca 773, fondamenta San Biagio (041 522 4844/www.cipriani.com). Vaporetto Sant' Eufemia. **Open** 10.30am-11pm Mon, Wed-Sun. Closed Nov-Mar. **Meals served** noon-3pm, 7-10.30pm Mon, Wed-Sun. **Average** €75. **Credit** AmEx, DC, MC, V. **Map** p328 C10 **49**
Arrigo Cipriani's second stronghold (after Harry's Bar; *see p185*), this open-air restaurant is only open when the weather allows. The cuisine is supposedly more summery than *chez* Harry, but in practice

I Figli delle Stelle.

many dishes are identical. What changes is the cost: prices here are two-thirds of those at the mother ship (though that's still a big dent in the wallet). Outside of mealtimes, you can order just a coffee and one of the delectable pastries made on the premises. Come prepared for mosquitoes.

Mistrà
Giudecca 212A, fondamenta del Ponte Lungo (041 522 0743). Vaporetto Palanca or Redentore. **Meals served** noon-3.30pm Mon; noon-3.30pm, 7.30-10.30pm Wed-Sun. Closed 2wks Jan & 2wks Aug. **Average** €45. **Credit** AmEx, DC, MC, V. **Map** p328 E12 ⑤⓪
Amid a sprawl of boatyards, a fire-escape staircase leads up to this first-floor trattoria with spectacular views over the lagoon. Mistrà is a word-of-mouth success among local foodies for its excellent fish menu (octopus and potato salad; baked fish with potatoes, cherry tomatoes and olives) and range of Ligurian specialities. They also do good steaks, if you're all fished out. Lunch is cheap and worker-oriented, dinner more ambitious and more expensive.

LIDO & LAGOON
Lido

★ € Al Mercà
Lido, via Enrico Dandolo 17A (041 526 4549). Vaporetto Lido. **Meals served** 10.30am-3pm, 6.30pm-midnight Tue-Sun. **Average** €40. **Credit** MC, V. **Map** p327 BB3 ⑤①
A success since its recent opening, Al Mercà is a great place for a light meal of fresh seafood. Charming hosts serve excellent mixed seafood *antipasti*, fishy pasta dishes and grilled fish to contented diners out on the portico of the former produce market.

La Favorita
Lido, via Francesco Duodo 33 (041 526 1626). Vaporetto Lido. **Meals served** 7.30-10.30pm Tue; 12.30-2.30pm, 7.30-10.30pm Wed-Sun. Closed Jan. **Average** €55. **Credit** AmEx, DC, MC, V. **Map** p327 CC2 ⑤②
With a lovely vine-shaded pergola for summer dining, this is an old-fashioned and reassuring sort of place that does textbook Venetian seafood classics like *spaghetti ai caparossoli* or *scampi in saor* (sweet-and-sour sauce), plus a few more audacious dishes such as pumpkin gnocchi with scorpion fish and radicchio. Service is professional, and the wine list has a fine selection of bottles from the north-east.

Murano

Busa alla Torre
Murano, campo Santo Stefano 3 (041 739 662). Vaporetto Faro. **Meals served** noon-3.30pm daily. **Average** €45. **Credit** AmEx, MC, V. **Map** p328 U2 ⑤③

THE BEST TRUE VENETIAN

For traditions revisited
Antica Adelaide. *See p171.*

For hearty and simple
Ca d'Oro (Alla Vedova). *See p172.*

For great *antipasti*
Vini da Gigio. *See p173.*

In summer, tables spill out into a pretty square opposite the church of San Pietro Martire. The service is deft and professional. The cuisine is reliable, no-frills seafood cooking, with excellent *primi* that might include ravioli filled with *branzino* (bream) in a spider-crab sauce, or tagliatelle with *canoce* (mantis shrimps). Note the lunch-only opening.
▶ *A perfect place for refuelling after resisting the hard sell at the island's glass workshops;* *see p136 Murano Glass.*

Burano & Mazzorbo

Alla Maddalena
Mazzorbo 7B (041 730 151). Vaporetto Mazzorbo. **Meals served** noon-3pm Mon-Wed, Fri-Sun. Closed 20 Dec-10 Jan. **Average** €35. **Credit** AmEx, DC, MC, V. **Map** p329 W1 ⑤④
Right opposite the jetty on the island of Mazzorbo is this lunch-only trattoria, which serves filling lagoon cuisine. During the hunting season, there's no better place for wild duck, sourced directly from local hunters; the rest of the year, seafood dominates. Book ahead for Sunday lunch in summer, when the waterside tables fill up with Venetians in the quiet garden behind fill up with Venetians. The house wine comes from the family's own vineyards.

Torcello

Locanda Cipriani
Torcello, piazza Santa Fosca 29 (041 730 150/ www.locandacipriani.com). Vaporetto LN to Torcello. **Meals served** noon-3pm Mon, Wed-Sun. Closed Jan. **Average** €80. **Credit** AmEx, DC, MC, V.
There is a lot to like about the high-class Locanda Cipriani, which was one of Hemingway's haunts. The setting, just off Torcello's pretty square, is idyllic; tables are spread over a large vine-shaded terrace during the summer. And although there is nothing remotely adventurous about the cuisine, it's good in an old-fashioned way. Specialities such as *risotto alla torcellana* (with seasonal vegetables) are done to perfection, and the desserts are tasty treats for rich kids. Dinner is served (7-9pm) on Friday and Saturday, by prior arrangement only.
▶ *If you want to stay at the locanda, see p163.*

Cafés, Bars & Gelaterie

Cappuccino, gelato, aperitivo – morning, noon and night.

Italians are assiduous frequenters of their local café for morning cappuccino and of their favourite bar for evening *aperitivi* (in fact, one establishment may answer to all their needs: the terms bar and café are generally interchangeable, and most are multi-purpose). But Venetians add another dimension to this with the traditional *bacaro*: a kind of wine bar with enough delicious bar snacks – *cicheti* – to turn a tipple into a meal.

That's not all that sets Venetians' bar-going habits apart. On a frosty winter morning, don't be surprised if you find locals adding a generous shot of warming grappa to their early-morning espresso. *Aperitivi*, on the other hand, are quite likely to be consumed in a *pasticceria* (cake shop), with some fruity, creamy pastry concoction as a chaser.

CONSUME

DRINK LIKE A VENETIAN

To the usual Italian breakfast, light snacks, pastries and alcoholic beverages routine, Venice contributes its own specialities: the *ombra* and the *spritz*. The former is a tiny glass of wine – *bianco* or *rosso* – which is knocked back in no time and is often the whole point of a *giro di ombre* – an *ombra*-crawl around selected *bacari* (the accent is on the first 'a'). A *spritz* is an *aperitivo* of white wine, Campari and a shot of seltzer or sparkling water; a sweeter version is made with low-alcohol Aperol. Also flowing freely into Venetian glasses are prosecco, the bubbly white made in the hills of the Veneto region, and *spento*, a bubble-free version of the same wine.

WHAT TO DRINK (AND EAT) WHEN

The Venetian day begins at the local bar with a cappuccino and *brioche* (pronounced the French way), preferably one baked on the premises.

Sweet things are consumed at other times too; many *pasticcerie* (cake shops) serve coffee and alcoholic beverages as well.

Gelato is an all-day stop-gap, indulged in by everyone during the hotter months. Quality varies greatly from place to place. A foolproof test of any shop is to eyeball the tub of banana ice-cream – if it's grey in colour, you know it's the real deal: bright yellow screams that the ice-cream's been made from a mix.

At *aperitivi* time, locals flock to wine bars: *bacari* or *enoteche*. The best offer an enormous selection of top-quality wines by the glass. Most have snacks, but in some, food and seated meals have become the whole point: these are included in the Eating Out chapter (*see pp164-181*). Where drinking remains the *raison d'être*, they are listed here.

For a list of local coffee varieties, *see p189* **Inside Track**. For the lowdown on regional vintages, *see p178* **Profile**.

About the author
American **Jill Weinreich** *has called Venice home for 13 years. She has a background in the visual arts, but currently works in import/export.*

➊ Green numbers given in this chapter correspond to the location of each café or bar on the street maps. *See pp320-329.*

ETIQUETTE

The practice in Italian bars is to decide what you want, pay at the till in advance, then display your receipt when you order at the counter. If you return to the same establishment sufficiently often to be considered a regular, you can pay afterwards. Remember that anything ordered at the counter must then be consumed at the counter.

If you want to sit at a café table, you should order from there (or at the very least indicate that you are planning to sit down when you pay); the privilege of occupying a table will push your bill up – a little in smaller, more hidden-away places but jaw-droppingly in, say, piazza San Marco, especially in the evening when a surcharge is added for the palm orchestras: horror tales of tourists paying €50 for a glass of mineral water may be urban legends, but they give the general idea – don't expect much (if any) change from a €10 note.

The routine changes in traditional *bacari*, where you generally order your drink, then begin dipping in to the array of *cicheti* (snacks) on the counter. Most bar staff have an uncanny gift for keeping track of who eats what, and totting up your bill accurately at the end. But it's polite to remember how much you've consumed in order to help them with their calculations.

Many bars that stay open late and/or have live music are listed in the Music & Nightlife chapter (*see pp231-236*).

(*see pp231-236*)

INSIDE TRACK
PROUST'S MOTHER

French novelist Marcel Proust used to take his mother to lunch at the **Quadri** (*see p185*), where the neoclassical first-floor restaurant is as expensive as it is elegant.

SAN MARCO

Cafés & bars

Bar all'Angolo

San Marco 3464, campo Santo Stefano (041 522 0710). Vaporetto Sant'Angelo. **Open** 6.30am-9pm Mon-Sat. Closed Jan. **No credit cards**. **Map** p323 F7 ❶

Secure a table outside and watch the locals saunter through the campo as you enjoy a coffee or *spritz*. Inside, you have your choice of standing at the usually crowded bar or relaxing in one of the comfy seats in the back where you'll find a mixed bag of locals and tourists being served good *tramezzini*, panini and fresh salads by friendly, if hurried, staff. There are certainly bigger bars in this busy campo, but none match the quality on offer here.

Caffè Florian

San Marco 56, piazza San Marco (041 520 5641/ www.caffeflorian.com). Vaporetto San Marco Vallaresso. **Open** *Apr-Oct* 10am-midnight daily.

Caffè Florian.

CONSUME

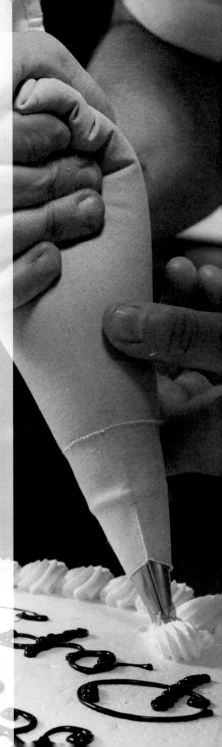

RosaSalva
Venezia
dal 1879

*Pastry, Cuisine, Banqueting
The best tradition in Venice
since 1879*

*Renowned Pasticceria
Rosa Salva
just a stone's throw from both
Rialto and Piazza San Marco,
creates traditional
mouth-watering cakes, biscuits
and luscious desserts beloved of
the sweet-toothed Venetians.*

Venezia
Calle Fiubera - San Marco 950
ph.0415210544
Mercerie - San Marco 5020
ph.0415227934
SS. Giovanni e Paolo - Castello 6779
ph.0415227949

Mestre
Via Cappuccina 17 ph.041988400

www.rosasalva.it
info@rosasalva.it

Nov-Mar 10am-11pm Mon, Tue, Thur-Sun. Closed 2wks Dec & 2wks Jan. **Credit** AmEx, DC, MC, V. **Map** p323 H8 ❷

Florian sweeps you back to 18th-century Venice with its mirrored, stuccoed and frescoed interior. Founded in 1720 as 'Venezia Trionfante', its present appearance dates from an 1859 remodelling. Rousseau, Goethe and Byron hung out here – the last in sympathy with those loyal Venetians who boycotted the Quadri (*see below*) across the square, where Austrian officers used to meet. Times have changed, and these days having a drink at Florian is more bank statement than political statement, especially if you sit at one of the outside tables, where not even a humble *caffè* costs less than €10.

Caffetteria Doria

San Marco 4578C, calle dei Fabbri (329 351 7367 mobile). Vaporetto Rialto. **Open** 6am-8.30pm Mon-Sat; 1-8.30pm Sun. **No credit cards. Map** p323 H7 ❸

Take a page from the locals and squeeze into this popular, standing-room-only bar for a delicious cup of coffee, mid-afternoon snack or one of the best *spritz* in town. Service is always friendly and welcoming. Knowledgeable owners Andrea and Riccardo stock a huge selection of wine and spirits.

Gran Caffè Quadri

San Marco 120, piazza San Marco (041 522 2105/www.quadrivenice.com). Vaporetto San Marco Vallaresso or San Zaccaria. **Open** *Apr-Oct* 9am-midnight daily. *Nov-Mar* 9am-11pm Tue-Sun. **Credit** AmEx, DC, MC, V. **Map** p323 H7 ❹

With its ornate stucco mouldings, 18th-century murals, huge mirrors and polished wooden furniture, Quadri is every inch the *caffè storico*. People have been drinking here since 1638, when it was called Il Rimedio. Giorgio Quadri was among the first to bring Turkish-style coffee to Venice when he took the place over in the late 18th century. Stendhal, Wagner and Balzac were habitués. In the evening, a palm orchestra competes out in the square with the one at Florian's (*see above*) opposite, and romantics pay small fortunes to sip cocktails under the stars.
▶ *Who else drank here? See p183 Inside Track.*

Harry's Bar

San Marco 1323, calle Vallaresso (041 528 5777/www.cipriani.com). Vaporetto San Marco Vallaresso. **Open** 10.30am-11pm daily. **Credit** AmEx, DC, MC, V. **Map** p323 H8 ❺

This historic watering hole, founded by Giuseppe Cipriani in 1931, has changed little since the days when Ernest Hemingway came here to work on his next hangover… except for the prices and the numbers of tourists. But despite the crush, a Bellini (peach juice and sparkling wine) at the bar is as much a part of the Venetian experience as a gondola ride (and at €15 far cheaper). At mealtimes, diners enjoy Venetian-themed international comfort food

---

THE BEST GRAND CAFES
For feeling Byronic **Caffè Florian.** *See p183.* **For a Proustian rush** **Gran Caffè Quadri.** *See p185.*

---

at steep prices (€120-plus for three courses). Stick with a Bellini, and don't even think of coming in here wearing shorts or ordering a *spritz*.

Gelaterie

Igloo

San Marco 3651, calle della Mandola (041 522 3003). Vaporetto Sant'Angelo. **Open** *Feb, Mar, Oct, Nov* 11.30am-7.30pm. *Apr-Sept* 11am-9pm daily. Closed mid Nov-Carnevale. **No credit cards. Map** p323 G7 ❻

Generous portions of handmade, creamy *gelato* in a wide range of varieties to please everyone is what Igloo is all about. In the summer months, fruit flavours such as fig or blackberry are made from the nearby market's freshest produce. Igloo is easily found by spotting the crowd of happy ice-cream eaters spilling out into the compact street.

Pasticcerie

Marchini Time

San Marco 4598, campo San Luca (041 241 3087). Vaporetto Rialto. **Open** 7am-8.30pm daily. **No credit cards. Map** p323 G7 ❼

This is the latest addition to the Marchini pastry empire, the oldest in *La Serenissima*. The renovated space lights up campo San Luca with its colourful windows displaying the latest cakes, cookies and chocolates. There's a dizzying array of *cornetti* to enjoy with your breakfast coffee – the raspberry jam-filled one is mouth-watering.
▶ *For another of the Marchini dynasty's confectionery outlets, see p203.*

CASTELLO
Cafés & bars

★ Angiò

Castello 2142, ponte della Veneta Marina (041 277 8555). Vaporetto Arsenale. **Open** *Feb-May, Oct-Dec* 7am-9pm Mon, Wed-Sun. *June-Sept* 7am-midnight Mon, Wed-Sun. **Credit** MC, V. **Map** p325 N8 ❽

Owned by siblings Andrea and Giorgia, Angiò is the finest stopping point along one of Venice's most tourist-trafficked spots – the lagoon-front riva degli Schiavoni. Tables line the water's edge, with a stunning view across to San Giorgio Maggiore;

CONSUME

www.treesforcities.org

Trees for Cities
Charity registration number 1032154

Travelling creates so
many lasting memories.

Make your trip mean
something for years to
come - not just for you
but for the environment
and for people living in
deprived urban areas.

Anyone can offset their
flights, but when you
plant trees with Trees for
Cities, you'll help create
a green space for an
urban community that
really needs it.

Leave
Your
Mark
Create a green future for cities.

ultra-friendly staff serve up pints of Guinness, freshly made sandwiches and interesting selections of cheese and wine. Music events are held here during the summer months on Saturday evenings.
► *If you're wondering how the view looks in reverse, climb the campanile at San Giorgio Maggiore; see p130.*

Vincent Bar

Sant'Elena, viale IV novembre 36 (041 520 4493). Vaporetto Sant'Elena. **Open** 7am-10pm Tue-Sun. **No credit cards. Map** p326 Q11
Sant'Elena is surely the only place in Venice you'll find more residents, trees and grassy expanses than tourists, churches and galleries. Grab a seat – and a drink – outside this bar and join the locals gazing lazily across the lagoon at passing boats or keeping a watchful eye on their *bambini* as they play in the park. The bar's ice-cream is made on the premises.

Zenzero

Castello 5902A, campo Santa Marina (041 241 2828). Vaporetto Rialto. **Open** 7.30am-4pm Mon; 7.30am-8pm Tue-Sat. **No credit cards. Map** p324 J6
Perfectly located in picturesque campo Santa Marina, Zenzero ('ginger' in Italian) is a café-bar serving food with a difference. The home-made pastries are light and extra flaky; the sandwiches are creative, and there are two pasta dishes each day for a light lunch. There are three tables inside, but the view from the pavement tables is to be preferred when the weather permits.
► *Zenzero is an offshoot of the nearby Osteria di Santa Marina; see p168.*

THE BEST WATERSIDE BARS

For enjoying the Zattere
Al Chioschetto. *See p191.*

For leafy lagoon calm
Vincent Bar. *See p187.*

For a Grand Canal perch
Taverna del Campiello Remer. *See p188.*

Gelaterie

★ Boutique del Gelato

Castello 5727, salizzada San Lio (041 522 3283). Vaporetto Rialto. **Open** *Feb-May, Oct, Nov* 10am-8.30pm daily. *June-Sept* 10am-11.30pm daily. Closed Dec-Jan. **No credit cards. Map** p324 J6
Most Venetians agree that some of the city's best *gelato* is served in this tiny outlet on busy salizzada San Lio. Be prepared to be patient though, because there's always a huge crowd waiting to be served. See it as quality assurance – it's worth the wait.

Pasticcerie

★ Da Bonifacio

Castello 4237, calle degli Albanesi (041 522 7507). Vaporetto San Zaccaria. **Open** 7am-8.30pm Mon-Wed, Fri-Sun. Closed 3wks Aug. **No credit cards. Map** p324 K7

CONSUME

Rosa Salva. *See p188.*

In a narrow calle behind the Danieli Hotel, this is a firm favourite with Venetians, whom you'll find outside the entrance in great numbers, waiting to squeeze inside for a coffee, drink and something from the cake cabinet. As well as a tempting array of snacks and traditional cakes such as *mammalucchi* (deep-fried batter cakes with candied fruit), Da Bonifacio is famous for its creative *fritelle* (with wild berry, chocolate, almond or apple fillings), which appear in January and remain through Carnevale.

Pasticceria Melita

Castello 1000-4, fondamenta Sant'Anna (no phone). Vaporetto Giardini. **Open** 8am-2pm, 3.30-8.30pm Tue-Sun. **No credit cards.** **Map** p326 P9 ⑬
Your senses will reel at the dizzying assortment of pastries on offer here. Don't let the brusqueness of the pastry chef put you off: he made pastries for the Hotel Danieli for 20 years before opening his own piece of sweet paradise here in the 1980s. There's no sitting down for a languorous coffee and cake session here: it's a stand-up or takeaway only kind of place, but is a local favourite.

★ Rosa Salva

Castello 6779, campo Santi Giovanni e Paolo (041 522 7949). Vaporetto Fondamente Nove. **Open** 7.30am-8.30pm Mon, Tue, Thur-Sun. **No credit cards.** **Map** p324 K5 ⑭
Take the time and pay the higher prices to sit down and savour the history that surrounds you in campo Santi Giovanni e Paolo while nursing one of the smoothest *cappuccini* in town and trying one of Rosa Salva's delicious cakes. If it's ice-cream you fancy, all their flavours are made on the premises. *Photo p187.*

Alaska. *See p191.*

CANNAREGIO

Cafés & bars

Ardidos

Cannaregio 2282, calle de Noal (041 894 6182). Vaporetto Ca' d'Oro. **Open** 7.30am-10pm daily. **No credit cards.** **Map** p321 G4 ⑮
Ardidos's owner Beatrice used to be an interior designer, based in Milan – and it shows: this recently opened café-bar with its glass, brick, ceramic and wood detailing manages to be warm and contemporary, casual yet elegant. The abundant happy hour buffet is one of the best in Venice. Breakfast, lunch and brunch are all served in addition to Beatrice's excellent mojitos. The candle-lit courtyard is a welcoming alternative when all of the inside tables are occupied.

Enoteche & bacari

La Cantina

Cannaregio 3689, campo San Felice (041 522 8258). Vaporetto Ca' d'Oro. **Open** 11am-10pm Mon-Sat. Closed 2wks Jan & 2wks July-Aug. **Credit** MC, V. **Map** p321 G4 ⑯
This wonderful place to indulge in a well-deserved *aperitivo* has snack offerings so substantial that a quick drink can easily turn into a full meal. The ambience indoors is warm and cosy. The outside tables are the perfect place for watching the world bustle by. The friendly staff will help you to order a plate (or two or three) piled high with mouthwatering *crostini*, made on the spot by Francesco with whatever's in season at local markets. There's a list of around 30 wines available by the glass; La Cantina also sells Gaston, a beer that's been brewed specially for the bar.

Un Mondo diVino

Cannaregio 5984A, salizada San Canciano (041 521 1093). Vaporetto Ca' d'Oro or Rialto. **Open** 10am-3pm; 5.30-10pm Tue-Sun. **Credit** MC, V. **Map** p324 J5 ⑰
This *bacaro* is a wonderful meeting-spot, full of Venetians and visitors throughout the day. The intimate interior, with its low, wooden-beamed ceiling, begs passers-by to stop inside. Over 40 fine wines are offered by the glass, and the large bar has a bewilderingly large selection of *cicheti*, including wonderful artichokes, *bacalà*, meatballs and *melanzane alla parmigiana* (aubergines with mozzarella). During warmer weather, enjoy your *aperitivo* and snacks outside beneath an awning provided to avert pigeon-damage.

★ Taverna del Campiello Remer

Cannaregio 5701, campiello Remer (349 336 5168 mobile). Vaporetto Ca' d'Oro or Rialto. **Open** 10.30am-3.30pm, 5.30pm-1am Mon, Tue, Thur-Sun. **Credit** MC, V. **Map** p321 H5 ⑱

Al Remer guarantees you a warm welcome – not always matched by good service. It's a cosy little *bacaro*, with good renditions of the usual *cicheti*. The traditional Venetian meal fare is nothing to write home about, and is expensive unless you opt for the lunchtime special. But what makes Al Remer unique (if you ever get there, because it's a devil to find) is its exquisite setting in a tiny square right on the Grand Canal. With drink in hand, there can be few finer places to soak in the glories of that waterway.

Gelaterie

Il Gelatone
Cannaregio 2063, rio terà Maddalena (041 720 631). Vaporetto San Marcuola. **Open** *Mid Jan-Apr, Oct-mid Dec* 11am-8pm daily. *May-Sept* 11am-10.30pm daily. **No credit cards. Map** p321 F3 ⑲
Follow the trail of overflowing ice-cream cones between the railway station and the end of strada Nuova and you'll find Il Gelatone. The luscious *gelato* comes in a number of gorgeous flavours and satisfyingly generous portions: the yoghurt-flavoured variety with sesame seeds and honey is especially good.

Pasticcerie

★ Boscolo
Cannaregio 1818, campiello de l'Anconeta (041 720 731). Vaporetto San Marcuola. **Open** 6.40am-8.40pm daily. **No credit cards. Map** p321 E3 ⑳
The bar at Boscolo's *pasticceria* is always packed; locals flock to enjoy an extra-strong *spritz al bitter* with one of the home-made *pizzette*. There is also an excellent assortment of Venetian sweets: *frittelle* during Carnevale, as well as *zaleti* and *pincia* (made with cornflour and raisins). Boscolo's range of chocolates in the form of interesting (and graphic) Kama Sutra positions have made this confectioner famous.

SAN POLO & SANTA CROCE
Cafés & bars

Bar ai Nomboli
San Polo 2717C, rio terà dei Nomboli (041 523 0995). Vaporetto San Tomà. **Open** 7am-9pm Mon-Fri. Closed 3wks Aug. **No credit cards. Map** p321 E6 ㉑
This bar, which is much loved by Venice's student population, has expanded its already impressive repertoire of sandwich combinations. You'll need to summon all of your decision-making skills when faced with a choice of more than 100 sandwiches and almost 50 *tramezzini*: try the 'Serenissima' with tuna, peppers, peas and onions or perhaps the 'Appennino' with roast beef, broccoli and pecorino – or ask them to build your own creation, using any of their fresh ingredients.

**INSIDE TRACK
CAFFE TALK**

Don't even think of ordering a Frappuccino in Venice (at the time of writing, there were no Starbucks here anyway). Instead, go for a **cappuccino**, **caffè latte**, or try one of these:

caffè espresso
caffè americano espresso diluted with hot water, served in a larger cup
caffè corretto espresso with a shot of alcohol (usually grappa)
caffè doppio double espresso
caffè lungo espresso made with slightly more water
caffè macchiato espresso with just a dash of milk
decaffeinato any of the above drinks but without the buzz

Caffè dei Frari
San Polo 2564, fondamenta dei Frari (041 524 1877). Vaporetto San Tomà. **Open** 8am-9pm Tue-Sun. Closed 2wks Aug. **No credit cards. Map** p321 E6 ㉒
A cosy bar with an even cosier mezzanine, which is often packed with students and lawyers. The walls feature art nouveau interpretations of 18th-century Venice. Sit back and relax in one of their comfortable booths and enjoy a tasty spread of snacks, which accompany all of the *aperitivi* and drinks.
▶ *This is the logical place to catch your breath after visiting the nearby Frari (see p109).*

★ Caffè del Doge
San Polo 609, calle dei Cinque (041 522 7787/ www.caffedeldoge.com). Vaporetto Rialto Mercato or San Silvestro. **Open** 7am-7pm Mon-Sat; 7am-1pm Sun. **No credit cards. Map** p321 G6 ㉓
Italians scoff at the idea of drinking cappuccino after 11am, but rules like this go by the board at the Caffè del Doge, where any time is good for indulging in the richest, creamiest, most luscious cup of coffee in Venice. Two signature blends and a variety of single-origin coffees are available to consume or purchase. Don't overlook the pastries, and watch out for the speciality coffees, for which a portion of each sale goes to *bambini del caffè* (Children of Coffee), a non-profit organisation that assists children who work on coffee plantations worldwide.

Muro Vino e Cucina
San Polo 222, campo Cesare Battisti già Bella Vienna (041 523 7495/www.murovenezia.com). Vaporetto Rialto or Rialto Mercato. **Open** 9am-3pm, 4pm-2am Mon-Sat. **Credit** MC, V. **Map** p321 G5 ㉔

CONSUME

Evening in the Market

Veg out at a bunch of cool drinking (and eating) spots.

The high-density retail zone at the north-western foot of the Rialto bridge used to be 'early to bed, early to rise' in the extreme: market traders would begin piling their stalls high with fruit, vegetables and fish well before the sun had risen, bustling through until around 2pm, after which campo Cesare Battisti (aka campo Bella Vienna), campo della Pescaria and the Naranzaria were eerily quiet.

There have always, of course, been bars and *bacari* in the area to slake the thirst of hungry market workers, but the last few years has seen an influx of hip new eateries and drinking dens, making this area an all-day (not to mention late-night) magnet.

The situation is ideal: there's hardly a single private house for streets around, allowing high decibel levels; and the setting is impossibly romantic, with unexpected vistas of the Grand Canal around each mysteriously shuttered-up corner.

It's a mixed crowd of mainly young(-ish), mainly professional locals, plus visitors in the know, who congregate here. Tipplers in a hurry – or those who don't mind about niceties such as somewhere to sit – grab a glass at **Al Marcà** (pictured; *see below*) and stand in campo Bella Venezia in the happy, noisy mêlée of *ombra* and *spritz* imbibers. **Muro**'s minimalist ground-floor bar (*see p189*) attracts a designy clientele, including a large student contingent, while foodies frequent the upstairs restaurant.

You can also segue from *aperitivi* and *cicheti* to fully fledged meals in **Naranzaria** (*see p176*) and **Bancogiro** (*see p175*). The former offers an upscale menu including sushi prepared by the Japanese co-owner; the latter has recently been taken over by the excellent Osteria San Marco (*see p165*), so expect interesting culinary developments. Both have a clutch of hotly contended tables looking out towards the Grand Canal in all its grandiose glory.

Stylish Muro is generally packed with throngs of sophisticated but thirsty *spritz*-seekers. There's something for pretty much everyone here – from *aperitivi* and *cicheti* at their spacious downstairs bar and outside tables, to eclectic fine dining on the first floor. In the colourful area around the historic Rialto markets, Muro's sleek, modern design is complemented by the friendly staff. The €7 self-service lunch on Saturdays in the campo outside is highly popular.

▶ *See also above Evening in the Market.*

With standing room only in the campo, Al Mercà has been serving Rialto marketgoers with their victuals since 1918. A recent change in ownership has brought young partners Gabriele, Marco and Giuseppe together behind the impossibly small counter. Packed into this tiny space is a snack-filled case with meatballs, artichoke hearts and mini-sandwiches, in addition to numerous options for panini toppings and a generous selection of wines by the glass.

▶ *See also above Evening in the Market.*

Enoteche & bacari

Al Marcà

San Polo 213, campo Cesare Battisti già Bella Vienna (347 100 2583 mobile). Vaporetto Rialto or Rialto Mercato. **Open** 9am-3pm, 6-9pm Mon-Sat; 6-9pm Sun. **No credit cards.** **Map** p321 G5 ㉕

Al Prosecco

Santa Croce 1503, campo San Giacomo dell' Orio (041 524 0222). Vaporetto San Stae. **Open** 8am-10pm Mon-Sat. Closed Jan & Aug. **No credit cards. Map** p321 E4 ㉖

Prosecco – whether sparkling or still (aka *spento*) – is second only to *spritz* in terms of daily Venetian consumption, and (as the name suggests) this bar is a good place for consuming it. The shaded outside tables are a fantastic vantage point for observing daily life in a lively campo, but the interior is just as convivial on cool days. Exceptional wines are served by the glass, accompanied by a first-rate choice of cheeses, cold meats, marinated fish and oysters.

Da Lele
Santa Croce 183, campo dei Tolentini (no phone). Vaporetto Piazzale Roma. **Open** 6am-2pm, 4-8pm Mon-Fri; 6am-2pm Sat. **No credit cards. Map** p320 C6 ㉗
Gabriele's (Lele's) place is the first authentic *osteria* for those arriving in Venice – or the last for those leaving; look for the two barrels outside and you've found it. It's so small in here, there isn't even room for a phone – but there are local wines from Piave, Lison and Valdobbiadene on offer, as well as rolls that are filled to order with meat and/or cheese.
▶ *For a primer on local wines, see p178 Profile.*

Do Mori
San Polo 429, calle dei Do Mori (041 522 5401). Vaporetto Rialto, Rialto Mercato or San Silvestro. **Open** 8.30am-8.30pm Mon-Sat. **No credit cards. Map** p321 G5 ㉘
Do Mori claims to be the oldest *bacaro* in Venice, dating back to 1462. Batteries of copper pans hang from the ceiling, and at peak times the narrow bar is a heaving mass of bodies lunging for the excellent mini-sandwiches and the vast selection of fine wines. Don't point to a label at random, as prices can sometimes be in the connoisseur bracket. You won't go far wrong if you stick to a glass of the classic *spento* – prosecco minus the bubbles.

Gelaterie

★ Alaska Gelateria-Sorbetteria
Santa Croce 1159, calle larga dei Bari (041 715 211). Vaporetto Riva de Biasio. **Open** *Apr-Oct* 11am-midnight daily. *Feb-Mar & Nov* noon-9pm daily. Closed Dec-Jan. **No credit cards. Map** p320 D4 ㉙
Carlo Pistacchi is passionate about making ice-cream and experimenting with new flavours using only the freshest natural ingredients. Stick to tried and true choices such as hazelnut or yoghurt, or branch out to sample seasonally changing exotic flavours, such as artichoke, fennel, asparagus or ginger. Multiple visits are in order, not only to experience a variety of flavours but also fully to enjoy the antics of AS Roma-supporter Carlo. *Photo p188.*

Pasticcerie

Pasticceria Rio Marin
Santa Croce 784, rio Marin (041 718 523). Vaporetto Riva di Biasio. **Open** 6.30am-8pm Mon, Tue, Thur-Sun. Closed Aug. **Credit** MC, V. **Map** p320 D5 ㉚

Just a short hop across the Grand Canal from the train station, Bianca and Dario's delicious cakeshop is a rewarding stopover on arrival in (or departure from) Venice – or at any other time, for that matter. There's a world of choice here. Individual portions can be consumed with a coffee or drink at one of the tables along the rio Marin. Alternatively, treats such as a wonderful creation with cream and fresh fruit can be purchased family-size to take away.

Rizzardini
San Polo 1415, campiello dei Meloni (041 522 3835). Vaporetto San Silvestro. **Open** 7am-8.30pm Mon, Wed-Sun. Closed Aug. **No credit cards. Map** p321 F6 ㉛
An eye-catching *pasticceria* with pastries, cookies and snacks to match. When owner Paolo is behind the bar, there's never a dull moment. It's especially good for traditional Venetian pastries, cookies, coffee, *frittelle* during Carnevale… anything, if you can manoeuvre up to the counter and place your order.

DORSODURO
Cafés & bars

Ai Do Draghi
Dorsoduro 3665, calle della Chiesa (041 528 9731). Vaporetto San Tomà. **Open** *Apr-Oct* 7.30am-2am daily. *Nov-Mar* 7.30am-11pm daily. **No credit cards. Map** p322 C7 ㉜
Throngs of cheerful *spritz* drinkers cram into the small calle off campo Santa Margherita where the entrance to Ai Do Draghi is located – and also on to its tables on the square – to enjoy draught beers, strong *spritz al bitter* and approximately 40 wines by the glass. Not only are the staff friendly and courteous, but the outdoor seating provides one of the best vantage points from which to observe the bustling pace of campo Santa Margherita. The indoor seating, a well-kept secret, is snug.

★ Al Chioschetto
Dorsoduro 1406A, fondamenta delle Zattere (348 396 8466 mobile). Vaporetto Zattere. **Open** *June-Sept* 7.30am-2am daily. *Oct-May* 7.30am-6pm daily. **No credit cards. Map** p322 C9 ㉝

THE BEST APERITIVO HAUNTS

For coolest design
Ardidos. *See p188.*

For an ombra on the hoof
Al Marcà. *See p190.*

For a drink with a view
Skyline Bar. *See p192.*

CONSUME

A much-loved spot not only for scrumptious panini and nibbles, but also for the tranquillity of sitting outside along the Giudecca Canal with a sweeping view from industrial Marghera to Palladian San Giorgio Maggiore. Seating is strictly outside, so take advantage of any sunny day throughout the year and head over here for your daily bar needs.

▶ *If you're tempted by the view, head over to San Giorgio Maggiore for a visit; see p130.*

★ Da Gino

Dorsoduro 853A, calle Nuova Sant'Agnese (041 528 5276). Vaporetto Accademia. **Open** 6am-7.30pm Mon-Sat. Closed Aug & 2wks Dec-Jan. **No credit cards. Map** p323 E9 ㉞
You will always be greeted with a smile by the Scarpa family, whether it's your first or your 100th visit; they take customer service seriously in a city where so many tourists make for some cranky hosts. Stop inside for a visit and you'll find Inter-fan Emilio expertly manning the coffee machine. Gino's serves some of the best *tramezzini* and made-to-order panini around.

▶ *Tables outside along the calle make excellent viewpoints for watching the flow of gallery-goers making their way between the nearby Accademia (see p122) and Guggenheim Collection (see p121).*

Enoteche & bacari

Cantinone (già Schiavi)

Dorsoduro 992, fondamenta Nani (041 523 0034). Vaporetto Accademia or Zattere. **Open** 8am-8.30pm Mon-Sat. Closed 2wks Aug. **No credit cards. Map** p322 D9 ㉟
Two generations of the Gastaldi family work here, filling glasses, carting cases of wine, and preparing huge panini with mortadella or more delicate *crostini* with, for example, creamy tuna spread with leeks. Give yourself ample opportunity to select from the day's offerings by coming before the crowds pour in at 1pm. When the bar itself is full, you'll be in good company on the bridge outside – a good setting for the Venetian ritual of *spritz* and prosecco consumption.

Gelaterie

Gelateria Lo Squero

Dorsoduro 989-90, fondamenta Nani (347 269 7921 mobile). Vaporetto Accademia or Zattere. **Open** 11am-9pm daily. **No credit cards. Map** p322 D9 ㊱
Simone Sambo makes some of the finest ice-cream in Venice. He's hard-pressed to pinpoint a favourite flavour, but can happily rattle off those in in his current repertoire – which always depends on the freshest ingredients available. His mousse series (blueberry, strawberry, chocolate and hazelnut, among others) is so light and creamy, it's served in a waffle cone so it doesn't fly away.

Grom

Dorsoduro 2761, campo San Barnaba (041 099 1751). Vaporetto Ca' Rezzonico. **Open** 11am-11.30pm Mon-Fri; 11am-11.30pm Sun. **No credit cards. Map** p322 D8 ㊲
Founded in Turin and spreading as far as New York, the Grom gelato empire has now reached Venice, serving their trademark ice-cream made with high-quality ingredients such as *sfusato* lemon from Amalfi, *tonda gentile* hazelnut from Lombardy, and pistachios from Bronte in Sicily. Note, though, that at €2.50 a scoop, the price is almost double that of any other gelateria in town.

Pasticcerie

Tonolo

Dorsoduro 3764, calle San Pantalon (041 523 7209). Vaporetto San Tomà. **Open** 7.45am-8pm Tue-Sat; 7.45am-1pm Sun. Closed Aug. **No credit cards. Map** p322 D6 ㊳
This Venice institution has been operating in the same spot since 1953. The coffee is exceptional. On Sundays, the place fills up with locals buying sweet offerings to take to lunch – don't be shy about asserting your rights or you may never get served. All the delectable pastries – which are candy for the eyes as well as the stomach – come in miniature sizes to make sampling a little bit easier.

LA GIUDECCA & SAN GIORGIO

Cafés & bars

Skyline Bar

Molino Stucky Hilton Hotel, Giudecca 810, campo San Biagio (041 272 3310). Vaporetto Palanca. **Open** noon-3.30pm, 5.30pm-1am daily. **Credit** AmEx, MC, V. **Map** p322 B10 ㊴
It's a hike across to the new Hilton Hotel (*see p144*) in the former Molino Stucky flour mill (*see p127*) – and the bar is an expensive extravagance – but sit out on the rooftop terrace and survey Venice beneath you, beyond the grand sweep of the Giudecca canal, and you'll certainly feel that it's all worth it. Full meals and light snacks are served but forget the expensive food and just savour the view, with a drink in hand. The Skyline opens evenings only in the winter months.

INSIDE TRACK
VENICE & COFFEE

Venice's relationship with coffee is a long and significant one. The city's very first *bottega del caffè* opened in 1683 in piazza San Marco. By the late 18th century, as many as 24 coffee shops graced this square alone.

Shops & Services

Truly unique gifts: lace, glass, masks and… plastic gondolas.

Venice was once the crossroads between East and West, and merchants from across Europe met those from the Levant here to trade. Nowadays, out-of-towners continue to be well catered for, though the products which dominate – sadly invading premises which once housed bakers and butchers and greengrocers – tend to be tacky souvenirs and factory-made masks.

In among the tourist tack, however, are some gems, including the creations of a handful of local craftspeople such as the Attombri brothers (*see p194* **Beads by Attombri**) and Vittorio Costantini (*see p207*). When seeking out the real Venetian thing, always bear this in mind: if it's cheap, it's almost certainly not genuine.

THE LOWDOWN

Venice is not shopping-centre friendly. If you are looking for a mall to fill all your needs, you'll have to journey to the mainland. The **Centro Barche** in Mestre offers everything from an H&M clothing store to the Feltrinelli International bookshop.

Most food shops are closed on Wednesday afternoons, while some non-food shops stay shut on Monday mornings. During high season (which in Venice includes Carnevale in February/March, Easter, the summer season from June to October, and the four weeks leading up to Christmas) many shops abandon their lunchtime closing and stay open all day, even opening on Sundays.

It pays to be sceptical about the hours posted on the doors of smaller shops: opening times are often determined by volume of trade or personal whim. If you want to be sure of not finding the shutters drawn, call before you set out.

TAX REBATES

If you are not an EU citizen, remember to keep your official receipt (*scontrino*) as you are entitled to a rebate on **IVA** (sales tax) paid on purchases of personal goods costing more than €155, as long as they leave the country unused and are bought from a shop that provides this service. Make sure that there is a sign displayed in the window and also ask for the form that you'll need to show at customs upon departure. For more information about customs, see the Italian government website (www.agenzia dogane.it), which has a section in English.

ART SUPPLIES

Arcobaleno
San Marco 3457, calle delle Botteghe (041 523 6818). Vaporetto Sant'Angelo. **Open** 9am-12.30pm, 4-7.30pm Mon-Fri; 9am-12.30pm Sat. **No credit cards. Map** p323 F7.
Arcobaleno stocks a vast assortment of artists' pigments. As well as art supplies, they carry all the basics in hardware, light bulbs and detergents.

Cartoleria Accademia
Dorsoduro 1044, campiello Calbo (041 520 7086). Vaporetto Accademia. **Open** 8am-1pm, 3.30-7pm Mon-Fri; 8am-1pm Sat. **No credit cards. Map** p323 E9.

CONSUME

Beads by Attombri

Venetian jewellery originals.

Underneath the arches at the north-western foot of the Rialto, jeweller-brothers Stefano and Daniele **Attombri** (*see p201*) have been peddling their sumptuous wares since the early 1990s; the showroom across the Grand Canal in campo San Maurizio is a recent addition.

These self-taught designers create intricate pieces combining metal wire and antique Venetian glass beads. Not only are the designs – ranging from minimalist bracelets to jaw-dropping necklaces – unique; branching out from their antiques-only creations, the brothers have taken to adding custom-made one-off blown glass cameos of their own design into their jewellery. The use of non-nickel metal means that even those with sensitive skin can indulge. Not content with confining themselves to trinkets and baubles, they also produce interior design pieces, including mirrors and lamps.

The showrooms may be small, but the brothers' stake in the market is expanding. Their work is sold from New York to California, and their creations adorn the necks of Hollywood stars. In 2005, they made their British TV debut, appearing on a Trinny and Susannah *What Not to Wear* holiday special, with the two sartorial despots waxing lyrical about Attombri gems. However, it's not just the BBC fashion police who love their work: in 2006, they garnered the New Talents award at the Milan Design Fair, thanks to their 'irreverent and transgressive' designs. Go to the store and let them drape their beady wonders around you.

In the business since 1810, small but well-stocked Cartoleria Accademia carries a wide range of artists' supplies. Open mornings only in August.
Other locations Dorsoduro 1097, rio di San Trovaso (041 528 5283).

Testolini
San Marco 4744-6, calle dei Fabbri (041 522 3085/www.testolini.it). Vaporetto Rialto.
Open 9am-7.30pm Mon-Sat. **Credit** AmEx, DC, MC, V. **Map** p323 H6.
Testolini carries stationery, backpacks, briefcases, calendars and supplies for both art and office. The staff can be on the cool side but the choice is huge... by Venetian standards.
▶ *For fine stationery as a gift idea, see p204.*

BOOKS & MAGAZINES
English-language

Most of the bookshops listed below have a limited selection of English books; **Libreria Mondadori** and **Cafoscarina 3** have the widest choice. International newspapers and magazines can be found at *edicole* (newsstands; *see p301* **Foreign press**).

General

★ Libreria Mondadori
San Marco 1345, salizada San Moisè (041 522 2193/www.libreriamondadorivenezia.it). Vaporetto San Marco Vallaresso. **Open** 10am-7.30pm Mon-Sat; 11am-7.30pm Sun. **Credit** AmEx, MC, V. **Map** p323 H7.
Venice's only mega-bookshop sprawls over three floors. The ground floor is reserved for exhibits, book signings, events and courses of various kinds. Upstairs, there's a selection of books in English.

Specialist

Alberto Bertoni – Libreria
San Marco 3637B, calle de la Mandola (041 522 9583/www.bertonilibri.com). Vaporetto Sant'Angelo. **Open** 9am-1pm, 3-7.30pm Mon-Sat. **Credit** MC, V. **Map** p323 G7.
Just off calle de la Mandola (look for the display case marking the turn-off), this well-hidden cavern is home to art books, exhibition catalogues and the like, all with significant reductions off cover prices.
Other locations San Marco 4718, calle dei Fabbri (041 522 4615).

Cafoscarina
Dorsoduro 3259, campiello degli Squellini (041 240 4801/www.cafoscarina.it). Vaporetto Ca' Rezzonico or San Tomà. **Open** 9am-1pm, 2.30-7pm Mon-Fri; 10am-1pm Sat. **Credit** MC, V. **Map** p322 D7.

CONSUME

Filippi Editore Venezia.

This is the official bookstore of the Università Ca' Foscari, selling mostly scholarly texts on a wide variety of topics. On the other side of the campiello (Dorsoduro 3224) is Cafoscarina 3, which stocks a good selection of books in English.
► *If you'd rather read without buying, visit the Università di Ca' Foscari library; see p301.*

Fantoni Libri Arte
San Marco 4119, salizada San Luca (041 522 0700). Vaporetto Rialto. **Open** 10am-8pm Mon-Fri; 10am-1pm, 4.30-7.30pm Sat. **Credit** AmEx, DC, MC, V. **Map** p323 G7.
Beautifully illustrated art, architecture, design, photography and textile books, mostly in Italian. There's also a small selection of cookbooks and works on Venice in English.

★ Filippi Editore Venezia
Castello 5284, calle Casseleria (041 523 6916). Vaporetto San Zaccaria. **Open** 9am-12.30pm, 3-7.30pm Mon-Sat. **Credit** MC, V. **Map** p324 J7.
Venice's longest-running publishing house has over 400 titles on Venetian history and folklore – all limited editions in Italian.
► *To read up on Venice's history, see pp14-26.*

Libreria Marco Polo
Castello 5469, salizada San Lio (041 522 6343/ www.libreriamarcopolo.com). Vaporetto Rialto. **Open** 9.30am-1pm, 3-7.30pm Mon-Sat. **Credit** AmEx, DC, MC, V. **Map** p324 J6.
This friendly bookstore specialises in travel, from guides and maps to works of fiction. There's a good selection of guidebooks and fiction in English.

Libreria Toletta
& Toletta Studio
Dorsoduro 1214, calle Toletta (041 523 2034).
Vaporetto Accademia or Ca' Rezzonico. **Open**
9.30am-7.30pm Mon-Sat; 3.30-7.30pm Sun.
Credit AmEx, DC, MC, V. **Map** p322 D8.
Toletta offers 20-40% off the usual retail prices.
Italian classics, art, cookery, children's books and
history (mostly in Italian) all feature, along with a
vast assortment of dictionaries and reference
books. Next door is the Toletta Studio, which specialises in architecture. Toletta Cube (address
below; closed at lunch, and Sun from June to Aug)
is their newest shop, just across the calle, and it carries art and photography books as well as posters,
cards and gadgets.
Other locations Dorsoduro 1175, calle Toletta
(041 241 5660).

Studium
San Marco 337C, calle Canonica (041 522
2382). Vaporetto San Zaccaria. **Open** 9am-
7.30pm Mon-Sat; 9.30am-1pm, 2-6pm Sun.
Credit AmEx, DC, MC, V. **Map** p324 J7.
This shop stocks a wide selection of works on
Venice, as well as travel books and novels in
English. The shop's true speciality is revealed as
you step into the back room, which is filled with
theology studies, icons and prayer books.

ELECTRONICS
& PHOTOGRAPHY

For information about mobile phone hire,
see p212 **Travellers' Needs**.

Interpress Photo
San Polo 365, campo delle Beccarie (041 528
6978). Vaporetto Rialto Mercato or San Silvestro.
Open 9am-12.30pm, 3.30-7.30pm Mon-Sat.
Credit DC, MC, V. **Map** p321 G5.
This is definitely one of the cheapest places in
Venice for film development. The shop also provides
one-hour service, passport photographs and photo-
copies. A small selection of authentic Murano glass
is on sale alongside sunglasses.

FASHION

All of the big-name fashion boutiques (such
as **Armani, Prada, Gucci** and so on) are
clustered around four streets in the vicinity
of piazza San Marco: calle Vallaresso; salizada
San Moisè and its continuation, calle larga
XXII Marzo; calle Goldoni; and the Mercerie
(*see p204* **Inside Track**). If you've seen it all
before, the shops listed below offer something
a little different.

For lace-work and linens, *see p212*.

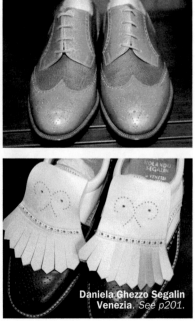

Daniela Ghezzo Segalin
Venezia. *See p201.*

CONSUME

Carteria Tassotti. See p204.

General

Araba Fenice
San Marco 1822, Frezzeria (041 522 0664).
Vaporetto Giglio or San Marco Vallaresso.
Open 9.30am-7.30pm Mon-Sat. **Credit** AmEx,
DC, MC, V. **Map** p323 H6.
A classic yet original line of women's clothing made
exclusively for this boutique, plus jewellery in ebony
and mother-of-pearl.
▶ *For more jewellery stores, see p199.*

Diesel
San Marco 5315-6, salizada Pio X (041 241 1937/
www.diesel.com). Vaporetto Rialto. **Open** 10am-
7.30pm Mon-Sat; 11am-7pm Sun. **Credit** AmEx,
DC, MC, V. **Map** p324 H6.
This well-known Veneto-based company's kooky,
club-wise, lifestyle-based styles have invaded
Europe and North America; its hipper-than-hip store
is a landmark on the Venetian shopping scene.

★ Hibiscus
San Polo 1060-61, ruga Rialto/calle dell'Olio
(041 520 8989). Vaporetto San Silvestro.
Open 9.30am-7.30pm Mon-Sat; 11am-7pm Sun.
Credit AmEx, DC, MC, V. **Map** p321 G6.
Viaggio nei colori – a voyage into colour – is the
Hibiscus motto, demonstrated in clothing, jewellery,
handmade scarves, bags and ceramics with an eth-
nic flair. Not cheap, but there are some unique finds.

★ Ottico Fabbricatore
San Marco 4773, calle dell'Ovo (041 522 5263/
www.otticofabbricatore.com). Vaporetto Rialto.
Open 9am-12.30pm, 3.30-7.30pm Mon-Sat;
11am-7pm Sun. **Credit** AmEx, DC, MC, V.
Map p323 H6.
See p206 **Profile**.

Pot-Pourrì
San Marco 1810, ramo dei Fuseri (041 241
0990/www.potpourri.it). Vaporetto San Marco
Vallaresso. **Open** 3.30-7.30pm Mon; 10am-1pm,
3.30-7.30pm Tue-Sat. **Credit** AmEx, DC, MC, V.
Map p323 G7.
Walking into this shop is like stepping into an elegant friend's bedroom. Clothes are draped over armchairs or hang from wardrobe doors while charming
knick-knacks cover the dressing table. This faux-
boudoir houses designers such as Cristina Effe and
Marzi as well as homewares. Open daily from May
to July and Sept to Oct.

Used & vintage

Laura Crovato
San Marco 2995, calle delle Botteghe (041 520
4170). Vaporetto Sant'Angelo. **Open** 4-7.30pm
Mon; 11am-1pm, 4-7.30pm Tue-Sat. **Credit** DC,
MC, V. **Map** p323 F7.

Nestling between expensive galleries and antique shops, Laura Crovato offers a selection of used clothes and a sprinkling of new items, including raw-silk shirts and scarves, costume jewellery and sunglasses.

FASHION ACCESSORIES & SERVICES

See also p198 **Hibiscus**.

★ 3856

Dorsoduro 3749, calle San Pantalon (041 720 595). Vaporetto San Tomà. **Open** 10am-7.30pm Tue-Sat. **Credit** AmEx, DC, MC, V. **Map** p32D6.
This boutique is particularly popular with fashion-conscious students. Jewellery, scarves and bags sit alongside clothes and Georgina Goodman shoes.

Monica Daniele

San Polo 2235, calle Scaleter (041 524 6242/www.monicadaniele.com). Vaporetto San Silvestro or San Stae. **Open** 9am-6pm Mon-Sat. **Credit** AmEx, MC, V. **Map** p321 E5.
This odd little shop specialises in *tabarri* (traditional Venetian cloaks) and hats, from panamas to stylish creations by the shop's owner.

ZaZú

San Polo 2750, calle dei Saoneri (041 715 426). Vaporetto San Tomà. **Open** 2.30-7.30pm Mon; 10am-1.30pm, 2.30-7.30pm Tue-Sat. **Credit** AmEx, DC, MC, V. **Map** p321 E6.
Clothing and jewels from the East that are very wearable in the West. There are handbags and other accessories as well.

Carnevale costume rentals

For shops selling masks, *see p207.*

Atelier Pietro Longhi

San Polo 2671, ramo secondo Saoner (041 714 478/www.pietrolonghi.com). Vaporetto San Tomà. **Open** 10am-12.30pm, 3-7.30pm Mon-Fri; 10am-12.30pm Sat. **Credit** AmEx, DC, MC, V. **Map** p321 E6.

THE BEST
CARNEVALE SUPPLIERS

For great costumes
Atelier Pietro Longhi. *See above.*

For authentic cloaks
Monica Daniele. *See above.*

For the essential mask
Tragicomica. *See p207.*

It costs between €160 and €600 to rent an outfit for the first day; each additional day is half-price. The shop offers discounts for groups.
▶ *For more about Venice's famous Carnevale celebrations, see p217 Profile.*

Nicolao Atelier

Cannaregio 2590, fondamenta della Misericordia (041 520 7051/www.nicolao.com). Vaporetto Guglie. **Open** 9am-1pm, 2-6pm Mon-Fri. **Credit** DC, MC, V. **Map** p321 G3.
A very simple costume rents from €150 per day; the more elaborate ones can go up to as much as €300 a day. There is, however, a reduction for each additional hire day thereafter.

Cleaning & repairs

Daniela Ghezzo Segalin Venezia and **Giovanna Zanella** (for both, *see p201*) also do shoe repairs. Many haberdashery shops will do clothing repairs.

Calzolaio Pietro Rizzi

Dorsoduro 3799B, calle della Scuola (340 932 4268). Vaporetto San Tomà. **Open** 8am-1pm, 3-7.30pm Mon-Fri. **No credit cards.** **Map** p322 D6.
One of the few remaining shops in Venice that repairs shoes: a heel job costs €6-€7 for women's heels and €12 for men's.

Centro Pulisecco

Cannaregio 6262D, calle della Testa (041 522 5011). Vaporetto Ca' d'Oro. **Open** 8.30am-12.30pm, 3-7pm Mon-Fri. **No credit cards.** **Map** p324 J5.
Centro Pulisecco offers dry-cleaning only. Trousers cost €3.20, jackets €4 and sweaters €2.50. An express service is available.
Other locations Cannaregio 1749, rio terà del Cristo (041 718 020).

Hats

See above **Monica Daniele**.

Jewellery

Shops such as **Nardi** and **Missiaglia** in piazza San Marco stock the city's most impressive and expensive jewellery, and **Cartier** (Mercerie San Zulian) and **Bulgari** (calle larga XXII Marzo) also have outlets in Venice. The smaller shops on the Rialto bridge offer more affordable silver and gold chains and bracelets sold by weight, and you will find handmade items in workshops far from the chi-chi areas of town.
For glass beads, *see p205. See also p207* **Marina & Susanna Sent**.

CONSUME

★ Attombri
*San Polo 74, sottoportego degli Orafi (041
521 2524/www.attombri.com). Vaporetto San
Silvestro.* **Open** 9.30am-1pm, 2.30-7pm Mon-Sat.
Credit AmEx, DC, MC, V. **Map** p321 H5.
See p194 **Beads by Attombri.**
Other locations San Marco 2668A, campo
San Maurizio (041 521 0789).

Laberintho
*San Polo 2236, calle del Scaleter (041 710 017/
www.laberintho.it). Vaporetto San Stae or San
Tomà.* **Open** 9.30am-1pm, 2.30-7pm Tue-Sat.
Credit AmEx, DC, MC, V. **Map** p321 E5.
A pair of young goldsmiths runs this tiny *bottega*,
which specialises in inlaid stones. In addition to
the one-of-a-kind rings, earrings and necklaces on
display, they will produce made-to-order pieces.
Other locations San Marco 5468, calle della
Bissa (041 522 5624).

Sigfrido Cipolato
*Castello 5336, Casselleria (041 522 8437).
Vaporetto Rialto.* **Open** 11am-12.30pm Mon;
11am-7.30pm Tue-Sat. **Credit** AmEx, DC,
MC, V. **Map** p324 J6.
This jeweller painstakingly carves ebony to recre-
ate the famous Moors' heads brooches and earrings.

Shoes & bags

The big names in leather – **Bruno Magli,
Fratelli Rossetti** and **Furla**, to name but
a few – are all located around piazza San Marco.
For something completely different, try one
of the following.

★ Daniela Ghezzo Segalin Venezia
*San Marco 4365, calle dei Fuseri (041 522
2115). Vaporetto Rialto or San Marco Vallaresso.*
Open 10am-12.30pm, 3-7pm Mon-Fri; 10am-1pm
Sat. **Credit** AmEx, DC, MC, V. **Map** p323 G7.
The shoemaking tradition that was established by
'the Cobbler of Venice', Rolando Segalin, continues

through his apprentice. Of the 250 or so models
handcrafted here a year, some of the most interesting creations are on display in the window, including an extraordinary pair of gondola shoes. A pair
of Ghezzo's creations will set you back anything
between €650 and €1,800. Repairs are done as well.
Photo p197.

Francis Model
*San Polo 773A, ruga Rialto/ruga del Ravano
(041 521 2889). Vaporetto Rialto Mercato or
San Silvestro.* **Open** 9.30am-7.30pm Mon-Sat;
10.30am-6.30pm Sun. **Credit** AmEx, DC, MC, V.
Map p321 G6.
Handbags and briefcases are produced in this tiny
bottega by a father-and-son team.

Giovanna Zanella
*Castello 5641, calle Carminati (041 523 5500).
Vaporetto Rialto.* **Open** 9.30am-1pm, 3-7pm Mon-
Sat. **Credit** AmEx, DC, MC, V. **Map** p324 J6.
Venetian designer-cobbler Giovanna Zanella creates
a fantastic line of handmade shoes in an extraordinary variety of styles and colours. A pair of shoes
costs €450 to €1,000. There are bags, hats and a line
of gloriously coloured clothes too.

★ Mori & Bozzi
*Cannaregio 2367, rio terà Maddalena (041 715
261). Vaporetto San Marcuola.* **Open** 9.30am-
7.30pm daily. Closed Sun in July & Aug. **Credit**
AmEx, DC, MC, V. **Map** p321 F3.
Shoes for the coolest of the cool: whatever the latest
fad – pointy or square – it's here. There are enough
trendy names and designer-inspired footwear to
please the Carrie Bradshaw in us all.

FOOD & DRINK
Drinks

Bacari and *enoteche*, where the focus is more
on sitting down to drink, are covered in the
Cafés, Bars & Gelaterie chapter; *see pp182-192.*

Bottiglieria Colonna
*Castello 5595, calle della Fava (041 528 5137).
Vaporetto Rialto.* **Open** 9am-1pm, 4-8pm Mon-
Sat. **Credit** MC, V. **Map** p324 H6.
Helpful staff will give advice on the extensive range
of local and regional wines on offer, and prepare
travel boxes or arrange for shipping.
▶ *For a primer on the vintages you're likely
to find, and the main labels in north-eastern
Italy, see p178 Profile.*

★ Vinaria Nave de Oro
*Dorsoduro 3664, campo Santa Margherita (041
522 2693). Vaporetto Ca' Rezzonico.* **Open** 9am-
1pm, 5-8pm Mon, Tue, Thur-Sat; 9am-1pm Wed.
No credit cards. Map p322 D7.

Cioccolato

Chocolate, chocolate, chocolate.

Although culinary Venice is famous for all things fishy, the sweet-toothed visitor needn't despair. You can feed your cocoa habit at two *ciocolaterie* that would put *Chocolat*'s Vianne Rocher to shame.

VizioVirtù (pictured; *see p204*), at the San Tomà vaporetto stop, serves up gluttonous pleasures. Here, you can witness chocolate being made while nibbling on a spicy praline or sipping an iced chocolate. This cornucopia of cocoa has unusual delights such as blocks of chocolate Parmesan, and cocoa *tagliatelle* (the chef recommends teaming it with game sauces). The shop also caters to diabetic chocaholics. If you're looking for something special, the Willy Wonka of Venice will tailor-make it for you.

Dolceamaro (the name translates as 'bitter-sweet'; *see p203*) is tucked away underneath the arches between campo San Bartolomeo and San Lio. Choc delights range from 100 per cent cocoa chocolate slabs for fundamentalists to a beautifully tailored man's shirt made entirely from milk chocolate. In colder weather, the hot chocolate is a must: get an espresso-sized shot of this dark gloopy delight to boost your energy levels after a deep midwinter sightseeing session. Run by the erstwhile owner of renowned bar Un Mondo diVino (*see p188*), the store also offers a range of fine wines. Pop in for a sweet, rather than bitter-sweet, experience.

Bring your own bottles here and the staff will fill them with anything from pinot grigio to merlot. For something different, try *torbolino*, a sweet and cloudy first-pressing white wine.
Other locations Castello 5786B, calle del Mondo Nuovo (041 523 3056); Cannaregio 1370, rio terà San Leonardo (041 719 695); via Lepanto 24D, Lido (041 276 0055).

Vino e... Vini

Castello 3565-6, salizada Pignater (041 521 0184). Vaporetto Arsenale. **Open** 9am-1pm, 5-8pm Mon-Sat. **Credit** AmEx, MC, V. **Map** p325 M7.

Vino e... Vini stocks a wide-ranging selection of major Italian wines, as well as French, Spanish, Californian and even Lebanese vintages.
▶ *For more about local vintages, see p178 Profile.*

General

Grocery shops (*alimentari*) offer all the usual staples from around Italy, as well as Venetian specialities such as *baccalà mantecato* (a delectable spread made with dried cod) and *mostarda veneziana* (a sweet-and-sour sauce made with dried fruit). Butchers and bakers are thin on the ground.

★ Aliani Gastronomia

San Polo 654, ruga Rialto/ruga vecchia San Giovanni (041 522 4913). Vaporetto Rialto Mercato or San Silvestro. **Open** 8am-1pm, 5-7.30pm Tue-Sat. **Credit** MC, V. **Map** p321 G5.

A traditional grocery that stocks a selection of cold meats and cheeses from every part of Italy, plus an assortment of prepared dishes and roast meats.

Billa

Dorsoduro 1491, Zattere (041 522 6187). Vaporetto San Basilio. **Open** 8.30am-8pm Mon-Sat; 9am-8pm Sun. **Credit** AmEx, MC, V. **Map** p322 C9.

Open seven days a week, this supermarket on the Zattere stocks fruit, vegetables and other staples at lower prices than most *alimentari*.

Other locations Cannaregio 3027M, calle delle Contiere (041 524 4786); Lido, Gran Viale (041 526 2898).

Coop

Santa Croce 506A, piazzale Roma (041 296 0621). Vaporetto Piazzale Roma. **Open** 8.30am-8pm daily. **Credit** MC, V. **Map** p320 B5.

The Coop supermarket offers goods at good prices. This branch caters to tourists, with a handy salad bar, snacks and Venetian specialities conveniently lumped together. The Coop also stocks organic and fair-trade products. The branches listed below are closed on Sunday.

Other locations Santa Croce 1493, campo San Giacomo dell'Orio (041 275 0218); Giudecca 484, calle dell'Olio (041 241 3381).

Punto Sma

Dorsoduro 3017, campo Santa Margherita (041 522 6780). Vaporetto Ca'Rezzonico. **Open** 8.30am-8pm Mon-Sat. **Credit** DC, MC, V. **Map** p322 D7.

Prices may not be all that competitive in this small, fully stocked supermarket, but its central location certainly makes it handy.

Markets

For fruit, vegetables, meat and fish, the market that's held Monday to Saturday morning at the north-western foot of the Rialto bridge (*see p98*) is difficult to beat.

The market that sets up halfway along via Garibaldi in the eastern Castello every morning (except Sunday) is a more sedate affair.

Specialist

Venetians are famous for their sweet tooth. There is, therefore, an extraordinary variety of calorific delights to devour while strolling through the *calli*; for cafés, bars, *pasticcerie* (where you can nibble your pastry with a coffee) and *gelaterie, see pp182-192.*

Cibele

Cannaregio 1823, campiello dell'Anconeta (041 524 2113). Vaporetto San Marcuola. **Open** 8.30am-12.45pm, 4-7.45pm Mon-Sat. **Credit** MC, V. **Map** p321 F3.

A full range of natural health foods, cosmetics and medicines are on sale here. Staff will also prepare blends of herbal teas and remedies.

Dolceamaro

San Marco 5415, sottoportego de la Bissa (041 241 3045). Vaporetto Rialto. **Open** 10.30am-7.30pm daily. **Credit** MC, V.
Map p321 H6.

See p202 **Cioccolato.**

★ Drogheria Mascari

San Polo 381, ruga degli Spezieri (041 522 9762). Vaporetto Rialto Mercato or San Silvestro. **Open** 8am-1pm, 4-7.30pm Mon-Sat. **No credit cards. Map** p321 G5.

Mascari is the best place in the city to find exotic spices, nuts, dried fruit and mushrooms, as well as oils and wines from different regions in Italy.

Kosher Tevà

Cannaregio 1242, campo del Ghetto Vecchio (041 524 4486). Vaporetto Guglie. **Open** 10am-6.30pm Mon-Fri, Sun. **No credit cards**. **Map** p321 E2.

In the heart of the Ghetto, Tevà produces excellent breads, biscuits and cakes… all kosher, exactly as the shop's name implies.

▶ *To find out about the history of the Ghetto and Venice's Jewish community, see p93.*

Marchini Pasticceria

San Marco 676, calle Spadaria (041 522 9109/www.golosessi.com). Vaporetto Rialto or San Zaccaria. **Open** 9am-8pm daily. Closed Tue in summer. **Credit** AmEx, DC, MC, V. **Map** p324 J7.

Probably Venice's most famous sweet shop, and certainly the most expensive, Marchini has exquisite chocolate, including *Le Baute Veneziane* – small chocolates in the form of Carnevale masks. Cakes can be ordered.

★ Pronto Pesce Pronto

San Polo 319, calle delle Beccarie, (041 822 0298). Vaporetto Rialto or Rialto Mercato. **Open** 9am-2.30pm, 5-8pm Tue-Sat. **No credit cards. Map** p321 G5.

It can be hard getting a table at the tiny and hopelessly popular Alle Testiere restaurant but don't despair. For this deli, the same team produces exquisite seafood pasta sauces and other specialities to take away. Stop in here for provisions for that gourmet picnic.

▶ *If you do want to chance getting a table, head across the Grand Canal to Alle Testiere; see p167.*

CONSUME

Rialto Bio Center

San Polo 366, campo delle Beccarie (041 523 9515). Vaporetto Rialto Mercato or San Silvestro. **Open** 8.30am-1pm, 4.30-8pm Mon-Sat. **Credit** AmEx, DC, MC, V. **Map** p321 G5.

A little bit of just about everything can be found in this small health food shop, from wholewheat pasta, grains, honey and freshly baked breads to natural cosmetics and incense.

Rizzo Regali

San Marco 4739, calle dei Fabbri (041 522 5811). Vaporetto Rialto. **Open** 9am-8pm Mon-Sat. **Credit** MC, V. **Map** p323 H7.

This old-fashioned shop sells traditional cakes, sweets and chocolates. For *pesce d'aprile* (April Fool's Day), you can buy bags of foil-wrapped chocolate goldfish. If you can't find the *torrone* (nougat) you're looking for here, then it doesn't exist.

VizioVirtù

San Polo 2898A, calle del Campaniel (041 275 0149/www.viziovirtu.com). Vaporetto San Tomà. **Open** 10am-7.30pm daily (with variations in July). **Credit** MC, V. **Map** p323 E7.
See p202 **Cioccolato.**

GIFTS & SOUVENIRS

For Carnevale masks, *see p207*; for lace-work and linens, *see p212*; for fabrics, *see p209*; for glass beads and other glassware, *see p205* and *p136* **Murano Glass.**

Carteria Tassotti

San Marco 5472, calle de la Bissa (041 528 1881/www.tassotti.it). Vaporetto Rialto. **Open** 10am-1pm, 2-7pm daily. **Credit** AmEx, MC, V. **Map** p323 H6.

This Bassano-based family business has a charming selection of greeting cards, decorative paper, diaries and notebooks. Wedding invitations and business cards can also be ordered. *Photo p198.*

★ Ebrû

San Marco 3471, campo Santo Stefano (041 523 8830/www.albertovallese-ebru.com). Vaporetto Accademia or Sant'Angelo. **Open** 10am-1.30pm, 2.30-7pm Mon-Wed; 10am-1pm, 2.30-7pm Thur-Sat; 11am-6pm Sun. **Credit** AmEx, MC, V. **Map** p323 F8.

Beautiful, marbled handcrafted paper, scarves and ties. These are Venetian originals, whose imitators can be found in other shops around town.
▶ *For more fashion accessories, see p199.*

Le Forcole di Saverio Pastor

Dorsoduro 341, fondamenta Soranzo de la Fornace (041 522 5699/www.forcole.com). Vaporetto Salute. **Open** 8.30am-12.30pm, 2-6pm Mon-Fri. **Credit** AmEx, MC, V. **Map** p323 F9.

The place to come when you need a new *forcola* or pair of oars for your favourite gondola. Saverio Pastor is one of only three recognised *marangon* (oar-makers) in Venice; he specialises in making the elaborate walnut-wood rests (*forcole*) that are the symbols of the gondolier's trade. There are also bookmarks, postcards and some books (in English) on Venetian boatworks.
▶ *To learn more about the boatbuilding trade, head to the Museo Storico Navale; see p85.*

Gilberto Penzo

San Polo 2681, calle II dei Saoneri (041 719 372/www.veniceboats.com). Vaporetto San Tomà. **Open** 9.30am-12.30pm, 3-6pm Mon-Sat. **Credit** MC, V. **Map** p321 E6.

Gilberto Penzo creates astonishingly detailed models of gondolas, sandolos, topos and *vaporetti*. Inexpensive kits are also on sale – if you would like to practise the fine art of shipbuilding yourself.

Il Pavone

Dorsoduro 721, fondamenta Venier dei Leoni (041 523 4517). Vaporetto Accademia. **Open** 9.30am-1.30pm, 2.30-6.30pm daily. **Credit** DC, MC, V. **Map** p323 F9.

This is a place to seek out for handmade paper with floral motifs in a variety of colours. Il Pavone also stocks boxes, picture frames, key chains and other objects, all decorated in the same style. Quality products at decent prices.
▶ *For everyday stationery, see p193 Art Supplies.*

★ Signor Blum

Dorsoduro 2840, campo San Barnaba (041 522 6367/www.signorblum.com). Vaporetto Ca' Rezzonico. **Open** 10am-7pm daily. **Credit** AmEx, DC, MC, V. **Map** p322 D8.

Mr Blum's colourful, handmade wooden puzzles of Venetian *palazzi*, gondolas and animals make great gifts for children and adults alike.

INSIDE TRACK
THE MAIN DRAG

The **Mercerie** (*see p72*) – the maze of crowded, narrow alleyways leading from piazza San Marco to the Rialto – and the streets known collectively as the **Frezzeria**, which wind between La Fenice (*see p76*) and piazza San Marco, have been the main retail areas in this city for the past 600 years or so.

The densest concentration of big-name fashion outlets can be found around calle larga XXII Marzo, just west of the piazza, where top names such as Prada, Fendi, Versace and Gucci have all staked territory for their boutiques.

Tragicomica. *See p207.*

Florists

Fioreia San Rocco

San Polo 3127, campo San Rocco (041 524 4271). Vaporetto San Tomà. **Open** 8.30am-12.30pm, 3.30-7.30pm Mon-Sat; 9am-12.30pm Sun. **Credit** AmEx, MC, V. **Map** p322 D6.
Alessandra Gallenda's shop can provide anything from a single rose to a hothouse plant. The shop is affiliated to Interflora and will deliver. Prices for a bouquet start at around €15.

Glass beads

Antichità Claudia Zaggia

Dorsoduro 1195, calle Toletta (041 522 3159). Vaporetto Accademia. **Open** 9.30am-1pm, 3.30-7pm Mon-Sat. **No credit cards.** **Map** p322 D8.
Beautiful handpainted antique glass beads that can be purchased individually or made into jewellery. There's also a good selection of antiques and lace.
▶ *For shops specialising in lace-work, see p212.*

Anticlea Antiquariato

Castello 4719A, calle San Provolo (041 528 6946). Vaporetto San Zaccaria. **Open** 10am-1.30pm, 2-7pm Mon-Sat. **Credit** AmEx, MC, V. **Map** p324 K7.
Packed with curious antique treasures, as well as an outstanding selection of Venetian glass beads.
▶ *For general antique shops, see p208.*

★ Perle e Dintorni

San Marco 3740, calle della Mandola (041 520 5068). Vaporetto Sant'Angelo. **Open** 9.30am-7.30pm Mon-Sat; noon-7pm Sun. **Credit** AmEx, DC, MC, V. **Map** p323 G7.
Here, you can buy bead jewellery or assemble your own unique pieces, choosing from a vast assortment of glass beads, most of which are new versions based on antique designs.

Glassware

Glass and Venice are well-nigh synonymous: the city was famous for its exquisite glassware even before the industry shifted to Murano in 1291. While much of the production takes place there, glass can still be purchased in Venice itself.

The shops identified in this chapter are all reputable outlets. Good Venetian glass is not cheap; anything you find for under €10 is probably made in China.

For information about glass factories and shops in Murano, *see p136* **Murano Glass**. For gallery information, *see p224*.

Canestrelli

Dorsoduro 1173, calle della Toletta (041 277 0617/www.venicemirrors.com). Vaporetto Accademia. **Open** 11am-1.30pm, 3.30-7.30pm Mon-Sat. **Credit** MC, V. **Map** p322 D8.
Designer-producer Stefano Coluccio specialises in beautifully framed convex mirrors.

Profile Ottico Fabbricatore

A one-stop shop for putting together a look of effortless Italian elegance.

Ever wandered around an Italian city, wondering how Italian women appear to pull off effortless elegance so, well, effortlessly? Ask an Italian for her secret and she will tell you that it is all about the cut and the quality of the fabric. A few key pieces seemingly thrown together will create a stylish look that's hard to emulate if your usual shopping haunts are budget high-street clothing shops.

These key pieces tend to include great sunglasses, something in cashmere and a fabulous bag. If this is the look you're after, then look no further than the über-stylish **Ottico Fabbricatore** (*see p198*). As the name suggests, this ultra-modern shop specialises in designer eyewear – the kind you won't find anywhere else in Italy, with extraordinary frames in anything from buffalo horn to titanium. Pop in for a pair of sunglasses, or bring along your prescription and treat yourself to glasses the likes of which chain-store opticians can only dream of.

Run by a husband-and-wife team – optician Francesco Lincetto and designer Marianna Leardini – the boutique also sells gossamer-like cashmere and sensual silk apparel. The couple have recently extended their store, adding an upstairs space dedicated to clothing, along with a selection of luxurious bags that

were designed by Marianna in materials ranging from calfskin to ostrich. Ottico Fabbricatore may not be able to turn you into a perfectly groomed Italian, but it will certainly help you make serious inroads into your holiday cash while trying.

Genninger Studio

Dorsoduro 2793A, calle del Traghetto (041 522 5565/www.genningerstudio.com). Vaporetto Ca' Rezzonico. **Open** 10am-1.30pm, 2.30-7pm Mon-Sat. **Credit** AmEx, MC, V. **Map** p322 D8.

Flame-worked and blown beads, custom jewellery, knick-knacks, lighting and mirrors designed by Leslie Ann Genninger. A contemporary take on Venetian luxury and decadence in beautiful surroundings on the Grand Canal.

L'Isola

San Marco 1468, campo San Moisè (041 523 1973/www.lisola.com). Vaporetto San Marco Vallaresso. **Open** 9am-7pm daily. **Credit** AmEx, DC, MC, V. **Map** p323 H8.

Carlo Moretti's showroom showcases his own elegant clear and coloured glass designs: some unique pieces and signed and numbered editions by Moretti and a few selected artists.

Marina & Susanna Sent

Dorsoduro 669, campo san Vio (041 520 8136). Vaporetto Accademia. **Open** 10am-6pm daily. **Credit** AmEx, MC, V. **Map** p323 F9.

Venice's best contemporary glass jewellery is created by the Sent sisters. There's also a good selection of the work of the contemporary design house Arcade.
► *See also p136 Murano Glass.*

★ Vittorio Costantini

Cannaregio 5311, calle del Fumo (041 522 2265/www.vittoriocostantini.com). Vaporetto Fondamente Nove. **Open** 9.15am-1pm, 2.15-5.30pm Mon-Fri. **Credit** MC, V. **Map** p324 J4.

Vittorio is internationally renowned as one of the most original Venetian lamp workers. His intricate animals, insects, fish and birds are instantly recognisable for their fine workmanship.

Masks

★ Ca' Macana

Dorsoduro 3172, calle delle Botteghe (041 520 3229/www.camacana.com). Vaporetto Ca' Rezzonico. **Open** 10am-6pm daily. **Credit** AmEx, DC, MC, V. **Map** p322 D8.

This workshop is packed with traditional papier-mâché masks from the *Commedia dell'arte* theatre tradition. Explanations of the mask-making process, as well as courses, are given by the artist in residence.
► *For more about Venice's famous Carnevale celebrations, see p217 Profile.*

Carta Alta

Dorsoduro 2808, campo San Barnaba (041 523 8313/www.venicemaskshop.com). Vaporetto Ca' Rezzonico. **Open** 10am-2.30pm, 3.30-6pm Mon-Sat. **Credit** MC, V. **Map** p322 D8.

Though essentially a mask shop, you can also find handcrafted products such as marionettes.

MondoNovo

Dorsoduro 3063, rio terà Canal (041 528 7344/ www.mondonovomaschere.it). Vaporetto Ca' Rezzonico. **Open** 10am-6pm Mon-Sat. **Credit** MC, V. **Map** p323 D7.

Venice's best-known *mascheraio* offers an enormous variety of masks, both traditional and modern. You can also see his work at the recently restored Fenice theatre, where he worked on the sculptures.

★ Papier Mâché

Castello 5175, calle lunga Santa Maria Formosa (041 522 9995/www.papiermache.it). Vaporetto Rialto. **Open** 9am-7.30pm Mon-Sat; 10am-7pm Sun. **Credit** AmEx, DC, MC, V. **Map** p324 K6.

This workshop uses traditional techniques to create contemporary masks inspired by the works of Klimt, Kandinsky, Tiepolo and Carpaccio. They stock ceramics and painted mirrors too.

Tragicomica

San Polo 2800, calle dei Nomboli (041 721 102/www.tragicomica.it). Vaporetto San Tomà. **Open** 10am-7pm daily. **Credit** AmEx, MC, V. **Map** p323 E6.

A spellbinding collection of masks: mythological subjects, Harlequins, Columbines and Pantaloons, as well as 18th-century dandies and ladies. *Photo p205.*

HEALTH & BEAUTY
Hairdressers & barbers

Prices are *à la carte* in Italy: each dab of styling foam or puff of hairspray pushes up the bill. Most salons are closed on Mondays.

Stefano e Claudia

San Polo 1098B, riva del Vin (041 520 1913). Vaporetto San Silvestro. **Open** 9am-5pm Tue-Sat. **Credit** AmEx, MC, V. **Map** p323 G6.

The Stefano e Claudia salon is easily the most contemporary on the lagoon. Prices are high and an appointment is a must. The real bonus is that as you're getting styled, you can enjoy a beautiful view of the Grand Canal.

Tocco di Gio'

Santa Croce 661A, campo della Lana (041 718 493). Vaporetto Ferrovia. **Open** 9am-6pm Tue-Sat. **No credit cards. Map** p320 C5.

For men and women. Get a good cut at a reasonable price in a friendly atmosphere.

Opticians

Most opticians will do minor running repairs on the spot and (usually) free of charge. Designer eyewear is also available from **Ottico Fabbricatore**; *see p206* **Profile**.

CONSUME

Ottica Carraro Alessandro

San Marco 3706, calle della Mandola (041 520 4258/www.otticacarraro.it). Vaporetto Sant' Angelo. **Open** 9.30am-1pm, 3-7.30pm Mon-Sat. **Credit** AmEx, DC, MC, V. **Map** p323 G7.

Get yourself some unique and funky eyewear – the frames are exclusively produced and guaranteed for life. Ottica Carraro Alessandro offers extraordinary quality at reasonable prices.

Punto Vista (Elvio Carraro)

Cannaregio 1982, campiello Anconeta (041 720 453). Vaporetto San Marcuola. **Open** 9am-7.30pm Mon-Sat. **Credit** DC, MC, V. **Map** p321 F3.

Punto Vista stocks eyeglasses, sunglasses, contact lenses and saline solution. They also undertake walk-in eye examinations and glasses repairs.

Pharmacies

See p300.

Shops

Cosmetics and toiletries can be found in the one-stop stores (*see p202*) or in *farmacie* (pharmacies; *see p300*), although prices tend to be higher at the latter. For designer names, try smaller, more specialised *profumerie*. For herbal products of any type, such as aromatherapy oils, head for an *erboristeria*. For health food shops, *see pp203-204*.

Il Bottegon

San Polo 806, calle del Figher (041 522 3632). Vaporetto San Silvestro. **Open** 9am-12.45pm, 4-7.30pm Mon-Sat. **Credit** AmEx, MC, DC, V. **Map** p321 G5.

You'll be so overwhelmed by how much is crammed into this tiny space: as well as cosmetics and toiletries, you'll find pots, pans, rugs and general hardware. **Other locations** Castello 1311, via Garibaldi (041 521 0780).

INSIDE TRACK
TRADING IN HISTORY

In past centuries, traders of different nations each had their own *fondaco* (also spelled *fontaco* or *fondego*), a warehouse-cum-lodging. So successful in their business – and so desirous of making an impression – were the German traders in Venice that their **Fondaco dei Tedeschi** was adorned with frescoes by Titian and Giorgione. Currently home to the main post office (*see p303*), their 16th-century palazzo was bought by the Benetton group in September 2008.

L'Erbania

San Polo 1735, calle dei Botteri (041 723 215). Vaporetto Rialto Mercato, San Silvestro or San Stae. **Open** 10am-7pm Tue-Sat. **Credit** DC, MC, V. **Map** p321 G5.

A quaint shop near the Rialto where a herbalist will mix up concoctions for you. Alternatively, choose from a variety of prepared creams and perfumes.

Spas & salons

Beauty Care

San Marco 3564, calle Caotorta (041 241 0767). Vaporetto Sant'Angelo. **Open** 10am-6.30pm Tue-Sat. **Credit** AmEx, MC, V. **Map** p323 F8.

This ultra-discreet beautician offers top-to-toe care, from facials to pedicures with a bikini wax in between. A manicure will set you back €20 and a bikini wax €12. The solarium costs €1 per minute.

Segreti di Donne

Santa Croce 2163-4, calle Longa (041 244 0123). Vaporetto San Stae. **Open** 9am-7pm Tue-Fri; 9am-3pm Sat. **Credit** AmEx, MC, V. **Map** p321 F5.

This beauty centre gives you the works, with a stone massage setting you back €75. A manicure is €13 and a well-earned pedicure costs €25. The girls are friendly and the parlour is clean and quietly elegant.

HOUSE & HOME
Antiques

Antique shops can be found throughout the city, though the concentration is greatest around campo San Maurizio and calle delle Botteghe (near campo Santo Stefano). Watch out for flyers for occasional antique fairs.

Antichità Marciana

San Marco 1864, campo San Fantin (041 523 5666/www.antichitamarciana.it). Vaporetto San Marco Vallaresso. **Open** 3.30-7.30pm Mon; 9.30am-1pm, 3.30-7pm Tue-Sat. **Credit** AmEx, MC, V. **Map** p323 G7.

Primarily a purveyor of (minor) Old Master paintings, this shop also has a tasteful selection of antique baubles and a range of soft furnishing made from richly painted velvets created by the owner in her workshop. A favourite among interior designers.

Antiquus

San Marco 2973, calle delle Botteghe (041 520 6395). Vaporetto Sant'Angelo. **Open** 10am-1pm, 2-7.30pm Mon-Sat. **Credit** AmEx, DC, MC, V. **Map** p323 F7.

This charming shop has a beautiful collection of Old Master paintings, furniture, silver and antique jewellery, including Moors' heads brooches and earrings. **Other locations** Dorsoduro 873A, Fondamenta Gerardini (041 241 3725).

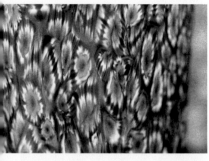

Kirei. *See p211.*

Guarinoni
San Polo 2862, calle del Mandoler (041 522 4286). Vaporetto San Tomà. **Open** 9am-noon, 3-7pm Mon-Sat. **Credit** MC, V. **Map** p323 E6.
An assortment of antique furnishings from as early as the 16th century is sold here. The shop also has a workshop that restores gilded ceilings.

Fabrics & accessories

See also p208 **Antichità Marciana.**

Arras
Dorsoduro 3235, campiello Squellini (041 522 6460/www.arrastessuti.com). Vaporetto Ca' Rezzonico. **Open** 9am-1pm, 3-7pm Mon-Sat.
Credit AmEx, DC, MC, V. **Map** p322 D7.
In this venture involving disabled people, a variety of handwoven fabrics are created in a vast range of colours and textures. These unique textiles are then worked into bags, clothing and scarves. Customised designs can be ordered.

★ Bevilacqua
San Marco 337B, ponte della Canonica (041 528 7581/www.bevilacquatessuti.com). Vaporetto San Zaccaria. **Open** 10am-7pm Mon-Sat; 10am-5pm Sun. **Credit** AmEx, DC, MC, V. **Map** p324 J7.
This diminutive shop offers exquisite examples of both hand- and machine-woven silk brocades, damasks and velvets. The Venetian textile tradition is kept alive by these local weavers, who use original 17th-century looms.
Other locations San Marco 2520, campo Santa Maria del Giglio (041 241 0662).

★ Fortuny Tessuti Artistici
Giudecca 805, fondamenta San Biagio (041 522 4078/www.fortuny.com). Vaporetto Palanca.
Open 9am-noon, 2-5pm Mon-Fri. **Credit** AmEx, MC, V. **Map** p322 B10.
This pared-back factory showroom space almost glows with the exquisite colours and patterns of original Fortuny prints. At €360 a metre, you may not be tempted to buy, but it's worth the trip just to see it.

★ Gaggio
San Marco 3441-51 calle delle Botteghe (041 522 8574/www.gaggio.it). Vaporetto San Samuele or Sant'Angelo. **Open** 10.30am-1pm, 4-6.30pm Mon-Fri; 10.30am-1pm Sat. **Credit** AmEx, DC, MC, V. **Map** p323 F7.
Emma Gaggio is a legend among seamstresses, and her sumptuous handprinted silk velvets (from €195 a metre) are used to make cushions and wall hangings as well as bags, hats, scarves and jackets.

Trois
San Marco 2666, campo San Maurizio (041 522 2905). Vaporetto Giglio. **Open** 4-7.30pm

CONSUME

Mon; 10am-1pm, 4-7.30pm Tue-Sat. **Credit** DC, MC, V. **Map** p323 F8.

This is one of the best places in *La Serenissima* to buy original Fortuny fabrics – and at considerable savings on the prices you'd find in the UK and the US (though this still doesn't make them particularly cheap). Made-to-order bead-work, masks and accessories are also available.

Venetia Studium

San Marco 2403, calle larga XXII Marzo (041 522 9281/www.venetiastudium.com). Vaporetto Giglio. **Open** 9.30am-7.40pm Mon-Sat; 10.30am-6pm Sun. **Credit** AmEx, DC, MC, V. **Map** p323 G8.

Venetia Studium stocks splendid silk pillows, lamps, scarves, handbags and other accessories in a marvellous range of colours. They're certainly not cheap, but they do make perfect gifts.

Other locations San Marco, Torre dell'Orologio (041 522 6791).

General

For glassware, *see p205*.

Ceramiche La Margherita

Santa Croce 2345, sottoportico della Siora Bettina (041 723 120/www.lamargherita venezia.com). Vaporetto San Stae. **Open** 9.30am-1pm, 3.30-7pm Mon-Sat. **Credit** AmEx, MC, V. **Map** p321 F5.

A delightful collection of handpainted terracotta designed by the owner. Plates, bowls, teapots, ornaments and mugs are all available in a variety of colours and patterns.

Cornici Trevisanello

Dorsoduro 662, campo San Vio (041 520 7779). Vaporetto Accademia. **Open** 9am-1pm, 3-7pm Mon-Fri; 9am-1pm Sat. **Credit** AmEx, MC, V. **Map** p323 F9.

This workshop is home to a father, son and daughter team that makes beautiful gilded frames, many with pearl, mirror and glass inlay. Custom orders and shipping are not a problem.

Fustat

Dorsoduro 2904, campo Santa Margherita (041 523 8504). Vaporetto Ca' Rezzonico. **Open** 9.30am-12.30pm Mon-Sat. **Credit** MC, V. **Map** p322 C7.

Madera.

The pottery is handmade by the owner in this small workshop/outlet. Demonstrations of the making of Raku (a type of Japanese pottery) and courses are also offered periodically.

★ Kirei

San Polo 219, campo Cesare Battisti (041 522 8158). Vaporetto San Silvestro. **Open** 10am-12.30pm, 4-7.30pm Mon-Sat. **Credit** AmEx, MC, V. **Map** p321 G5.

This elegant shop sells exquisite accessories for the kitchen and dining room, from Versace dinner services to Riedel glassware. *Photo p209.*

★ Madera

Dorsoduro 2762, campo San Barnaba (041 522 4181/www.maderavenezia.it). Vaporetto Ca'

Rezzonico. **Open** 10.30am-1pm, 3.30-7.30pm Tue-Sat. **Credit** AmEx, DC, MC, V. **Map** p322 D8.

Fusing minimalist design with traditional techniques, the young architect and craftswoman behind Madera creates unique objects in wood. She also sells exceptional lamps, ceramics, jewellery and textiles by other European artists.

Sabbie e Nebbie

San Polo 2768A, calle dei Nomboli (041 719 073). Vaporetto San Tomà. **Open** 10am-12.30pm, 4-7.30pm Mon-Sat. **Credit** AmEx, MC, V. **Map** p323 E6.

A beautiful selection of Italian ceramic pieces are on display here, as well as refined Japanese works. The shop also sells handmade objects (such as lamps and candlesticks) by Italian designers.

Ye Olde Shoppers

Venetian retail therapy, Renaissance-style.

If price tags in the luxurious shops around St Mark's square are making you wince, and your credit card is melting, you can take comfort in the knowledge that retail therapy was just as painful for many a shopper in Renaissance Venice.

Just like today, keeping up with fashion was a problem for cash-strapped women in *über*-trendy 16th-century Venice. One way around this was recycling expensive fabrics and clothes, à la Scarlett O'Hara, to create more up-to-date pieces. Less talented needlewomen, on the other hand, could buy on credit – but creditors often lured women who couldn't keep up with repayments into prostitution to recoup their money.

Just as you might hire a snazzy outfit for Carnevale today, Renaissance women would rent spectacular outfits for special occasions. Men also rented sumptuous get-ups, and it didn't end with clothes. Sir Henry Wotton, English ambassador to Venice in the 17th century, rented everything from a billiards table to bed sheets.

Pawnbrokers and secondhand dealers did a roaring trade in Venice. And it wasn't only the poor who tried to pawn or sell goods, though they did so in more dramatic fashion: records show impoverished men pledging their wives and children against loans. Patrician families would furnish their servants' rooms with secondhand furniture, and sometimes their own living areas as well. They also pledged or re-mortgaged more valuable items, from fine linen to jewellery, in order to rustle up some ready cash.

The position that women held in the marketplace was very different in Venice than in many other places at that time. Traveller Thomas Coryat noted in the early 17th century: 'I have observed a thing amongst Venetians that I have not a little wondered at, that their Gentlemen and greatest Senators... will come into the market, and buy their flesh, fish, fruites and other things.'

His wonderment was countered by a Venetian ambassador's astonishment when visiting London later that century: he remarked in particular on English women's 'great freedom to go out of the house without menfolk.'

Though Venetian women were often left out of the shopping experience, one woman whose shopping exploits would make a WAG weep was Isabella d'Este (1474-1539), marchioness of Mantua and a frequent visitor to Venice. As a young bride, she asked a friend in Paris to purchase jewels and fabrics on her behalf – one of the first records of mail-order shopping.

She also had a personal shopper trawling the shops in Venice for her. One thing that caught her eye on a visit to the Sensa market in St Mark's Square was 'a magnificent show of beautiful glass'; other acquisitions included gems and luxurious fabrics. Although viewed as greedy and acquisitive, her purchasing power was a sign of political and financial clout, making her one of history's most remarkable and formidable shopaholics.

CONSUME

Lace & linens

Lace can be bought on the island of Burano
(see p134), where you can watch the women
making it. Remember: if it's cheap, it's machine
made, and if it's very cheap, it almost certainly
hails from the Far East.

★ Annelie
*Dorsoduro 2748, calle lunga San Barnaba (041
520 3277). Vaporetto Ca' Rezzonico.* **Open**
9.30am-1pm, 4-7.30pm Mon-Sat. **Credit** AmEx,
DC, MC, V. **Map** p325 E2.
A delightful shop run by a delightful lady who has
a beautiful selection of sheets, tablecloths, curtains,
shirts and baby clothes, either fully embroidered or
with lace detailing. Stocks antique lace too.

Cristina Linassi
*San Marco 3537, campo Sant'Angelo (041
523 0578/www.cristinalinassi.it). Vaporetto
Sant'Angelo.* **Open** 9.30am-1pm, 2.30-7.30pm
Mon-Sat; 9.30am-1pm, 2.30-7pm Sun. **Credit**
AmEx, MC, V. **Map** p323 F7.
This tiny boutique sells hand-embroidered night-
gowns, towels and sheets made in its own workshop.
The catalogue has designs for made-to-order items.

Martinuzzi
*San Marco 67A, piazza San Marco (041 522
5068). Vaporetto San Marco Vallaresso.* **Open**
9am-7pm Mon-Sat. **Credit** AmEx, DC, MC, V.
Map p324 H8.
The oldest lace shop in Venice, Martinuzzi has
exclusive designs for bobbin lace items such as place
mats, tablecloths and linens. If you have an odd-sized
bed, not to worry – Martinuzzi will create a sheet set
especially for you. Also open Sunday in summer.

MUSIC & ENTERTAINMENT

The **Museo della Musica** sells recordings
by Vivaldi and other composers; see p76.

Nalesso
*San Marco 5537, salizada fontego dei Tedeschi
(041 522 1343). Vaporetto Rialto.* **Open** 10am-
7.30pm Mon-Sat; 11am-7pm Sun. **No credit
cards. Map** p321 H5.

INSIDE TRACK TACK

Devotees of kitsch should not miss the
stalls and shops near the train station,
where plastic gondolas, illuminated
gondolas, flashing gondolas, musical
gondolas and even gondola cigarette
lighters reign supreme. Stalls at both ends
of the Rialto bridge are also a good bet.

Specialising in classical Venetian music, Nalesso
also sells concert tickets for the Fenice and Malibran
theatres as well as for concerts in various churches.
▶ *For details of churches that regularly hold
concerts, see p240.*

TICKETS

Tickets for most events can be purchased at
Hellovenezia (041 2424) offices inside the
railway station and at piazzale Roma. Tickets
for many cultural events are sold at the **APT**'s
Palazzina Santi office (see p305). **Nalesso** also
sells tickets; see above.

Bassani
*Dorsoduro, San Basilio Fabbricata 17 (041 520
3644/www.bassani.it). Vaporetto San Basilio
or Santa Marta.* **Open** 9am-1pm, 2-6pm Mon-
Fri; 9.30am-12.30pm Sat. **Credit** AmEx, MC, V.
Map p322 A8.
Inside the port authority complex (located at the
western end of Dorsoduro), Bassani sells tickets for
concerts held in churches around town and organises walking tours, gondola rides and visits to the
islands of the lagoon. The company also functions
as a regular travel agency.
▶ *For a list of guided tour companies, see p297.*

TRAVELLERS' NEEDS

For couriers and shippers, see p298. For artists'
supplies, see p193. See also above **Bassani**.
If you need to rent a mobile phone during
your stay, try **Cellhire** (www.cellhire.com),
which can deliver phones to your hotel in
advance of your stay. However, mobile phone
companies offer cheap or free SIM cards, and
pay-as-you-go deals are quite cheap. (For more
information about mobile phones, see p304.)

CTS (Centro Turistico Studentesco)
*Dorsoduro 3252, fondamenta del Tagliapietra
(041 520 5660/www.cts.it). Vaporetto Ca'
Rezzonico or San Tomà.* **Open** 9.30am-1.30pm,
2-6pm Mon-Fri. **Credit** MC, V. **Map** p322 D7.
This travel agency caters to its own members (membership €30) and to students in general, offering dis-
count air fares and train tickets. ISICs cost €10: bring
a passport photo and a document proving you are a
student. It also has tickets to concerts, exhibitions and
the theatre at discounted prices for members.

Park View Viaggi
*Dorsoduro 3944, calle San Pantalon (041 520
0988/www.parkviaggi.it). Vaporetto San Tomà.*
Open 9am-7pm Mon-Fri. **Credit** AmEx, MC,
DC, V. **Map** p322 C6.
The staff at this travel agency are both friendly and
highly efficient. Park View has a money-changing
service too. You can purchase train tickets up to 6pm.

Arts & Entertainment

Canottieri Giudecca. *See p244.*

| Calendar | 214 |
| Profile Carnevale | 217 |

| Children | 218 |
| Lion Hunting | 219 |

| Film | 221 |
| Six Degrees of Animation | 222 |

| Galleries | 224 |

| Gay & Lesbian | 229 |

Music & Nightlife	231
Summer Festivals	232
Sounds of the Lagoon	234

Performing Arts	237
Baroque Without the Tinkle	238
Fenice Firsts	242

| Sport & Fitness | 244 |
| Shipshape | 245 |

Calendar

On land and on the water, there's a lot to celebrate in Venice.

Napoleon suppressed more than just the monasteries during his Venetian rule in the early 19th century: many traditional festivities in what had been Europe's party capital were stamped out. By that time, Venice's celebrations had become frantic and excessive, the tawdry death-throes of a city in terminal decline.

The revelries that were resuscitated in the late 20th century – **Carnevale**, being the most famous example, and the almost as colourful **Regata Storica** – were done so by a city council with an eye firmly on tourist revenue.

LOCAL TRADITION

Despite the tourist focus of Venice's big events, the locals haven't lost the knack of enjoying themselves, and residents enter enthusiastically into these revamped shindigs, especially if they take place on the water. There are more than 120 regattas in the lagoon each year. The Regata Storica (*see p216*) may look like it's funded by the tourist board, but Venetians get seriously involved in the races; the **Vogalonga** (*see p215*) is a remarkable display of the Venetian love of messing about in boats.

In fact, from the earliest days of the Republic, festivals, processions and popular celebrations were an intrinsic part of the city's social fabric. The government used pageantry both to assert the hierarchical nature of society and to give the lower orders the chance to let off steam. The government declared official celebrations in honour of anything from the end of plague to a naval battle – and there was no shortage of local saints' days to celebrate. For the working classes, there were the *corse al toro* (bullfights) in campo Santo Stefano, or bloody battles between rival sections of the populace.

For public holidays and religious days, *see p305*. For a full list of events, see the City of Venice website: www.comune.venezia.it.

SPRING

★ Carnevale
Date 10 days ending on Shrove Tuesday.
See p217 **Profile.**
▶ *For Carnevale costume hire, see p198.*

Su e Zo per i Ponti
Information: 041 590 4717/
www.tgseurogroup.it/suezo.
Date one Sunday in March or April.
Literally 'Up and Down the Bridges', this excursion is inspired by the traditional *bacarada* (bar crawl). It is an orienteering event in which you are given a map and a list of checkpoints to tick off in the city of Venice. Old hands take their time checking out the *bacari* along the way. Individuals can register at the starting line in piazza San Marco on the morning of the event, while groups should phone ahead. Costumes, music and dancing liven up the route.
▶ *If you want to try your own bar crawl, read our reviews of Venice's best bacari on pp182-192.*

Benedizione del Fuoco
Basilica di San Marco (041 522 5205).
Vaporetto San Marco Vallaresso or San Zaccaria.
Date Maundy Thursday. **Map** p324 J7.
At around dusk on the eve of Good Friday, all the lights are turned off inside St Mark's basilica (*see p61*) and a fire is lit in the narthex (entrance porch). Communion is celebrated and the four elements are blessed: earth is represented by the faithful masses, fire by the large altar candle, water at the baptismal font and air by the surrounding environment.

Festa di San Marco
Bacino di San Marco. Vaporetto San Marco Vallaresso or San Zaccaria. **Date** 25 Apr.
Map p324 J-K8.
The traditional feast day of Venice's patron saint is a surprisingly low-key affair. In the morning, there is a solemn Mass in the basilica, followed by a gondola regatta between the island of Sant'Elena

(*see p84*) and the Punta della Dogana (*see p120*) at the entrance to the Grand Canal. The day is also known as *La Festa del boccolo* ('bud'): red rosebuds are given to wives and lovers.

Festa e Regata della Sensa

San Nicolò del Lido & Bacino di San Marco (information: 041 529 8711/041 274 7737).
Date Ascension Day (5th Thur after Easter).
Back in the days of the Venetian Republic, the doge would board the glorious state barge, the Bucintoro, and be rowed out to the island of Sant'Andrea. After he arrived, he would throw a gold ring overboard, to symbolise *lo sposalizio del mare* – Venice's marriage with the sea.

Today, the mayor does the honours, the Bucintoro looks like a glorified fruit boat and the ring has become a laurel wreath. The ceremony is now performed at San Nicolò, on the Lido, and is followed by a regatta. If it rains, local lore says it'll tip down for the next 40 days. ('*Se piove il giorno della Sensa per quaranta giorni non semo sensa.*')
▶ *There's a model of the Bucintoro in the Museo Storico Navale; see p85.*

Mare Maggio

Information: 041 533 4850/www.maremaggio.it.
Date mid-May.
This new annual festivity allows a three-day glimpse inside the towering walls of the military zone inside the Arsenale (*see p84*). There are historical re-enactments, homages to Venice's boat-building traditions, promotion of local water-borne tourism and much naval self-glorification.

★ Vogalonga

Information: 041 521 0544/www.vogalonga.it.
Date one Sunday in May or early June.
For one chaotically colourful day, Venetians (or at least those with strength enough to complete the 33km/20.5 mile route) protest against motorboats and the damage they do by boarding any kind of rowing craft and making their way through the lagoon and the city's two main canals in this annual free-for-all on the water. They are joined by a host of out-of-towners and foreigners: in 2007, 5,832 registered rowers participated, 2,833 of whom came from outside Italy. Boats set off from in front of the Doge's Palace at 8.30am.

Veneto Jazz

Information: via Corriva 10, Cavasagra di Vedelago (0423 452 069/www.venetojazz.com).
Box office at venues before performances.
Date Jan-Apr & June-Aug. **Credit** (online bookings only) MC, V.
Giants of the jazz scene perform alongside lesser-known talents in various venues around Venice and further afield in the Veneto.
▶ *For more annual music events, see p232 Summer Festivals.*

SUMMER

★ Biennale d'Arte Contemporanea & Architettura

Giardini di Castello (041 521 8711/ www.labiennale.org). Vaporetto Giardini.
Date *Art* (odd years) June-Nov. *Architecture* (even years) Sept-Nov. **Map** p326 P10.
The Biennale d'Arte, established in 1895, is the *Jeux sans Frontières* of the contemporary art world; its architectural counterpart draws a strong crowd.
▶ *For an in-depth look at all the Biennale has to offer, see pp47-49.*

Palio delle Antiche Repubbliche Marinare

Bacino di San Marco. Vaporetto San Marco Vallaresso or San Zaccaria. **Date** June or July.
This competition takes place in Venice once every four years (2003, 2007, and so on; at other times it's in Amalfi, Genoa or Pisa). The 2,000m race starts at the island of Sant'Elena and finishes at the Doge's Palace. Before the race, 400-odd boats carrying costumed representatives of the four Marine Republics parade along the riva dei Sette Martiri and the riva degli Schiavoni.

Festa di San Pietro

San Pietro in Castello. Vaporetto Giardini.
Date week ending 29 June. **Map** p326 Q8.
The most lively and villagey of Venice's many local festivals in celebration of San Pietro Martire. A week of events centres on the church green of San Pietro (*see p87*): there are competitions, concerts, food stands and bouncy castles.

Venezia Suona

Information: 041 275 0049/www.veneziasuona.it.
Date one weekend in July.
The name means 'Venice plays'… and that it does, with hundreds of bands playing anything from rock to folk to reggae to jazz. Music can be heard from about 4pm onwards in *campi* all over the city.

Festa di San Giacomo dell'Orio

Campo San Giacomo dell'Orio. Vaporetto Riva di Biasio or San Stae. **Date** week ending 25 July.
Map p321 E5.
Concerts, a barbecue and a charity raffle make up this local fair: it provides a great occasion to 'do as the Venetians do' in a truly beautiful campo.

★ Arena di Campo San Polo

Campo San Polo (information: 041 524 1320/ www.comune.venezia.it/cinema). Vaporetto San Silvestro or San Tomà. **Date** late July-early Sept.
Map p321 F6.
A huge outdoor theatre is set up in campo San Polo to show current films, usually dubbed into Italian, occasionally with English subtitles.
▶ *For box office details, see p222.*

ARTS & ENTERTAINMENT

★ Festa del Redentore

Bacino di San Marco, Canale della Giudecca.
Date 3rd weekend of July.

The Redentore is the oldest continuously celebrated date on the Venetian calendar. At the end of a plague epidemic in 1576, the city commissioned Andrea Palladio to build a church on the Giudecca – Il Redentore (the Redeemer). Every July, a pontoon bridge is built across the canal that separates the Giudecca from Venice proper, so people can make the pilgrimage to the church. But, while the religious part of the festival falls on Sunday, what makes this weekend so special are the festivities on Saturday night. Boats of every shape and size gather in the lagoon between St Mark's, San Giorgio, the Punta della Dogana and the Giudecca, each holding merry-makers supplied with food and drink. This party culminates in an amazing fireworks display.

Ferragosto – Festa dell'Assunta

Date 15 Aug.

If you want Venice without Venetians, this is the time to come, as everyone who can leaves the city. Practically everything shuts down and people head to the beach. There is usually a free concert in the cathedral of Santa Maria Assunta (*see p140*), on the island of Torcello, on the evening of the 15th. Tourist offices (*see p305*) have more information.

★ Regata Storica

Grand Canal. **Date** 1st Sun in Sept.

This event begins with a procession of ornate boats down the Grand Canal (*see pp52-59*), rowed by locals in 16th-century costume. Once this is over, the races start – which is what most locals have come to see. There are four: one for young rowers, one for women, one for rowers of *caorline* – long canoe-like boats in which the prow and the stern are identical – and the last, the most eagerly awaited, featuring two-man sporting *gondolini*. The finish is at the sharp curve of the Grand Canal between Palazzo Barbi and Ca' Foscari: here, the judges sit in an ornate raft known as the *machina*, where the prize-giving takes place.

★ Mostra Internazionale D'Arte Cinematografica (Venice International Film Festival)

For listings and review, *see p222*.
▶ *For an in-depth look at the festival's history and all the Biennale has to offer, see pp47-49*.

AUTUMN

Sagra del Pesce

Island of Burano. Vaporetto 12. **Date** 3rd Sun in Sept. **Map** p329.

Fried fish and lots of white wine are consumed in this feast, in the *calli* between Burano's brightly painted houses. Those rowers who are not legless then take part in the last regatta of the season.

Sagra del Mosto

Island of Sant'Erasmo. Vaporetto 13 to Chiesa.
Date 1st weekend in Oct.

This festival is a great excuse for Venetians to spend a day 'in the country' on the island of Sant'Erasmo (*see p140*), getting light-headed on the first pressing of wine. The salty soil does not lend itself to superior wine – which is why it's best to down a glass before the stuff has had much chance to ferment. Sideshows, grilled sausage aromas and red-faced locals abound.

Venice Marathon

Information: 041 532 1871/www.
venicemarathon.it. **Date** 4th Sun in Oct.
The marathon starts in the town of Stra, east of Padua, follows the Brenta Canal, and then winds through Venice to end on the riva Sette Martiri.

WINTER

Festa di San Martino

Date 11 Nov.

Kids armed with *mamma*'s pots and spoons raise a ruckus around the city, chanting the saint's praises and demanding trick-or-treat style tokens in return for taking their noise elsewhere. Horse-and-rider shaped San Martino cakes, with coloured icing dotted with silver balls, proliferate in cake shops.

Festa della Madonna della Salute

Church of Madonna della Salute. Vaporetto Salute. **Date** 21 Nov. **Map** p323 G9.

In 1630-31, Venice was 'miraculously' delivered from the plague, which claimed almost 100,000 lives – one in three Venetians. The Republic commissioned a church from Baldassare Longhena, and his Madonna della Salute (literally, 'good health') was completed in 1687.

On this feast day, a pontoon bridge is strung across the Grand Canal from campo Santa Maria del Giglio to La Salute so that a procession led by the patriarch (archbishop) of Venice can make its way on foot from San Marco. Along the way, stalls sell cakes and candyfloss, and candles for pilgrims to light inside the church. Then everybody eats *castradina* – cabbage and mutton stew – which tastes nicer than it sounds.
▶ *For further details about the Salute, see p123*.

Christmas, New Year & Epiphany (La Befana)

Venice's Yuletide festivities are low-key affairs. There are two events: the New Year's Day swim off the Lido (www.lidovenezia.it) for hardy swimmers, and the *Regata delle Befane* (www.bucintoro.it) on 6 January, a rowing race along the Grand Canal in which the competitors, all aged over 50, are dressed up as *La Befana* – the ugly witch who gives sweets to good children and pieces of coal to bad ones.
▶ *Venice's public holidays are listed on p305*.

Profile Carnevale

The world's largest and most famous masked ball.

Venice's pre-Lenten **Carnevale** had existed since the Middle Ages, but it came into its own in the 18th century. As the Venetian Republic slipped into terminal decline, the city's pagan side began to emerge. Carnevale became an outlet for all that had been prohibited for centuries by the strong and sober arm of the doge. Elaborate structures would be set up in piazza San Marco as stages for acrobats, tumblers, wrestlers and other performers. Masks served not only as an escape from the drabness of everyday life but to conceal the wearer's identity – a useful ploy for nuns on the lam or slumming patricians.

The Napoleonic invasion in 1797 brought an end to the fun and games, and Carnevale was not resuscitated until the late 1970s. When it was reintroduced, it was predominantly with money-earning in mind: the city authorities and hoteliers'

association saw the potential, and today the heavily subsidised celebrations draw revellers from all over the world.

But if Carnevale fills Venetian hotels and coffers, it also gives the locals with a chance for fun and games. Visitors flock to piazza San Marco, where professional *poseurs* in ornate (and exorbitant) costumes occupy prime spots and wait for the world's press photographers to immortalise them. Venetians, on the other hand, organise private masked and costumed celebrations, or gather in smaller squares: the 40xVenezia association (*see p31*), for example, turned campo Bella Venezia into a joyous Indian reserve for Carnevale 2009.

The party starts ten days before *martedì grasso* (Shrove Tuesday), though plans are afoot to kick off the festivities even earlier. Tourist offices (*see p305*) can provide full Carnevale programmes.

READY? GET SET... All you need for Carnevale.

Masks They also make great souvenirs. *See p207.*

Cloaks Visit Monica Danieli to get covered. *See p198.*

Costume hire What to wear, what to wear? *See p198.*

Gondola hire Pricey but memorable. *See p297.*

ARTS & ENTERTAINMENT

Children

In a city designed like a puzzle, you'll find plenty for kids to do.

With its labyrinthine geography, its hundreds of crooked bridges and its omnipresent winged lions, Venice is intrinsically weird enough to keep almost any youngster's interest alive. Of course, a solid diet of Baroque churches and interminable art galleries may quell their curiosity. But Venice has so much more than that to offer children.

Plan your day's activities with imaginative foresight, allow for a good deal of walking and make sure you factor in plenty of ice-cream stops. You'll be surprised, too, how much you'll learn by letting your offspring take the lead: bedazzled by the wonder of it all, they may well end up enlightening you on fascinating aspects of the city that might otherwise have passed you by.

SIGHTSEEING

Little ones are amazed by the sheer mechanics of the place: exploit it, and remember that hours hanging over bridges spotting fish-finger delivery boats is part of the Venetian experience too. Older kids may be inveigled into the right frame of mind with a pre-emptive gift of Cornelia Funke's novel, *The Thief Lord*; if that intrigues them, a visit to **campo Santa Margherita** (*see p116*) will be indispensable.

When you're done watching boats slipping under the city's 400-plus bridges, offer your kids a glimpse of illustrious craft of the past at the **Museo Storico Navale** (*see p85*), where Venice's maritime history is charted in scale models of ships built in the Arsenale over the centuries.

Venetians have always devoted much time to games and sport; visit the **Museo Querini Stampalia** (*see p78*), where a collection of 18th-century scenes includes some very unlikely amusements: one painting, *La Guerra dei Pugni* by Antonio Strom, shows one of the mass boxing matches that occurred frequently on bridges. The initial four competitors – before proceedings degenerated into a free-for-all – started out with one foot on the white inlaid footprints on the corners of the top step.

About the author

Patrizia Lerco is from Verona and has lived in Venice since 1983. She works as a translator and tour manager.

Don't forget to introduce your kids to the most famous Venetian game of all. With the lagoon behind you, and the lagoon-facing façade of the Doge's Palace in front of you, make your way to the third column from the left. Place your back firmly against it, then walk round it, all the way. Can you circumnavigate it without holding onto the pillar and without slipping off the shoe-worn marble pavement?

Most of Venice's museums are singularly hands-off, but some may still appeal to kids. If the vast Tintorettos and echoing halls of the **Palazzo Ducale** (*see p67*) inspire only yawns, combine your visit there with a tour of the palace's secret corridors, the *Itinerari Segreti* (not advisable for toddlers; *see p69*),

---

INSIDE TRACK
PUNCH-UP

When you've seen how it's done in Antonio Strom's painting in the **Museo Querini Stampalia** (*see p78*), try out a traditional Venetian fist-fight on **ponte dei Pugni** (*see p116*) near campo San Barnaba (map p322 D8), **ponte della Guerra** near campo San Zulian (map p324 J6) or **ponte di Santa Fosca** near the campo of the same name (map p321 G3), all of which have white footprints on their pavements marking the starting points.

---

which will take you into dungeons and torture rooms. Only two rooms are currently open at the **Museo di Storia Naturale** (*see p104*) but they are home to an aquarium and some very impressive fossils.

Break your children into art with visits to less demanding exhibits, such as the **Scuola di San Giorgio degli Schiavoni** (*see p87*), where Vittorio Carpaccio's *St George* cycle is packed with fascinating detail. The grand Tintorettos in the **Madonna dell'Orto** (*see p95*), particularly *The Last Judgement*, are full of the kind of gruesome details – such as

bodies with skulls for heads scrabbling their way out of the earth – likely to appeal to kids.

Don't be scared off from big galleries such as the **Accademia** (*see p122*): you may link up with one of the gallery's more child-friendly guides, who will bend over backwards to interest your offspring in the collection. The **Musei Civici** (*see p66*) organise family events, usually on Sunday afternoons (in Italian only at present); it's €10 for a family of four.

To win a little picture-viewing time in churches, try pointing out to your kids that the red marble used in so many church floors

Lion Hunting

St Mark's square and vicinity provides an ideal arena for a game of I-Spy.

Subjects for I-Spy games are manifold in Venice: bell towers are always a good bet, but lions are a little trickier to spot. The winged lion has been a symbol of the city since the early ninth century (for the story of how this happened – and another picture clue – *see p18*).

You'll find that piazza San Marco and its adjoining *piazzette* offer a fine pride, ranging from the ancient and exotic (Syrian,

Persian or Chinese) to the pink and cuddly (the porphyry statues in piazzetta dei Leoncini). Below are pictures of just a few of them to get you started on your quest.

For a more challenging treasure hunt, which will have you criss-crossing the city, older kids might prefer to try finding all of the well-heads we've identified as unusual or interesting; *see p86* **The Well-heads of Venice**.

contains amazing fossils. While they embark on mini-palaeontological excursions, you can concentrate on the artworks.

When the culture all gets too much, take Junior up a **campanile** for a bird's-eye view of the city. The one in piazza San Marco (*see p65*) is the highest; **San Giorgio Maggiore**'s (*see p130*) affords a more detached vantage point. Time your ascent to coincide with the striking of an hour – midday is particularly deafening. As this guide went to press, the gracious, smaller-scale **Scala del Bòvolo** (*see p76*) was closed for restoration; but if it's open when you visit, this lift-less climb will give the kids the satisfaction of making their own panting way up to the top. As does the campanile at the basilica on **Torcello** (*see p139*), though it's via steep sloping ramps rather than stairs; a fine view over the lagoon is the reward.

PARKS, BEACHES & ENTERTAINMENT

Most Venetian kids spend their free time in their local *campi*. Ball games are officially forbidden there, but you will find them going on in most of them anyway, particularly in the larger ones like campo Santa Maria Formosa and campo San Polo. Venetian kids are used to letting foreign visitors join in. In campo Santa Maria Formosa and campo Santo Stefano, small play areas for toddlers have been set up next to the churches.

Although well hidden, there are public parks in the city too, and most of them – including the **giardini pubblici** (*see p84*) and the **Parco Savorgnan** (*see p88*) – have been fitted up with swings and slides. Out in **Sant'Elena** (*see p84*), things improve with a grassy play area along the lagoon, and a roller skating/cycling rink.

On the mainland, the brand new **Parco San Giuliano** (bus 12 from piazzale Roma) is one of Italy's largest urban parks. The recently planted trees don't offer much shade on a blazing summer day, but there are play areas, football pitches, a lake and a roller skating rink.

In summer, break up the culture with a trip to the **Lido** and its beaches (*see p131*). Most of the main ones are sewn up by the big hotels, which will charge you for a small stretch of sand, sometimes with deckchair and umbrella, and certainly with huge numbers of near neighbours. Pleasant **Sant'Erasmo** (*see p140*) – a large, rural island – can be cycled around in an hour or so. There's a small beach straight across the island from the ferry landing stage. Alternatively, head for the beaches of **Lido di Jesolo** (*see p236*).

Local feast days may also provide entertainment for your children, usually in the shape of puppet theatres. Watch walls around the city for posters announcing *feste*. Particularly picturesque is the feast of Saints Peter and Paul in the parish of **San Pietro in Castello** (*see p87*), celebrated on 29 June.

GETTING AROUND

The frequent absence of barriers between pavement and canal presents a problem for mobile toddlers: safety reins might not be a bad idea here. Pre-walkers present another dilemma. After heaving a pushchair over the umpteenth bridge in a day, a baby backpack may seem like a gift from heaven.

Vaporetto travel is far from cheap. Children under five travel free; after that they pay full fare, although discounted passes are available (*see p6 and p296*). But if you look on the means of transport as a Venetian experience in itself, the cost will not seem so outrageous. It is perfectly acceptable to take your pram or pushchair onto the vaporetto at no extra cost – although it is probably better to avoid doing this on the smaller boats at rush-hour. A complete circle on line 2 (red) from the riva degli Schiavoni will take your fascinated offspring across to the Giudecca, then up to the station and port areas, giving them a glimpse of Venice's industrial underbelly as well as a triumphal march down the Grand Canal.

BOOKS

The excellent children's guide (in English) *VivaVenice* by Paolo Zoffoli and Paola Scibilia (Elzeviro, 2002) has games, informative illustrations and interesting facts. *Venice for Kids* by Elisabetta Pasqualin (Fratelli Palombi, 2004) belongs to a series of books on Italian cities.

On the fiction front, Terry Jones's fantasy story *Nicobobinus* and Anthony Horowitz's *Scorpia* both begin with exciting scenes set in Venice. And the city's alleys, *campi* and canals provide an important backdrop for the scamps of Cornelia Funke's *The Thief Lord*.

INSIDE TRACK
ALMOST A GONDOLA

Most children will demand a gondola trip. Remember that this expensive experience (*see p297*) can be substituted by – or supplemented with – rides on the humbler but more useful *traghetti* (*see p296*) that ply across the Grand Canal at points distant from bridges. Let your kids stand up in the boat like real Venetians.

Film

One feature-length festival and a very few shorts.

Venice may be home to the world's longest-running **film festival** (*see p222*), but outside the once-a-year movie jamboree, the city has great difficulty enticing its populace into its cinemas. Many former picture palaces now house supermarkets, a pretty accurate reflection of local demand, with a diminishing population translating into decreasing numbers of moviegoers.

Besides the festival at the beginning of September, when the Lido's bikini-clad hordes rub shoulders with journalists, photographers and a constellation of international stars, the only other ray of hope is **Circuito Cinema**, a film promotion initiative that runs and programmes a group of local arthouse cinemas.

WHERE TO GO, WHAT TO SEE

The Circuito's cinemas are the **Giorgione Movie d'Essai**, **Multisala Astra** on the Lido, the **Mignon Arthouse** in Mestre and the **Aurora Movie d'Essai** in Marghera. The plush **Sala Perla**, housed in the former Casinò on the Lido (lungomare Marconi, 041 524 1320), completes the set and now runs a Friday evening series of first-run films, as well as Sunday afternoon theatre productions.

In Italy, the dubber is king, and the dearth of original-language films infuriates cinema buffs. The Giorgione and the Astra offer a limited selection of films in the *versione originale.*

ASSOCIATIONS

Circuito Cinema
Information: Palazzo Mocenigo, Santa Croce 1991, salizada San Stae (041 524 1320/www. comune.venezia.it/cinema). Vaporetto San Stae. **Map** p321 F4.
The Circuito Cinema operates as a publisher and as a cine-club organising a series of themed seasons and workshops. It also airs original-language films, mostly classics or arthouse movies. Its annual (July-June) *CinemaPiù* card (€30; €20 for

students) gives discounts to all of Venice's cinemas. It can be bought from the Giorgione and Astra cinemas (for both, *see below*), and in the summer at the San Polo open-air cinema (*see p222*).

CINEMAS

Giorgione Movie D'Essai
Cannaregio 4612, rio terà dei Franceschi (041 522 6298). Vaporetto Ca' d'Oro.
No credit cards. Map p324 H4.
This two-screener run by Circuito Cinema (*see above*) combines the usual fare with themed seasons and kids' films (on Saturday and Sunday at 3pm).

Multisala Astra
Via Corfù 9, Lido (041 526 5736). Vaporetto Lido. **No credit cards. Map** p327 BB3.
The council-run Astra is a two-screener usually offering the same fodder as the Giorgione (*see above*)

INSIDE TRACK
BOND IN VENICE

To the east of campo Santo Stefano (*see p74*), campiello Pisani is overlooked by the impressive 17th-century **Palazzo Pisani**, now the music conservatory. The palace was used for the shoot-out at the end of the 2006 James Bond film *Casino Royale.* An earlier Bond came to blows in the **Torre dell'Orologio**; *see p71.*

About the author
Jo-Ann Titmarsh *has lived in Venice since 1992. She is the author of* Venice Walks *(Duncan Petersen Publishing, 2009) and is a regular contributor to* Time Out Venice.

a week before or after. During the Film Festival, the Astra is also home to the Venice Film Meeting, which promotes locally made films.

OPEN-AIR CINEMA

★ Arena di Campo San Polo

Campo San Polo. Vaporetto San Silvestro or San Tomà. **Date** late July-early Sept. **Box office** from 7.30pm. **Tickets** €5-€8; €24 for 6 films (excluding special screenings and events). **No credit cards. Map** p321 F6.

This large square is home to Venice's second most important cinematic event. Around 1,000 cinema-goers a night brave the mosquitoes to fill this open-air arena. Films are generally reruns of the previous season's blockbusters, plus the odd pre-view. During the Film Festival, you can catch some original-language films a day or two after their Lido screening. For programme details, see the city council website: www.comune.venezia.it.

VIDEOTHEQUES

Videoteca Pasinetti/Casa del Cinema

Palazzo Mocenigo, Santa Croce 1990, salizada San Stae (041 524 1320). Vaporetto San Stae. **Open** *Video archive* 8.30am-1.30pm Mon-Fri. **Shows** *Video-projected cinema classics* 6pm, 9pm

Tue, Fri. **Admission** by membership card (€30), valid July-June. **No credit cards. Map** p321 F4.

This council-run video archive was founded in 1991 to collect and conserve an incredible volume of audio-visual material concerning Venice, in all formats: feature film, TV documentary, newsreel, amateur video, and so on. More than 3,000 videos are kept here, and there's a screening room where brief film seasons are held.

FESTIVALS

Circuito off – Venice International Short Film Festival

Information: Incubatore CNOMV, Giudecca 212, fondamenta delle Zitelle (041 244 6979/www. circuitooff.com). Vaporetto Redentore. **Date** 1st wk Sept. **Admission** non-professional accreditation €10. **Map** p329 H11.

This short-film festival, run by the Associazione Artecolica, includes competitions, retrospectives and videos. In 2008, it was held on San Servolo.

★ Mostra Internazionale d'Arte Cinematografica (Venice International Film Festival)

Palazzo del Cinema, lungomare Marconi 90, Lido (041 521 8711/www.labiennale.org). Vaporetto Lido. **Date** 11 days, starting late Aug/early Sept.

Six Degrees of Animation

The Venice Film Festival takes animated films seriously.

The 2009 Venice International Film Festival saw a Lifetime Achievement gong awarded to prolific Pixar filmmaker **John Lasseter**. Festival director Marco Müller proclaimed that the director of *Toy Story* and the extraordinary 3-D *Bolt* was 'one of the great expressive forces of the new millennium.'

Lasseter was not the first animator to be presented with a Golden Lion for his life's work. The same award was bestowed on Japanese animation maestro **Hayao Miyazaki** in 2005. His most recent masterpiece of hand-drawn animation, *Ponyo*, was screened at the 2008 edition of the Venice festival. Rather sweetly, Miyazaki was concerned that the Lifetime Achievement recognition might make it look like he was coming to the end of his career, but commented that if the indefatigable Clint Eastwood was prepared to accept the prize (way back in 2000), then so was he.

Miyazaki and Lasseter are close friends, the latter overseeing the dubbing of Miyazaki's movies in the US and acting as executive producer on some of his films.

However, Lasseter's relationship with animators lauded at the Venice Festival doesn't stop there. He and **Tim Burton** were both students together at CalArts, the art school founded by a certain Walt Disney. Tim Burton has also enjoyed great acclaim in Venice, garnering the same Lifetime Achievement Award at the 64th Festival; his stop-motion *Corpse Bride* was screened in honour of the nomination.

So, what does this tell us about the Venice Film Festival? That it's long been a champion of animation and is ready to praise the genre's most adept purveyors. As animation remains one of the film industry's biggest money-makers and becomes ever more accepted as a contender for serious consideration (*Wall-E* earning Academy Award nominations, for example) – while constantly pushing the boundaries of filmmaking – the Venice Film Festival's appreciation of the doyens of this field show that it is no Mickey Mouse organisation.

Casino Royale (2006).

Tickets *Season tickets for Sala Grande or PalaLido* €130-€1,100. *Individual screenings* €10-€38. **Credit** AmEx, DC, MC, V. **Map** p327 CC5.
The 11-day Venice Film Festival takes place along the main, sea-facing Lido esplanade, between the Hotel des Bains (*see p163*) and the Excelsior (*see p162* **Inside Track**). Between these two grand hotels is the marble-and-glass Palazzo del Cinema, where official competition screenings take place in the Sala Grande. Other festival screens can be found in the gargantuan PalaLido, inside the Casinò and at the Palabiennale marquee. In 2008, big names such as Jonathan Demme, with *Rachel's Getting Married*, and Darren Aronofsky's *The Wrestler* contended for the Golden Lion award.

Press accreditation guarantees virtually unlimited access to the festival; the press pass costs €50 and permits priority entry to a number of special screenings, mostly in the morning and early evening. Arrange this at least two months in advance by contacting the Biennale press office (041 521 8857, www.labiennale.org).

'Cultural' accreditation is another option; it allows access to a more restricted range of screenings. This should be arranged before the end of June. A special deal for people under 26/over 60 offers a six-day (€100) or 11-day (€130) festival pass. Individual tickets are available on the day before screenings from the ticket office at piazzale Casinò (lungomare Marconi, Lido, open 8am-midnight daily); Palabiennale (via Sandro Gallo, open 8am-midnight); and at the offices of La Biennale (Ca' Giustinian, San Marco 1365A, calle del Ridotto,

open 8am-1.30pm, 3.30-6pm). Same-day tickets are occasionally available. Note that we have given approximate prices; no information on possible increases was available as this guide went to press.
► *For more on the film festival, and the other elements of the Biennale, see pp47-49.*

Further afield

Asolo Art Film Festival
Information: Foresto Vecchio 8, Asolo (0423 199 5235/www.asolofilmfestival.it). **Date** late Aug-early Sept. **No credit cards**.
As well as being a leading protagonist in Liliana Cavani's *Ripley's Game*, Asolo also holds its own film festival, focusing on art and artists. Films are screened at the Teatro Duse (in piazzetta E Duse); other sites around the town host related events.
► *For where to stay and eat in Asolo, see p289.*

Le Giornate del Cinema Muto
Information: Cineteca del Friuli, Palazzo Gurisatti, via Bini 50, Gemona (0432 980 458 /www.giornatedelcinemamuto.it). **Date** early Oct. **No credit cards**.
In Europe's most prestigious silent-movie festival, highlights include an international forum of musicians for silent movies, retrospectives and films such as the British documentary *The Battle of the Somme* (1916). Accreditation costs €30 and allows unlimited viewings (except opening and closing nights, when a silent movie with musical accompaniment costs €13). Non-accredited viewers pay €5 per screening.

Galleries

A contemporary scene that lives up to Venice's glorious art history.

Not content with its large share of the world's Old Masterpieces, Venice is becoming an ever more important player on the high-brow contemporary scene too. An impressive 77 nations (including, for the first time, the Vatican and Abu Dhabi) were expected to send works by over 90 artists to the 2009 **Biennale** (*see pp47-49*), a two-yearly artistic bunfight where deals are hatched and hopefuls vie with big names for a piece of the action.

But *La Serenissima* continues to improve steadily on the modern and contemporary public exhibition front too, culminating in the June 2009 openings of François Pinault's Punta della Dogana gallery (*see p124* **The Whole Punta**) and the Renzo Piano-designed **Fondazione Vedova** gallery (*see p126*).

THE SCENE

The momentum of Venice's contemporary art scene has been growing for quite a while. The **Peggy Guggenheim Collection** (*see p121* **Profile**) of 20th-century masters, in its delightful Grand Canal palazzo, has long been the city's third most visited attraction. Challenging it – as of 2006 – is **Palazzo Grassi** (*see p75*), where new owner, the French industrial magnate François Pinault, has exhibited some of his own extensive contemporary collection between crowd-pleasers such as a show on the Barbarians.

Pinault's influence on Venice's art scene increased exponentially in 2009 when he opened his new space at the Punta della Dogana, the bonded warehouses of the old customs house right across the lagoon from St Mark's. Pinault fought off counter-bids by the Guggenheim foundation (among others), then brought Tadao Ando – the Japanese architectural superstar, who also worked at Palazzo Grassi – to craft a space in which to hang his collection.

The first decade of the millennium has seen great changes at the Biennale: the **Italian Pavilion** has been shifted to a space inside the Arsenale (*see p84*), with a new bridge linking the Biennale *giardini* to the *Padiglione Italia*, and the old Italian Biennale HQ has become a year-round exhibition centre. It will become home,

eventually, to the **ASAC** (*Archivio Storico delle Arti Contemporanee; see p301*), which for years has been housed in a sadly dysfunctional location in industrial Marghera.

Arts activity on the mainland continues to languish, though the **Centro Culturale Candiani** (*see p240*) is slowly learning how to create decent programming – an indication that Venice has not only kept afloat but is learning how to swim in the ever-changing world of contemporary artistic practices.

As well as the Biennale's new efforts at interaction with the city, plenty is being done to keep Venice on the international arts map by the Arts and Design faculty of the **Università IUAV di Venezia** (architecture university; *see p303*), which holds workshops run by internationally renowned artists, and the ever-green **Bevilacqua La Masa** (*see p227*) with its restructured artists in residence programme.

These initiatives have also begun to revive 'local' artistic production at last. To make up for a slump in the **Querini Stampalia** foundation's activities (*see p78*), and the **Academy of Fine Arts**' apparent inability to take advantage of its new headquarters in the former Ospedale degli Incurabili in Dorsoduro, a few interesting new galleries have opened in the past few years.

If you are inspired by Venice to take up a brush yourself, there are a number of places where you can pick up paints; *see p193*.

SAN MARCO

A+A

*San Marco 3073, calle Malipiero (041 277 0466/
www.aplusa.it). Vaporetto San Samuele.* **Open**
11am-2pm, 3-6pm Tue-Sat. **No credit cards.**
Map p323 E7.
A lively – and at times experimental – non-profit
exhibition space sponsored by the Slovenian ministry of culture. It hosts numerous shows, events,
conferences, and curatorial classes too, organised
in collaboration with Slovenian-related or local
institutions. It is home to the Slovenian Pavilion
during both the contemporary art and architecture
editions of the Biennale.
▶ *To find out more about the different elements
of the Biennale, see pp47-49.*

Bugno Art Gallery

*San Marco 1996D, campo San Fantin (041 523
1305/www.bugnoartgallery.it). Vaporetto San
Marco Vallaresso.* **Open** 4-7.30pm Mon, Sun;
10.30am-7.30pm Tue-Sat. **Credit** AmEx, DC,
MC, V. **Map** p323 G7.
Large windows overlooking the Fenice opera house
reveal a large space devoted to artists working in all
types of media. Well-known local artists are also
included in the gallery's collection. So packed is the
exhibition calendar that shows often spill over into
a smaller exhibition space nearby.
▶ *The Jarach Gallery is also located in this
campo; see p228.*

Il Capricorno

*San Marco 1994, calle dietro la Chiesa (041 520
6920). Vaporetto Giglio or San Marco Vallaresso.*
Open 11am-1pm, 5-8pm Mon-Sat. **No credit
cards. Map** p323 G7.
Many artists who are now basking in the national
or international limelight showed in this small, low-
profile gallery in the early stages of their careers.
Various shows each year are dedicated to younger
international artists.

Caterina Tognon

*San Marco 2746, Palazzo da Ponte, calle del
Dose (041 520 7859/www.caterinatognon.com).
Vaporetto Giglio.* **Open** 10am-1pm, 3-7pm Tue-
Sat. **Credit** MC, V. **Map** p323 F8.
Following the success of her first gallery, which she
opened in Bergamo in 1992, renowned curator
Caterina Tognon created this Venetian showcase
for contemporary art in glass in 1998. In 2004, the
gallery expanded on to the first floor of the palazzo
it occupies. Various shows take place each year by
emerging and renowned artists.
▶ *For information about Venice's famous glass-
makers, see p136 Murano Glass.*

Contini Galleria d'Arte

*San Marco 2765-69, calle dello Spezier (041
520 4942/www.continiarte.com). Vaporetto
Accademia or Giglio.* **Open** 10.30am-1pm,
2.30-7pm daily. **Credit** AmEx, DC, MC, V.
Map p323 F8.

ARTS & ENTERTAINMENT

The Biennale. *See pp47-49.*

A very large space (by Venetian standards) stretching along both sides of the street, the Contini is home to a large selection of 20th-century art. International masters are exhibited next to world-renowned Italian artists. The Tuscan-born Continis have run sister galleries in Cortina d'Ampezzo for years.

▶ *For details about visiting Cortina d'Ampezzo, see p291.*

Flora Bigai Arte Moderna e Contemporanea

San Marco 1652, piscina di Frezzeria (041 521 2208). Vaporetto San Marco Vallaresso. **Open** 3.30-7.30pm Mon; 10am-1pm, 3.30-7.30pm Tue-Sat. **Credit** AmEx, DC, MC, V. **Map** p323 G7.

Less active than its sister gallery in Tuscany, this large space presents a couple of exhibitions a year though with a rather irregular calendar. It tends to focus on international artists, and representatives of Pop Art in particular.

Fondazione Bevilacqua la Masa

Exhibition space *San Marco 71C, piazza San Marco (041 523 7819/www.bevilacqualamasa.it). Vaporetto San Marco Vallaresso.* **Open** (during exhibitions only) 10.30am-5.30pm Mon, Wed-Sun. **Map** p324 H8.

Offices & exhibition space *Dorsoduro 2826, fondamenta Gherardini (041 520 7797). Vaporetto Ca' Rezzonico.* **Open** *Office* 10am-6pm Mon-Fri. *Exhibition space* days and times vary. **Map** p322 C8.

The Fondazione Bevilacqua la Masa was founded more than a century ago by Duchess Felicita Bevilacqua La Masa, who left her palace of Ca'

Pesaro (*see p103*) to the city in order to give local artists a space in which to explore new trends.

This institution – now housed in separate headquarters – is very active in organising exhibitions, collaborating with the Arts and Design faculty of the IUAV (architecture university), and with other organisations working to foster new art in Italy. There are talks, performances, an archive and an artist-in-residence programme on the Giudecca (041 520 7797, open by appointment only). The annual *esposizione collettiva* is dedicated to artists based in the Veneto area under the age of 30.

Galerie Bordas

San Marco 1994B, calle dietro la Chiesa (041 522 4812/www.galeriebordas.com). Vaporetto San Marco Vallaresso. **Open** 11am-1pm, 4.30-7.30pm Mon-Sat. **Credit** AmEx, MC, V. **Map** p323 G7.

The only gallery dealing in serious graphics by internationally renowned masters such as Asger Jorn. The space is small but the collection of artists' books held here is huge.

La Galleria

San Marco 2566, ramo Calegheri (041 520 7415/www.galerie.vanderkoelen.de). Vaporetto Giglio. **Open** 10am-12.30pm, 3.30-6.30pm Mon-Sat. **Credit** AmEx, DC, MC, V. **Map** p323 F8.

La Galleria has a longstanding reputation – owing partly to its German owner's scholarly publications and partly to the sister gallery in Mainz, which was founded three decades ago – that makes this intimate space a must for viewing artworks and artists' books by well established names.

Galleria Michela Rizzo. *See p228.*

Galleria Marina Barovier

San Marco 3202, campo San Samuele (041 523 6748/www.barovier.it). Vaporetto San Samuele. **Open** (by appointment) 10am-12.30pm, 3.30-7.30pm Mon-Sat. **No credit cards.** **Map** p323 E8.

Marina Barovier hosts a collection of classic masterpieces of Venetian 20th-century works in glass and represents numerous renowned artists (local and international) working in glass. It stages a few shows a year. As this guide went to press, Marina Barovier was planning to move her gallery; check the website for details.

Galleria Michela Rizzo

San Marco 2597, fondamenta della Malvasia Vecchia (041 241 3006/www.galleriamichela rizzo.net). Vaporetto Giglio. **Open** 10am-12.30pm, 3.30-7pm Tue-Sat. **No credit cards.** **Map** p323 F8.

A fairly recent addition – and a rising star – on the Venetian scene, Michela Rizzo focusses on conceptual and more cutting-edge artists and performers in a packed programme of exhibitions and events. *Photo p225.*

Galleria Traghetto

San Marco 2543, campo Santa Maria del Giglio (041 522 1188/www.galleriatraghetto.it). Vaporetto Giglio. **Open** 3-7pm Mon-Sat. **Credit** AmEx, DC, MC, V. **Map** p323 G8.

This gallery with a 30-year history of dealing with Venetian 20th-century abstracts is a point of reference for established artists and for contemporary emerging artists working in all media.

Galleria Venice Design

San Marco 3146, salizada San Samuele (041 520 7915/www.venicedesignartgallery. com). Vaporetto San Samuele. **Open** 10am-1pm, 3-7pm daily. **Credit** AmEx, DC, MC, V. **Map** p323 E7.

As one of the historical landmarks of contemporary art in Venice, this gallery deals especially in sculpture by established artists, both Italian and international. It also focuses on artists' jewellery pieces and interior design. This gallery's other branch (*see below*) is open 10am-7.30pm Saturday and Sunday. **Other locations** San Marco 1310, calle Vallaresso (041 523 9082).

Jarach Gallery

San Marco 1997, campo San Fantin (041 522 1938/www.jarachgallery.com). Vaporetto Giglio. **Open** (mornings by appointment only) 10.30am-2pm, 3-7.30pm Tue-Sun. **Credit** AmEx, DC, MC, V. **Map** p323 G7.

This large space – tucked into a courtyard opposite the Fenice opera house – is one of the more recent additions to the Venetian scene. It mainly deals with photography, but also hosts literary presentations.

Tornabuoni Arte

San Marco 2663, campo San Maurizio (041 523 1201/www.tornabuoniarte.it). Vaporetto Giglio. **Open** 10.30am-1pm, 2.30-7.30pm Tue-Sun. **No credit cards.** **Map** p323 F8.

The first Tornabuoni gallery opened a quarter of a century ago in chic via Tornabuoni in Florence. This is the latest, and a newcomer on the Venetian gallery scene. It organises various shows dedicated to masters of Italian and international post-war art.

CASTELLO

Spiazzi

Castello 3865, campo San Martino (041 523 9711/www.spiazzi.info). Vaporetto Arsenale. **Open** 2-6pm Mon-Fri. **No credit cards.** **Map** p325 M7.

This former carpenter's workshop has been transformed into a non-profit space in which exhibitions of very young, mainly local, artists are organised. It offers a darkroom facility and is responsible for various craft workshops, and sometimes hosts overspill from both the Art and the Architecture editions of the Biennale.

▶ *For an overview of the Biennale, see pp47-49.*

DORSODURO

See also p227 **Fondazione Bevilacqua la Masa.**

Galleria d'Arte l'Occhio

Dorsoduro 181, calle San Gregorio (041 522 6550/www.gallerialocchio.net). Vaporetto Salute. **Open** 10am-6pm Mon, Wed-Sat. **Credit** AmEx, MC, V. **Map** p323 G9.

This intimate, friendly gallery has been around for 15 years but recently expanded its premises and can now stage 'true' exhibitions. It focuses mainly on established younger artists, many of them local. ▶ *Dorsoduro has one of the world's greatest concentrations of contemporary art, especially with the opening of the new Punta della Dogana; see p124 The Whole Punta.*

LA GIUDECCA & SAN GIORGIO

Nuova Icona

Giudecca 454, calle dell'Olio (041 521 0101/ www.nuovaicona.org). Vaporetto Palanca. **Open** (during exhibitions) 4-8pm Thur-Sun; by appointment at other times. **No credit cards.** **Map** p328 D11.

Nuova Icona organises a packed calendar of shows, performances and other artistic events, often collaborating with national exhibits at the Art Biennale. It holds some events in the Oratorio San Ludovico, near the church of San Sebastiano (Dorsoduro 2552, corte dei Vecchi, contact gallery for opening times), and with Michela Rizzo (*see above*).

Gay & Lesbian

Venice may be romantic, but you'll struggle to find a date.

Venice is for culturally inclined romantics…
so don't come looking for a fast-paced scene.
The atmosphere heats up – a little – in summer,
when the city is crowded; though even then, you'll
need some imagination to make out any real action.
Imagination, or transport to *terra ferma*: there
is a much more keenly felt urban restlessness to
Mestre and Marghera, the mainland counterpart
to Venice, where newer, flashier clubs and bars
pull in the younger crowd from the province.
And Padua, too, offers something lacking, alas,
in Venice's *centro storico*: real nightlife.

GENERAL INFORMATION

The national gay rights group **ArciGay**
(www.arcigay.it) sponsors activities, festivals,
counselling and AIDS awareness. ArciGay
membership (€15) is needed to enter several
venues listed below; this can be purchased
at the door of venues requiring it.

VENICE & AROUND
City to sand

In the old city centre, with its laid-back, quiet
gay scene tucked away in the private sphere,
dinner parties or quiet drinks at the local
bacaro define the way the city's gay community
go about their business. Out in the lagoon,
gay-friendly B&Bs are seductively hidden
away on islands such as Sant'Erasmo (**Il Lato
Azzurro**) and Torcello (**Casa d'Artista
Lucio Andrich Bed & Breakfast**).
　　The summer provides more scope for fun,
when gay visitors in large numbers descend
on the rather secluded **Alberoni Beach**
and surrounding dunes, which indulge nude
sunbathing and cruising. **Il Muro**, one of the
city's oldest cruising institutions, is no longer
as popular as it once was, but still attracts
a number of discreet post-midnight visitors.

Open-air

Il Muro (The Wall)
Vaporetto San Marco Vallaresso. **Map** p324 H8.
Behind the Procuratie Nuove, by the Giardinetti
Reali (at the lagoon end of the piazzetta di San

Marco; turn right and keep on walking), Il Muro has
seen better days as the city's after-dark cruising
area. Now rarely frequented from October to May,
it can still pull a crowd during summer. But even
with no one about, the place has a romantic charm
all its own, and is worth a visit just for the view it
affords of San Giorgio Maggiore across the canal.
▶ *Rather just visit in the daytime? See p61.*

Alberoni Beach, Lido
Vaporetto Lido then bus. **Map** off p327 CC2.
Now an almost exclusively gay beach, Alberoni is
the place to cruise in summer. The dunes and pine
forest are where the action is. If the weather's good,
cruising starts as early as April; but if you enjoy
being spoilt for choice, go for Saturdays and Sundays
in July and August. Take the B/ bus (Alberoni
Spiaggia) from Santa Maria Elisabetta to the last
stop, then turn right and walk about ten minutes.
▶ *For more about Lido bus routes, see p132.*

Where to stay

Il Lato Azzurro
*Via Forti 13, Sant'Erasmo (041 523 0642/
www.latoazzurro.it). Vaporetto 13 to Sant'
Erasmo-Capannone.* **Rates** €70-80 double.
Credit AmEx, MC, DC, V.
This gay-owned and operated guest house on the
vegetable-garden island of Sant'Erasmo (*see p140*)
is the ideal place to stay if you want a really quiet
retreat. If you prefer something more urban, Il Lato
Azzurro has B&B rooms in Venice itself (Cannaregio
6057, calle Widman, €90 double) and two apartments (€800 a week each) at Santa Maria Nova (map
p324 J5). Both places have triple rooms too. Dinner
at the Sant'Erasmo house costs €20.

Casa d'Artista Lucio Andrich Bed & Breakfast

Via Borgognoni 4L, Torcello (041 735 292/ www.lucioandrich.com). Vaporetto LN to Burano, then T to Torcello. **Rates** €60 single (Stanza del Sottotetto, in main house); €80 double (Stanza Carciofi, in converted fisherman's cottage); €120 double (Stanza del Maestro, in main house); €160 quadruple (Stanza Palude della Rosa, in converted fisherman's cottage). **No credit cards**.

This bed and breakfast on Torcello caters to an exclusive clientele, and is just the thing if you need to get away from it all. The guest rooms, located in the main house and in the *cason* (fisherman's cottage), afford incredible views. The owner, Paolo, also rents boats (€50 for a three-hour tour with Paolo at the helm) if you're interested in exploring the lagoon.

Where to eat & drink

Campo Santa Margherita (map p322 C-D7; *see p116*) is the focal point for the trendier young Venetians. Its bars and *pizzerie* are all extremely busy during summer. Not the cruisiest of places, but certainly friendly.

There's plenty of evening life in the bars around the north-western foot of the Rialto bridge (*see p190* **Evening in the Market**). **Alla Zucca** (*see p173*), ten minutes' or so walk to the north-west, is one of Venice's most gay-friendly restaurants.

PDM Bar Porto de Mar

Via delle Macchine 41-3, Marghera (041 921 247/www.portodemar.com). Bus 2 or 7 from piazzale Roma/train to Mestre station, then 10mins walk. **Open** 10.30pm-4am Fri, Sat; 10.30pm-2am Sun. **Admission** (with ArciGay membership; *see p229*) €5; €10 for special events. **Credit** MC, V.

The Venetian expression '*porto de mar*' loosely translates as hubbub, but literally means sea port. This new venue, with darkroom, bar and outside area used for cruising in summer, is worth the trip just for a glimpse of the old port before it is fully regenerated. The bar's popular with a younger crowd, but is also very welcoming if you're the wrong side of 40.

Saunas

Metrò Venezia Club

Via Cappuccina 82B, Mestre (041 538 4299/ www.metroclub.it). Bus 2 or 7 from piazzale Roma/train to Mestre, then 5mins walk. **Open** 2pm-2am daily. **Admission** (with ArciGay membership; *see p229*). *Before 9pm* €15; €12 under-26s. *After 9pm* €12. **Credit** MC, V.

The first gay venue to open in the Venice area, Metro has a bar, a dry sauna, steam sauna, private rooms, darkroom and solarium. Massage and hydro-massage are also available. Trade here is very brisk.

Tours

Venice à la Carte

041 296 0425/349 144 7818 mobile/www. tourvenice.org. **Rates** varies according to tour. **No credit cards**.

Tailor-made tours of Venice and the Veneto villas, catering for a wide variety of cultural interests and credit limits, organised by Alvise Zanchi, a native Venetian and expert tour guide.

▶ *For other guided tours of Venice, see p297.*

PADUA

The following list contains only those gay places that are most easily accessible by public transport or taxi (*see p264* and *pp295-296*) from Venice or Mestre. Cruising continues to be very risky, especially around Padua station, and should be avoided, even during the day.

For general tourist information about Padua, and where to stay and eat, *see pp255-264*.

Nightlife

Flexo Club

Via D Turazza 19, int. 3 (049 807 4707/ www.flexoclub.it). **Open** 10pm-2am Wed-Sun. **Admission** (with ArciGay membership; *see p229*) €15. **Credit** MC, V.

Flexo has a cocktail bar, disco, solarium, cruising area, darkrooms, gym, beauty centre, hydro-massage and a large cruising garden – pretty much everything you could ever want. It has also softened its no-women policy, though Saturdays are men-only. The first Saturday of every month is bears night, and Thursdays have been set aside for naked parties in a cordoned-off section of the club.

Pixelle

Via D Turazza 19, int. 4 (346 611 3972 mobile/www.pixelle.it). **Open** 9pm-4am Wed-Sat. Closed June-Sept. **Admission** (with ArciGay membership; *see p229*) free; €3 for special events. **No credit cards**.

Since 2006, this women's (but not women-only) bar/club has been arranging cultural events, book presentations, performances and concerts.

Saunas

Metrò Sauna

Via D Turazza 19, int. 1 (049 807 5828/ www.metroclub.it). **Open** 2pm-2am daily. **Admission** (with ArciGay membership; *see p229*). *Before 9pm* €16.50 Mon-Fri; €17 Sat, Sun; €12 under-26s. *After 9pm* €12. **Credit** MC, V.

Large, modern and well-equipped, this place has a proper work-those-pores Finnish sauna. It also has well-earned rest and private massage facilities.

Music & Nightlife

Venice is a lovely place for drinks – but head elsewhere for clubbing

In centuries past, visitors flooded Venice for
its party scene. These days, you're going to
have to settle for something a little more sedate.
Which isn't to say it's not there: just be prepared
for a different pace.

A typical Venetian night out starts with a
post-work and pre-prandial *spritz* in one of
the bars around the Rialto market area, which
might develop into a *giro de ombre*, a bar-crawl
Venetian style. And for those still standing when
the traditional *bacari* close, there's a network of
late-opening bars hidden away all over town –
at Rialto, or Cannaregio's 'party' fondamenta della Misericordia, or Dorsoduro's
'alternative' drawing room of campo Santa Margherita.

THE SCENE

Live music

Stringent noise pollution regulations and lack
of adequate venues have effectively pulled the
plug on large music events, **Carnevale** (*see
p217* **Profile**), **Venezia Suona** (*see p215*)
and the other summer events (*see p232*
Summer Festivals) being the exceptions.
Rock 'n' roll royals who do dates in Venice are
usually confined to the extremely formal setting
of one of the local theatres. There's better
news for serious jazz heads as regular series
of high-quality jazz and experimental music
are organised by local cultural organisations
such as **Caligola** (www.caligola.it) and
Vortice (www.vortice.provincia.venezia.it),
which has managed to pull such avant-jazzers
as Larry Ochs, Dave Douglas and Elliot Sharp.

Thanks to the tenacity of the handful of bar
owners still willing to wrestle with red tape and
persist in the face of party-pooper petitioning
neighbours, it's still possible to play and hear
live music in various *locali* around town.
Venetian vibes tend to be laid-back, and these
small, free gigs are almost always reggae, jazz
or blues – with the occasional rock, Latino or
world session. Clubs and venues on the nearby
mainland draw bigger acts.

About the author

*Kate Davies has lived in Venice for ten years
and is a regular contributor to* Time Out Venice.

Club culture

For serious club culture, make for the mainland.
In the winter, a short bus or train ride to Mestre
or Marghera (just across the bridge and well
served by night buses) is all it takes to dance
until dawn. In the summer, most of the dance
action moves out to the seaside resort of **Lido
di Jesolo** (*see p235*), the place to be for house
and techno, with a smattering of Latino.

Information & tickets

Day-to-day listings are carried by the two local
papers, *Il Gazzettino* and *La Nuova Venezia*. For
a fuller overview of concerts and festivals, with
English translations, monthly listings magazine
Venews is indispensable. Also keep your eyes
peeled for posters advertising upcoming gigs
and events. Tickets are usually available at
the venue but in some cases they can be bought
in advance at the CD shop **Parole e Musica**,
Castello 5673, salizada San Lio (041 521 2215) or
via the national ticket agency www.boxoffice.it.

Unless specified, the bars listed below have
no extra charge for music. Note that smoking is
strictly forbidden in indoor public spaces except
in designated rooms with extraction systems.

LATE BARS & MUSIC BARS

Many of the drinking establishments listed
in the Cafés, Bars & Gelaterie chapter are also
open well into the evening; *see pp182-192.*

San Marco

★ Aurora

San Marco 48-50, piazza San Marco (041 528 6405/www.aurora.st). Vaporetto San Marco Vallaresso. **Open** 8pm-2am Wed-Sun. **Credit** AmEx, DC, MC, V. **Map** p324 J8.

The evening management of this classic café right by the campanile in St Mark's square is trying to bring Venetians of all ages back to their piazza by organising art exhibitions, video projections and DJ sets to go with affordable cocktails and that favourite of Venetian tipples, *spritz* (€3 inside, €7 at a table in the square).

Bacaro Jazz

San Marco 5546, salizada del Fontego dei Tedeschi (041 528 5249/www.bacarojazz.com). Vaporetto Rialto. **Open** noon-2am Mon, Tue, Thur-Sun. **Credit** AmEx, DC, MC, V. **Map** p324 H5.

Venice's most central late-night watering hole, Bacaro Jazz is a place to mingle with fellow tourists or foreign students rather than meet the locals. It hots up during happy hour (4-7pm), and the background jazz and wide range of killer cocktails keep the party going into the early hours.

▶ *For live jazz, head to Venice Jazz Club; see p235.*

Centrale Restaurant Lounge

San Marco 1659B, piscina Frezzeria (041 296 0664/www.centrale-lounge.com). Vaporetto San Marco Vallaresso. **Open** 7pm-2am daily. **Credit** AmEx, DC, MC, V. **Map** p323 H7.

Only the exposed bricks of the original 16th-century palazzo's walls will remind you you're in Venice: this cool, contemporary restaurant and lounge bar is more New York or London. Owner Franco lays on events like live drum 'n' bass and jazz sessions or a regular international gay night, and serves a full, fresh à la carte menu right until closing time.

Summer Festivals

In Venice and the Veneto, music fills the air.

As winter loosens its grip, stages are set up in squares, parks and villas to host concerts in Venice, on the islands and the nearby mainland. There is a wealth of other festivals in the region – look out for the posters around town. *See also pp214-217.*

Festa di Liberazione

San Polo, campo dell'Erberia (www. prcvenezia.org). Vaporetto Rialto Mercato. **Date** late Aug-early Sept. **Map** p321 H5.

Rally meets rave at Rialto for the Rifondazione Comunista party's festival. Serious debates and films are followed by nightly concerts with salsa, rock, blues, reggae and world music.

Marghera Village Estate

Via Orsato 9, Panorama car park, Marghera (333 786 5622 mobile/www.villagestate.it). Bus 6/ from piazzale Roma. **Date** June-Aug **Open** 6pm-2am daily. *Concerts* 9.45pm. **Admission** free.

The Village's setting – a scrap of grass amid hypermarkets – may not be awe-inspiring, but this is where Venetians and *mestrini* of all ages spend their summer nights. Free nightly live music is followed by dancing and DJ sets, as well as a host of bars and food stalls to keep the party going.

Venice Airport Festival

Forte Bazzera, via Bazzera, Tessera (333 973 4330 mobile/www.myspace.com/ veniceairportfestival). Bus 5 from piazzale Roma to Tessera church stop. **Date** late July/early Aug. **Open** 7pm-2am daily. *Concerts* 9pm. **Admission** free; €10 for special events. **No credit cards.**

Strictly no cover bands: this festival hosts nightly gigs by top quality Italian and international indie rock bands, drawing fans from all over the region. Concerts are followed by DJ sets and off-beat film screenings.

Veneto Jazz

Via Corriva 10, Cavasagra di Vedelago (0423 452 069/www.venetojazz.com). **Box office** at venues before performances or www. boxofficeitalia.com. **Date** Jan-Apr & June-Aug. **Credit** (online bookings) MC, V.

Jazz giants such as Herbie Hancock, Keith Jarrett and Chick Corea perform alongside lesser-known talents against the backdrop of Verona's Teatro Romano (*see p271*), a castle in Bassano, or in cloisters, parks and squares all over the Veneto.

Venezia Suona

Cannaregio 3546, fondamenta dell'Abbazia (041 275 0049/www.veneziasuona.it). **Date** 3rd or 4th Sun in June or last weekend in July. **Admission** free.

'Venice Plays' with anything from a cappella choirs and jazz quartets to punk or Zappa revival bands, who jam in *campi* and by canals all over the city.

Santo Bevitore. See p234.

ARTS & ENTERTAINMENT

Alternatively, go after dinner to sink into one of the designer armchairs, explore the cocktail menu and chill out to lounge and house sounds.

Torino@Notte
San Marco 4591, campo San Luca (041 522 3914). Vaporetto Rialto. **Open** 9pm-1am Tue-Sat. **No credit cards. Map** p323 G7.
This dreary daytime snack bar switches management after dark and transforms into a happening hotspot. DJ sets and live music (some Wednesdays, and sometimes at weekends) keep the mix of students and older musos grooving to acid jazz, fusion and funky tunes, while Carnevale brings a week of live gigs in the campo outside.

Castello

Inishark
Castello 5787, calle del Mondo Novo (041 523 5300). Vaporetto Rialto. **Open** 6pm-1.30am Tue-Sun. **No credit cards. Map** p325 J6.
Tucked away in a small calle near Santa Maria Formosa, this Irish-style pub has the best Guinness on tap in town and great snacky food to soak up the black stuff – we recommend the roast suckling pig and mustard sandwiches. Satellite TV packs in the fans for Champions League football.

★ La Mascareta
Castello 5183, calle lunga Santa Maria Formosa (041 523 0744). **Open** 7pm-2am daily. **Credit** MC, V. **Map** p324 K6.

Genial, bow-tied Mauro Lorenzon keeps hundreds of wines – including some rare vintages – in his cellars, serving them up by the bottle or glass along with plates of cheeses, seafood, cold meats or *crostini*. There are also more filling options – hearty soups, for example – every evening.

Cannaregio

★ Dogado Lounge
Cannaregio 3660A, strada Nuova (041 520 8544/www.dogadoclub.com). Vaporetto Ca' d'Oro. **Open** noon-4am daily. **Admission** (incl 1st drink) €10. **No credit cards. Map** p321 G4.
The huge terrace of the Dogado Lounge, above the Billa supermarket on strada Nuova, is a great place to stop off for a drink or bite to eat during the day. But this café-restaurant has also become Venice's newest place to dance – and the most popular with young Venetians. The current regime is: salsa nights on Thursdays, regular disco nights on Fridays and Saturdays, and tango nights on Sundays.

Fiddler's Elbow Irish Pub
Cannaregio 3847, corte dei Pali già Testori (041 523 9930). Vaporetto Ca' d'Oro. **Open** 5pm-1am daily. **Credit** AmEx, MC, V. **Map** p321 G4.
Expats, locals and tourists of all ages prop up the bar in Venice's oldest Irish pub. Party-pooping neighbours have put a stop to regular live music nights, but local bands still play on special occasions such as Hallowe'en and St Patrick's Day. Big sports events are screened in the campo outside.

Iguana

Cannaregio 2515, fondamenta della Misericordia (340 376 5417 mobile). Vaporetto San Marcuola. **Open** 6pm-2am daily. **Credit** MC, V. **Map** p321 G3.

With tacos, tequila and tecate – in addition to mescal and margaritas – the Misericordia's Mexican bar swings to salsa sounds till late at night. It's no surprise that the summer *spritz* hour (6-8pm June-Sept, €2 a *spritz*) packs in the students.

Paradiso Perduto

Cannaregio 2540, fondamenta della Misericordia (041 720 581). Vaporetto San Marcuola. **Open** 6pm-1am Mon, Wed, Thur; 11am-2am Fri-Sun. **No credit cards. Map** p321 G3.

Probably the most famous Venetian haunt after Harry's Bar (*see p185*), this 'Paradise Lost' is well worth finding. Arty types of all ages take their places at the long *osteria* tables for the mix of seafood and succulent sounds (mainly jazz and salsa), which go live two or three Sundays a month.

Santo Bevitore

Cannaregio 2393A, campo Santa Fosca (041 717 560/www.ilsantobevitorepub.com). Vaporetto Ca' d'Oro or San Marcuola. **Open** 9.30am-1.30am Mon-Sat. **No credit cards. Map** p321 G3.

This friendly pub-café on campo Santa Fosca, just off strada Nova, has consistently proved popular

with both Venetian locals and visitors, who drop in to munch *cicheti* during the day or come to while away the evening over a beer or a glass of wine. The quality background music goes live on the first Monday of the month. *Photo p233.*

San Polo & Santa Croce

See also p189 **Muro Vino e Cucina**.

Al Pesador

San Polo 125-6, campo San Giacomo di Rialto (041 523 9492). Vaporetto Rialto or Rialto Mercato. **Open** 6.30pm-2am Tue-Sun. **Credit** MC, V. **Map** p321 H5.

This beautiful *bacaro*-style bar was once the place where fruit and veg were weighed for the local market. These days, crowds of students cram inside or hang out at the back, overlooking the Grand Canal.
► *For more on the area's drinking scene, see p190 Evening in the Market.*

Ai Postali

Santa Croce 821, fondamenta Rio Marin (no phone). Vaporetto Riva di Biasio or San Tomà. **Open** 7.30pm-2am Mon-Sat. Closed Aug. **No credit cards. Map** p320 D5.

This long-established *osteria* is a firm Venetian favourite. Local drinkers moor their boats beneath the outside terrace to pop in for a drink.

Sounds of the Lagoon

Local heroes keep the beat going.

'In every house someone plays a musical instrument, someone sings, someone accompanies. Everywhere someone makes music or rushes to hear it,' commented a French visitor to Venice in the 18th century. The Serene Republic of Music was once renowned around the world for its composers and musicians, for its instrument-makers and music printing. Such an illustrious musical tradition now lies firmly in the past.

In the 1960s, **Pino Donaggio** – now a prolific film and TV soundtrack composer, teaming up with the likes of Brian De Palma – was Venice's Dear of Pop, writing '*Lo che non vivo*', which was translated into English as 'You Don't Have to Say You Love Me' for Dusty Springfield and later sung by Elvis; and sultry crooner **Patty Pravo** played the dogaressa. Since then, few of the lagoon city's productions have hit the world stage.

Cover bands abound today. Great fun to catch when they play in Venice are **Discofever**, whose tongue-in-cheek

renditions of '70s hits (with platforms and wigs) bring Chic and Co to the campo to make a great '70s night party.

Yet while the local music scene is small, it is by no means dormant. Internationally known home-grown talent includes Groove Jet producer and DJ **Spiller** and Treviso-born **Tolo Marton**, 'Italy's Hendrix'. The vast majority of Venetian vibes, however, have their roots in Kingston Town and local musicians and the music-going public love to 'Lively Up Themselves' to roots reggae. Venetians started skanking to **Pitura Freska**, whose unlikely mix of Venetian dialect and reggae shot them to national fame and brought two rare platinum discs back to the Lagoon; since the band split, frontman **Sir Oliver Skardy** has gone solo. And gigs by **Gialloman** and **Caraibi Near** always draw droves of dread-nodding fans. Catering to a younger Jah-loving generation, ska band **Fahreheit 451**'s hit *Veleno* has made them a household name and the outstanding musicians forming

Dorsoduro

Café Blue

Dorsoduro 3778, crosera San Pantalon (041 522 7613). Vaporetto San Tomà. **Open** 10am-2am daily. **No credit cards. Map** p322 D6.

This pub-style boozer bulges with students and an older international set well into the small hours. Chill out to the occasional DJ set or live gig.

Café Noir

Dorsoduro 3805, crosera San Pantalon (041 528 0956). Vaporetto San Tomà. **Open** 8am-2am Mon-Sat; 7pm-2am Sun. **No credit cards. Map** p322 D6.

Warm and intimate Café Noir is a winter favourite among the university and twentysomething crowd, who while away their days over panini and hot chocolate. As it livens up later, it fills up inside and out with imbibers of *spritz* and alcopops.

★ Il Caffè

Dorsoduro 2963, campo Santa Margherita (041 528 7998). Vaporetto Ca' Rezzonico. **Open** 7am-1am Mon-Sat. **No credit cards. Map** p322 C7.

Relaxed and bohemian, the campo's oldest bar is universally known as 'Caffè Rosso'. It attracts a mixed crowd of all ages who spill out from its single room to sip a *spritz* in the campo or to choose from the impressive wine list. Occasional live music.

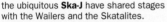

the ubiquitous **Ska-J** have shared stages with the Wailers and the Skatalites.

A low-key but often high-calibre jazz scene has produced some very fine musicians, including brothers **Pietro** and **Marcello Tonolo** and the genre's rising star, bassist **Andrea Lombardini**, while the various formations revolving around the **Suono Improvviso** project often play during local festivals such as Carnevale and the Redentore. Smooth sounds are also the speciality of non-native but Venice-based **Nossa Alma Canta**, whose Brazilian beats often rouse their adopted hometown.

The mainland has a far more varied scene, with bands like the highly talented **Good Morning Boy** and **Grimoon**, who make their own short films to accompany each song. Their haunting melodies blend pop, rock and folk with *chansons françaises* and have earned them success both locally and internationally. Catch them if you can.

Impronta Café

Dorsoduro 3815, crosera San Pantalon (041 275 0386). Vaporetto San Tomà. **Open** 7am-2am Mon-Sat. Closed 3wks Aug. **Credit** AmEx, DC, MC, V. **Map** p322 D6.

Modern and minimalist, Impronta is packed until the small hours with students during the winter, and is busy throughout the year with anyone looking for an affordable bite to eat, cool cocktails or a night cap.

★ Orange

Dorsoduro 3054A, campo Santa Margherita (041 523 4740). Vaporetto Ca' Rezzonico. **Open** 9am-2am Mon-Fri; 10am-2am Sat, Sun. **No credit cards. Map** p322 D7.

The newest and coolest kid on the campo, Orange's sleek, stylish design, creative cocktails and friendly staff have made it a roaring success with a hip mixture of young locals and students. In winter, smokers huddle around heaters in the internal garden, while in summer everyone grabs a table on the campo.

La Giudecca & San Giorgio

See p192 **Skyline Bar**.

CLUBS

See also p233 **Dogado Lounge**.

Piccolo Mondo

Dorsoduro 1056A, calle Contarini-Corfù (041 520 0371). Vaporetto Accademia. **Open** 10.30pm-4am daily. **Admission** free. **Credit** AmEx, DC, MC, V. **Map** p323 E8.

Called 'El Souk' in better days, this 'small world' remains one of the few places to dance in Venice proper. You may, therefore, find yourself on its dancefloor. If you do, you'll be mixing with ageing medallion men, lost tourists and foreign students so desperate to dance, they'll go anywhere.

★ Venice Jazz Club

Dorsoduro 3102, fondamenta dei Pugni (041 523 2056/340 150 4985 mobile). Vaporetto Ca' Rezzonico. **Open** 7pm-2am Mon-Sat. **Admission** (incl 1st drink) €20. **Credit** MC, V. **Map** p322 C8.

The intimate setting and nightly live music make this club, just behind campo Santa Margherita, a perfect place for a night out for fans of high-quality jazz. Concerts start at 9pm.

FURTHER AFIELD

Lido di Jesolo

Most of Jesolo's clubs open at 11pm, but nobody who's anybody shows up until 1am. Save money (rather than face) by picking up flyers offering reduced entrance before 1am. The clubs listed below are perennial favourites.

GETTING TO LIDO DI JESOLO

The Lido di Jesolo bus (information 0421 380 035) leaves from piazzale Roma, but it's more fun to get the double-decker *motonave* from San Zaccaria-Pietà, on the riva degli Schiavoni, to Punta Sabbioni and bus it from there. There are regular boats making the return journey, with a change at Lido between 1am and 6am. Note that if you drop before dawn, you'll need a lift or taxi (0421 372 301, approximately €40) back to the boat stop at Punta Sabbioni as no buses link up with the boats between 12.30am and 5.10am.

Il Muretto

Via Roma Destra 120, Lido di Jesolo (0421 371 310/www.ilmuretto.net). **Open** *Apr-Sept* 11pm-4am Wed, Fri, Sat, Sun. **Admission** €20-€50. **Credit** MC, V.

The home of Italian house – and a Jesolo legend – Il Muretto has been going for over 40 years but remains super-trendy. A mass of ecstatic youth floods the dancefloor for serious house music expertly spun by highly respected resident DJs and guests who are living legends in clubland: Rampling, Oakenfold, Kevorkian, Tenaglia and the Chemical Brothers to name just a few.

★ Terrazza Mare Teatro Bar

Vicolo Faro 1, Jesolo (0421 370 012/www.terrazza mare.com). **Open** *Apr-Sept* 6pm-4am daily. **Admission** free-€10. **Credit** MC, V.

This once-humble beach bar by the lighthouse is more of a cultural space than a club, organising music, exhibitions, and theatre and dance productions, in addition to club nights. With free entry (except special events), no heavy-handed bouncers or label-led dress code, the informal atmosphere attracts a mixed group of groovers, who flock here in their thousands.

Vanilla Club

Via Buonarroti 15, Lido di Jesolo (0421 371 648/ www.vanillaclub.eu). **Open** *June* 11pm-5am Sat, Sun. *July-Sept* 11pm-5am daily. **Admission** €7-€20. **Credit** AmEx, MC, V.

House, hip hop and R&B are the resident sounds in the Vanilla Club, located in the Acqualandia complex. There might also be a dash of disco sounds to boogie to under the palm trees.

Mestre & Marghera

Area Club

Via Don Tosatto 9, Mestre (348 461 1461 mobile/ www.infoprenotazioni.com/areavenezia). Train to Mestre, then bus 3. **Open** 11.30pm-4am Fri-Sat. **Admission** €15-€30. **Credit** DC, MC, V.

The first venue in the Venice region to specialise in hardcore techno; it plays host to big-name DJs and attracts well-heeled clubbers.

Molo 5

Via dell'Elettricità 8, Marghera (041 538 4983/ www.blunotte.it). Bus 2, 4, 4/, 6 or 6/ from piazzale Roma. **Open** *May-Sept* 8pm-2am Wed; 8pm-midnight Thur, Sun; 8pm-4am Fri, Sat. **Admission** (incl 1st drink) €13-€16. **Credit** AmEx, MC, V.

Molo 5 attracts reality TV stars, who come to dine and strut their designer tans to house, commercial and Latino sounds. The restaurant is open all year.

TAG Club

Via Giustizia 19, Mestre (334 824 5710 mobile). Train to Mestre. **Open** *Sept-May* 10pm-8am Fri, Sat. **Admission** (incl 1st drink) €10. **No credit cards**.

A small but lively club just behind the train station in Mestre that puts on an eclectic range of concerts and exhibitions and pop/rock nights. 'Afterhours' parties follow, starting after 3am and featuring house music mixed by well-known DJs – among them local boy Spiller.

▶ *For more on local DJs and musicians, see p234 Sounds of the Lagoon.*

★ Al Vapore

Via Fratelli Bandiera 8, Marghera (041 930 796/www.alvapore.it). Train to Mestre, or bus 6 or 6/ from piazzale Roma. **Open** 7.30am-3pm, 6pm-2am Tue-Fri; 6pm-2am Sat, Sun. **Admission** Tue-Fri free; Sat (incl 1st drink) €10. **No credit cards**.

This music bar has been putting on jazz, blues, soul and rock gigs for years and is very active on the local scene. Popular Jazz Buffet nights take place in the week with funky DJ sets and a free buffet. At weekends, well-known Italian and international musicians perform on the tiny stage. There's no charge on Fridays, but drinks cost more. Over summer, Al Vapore moves to Marghera Village Estate (*see p232* **Summer Festivals**).

The Veneto

For clubbing in the Padua area, *see p263*.

New Age Club

Via Tintoretto 14, Roncade, Treviso (0422 841 052/www.newageclub.it). Venice–Trieste motorway, exit Quarto d'Altino; follow signs for Roncade. **Open** *Oct-May* 9.30pm-5am Fri; 11.30pm-5am Sat. **Admission** *Disco* free after 12.30am for ARCI members Fri (annual membership €9 at the door); €9 (incl 1st drink) Sat. *Concerts* €8-€25. **No credit cards**.

You'll need a car to get to this spot but if you're a pop, rock or metal fan it can be well worth it for some of the big acts that pass through to play on its small stage. Interpol, the Veils, Supergrass and Black Rebel Motorcycle Club have been among recent guests. A rock disco follows the gigs.

Performing Arts

Living largely in the past – but what a past.

The days – in the 18th and 19th centuries – when Venice boasted no fewer than 18 hyperactive theatres are long gone, as is the community of playwrights working flat out to produce dramas and operas to keep an entertainment-hungry public sated. In the 1750-51 season, for instance, Venetian scribbler Carlo Goldoni produced 16 major works; a century later, Verdi's operas *Rigoletto* and *La Traviata* premiered here (*see p242* **Fenice Firsts**).

Today's local theatre-going public is less demanding, and visitors are all too happy to settle for costumed renditions of Vivaldi's greatest hits. But the growth and revamping in recent years of small theatres have finally given a little more space for experiments in the avant-garde.

THE SCENE

Limited in quantity it may be, but – Vivaldi renditions aside – Venice's serious performance scene today is high on quality, thanks largely to the efforts of the Biennale arts umbrella organisation (*see also pp47-49*). Stages here tend to be multi-purpose, with **La Fenice** (*see p239*), for instance, hosting opera, dance and other performances, and the **Teatro Malibran** (*see p239*) offering classical music and ballet.

THEATRICAL TRADITIONS

The popular *Commedia dell'arte* offerings of playwrights Pietro Chiari and Carlo Gozzi – who went on to produce fairy-tale works including the original *Turandot* – were ousted from centre stage when the city's most enduringly popular playwright, Carlo Goldoni, came on the scene in the mid 18th century. A law student who ran away from school to join a band of travelling players, Goldoni reformed the genre by bringing to the stage his satirical observations, usually in dialect, of Venetians and their foibles.

So popular was opera in *La Serenissima* that, it's been calculated, almost 1,300 operas were produced in Venice in just over a generation. After the fall of the Republic, composers such as Donizetti, Bellini and Rossini regularly provided new works for the La Fenice opera house. Besides Verdi's *Rigoletto* and *La Traviata*, La Fenice hosted premières

of Benjamin Britten's *The Turn of the Screw* and Igor Stravinsky's *The Rake's Progress*. In the 20th century, Luciano Berio and Venice's greatest modern composer, Luigi Nono, were commissioned to write for the opera house.

The **Teatro Carlo Goldoni** (*see p239*) in Venice and the **Teatro Toniolo** (*see p240*) in Mestre tend to serve up standard theatrical fare. You can find more cutting-edge work in Venice's smaller theatres: the **Teatro Fondamenta Nuove** (*see p239*), which initially opened for contemporary dance productions but has now branched out into all forms of experimental expression; the **Teatrino Groggia** (*see p239*); and the **Teatro Junghans** (www.teatrojunghans.it), on the Giudecca, which has curtailed operations recently but still hosts occasional festival productions; as well as at Mestre's **Teatrino della Murata** (*see p240*). The **Teatro**

INSIDE TRACK
MALIBRAN IN MEMORIAM

Originally the Teatro San Giovanni Crisostomo, the **Teatro Malibran** (*see p239*) was renamed in 1835 after the famous Spanish soprano Maria Garcia Malibran gave a free recital there. The singer fell to her death from a horse, in Manchester, when she was 28.

a l'Avogaria (*see p239*) explores the outer reaches of Venetian and Italian theatre, often using theatre for didactic purposes, while the **Centro Culturale Candiani** (*see p240*), in Mestre, puts on contemporary pieces.

The summer provides welcome relief in terms of contemporary theatre, dance and music, when performances abound during the **Biennale di Venezia, Danza-Musica-Teatro** (*see p243*), which brings high-quality international productions and artists.

DANCE

The Teatro Fondamenta Nuove hosts an annual dance festival in the autumn, but most dance events are limited to the summer months, when the Biennale provides contemporary performances. The Teatro Toniolo and Centro Culturale Candiani also have fairly mainstream contemporary dance offerings. The seasons at La Fenice and Teatro Malibran always include classical ballet features. In the summer, tango aficionados can watch or even join performances in campo San Giacomo dell'Orio, on the steps of the station or in front of the Salute basilica (www.tangoaction.com).

CLASSICAL MUSIC & OPERA

Venice has become a victim of its own musical tradition, with Vivaldi pouring out of its *scuole* and churches, usually performed by bewigged and costumed players. For many, experiencing Vivaldi in Venice is an absolute must. But more discerning music-lovers might feel somewhat Baroqued out by the predictable programmes performed by local groups, whose technical ability rarely goes beyond the so-so to fairly good range. Exceptions are the **Venice Baroque Orchestra**, a global success (*see below* **Baroque Without the Tinkle**), and the orchestra of La Fenice, one of the best in the country. As well as its opera and ballet seasons, La Fenice has at least two concert seasons a year. The Teatro Malibran shares the Fenice's programmes and also has its own chamber music season, with performances by the **Società Veneziana dei Concerti**. Mestre's Teatro Toniolo also has a symphony and chamber music season. Most other musical events take place in Venice's churches or *scuole* (*see p240*).

St Mark's basilica holds a smattering of ceremonial concerts throughout the year, with the patriarch deciding who is to attend.

Baroque Without the Tinkle

The Venice Baroque Orchestra gives a fresh sound to timeless music.

Once upon a time, lucky music-lovers could catch the award-winning, globetrotting **Venice Baroque Orchestra** at the Scuola Grande di San Rocco (*see p112*). Nowadays, you're best off buying one of their excellent Deutsche Grammophon recordings and experiencing Venice with them as your iPod-provided soundtrack.

Formed in 1997 by conductor, harpsichordist, organist and Baroque scholar Andrea Marcon, this ensemble rediscovers neglected works of the Venetian Baroque, and performs them on period instruments. Its size and composition varies from a small chamber group to a classic orchestra as the repertoire demands. It has won widespread acclaim for its performances of previously unpublished works by Claudio Monteverdi and Antonio Vivaldi, and for its revival of lost operas including Handel's *Siroe* (in 2000), *L'Olimpiade* by Baldassare Galuppi (in 2006) and the Venetian serenata *Andromeda liberata* (2004), which was composed at least in part by Vivaldi.

The orchestra's revolutionary playing technique does away with the mechanical, tinkly, so-called 'sewing machine' style that is usually used for Baroque music: the brilliant violinist Giuliano Carmignola can make it seem like you're hearing even *The Four Seasons* for the very first time.

Antonio Vivaldi.

But lovers of sacred music should catch one of two regular Sunday appointments: the sung Mass at St Mark's (10.30am) and the Gregorian chant on the island of **San Giorgio** (11am).

Visiting music groups often come to town to give one-off, free performances in Venice's churches; look out for posters around town. The city has two resident gospel choirs, the **Venice Gospel Ensemble** (www.venicegospel.com) and the **Joy Singers of Venice** (www.joysingers.it), who perform frequently at various venues around town.

THE SEASON

Venice's theatre and dance season stretches from November to June – though La Fenice keeps on going most of the year, closing only for August. Tourist-oriented classical music concerts are held all year. Smaller theatre groups take advantage of the summer temperatures from June onwards and move into Venice's open spaces (*see pp214-217*).

But the colder months are not without their serious attractions: look out for concerts held throughout the city during late December to provide some Christmas sparkle.

INFORMATION & TICKETS

Tickets for concerts and performances can usually be purchased at theatre box offices immediately prior to shows; the tourist information office near piazza San Marco (*see p305*) and Hellovenezia offices (*see p212*) sell tickets for 'serious' events; most travel agents and hotel receptions will obtain tickets for classical music concerts.

For high-profile or first-night productions at prestigious venues such as La Fenice, Teatro Carlo Goldoni, Teatro Malibran or Teatro Toniolo, the limited number of seats not taken by season-ticket holders will sell out days or even weeks in advance: tickets should be reserved at the theatres themselves or on their websites at least ten days before performances.

Local newspapers *Il Gazzettino* and *La Nuova Venezia* carry listings of theatrical events, as does the bilingual monthly *Venews*.

THEATRES

Teatrino Groggia

Cannaregio 3150, Parco di Villa Groggia (041 524 4665/www.comune.venezia.it/teatrinogroggia). Vaporetto Sant'Alvise. **Box office** 1hr before shows. **Shows** 9pm, days vary. **No credit cards. Map** p321 E1.

Tucked away in the trees, this excellent little space in the northern part of Cannaregio has earned a firm following for its variety of multimedia performances, experimental music and drama, and shows for children in the beautiful garden.

Teatro a l'Avogaria

Dorsoduro 1607, corte Zappa (041 520 9270/ www.teatroavogaria.it). Vaporetto Ca' Rezzonico or San Basilio. **Shows** 8.30pm Mon-Sat; 5pm Sun. **Tickets** by donation. **No credit cards. Map** p322 C8.

This experimental theatre (entry to which is by voluntary donation) was founded in 1969 by renowned director Giovanni Poli. It was at the Teatro a l'Avogaria that he continued the experimental approach he developed in the 1950s. Since his death in 1979, Poli's disciples have pressed on with his experiments, staging works by lesser-known playwrights from the 15th to 19th centuries. Places must be booked at the number above between 2.30 and 4.30pm. The theatre opens its doors 15 minutes before performances.

Teatro Carlo Goldoni

San Marco 4650B, calle Carbonera (041 240 2011/www.teatrostabileveneto.it). Vaporetto Rialto. **Box office** 10am-1pm, 3-6.30pm Mon-Fri & 1hr before shows. **Shows** 8.30pm Tue, Wed, Fri, Sat; 4pm Thur, Sun. **Credit** MC, V. **Map** p323 G6.

The Goldoni regularly serves up Venetian classics by its namesake and 20th-century classics regularly feature on the programme, as do, more recently, more contemporary Italian pieces.

Teatro Fondamenta Nuove

Cannaregio 5013, fondamenta Nuove (041 522 4498/www.teatrofondamentanuove.it). Vaporetto Fondamente Nove. **Box office** 1hr before shows. **Shows** 9pm, days vary. **No credit cards. Map** p322 C3.

Opened in 1993 in an old joiner's shop, the Teatro Fondamenta Nuove stages contemporary dance and avant-garde drama, including works by Crimp and Copi, as well as high-quality experimental music performances. It also organises film festivals, symposiums, exhibitions and workshops.

★ Teatro La Fenice

San Marco 1965, campo San Fantin (041 2424/ 041 786 654/www.teatrolafenice.it). Vaporetto Giglio. **Box office** Hellovenezia (*see p212*). **Credit** AmEx, MC, V. **Map** p323 G8.

Newly restored and positively gleaming, La Fenice is back in business offering opera, ballet and concert seasons. Rehearsals allowing, 40-minute tours (€7; €5 reductions) can be booked at the box office. Photos pp240-241.

► *For more information about tours, see p76. For the theatre's history, see p242 Fenice Firsts.*

★ Teatro Malibran

Cannaregio 5873, calle dei Milion (041 786 603/ www.teatrolafenice.it). Vaporetto Rialto. **Box office** 1hr before shows; Hellovenezia (*see p212*). **Shows** 7 or 8pm, days vary; 3.30pm Sat, Sun. **Credit** AmEx, MC, V. **Map** p324 H5.

Teatro La Fenice. *See p239.*

Inaugurated in 1678 as Teatro San Giovanni Crisostomo, this 900-seater was built on the site where Marco Polo's family palazzo once stood. The theatre now shares the classical music, ballet and opera season with La Fenice; in addition, it has its own chamber music season.

Further afield

For details of opera performances in Verona's Roman **Arena**, *see p272* **From Callas to Camels....** And for that city's **Teatro Romano**, *see p270*.

★ Centro Culturale Candiani
Piazzale Candiani 7, Mestre (041 238 6111/ www.centroculturalecandiani.it). Bus 2 from piazzale Roma. **Box office** 3-10pm Mon; 10am-1pm, 3-10pm Tue-Sun. **No credit cards**.
This 1970s arts centre contains an auditorium, video library, exhibition space and outdoor arena. Alfresco performances are held from June to September. Entertainment ranges from Bach to *The Vagina Monologues*, plus mini film festivals.

Teatrino della Murata
Via Giordano Bruno 19, Mestre (041 989 879/ www.teatromurata.it). Bus 2 from piazzale Roma. **Box office** 30mins before shows. **Shows** 9pm Mon-Sat; 5pm, 9pm Sun. **No credit cards**.
The tiny Teatrino della Murata (which contains a mere 70 seats) is situated in a former warehouse under the remains of the ancient city walls. Funded by the city and regional councils, it specialises in showcasing multicultural theatre.

Teatro Toniolo
Piazzetta Battisti 1, Mestre (041 396 9222/ box office 041 971 666/www.culturaspettacolo venezia.it). Bus 2 or 7 from piazzale Roma. **Box office** 11am-12.30pm, 5-7.30pm Tue-Sun. **No credit cards**.
Founded in 1913, the Teatro Toniolo serves up an assortment of performances, from vernacular favourites to contemporary plays. With its new stagings of Italian and foreign classics, musicals, cabaret, classical and pop music concerts, and contemporary dance and ballet, there is definitely something to suit all tastes.

CHURCHES, SCUOLE & PALAZZI

For information on musical events in Venice's churches, check the local press (*see p301*).

Ateneo San Basso
San Marco 315A, piazzetta dei Leoncini (041 528 2825/www.virtuosidivenezia.com). Vaporetto San Marco Vallaresso. **Box office** 10am-1pm, 2-8.30pm Mon-Sat. **Shows** 8.30pm Mon-Sat. **Tickets** €25; €20 reductions. **No credit cards**. **Map** p324 J7.
Just off St Mark's square, the Ateneo puts on the *Four Seasons* and other Vivaldi works played by the St Mark's Chamber Orchestra.

★ Basilica dei Frari
San Polo, campo dei Frari (041 719 308/ www.basilicadeifrari.it). Vaporetto San Tomà. **Map** p321 E6.

The lofty Gothic Frari is one of the best venues in Venice for catching high-standard performances of sacred music. It has regular seasons in the autumn and spring; organ recitals and a number of free or low-cost afternoon concerts are held especially over Christmas and the New Year. If you go to one of the winter concerts, wrap up warm.
▶ *For further information on this magnificent basilica, see p109.*

Palazzo Barbarigo Minotto
San Marco 2504, fondamenta Duodo o Barbarigo (340 971 7272/www.musicapalazzo. com). Vaporetto Giglio. **Box office** 30mins before shows. **Shows** 8.30pm daily. **Tickets** €50. **No credit cards.** **Map** p323 F8.
In the beautiful surroundings of a 17th-century palazzo, performances include a variety of classic opera arias, Neapolitan songs and complete operas with few instruments and a piano to accompany the singers. During the evening, the small audience follows the performers around the salons of the palazzo, from the frescoed Sala Tiepolo on to the bedroom for the more intimate 'love duets'.

Palazzo delle Prigioni
Castello 4209, ponte della Paglia (041 984 252/www.collegiumducale.com). Vaporetto San Zaccaria. **Box office** 10.30am-8.30pm on performance days. **Shows** 9pm Mon, Wed, Fri, Sun. **Tickets** €25; €20 reductions. **No credit cards.** **Map** p324 J8.
Just over the Bridge of Sighs from the Doge's Palace, the prisons host concerts by the Collegium Ducale Orchestra – which performs its Venetian

Baroque and German Romantic repertoires several times a week – and also jazz evenings courtesy of the Venice Jazz Quartet.

San Giacomo di Rialto
San Polo, campo di San Giacomo (041 426 6559/ www.ensembleantoniovivaldi.com). Vaporetto Rialto or Rialto Mercato. **Box office** 10am-6pm; 10am-8.45pm on performance days. **Shows** 8.45pm Wed, Fri, Sun. **Tickets** €25; €20 reductions. **Credit** MC, V. **Map** p321 H5.
One of the oldest churches in Venice, affectionately known as San Giacometto, it hosts concerts by the Ensemble Antonio Vivaldi. *See also p99.*

Santa Maria Formosa
Castello, campo Santa Maria Formosa (041 984 252/www.collegiumducale.com). Vaporetto Rialto. **Box office** 10.30am-8.30pm on performance days. **Shows** 9pm, days vary. **Tickets** €25; €20 reductions. **No credit cards.** **Map** p324 J6.
This charming church in western Castello is the alternative venue for performances by the Collegium Ducale Orchestra and also hosts free concerts by visiting foreign choirs.
▶ *For further information on this church, see p82. The Collegium also performs at the Palazzo delle Prigioni; see above.*

Santa Maria della Salute
Dorsoduro, campo della Salute (041 274 3928/ www.marcianum.it/salute). Vaporetto Salute. **Shows** 4pm Sun. **Map** p323 G9.
The lofty Baroque Salute church (*see p123*) hosts free Sunday afternoon organ recitals at 4pm.

San Vidal

San Marco 2862B, campo San Vidal (041 277 0561/www.interpretiveneziani.com). Vaporetto Accademia. **Box office** 9.30am-8.30pm Mon-Sat; 10am-6pm Sun. **Shows** 9pm Mon-Sat (8.30pm in winter). **Tickets** €24; €19 reductions. **Credit** MC, V. **Map** p323 E8.

For highly professional renditions of Venice's favourite composer, Vivaldi, visit the church of San Vidal (*see p75*), where the no-frills *Interpreti veneziani* play to a backdrop of Carpaccio's San Vitale on a white horse over the high altar.

Scuola Grande di San Giovanni Evangelista

San Polo 2454, campiello della Scuola (041 718 234/www.scuolasangiovanni.it). Vaporetto San Tomà. **Box office** 10am-5pm Mon-Fri & from 6pm on performance days. **Shows** 9pm, days vary. **Tickets** €30-€35; €25-€30 reductions. **No credit cards.** **Map** p320 D5.

This 14th-century *scuola*, with an imposing marble staircase and paintings by Tintoretto and Tiepolo, hosts *Musica in maschera*, an orchestra and choir performing shrink-wrapped opera. *See also p111.*

Fenice Firsts

The glory days of Venice's opera house.

When the curtain first went up in 1792 at **La Fenice** – today Venice's one and only opera house – it had seven or eight rivals in a city that boasted an opera tradition stretching back over a century and a half. It was built to replace the Teatro San Benedetto, which burnt down in 1774. Living up to its name (*fenice* means phoenix), it has burned to the ground twice since opening and has twice risen from the ashes, most recently in 2003 after a devastating fire in 1996. The latest rebuilding restored it to its former glory, with the bonus of updated stage machinery and surtitles for the audience.

The 20th century saw significant musical milestones with both Britten's *The Turn of the Screw* and Stravinsky's *The Rake's Progress* premiering here, but it was in the 19th century that the theatre's reputation glittered as brightly as its opulent gilded interior. The greatest composers of the age wrote for La Fenice: Bellini, Donizetti and Rossini, whose *Tancredi* and *Semiramide* both had their premières here. But from the 1840s on, it was Verdi who stole the show. After his *Attila* premiered in 1846, the theatre directly commissioned *Rigoletto* (1851), *La Traviata* (1853) – which flopped miserably – and *Simon Boccanegra* (1857).

The *Traviata* fiasco was easily forgotten as La Fenice was also the focal point for revolutionary struggles for Italian unity and anti-Austrian protest in this period, and Verdi was their standard bearer. The Fenice audience would join in his operas' rallying, patriotic choruses. They would also throw bouquets of red, white and green, the colours of Italy's tricolour, on to the stage with cries of '*Viva Verdi*' – the composer's name but also an acronym for *Vittorio Emanuele, Re d'Italia*, (Vittorio Emanuele, King of Italy). When the Austrians got wise to this, the Italian colours were banned and forcibly replaced by Austria's black and yellow: performers left these bouquets where they landed in disdain.

Madama Butterfly at La Fenice.

Scuola Grande di San Teodoro
*San Marco 4810, salizzada San Teodoro (041
521 0294/www.imusiciveneziani.com). Vaporetto
Rialto.* **Box office** 10am-7pm daily. **Shows**
8.30pm Tue-Sun. **Tickets** €25-€35; €20-€30
reductions. **No credit cards. Map** p324 H6.
If your heart is set on performers in wigs, head for
the Scuola Grande di San Teodoro, where the local
I Musici Veneziani orchestra dishes up Vivaldi and
a medley of opera arias.

OTHER MUSIC VENUES

Fondazione Querini Stampalia
*Castello 5252, campo Santa Maria Formosa
(041 271 1411/www.querinistampalia.it).
Vaporetto Rialto.* **Shows** 5pm, 8.30pm Fri, Sat.
Tickets €8; €6 reductions. **Credit** AmEx, DC,
MC, V. **Map** p324 J6.
The soirées that are organised by this enterprising
museum and cultural foundation (*see p78*) take the
form of a half-hour recital of lesser-known works,
usually from the Renaissance or Baroque periods.

Fondazione Cini
*Isola di San Giorgio (041 528 9900/www.cini.it).
Vaporetto San Giorgio.* **Map** p329 K10.
The foundation draws on its impressive archives to
organise music seminars, workshops, masterclasses
and concerts of rare or neglected music. Concerts are
held at the Fondazione HQ on San Giorgio or at
Palazzo Cini (Dorsoduro 864, piscina del Forner, 041
521 0755). Just turn up at the venues in time for the
concerts, which are free.
▶ *For more about the Cini Foundation, see p129.*

FESTIVALS

For the **Venezia Suona** festival, *see p215.*

Biennale di Venezia, Danza-Musica-Teatro
*Ca' Giustinian, San Marco 1364, calle del Ridotto
(041 521 8711/www.labiennale.org). Vaporetto
San Marco Vallaresso.* **Box office** Hellovenezia
(*see p212*). **Date** *Dance* mid-late June. *Theatre*
July. *Music* late Sept-mid Oct. **Map** p323 H8.
Venice's Biennale festival umbrella has recently
allotted new funds to its dance, music and theatre
department. The programme remains restricted to
the summer months and is staged in newly restored
venues inside the Arsenale (*see p84*): the Teatro
Tese, the Tese alle Vergini and the smaller Teatro
Piccolo Arsenale (all open for Biennale performances
only), as well as squares and venues around the city.
▶ *For much more on the Biennale, see pp47-49.*

Festival Galuppi
041 522 1120/www.culturaspettacolovenezia.it.
Box office at venues 2hrs before performance;
Hellovenezia (*see p212*). **Date** late Aug-mid Oct.

This festival is dedicated to the Venetian composer
Baldassarre Galuppi (*see p135* **Music of the
Islands**). Listen to 18th-century classical music in
otherwise inaccessible venues, such as the islands of
San Francesco del Deserto and Lazzaretto Nuovo.

Le Giornate Wagneriane
*Associazione R Wagner, Palazzo Albrizzi,
Cannaregio 4118, fondamenta Sant'Andrea
(041 523 2544/www.acitve.com).* **Box office**
see below. **Date** 16 Oct-26 Nov. **Map** p321 H4.
Wagner is the star of a series of world-class concerts
organised by the Associazione R Wagner; the
Giornate Wagneriane also includes conferences on
the great man, and visits to the house he occupied
while in Venice. Concerts are free, and by invite only,
though these are easily obtainable: call 041 526 0407
(9.30am-12.30pm Mon-Fri) from October or email
arwv@libero.it. Venues include the Palazzo Albrizzi;
Fondazione Cini (*see above*) and Fondazione Levi
(San Marco 2893, calle Giustiniani).

Teatro in Campo
*041 522 1740/bookings 340 844 4117/www.
pantakin.it/www.destateincampo.it.* **Box office**
at venue from 6pm on performance days;
Hellovenezia (*see p212*). **Date** late July-mid Aug.
The Teatro in Campo festival graces campo Pisani
(map p323 E9) near the Accademia, with good
drama and opera. The programme also includes free
performances on the islands of the lagoon.

Further afield

OperaEstate
*Via Vendramin 35, Bassano del Grappa (0424
217 819/box office 0424 524 214/www.opera
estate.it).* **Box office** 9.30am-12.30pm, 4-6.30pm
Mon-Sat. **Date** July-Sept.
The Bassano town council organises this summer
feast of dance, theatre, opera, music and cinema in
Bassano and more than 30 other towns around the
Veneto, including the breathtakingly beautiful
Asolo (*see p288*), the chessboard town of Marostica
and Montecchio Maggiore. Jazz and classical music
are on offer through the summer, with international
performers such as Sarah Jane Morris. You can also
catch dance performances – with recent guests
including Royal Ballet soloists, Israel's dance star
Talia Paz and Moses Pendleton with Momix – and
a bag of treats in the theatre.

Settimane Musicali al Teatro Olimpico
*Contrà San Pietro 67, Vicenza (347 492 5005/
www.olimpico.vicenza.it).* **Box office** *April-June*
at the Teatro Olimpico 10am-1.30pm, 4.30-7.30pm
Mon-Sat. **Date** first 2wks June.
In the sumptuous setting of Palladio's masterpiece,
the Teatro Olimpico (*see p279*), Vicenza's annual
music festival focuses on a theme or composer each
year, with conferences and concerts as well as films.

ARTS & ENTERTAINMENT

Sport & Fitness

As if Venice's built-in step classes weren't enough to keep you fit...

With more than 400 stone-stepped bridges and no viable alternative to tramping its endless miles of pedestrian thoroughfares, Venice comes with a punishing built-in exercise programme. But watery pursuits are what web-footed Venetians really like best. Traditional water-borne competitions have stood the test of time, with the **Regata Storica** taking place since the 15th century and still going strong, and the **Vogalonga** attracting more participants every year. Over 120 regattas are held annually, clearly demonstrating Venice's love for all things aquatic.

SAILING THE SEVEN SEAS

Two activities dominate on the mosquito-infested lagoon: Venetian rowing (*voga alla veneta*) and three-sail sailing (*vela al terzo*).

In *voga alla veneta* the rower stands up, facing the direction of travel. There are various types of *voga alla veneta* – team rowing is one, and the impressive solo, cross-handed, two-oar method known as *voga alla valesana* is another. But the most famous type is *voga ad un solo remo* (one-oar rowing) – one of the most difficult rowing strokes of all – as practised by Venetian gondoliers. The gondolier only ever puts his oar in the water on the right side of the boat. Pushing on the oar makes the craft turn to the left; the downstroke corrects the direction. In theory, a gondolier uses the same energy rowing a half-tonne gondola as the average person does walking, though that doesn't quite explain how they get those biceps…

Vela al terzo was once the means of transporting goods for trade throughout Venice's Adriatic dominions. But the city's traditional wooden flat-bottomed sailing craft is now found only in the lagoon, being used exclusively for pleasure and sport.

SPECTATOR SPORTS
Football

Venetians are just as *calcio*-crazed as their land-dwelling compatriots. On match days, supporters sail to the football stadium at Sant'Elena (map off p326 Q10). Home matches take place on alternate Saturdays or Sundays, from September to June. Tickets cost €10-€35 in the stands (reductions for under-18s/over-60s; under-10s pay €3.20 if accompanied by an adult) and are on sale at the ground, at main Hellovenezia (*see p212*) ticket offices, and at the train station (8.30am-6.30pm). For further information, check www.veneziacalcio.it.

Rowing races

The most sumptuous of all the Venetian regattas is the **Regata Storica** (*see p216*) on the first Sunday in September. Perhaps even more spectacular is the **Vogalonga** (*see p215*), which follows a 30-kilometre (18-mile) route around Venice and the northern lagoon. The race is held in June and is open to anyone with a boat and an oar. Rowers descend from all over the country and further afield.

ACTIVE SPORTS & FITNESS
Boating

Canottieri Giudecca
Giudecca 259, fondamenta Ponte Lungo (041 528 7409/www.canottierigiudecca.com).
Vaporetto Palanca. **Open** *Office* 4-6pm Tue, Thur. *Lessons* 2.30-7.30pm Mon; 8.30am-12.30pm, 2.30-7.30pm Tue-Sat; 9am-12.30pm Sun.
Rates €26 enrolment; €5 insurance; €156 yearly membership; €13 monthly membership; €6 per lesson. **No credit cards. Map** p328 E11.
Options here include Venetian rowing in *mascarete* (small, sporty, gondola-like craft), as well as canoes

Shipshape

Take to the waves for fishing or just lazy cruising.

Fishing is a time-honoured Venetian pastime, the Giardini embankment (*see p84*) and the Zattere (*see p125*) being two popular haunts. Angling requirements can be purchased at **Nautica & Pesca** (San Polo 3137, campiello San Rocco, 041 277 0919, www.ferramentadeluca.com), which sells everything from lugworms to wellies – though they don't hire out tackle.

Armed with your rod and worms, you may have a yen for a boat. **Cristiano Brussa** has hire shops in Cannaregio (fondamenta di Cannaregio 1030, 041 275 0196, www.cristianobrussa.com, open 7.30am-5.30pm Mon-Fri) and Castello (fondamenta dei Greci 5030, 041 528 4333, open 7.30am-5.30pm daily) with boats available by the hour or the day. No licence is needed, but they will take you on a test run. A six-person boat costs €20 per hour or €120 per day, petrol included. A valid document must be left at the hire shop while renting. They do not accept credit cards.

If you envisage yourself battling it out with the big boys on the high seas, contact **Big Game Fishing** (campo Stringari 13, Sant'Elena, 041 528 5123, www.biggame sportfishing.it). Staff will rig you out and escort you to the Adriatic. Smaller catches like mackerel make up the normal fare but tuna, shark and other monsters of the deep are possible. Day trips cost €100 per person (minimum four, maximum ten people; novices welcome) and the staff prefers a week's notice. No credit cards.

If, on the other hand, you fancy messing about on the water without expending energy, contact Alfredo Zambon (335 623 3328 mobile, www. ilnuovotrionfo.it) to experience life on board the **Nuovo Trionfo**, a traditional *trabacolo* built in 1926. The boat – a two-masted, 30-metre (98-foot) vessel once common on the Adriatic but now the only one of its kind left – has been beautifully restored by an association that aims to preserve and promote the traditional wooden boats of Venice. Year-round, and from April to October in particular, an extensive range of activities is offered in the lagoon for up to 30 people: from a cruise or a sailing excursion, to special events, dinners or tours of the main islands of the lagoon. A half-day tour on the *trabacolo* will set you back around €800, while the full-day experience costs €1,300. The **Guide to Venice** tour company (*see p297*) can arrange to have an English-speaking guide for your sailing trip.

ARTS & ENTERTAINMENT

and sailboats, plus use of the gym. All rowers must pay the enrolment and insurance fees; short-stay visitors will be charged the monthly membership fee.

Reale Società Canottieri Bucintoro

Dorsoduro 10, 15 & 261, Zattere (041 520 5630/041 523 7933/www.bucintoro.org). Vaporetto Salute or Zattere. **Open** *Office* 10am-noon Tue-Sat. *Lessons* 9am-5pm Tue-Sat; 9am-1pm Sun.* **Rates** *Annual membership* €250 men, €200 women. *Rowing lessons* €100 each. **No credit cards. Map** p323 G10.

Founded in 1882, the Reale Società Canottieri Bucintoro is one of Italy's oldest sports clubs, and boasts a slew of Olympic rowing records. The club offers canoeing, kayaking and Venetian rowing, plus a well-equipped gym. Call for special visitors' rates.

Remiera Canottieri Cannaregio

Cannaregio 3161, campo Sant'Alvise (041 720 539/www.remieracanottiericannaregio.it). Vaporetto Sant'Alvise. **Open** 8.30am-12.30pm, 2.30-6pm Tue-Sun. **Rates** €30 enrolment; €10 monthly membership. **No credit cards. Map** p321 E1.

This boat club offers beginners' *voga alla veneta* courses by arrangement. There's a good gym, which remains open until 9pm.

Società Canottieri Francesco Querini

Castello 6576D, fondamenta Nuove (041 522 2039/www.canottieriquerini.it). Vaporetto Ospedale. **Open** 8am-7pm Tue-Sat; 8am-1pm Sun. **Rates** €26 enrolment fee; €26 monthly fee; €100 for 8 lessons. **No credit cards. Map** p324 L5.

Venice's second-oldest boat club, the Querini also has a good gym. The club offers rowing, canoeing and Venetian rowing.

Golf

Circolo Golf Venezia

Strada Vecchia 1, Alberoni-Lido (041 731 333/ www.circologolfvenezia.it). Vaporetto Lido, then bus A or B to Alberoni. **Open** *Apr-Sept* 8am-8pm Tue-Sun. *Oct-Mar* 8.30am-6pm Tue-Sun. **Rates** (under-21s 50% reduction) €72 Tue-Fri; €84 Sat, Sun. **Credit** AmEx, DC, MC, V. **Map** off p327 BB6.

The Lido links have three practice courses as well as a full 18-hole course. It's open to non-members, though only to those with proof of membership of golf clubs elsewhere.

► *If you want to practice your swing within reach of your hotel room, check in to the San Clemente Palace; see p163.*

Canottieri Giudecca. *See p244.*

Gyms

For rowing clubs equipped with gyms, *see p244*.

ASD Novafit
Cannaregio 5356, calle Stella (041 522 8636).
Vaporetto Fondamente Nove. **Open** 8.30am-
9.30pm Mon-Fri; 8.30am-12.30pm Sat. **Rates**
€30 annual enrolment; €70/month lessons with
instructor; €95/month (€255/quarter) lessons with
personal trainer. **No credit cards. Map** p324 J4.
This gym, tucked away behind Palazzo Widman,
has an air-conditioned fitness room, with equally
breezy instructors. Courses include Pilates and yoga.

Eutonia Club
Dorsoduro 3656, calle Renier (041 522 8618/
www.eutoniaclub.it). Vaporetto Ca' Rezzonico
or San Tomà. **Open** 8am-10.30pm Mon-Fri; 9am-
12.30pm Sat. **Rates** €34.50 annual enrolment or
€14 daily entrance fee for use of the gym; €49 for
8 sessions (valid 1 month); €42/hr with a personal
trainer. **No credit cards. Map** p322 C7.
This gym has three well-lit rooms and friendly staff
to put you through your paces. Courses range from
kali filipino to belly dancing.

Running

The best time for '*footing*' along the Venetian
streets is early morning. Popular spots include
wider pavements on the Zattere, the fondamenta
by the Giardini vaporetto stop, or further east
under the shady *pineta* of Sant'Elena.

The **Venice Marathon** (*see p216*) takes
place in October. The starting line is at the Villa
Pisani at Strà; the race passes along the Brenta
Canal (*see p260*), over the bridge to Venice, then
by a specially erected pontoon over the lagoon
to the finishing line on the riva degli Schiavoni.
The less competitive **Su e Zo per i Ponti**
(*see p214*) takes place in March.

Swimming

Although often lukewarm and jellyfish infested,
the Lido's Adriatic water draws locals in their
thousands to its public beaches; *see p131*.

There are three public pools, though
Byzantine timetables and lengthy holiday
closures leave few windows for a spontaneous
quick dip. Swimming caps in the water and
poolside flip-flops are obligatory. The hours
given below are for 'free' swimming (when
the pool is not booked for courses).
See also below **Tennis Club Ca' del Moro.**

Piscina Comunale Sant'Alvise
Cannaregio 3163, calle del Capitello (041 715
650). Vaporetto Sant'Alvise. **Open** 1-2.30pm,
9-9.45pm Mon, Thur; 1-4pm, 8.15-9pm Tue, Fri;

1-2.30pm, 6.15-9pm Wed; 9am-noon, 6-7.30pm
Sat; 10am-noon Sun. **Rates** €6/session; €50 for
10 sessions. **No credit cards. Map** p321 E1.
Courses for all, plus a warm mini-pool for small fry.
Opening times vary during summer holidays.

Piscina Comunale Sacca Fisola
Giudecca, San Biagio-Sacca Fisola (041 528 5430).
Vaporetto Sacca Fisola. **Open** 9.45am-noon,
1-2.30pm, 7.15-8.45pm Mon, Tue, Thur, Fri; 3.30-
5pm, 6.30-7.15pm Wed; 3.30-6pm Sat; 3-6pm Sun.
Rates €5.70/session; €48 for 10 sessions (valid
3 months). **No credit cards. Map** off p322 A10.
This pool is for serious swimmers. No mini-pool.

Piscina Ca' Bianca
Ca' Bianca, via Sandro Gallo, Lido (041 526
2222). Vaporetto Lido, then bus A or B towards
Malamocco. **Open** 10.45-11.30am, 8.30-9.15pm
Mon, Tue, Thur; 10.45am-12.30pm, 7.45-9.15pm
Wed; 10.45am-12.30pm, 7.45-8.30pm Fri; 4.45-
5.30pm Sat. **Rates** €5.50/session. **No credit
cards. Map** off p327 BB6.
The newest pool in town, this is very popular with
the inhabitants of the Lido. No mini-pool though.

Tennis

Tennis Club Ca' Del Moro
Via Ferruccio Parri 6, Lido (041 770 965).
Vaporetto Lido, then bus V. **Open** 8.30am-9pm
Mon-Fri; 8.30am-8pm Sat, Sun. **Rates** *Tennis*
€11/hr per person; €44/court for 4 people
for 90mins. *Pool* €9 half day; €18 full day.
No credit cards. Map off p327 BB6.
This sports centre on the Lido has ten tennis courts,
a gym, swimming pool and football pitches.

Yoga & shiatsu

Yoga Studio di Paola Venturini
San Polo 2006, campo San Polo (348 293 6522/
www.yogastudeiovenezia.it). Vaporetto San
Silvestro or San Tomà. **Rates** €20/session
(1hr 45mins); private sessions by arrangement.
No credit cards. Map p321 F6.
Iyengar yoga predominates in Venice. Though not
as energetic-looking as ashtanga, a session with
Paola Venturini will still put you through your paces.

Offset your
flight with
Trees for Cities
and make your
trip mean
something for
years to come

www.treesforcities.org/offset

Trees for Cities
Charity registration number 1032154

The Veneto

Villa Barbaro a Maser. *See p287.*

Getting Started	**251**
Walk Chioggia	252
Map The Veneto	253
Not Venice but Trying	254
Padua	**255**
Map Padua	257
The Brenta Canal	261
Verona	**265**
Map Verona	267
Star-crossed Weddings	271
From Callas to Camels…	272
Vicenza	**275**
Map Vicenza	277
Profile Andrea Palladio	280
Drive Villa Jaunts	285
Treviso & the Northern Veneto	**286**
Moving Mountains	288
The Hills are Alive…	292

Bags packed, milk cancelled, house raised on stilts.

You've packed the suntan lotion, the snorkel set, the stay-pressed shirts. Just one more thing left to do – your bit for climate change. In some of the world's poorest countries, changing weather patterns are destroying lives.

You can help people to deal with the extreme effects of climate change. Raising houses in flood-prone regions is just one life-saving solution.

Climate change costs lives.
Give £5 and let's sort it *Here & Now*

www.oxfam.org.uk/climate-change

Be Humankind Oxfam

Getting Started

Roman remains, Palladian villas and the dramatic Dolomites.

Competing against Venice is not easy, but there are one or two areas where the Veneto region, over on the mainland, beats its gracious capital. For Roman ruins, head for **Verona** (*see p265*), with its magnificent Arena. Giotto's works in the Scrovegni Chapel in **Padua** (*see p255*) are the *nec plus ultra* of the Renaissance fresco cycle by a maestro who hardly got a look-in over in *La Serenissima*.

And though Venice boasts some great churches by Palladio, you'll have to visit his Basilica Palladiana in **Vicenza** (*see p275*) to experience the great architect's take on urban restyling, and the villas (*see pp280-285*) of the countryside around Vicenza for his stately rural retreats. Venice, moreover, is a little short on natural beauties: the mainland's the place to go for landscape and greenery, rising to dramatic mountains north of **Treviso** (*see p286*).

TERRA FERMA BREAKS

The environmental ravages of the economic miracle (*see pp29-30*) have spared some lovely untouched and under-visited corners of the Veneto, particularly in the hills and mountains: the Colli Euganei beyond Padua and the Colli Berici south of Vicenza roll pleasantly above the industrial sprawl. But the Veneto is largely defined by its towns.

Treviso has frescoed *palazzi* and an economic vitality – of which the Benetton empire is the most famous flag-bearer – that gives it a lively, dynamic feel. Beyond, in the gentle foothills of the Dolomites, are the wine-producing centres of **Conegliano** and **Valdobbiadene** (for both, *see p290*); **Asolo** and **Possagno** (for both, *see p288*), given up respectively to the leisured laziness of *il dolce far niente* (literally, 'sweet doing nothing') and the cold neoclassical visions of Antonio Canova; and **Bassano del Grappa** (*see p288*), home of the fiery spirit of that name. (For more on the region's wines, *see p178* **Profile**).

Beyond **Belluno** (*see p291*), the mountains begin in earnest, bringing hordes of *beau monde* skiers to the elegant resort of **Cortina d'Ampezzo** (*see p291*) and queues of summer hikers to attempt one of the numerous *alte vie* (high-altitude footpaths) that traverse the pink-granite Dolomites.

Heading north-east from Venice, a straggle of seaside resorts with high-density beach umbrellas, campsites and discos stretches all the way from **Lido di Jesolo** (*see p235*) to the border of the Veneto.

But for many visitors – especially those who don't read the small print on their travel itinerary – the first experience of the Veneto is **Mestre** (*see p254* **Not Venice but Trying**) or **Chioggia** (*see p252* **Walk**). At the southern end of the lagoon, Chioggia is half fishing port and half high-rise tourist resort. Industrial Mestre – with its plethora of modern overspill hotels – is not as bleak a prospect as it first appears: it has nightlife, cinemas, theatre… and there's plenty of transport across the lagoon back to Venice.

GETTING AROUND

By train

Padua (30 minutes from Venice), Vicenza (55 minutes) and Verona (85 minutes) are all connected to Venice by frequent, fast Intercity or Eurostar trains on the Venice–Milan–Turin line. There are also slower *regionali* services.

Heading north from Venice is not quite as straightforward. Treviso (20-30 minutes) and Conegliano (40-50 minutes) are on the main line from Venice to Udine, and are served mainly

Walk Chioggia

Venice in miniature.

A small town of Roman origin at the southern end of the lagoon, the fishing port of **Chioggia** spreads over a rectangular island split down the middle by the Canal Vena; to the east is the long arm of the beach resort of Sottomarina. From piazzeta Vigo, the long, wide corso del Popolo extends the whole length of the island, parallel to the canal. On either side, narrow lanes lead off to the lagoon.

The only sight not on the corso is the church of **San Domenico** (open 8am-noon, 2.30-5.30pm daily), on its very own island at the end of the street that begins across a balustraded bridge from piazzetta Vigo, where the ferry ties up. A barn-like, 18th-century reconstruction, it houses Vittore Carpaccio's last recorded work, a graceful poised *St Paul* (after the second altar on the right; 1520). Other works of note are a huge wooden crucifix – possibly a German work of the 14th century – and a Rubens-like Tintoretto. More charming is the collection of naïve ex-voto paintings placed by grateful fishermen in a side chapel.

Halfway down the corso is the **Granaio**, the former municipal granary, built in 1322 but heavily restored in the 19th century; it now hosts the fish market (open 8am-noon Tue-Sun). Nearby, the church of **San Giacomo** (open 7am-noon, 4-6.30pm daily), has a high altar in elaborate faux-Baroque (1907), which contains the *Madonna della Navicella*, an image of the Virgin as she appeared to a Sottomarina peasant in 1508.

Just beyond the Granaio is the small piazza XX Settembre. Here stands the church of the **Santissima Trinità** (10am-1pm Thur; 5-8pm Fri, Sun). which has been restored and converted into a museum. The church is a small but elegant 18th-century building by Andrea Tirali. Some interesting paintings have been moved here since the restoration, including two large 17th-century works on the life of St Nicholas: the *Consecration of St Nicholas* by Pietro Damini is especially splendid, offering a fine display of colourful clerical robes.

More interesting than the church itself is the grandiose Oratorio dei Battuti, which begins just behind the high altar. This large space, built for a philanthropic confraternity of laymen devoted to the Madonna (and originally to flagellation), was decorated with a grandiose cycle of ceiling paintings by a number of the major names of 17th-century Mannerist painting in Venice. Particularly fine is the *Resurrection* by Alvise del Friso.

Leaving the church, cross the bridge to your right, and you will come to the church of the **Filippine**, an 18th-century building (open for services only) with an extraordinary Chapel of Reliquaries (third on the right).

Near the end of the corso, two churches stand side by side on the right. The smaller one is **San Martino** (open for services only), a Venetian Gothic jewel built in 1393. Next door, the huge 17th-century **Duomo** (10.30am-noon, 3.30-6pm daily) was built to a design by Baldassare Longhena after a fire destroyed the original tenth-century church. Only the 64-metre (210-foot) campanile across the road remains from the earlier structure (though it was completed in the 14th-century). Inside the Duomo, the chapel to the left of the chancel contains a series of grisly 18th-century paintings depicting the torturously prolonged martyrdom of the two patron saints of Chioggia, Felix and Fortunatus (Lucky and Happy).

The road to the left of the Duomo leads to the **Museo Diocesano** (9am-noon Thur; 3-6pm Fri; 3-6.30pm Sun). It contains a collection of religious art, including two fine polyptychs by Paolo Veneziano.

The **Torre di Santa Maria** marks the end of the old town; just beyond, in campo Marconi, is the deconsecrated church of San Francesco, which has been turned into the **Museo Civico della Laguna Sud** (9am-1pm Tue, Wed; 9am-1pm, 3-6pm Thur-Sat; 7.30-11pm Sun – yes, that's evening only on Sundays). The museum provides a good introduction to aspects of lagoon life. On the top floor is an exhaustive collection of model fishing boats, plus a small gallery with an attractive triptych by Ercole del Fiore (1436), *Justice between Saints Felix and Fortunatus*.

GETTING THERE

Twice-hourly bus-plus-boat services leave Santa Maria Elisabetta vaporetto stop on the Lido for the picturesque trip to Chioggia (1hr30mins). Alternatively, bus 80 leaves piazzale Roma every 30 minutes for the 50-minute road trip.

THE VENETO

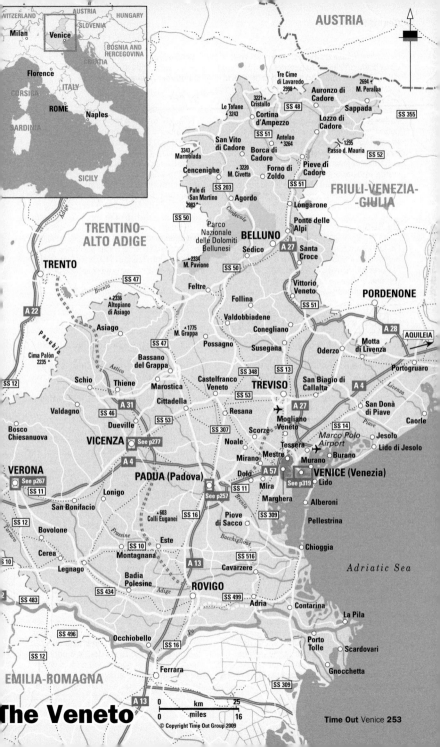

The Veneto

by *interregionale* trains. To the north-west, Castelfranco Veneto (40 minutes) and Bassano del Grappa (60 minutes) are served by a local line with around 15 trains a day. Around seven local trains a day make the agonisingly slow but very pretty haul up the Piave valley from Padua to Feltre (90 minutes) and Belluno (two hours); some then proceed further, to Calalzo-Pieve di Cadore (three hours), which is connected by bus to Cortina d'Ampezzo. For more resort and travel information in this area, consult the skiing website www.dolomitisuperski.it.

See the individual chapters in this section for further details of specific routes. For general information on rail travel in Italy, *see p295*.

By bus

On mountain routes, buses are often the only mode of public transport. The ski resort of Cortina d'Ampezzo, for example, is best reached by bus (*see p292*). Many destinations can be reached by combining train and bus

journeys. See individual chapters in the Veneto section for details of bus services. Note that Sunday services are limited.

By car

The larger towns in the Veneto are connected to Venice by fast motorway links – but be warned that tolls on Italian motorways are not cheap. Main highways (equivalent to the UK's A-roads), identified as *strade nazionali* or *strade statali* (prefix 'N' or 'SS' followed by a number), are not always good and often take a direct route right through the centre of towns (with a consequently high risk of encountering traffic confusion) rather than simply bypassing them.

For more out-of-the-way destinations and mountain roads, a good map is essential; those in the 1:200,000-scale series published by the Touring Club Italiano (TCI) have plenty of detail and are available in most bookshops and in motorway service stations.

For car-hire information, *see p297*.

Not Venice but Trying

Venice's mainland gateway tries in vain to live up to its glamorous neighbour.

Facing Venice from the mainland, **Mestre** was an insignificant walled town from the tenth century (the only notable remnant of these medieval fortifications is the tower in its main piazza). It began to grow exponentially only in the last century, with the creation of the industrial port of **Marghera** when the lure of jobs attracted workers from all over Italy. From the 1950s, lagoon-dwelling Venetians began to move here too, fleeing high house prices in Venice itself, or simply seeking 'luxurious' trappings such as cars and supermarkets. Though psychologically a big move, it's only a ten-minute bus or train ride from Venice.

As Mestre's population expanded, the town galloped outwards and upwards in grim concrete. Defined by what it is not (that is, Venice), Mestre has only recently begun to strive for its own identity. An evening visit to **piazza Ferretto** – the attractive square at Mestre's heart – will give you a sense of the extent to which Mestre is youth-oriented. Mestre has more cinemas than Venice; both the centre and the environs are home to some great clubs, gay and straight (*see p230 and p236*).

It is also fair to say that the ugliness of Mestre has been somewhat exaggerated. Pedestrianised piazza Ferretto is as fine a central piazza as you will find in many small

Italian towns, and there are attractive arcaded streets to the north (via Palazzo) and a pleasant market area to the east of the square. The churches of **San Rocco** (open Sept-June 10am-noon, 4-7pm Mon-Sat, 9am-noon Sun, with mass in Romanian at 10am) with its 18th-century decorations, and **San Girolamo** (open 9am-noon, 4-6.30pm Mon-Sat), with its restored Gothic interior, are worth a look. There are also some fine classical villas, particularly in the greener areas north of town.

In recent years, Mestre has established some cultural independence from Venice: its theatres (*see p240*) provide musical and dramatic seasons that rival almost anything the lagoon city has to offer (opera excluded). The **Centro Culturale Candiani** (*see p240*) has spaces for exhibitions, workshops and multimedia events.

In 2004, dreary Mestre's desire for green space was answered by the opening of **Parco San Giuliano**, a 70-hectare (175-acre) area of former wasteland between the town and the lagoon, with bicycle tracks, woods, canals, play areas, a roller-skating rink and lake. A pedestrian bridge crosses the busy ringroad to connect the park to the centre. The walk across the park is worth it for the view over the lagoon to Venice – and that, of course, sums up Mestre's problem.

Padua

Now emerged from Venice's shadow, Padua quietly thrives.

Padua spent almost 400 years under the Venetian yoke and struggled, for decades after, to find an identity for itself. It wasn't until the north-eastern economic miracle of the 1960s and '70s, in fact, that this elegant city of some 200,000 souls truly found its feet, contributing to the upsurge and furnishing itself with all the designer shops and smart accoutrements of well-heeled Veneto life.

But Padua has much to offer besides: a university that has been going strong since the 13th century; Europe's oldest botanical garden; the spectacular **Il Santo** basilica, dedicated to the city's patron (St Anthony); not to mention Giotto's great fresco cycle in the **Cappella degli Scrovegni**, surely one of the world's greatest masterpieces.

HISTORY

Agricultural communities lived in the Padua area from around 1200 BC, but it was the Romans who transformed this fertile spot into the thriving town of Patavium; the ruins of their Arena lie just outside the Musei Civici complex. Little else survived the attacks of Attila and his Huns in 452. After becoming an independent republic in 1164, the city's political and cultural influence peaked under the Carrara family (1338-1405). Venice (1405-1797), Austria, Napoleon and again Austria had their turns ruling; however, Paduans played an active role in freeing northern Italy from foreign dominion. In 1866 the Austrians were banished, and Padua and the Veneto were annexed to the united Kingdom of Italy.

SIGHTSEEING

If you only see one sight, make it the dazzling **Cappella degli Scrovegni** (Scrovegni Chapel; *see p256*), Giotto's masterpiece. It's part of the **Complesso Eremitani**, also encompassing the Pinacoteca (picture gallery), Museo Archeologico, and a museum of applied arts. Nearby, the church of **Gli Eremitani** (*see p257*) has frescoes by Mantegna.

Towards the city centre, corso Garibaldi becomes pedestrianised and more pleasant, arriving at **Gran Caffè Pedrocchi** (*see p258 & p262*), with the university HQ at **Palazzo del Bò** (*see p259*) opposite. To the west lie

Padua's three main *piazze*, ringed and linked by attractive cobbled streets, boutiques and shady loggias. Between piazza della Frutta and piazza delle Erbe is the **Palazzo della Ragione**, which houses the huge public chamber known to locals as **Il Salone**. Piazza dei Signori is dominated by the **Palazzo del Capitanio**. To the south lies the underwhelming **Duomo** (*see p257*), Padua's cathedral, and its fabulously frescoed 12th-century **baptistry**.

Between piazza del Duomo and via VIII Febbraio is the tranquil old **Ghetto** (*photos pp258-259*), now a beautifully renovated pedestrian zone with shops and bars lining the cobbled streets. The area was closed off in 1603 by four gates restricting its Jewish inhabitants' movements, and remained that way until 1797. One synagogue remains on via Solferino; beneath the 16th-century loggia in Nanto stone is a plaque commemorating the deaths of 46 Paduan and 8,000 Italian Jews during the Holocaust. All that is left of the Sinagoga Tedesca (German Synagogue) – the city's oldest synagogue, destroyed in 1943 by anti-Semitic *padovani* – is a plaque on via delle Piazze.

Back on via VIII Febbraio, as you continue south the street becomes via Roma, passing **Santa Maria dei Servi** (1393). The church is only open for mass, but look out for the beautifully carved wooden door (1511) by Bartolomeo Campolongo.

Via Roma becomes via Umberto I before reaching the **Prato della Valle**. The extensive Prato claims to be the largest public square in

Italy, its elliptical shape reflecting that of the Roman theatre which once stood on the site. Immediately left on entering the Prato is the delightful **Museo del Precinema** (see p259). Further south towards the river is the beautiful medieval complex housing **La Specola** (see p259), the observatory.

Facing the Prato to the south is the church of **Santa Giustina** (see p260). Where via Belludi meets the Prato is the Drogheria Preti, a delightful former *spezzeria* (an apothecary selling herbs and spices for medicinal use) that has changed little in the past century. A stone's throw away is **Il Santo** (see p260), whose economic name belies an awe-inspiring interior; pilgrims flock to the reliquary containing St Anthony's tongue, and the prospect of touching his sarcophagus. The little **Scoletta del Santo** and **Oratorio di San Giorgio**, both in piazza del Santo, offer interesting frescoes on a smaller scale. Next door is the **Orto Botanico** (Botanical Garden; see p259) and on the other side a fine work by Falconetto, the **Loggia e Odeo Cornaro** (see p258).

★ **Complesso Eremitani:**
Scrovegni Chapel & Musei Civici
Piazza Eremitani 8 (049 820 4551/049 201 0020/www.cappelladegliscrovegni.it). **Open** *Museums* 9am-7pm Tue-Sun. *Chapel* 9am-7pm Mon; 9am-10pm Tue-Sun. **Admission** (plus €1 booking fee for Scrovegni chapel) *Museums & chapel* €11; €5-€8 reductions. *Museums only* €10; €5-€8 reductions. *Chapel only* €7-€11. **Credit** (online bookings only) MC, V. **Map** p257 C1/2.

The Complesso Eremitani includes the Cappella degli Scrovegni (Scrovegni Chapel) and the Musei Civici (city museums): the Pinacoteca (picture gallery), Museo Archeologico (archeological museum) and the Museo di Arti Applicate (museum of applied arts) housed in Palazzo Zuckermann.

Booking is obligatory for the Scrovegni Chapel and should be done at least 24 hours in advance. You can book online by credit card or directly at the Musei Civici. Although the chapel is included on the

Padovacard (see below **Inside Track**), a reservation must still be made and the €1 booking fee paid. Evening visits (7-10pm) cost €7 (plus booking fee) for a regular 20-minute evening visit or €11 (plus booking fee) for a 40-minute stay. After this complicated procedure, you generally only get a mere 15-20 minutes to admire the masterpiece. But one look and it will seem worth the hassle.

Cappella degli Scrovegni (Scrovegni Chapel)
This externally unassuming building was commissioned by Enrico Scrovegni, and construction began in 1303. Dante immortalized Enrico's father, Reginaldo, in his *Inferno*, accusing him of usury. It is said that Enrico commissioned the chapel in order not to secure himself the same fate. Enrico is pictured, dressed in violet – the colour of penitence – offering the chapel to Mary in the *Last Judgment* fresco at the far end. The chapel, consecrated in 1305, was originally connected to the Scrovegni palace, which stood inside the area of the Arena, but was demolished in 1827. Centuries of neglect left the frescoes in a state of disrepair, but in 2002, after extensive restoration work, the chapel reopened to the public looking as magnificent as ever.

The two sculptures on the altar, *Two Angels* and *The Virgin and Child*, are by Giovanni Pisano. But it's Giotto's magnificent fresco cycle that utterly dominates the interior. Painted c1304-13, it tells the story of mankind's salvation through the lives of the Virgin, Christ, and depictions of stories of Mary's parents Joachim and Anne. The story of Christ unfolds in the middle and lower rows, with the middle of the right-hand wall dominated by the scene of Judas's kiss.

The high dado at the base of the walls is decorated with fine grisaille paintings of the seven Virtues and Vices. Particularly striking are the figures of Envy blinded by her own serpentine tongue and Prudence equipped with pen and mirror. In the huge *Last Judgment*, covering the west wall of the Chapel, suffering souls are tortured by the kind of demonic beasts that Enrico hoped to avoid, still as hellishly captivating as they must have been 700 years ago.

Pinacoteca & Museo Archeologico
These moderately interesting civic collections are housed in the cloisters of the Eremitani church (see p257). The archeological wing on the ground floor contains some fine pieces, including remains from Roman Padua in room 5. A fifth-century AD skeleton of a young man and his horse is unusual: the animal may have been sacrificed and buried alongside him to speed him on his voyage into the afterlife.

Upstairs, the Pinacoteca-Museo d'Arte Medioevale e Moderna starts with Giovanni Bellini's intriguing *Portrait of a Young Senator*. Works by Titian, Palma il Vecchio, Domenico Tintoretto, Veronese and the collection's only female artist, Chiara Varotari (1584-1663) follow. Next up is a Giotto *Crucifixion* that originally hung in the

INSIDE TRACK
PACKAGE DEALS

The **Padovacard** (€15 for 48 hours; €20 for 72 hours) allows free access for one adult and one child (under 12) to virtually all of Padua's attractions. It can be purchased at the sights covered by the ticket, and at the town's tourist offices (see p264). Further discounts are included, plus free travel on APS buses. For further information, see www.padovacard.it or call 049 876 791.

THE VENETO

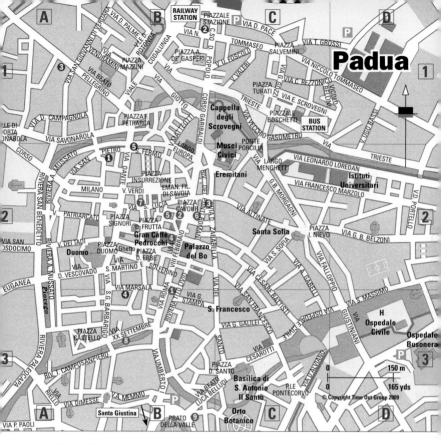

Scrovegni Chapel. There are also fine works by the Bassano family, Pozzoserrato and Luca Giordano, altarpieces by Romanino and Tintoretto, and several sculptures by Canova. The final painting, by Giorgio Fossati (1706-85), is a bird's-eye view of the Prato della Valle (see p255), showing how the city looked in the 18th century when the area was used as a fair.

Museo di Arti Applicate

Housed since 2004 in Palazzo Zuckermann, with its entrance at corso Garibaldi 33, this section of the civic museums contains a small collection of ceramics, furniture, lace, clothes and jewellery. A set of 1781 printing plates shows a map (in mirror-version, of course) of Padua before the fall of *La Serenissima*.

FREE Duomo

Piazza Duomo (church 049 662 814/baptistry 049 656 914). **Open** *Church* 7.30am-noon, 3.45-7.30pm Mon-Sat; 7.45am-1pm, 4-8.30pm Sun. *Baptistry* 10am-6pm daily. **Admission** *Church* free. *Baptistry* €2.80; €1.80 reductions. **No credit cards. Map** p257 A2.

The first church on this site was destroyed in 899 by rampaging Huns; its Romanesque replacement, consecrated in 1075, is pictured in the frescos of the baptistry next door. In 1551, Michelangelo won a competition with his design for the new church, but it's clear from the uninspiring final form that his plans were not adhered to. Construction wasn't completed until 1754. Inside are paintings by Stefano dell'Arzere, Tiepolo, Paris Bordone and a panel painting of a Byzantine-style *Virgin and Child,* a copy of an original by Giotto. The real jewel is the 12th-century baptistry next door, frescoed from floor to ceiling by the 14th-century Florentine Giusto de Menabuoi.

FREE Gli Eremitani

Piazza Eremitani 9 (049 875 6410). **Open** 8.30am-12.30pm, 3.30-7pm Mon-Sat; 10am-12.30pm, 4-7pm Sun. **Map** p257 C2.

The original building, dating from 1276, was bombed on 11 March 1944, then meticulously restored. The reconstructed wooden ceiling (finished at the start of the 14th century) was designed by Friar Giovanni degli Eremitani, who was also

THE VENETO

responsible for the imposing vaulted ceiling of il Salone (the Palazzo della Ragione; *see p260*). The church's most valuable treasures – frescoes by Mantegna, who began the work in 1448 when he was just 17 years old – were almost totally destroyed.

Fortunately, the *Martyrdom of St Christopher*, the *Carrying of the Body of St Christopher* and *Our Lady of the Assumption* survived the bombing raids, having been removed some decades earlier; colour photographs taken just before the war have enabled the restoration of the *Martyrdom of St James* and *St Christopher Converts the Knights* from fragments found in the rubble. The tomb of Jacopo da Carrera (workshop of Andriolo de' Santi, 1345-50) features an inscription of Latin verses that the poet Francesco Petrarch dedicated to a friend. Bizarrely enough, the church was the original home of the tomb of the very Protestant Prince Frederick William of Orange, who died in Padua in 1799. It was removed to a more appropriate spot in Delft, Holland, in 1896, but a bronze copy of the marble *Pietà* (1806-08) by Antonio Canova that adorns the tomb can still be seen in the vestibule opposite the chapel.

Gran Caffè Pedrocchi

Via VIII Febbraio 15, entrance from piazzetta Pedrocchi (049 878 1231/www.caffepedrocchi.it). **Open** *Architectural rooms and Museo del Risorgimento e dell'Età Contemporanea* 9.30am-12.30pm, 3.30-6pm Tue-Sun. **Admission** €4; €2.50 reductions. **No credit cards.** **Map** p257 B2.

Antonio Pedrocchi's vision to build a café that was 'the most beautiful on the face of the Earth' lives on today in his Gran Caffè Pedrocchi, a unique combination of architectural styles and interior designs. Opened to the public in 1831, it soon became known as 'the café without doors' because it was open 24/7.

Other than the opening hours, little has changed in the café. The great Venetian architect Giuseppe Jappelli was chosen by Pedrocchi to realize his vision, and work commenced in 1826. When the upper floor, designed to serve as a Ridotto (a club for gambling and dancing), was opened in 1842, the frescoes were still wet. It contains a condensed tour of Western culture: the Etruscan, Greek, Roman, Herculaneum, Renaissance, Moorish and Egyptian rooms, all lavishly decorated, surround the ballroom, or Sala Grande. Also known as the Rossini Room, the ballroom is twice the height of the others and features a balcony where performances and recitals were staged. Pedrocchi liked to look down, unseen, on the gambling nobles from one of the windows situated high in the walls. The Caffè Pedrocchi's first-floor rooms also house the Museo del Risorgimento e dell'Età Contemporanea, with military memorabilia from 1797 to 1945. *Photo p260.*

▶ *For café and restaurant hours, see p262.*

Loggia e Odeo Cornaro

Via Cesarotti 37 (335 142 8861). **Open** 10am-1pm Tue-Fri; 10am-1pm, 3-6pm Sat, Sun. **Admission** €3; €2 reductions. **No credit cards.** **Map** p257 C3.

Ghetto. *See p255.*

This Renaissance gem was once the home of Alvise Cornaro, a wealthy Venetian and patron of the arts, who commissioned his friend – the Veronese architect Giovanni Maria Falconetto (who stayed at the house as Cornaro's guest for 21 years) – to design the loggia in the internal courtyard for theatrical performances. Completed in 1524, this was Falconetto's first architectural work, followed in 1530 by the Cornaro Odeum, a frescoed octagonal room. The house became popular as a theatre and intellectual salon; Palladio's villa designs are said to have been inspired by visits to the house. *Photos p263.*

Museo del Precinema (Collezione Minici Zotti)
Prato della Valle 1A (049 876 3838/www.minici zotti.it). **Open** 10am-4pm Mon, Wed-Sun. Closed 2wks Aug. **Admission** €3; €2 reductions. *Guided tours* €5. **No credit cards. Map** p257 B3.
This minute museum houses a collection of optical curiosities. The delightful display of magic lanterns (precursors to photo and film) includes hand-painted glass slides, optical instruments, and a Javanese puppet theatre. Some of them are in such good order that they may be operated by visitors. *Photo p264.*

Orto Botanico (Botanical Garden)
Via Orto Botanico 15 (049 827 2119/www. ortobotanico.unipd.it). **Open** *Apr-Oct* 9am-1pm, 3-7pm daily. *Nov-Mar* 9am-1pm Mon-Sat **Admission** €4; €1-€3 reductions. **No credit cards. Map** p257 C3.

This compact botanical garden, founded in 1545 (the first of its kind in Europe), is home to an impressive 4,000 species. Originally a garden of simples (medicinal herbs) supplying the raw materials for the university's medical faculty, it now provides a tranquil refuge from the surrounding bustle. It also contains exquisite freshwater habitats.

Osservatorio Astronomico – Museo La Specola
Vicolo dell'Osservatorio 5 (049 829 3469/www. pd.astro.it/museo-laspecola). **Open** (guided tours only) *Oct-Apr* 4pm Sat, Sun. *May-Sept* 6pm Sat, Sun. **Admission** €7; €5 reductions. **No credit cards. Map** p257 A3.
This beautifully situated medieval tower overlooking the river was made into an observatory by the city's Venetian overlords in 1761. A guided tour takes you up the tower to the observatory rooms and finally to the figures room, an octagonal chamber whose walls were frescoed in the 18th century with life-size portraits of eight eminent astronomers. There's also a collection of antique telescopes, quadrants, sextants and other heavenly paraphernalia.
▶ *Tickets must be purchased in advance from the Oratorio di San Michele, opposite the Specola at piazzetta San Michele 1.*

Palazzo del Bò (University of Padua)
Via VIII Febbraio 2 (049 827 3047/www.unipd. it). **Open** (guided tours only; times are liable to change without warning) *Mar-Oct* 3.15pm, 4.15pm, 5.15pm Mon, Wed, Fri; 9.15am, 10.15am, 11.15am Tue, Thur, Sat. *Nov-Feb* 3.15pm, 4.15pm Mon, Wed, Fri; 10.15am, 11.15am Tue, Thur, Sat. **Admission** €5; €2-€3.50 reductions. Tickets on sale at the office in the Atrium 15mins before each tour. **No credit cards. Map** p257 B2.
The second-oldest university in Italy (after Bologna) was officially founded in 1222, but didn't move to its current location, Palazzo del Bò (bull) – named after the butchers' inn that used to stand on the site – until 1493. The Old Courtyard, designed by Andrea Moroni, is decorated with the coats of arms and family crests of illustrious rectors and students. University alumni include Copernicus, Sir Francis Walsingham and Oliver Goldsmith, all of whom are remembered in the Sala dei Quaranta, where you can

---

INSIDE TRACK
EARLY HOURS

The façade of the **Palazzo del Capitanio**, on Piazza dei Signori, may date from 1532 but it supports an elaborate mechanical clock built a century earlier. Installed in 1437, to a design by Maestro Novello, it's a reproduction of the first clock made in Italy (1344).

THE VENETO

also see Galileo's lectern (he taught here from 1592 to 1610). The university attracted students from all communities, and in the mid 14th century its medical faculty became the first in Europe to accept Jewish students (albeit on payment of double fees). In 1678, Elena Lucrezia Cornaro Piscopia became the first woman graduate (philosophy) in Europe; there is a statue dedicated to her on the stairway. The magnificent oval wooden-benched anatomy theatre, the first of its kind in the world, built by Girolamo Fabrizi Aquapendente in 1594, marked the beginnings of empirical modern medicine.

▶ *You can visit the tomb of Elena Lucrezia Cornaro Piscopia inside Santa Giustina; see right.*

Palazzo della Ragione

Via VIII Febbraio (049 820 5006). **Open** 9am-6pm Tue-Sun. **Admission** €4; €2 reductions; extra charges apply for special exhibitions. **No credit cards**. **Map** p257 B2.

Il Salone, as locals call it, was originally built in 1218-19 to provide the city with a prison and public offices. Between 1306 and 1309 it was converted to accommodate the law courts, and the external loggia of the piano nobile was added. The impressive ship's-keel roof, said to have been painted with over 7,000 stars and planets by Giotto and assistants (1315-17), was destroyed by fire in 1420 and promptly rebuilt. But the doomed ceiling was again destroyed, in 1756, this time ripped off by a hurricane, and again reconstructed to the original design, in 1759.

Inside, the Salone is frescoed with representations of the zodiac, months and seasons, but is mostly empty apart from a huge wooden horse, created for a tournament in 1466. In the north-east corner of the hall sits the *Pietra del vituperio* (stone of shame) where, according to 1261 statutes, insolvent debtors had to sit in their underwear, repeating the words *cedo bonis* (I renounce my worldly goods) before being banished. Those who tried to return risked a repeat of the punishment – plus having three buckets of water poured over their heads.

▶ *Enter by the staircase in piazza delle Erbe, or from via VIII Febbraio for wheelchair users.*

FREE Santa Giustina

Prato della Valle (049 822 0411). **Open** 7.30am-noon, 3-7pm daily. **Map** off p257 B3.

The vast, sparse basilica of Santa Giustina, built 1532-79, houses paintings by Palma il Giovane, Luca Giordano and Carlo Loth, and an altarpiece by Veronese depicting the martyrdom of St Justine. Among the relics in the corridor of the martyrs are bits of St Luke the Evangelist and St Matthias. To the right of the high altar is St Luke's Chapel, which contains the tomb of Elena Lucrezia Cornaro Piscopia (1646-84), the first woman in the world to get a university degree; ask one of the friendly monks if you want to go in.

★ FREE Il Santo (Basilica di Sant'Antonio)

Piazza del Santo (049 878 9722/www.basilicadel santo.org). **Open** 6.20am-7pm Mon-Fri; 6.20am-7.45pm Sat, Sun. **Map** p257 C3.

Although St Anthony was a preacher who rejected worldly wealth, the *padovani* built one of Christendom's most lavish churches to house his

Gran Caffè Pedrocchi. *See p258.*

The Brenta Canal

Take a cruise from Venice to Padua, passing a few of Palladio's villas.

Stretching for 36 kilometres (22 miles) between Venice and Padua, the Brenta waterway was canalised in the 16th century. Goethe fondly remembered cruising down the canal in 1786, enjoying 'the banks studded with gardens and summer houses.' Nowadays, though, many of the gardens and summer houses have long since been replaced by housing estates and industrial sites.

A number of Palladian villas still grace the canal, part of which can be navigated in a boat, *Il Burchiello*, that chugs up the Brenta from Venice as far as Strà. The boat journey includes the *ville* Widmann, Pisani and Foscari.

Villa Foscari, aka 'La Malcontenta' (via dei Turisti 9, Malcontenta, 041 520 3966, www.lamalcontenta.com) is one of the most acclaimed creations of Andrea Palladio. The origin of the villa's nickname is hotly disputed, but is said to refer to an unhappy ('malcontenta') woman who was housed there in isolation. Some say she was a disgraced Foscari wife; others that when the family abandoned the villa shortly after the fall of the Venetian Republic in 1797, rumours of a mysterious, outcast woman arose to keep undesirables away. With its double staircase and elegant Greek temple façade, the Villa Foscari has been the inspiration for thousands of buildings throughout Europe and America.

The boat trip ends at the **Villa Pisani** (via Doge Pisani 7, Strà, 049 502 074, www.villapisani.beniculturali.it), a remarkable design of the early to mid 18th century.

The budget traveller can enjoy a similar route at a fraction of the price by taking ACTV's 53 bus (bound for Padua) from piazzale Roma, leaving at 25 and 55 minutes past the hour.

SITA – Divisione Navigazione 'il Burchiello'
Via Orlandini 3, Padua (049 820 6910/ www.ilburchiello.it). **Services** (Mar-Oct) *Venice–Padua* departure from Pietà boat stop (near San Zaccaria, Venice) at 9am Tue, Thur, Sat. *Padua–Venice* departure from piazzale Boschetti at 8.15am on Wed, Fri, Sun. Booking online advisable. **Rates** (incl entrance to Villa Foscari, to Barchessa Valmarana or Widmann, to Villa Pisani and return bus journey) €79; €37-€52 reductions. **Credit** MC, V.

THE VENETO

remains. Popularly known as Il Santo, the basilica is one of Italy's most important pilgrimage churches. Work on the church began soon after the saint's death (1231) and canonisation (1232), although the main structure remained unfinished until around 1350, when his body was moved to its present tomb in the Cappella dell'Arca. This chapel also contains some of the basilica's great artistic treasures: a series of marble bas-reliefs of scenes from the life of the saint by Jacopo Sansovino, Tullio Lombardo and Giovanni Minello. The chapel's ceiling, by architect Giovanni Maria Falconetto, dates from 1533. Unfortunately, visitors are kept away from the high altar, which supports Donatello's bronze panels and crucifix (1444-45); behind the altar, his stone bas-relief of the Deposition is more visible, as are two of the bronzes: a bull and a lion, representing the evangelists St Mark and St Luke.

Other works of interest include Altichiero's late 14th-century frescoes in the Cappella di San Felice (on the south wall), Giusto de Menabuoi's frescoes in the Cappella del Beato Luca Belludi, and two fine funeral monuments – to Alessandro Contarini (d.1553) and Cardinal Pietro Bembo (d.1547) – both by Michele Sanmicheli. At the back of the apse is the florid Cappella del Tesoro, to which Anthony's 'miraculous' relics were transferred in 1745 for safe-keeping. Here you can inspect the reliquary containing the saint's tongue, his original coffin and fragments of his robes, all housed in their specially built, garish Baroque setting.

In the piazza in front of the church stands the great Renaissance masterpiece, Donatello's monument to the famous *condottiere* (mercenary soldier) Erasmo da Narni (d.1443), aka Gattamelata, who is buried inside the basilica. Commissioned by the *condottiere*'s family in 1453 and cast the same year, it was the first full-size equestrian bronze to be made since antiquity.

▶ *Donatello is known to have inhabited the house at piazza del Santo 19, between 1444 and 1454.*

Scuola del Santo & Oratorio di San Giorgio

Piazza del Santo 11 (049 875 5235). **Open** *Oratorio* 9am-12.30pm, 2.30-5pm daily. *Scuola* 10am-noon, 3-5pm daily. **Admission** €4; €3.50 reductions. **No credit cards**. **Map** p257 C3.
The Scuola del Santo contains 16th-century frescoes, some of which Titian is said to have had a hand in. The oratory, constructed in 1377 for the Lupi di Soragna family, contains a cycle of frescoes by

Altichiero (1379-84) depicting scenes from the lives of Saints Catherine and George. Altichiero is at his best here, and this place is worth a visit even after the long hike around the basilica (*see p260*).

WHERE TO EAT & DRINK

If you're on a tight budget, the morning markets in piazza delle Erbe or piazza della Frutta (and the shops in the arcades around them) offer a wide range of local produce for picnics. If DIY sandwiches are not your thing, take a seat and watch the passing Paduans from one of the many reasonably priced cafés on via Roma, whose seating and umbrellas fill the street.

Bar Fuji

Via Roma 53 (049 875 9485). **Open** 9am-12.30am daily. **Average** €12. **Credit** MC, V. **Map** p257 B3 ❶

A great place to pop in for lunch, this café serves the usual *panini* and *tramezzini*, but the highlight is sushi. They serve an excellent-value fixed-menu plate for €6 (four pieces of sushi plus rice) or a ten-piece platter for €10.

★ Caffè Cavour

Piazza Cavour 10 (049 875 1224/www.caffe cavour.com). **Open** 7.30am-midnight Mon, Wed-Sun. **Average** €25. **Credit** AmEx, MC, V. **Map** p257 B2 ❷

This elegant pâtisserie is home to world-renowned pastry chef Emanuele Saracino. Incredibly intricate – and unmissable – cakes and pastries are on offer on the ground floor, while upstairs you can savour a pleasant meal overlooking the square.

★ Le Calandre

Via Liguria 1, Sarmeola di Rubano (049 630 303/www.calandre.com). **Meals served** noon-2pm, 8-10pm Tue-Sat. Closed 3wks Dec/Jan, 3wks Aug. **Average** €130. **Credit** AmEx, DC, MC, V.

This restaurant, 4km (2.5 miles) west of the city, boasts the youngest chef to have been awarded three Michelin stars. Local boys Massimiliano and Raffaele Alajmo serve up such delights as toasted king prawns with broad bean, radish and apple 'cheese', and beef medallions with aromatic herbs and liquorice. After washing it all down with wine from a superlative list, a lime and celery sorbet with

passion fruit *jus* is all you need to cleanse the palate. Break the bank (and your diet): Le Calandre is not to be missed. Booking is essential.

Ciocco Gelateria Venchi

Via Ponte Altinate 6 (049 876 4706). **Open** 11am-9pm Mon-Thur, Sun; 11am-midnight Fri, Sat. **No credit cards**. **Map** p257 B2 ❸

This friendly ice-cream parlour serves *gelati* and *granite* (crushed water-ice) made on the premises with no artificial preservatives or flavourings.

★ Gran Caffè Pedrocchi

Via VIII Febbraio 15/piazzetta Pedrocchi (049 878 1231/www.caffepedrocchi.it). **Open** 9am-9pm Mon-Thur; 9am-midnight Fri, Sat. **Meals served** 12.30-2pm Thur-Tue. **Average** €35. **Credit** AmEx, DC, MC, V. **Map** p257 B2 ❹

For centuries Padua's most elegant watering hole, and now restored to its former glory, Pedrocchi's is a landmark in its own right. Try the speciality, a cappuccino with a wicked twist. *Photo p260.*

▶ *For details of the café's history and design, and to visit the architectural rooms, see p258.*

Graziati

Piazza della Frutta 40 (049 875 1014/www. graziati.com). **Open** 7.30am-8.30pm Tue-Sun. **Meals served** noon-2.30pm Tue-Sun. **Average** €25. **Credit** MC, V. **Map** p257 B2 ❺

Graziati is essentially a day-long *pasticceria*, specialising in a calorific range of tantalising millefeuille pastries. For something more substantial, the subterranean restaurant serves hearty lunches. On display is a beautiful 14th-century wooden door rediscovered during restoration.

PePen

Piazza Cavour 15 (049 875 9483/www.pepen.it). **Meals served** noon-2.45pm, 6.30pm-12.30am Mon-Sat. Closed 3wks Aug. **Average** €45. **Credit** AmEx, DC, MC, V. **Map** p257 B2 ❻

This popular haunt for the young and lovely at lunchtime has great outdoor seating in summer. As well as pizza, the menu offers a selection of meat and fish dishes, along with an extensive wine list.

Rosso Pomodoro

Via Santa Lucia 68 (049 875 1645). **Meals served** 12.30-3pm, 7.30pm-midnight daily. **Average** €18. **Credit** AmEx, DC, MC, V. **Map** p257 B2 ❼

Good, family-friendly Neapolitan pizzeria.

Sottosopra Bar Tea Room

Via XX Settembre 77 (049 664 898). **Open** 11am-3pm, 7pm-1am Tue-Sat; 7pm-1am Sun. **Credit** MC, V. **Map** p257 B3 ❽

A studenty café with a laid-back vibe. There's a good selection of herbal teas, and salads for around €10.

THE VENETO

THE VENETO

Loggia e Odeo Cornaro. *See p258.*

Zairo

Prato della Valle 51 (049 663 803). **Meals served** noon-2.30pm, 7pm-1am Tue-Sun. **Average** €30. **Credit** AmEx, DC, MC, V. **Map** p257 B3 ❾

Its outdoor seating, with views over the Prato (*see p255*), and its late hours make Zairo a popular spot.

NIGHTLIFE

Many venues above stay open until midnight or later; in particular, Gran Caffè Pedrocchi and Sottosopra Bar Tea Room are late-evening spots. For gay and lesbian venues, *see p230*.

Villa Barbieri

Via Venezuela 11 (049 870 3223). **Open** 8.30pm-4am Wed, Fri, Sat. **Admission** €15 (men); €11 (women). **Credit** AmEx, MC, V.

This summer haunt for Paduan night owls is set in beautiful grounds buried within the city's industrial outskirts. It's actually a fair hike to get there: follow signs for Padova Est to the Sheraton roundabout and then take the motorway towards Bologna, exiting at corso Stati Uniti, which leads to via Venezuela. The music is mainly house and revival, with live music on some nights; you'll be turned away if you look scruffy.

WHERE TO STAY

Albergo Dante
Via San Polo 5 (049 876 0408). **Rates** €47-€59 double. **Credit** MC, V. **Map** p257 B2 ❶
Seriously cheap, this hotel has rather bare rooms, several without their own bathroom, but nicely situated north of the Duomo, near the river. Breakfast is not included.

Grand'Italia
Corso del Popolo 81 (049 876 1111/www. hotelgranditalia.it). **Rates** €130-€226 double. **Credit** AmEx, DC, MC, V. **Map** p257 B1 ❷
This art nouveau hotel is ideally situated close to the train station and major sights of the city centre. The recently restored rooms are quiet and comfortable, and many have balconies.

Hotel Piccolo Vienna
Via Beato Pellegrino 133 (049 871 6331/www. hotelpiccolovienna.it). **Rates** €50-€66 double. Breakfast €3. **Credit** MC, V. **Map** p257 A1 ❸
For the cash-strapped traveller, this hotel in the historic centre of the city provides clean – if cramped – rooms (some without WC).

Majestic Toscanelli
Via dell'Arco 2 (049 663 244/www.toscanelli. com). **Rates** €139-€178 double. **Credit** AmEx, DC, MC, V. **Map** p257 B3 ❹

Museo del Precinema. *See p259.*

All the rooms in this quiet hotel offer attractive views over the quaint streets of the Ghetto, just one minute's walk away from the town's main squares.

Sant'Antonio
Via San Fermo 118 (049 875 1393/www. hotelsantantonio.it). **Rates** €94 double. Breakfast €7. **Credit** MC, V. **Map** p257 B2 ❺
Sant'Antonio is centrally located and good value for money, unless you get one of the rooms overlooking a street corner (busy very early in the morning).

GETTING THERE

By train All trains bound south-west from Venice stop at Padua. Journey time 25-35mins.
By bus From Venice's piazzale Roma bus terminus, orange **ACTV** buses saunter slowly to Padua. Blue **SITA** buses (049 820 6811) speed along the motorway. In Padua, both stop at the bus station in piazzale Boschetti.
By car Padua is on the A4 La Serenissima motorway.

GETTING AROUND

By bus Buses in Padua are operated by **APS** (049 20111, www.apsholding.it); tickets must be purchased before boarding, cost €1 and are valid for 75 minutes.
By bicycle Bicycle hire (348 701 6373 mobile) is available from a small kiosk (open 24 hours daily) at the station. It costs €3 for the first hour and €1 for each successive hour, or €6 per day. A deposit of €50 (cash only) is required for each individual bike.

TOURIST INFORMATION

There are three tourist offices in the city. Alternatively, see www.turismopadova.it.

IAT *Padua railway station (049 875 2077).* **Open** 9.15am-6.30pm Mon-Sat; 9am-noon Sun. **Map** p257 B1.
IAT *Galleria Pedrocchi, next to Gran Caffè Pedrocchi (049 876 7927).* **Open** 9am-1.30pm, 3-7pm Mon-Sat. **Map** p257 B2.
IAT *Piazza del Santo, opposite the basilica (049 875 3087).* **Open** 10.30am-1pm, 3-6pm Mon-Sat; 3-6pm Sun. Closed Nov-Mar. **Map** p257 C3.

> ### INSIDE TRACK
> ### PALLADIO NEAR PADUA
>
> Palladio's **Villa Cornaro** in Piombino Dese, north of Padua, is one of the architect's most satisfying designs. For information, *see p283.*

Verona

From ancient Roman theatres to Shakespeare's stage set.

Verona may be synonymous for many with
Romeo and Juliet, but lovers' laments had rung
out from the city long before the Bard made it his.
It was here that Dante completed *Paradiso*, in
which he finally meets his divine Beatrice. The
poet Petrarch lamented the death of Laura 'while
I was in Verona, alas ignorant of my fate'.

The attraction today known as **Juliet's House**
pales in comparison with the other glories that
Verona has to offer. If, across the lagoon, Venice
lacks any ancient remains, Verona more than
makes up for it. There's a Roman amphitheatre –
the **Arena** – and theatre, both of which host cultural extravaganzas in the warmer
months, the Arena opera season being world-famous.

HISTORY

After being colonised by the Romans back
in 89 BC, Verona became a frequent prize of
conquest. By the 12th century, however, it
had settled down somewhat, and had become
an independent city-state. Verona eventually
reached its zenith in the 13th and 14th
centuries, when the home-grown Della Scala
(or Scaligero) dynasty (hence the ladder
in local coats-of-arms – *scala* in Italian means
'ladder') brought a period of peace to a city
that had long been racked by Montague and
Capulet-style family feuding.

Patronage of the arts went hand in hand
with the Della Scala lust for power. However,
the dynasty fell in 1387 and was replaced by
Milan's Viscontis, superseded in turn by the
Venetian Republic. Renaissance Verona lent
its Venetian overlords its refined architect
Sanmicheli and his protégé, Paolo Veronese.
Only in 1866 did Verona rid itself of foreign
rulers, when it joined the newly united
Kingdom of Italy.

SIGHTSEEING

Dominating the entrance to the old town in
piazza Brà is the magnificent Roman **Arena**
(*see p266*). The Teatro Romano and ponte
Pietra are further signs of the ancients. Many
modern buildings stand on Roman foundations;
some have fragments of Roman marble-work
in their fabric.

Verona's medieval architecture dates
mostly from after the great earthquake of
1117. In the building boom that followed,
the city was adorned with some of its finest
buildings: the basilica of **San Zeno** (*see p270*),
the **Duomo** (*see p269*) and the Gothic churches
of **Sant'Anastasia** and **San Fermo** (for both,
see p269). Ancient, medieval and modern
are knitted together with the ever-present
pink-tinged stone and marble.

The old town, nestling in the loops of the
meandering Adige River, stretches out from
piazza Brà. Overshadowed by the magnificent
Arena, this large square is home to a number
of cafés on the *Liston*, the Veronese promenade,
and the **Museo Lapidario** (1.30-7.30pm Mon,
8.30am-7.30pm Tue-Sun), a small collection of
Greek and Roman fragments and inscriptions.
A short walk north-east from piazza Brà along
via Mazzini takes you to the heart of the city –
the adjoining squares of **piazza delle Erbe**
and **piazza dei Signori**.

Once the site of the Roman forum, piazza
delle Erbe today is home to a somewhat
tacky market (Mon-Sat), which nevertheless
can't detract from the stunning surrounding
buildings (all closed to the public). At the
northern end is the huge 14th-century **Casa
Mazzanti** with its splendid late Renaissance
frescoes on the outer façade, the highly
ornamented **Palazzo Maffei** and the **Torre
Gardello** clock tower, built in 1370. Dotted
among the stalls are the gleaming 16th-century
Berlina, under which public officials were

invested with their office, and a fountain (1368), whose basin is of Roman origin, as is the body of the statue known as the 'Madonna Verona', which stands above it. The tall houses at the square's southern end once marked the edge of the Jewish ghetto.

A detour south-east out of piazza delle Erbe along via Cappello leads to **Casa di Giulietta** (Juliet's House; *see p268*). Further down via Cappello is the **Porta Leoni**, a fragment of a Roman city gate and now part of a medieval house; excavations have exposed the full extent of the towered and arched structure. Just over the bridge from here is the district from which artist Paolo Veronese came; the modern church of **San Paolo** (via XX Settembre 2, open 9-11.30am, 4.30-6pm daily) has one of his early works, the *Madonna and Saints*.

Piazza dei Signori, the heart of medieval Verona's governance and finance, contains the 15th-century **Loggia del Consiglio** (closed to the public) topped by statues of illustrious *veronesi*, including Catullus. Linking *piazze* delle Erbe and dei Signori is the 12th-century **Palazzo della Ragione**, recently restored and now functioning as an exhibition space.

A gateway on the piazza dei Signori side of the palazzo leads into the **Mercato Vecchio** courtyard, with its huge Romanesque arches and magnificent outdoor Renaissance staircase. The palazzo is dominated by the 83-metre (272-foot) **Torre dei Lamberti** (1462). From the next courtyard on the right you can descend into the archeological site of the **Scavi Scaligeri** (*see p271*). At the eastern exit from piazza dei Signori are the **Della Scala family tombs** (*tombe* or *arche scaligere*; *see p271*).

Moving northwards, the peaceful, narrow streets are a captivating labyrinth dotted with medieval and Renaissance *palazzi*. In via Pigna, take a look at the carved marble Roman pine cone (*pigna*) before heading north down via San Giacomo alla Pigna towards the Duomo, or south towards the imposing church of Sant'Anastasia. Close by, **ponte Pietra** is Verona's oldest bridge and, for centuries, was the only link between the city centre and the suburbs beyond. The two stone arches on the left bank of the river are Roman

and date back to before 50 BC. The other three brick arches date from between 1200 and 1500. The bridge was reconstructed using original stones in 1957 after being destroyed by retreating Germans.

The ponte Pietra leads across the river to some of Verona's most beautiful churches – including **San Giorgio in Braida** and **Santa Maria in Organo** (for both, *see p269*) – as well as the **Museo Archeologico** (*see p269*) and the remains of the **Teatro Romano** (*see p271*). The area around Castel San Pietro (closed to the public) – part of the city's medieval and Renaissance fortifications, heavily redesigned by Austrian occupiers in the mid 19th century – offers a bird's-eye view of the city. Head south-east from the bridge along regaste Redentore and its continuations to the pretty **Giardino Giusti** (*see p269*). Back towards the river is the church of San Tommaso, where Mozart, aged 13, played the organ on his visit to the city, birthplace of his future archrival, Salieri.

Corso Porta Borsari, Roman Verona's busy main street, leads out of the north end of piazza delle Erbe towards the **Porta Borsari**, the best-preserved of the city's Roman gates; it probably dates from the reign of Emperor Claudius (AD 41-54). In a small garden along corso Cavour is the **Arco dei Gavi**, a triumphal arch attributed to Vitruvius, dating from about 50 BC. The medieval fortress of **Castelvecchio** (*see p268*), adorned with swallow-tail battlements, hosts a museum and gives on to the ponte Scaligero, the other stone bridge crossing the Adige.

The stunning basilica di San Zeno, home to Verona's patron saint, is located outside the centre, to the west of piazza Brà.

TICKETS & PASSES

An admission fee is charged by some churches and all museums in Verona. Cut costs by buying a **Verona Card** (www.veronacard.it, €10 for one day, €15 for three days), valid for all the sights that charge. It can be bought at the exchange office in the station or the ticket offices of any of the churches or museums participating in the scheme, and includes bus fares around the city. No credit cards accepted.

A second scheme (the *itinerario completo*) offers entrance to five of Verona's churches (San Zeno, San Lorenzo, Sant'Anastasia, San Fermo and the Duomo) for €5 (€4 reductions).

★ **Arena**
Piazza Brà (045 800 3204). **Open** 1.45-7.30pm Mon; 8.30am-7.30pm Tue-Sun (closes at 4.30pm during opera season). **Admission** €6; €4.50 reductions. **No credit cards**. **Map** p267 B4.
The largest Roman amphitheatre in northern Italy, Verona's Arena was capacious enough to seat

---

INSIDE TRACK WHALE BONE

From one of the eight elegant arches in piazza dei Signori – **Arco della Costa** – hangs a whale bone. According to local legend, it will fall if an adult virgin passes beneath it.

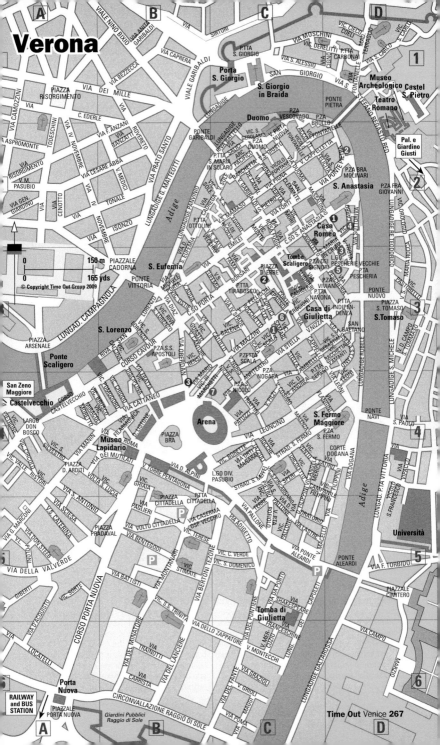

Verona

Views from the **Museo Archeologico**.

the city's whole population of 20,000 when it was constructed in about AD 30. The 44 tiers of stone seats inside the 139m by 110m (456ft by 361ft) amphitheatre are virtually intact, as is the columned foyer. After the earthquake of 1117 destroyed most of the Arena's outer ring (the remaining four arches are known as the 'ala'), the city repaired the damage almost immediately.

Originally the site of gladiatorial games and – filled with water – naval battles, it was used by post-Roman inhabitants as a shelter during fifth- and sixth-century Barbarian invasions. Medieval *veronesi* treated it as a red-light district and it was home to the city's cut-throats. Later, city masters used the Arena as a law court and site of the occasional execution. It functioned as a theatre in the 17th and 18th centuries, hosted circuses and hot-air balloon launches in the 19th, and became a football stadium in the early 20th century. It now provides a spectacular setting for summer operas.

▶ *For more on operas here (and booking details), see p272* **From Callas to Camels...**.

Casa di Giulietta (Juliet's House)
Via Cappello 23 (045 803 4303). **Open** 1.30-7.30pm Mon; 8.30am-7.30pm Tue-Sun. **Admission** €6; €4.50 reductions. **No credit cards. Map** p267 C3.
See p271 **Star-crossed Weddings**.

Castelvecchio
Corso Castelvecchio 2 (045 806 2611/www. comune.verona.it/castelvecchio/cvsito). **Open** 1.30-7.30pm Mon; 8.30am-7.30pm Tue-Sun. **Admission** €6; €4.50 reductions. **No credit cards. Map** p267 A4.
The Della Scala family came to power in the 13th century as a result of the Guelf-Ghibelline conflicts that shaped so much of northern Italian politics in the Middle Ages. By the time Duke Cangrande II began building this castle in 1355, the family needed a fortress for waging war and as a refuge from over-taxed Veronese citizens: ponte Scaligero, the magnificent fortified medieval bridge, was intended as an emergency escape route.

The castle is now a museum and exhibition venue, with interiors beautifully redesigned in the 1960s by Venetian architect Carlo Scarpa. The museum itself contains important works by Mantegna, Crivelli, Pisanello, Giovanni Bellini, Veronese, Tintoretto, Giambattista Tiepolo, Canaletto and Guardi, plus a magnificent collection of 13th- and 14th-century Veronese religious statuary. An armoury and an assortment of local jewellery complete the collection.
▶ *To see where the Della Scala clan ended up, check out the family tombs; see p271.*

Duomo
Piazza Duomo (045 592 813/www.chiese verona.it). **Open** 10am-1pm, 1.30-4pm Tue-Sat; 1-5pm Sun. **Admission** €2.50. **No credit cards**. **Map** p267 C2.
Verona's cathedral, begun in 1139, is Romanesque downstairs, Gothic upstairs and Renaissance at the top half of the bell tower. The elegant front portico is decorated with Romanesque carvings of the finest quality, showing Charlemagne's paladins Oliver and Roland (featured in the medieval epic *Chanson de Roland*). Inside, the first chapel on the left has a magnificent *Assumption* by Titian and an altar by Jacopo Sansovino. In the same complex is the ancient church of Sant'Elena, with the remains of an earlier Christian basilica and Roman baths. And, at the back of the cathedral, to the right of its graceful apse, is the chapel of San Giovanni in Fonte, with a large, carved, octagonal, Romanesque baptismal font.
▶ *On the right as you leave is the Biblioteca Capitolare, one of the oldest libraries in the world; Petrarch discovered letters by Cicero here.*

★ Giardino Giusti
Via Giardino Giusti 2 (045 803 4029). **Open** 9am-7pm daily. **Admission** €6. **No credit cards**. **Map** off p267 D2.
The façades that front one of Verona's most traffic-clogged streets hide one of the finest Renaissance gardens in Italy. Tucked behind the great Renaissance townhouse of the Giusti family – the Palazzo Giusti del Giardino – the statue-packed gardens with their tall cypresses were laid out in 1580. The wild upper level climbs the steep slopes of the hill behind, which offers superb viewing and picnic opportunities.

Museo Archeologico
Regaste Redentore 2 (045 800 0360/ www.comune.verona.it/castelvecchio/cvsito). **Open** 1.30-7.30pm Mon; 8.30am-7.30pm Tue-Sun. **Admission** €4.50; €3 reductions. **No credit cards**. **Map** p267 D1.
This small museum contains a fine collection of Roman remains. Situated in a former monastery, the museum offers incomparable views over Verona and the River Adige.
▶ *Admission to the Teatro Romano is included with the museum entrance fee; see p271.*

San Fermo Maggiore
Stradone San Fermo (045 592 813/www. chieseverona.it). **Open** 10am-4pm Tue-Sat; 1-5pm Sun. **Admission** €2.50. **No credit cards**. **Map** p267 D4.
At San Fermo, you get two churches for the price of one: the intimate and solemn lower church is Romanesque; the upper church, towering and full of light, is Gothic. Its wooden ceiling resembles an upturned Venetian galleon. Among the important frescoes is an *Annunciation* by Antonio Pisanello, to the left of the main entrance.

FREE San Giorgio in Braida
Piazzetta San Giorgio 1 (045 834 0232). **Open** 8-11am, 5-7pm Mon-Sat; 9.15-10.30am, 5-6.30pm Sun. **Map** p267 C1.
This great domed Renaissance church, probably designed by the Veronese military architect Michele Sanmicheli between 1536 and 1543, contains some of the city's greatest treasures. Shining in this light-filled masterpiece are a *Baptism of Christ* by Tintoretto, above the entrance door, and a moving *Martyrdom of St George* by Paolo Veronese. But even these greats are put in the shade by a serene *Madonna and Child with Saints Zeno and Lawrence* by local dark horse Girolamo dai Libri.

FREE Santa Maria in Organo
Piazzetta Santa Maria in Organo (045 591 440). **Open** 8-11.30am, 2.30-5.30pm Mon, Tue, Thur, Sat, Sun; 8am-noon Wed, Fri. **Map** off p267 D2.
This Renaissance church has a host of frescoes by local painters. Pass them by and make your way to the apse and sacristy to see what Giorgio Vasari described as the most beautiful choir stalls in Italy. A humble monk, Fra Giovanni da Verona (d.1520), worked for 25 years cutting and assembling these infinitely complex, coloured, wooden images of animals, birds, landscapes, cityscapes, religious scenes and musical and scientific instruments in dozens of intricate intarsia panels.

Sant'Anastasia
Piazza Sant'Anastasia (045 592 813/www. chieseverona.it). **Open** 10am-4pm Tue-Sat; 1-5pm Sun. **Admission** €2.50. **No credit cards**. **Map** p267 D2.

INSIDE TRACK
PARADISE FOR A TOP DOG

Verona is quietly boastful about the fact that the poet Dante lived in exile at the court of the Della Scala family from 1304. He dedicated his *Paradiso* to one of the city's 'top dogs', Cangrande I (*see p271*).

Arche Scaligere.

Dedicated to Thomas à Becket, the martyred arch-bishop of Canterbury, this 16th-century church was designed by Sanmicheli, who is buried here. It contains works by local artists and the Bonatti organ, which the young Mozart played in 1770.

★ San Zeno Maggiore

Piazza San Zeno 2 (045 592 813/www.chiese verona.it). **Open** 10am-4pm Tue-Sat; 1-5pm Sun. **Admission** €2.50. **No credit cards**. **Map** off p267 A4.

One of the most spectacularly ornate Romanesque churches in northern Italy, San Zeno Maggiore was built between 1123 and 1138 to house the tomb and shrine of San Zeno, an African who became Verona's first bishop in 362 and is now the city's much-loved patron saint.

The façade, with its great rose window and porch, is covered with some of Italy's finest examples of Romanesque marble sculpture. Scenes from the Old Testament and the life of Christ mingle with hunting and jousting scenes, attributed to the 12th-century sculptors Nicolò and Guglielmo. The graceful porch is supported by columns resting on two carved marble lions; they serve as a frame for the great bronze doors of the basilica. Nicknamed 'the poor man's bible', the doors' 48 panels have scenes from the Bible and from the life of San Zeno, and a few that experts have been hard-pressed to pin down, including a woman suckling two crocodiles. The panels on the left-hand door date from about 1030 and came from an earlier church.

Inside the lofty church (note the magnificent ceiling built in 1386), a staircase descends into the crypt, which contains the tomb of San Zeno. The magnificent Mantegna triptych that dominated the altar has, alas, been packed off to Florence and isn't expected to return until 2010.

The enduring love affair between San Zeno and the city that adopted him may have something to do with the huge, early 12th-century marble statue of the African bishop having a grand old chuckle, which is found in a niche to the left of the apse. His black face, with its distinctly African features, is unique in Italian religious statuary. When he wasn't converting Veronese souls to Christianity, he is held to have spent his time fishing in the River Adige, seated on a rock in front of the San Zeno Minore church nearby. Covering the inside walls of the basilica are frescoes dating from the 12th to the 14th centuries, but perhaps more interesting than the paintings themselves is the 15th- to 17th-century graffiti scratched into them.

To the right of the church is a massive bell tower, 72m (236ft) high, begun in 1045. To the left is a lower tower, which is all that remains of the Benedictine monastery that stood on the site before the basilica was built, and which, according to local lore, stands over the grave of Pepin, Charlemagne's disinherited hunchback son. Behind is a Romanesque cloister. Stays open through the day in summer.

This imposing brick Gothic church is best visited early in the morning, when sunlight streams in to illuminate Antonio Pisanello's glorious fresco (1433-38; above the terracotta-clad Pelligrini chapel) of St George girding himself to set off in pursuit of the dragon that has been pestering the lovely princess of Trebizond. Carved scenes from the life of St Peter Martyr adorn the unfinished façade, while inside, two delightful *gobbi* (hunchbacks) crouch down to support the holy water font; the one on the left was carved by Paolo Veronese's father in 1495. On the left of the church stands the tiny, deconsecrated San Pietro in Martire (San Giorgetto dei Domenicani), with three Gothic funerary monuments on its exterior. It is sometimes opened by volunteers to let the public see the fragments of frescoes inside in summer. There's no lunch time closing in summer.

FREE San Tomaso Cantuariense

Piazza San Tomaso 1 (045 803 356). **Open** 8am-noon; 4-7.30pm daily. **Map** p267 D3.

Scavi Scaligeri

Corte del Tribunale, piazza Viviani (045 800 7490/www.comune.verona.it/scaviscaligeri).
Open 10am-7pm Tue-Sun. **Admission** €5.
No credit cards. Map p267 A2.

These excavations are a good place to get a feel for the city's historical layering, as you move between Roman mosaics and roads, interspersed at random with medieval and Lombard remains.

Teatro Romano

Regaste Redentore 2 (045 800 0360/www. comune.verona.it/castelvecchio/cvsito). **Open** 1.30-7.30pm Mon; 8.30am-7.30pm Tue-Sun.
Admission (incl Museo Archeologico; *see p269*) €4.50; €3 reductions. **No credit cards.**
Map p267 D1.

The Roman theatre, dating from around the first century BC, was buried under medieval houses until the late 19th century. The theatre offers beautiful views over the city and is an evocative venue for an annual festival of theatre (Shakespeare is a perennial favourite), ballet and jazz.
▶ *For programme and booking details, contact Estate Teatrale Veronese (045 807 7201, www. estateteatraleveronese.it). Tickets (€7-€26) can also be bought at the teatro before performances.*

★ FREE Tombe or Arche Scaligere (Della Scala family tombs)

Via Santa Maria in Chiavica. **Closed** to the public, though visible from outside.
Map p267 C3.

The Gothic tombs of medieval Verona's 'top dogs', the Della Scala family, date from 1277 to the final years of the 14th century and give a good idea of the family's sense of its own importance. Carved by the most sought-after stonemasons of the era, the more lavish tombs are topped with spires. Note the family's odd taste in first names. The monument to Cangrande (Big Dog, d.1329), above the doorway to the church of Santa Maria Antica, shows the valiant duke smiling in the face of death, guarded by crowned dogs. (This is a copy; the original is in the Castelvecchio; *see p268.*) Poking out from above the fence are the spire-topped final resting places of Cansignorio (Lord Dog, d.1375) and Mastino II (Mastiff the Second, d.1351). Among the less flamboyant tombs is that of Mastino I (d.1277), founder of the doggy dynasty.

Next door, the intimate church of Santa Maria Antica (open 7.30am-noon, 3.30-7pm daily) was the Della Scala family chapel. Indirectly, the church has loaned its name to Milan's famous opera house, *La Scala.* When Beatrice Regina della Scala married and

---

Star-crossed Weddings

Daring lovers can tie the knot below Juliet's balcony.

The *veronesi* may believe that **San Zeno** (*see p270*) is the city's symbol. Millions of tourists think otherwise. Generations of visitors have crowded the courtyard of a pretty 13th-century palazzo, gazing enraptured at a balcony cunningly tacked on to the first floor in the 1920s, leaving their entwined signatures on graffiti-covered walls and having a furtive rub of the shiny right breast of a 20th-century bronze of Shakespeare's best-loved heroine. But it wasn't until 2009 that Verona's town council had the bright idea of turning the so-called **Casa di Giulietta** (Juliet's House; *see p268*) into the world's most sought-after wedding location... at a price.

Disentangling myth and history is difficult in Verona, where locals have been milking their *Romeo and Juliet* connections for centuries. The Montagues and Capulets may have been real enough but young Juliet Capulet was not laid to rest in the Roman sarcophagus in the former convent of **San Francesco al Corso** (via del Pontiere 35), where Mme de Stael and Lord Byron went into Romantic raptures (and which Charles Dickens, more prosaically,

described as 'a sort of drinking trough'). And the Capulets certainly never lived in what's now known as the Casa di Giulietta. This doesn't stop starry-eyed visitors in droves paying for a ticket (*see p268*) that allows them into a rather stark interior, where they can pen and post their letters to Juliet before taking a quick bow on the famous balcony.

Now, however, for a fee ranging from €600 (for local residents) to €800 (for EU citizens) or even €1,000 (for those from outside the EU), lovers can tie the knot in the courtyard beneath the balcony. The various tariffs, the city council insists, reflect the different costs of the paperwork involved in getting people wed. And they're a bargain compared to civil services in Venice, where EU citizens can pay anything up to €1,800 and those from outside the EU up to €4,200.

For the record, **Romeo's house** – which at least may have actually belonged to the Montague family – is, tastefully, not open to the public. It's just across from the Della Scala tombs (*see above*), at Arche Scaligere 4.

THE VENETO

From Callas to Camels...

The show goes on at Verona's Arena.

While the bloodshed and torment that filled Verona's **Arena** (*see p266*) over 2,000 years ago are now purely theatrical, the spectacle has remained, with stagings of classics by Puccini, Bizet, Verdi and co every night from June to September. The best to see are the grand-scale productions with huge choruses and spectacular sets. The atmosphere is charged with excitement as music-lovers start squeezing onto the (unnumbered) stone terraces a good two hours before the performance begins.

Some might have already eaten at the self-service restaurant **Brek** (045 800 4561, average €15, kids' menu €4.40), directly opposite, in piazza Brà. Others stock up at the local supermarket (**PAM**, at via dei Mutilati 3, is open until 9pm daily) and settle down with their picnics. All bring or rent (€2) a cushion as a night perched on a two-millennia-old piece of marble can seem long and painful. Occupants of the *poltronissime*, the red-cushioned stalls seats, can saunter in

just before the show commences, perhaps after having tucked into one of the pre-opera menus (€45 without wine, served from 6.30pm) in the courtyard of the baroque **Ristorante Maffei** (045 801 0015, www.ristorantemaffei.it, closed Sun from Oct to Mar), in nearby piazza delle Erbe. Armani-clad industrialists show off their expensive seats and their even more expensive consorts. Differences dissipate as darkness descends; a hush falls over the 15,000-capacity crowd as the overture is played to the flickering of *mocoleti*, the candles traditionally lit all around the amphitheatre for the prelude.

In the Arena's 80-plus-year operatic history, divas such as Renata Tebaldi, Angela Gheorghio and Maria Callas – who made her international debut here as La Gioconda in 1947 – have all trod the boards, together with tenors from Beniamino Gigli to José Carreras. Scenic extravaganzas have been staged, with designers such as Franco Zeffirelli called

upon to recreate the River Nile or Sevillian mountains. Casts of hundreds for such shows have included horses, elephants and even camels, one of which managed to escape one year and lope off around town.

Centre-stage drama once turned into a backstage fracas when director Roberto Rossellini conjured up over-realistic smoke effects during a performance of *Othello*, nearly choking the leading man, tenor Mario del Monaco. The fuming *divo* won the day and Rossellini was sent packing before the show would go on. Fully front-stage tragedy turned to comedy more recently when a voluptuous 'calamity' Carmen fell out of her costume, taking the puff out of her dying gasp.

But even the rare glitches can't detract from the show; hours of magical music with natural acoustics and the stunning setting make a night in the world's largest open-air opera house a matchless experience.

After the final curtain, the crowd go their separate ways with the final notes still ringing in their ears; some go off to star-spot at the **Liston** (via Dietro Liston 19, 045 800 4515, closed Wed, average €30), where cast and conductors are known to eat after the show. Others dive into the narrow street behind the Arena for dinner at **Trattoria Tre Marchetti** (*see p274*), which has served meals since 1291, or to the simpler **Bacaro dell'Arena** (045 590 503, closed Mon, average €25), further down at 1B vicolo Tre Marchetti; it's also open until 2am on opera nights. Those who've already booked at the **Bottega del Vino** (*see right*), will have Veronese dishes awaiting them and a choice of over 3,000 wines to uncork as they discuss the show. Wherever they go, all will agree that the evening under the stars in a 2,000-year-old theatre can only be described as pure magic.

Fondazione Arena di Verona
Via Dietro l'Anfiteatro 6B (045 800 5151/www.arena.it). **Performances** *June-Aug* 9pm Tue-Sun. **Tickets** €21-€198. **Credit** AmEx, DC, MC, V. **Map** p253 B3. Seats are sometimes available on the day of the show, especially midweek.

moved to Milan, she had her own prayer chapel built on the site of the future opera house in 1381; it was modelled on and named after this chapel.
▶ *You can visit the Della Scala family's old home, the Castelvecchio; see p268.*

WHERE TO EAT & DRINK

Verona's cuisine is a mix of Middle European heft and Italian sensibility. Boiled and roasted meats are popular, served up with *cren*, the local take on horseradish sauce, and *pearà*, made of bone marrow, bread and pepper. Braised horse meat (*pastissada de caval*) is another local speciality, as is donkey *ragù*. Vegetarians take heart: *bigoli*, a sort of thick spaghetti, is often served with meat-free sauces. Pumpkin-stuffed ravioli is a speciality.

The vineyards around Verona produce some of Italy's most recognisable wine exports: Soave, Bardolino and Valpolicella (*see p178* **Profile**). But the Veronese take wine very seriously (the ultra-serious **Vinitaly** takes place here every spring; see www.veronafiere.it for information), keeping the lightweight export names for everyday use and the better-kept secrets like Amarone and Valpolicella Classico for special occasions.

For pre- and post-theatre dining near the Arena, *see left* **From Callas to Camels....**

Bottega del Vino
Via Scudo di Francia 3 (045 800 4535/ www.bottegavini.it). **Meals served** noon-3pm, 6pm-midnight Mon, Wed-Sun. **Average** €45. **Credit** AmEx, DC, MC, V. **Map** p267 C3 ❶
Open the heavy wooden door to find a bustling, flamboyantly decorated dining room that serves up excellent local dishes, including *pastissada de caval*, and an amazing selection of wines.

Cappa Café
Piazzetta Brà Molinari 1A, corner of via Ponte Pietra (045 800 4516/www.cappacafe.it). **Open** 7.30am-2am daily. **Credit** AmEx, DC, MC, V. **Map** p267 D2 ❷
The Cappa Café is a great place for an early-evening drink on the terrace, with views of the ponte Pietra and across the Adige to the Teatro Romano and cypress-clad hillside above. It livens up later on with a young crowd.

Hostaria La Vecchia Fontanina
Piazzetta Chiavica 5 (045 591 159). **Meals served** noon-2.30pm, 7-10.30pm Mon-Sat. **Average** €25. **Credit** AmEx, DC, MC, V. **Map** p267 D3 ❸
Popular with savvy locals and a good option for non-donkey-eating vegetarians, this place serves a varied menu of creative versions of local specialities, including *bigoli* with nettles.

THE VENETO

THE VENETO

Ostaria Sottoriva

Via Sottoriva 9A (045 801 4323). **Meals served** noon-3.30pm, 6.30-10.30pm Mon, Tue, Thur-Sun. **Average** €20. **Credit** MC, V. **Map** p267 D2 ❹

Under the porticoes in a picturesque street, this traditional Veronese *osteria* is proud of its venerable status. The menu is simple and traditional, and there's a good selection of wines.

Ristorante Al Cristo

Piazzetta Pescheria 6 (045 594 287/www. ristorantealcristo.it). **Meals served** noon-2.30pm, 7-11pm Tue-Sun. **Average** €80. **Credit** AmEx, DC, MC, V. **Map** p267 D3 ❺

Seafood fiends can feast on sushi and sashimi, oysters and Iranian caviar. It can get busy, and booking is advisable at weekends.

★ Ristorante Greppia

Vicolo Samaritana 3 (045 800 4577/www. ristorantegreppia.it). **Meals served** noon-2.30pm, 7-10.30pm Tue-Sun. Closed 2wks June. **Average** €35. **Credit** AmEx, DC, MC, V. **Map** p267 C3 ❻

Off via Mazzini, this Verona institution serves up some of the best renditions in town of local classics.

★ Trattoria Tre Marchetti

Vicolo Tre Marchetti 19B (045 803 0463). **Meals served** *Sept-June* noon-2.30pm, 7-10.30pm daily. *July, Aug* noon-2.30pm, 6.30pm-2am Tue-Sun. Closed 2wks June. **Average** €50. **Credit** DC, MC, V. **Map** p267 C4 ❼

Meals have been served on these premises since 1291, making it one of the most ancient eateries in Europe. It has lost none of its allure over the centuries: informal and crowded, and now serves specialities of *bigoli* with duck, *pastissada de caval* and *baccalà* (cod) *alla vicentina*. Booking is advisable.

WHERE TO STAY

Hotels fill up during the opera season, so it's best to book in advance. **CAV** (via Patuzzi 5, 045 800 9844, www.cav.vr.it, open 10am-7pm Mon-Sat) runs a free hotel-booking bureau.

Campeggio Castel San Pietro

Via Castel San Pietro 2 (045 592 037/www. campingcastelsanpietro.com). Bus 41 or 95 from the station, get off at first stop in via Marsala. **Rates** €5-€15 per plot; €6.50 per person; €4.50 under-8s. Closed mid Oct-Apr. **No credit cards.**

This campsite is in a stunning position 15 minutes' walk from the centre of Verona.

Due Torri Hotel Baglioni

Piazza Sant'Anastasia 4 (045 595 044/www. baglionihotels.com). **Rates** €230-€550 double. **Credit** AmEx, DC, MC, V. **Map** p267 D2 ❶

This celebrated hotel (Beethoven, Mozart and Goethe have been among its guests) is widely considered to be the city's finest. Some of the rooms let guests go eyeball to eyeball with Gugliemo di Castelvarco, whose tomb tops the archway across from the hotel.

Hotel Aurora

Piazza delle Erbe 2 (045 594 717/www.hotel aurora.biz). **Rates** €100-€150 double. **Credit** AmEx, DC, MC, V. **Map** p267 C3 ❷

This simple hotel is friendly and efficiently run and has a great terrace for people-watching.

Hotel Bologna

Piazzetta Scalette Rubiani 3 (045 800 6830/www. hotelbologna.vr.it). **Rates** €100-€220 double. **Credit** AmEx, DC, MC, V. **Map** p267 B4 ❸

A comfortable hotel in a perfect spot for exploring.

Residence Antico San Zeno

Via Rosmini 15 (045 800 3463/www.residence anticosanzeno.it). **Rates** €90-€170 double. **Credit** AmEx, DC, MC, V. **Map** off p267 A4 ❹

Just around the corner from the church of San Zeno, this quiet and beautifully restored hotel has enormous rooms and mini-apartments for up to five people, all with their own cooking facilities. During the opera season and important trade fairs, prices here almost double.

GETTING THERE

By air Valerio Catullo Airport (*see p295*).
By train There are regular services from Milan and Venice (75-90mins).
By car Take the A4 La Serenissima motorway.

GETTING AROUND

By bus The orange buses are run by **AMT** (045 887 1111, www.amt.it); most start and terminate at Porta Nuova. Tickets can be purchased at any tobacconist. A €1 ticket is valid for one hour and should be punched on each bus boarded.
By bicycle The tourist office at the train station (*see below*) offers bikes for free. Leave a passport or another document and get the bike back before the office closes.

TOURIST INFORMATION

For information, see www.tourism.verona.it.

IAT *Via degli Alpini 9 (045 806 8680).* **Open** 9am-7pm Mon-Sat; 9am-3pm Sun. **Map** p267 B4.
IAT *Railway station, piazzale XXV Aprile (045 800 0861).* **Open** 10am-7pm Mon, Tue; 10am-5pm Wed-Sun. **Map** off p267 A6.
IAT *Valerio Catullo Airport (045 861 9163).* **Open** 9am-6pm Mon-Sat.

Vicenza

Where architectural legend Andrea Palladio made his mark.

Vicenza was a Roman settlement, and the city's ancient layout is still virtually intact. It became an important Lombard and Frankish centre, but was destroyed by Magyar ravagers in 899, only to flourish again later in the Middle Ages when astute locals took advantage of their strategic position as the link between two rivers. In 1404, Vicenza came under the rule of Venice, and a veritable building boom began.

Vicenza's leading families assuaged their hurt feelings – and proclaimed their superiority – by commissioning sumptuous townhouses and country *ville*. Additionally, Venetian nobles were encouraged to develop country estates in order to strengthen the Republic's grip on the surrounding territory. It was into this cauldron of Renaissance one-upmanship that **Andrea Palladio** (*see pp280-281*) fell in the 1540s. The mark he left here would influence architecture the world over for centuries to come.

The City

SIGHTSEEING

A major hub of the north-eastern economic miracle, Vicenza oozes wealth. The city is home to Italy's precious metal working industry, and the **VicenzaOro** trade fair (www.vicenzaoro.org) takes place here several times a year. The city's two main claims to fame – Palladio and gold – come together along the streets of the *centro*, where shop windows in ground floors of glorious Palladian *palazzi* glisten with world-class jewels, exorbitant geegaws and designer togs.

Despite its Roman origins, Vicenza's character is very much medieval and Renaissance. Just outside the town walls, to the west of the centre, is the statue-dotted **Giardino Salvi**. This pleasant public park houses Andrea Palladio's **Loggia Valmarana**, a Doric-style temple spanning the waters of a canal. Nearby is a Baroque loggia by Baldassare Longhena.

Inside the walls, piazza del Castello takes its name from a castle built in 1337-38 by the Della Scala family, who ruled here from 1311 to 1404. The tower in the corner of the piazza is all that remains of the castle. The adjoining gate, **Porta Castello**, was constructed in 1343 on the site of

the city's Roman gate. The piazza is home to the odd-looking **Palazzo Porto Breganze**, a tall awkward fragment in the southern corner, designed by Palladio but never finished.

Palladio had a hand in five of the grandiose *palazzi* lining corso Palladio (all are closed to the public). The first palazzo of note, on the left-hand side as you exit piazza del Castello, is the magnificent **Palazzo Thiene Bonin Longare**, begun in 1562. At no.45 is **Palazzo Capra**, almost certainly designed by the young Palladio between 1540 and 1545.

A quick turn right into contrà Battisti (streets in Vicenza's centre are called 'contrà' instead of 'via') leads to the **Duomo** (*see p278*), which is the entrance to the **Criptoportico Romano** (*see p277*), the only surviving remnant of Roman Vicetia. Back on corso Palladio, a detour to the left leads to the Gothic brick church of **San Lorenzo** (*see p278*), while at no.92 is **Palazzo Pojana** (1564-66), which consists of two separate buildings cunningly joined together by Palladio. **Palazzo Trissino Baston**, at no.98, was designed in 1592 by Palladio's student Vincenzo Scamozzi but not completed until 1667; the interior can be visited (by appointment only, 0444 221 111).

In the vast and elegant piazza dei Signori, south of the corso, is the 82-metre (269-foot) **Torre di Piazza** clock tower, which dates from the 12th century. Tacked gracefully on to the Gothic Palazzo della Ragione assembly hall (known as the **Basilica Palladiana**, in the Roman sense of the word *'basilica'* – a public place where justice is dispensed) is Palladio's marvellous loggia (*see p277*). Opposite this is his **Loggia del Capitanato**, a fragment of a building, built to celebrate Venice's victory over the Turks in the Battle of Lepanto in 1571. On the same side is the complex of the **Monte di Pietà**, the city's 16th-century pawn shop.

Piazza delle Erbe is dominated by a medieval tower where wrongdoers were taken to be tortured. In the labyrinth of streets to the south of piazza delle Erbe is the **Casa Pigafetta** (contrà Pigafetta 9). Dating from 1444 and built in late Spanish Gothic style, this strange, highly decorated townhouse was the birthplace of Antonio Pigafetta, who was one of only 21 survivors of Magellan's epoch-making circumnavigation of the globe (1519-22).

Coming off corso Palladio to the north of piazza Signori is contrà Porti, a real palazzo feast. The clannish Porto family all built their houses in one street. At no.11 is the **Palazzo Barbaran Da Porto**, designed and built by Palladio (1569-71), with an interior by Lorenzo Rubini. After a 20-year restoration, it is now home to the **Museo Palladiano** (*see p277*).

Casa Porto (no.15) is an undistinguished 15th-century building that was badly restored in the 18th century but is of interest as the home of Luigi Da Porto (d.1529), writer of the first known account of the Romeo and Juliet story. At no.19 the exquisite, late-Gothic **Palazzo Porto Colleoni** is a typical 15th-century attempt to beat the Venetians at their own game. **Palazzo Iseppo Da Porto**, at no.21, is one of Palladio's earliest creations; its interior is decorated with frescoes by Tiepolo, but, again, it's not open to the public.

At the end of the street, over the Bacchiglione river, contrà San Marco is a wide street lined with fine 16th- and 17th-century *palazzi*, including **Palazzo Da Schio**, an elegant

townhouse designed by Palladio in the 1560s. Back on corso Palladio, **Palazzo Caldogno Da Schio** (no.147) is a flamboyant 14th-century jewel, which once had gilded capitals – hence its other name, *Ca' d'Oro*. Under the portico is a lapidarium of stone fragments collected by Giovanni da Schio (1798-1868).

The **Gallerie di Palazzo Leoni Montanari** (*see p278*), in contrà Santa Corona, just off the corso, contains charming 18th-century genre paintings by Pietro Longhi. Also in contrà Santa Corona is the **Museo Naturalistico Archeologico** (entry with Biglietto Unico only; *see below* **Tickets & Passes**). On the corner of this street and the corso, the great Gothic church of **Santa Corona** (*see p278*) was completed in 1270 and is Palladio's final resting place. Just a stone's throw away is the tiny **Casa Cogollo** (no.167), attributed to Palladio (1560-70).

The main street ends in piazza Matteotti, where two of Vicenza's real artistic treats await: Palazzo Chiericati (1550), one of Palladio's finest townhouses, now the city's art gallery (**Museo Civico**; *see p278*); and the architect's final masterpiece, the **Teatro Olimpico** (*see p279*).

Perched on one of the hilltops that surround Vicenza to the south is the charming **Santuario di Monte Berico** (*see p278*). Fantastic views over the city and across to the Alps await those who make the 20-minute journey up the hill in the shade of the handy 18th-century loggia that lines Viale X Giugno. Further along the same road is the **Museo del Risorgimento e della Resistenza** (entry with Biglietto Unico only; for details, *see below* **Tickets & Passes**).

To the south-east of the centre, at the end of viale Risorgimento, Palladio's **Arco della Scalette** stands at the foot of 192 steps leading to **Villa Valmarana 'Ai Nani'** ('of the dwarves'; *see p279*). Further along the same path is the Villa Capra Valmarana, better known as **Villa Rotonda** (*see p279*), possibly the most famous of all Palladio's buildings. Even if the villa is closed, you can still admire the exterior from the garden.

INSIDE TRACK
PALLADIO CARD

For 2009, a €10, ten-day **Palladio Card** was introduced, allowing admission to six of Palladio's best-known villas, plus reduced entrance charges to another four. Hopefully, the pilot scheme will continue for the future. You can buy it at participating villas, at CISA (*see right*) or online (www.palladiocard.it). The excellent website has information on all the villas, plus clear maps showing how to find them.

TICKETS & PASSES

Admission to the Civic Museums of Vicenza (www.museicivicivicenza.it) – Museo Civico, Museo Naturalistico Archeologico, Museo del Risorgimento e della Resistenza, as well as the Teatro Olimpico – is by **Biglietto Unico** only. Tickets, valid for three days, can only be bought at the Teatro Olimpico (*see p279*) and cost €8 (€6 reductions, €12 family). Credit cards aren't accepted.

The **Palladio Card** gives free or reduced entry to a number of the architect's works; *see left* **Inside Track**.

★ Basilica Palladiana
(Palazzo della Ragione)

Piazza dei Signori (0444 323 681). **Open** during exhibitions. **Admission** varies. **Map** p277 C2.

'It is not possible to describe the impression made by Palladio's Basilica…' gushed Goethe about Palladio's most famous piece of urban restyling. The Palazzo della Ragione, seat of city government, was built in the 1450s; but the loggia that surrounded it collapsed in 1496. The city fathers canvassed the leading architects of the day; luckily for Palladio, who was only 17 at the time, they dithered for 20 years before accepting the audacious solution he proposed in 1546. Palladio's double-tiered loggia, comprising Serlian windows, encases the original Gothic palazzo in a unifying Renaissance shell. The basilica is now used as an exhibition space and is only open for shows, many of which are free.

CISA (Museo Palladiano)

Palazzo Barbaran Da Porto, contrà Porti 11 (0444 323 014/www.cisapalladio.org). **Open** during exhibitions 10am-6pm Wed-Sun. Closed Nov-Mar. **Admission** €5; €3 reductions. **Credit** MC, V. **Map** p277 B1.

This palazzo houses the International Centre for the Study of the Architecture of Andrea Palladio, which hosts irregular temporary exhibitions on architectural themes. The main draw is the palazzo, though it's only open when exhibitions are on. *Photo p278.*

FREE Criptoportico Romano

Piazza Duomo (0444 226 626). **Open** (guided tours only) 10am-11.30am Sat. **Admission** free. **Map** p277 B2.

This incredibly preserved structure, all that remains of a large, first-century *domus* (Roman townhouse), is now substantially buried after 2,000 years of rising ground levels. Builders stumbled upon it in 1954. The 90m (295ft) of vaulted tunnels formed part of the foundations supporting a walled internal garden. Well ventilated in summer, and possibly heated in winter, the space was most likely used for the storage of food and wine.

FREE Duomo

Piazza Duomo 8 (0444 320 996). **Open** 8am-noon, 3.30-6.30pm Mon-Fri; 10.30am-noon Sat; 3.30-7pm Sun. **Map** p277 B2.

The history of Vicenza's cathedral is perhaps more interesting than the building that stands today. The site is believed to have been occupied from around the fifth century by a Christian basilica, modified in the ninth century, tenth and 11th centuries. Its present form is the result of reconstruction carried out between 1267 and 1290, but it suffered extensive damage during World War II. The Palladian dome has been restored, as has the Gothic pink marble façade, attributed to Domenico da Venezia (1467). The banal brick interior contains an important polyptych by Lorenzo Veneziano, dated 1366.

Gallerie di Palazzo Leoni Montanari

Contrà Santa Corona 25 (0444 991 291/www.palazzomontanari.com). **Open** 10am-6pm Tue-Sun. **Admission** €4; €3 reductions. **Credit** MC, V. **Map** p277 C1.

A curious collection of two very different fields of art. On permanent display are 14 masterpieces by the 18th-century Venetian genre painter Pietro Longhi, plus several other paintings of Venice, including an interesting Canaletto. There's also an extraordinary collection of ancient Russian icons. The museum is worth a visit for the magnificent interiors alone, especially in the Galleria della Verità. Temporary exhibitions rotate every few months.

Museo Civico

Palazzo Chiericati, piazza Matteotti 37-39 (0444 321 348/www.museicivicivicenza.it). **Open** 9am-5pm Tue-Sun. **Admission** by Biglietto Unico only *(see p276).* **Map** p277 C1.

The art gallery in this Palladian palazzo contains a fascinating collection of works by local painters, and Bartolomeo Montagna (1450-1523) in particular. The highlight is a 1489 Cima da Conegliano alterpiece, *Madonna Enthroned with Child between Saints Giacomo and Girolamo* (James and Jerome). It also houses works by the likes of Van Dyck, Tintoretto, Veronese, Tiepolo, and a *Crucifixion* by the Flemish master Hans Memling, the central part of a triptych whose side panels are in New York.

FREE San Lorenzo

Piazza San Lorenzo (0444 321 960/www.sanlorenzo.vi.it). **Open** 7.30am-noon, 3.30-6.30pm daily. **Map** p277 A1.

The exterior of this sparse Gothic church, is the highlight; the magnificent marble portal encases an exquisite 14th-century lunette depicting the *Madonna and Child.* Inside, the Poiana altar in the right transept is a late Gothic assemblage of paintings and frescoes by various artists, including a 1500 frescoed lunette of the crucifixion by Bartolomeo Montagna. The peaceful 16th-century cloister contains a medieval well-head. *Photo p283.*

★ FREE Santa Corona

Contrà Santa Corona (0444 321 924). **Open** 8.30am-noon, 3-6pm Tue-Sat; 3-5pm Sun. **Map** p277 C1.

This magnificent Gothic brick church was built between 1260 and 1270, to house a thorn from Christ's crown. Its interior, consisting of three unequally sized naves, contains an *Adoration of the Magi* (1573) by Paolo Veronese in the third chapel on the right. In the crypt is the Valmarana Chapel, designed by Palladio. The beautifully elaborate high altar (1670) by Francesco Antonio Corberelli is a masterpiece of intricate marble inlay. The church's highlight, however, in the fifth chapel on the left of the nave, is a beautiful 1502 *Baptism of Christ* by Giovanni Bellini. As this guide went to press, the church was about to undergo a lengthy restoration.

▶ *Major artworks from Santa Corona can be seen at the Museo Diocesano (piazza del Duomo 12) while the church is being restored.*

FREE Santuario di Monte Berico

Viale X Giugno 87 (0444 559 411/www.monteberico.it). **Open** 7am-12.30pm, 2.30-7pm Mon-Sat; 6am-7pm Sun.

CISA (Museo Palladiano). *See p277.*

The Santuario di Monte Berico is a breathtakingly beautiful spot with fantastic views. The church itself was largely rebuilt in the 18th century; its interior contains Veronese's *Supper of St Gregory the Great* (1572) in the refectory, as well as a moving *Pietà* by Bartolomeo Montagna and a fine collection of fossils. The Virgin is said to have appeared twice here – in 1426 and 1428, making it a popular destination with pilgrims. An attractive 18th-century loggia built by Francesco Muttoni leads up Viale X Giugno to the church. There's a dedicated bus service (no number – ask at the stop) from the station Mon-Sat, though it is irregular.

★ Teatro Olimpico

Piazza Matteotti 11 (0444 222 800/www.musei civicivicenza.it). **Open** 9am-5pm Tue-Sun. May close occasionally in spring and autumn for rehearsals. **Admission** by Biglietto Unico only (*see p276*). **Map** p277 C1.

The remarkable Teatro Olimpico was Palladio's final masterpiece. Designed in 1579-80, just a few months before the architect's death, it was the first permanent indoor theatre to be built in Europe since the fall of the Roman Empire. His son Silla and his star pupil Vincenzo Scamozzi took over, and the two took considerable liberties with the original blueprint. The decorative flamboyance of the wood-and-stucco interior contrasts notably with its modest entrance and severe external walls. Based on Roman theatres described by Vitruvius, it has 13 semicircular wooden steps, crowned by Corinthian columns holding up an elaborate balustrade topped with elegant 'antique' sculpted figures. The permanent stage set, designed by Scamozzi, with its seven trompe l'œil street scenes, represents the city of Thebes in Sophocles' *Oedipus Rex*, which was the theatre's first performance, on 3 March 1585.

The elaborately frescoed antechambers to the theatre were also designed by Scamozzi and were used for meetings and smaller concerts of the Accademia Olimpica, the learned society of humanists that commissioned the place. Don't miss the chiaroscuro fresco in the entrance hall depicting a delegation of Japanese noblemen who visited Vicenza in 1585.

Performances were brought to a halt by Counter-Reformation censorship. It wasn't until after World War II that the theatre once again realised its potential as a venue. A season of classical dramas in September and October usually includes a staging of *Oedipus Rex* (in Italian). Concerts take place mainly in May and June. *Photo p284*.

▶ *For concert information, contact the tourist office (see p283) or visit www.comune.vicenza.it.*

★ Villa Rotonda

Via della Rotonda 45 (0444 321 793). Bus 8 or 13 from train station. **Open** *Gardens* Mar-Nov 10am-noon, 3-6pm Tue-Sun. *Interior* mid Apr-early Nov 10am-noon, 3-6pm Wed. **Admission** *Gardens* €5. *Interior* €10. **No credit cards**.

One of the most famous buildings in Western architecture, La Rotonda – designed by Palladio between 1567 and 1570, but not completed until 1606 – is not strictly speaking a villa at all, but a pleasure pavilion for retired cleric Paolo Almerico. The Rotonda (officially the Villa Almerico-Capra Valmarana) was the first to be given a dome, a form previously associated with churches. Opening hours for the interior are short, but it's worth seeing the grandiose exterior and the garden, described by Palladio as 'one of the most agreeable and delightful sites that one could hope to find.' If you're walking to the villa, get a free map from one of the tourist offices (*see p283*).

▶ *There are plenty of Palladian villas in the surrounding countryside; see pp283-285.*

Villa Valmarana ai Nani

Via dei Nani 8 (0444 321 803/www.villa valmarana.com). Bus 8 from viale Roma. **Open** *Mid Mar-mid Nov* 10am-noon, 3-6pm Tue-Sun. *Mid Nov-mid Mar* 10am-noon, 2.30-4.30pm Sat, Sun. **Admission** €8. **No credit cards**.

It's not known who designed this delightful villa, built in 1688, which still belongs to the Valmarana family. It's the interior that is the main attraction, thanks to a remarkable series of frescoes painted by Giambattista Tiepolo and his son Giandomenico in 1757. The statues of dwarves (*nani*) lining the wall to the right of the main villa were added in 1785 by Elena Garzadori, who redesigned the garden. Legend has it that the family built the statues in order to give their own dwarf daughter friendly familiars to gaze upon. The walk from the centre to this villa takes about 30 minutes. A free map is available from the tourist office (*see p283*).

WHERE TO EAT & DRINK

Antica Casa della Malvasia

Contrà delle Morette 5 (0444 543 704). **Meals served** noon-3pm, 7-11.30pm Tue-Sat. **Average** €25. **Credit** AmEx, MC, V. **Map** p277 C1 ❶

This centrally located *osteria* offers an excellent value lunch, and a good variety of wines, but lacks atmosphere at dinner time. The attractive tables outside are a pleasant place for an *aperitivo*.

Bella Vicenza Pizzeria

Via G De Proti 12 (0444 546 192). **Meals served** 6.30-11pm Wed-Sun. **Average** €15. **Credit** AmEx, DC, MC, V. **Map** p277 C2 ❷

This basic but adequate pizzeria offers great-value pizzas, plus limited other dishes.

De Gobbi

Via Olmo 52, Creazzo (0444 520 509). **Meals served** 12-2.30pm, 7.30-10.30pm Mon-Thur, Sun; 7.30-10.30pm Sat. Closed 3wks Aug. **Average** €30. **Credit** AmEx, DC, MC, V.

This restaurant, located a few kilometres outside Vicenza, serves a great *bollito misto*.

Profile Andrea Palladio

The father of all Palladian architects.

Teatro Olimpico.

Arguably the most influential figure in Western architecture, Andrea Palladio had an unremarkable start. He was born in Padua on 30 November 1508 and baptised Andrea di Pietro della Gondola. His father apprenticed him at the age of 13 to Giovanni da Porlezza, a stonecarver in Vicenza. Recognising his talent, the workshop put up the money for Andrea's guild entrance fee. He learned to design and carve church altars, tombs and architectural elements, many commissioned by local nobility.

While working on a villa on the outskirts of Vicenza between 1530 and 1538, he met its owner, Count Giangiorgio Trissino, the wealthy leader of a group of Humanist intellectuals dedicated to reviving classical culture. This chance meeting was to change the course of Western architecture.

Trissino set about turning Andrea into a worthy heir to Vitruvius, the ancient architect whose treatise *De Architectura*

underpinned the return to classical models in the Italian Renaissance. He also gave Andrea a more suitable name: 'Palladio' resonated with classical associations, and was the name of a helpful angel in Trissino's epic poem *Italia liberata dai goti* ('Italy Liberated from the Goths'). Trissino also gave Palladio time off and funds to study Roman antiquities in Verona and Padua, and took him to Rome three times between 1540 and 1550. Palladio studied, measured and sketched all the major classical remains, as well as the buildings and plans of Renaissance greats throughout Italy. In 1554, he published *Le antichità di Roma* (*The Antiquities of Rome*), a sort of predecessor to the guidebook.

Palladio's early patrons were part of the Trissino circle, who provided both work and intellectual stimulation after Trissino died in 1550. Among these enlightened Vicentine nobles were Pietro Godi, whose **Villa Godi Valmarana ora**

Malinverni (*see p284*) was Palladio's first independent commission, completed by 1542 and one of his most radical, pared-back designs. The Barbaro brothers encouraged Palladio to create one of his masterpieces, the **Villa Barbaro a Maser** (1550-57; *see p289*). Another patron, Girolamo Chiericati helped give the architect his first big break, in 1549: restructuring Vicenza's town hall (the **Basilica Palladiana**; *see p276*), which established Palladio as one of the leading architects of his day.

Palladio also benefited from good timing. In the 16th century, the Venetian government insisted that nobles build villas on the *terra ferma* (mainland) in order to boost agricultural production and increase *La Serenissima*'s control over the countryside. Commissions for villas were thus plentiful throughout the Veneto. In 1570, Palladio moved to Venice, to become unofficial chief architect, with prominent churches such as **San Giorgio Maggiore** (*see p130*) and the **Redentore** (*see p129*) reinforcing his fame. His influential treatise, *I quattro libri dell'architettura* (*The Four Books of Architecture*, 1570), spread his name further.

The pared-back design for which Palladio became so famous was certainly inspired by Roman and Greek architecture, but was never copied from it; Palladio used classical motifs, creating a style that defined elegance. The most recognisable feature of his buildings was the use of the Greco-Roman temple front as a portico; equally innovative were the dramatic high-relief effects on façades. The floor plans usually emphasised a strong central axis and symmetrical wings, with the proportions of the rooms determined mathematically to create harmonic spaces,

typically with high ceilings. Though always unmistakably his, each of Palladio's buildings is startlingly different – from the stark simplicity of **Villa Pisani** (1540; *see p284*) at Bagnolo di Lonigo to the vast complexity of the statue-crowned **Palazzo Chiericati** (now the Museo Civico; *see p278*) in Vicenza.

In his day, Palladio's domestic villa architecture largely overshadowed his other accomplishments. His country residences uniquely combined both a working farmhouse and elegant country retreat, with much of the decoration serving a function: the gracious entrance ramp at the **Villa Emo** (*see p289*) was also intended as a platform for threshing grain.

Palladio's designs also encompassed other practical functions: stables, cellars, granaries and dovecotes were located within the compounds and were intrinsic to the villa as a whole. Never ostentatious, overbearing in size or using costly materials, they make subtle statements through a dignified classical vocabulary, harmony of proportions both external and internal, and a human scale. Palladio's inventiveness and sensitivity extended to the aspect and location of villas, which he regarded as highly important in their function as an antidote to the stresses of urban life. Building near a river or canal was recommended; as well as allowing easy access by boat, water guaranteed cool breezes during the hot summer months, irrigated the gardens and, not incidentally, 'will afford a beautiful prospect.'

Palladio's revival of ancient Greek and Roman architecture created a style that was to be copied throughout Europe for centuries.

FOUR TO SEE

His first
Villa Godi Valmarana ora Malinverni; *see p284*.

His grandest
San Giorgio Maggiore; *see p130*.

His most famous
Villa Rotonda; *see p279*.

His last
Teatro Olimpico; *see p279*.

THE VENETO

★ Osteria Il Cursore
Stradella Pozzetto 10 (0444 323 504).
Open 11am-3pm, 6pm-1am Mon, Wed-Sun.
Closed 3wks July-Aug. **Meals served** noon-
3pm, 7.30-10.30pm Mon, Wed-Sat; 7.30-10.30pm
Sun. **Average** €28. **Credit** AmEx, MC, V.
Map p277 C2 ❸
This old-fashioned *vicentino* drinking den is across
the arched ponte San Michele. There are bar nibbles
and, for larger appetites, the kitchen turns out excellent versions of local specialities such as *bigoli con
sugo di anatra* (fat spaghetti with duck sauce) or *baccalà alla vicentina*.

★ Osteria i Monelli
*Contrà Ponte San Paolo 13 (0444 540 400/
www.osteriaimonelli.it).* **Open** 10.30am-3.30pm,
6.30pm-2am Tue-Sun. **Meals served** 12.30-3pm,
7.30-11pm Tue-Sun. Closed 2wks July. **Average**
€35. **Credit** DC, MC, V. **Map** p277 C2 ❹
A lively *osteria* near piazza delle Erbe serving excellent quality food, primarily meat dishes, including
filetto di struzzo (ostrich steak).

Pasticceria Sorarù
Piazzetta Palladio 17 (0444 320 915). **Open**
8.30am-1pm, 3.30-8pm Mon, Tue, Thur-Sun.
No credit cards. **Map** p277 C2 ❺
This charming *pasticceria* is worth a look even if you
don't have a sweet tooth. The columns, marble counters and ornate wooden shelves backed with mirrors
are all 19th-century originals; the cakes, firmly in the
Austro-Hungarian tradition, are a tad fresher.

★ Remo
*Contrà Caimpenta 14 (0444 911 007/www.
daremoristorante.it).* **Meals served** noon-
2.30pm, 7.30-10.30pm Tue-Sat; noon-2.30pm Sun.
Closed Aug, 2wks Dec-Jan. **Average** €35.
Credit DC, MC, V.

INSIDE TRACK
DINE LIKE A VICENTINE

The *vicentini* have been eating *baccalà
alla vicentina* – dried cod stewed in milk
and oil – since at least 1269. Another
firm favourite in the Veneto is *bollito misto*
(mixed boiled meat), which is far more
appetising than it sounds. Expect to
see some combination of sausage
(*cotechino*), whole hen (*gallina*) or chicken
(*pollo*), veal's tongue (*lingua*), calf's
head (*testina*) and a cut of beef (*manzo*).
This is served with various sauces: *salsa
verde* (parsley and capers), *mostarda*
(spicy preserved fruit), *cren* (horseradish)
and *peàra* (a combination of breadcrumbs
and bone marrow).

This country restaurant in an old farmhouse offers
some of the best cooking you'll find anywhere in the
Vicenza area. The boiled and roasted meats trolley
is a fixture, and Remo's *baccalà alla vicentina* is spectacular. Excellent sweets and house wine.

Ristorante Tre Visi Vecchia Roma
*Corso Palladio 25 (0444 324 868/www.trevisi.
vicenza.com).* **Meals served** 12.30-2.30pm,
7-10.30pm Tue-Sat; 12.30-3pm Sun. Closed 2wks
July. **Average** €35. **Credit** AmEx, MC, V.
Map p277 B2 ❻
A good place to pop into when Palladio's genius gets
a bit too much. Try for the outside courtyard.

WHERE TO STAY

See also p284 **Villa Saraceno**.

Albergo San Raffaele
*Viale X Giugno 10 (0444 545 767/www.albergo
sanraffaele.it).* **Rates** €65 double. **Credit** AmEx,
DC, MC, V.
Situated on the hill just below the Santuario di
Monte Berico (*see p278*), this hotel has fantastic
views over the city and is a real bargain for those on
a budget. Rooms are clean and simple, but comfortable; free parking included.

Camping Vicenza
Strada Pelosa 239 (0444 582 311). **Closed** Oct-
Mar. **Rates** €3-€7.40 per person; €6-€14.60 per
camper/tent. **Credit** AmEx, DC, MC, V.
Situated near the Vicenza Est exit of the A4
Milan–Venice motorway, this upmarket campsite is
well equipped; but be warned that it is a serious hike
from the city centre.

Hotel Castello
*Contrà Piazza Castello 24 (0444 323 585/www.
hotelcastelloitaly.com).* **Rates** €120 double.
Credit AmEx, DC, MC, V. **Map** p277 B2 ❶
This unpretentious hotel with 1980s-style interiors
is in the city centre close to corso Palladio and all the
main sights. Free parking is provided.

Hotel Cristina
*Corso Santi Felice e Fortunato 32 (0444 323
751/www.hotelcristinavicenza.it).* **Rates** €103-
€113 double. **Credit** AmEx, DC, MC, V.
Map off p277 A2 ❷
Located just a few steps outside the Porta Castello
gate, the environmentally friendly Hotel Cristina
offers special weekend packages for tourists.

Hotel Giardini
*Viale Giuriolo 10 (0444 326 458/www.hotel
giardini.com).* **Rates** €114 double. **Credit**
AmEx, DC, MC, V. **Map** p277 D1 ❸
This small, modern hotel is located across piazza
Matteotti from Palladio's Teatro Olimpico (*see p279*).

San Lorenzo. *See p278.*

GETTING THERE

By train Reaching Vicenza by rail is easy: there are regular trains to and from Venice (55mins) and Verona (30mins).
By bus FTV (0444 223 111, www.ftv.vi.it) buses run from Padua to Vicenza, near the railway station.
By car Take the A4 *La Serenissima* motorway from Venice towards Milan.

GETTING AROUND

By bus Vicenza's buses are operated by **AIM** (0444 394 909, www.aimvicenza.it). A ticket valid for any number of trips in 90mins costs €1.20.

TOURIST INFORMATION

As well as the tourist offices below, you can get information from www.vicenzae.org.

IAT *Piazza Matteotti 12 (0444 320 854).* **Open** 9am-1pm, 2-6pm daily. **Map** p277 D1.
IAT *Piazza dei Signori 8 (0444 544 122).* **Open** 10am-2pm, 2.30-6.30pm daily. **Map** p277 C2.

Villas Around Vicenza

PALLADIAN VILLAS

The countryside where Andrea Palladio (*see pp280-281* **Profile**) set his masterpieces once compared favourably with the Tuscan hills, but light industry and large-scale retail has put paid to that. Many of the visitable *ville* have their own parks and gardens which act as a buffer.

What follows is a selection of Palladio's most important villas. Entry to a number of these is free or at a reduced rate with the Palladio Card (*see p276* **Inside Track**). Unless otherwise stated, all transport instructions apply from central Vicenza, where services depart from the rural FTV bus terminal (information 0444 223 111, www.ftv.vi.it) in front of Vicenza station.

Palladio also designed villas outside the Vicenza area. For his **Villa Foscari 'La Malcontenta'**, *see p261*; for **Villa Emo** and **Villa Barbaro a Maser**, *see p289*.

Villa Cornaro

*Via Roma 92, Piombino Dese (049 936 5017).
SITA bus from Padua (piazzale Boschetto) for*

Trebaseleghe. Train to Piombino Dese from Padua or Venice (from Vicenza, change at Castelfranco Veneto). **Open** *May-Sept* 3.30-6pm Sat; other times by appointment for groups only. **Admission** €5. **No credit cards**.
Constructed in 1552-53, this villa introduced to Western architecture the two-storey projecting portico-loggia motif and the aesthetically pleasing golden ratio.

Villa Godi Valmarana ora Malinverni
Via Palladio 44, Lugo di Vicenza (0445 860 561/www.villagodi.com). *Bus to Thiene; change at Thiene to bus for Lugo di Vicenza.* **Open** *Apr-Sept* 3-7pm Tue, Sat, Sun. *Mar, Oct, Nov* 2-6pm Tue, Sat, Sun. **Admission** €6. **No credit cards**. *See pp280-281* **Profile**.

Villa Piovene Porto Godi
Via Palladio 51, Lugo di Vicenza (0445 860 613). *Bus to Thiene; change at Thiene to hourly bus for Lugo di Vicenza.* **Open** (gardens only) *Apr-Oct* 2.30-7pm daily. *Nov-Mar* 2-5pm daily. **Admission** €4.50. **No credit cards**.
A late commission, the formulaic style suggests to some critics that self-parody was beginning to set in. Only the central block is plausibly by Palladio.

Villa Pisani
Via Risaie 1, Bagnolo frazione di Lonigo (0444 831 104). *Bus for Cologna Veneta.* **Open** *Apr-Nov* by appointment. **Admission** €7; €6 reductions. **No credit cards**. *See pp280-281* **Profile**.

Teatro Olimpico.
See p279.

Villa Pojana
Via Castello 41, Poiana Maggiore (0444 898 554). *Bus for Noventa Vicentina.* **Open** *Apr-Oct* 10am-1pm, 2-6pm Wed-Sun. *Nov-Mar* by appointment. **Admission** €5; €3 reductions. **No credit cards**.
This villa demonstrates Palladio's skill as an architect of smaller dwellings. Completed around 1550, its façade is dominated by a Serlian arch (a central arched opening flanked by two rectangular ones) topped by telephone-dial openings. The interior has frescoes by Bernardino India and Anselmo Canera.

Villa Saraceno
Via Finale 8, Finale di Agugliaro (0444 891 371/www.landmarktrust.org.uk). *Bus for Noventa Vicentina; change at Ponte Botti for local service.* **Open** *Apr-Sept* 2-4pm Wed. *Oct-Mar* by appointment. **Admission** by donation.
In 1988, the lovely Villa Saraceno (1550) was bought by the British Landmark Trust and restored. It was built for a gentleman farmer, and has an attic-granary lit by large grilled windows, so that the wheat was kept ventilated.
▶ *Villa Saraceno is available as self-catering accommodation, offering a unique chance to stay in a Palladian villa. See the website for details.*

FREE Villa Thiene
Piazza IV Novembre 2, Quinto Vicentino (0444 584 211). *Bus 5 (for Quinto or Lanzé) from Vicenza (piazza Matteotti)*. **Open** 9.30am-12.45pm, 5.30-6.45pm Mon, Thur; 9.30am-12.45pm Fri. Groups by appointment only. **Admission** free.
Now the town hall of the unremarkable town of Quinto Vicentino, imposing Villa Thiene is only a fraction of what was to be an even more immense villa, designed by Palladio in 1546. The interior was frescoed in the mid 16th century by Giovanni De Mio and Bernardino India. Visitors can only visit a couple of rooms and the gardens, subject to permission.

OTHER ARCHITECTS' VILLAS

Andrea Palladio was not the only gainfully employed architect in Vicenza. Below is a selection of the *other* most important country villas in Vicenza province.

Villa Cordellina Lombardi
Via Lovara 36, Montecchio Maggiore (0444 908 141/www.provincia.vicenza.it/pdv/ville). *Bus to Recoaro.* **Open** *Apr-Oct* 9am-1pm Tue-Fri; 9am-noon, 3-6pm Sat, Sun. **Admission** €2.10. **No credit cards**.
This beautifully restored villa, built between 1735 and 1760 in the grand Palladian style, contains some flamboyant frescoes by Giambattista Tiepolo. There is also a charming French-style park, and a garden. Call ahead as opening hours vary.

Villa Pisani Ferri 'Rocca Pisana'

Via Rocca 1, Lonigo (0444 831 625). Bus to Lonigo. **Open** by appointment only. **Admission** €5. **No credit cards.**

Built in 1576 on the ruins of a medieval castle, this villa was designed by Palladio's pupil Vincenzo Scamozzi. Like La Rotonda (*see p279*), La Rocca has four main windos facing the four compass points, and a dome with a hole. But whereas the Rotonda hole is covered with glass, the hole here is open, allowing air to circulate.

Villa Trissino Marzotto

Piazza GG Trissino 2, Trissino (0445 962 029). Bus to Recoaro. **Open** *Mar-July, Sept, Oct* 9am-noon Wed, Sat. *Aug, Nov-Feb* appointment only. **Admission** *Villa* €5. *Garden* €5. **No credit cards.**

This elaborate complex is set in one of the most charming of Italy's private parks. The upper villa and the park were designed by Francesco Muttoni between 1718 and 1722. The garden is a typically 18th-century mixture of art and nature; the lower villa acts as a theatrical focal point.

Drive Villa Jaunts

Discover Palladio's grand designs in the countryside.

These driving itineraries take in several villas apiece, in trips from Vicenza. Local tourist offices (*see p283*) provide excellent road maps and their own villa information. The majority of villas are private homes, so opening hours are subject to change at short notice; phone ahead. Entry to several is free or at a reduced rate with the Palladio Card (*see p276* **Inside Track**).

NORTH-EAST OF VICENZA

It's quite a hike up to Lugo di Vicenza, home to magnificent Palladian villas, so allow a generous half-day. Head north-east out of Vicenza on the SS53. About four kilometres out of town, beyond a motorway flyover, the SP29 branches right towards Quinto Vicento, where Palladio's **Villa Thiene** (*see p284*) is now the town hall.

Backtrack on the SS53 towards Vicenza for about 500 metres, then join the A31 heading north towards Thiene. Where the motorway ends, veer right and follow the SP68 to Caltrano, then Lugo di Vicenza. In the centre of the village, via Giacomo Matteotti becomes via Palladio, which has two fine villas by the architect: **Villa Godi Valmarana ora Malinverni** and **Villa Piovene Porto Godi** (*see p284*). For a luxury lunch break or indulgent dinner, get back on the SP68, head for Zugliano, then Sarcedo, and continue on the SP63 to Montecchio Precalcino, home to the excellent **Locanda di Piero** (via Roma 32, 0445 864 827, www.lalocandadipiero.it). Vicenza is about ten kilometres south of here on the SP248.

NORTH-WEST OF VICENZA

If you're making this an afternoon drive, you could set out after a lunch at the **Antica Trattoria Monterosso** (via Roma 40, 0444 371 362, www.trattoriamonterosso.it)

in Alta Villa Vicentina. Take the SR11 south-west out of Vicenza, following the railway line towards Verona. The restaurant is in the village centre, by the motorway.

Back on the SR11, continue west to Montecchio Maggiore, home to the charming **Villa Cordellina Lombardi** (*see p284*) and its gardens. From here, the SP246 goes north to Valdagno; about seven kilometres outside Montecchio is Trissino, where you can visit the gardens and interiors of **Villa Trissino Marzotto** (by appointment only; *see above*).

SOUTH OF VICENZA

This whole-day circuit takes in four villas and a wonderful rural restaurant. From Vicenza, head due south on the SP247 towards Noventa Vicentina for about 15 kilometres. Palladio's **Villa Saraceno** (*see p284*) is located on via Finale, off the SP247 to the left, two kilometres before Noventa. Pioana Maggiore, home to Palladio's beguilingly modern-looking **Villa Pojana** (*see p284*), lies three kilometres beyond Noventa Vicentina.

Next, take the SP4 north out of Poiana Maggiore, taking a right on to the SP14 towards Lonigo after about two kilometres. Just outside Lonigo, perched on a hill overlooking the town, is **Villa Pisani Ferri 'Rocca Pisana'** (*see above*), designed by Palladio's protégé Vincenzo Scamozzi. Those with rumbling tummies and a generous credit facility should try luxurious **La Peca** (via A Giovannelli 2, 0444 830 214, www.lapeca.it) in Lonigo.

Continue by following the SP500 directly south out of town in the direction of Cologna Veneta for about a kilometre. Take the first right at the tiny hamlet of Bagnolo-Frazione di Lonigo. The next left leads to the classic Palladian **Villa Pisani** (*see p284*).

THE VENETO

Treviso & the Northern Veneto

Head for the hills.

North of Venice, the Veneto is a land of extremes, incorporating regimental rows of beach huts, fenlands spattered with small industries and dramatic Alpine mountain ranges. There is a plethora of day-trip opportunities: craggy mountains, Alpine meadows, mighty forests, tower-dotted hills and walled towns each with one or two points of interest. For outdoor types, a day may not be enough to enjoy what the mighty Dolomite mountains have to offer in this dramatic corner of northern Veneto.

Treviso

SIGHTSEEING

Some 25 kilometres (16 miles) north of its ostentatious neighbour, Treviso likes to fashion itself as 'little Venice'. This pretty town, with its painstakingly restored *palazzi* (damaged during intensive World War II bombing) and stunning frescoed churches, is an underrated beauty. It offers Venice's romantic canalside walks, Renaissance architecture and great art, but all on a much smaller scale and without the tourist mass to mar your visit.

While the Venetians are responsible for the walls guarding the old town, Treviso was important long before they muscled in during the 14th century. Originally the Roman town of Tarvisium, the city was also the seat of a Lombard duchy. The Venetian walls, dating back to 1509, protect three sides of the old town. The fourth is guarded by the Sile River. Once, Treviso's stream-fed canals were used by the city's dyers, tanners and paper mills; today, their mossy walls and small bridges offer a bucolic touch to the *osterie* ranged alongside.

Treviso is famous for its millionaires, the product of its family-run businesses. The most renowned – Benetton – has branched out from the home-knitted jumpers of Giuliana Benetton to less fashionable assets, like a sizeable chunk of Italy's motorway system.

Around the corner from the oversized Benetton store in piazza Indipendenza are piazza dei Signori and the **Palazzo dei Trecento**, the town hall which dates back to 1217. Across from the palazzo, in piazza Duomo, the **Duomo** (open 9am-noon, 3.30-6.30pm daily) contains an *Annunciation* (1570) by Titian and a beautiful *Adoration of the Magi* (1520) by Pordenone. Two other churches in nearby piazza San Vito – **San Vito** and **Santa Lucia** (both open 8am-noon daily) – offer splendid frescoes by Tommaso da Modena (1325-79), considered by some to be the greatest 14th-century artist after Giotto.

More works by Da Modena, including his masterpiece, *The Life of St Ursula*, are tucked away in **Santa Caterina** in piazza Giacomo Matteotti (open during exhibitions only). The privately run **Casa dei Carraresi** (0422 513 161) at via Palestra 33-5 is an exhibition space with world-class pretensions.

For a fresco fest, head to the church of **San Francesco** (open 7am-noon, 3-7pm daily). Work on the ceiling of the main chapel includes the wonderful *St Francis with Stigmata*, by an anonymous 14th-century painter, though some argue it should be attributed to Da Modena. Da Modena pops up yet again with a series of frescoes in the chapter house of the Dominican monastery adjoining the Romanesque-Gothic church of **San Nicolò** on via San Nicolò (open 8am-noon, 3.30-6pm daily).

WHERE TO STAY & EAT

Toni del Spin (via Inferiore 7, 0422 543 829, www.ristorantetonidelspin.com, closed lunch Mon, all Sun and mid July-mid Aug, average €30) is a pretty, intimate *osteria* serving local specialities at reasonable prices. **Trattoria Due Mori** (via Bailo 9, 0422 540 383, www. trattoria2mori.com, closed Wed, average €25) dishes up no-frills fare and alfresco seating in the centre of town. A young crowd can be found at **Osteria ai Filodrammatici** (via Filodrammatici 5, 0422 580 011, closed Mon, average €20). **Muscoli** (via Pescheria 23, 0422 583 390, closed Sun year-round, Wed from Apr to Oct, average €15) is the place to go for a reviving *ombra* (glass of wine) and outstanding nibbles. **Albergo Il Focolare** (piazza Ancilotto 4, 0422 56 601, www.albergo ilfocolare.net, €100 double) offers good service right in the heart of town.

GETTING THERE

By train There are regular Venice–Treviso services (25 mins).
By bus ACTV and ATVO (for both, *see p295*) buses run regularly from Venice's bus terminus in piazzale Roma.
By car Take the Treviso Sud exit from the A27 motorway; alternatively, take the SS13 from Venice/Mestre.

TOURIST INFORMATION

IAT *Piazza Monte di Pietà 8 (0422 547 632/ www.turismo.provincia.treviso.it).* **Open** 9am-1pm Mon; 9am-1pm, 2-6pm Tue-Fri; 9am-12.30pm, 3-6pm Sat; 9.30am-1pm, 3-6pm Sun.

West from Treviso

Between Treviso and Castelfranco are two fine villas by Andrea Palladio (*see p280* **Profile**): the magnificent Villa Barbaro a Maser and Villa Emo. **Villa Barbaro a Maser** is an out-and-out exercise in rural utopianism. It derives partly from Palladio's intellectual communion with the Barbaro brothers – for whom it was designed and built between 1550 and 1557 – and partly from the quality of the decoration. For only in this villa did the architect find a painter, Paolo Veronese, capable of matching his genius. The light, airy rooms house the artist's sumptuous trompe l'œil frescoes. Two traditional parts of the Veneto farmhouse have been dressed up in a new classical disguise: those two arcaded wings flanking the main porticoed building are actually *barchesse*, or farmhouse wings; while the mirror-image, sundial-adorned chapel fronts on either end are in fact dovecotes. Behind these is a nymphaeum – a semicircular pool surrounded by statues.

Treviso's city walls.

A tad more rustic, **Villa Emo** (*see also p280* **Profile**) contains joyous frescoes by Giambattista Zelotti, one of the major fresco artists of the late Italian Renaissance.

In **Castelfranco Veneto**, the **Duomo** (open 9.30-11.45am, 3.15-5.45pm Mon-Sat) is home to *Madonna and Child with Saints Liberal and Francis* (1504), one of the few surviving masterpieces of local artist Giorgio Barbarella, better known as Giorgione. The moats and 13th-century fortified red-brick wall provide a picturesque backdrop to the town.

Another local boy is featured in the tiny village of **Possagno**. Inside the family home of sculptor Antonio Canova (1757-1822) is the **Gipsoteca Canoviana**. The museum has many works, including the striking black-tack-studded plaster models for the finished statues. Modernist architect Carlo Scarpa designed the museum's extension (1955-57).

For more Scarpa, head to the cemetery (open 9am-7pm daily) in **San Vito d'Altivole**. Among the more mundane remembrances is the massive *Tomba Brion* – 2,200 square metres (23,656 square feet) of pure Scarpa, who spent the nine years before his death in 1978 constructing the monster. He is also buried here.

Robert Browning fell so deeply in love with the picture-postcard landscape of **Asolo** that he named his last collection of verse after the town (*Asolando*, 1889). Set among rolling hills covered with cypress trees, olive groves and vineyards, the town is not so much for sight-seeing as for window-shopping, a long lunch and a leisurely walk with the town's illustrious ghosts: Caterina Cornaro, the exiled Venetian-born Queen of Cyprus, who set up court in Asolo in 1489, and the 19th-century actress Eleonora Duse.

To the west of Asolo, **Bassano del Grappa** sits astride the Brenta river. Monte Grappa, a few kilometres outside of town, gives its name to both the town and Italy's fiery after-dinner drink. Technically a pomace brandy, grappa is a way of getting the most out of the vines. After the grapes are pressed for wine, the skins, seeds and stems are distilled into grappa.

The oldest and most famous name in grappa is **Nardini** (Ponte Vecchio 2). Another famous name, **Poli**, can be found at via Gamba 6, at the foot of Bassano's showpiece, the **Ponte degli Alpini**. Though the original bridge was probably constructed in the 1150s, what we see now is a faithful copy of Palladio's magnificent

Moving Mountains

The tragic history of a World War I front line.

Behind the town of **Cortina d'Ampezzo**'s glam sophistication and breathtaking natural surroundings lies a bleak heritage of wartime suffering. The town had been part of the Habsburg empire from 1511, but when Italy entered World War I in 1915, the Austro-Hungarians swiftly abandoned it.

They beat a hasty retreat into the nearby mountains, where their defences stopped the advance of the Italian forces. As winter approached, both sides began digging into a platform high up stark, rugged **Monte Lagazuoi** (2,752m/9,029ft). Temperatures that fell to –30°C (–22°F) and snow nine metres (30 feet) deep meant that thousands of men died not in combat but from hypothermia, disease and starvation.

The tunnels, open emplacements and trenches that witnessed those chilling events are now being restored and opened to the public in an EU-financed project run by Cortina in partnership with the Austrian town of Innsbrück. Spread over a swathe of bitterly contested mountainside to the west of Cortina, the open-air **Museo della Grande Guerra** (Great War Museum) comprises three sites (Monte Lagazuoi,

Monte Cinque Torri and the **Tre Sassi Fort**) within an eight-kilometre (five-mile) radius, each furnished with well sign-posted walking tracks and information panels.

PRACTICALITIES

The Museo della Grande Guerra (www.grandeguerra.dolomiti.org) is open all year, and is free to visit. You can hire audio guides for the mountain excursions at the Monte Cinque Torre chairlift or Lagazuoi cable-car ticket offices.

Tickets for the Cinque Torri chairlift and Lagazuoi cable-car cost €8.50 uphill, €6 downhill and €11.50 round trip. The Freepass day ticket costs €16 and comprises entry to the Tre Sassi museum, plus cable car/chairlift return trips on the two mountains. No credit cards.

All the sites can be reached by bus from Cortina; the tourist office (*see p292*) has timetables. Take torches if you're planning to explore the tunnels on Monte Lagazuoi. Guided tours are available all year round; contact the **Gruppo Guide Alpine Cortina** (corso Italia 69, 0436 868 505, www.guidecortina.com).

covered wooden bridge built in 1586 (Palladio's was blown up by retreating German troops at the end of World War II). In piazza Garibaldi is the **Museo Civico**, located inside the beautiful convent and cloistered gardens of the 14th-century church of San Francesco. The museum contains a fine collection of ceramics – Bassano is also known for its ceramics industry – and an archaeological section devoted to the city's Roman origins. Piazza Libertà is dominated by the medieval **Palazzo Municipale**, which is covered with faded frescoes. The **Museo degli Alpini**, with its collection of World War I memorabilia, stands at the far end of the ponte degli Alpini.

★ Gipsoteca Canoviana
Piazza Canova 74, Possagno (0423 544 323/www. museocanova.it). **Open** 9.30am-6pm Tue-Sun. **Admission** €7; €5 reductions. **No credit cards**.

Museo Civico
Piazza Garibaldi, Bassano (0424 519 450/www. museobassano.it). **Open** 9am-6.30pm Tue-Sat; 10.30am-1pm, 3.30-6.30pm Sun. **Admission** €4; €3 reductions. **No credit cards**.

FREE Museo degli Alpini
Via Angarano 2, Bassano (0424 503 662). **Open** 9am-8pm Tue-Sun. **Admission** free.

★ Villa Barbaro a Maser
Via Cornuda 7, Maser (0423 923 004/www. villadimaser.it). **Open** *Mar-Oct* 10am-6pm Tue, Sat; 11am-6pm Sun. *Nov-Feb* 2.30-5pm Sat, Sun. Other days by appointment for groups (20+) only. **Admission** €5. **No credit cards**. *Photo p290.*
▶ *For further information about this villa and its architect, Andrea Palladio, see p280 Profile.*

Villa Emo
Via Stazione 5, Fanzolo di Vedelago (0423 476 334). **Open** *Apr-Oct* 3-7pm Mon-Fri; 10am-12.30pm, 3-6.30pm Sun. *Nov-Mar* 2-4pm Mon-Fri; 2-5.30pm Sat, Sun. **Admission** €5.50; €3 reductions. **No credit cards**.
▶ *For more on this villa, see p280 Profile.*

WHERE TO STAY & EAT

In Asolo, the **Hotel Duse** (via Browning 190, 0423 55241, www.hotelduse.com, €110-€130 double, €8 breakfast) is a comfortable three-star option in the centre of town. **Ca' Derton** (piazza d'Annunzio 11, 0423 529 648, closed lunch Mon, dinner Sun and 2wks Aug, average €45) is a firm favourite with Italian foodies. Nearby, in the same piazza, **Ristorante Due Mori** (piazza d'Annunzio 5, 0423 952 256, closed Wed, average €35) is more casual but equally delicious.

In Bassano, **Al Castello** (via Bonamigo 19, 0424 228 665, www.hotelalcastello.it, €70-€100 double) is a reasonably priced three-star. **Birraria Ottone** (via Matteotti 50, 0424 522 206, closed dinner Mon, all Tue, average €25), serves mainly regional and Austrian dishes.

GETTING THERE

By train Frequent Venice–Bassano trains, which also stop at Castelfranco.
By bus Bus operator **La Marca** (0422 577 311) runs services from Treviso to Castelfranco and Bassano, and to Villa Barbaro a Maser. The bus for Montebelluna from Castelfranco station passes by Villa Emo.
By car From Treviso, SS53 will take you directly to Castelfranco Veneto. For Asolo, take SS348 to Montbelluna, then take SS248, which continues to Bassano del Grappa. Possagno is located a short distance from Asolo on minor roads.

TOURIST INFORMATION

IAT Asolo *Piazza Garibaldi 73 (0423 529 046/ www.turismo.provincia.treviso.it).* **Open** 9am-12.30pm Tue-Wed; 9am-12.30pm, 3-6pm Thur-Sun.

Santa Caterina, Treviso. *See p286.*

IAT Bassano *Largo Corona d'Italia 35 (0424 524 351/www.vicenzae.org).* **Open** 9am-1pm, 2-6pm daily.

IAT Castelfranco Veneto *Via Francesco Maria Preti 66 (0423 491 416/www.turismo.provincia. treviso.it).* **Open** *Apr-July, Sept, Oct* 9.30am-12.30pm Wed, Thur; 9.30am-12.30pm, 3-6pm Fri-Sun. *Jan, Mar, Aug, Nov* 9.30am-12.30pm Tue-Thur; 9.30am-12.30pm, 3-6pm Fri, Sat.

North from Treviso

Sheltered from cold northerlies by the nearby range of the Dolomites and enjoying warmer air sweeping up the Adriatic, the area between Conegliano and Valdobbiadene is home to sparkling prosecco and to Italy's *Strada del Prosecco*, an itinerary built around vineyards and wine outlets.

The town of **Conegliano** is pleasant if unchallenging. The 14th-century **Duomo** (open 9am-noon, 4-7pm daily) is home to a painting of the *Virgin and Child with Saints and Angels* by the town's most famous son, Giambattista Cima, known as Cima da Conegliano. Conegliano's cultural treasures end here, but visit the **Sala dei Battuti** (open Apr-Sept 3.30-7pm Sun, Oct-Mar 3-6.30pm Sun) next to the Duomo: dedicated to a brotherhood of flagellants, it's decorated with some truly odd 15th- and 16th-century biblical frescoes.

The hills change to mountains as you near **Vittorio Veneto**. Originally two smaller towns called Ceneda and Serravalle, Vittorio Veneto was formed and named in 1866, to commemorate the unification of Italy under King Vittorio Emanuele II. Serravalle has a well-preserved medieval *borgo* (quarter), which is unfortunately situated right on the busy *strada statale*. It's worth braving the exhaust fumes for a brief walk through the *borgo* and a glance at the frescoed **Loggia Serravallese**, which dates from 1462.

Both Conegliano and Vittorio Veneto offer access to Valdobbiadene; the road from Vittorio Veneto (take the SS51 out of town then follow signs) has the advantage of passing through **Follina**. Here, nestled among the hills of the *prealpi* and the sleepy town centre is one of the jewels of the Veneto, the **Abbazia Santa Maria** (open 6.30am-noon, 2.30-9.30pm daily). The Romanesque abbey dates back to the 12th century and features one of the most peaceful cloisters you'll ever see.

The town of **Valdobbiadene** is the headquarters for the production of prosecco, a native grape that fills 33 million bottles a year. An annual *spumante* fair takes place in September (www.forumspumantiditalia.it). The tourist office in the town (*see p292*) provides a complete list of producers on request. **Azienda Bisol**, in the neighbouring village of Santo Stefano (via Fol 33, 0423 900 138), produces one of the best *prosecchi*.

Villa Barbaro a Maser. *See p287.*

THE VENETO

Take the *Strada d'Alemagna* – the main road (SS51) from Vittorio Veneto to **Belluno** – and it's hard not to rhapsodise about the area. There's no shortage of awe-inspiring views, or trails (maps available from the IAT in Belluno; *see p292*) to view them from.

Like Treviso, the medieval town of Belluno invites comparisons with Venice. 'The Venice of the Alps' occupies a rocky terrace overlooking the Piave and Ardo rivers. An escalator carries visitors from the Lamboi car park to the main piazza, emerging on to a scene that is pure enchantment. Against a beautiful backdrop of mountains and tranquillity, the 15th-century **Palazzo dei Rettori** (once home to the town's Venetian rulers; not open to the public) and 16th-century **Duomo** (open 7am-12.30pm, 3.30-7.30pm daily) recall the architecture along the Grand Canal. The **Baptistry** (variable hours), across from the Duomo, contains an early 18th-century carving of John the Baptist by Andrea Brustolon.

In the mountains beyond Belluno is the jet-set capital of the Dolomites, **Cortina d'Ampezzo** – beautiful, but expensive. Summer sport pursuits range from the obvious climbing and hiking to riding and fishing. For those with thighs of thunder and butts of steel, mountain bikes can be hired from **2UE & 2UE** (via Roma 70, 0436 4121, www.dueduecortina.com). Half a day will set you back €14. For would-be Reinhold Messners, check out the *scuola roccia* (rock-climbing school; corso Italia 69B, 0436

868 505, www.guidecortina.com), which offers individual lessons, group excursions and guided solo climbs.

To the west of Belluno, **Feltre** was once a Roman fortress on the banks of the river Piave. Today, it is a perfectly preserved 16th-century town. Among the cobbled streets and frescoed *palazzi*, the sharp-eyed visitor will notice that many of the lapidaries are chipped clean. *La Serenissima* financed a well-endowed rebuilding programme after the town was destroyed in 1510 by the troops of the Holy Roman Emperor Maximilian I. Many of the stone markers praised Venice for its aforementioned munificence. When Napoleon rolled in he took umbrage at all the praise directed towards his enemies, and ordered the words destroyed. Despite Napoleon's enmity, paintings and statues of the lion of St Mark are everywhere. Many of the *palazzi* along Feltre's high street, via Mezzaterra, are frescoed by local artist Lorenzo Luzzo (1467-1512).

WHERE TO STAY & EAT

For good-value local cuisine in Conegliano, try the **Trattoria Stella** (via Accademia 3, 0438 22178, closed Sun and 3wks Aug, average €25). Alternatively, for something more upmarket, head for **Ristorante al Salisà** (via XX Settembre 2, 0438 24288, www. ristorantealsalisa.com, closed dinner Tue, all Wed, average €35) and indulge in a bottle from its excellent wine list.

On the same street you will find the **Hotel Canon d'Oro** (via XX Settembre 131, 0438 34246, www.hotelcanondoro.it, €80-€175 double). The **Hotel dei Chiostri**, in Follina (piazza IV Novembre 20, 0438 971 805, www. hoteldeichiostri.com, €135-€165 double), is a super-swanky hotel right across the street from the Abbazia (*see p290*).

At the lovely **Trattoria alla Cima** in Valdobbiadene (via Cima 13, 0423 972 711, closed dinner Mon, all Tue, average €30), you can enjoy excellent grilled meats.

Belluno's rustic **Al Borgo** restaurant (via Anconetta 8, 0437 926 755, closed dinner Mon, all Tue and 2wks Jan, average €30)

THE VENETO

offers smoked ham and sausages, in addition to unusual, filling pasta dishes. If you're looking for accommodation, try the centrally located **Albergo delle Alpi** (via Tasso 13, 0437 940 545, www.dellealpi.it, €110 double).

East of Belluno, the **Locanda San Lorenzo**, in the small town of Puos d'Alpago (via IV Novembre 79, 0437 454 048, www.locandasan lorenzo.it, closed Wed and 3wks Jan-Feb, average €55), offers some of the Veneto's best food, and doubles as an excellent hotel (€95 double).

In Cortina, the **Baita Fraina** (località Fraina 1, 0436 3634, closed Mon and 2wks Jan & 2wks July, average €30) serves hearty fare on a panoramic terrace. The **Hotel Menardi** (via Majon 110, 0436 2400, www. hotelmenardi.it, €103 double) has excellent modern facilities in a rustic setting.

In Feltre, the **Belle Epoque** (piazza Maggiore, 0439 80193, closed Mon and 2 wks Jan, average €25) serves up comforting food under the porticos of the town's main square.

GETTING THERE

By train Fast Venice–Udine trains stop at Conegliano; local Venice–Belluno trains call at Conegliano and Vittorio Veneto as well. There's a local train service from Treviso to Feltre. For Cortina, take the train to Calalzo, where there are bus connections to the town.
By bus Services from Venice's piazzale Roma to Belluno run during the summer, stopping at Conegliano and Vittorio Veneto. **La Marca** (0422 577 311) runs services from Treviso's bus station to the three towns, as well as Feltre.

There's an **ATVO** (0421 383 671) bus from piazzale Roma to Cortina d'Ampezzo at 7.50am (daily through summer; Sat & Sun only for most of the rest of the year, except peak skiing weeks; consult www.atvo.it); the journey takes three-and-a-half hours. The return service leaves Cortina at 3.15pm and will, on request, proceed to Venice airport after reaching piazzale Roma at 6.15pm.
By car From Treviso, take the SS13 to Conegliano, then the SS51 to Vittorio Veneto and Belluno. The three towns can also be reached by the A27 motorway. To get to Feltre from Belluno, take SS50. For Cortina, continue on SS51.

TOURIST INFORMATION

For information on ski resorts in the region, consult www.dolomitisuperski.it.

IAT Belluno *Piazza Duomo 2 (0437 940 083/ www.infodolomiti.it).* **Open** 9am-12.30pm, 3.30-6.30pm daily. Closed Sun afternoon Oct-Mar.
IAT Conegliano *Via XX Settembre 61 (0438 21 230/www.turismo.provincia.treviso.it).* **Open** 9.30am-12.30pm Mon-Wed, Sun; 3-6pm Fri, Sat.
IAT Cortina *Piazzetta San Francesco 8 (0436 323/www.infodolomiti.it).* **Open** 9am-12.30pm, 3.30-6.30pm daily.
IAT Feltre *Piazzetta Trento e Trieste 9 (0439 2540/www.infodolomiti.it).* **Open** 9am-12.30pm, 3.30-6.30pm daily.
IAT Valdobbiadene *Via Piva 53 (0423 976 975/ www.valdobbiadene.com).* **Open** 9.30am-12.30pm, 3-6pm Mon-Sat.

The Hills are Alive…

…with the sound of 'Action!'

Cortina and the mountains and forests of the **Dolomites** have provided the backdrop for countless cinematic gems (and howlers). Though ostensibly set in Colorado, Renny Harlin's *Cliffhanger* cliff-edge scenes were predominantly shot in the more dramatic Dolomites. Practised climbers bad-mouthed the film for its inaccurate depiction of the sport, but Sly Stallone saving the day offers spectacular shots of these craggy peaks.

Jean-Jacques Annaud's *The Bear,* also set in North America, was filmed in the Dolomites natural park. Not nearly as gory as *Grizzly*, this is an eco-friendly fable about an orphan bear cub hooking up with an older male for company and protection against us nasty humans.

Two big films taking even bigger advantage of Cortina and her environs are *The Pink Panther* and *For Your Eyes Only*. The first sees the hapless Inspector Clouseau (Peter Sellers) pursuing the elusive Phantom (David Niven); watching these movies, anyone who has ever tried to reach Cortina using public transport might gasp at the sight of a working train station in the town, while skiers will weep at the sight of the unpopulated slopes. *For Your Eyes Only* makes full use of all that Cortina has to offer. The town centre, with the snow sculptures from its annual competition, was 'enhanced' with truckloads of snow brought down from the slopes. The Olympic stadia (Cortina hosted the Winter Olympics in 1956) take centre stage. Part of the plot revolves around a figure skater; we catch her dancing in the Olympic ice stadium. Further stunning stunts are shot on local ski-runs and the dramatically sculptural Olympic ski-jump. With a cliffhanger shot on top of one of the Tofane mountains, the film is a hymn to the dazzling beauty of this Dolomite diamond.

THE VENETO

Directory

Getting Around	**295**
Resources A-Z	**298**
Travel Advice	298
The Local Climate	306
Glossary	**307**
Vocabulary	**308**
Further Reference	**309**
Index	**310**
Advertisers' Index	**316**

Getting Around

ARRIVING & LEAVING

By air

Low-cost carriers fly visitors to Venice through Venice, Treviso and Verona airports. National carriers fly principally to Venice, although some have services to Verona.

Venice Marco Polo Airport
switchboard 041 260 6111/flight & airport information 041 260 9260/www.veniceairport.it.
You can get a bus or taxi (*see below*) to piazzale Roma, but you may find that the **Alilaguna boat service** drops you nearer your hotel. The dock is seven minutes' walk from arrivals; porter service costs €4.50. Various Alilaguna (041 523 5775, www.alilaguna.com) services call at San Marco, Rialto, Fondamenta Nove, Guglie, Zattere and Madonna dell'Orto vaporetto stops: check which is handiest for your final destination. Main services are hourly, others less frequent. Tickets (€13; reductions for Venice Card holders; *see p6*) can be purchased at Alilaguna's counter in the arrivals hall or on board. Allow 70mins from or to San Marco. The non-stop service to San Marco takes 20mins but costs €25 (no reductions).

Two **bus** companies operate services from the airport. The slower bus 5, run by **ACTV** (0421 383 672, timetable information 041 24 24, www.actv.it), travels between the airport and piazzale Roma, leaving every 30mins; journey time 35-40mins. Buy tickets (€2.50; included with transport passes; *see p296*) on board.

The quicker bus service (20mins) between the airport and piazzale Roma is run by **ATVO** (0421 383 672, www.atvo.it). Buy tickets (€3; €5.50 return) from the ATVO counter at the airport, or at their piazzale Roma office. You may also be able to just pay the driver directly if you have exact change.

A **taxi** from the airport to piazzale Roma costs €33 and takes about 20mins. You can pay in advance by credit card in the arrivals hall at the **Cooperativa Artigiana Radio Taxi** (041 541 6363, info 041 595 1402) desk.

The most luxurious way to reach the centre is by **water taxi**.

Consorzio Motoscafi Venezia (041 541 5084) charges upwards of €98 for the 25-30 minute crossing. *See also p296* **Water Taxis**.

Treviso Sant'Angelo Airport
airport information 0422 315 111/www.trevisoairport.it.
ATVO (0422 315 327, www.atvo.it) **bus** services run from piazzale Roma and back to coincide with flights – if the flight arrives late, the bus will wait. The journey takes about 70mins, and costs €6 one way, €10 round trip (valid seven days). Buses from piazzale Roma leave ridiculously early so ensure your timely arrival. Alternatively, take a **train** from Venice to Treviso (35mins) and then a bus or taxi (**Cooperativa Radiotaxi Padova**, 049 651 333) to the airport. **ACTT** (0422 3271) bus 6 does the 20-minute trip from in front of Treviso train station to the airport at frequent intervals throughout the day and costs €1.

Valerio Catullo Airport (Verona) *045 809 5666/ www.aeroportoverona.it.*
A **bus** (0458 057911) runs every 20mins to the Verona train station, from 6.35am to 11.35pm. The 20min journey costs €4.50 (pay on board).

Major airlines

Alitalia *06 2222/www.alitalia.it.*
British Airways *199 712 266/ www.britishairways.com.*
Easyjet *848 887 766/ www.easyjet.com.*
Ryanair (Treviso Airport) *0422 315 331/premium-rate booking line 899 678 910/www.ryanair.com.*

By train

Most trains arrive at **Santa Lucia** station in Venice (map p320 C4), though a few will only take you as far as Mestre on the mainland; if so, change to a local train (every ten minutes or less during the day) for the short hop across the lagoon. *See also p296.*

Trenitalia's national rail information and booking number is 89 20 21, or 199 166 177 from mobile phones (both 7am-9pm daily). From a land line, press 1 after the recorded message, then

say '*altro*' to speak to an operator (who may not speak English).

The information office in the main hall of the station is open 7am-9pm daily. Buy tickets from the ticket windows (open 6am-9pm daily, all major credit cards accepted), vending machines in the station, travel agents around the city bearing the Trenitalia logo or on line at www.trenitalia.it.

The Trenitalia website gives exhaustive information on timetables, in English as well as Italian. Tickets can be booked through the website with a credit card and picked up from automated dispensers. Some of the routes are ticketless; take your email booking printout with you.

The slowest trains are prefixed R (Regionale); supplements are charged for high-speed trains: ES (Eurostar), IC (Intercity) or EC (Eurocity – which crosses a national border). Seat bookings are obligatory (and included in the price) on ES trains. Always consider reserving a seat on IC trains on Friday and Sunday evenings. **You must stamp your ticket** – and any supplement – in the yellow machines on each platform before boarding or face a fine. If you forget to stamp your ticket, locate the inspector as soon as possible to waive the fine.

By bus

Buses to Venice all arrive at piazzale Roma. For bus services on mainland Venice and the Lido, *see p296*; to other destinations in the Veneto, see the relevant chapters beginning on p251.

By car

Prohibitive parking fees make cars one of the least practical modes of arrival. Many Venetian hotels offer their guests discounts at car parks, and Venice Connected (*see p6*) has discounts. Main car parks (all open 24hrs) are listed below.

Autorimessa Comunale *Santa Croce 496, piazzale Roma (041 272 7301/www.asmvenezia.it).* Vaporetto *Piazzale Roma.* **Rates** €24 per 24hrs or part thereof. **Credit** AmEx, DC, MC, V. **Map** p320 A5.

Covered parking for over 2,300 cars, automatic number-plate reader and 200 CCTV cameras. Reservation online recommended.

Marco Polo Park *Venice Marco Polo Airport (041 541 5913/www.veniceairport.it). Bus 5 from piazzale Roma/free shuttle bus from main entrance of Venice airport.* **Rates** €12.50/day (discounts for longer periods). **Credit** AmEx, DC, MC, V.

Parking Stazione *Viale Stazione 10, Mestre (041 938 021). Bus 2 from piazzale Roma or train to Mestre station.* **Rates** €8/day Mon-Fri; €12/day Sat, Sun, public hols. **Credit** AmEx, DC, MC, V.

Venezia Tronchetto Parking *Isola Nuova del Tronchetto 1 (041 520 7555/www.veniceparking.it). Vaporetto Tronchetto.* **Rates** €3/hour; €21/day. **Credit** AmEx, MC, V. **Map** off p320 A4.

PUBLIC TRANSPORT

Public transport – including *vaporetti* (water buses) and local buses – in Venice itself and in some mainland areas is run by **ACTV** (www.actv.it).

ACTV's **Hellovenezia** outlets sell vaporetto public transport tickets and passes. If you're lucky, you can also pick up one of the free transport timetable booklets, but these are published at the start of the season and tend to run out swiftly (you can download them at www.hellovenezia.it/orari). Hellovenezia's extremely helpful call centre (041 2424) can provide you with information on ACTV vaporetto and bus schedules, and on events and tourist sights, in English. Hellovenezia shops and booths can be found at the airport, in piazzale Roma and at most vaporetto stops. Outlets at the larger stops (Accademia, Rialto, San Marco Vallaresso, San Zaccaria) sell Venice Card passes (*see p6*); those at the train station, Tronchetto and piazzale Roma also sell tickets for events.

ATVO (0421 383 671, www.atvo.it) runs more extensive bus services to numerous destinations on the mainland. These services, along with those of many other local companies, are described in the Veneto section of this guide, which begins on p251.

Vaporetti

Venice's *vaporetti* (water buses) run to a very tight schedule, with sailing times for each line marked clearly at stops. Strikes are frequent, but always announced in advance; look out for notices posted inside vaporetto stops bearing the title *sciopero* (strike). Regular services run from about 5am to around midnight, after which a frequent night service (N) follows the route taken by Line 2 during the day.

Taking a boat in the wrong direction is all too easy. Remember: if you're standing with your back to the station and want to head down the Grand Canal, take Line 1 (slow) or Line 2 (faster) heading left.

Fares Vaporetto tickets can be purchased at most stops, at *tabacchi* (*see p303*) and at Hellovenezia offices (*see above*). On board, you can only buy single tickets. Tickets are for single trips (€6.50 – valid 60mins on multiple boats), 12hrs (€16), 24hrs (€18), 36hrs (€23), 48hrs (€28), 72hrs (€33) or seven days (€50). The fare for a shuttle journey (ie one stop across the Grand Canal, the hop across to the Giudecca, or from Sant'Elena to the Lido) is €2.

Tickets must be validated prior to boarding the vaporetto, by stamping them in the yellow machines at the entrance to the jetty. Note that for multiple journey tickets you need only stamp your ticket once, at the start of the first journey.

Venice Connected (*see p6*) offers discounts on travel passes of up to 25 per cent, if booked online at least seven days in advance. You should flash your Venice Connected card at the machines by landing stages before boarding your boat.

Traghetti

The best way to cross the Grand Canal when you're far from a bridge is to hop on a *traghetto*. These unadorned *gondole* are rowed back and forth at fixed points along the canal. At just 50¢, it's the cheapest gondola ride in the city; Venetians make the three-minute hop standing up. *Traghetti* ply between the following points:

San Marcuola–Fontego dei Turchi Closed at time of going to press (restoration). **Map** p321 E3-4.
Santa Sofia–Pescheria 7.30am-7.45pm Mon-Sat; 8.45am-7pm Sun. **Map** p321 G4-5.
Riva del Carbon–riva del Vin 8am-2pm Mon-Sat. **Map** p321 G6.
Ca' Garzoni-San Tomà 7.30am-7.45pm Mon-Sat; 8.30am-7.15pm Sun. **Map** p323 E7.
San Samuele–Ca' Rezzonico 7.40am-1.30pm Mon-Sat. **Map** p323 E7.

Santa Maria del Giglio–Santa Maria della Salute 9.30am-6pm daily. **Map** p323 F8-9.

Buses

ACTV buses operate to both Mestre and Marghera on the mainland, as well as serving the Lido (*see p132*), Pellestrina and Chioggia. Services for the mainland depart from piazzale Roma (map p320 B5). From midnight until 5am, buses N1 (leaving every 30mins) and N2 (leaving every hour) depart from Mestre for piazzale Roma and vice versa. There are also regular night buses from the Lido (departing at least hourly) to Malamocco, Alberoni and Pellestrina.

Fares Bus tickets, costing €1.10 (also available in blocks of 10 tickets for €10), are valid for 75mins, during which you may use several buses, though you can't make a return journey on the same ticket. They can be purchased from ACTV ticket booths or from *tabacchi* (*see p303*) anywhere in the city. They should be bought before boarding the bus and then stamped on board.

Trains

Santa Lucia (map p320 C4) is Venice's main station. Most long-distance trains stop here; though some only go as far as Mestre on the mainland. Local trains leave Mestre for Santa Lucia every ten minutes or so. For information on rail travel in Italy, *see p295*.

WATER TAXIS

Water taxis are hugely expensive: expect to pay upwards of €98 from the airport (*see also p295*) directly to any single destination in Venice, and more for multiple stops. The minimum possible cost for a 15-minute trip from hotel to restaurant, for a single person is €50, with most journeys averaging €110 once numbers of passengers and baggage have been taken into account. Between the hours of 10pm and 7am there is a surcharge of €10.

Taxi pick-up points can be found at piazzale Roma, outside the train station, next to the Rialto vaporetto stop, and next to San Marco Vallaresso vaporetto stop (in front of the Giardini ex Reali), but it's more reliable to call and order yourself. Avoid asking your hotel to book a taxi for you, as they frequently add a 10% mark-up. Beware of unlicensed taxis, which charge even more than authorised ones. The latter have a black number on a yellow background.

Venezia Motoscafi *041 716 922 (24hrs); 041 716 000/041 71 124/ 041 715 544/041 716 949/www. venezianamotoscafi.it*. **Open** 24hrs daily. **No credit cards**.

GONDOLAS

Official gondola stops can be found at (or near) the following locations:
Fondamenta Bacino Orseolo Map p324 H7.
Riva degli Schiavoni in front of the Hotel Danieli. **Map** p324 K8.
San Marco Vallaresso vaporetto stop. **Map** p323 H8.
Santa Lucia railway station. Map p320 C4.
Piazzale Roma bus terminus. Map p320 C5.
Santa Maria del Giglio vaporetto stop. **Map** p323 F8.
Piazzetta San Marco jetty. Map p324 J8.
Campo Santa Sofia near Ca' d'Oro vaporetto stop. **Map** p321 G4.
San Tomà vaporetto stop. Map p323 E7.
Campo San Moisè by the Hotel Bauer. **Map** p323 G8.
Riva del Carbon at the southern end of the Rialto bridge, near the vaporetto stop. **Map** p323 G6.

Fares are set by the Istituzione per la Conservazione della Gondola e Tutela del Gondoliere (Gondola Board; 041 528 5075, www.gondola venezia.it); in the event that a gondolier tries to overcharge you – and it does happen: be prepared to stick to your guns – complain to the Gondola Board. Prices below are for the hire of the gondola, for six passengers or less. Having your own personal crooner will push the fare up.
8am-7pm €80 for 40mins; €40 for each additional 20mins.
7pm-8am €100 for 40mins; €50 for each additional 20mins.

DRIVING

Driving is an impossibility in Venice: even if your vehicle was capable of going up and down stairs and squeezing through the narrowest of alleyways, it wouldn't be legal for you to do so. Instead, you'll need to park on the outskirts and walk or use alternative means of transport. For car parks, *see p295*.

You can, on the other hand, drive on the Lido but there aren't many places to go. A car ferry (route 17)

leaves from the Tronchetto–Ferry Boat stop for Lido–San Niccolò every 50mins and costs €10 per car, plus a regular vaporetto ticket (*see p296*) per person.

It's certainly worth hiring a car, however, if you are planning to visit the Veneto countryside and its fine villas. For route information, see the relevant chapters, which start on p251. If you decide to rent a car, motorcycle or moped while in Italy, make sure you pay the extra charge to upgrade to comprehensive insurance cover.

Car breakdowns (Automobile Club d'Italia) *803 116*.
CISS traffic news *1518*.

Car hire

Avis *041 523 7377/ www.avisautonoleggio.it*.
Europcar *041 523 8616/ www.europcar.it*.
Hertz *041 528 4091/www.hertz.it*.
Maggiore National *041 935 300/ www.maggiore.it*.
Mattiazzo *041 522 0884/ www.mattiazzo.it*.
Chauffeur-driven limousine hire.

Parking

For a list of car parks, *see p295*.

CYCLING

Bikes are banned – and otiose – in Venice itself. One of the best ways to explore the Lido, however, is by bicycle, but be prepared to fight off hordes of journalists and film critics during the Film Festival in early September (*see p222*).

Cycle hire

For cycle hire on the island of Sant'Erasmo, *see p140*.

Venice Bike Rental *Gran viale Santa Maria Elisabetta 79A, Lido (041 526 1490)*. **Open** *Mar-Oct* 8.30am-8pm daily. **Rates** €3/hr; €9/day. **No credit cards**. Map p327 CC3.
Lido on Bike *Gran Viale 21B, Lido (041 526 8019/www.lidoonbike.it)*. **Open** *Mar-Sept* 9am-7pm daily. **Rates** €3/day; €42/wk; €120/mth. **Credit** MC, V. **Map** p327 BB3.

WALKING

Most of your Venetian sightseeing will be done on foot. Be aware that there are over 400 bridges, all with

steps. For etiquette tips and how to traverse Venice when it floods, *see p72* **Wet & Dry**; for getting around with children, *see p219*.

GUIDED TOURS

Unlike most tourist-oriented cities, there are no large organised tours of Venice. You can create a tour for yourself by simply wandering around, or see the city from a different (and very expensive) perspective by gondola or water taxi (*see above*). For the Grand Canal itself, nab a seat on the exterior deck of a vaporetto and read our Grand Canal chapter (*see pp52-59*) as fast as you can.

The **APT** tourist office website (*see p305*) provides information on guides by language and area, or try one of the following.

Context

www.contexttravel.com/venice. The university professors and experts at Context take groups of maximum six visitors on customised and/or themed tours. Prices vary according to length and number of participants.
Cooperativa Guide Turistiche *San Marco 750, calle Morosini de la Regina (041 520 9038/www. guidevenezia.it)*. Vaporetto San Zaccaria. **Open** *June-Aug* 9am-1pm, 2-6pm Mon-Fri; 9am-1pm Sat. *Sept-May* 9am-5pm Mon-Fri; 9am-1pm Sat. **Rates** €130 for 2hr tour for groups of up to 30 people; €4 for every extra person. **No credit cards**. **Map** p323 H7.
This cooperative has around 100 guides on its books, and offers made-to-measure tours in English and other languages. In high season, book at least a week in advance.
See Venice (Luisella Romeo) *041 590 2737/349 084 8303 mobile/ www.seevenice.it*.
Organises guided tours for groups of up to ten people (€113 per group for a two-hour tour).
Guide to Venice (Martino Rizzo) *041 526 5307/328 948 5671 mobile/www.guidetovenice.it*.
This historian specialises in tours of the islands, including cruises on traditional boats such as the *Nuovo Trionfo* (*see p245*); prices range from €40 to €70 per person. He also runs tours of Venice itself.
Venice with a Guide *www.venicewithaguide.com*.
The qualified guides charge €130 for their two-hour trips.
Venice Walks and Tours *www.tours-italy.com*.
Offers a selection of themed tours.

Resources A-Z

DIRECTORY

ADDRESSES

Postal addresses in Venice consist of the name of the *sestiere* (see p8) plus the house number. With only this information, you will likely never reach your destination.

For convenience, we have also given the name of the *calle* (street) or *campo* (square), etc where each place is located. But finding your way around remains a challenge, especially as matters are sometimes complicated by there being an official Italian and several unofficial Venetian dialect names in use for the same location. When asking for directions, make sure you ascertain the nearest vaporetto stop, church, large square or other easily identifiable local landmark.

AGE RESTRICTIONS

Buying/drinking alcohol 16.
Driving 18.
Sex (hetero- & homosexual) 16.
Smoking 16.

ATTITUDE & ETIQUETTE

For advice on navigating Venice's pedestrian-clogged streets, see p72 **Wet & Dry**. For drinking etiquette, see p182.

BUSINESS

If you are planning to do business in Venice, a call to your embassy's commercial sector in Rome (see p299) is always a good idea.

Conventions & conferences

Venice has many facilities on offer for business conferences and congresses. Palladian villas and other historic landmarks

in the surrounding areas also make great venues for all sorts of events.

For information on trade fairs in Venice, contact **Venezia Fiere** (San Polo 2120, campo San Polo, 041 714 066, www.veneziafiere.it).

Most of the organisers listed below are able to book hotels, transportation, and other facilities.

Codess Cultura *San Polo 2120, campo San Polo (041 710 200/ www.codesscultura.it).* **Map** p321 F6.
Endar *Castello 4966, fondamenta de l'Osmarin (041 523 8440/www.endar.it).* **Map** p324 K7.
Nexa *San Marco 3571C, campo San Luca (041 521 0255/www.nexaweb.it).* **Map** p323 G7.
Studio Systema *San Polo 699, calle del Paradiso (041 520 1959).* **Map** p321 G6.
Venezia Congressi *San Marco 4606, calle del Teatro Goldoni (041 522 8400/www.venezia congressi.com).* **Map** p323 G6.

Couriers & shippers

Bartolini *041 531 8944/ www.bartolini.it.*
DHL *199 199 345/www.dhl.it.*
Executive *041 508 4811/ www.executivegroup.com.*
FedEx *800 123 800/ www.fedex.com/it.*
Pony Express *041 532 1077/ www.pony.it.*
UPS *800 877 877/www.ups.com.*

Translators & interpreters

Most of the conference organisers listed above will also be able to provide you with interpreters.

Lexicon Translations
Viale Garibaldi 7, Mestre (041 534 8005/www.lexiconline.it).

TER Centro Traduzioni
Cannaregio 1076C, ramo San Giovanni (041 524 2538/www. ter-traduzioni.com). **Map** p320 D2.

CONSUMER

Tourism-related complaints are handled by the **APT**'s (see p305) Tourist Mediation Counter (phone 041 529 8710 or send an email to complaint.apt@turismovenezia.it).

CUSTOMS

If you arrive from an EU country you are not required to declare goods imported into or exported from Italy as long as they are for personal use.

For people arriving from non-EU countries the following limits apply:
● 200 cigarettes or 100 cigarillos or 50 cigars or 250 grams of tobacco
● one litre of spirits or two litres of wine
● one bottle of perfume (50 ml/ 1.76 oz), 250ml of eau de toilette
● gift items not exceeding €175 (€95 for children under 15)

Anything above these limits will be subject to taxation at the port of entry. For more information, call customs (*dogana*) at Marco Polo Airport on 041 269 9311 or consult www.agenziadogane.it.

For tax refunds, see p193.

DISABLED

The very things that make Venice unique – narrow streets, bridges (around 400), no barriers between pavements and canals – make the city an extra-difficult destination for travellers with impaired mobility or vision. Despite this, Venice should not be crossed off the holiday list altogether, as there has been an effort in recent years to make the city more negotiable for disabled travellers. The Comune di Venezia's **Informahandicap** service (*see below*) is a vital one-stop shop for information.

APT offices (*see p305*) provide a map (which can be downloaded at www.comune.venezia.it/informahandicap, then follow the links 'Venezia Accessibile', 'La Mobilità' and 'Mappa della Venezia Accessibile') showing the (very few) bridges with wheelchair ramps, and accessible public toilets (though the APT will be the first to tell you that these latter don't always work). It also indicates the parts of the city that are accessible to wheelchair users. Keys for operating automated ramps are also available at APT offices.

Informahandicap
www.comune.venezia.it/handicap.
Venice office *Ca' Farsetti, San Marco 4136, riva del Carbon (041 274 6144). Vaporetto San Marco Vallaresso.* **Open** 9am-noon Tue, Fri. **Map** p321 G6.
Mestre office *Centro Culturale Candiani, piazza Candiani 5, Mestre (041 274 6144).*
Open 9am-1pm Wed.
Set up by the city council, this service has an excellent website with travel information for the disabled, although only some pages have an English translation. Super helpful English-speaking staff can answer queries over the phone and send information on accessible hotels, restaurants and museums in Venice and the Veneto.
CO.IN. *800 271 027/www.coin sociale.it.* **Open** 9am-5pm Mon-Fri; 9am-1pm Sat.
This Rome-based organisation provides a tollfree telephone information line (from inside Italy only), with English speaking operators to advise visitors on the accessibility of hotels, museums and other disabled facilities.

Transport

Public transport is one area where Venice scores higher than many other destinations, as standard *vaporetti* and *motonavi* have a reasonably large, flat deck area and there are no steps or steep inclines on the route between quayside and boat, enabling easy travel along the Grand Canal, on lines 1 and 2. Lines that circle the city use *motoscafi*; some of their older models have not yet been adapted to accommodate wheelchairs, although the onboard

ACTV personnel are unerringly helpful. The vaporetto lines that currently guarantee disabled access (though peak times should be avoided if possible) are 1, 2, LN and N. Some of the buses that run between Mestre and Venice also have wheelchair access.

For further information, consult the Informahandicap site or phone:

Buses and vaporetti ACTV *041 24 24.*
Trains Trenitalia *199 303 060.*
Planes Marco Polo Airport *041 260 9260.*

DRUGS

Anyone caught in possession of any quantity of drugs of any kind will be taken before a magistrate. There is no distinction between possession for personal use and intent to supply. All offenders are therefore subject to stiff penalties, including lengthy prison sentences. Foreigners can expect to be swiftly deported. Couriering or dealing can land you in prison for up to 20 years.

ELECTRICITY

Italy's electricity system runs on 220/230V. To use British or US appliances, you will need two-pin adaptor plugs: these are best bought before leaving home, as they tend to be expensive in Italy and are not always easy to find. If you do need to buy one here, try any electrical retailer (look for *Casalinghi* or *Elettrodomestici* in the yellow pages).

EMBASSIES & CONSULATES

There are a handful of diplomatic missions in Venice. But for most information, and in emergencies, you will probably have to contact offices in Rome or Milan.

British Consulate *Piazzale Donatori di Sangue 2, Mestre (041 505 5990). Bus 7 from piazzale Roma.* **Open** 10am-1pm Mon-Fri. Outside of these hours, refer to the duty officer at the Milan consulate on 02 723 001.

Consulates in Milan

Australia 02 777 041.
Ireland 02 5518 7569.
New Zealand 02 7217 0001.
South Africa 02 885 8581.
United Kingdom 02 723 001.
United States 02 290 351.

Embassies in Rome

Australia 06 852 721.
Canada 06 854 441.
Ireland 06 697 9121.
New Zealand 06 853 7501.
South Africa 06 852 541.
United Kingdom 06 4220 0001.
United States 06 46741.

EMERGENCIES

See also p303 **Safety & security**. For hospitals, *see below* **Accident & emergency**.

Thefts or losses should be reported immediately at the nearest police station (either the Polizia di Stato or Carabinieri; *see p302*). Report the loss of your passport to the nearest consulate or embassy (*see above*). Report the loss of credit cards or travellers' cheques to your credit card company (*see p302*).

Ambulance 118.
Coast Guard 1530 or 041 240 5711.
Fire 115 or 041 257 4700.
Infant emergency 114.
Police – Carabinieri 112.
Police – Polizia di Stato 113.

GAY & LESBIAN

For information, *see pp229-230*.

HEALTH

The *pronto soccorso* (casualty department) of public hospitals provide free emergency treatment for travellers of any nationality.

EU citizens are entitled to reciprocal medical care if they have an EHIC (European Health Insurance Card) card, which, in the UK, can be applied for online (www.dh.gov.uk) or by post using forms that you can pick up at any post office. For minor treatments, take your EHIC card with you to any doctor for a free consultation. Drugs they prescribe can be bought at chemists at prices set by the health ministry. Tests or appointments with specialists in the public system (*Sistema sanità nazionale*, SSN) are charged at fixed rates (*il ticket*) and a receipt issued.

Non-EU citizens should review their private health insurance plans to see if expenses incurred while travelling are covered. If not, some form of health insurance is advisable.

Accident & emergency

For urgent medical advice from local health authority doctors during the night, call 041 529 4060

DIRECTORY

in Venice, 041 526 7743 on the Lido and 041 951 332 in Mestre (8pm-8am Mon-Fri; 10pm Sat-8am Mon).

The public relations department of Venice's **Ospedale Civile** (041 529 4588) can provide general information on being hospitalised in Venice.

The hospitals below all have 24-hour *pronto soccorso* (casualty) facilities. For an ambulance boat, telephone 118.

Ospedale dell'Angelo
Via Tosatto, Mestre (041 965 7111). A huge new hospital in the outskirts of Mestre.
Ospedale Civile *Castello 6777, campo Santi Giovanni e Paolo (041 529 4111/casualty 041 529 4516). Vaporetto Ospedale.* **Map** p324 K5. Housed in the 15th-century Scuola di San Marco, Venice's main civic hospital has helpful staff and doctors who are quite likely to speak English.
Ospedale di Padova
Via Giustiniani 2, Padua (049 821 1111).
Ospedale di Verona *Piazzale Stefani 1, Verona (045 812 1111).*

Contraception & abortion

Condoms are on sale near the checkout in supermarkets, or over the counter at chemists; the contraceptive pill is freely available with a prescription at any pharmacy.

Consultori familiari (family-planning clinics) are run by the local health authority; EU citizens with an EHIC (*see p299*) form are entitled to use them, paying the same low charges for services and prescriptions as locals. Non-EU citizens may use the service and, depending on their insurance plan, claim refunds. The *consultori* are staffed by good gynaecologists – book ahead for a visit. Abortions are legal when performed in public hospitals.

Dentists

Dental treatment in Italy is expensive; your insurance may not cover it. For urgent dental issues, go to the **Ambulatorio Odontostomatologico** at the Ospedale Civile (*see above*).

Hospitals

See p299 **Accident & emergency**.

Opticians

See p207.

Pharmacies

Pharmacies (*farmacie*), identified by a green or red cross above the door, are run by qualified chemists who will dispense informal advice on, and assistance for, minor ailments, as well as filling prescriptions. Over-the-counter drugs are much more expensive in Italy than in the UK or US. They can be purchased in some supermarkets.

Most chemists are open 9am-12.30pm, 3.45-7.30pm Mon-Fri and 9am-12.45pm Sat. A small number remain open on Saturday afternoon, Sunday and at night on a duty rota system, details of which are posted outside every pharmacy and published in local papers (*see p301*).

Most pharmacies carry homeopathic medicines. All will check your blood pressure. If you require regular medication, bring adequate supplies with you. Ask your GP for the generic rather than the brand name of your medicine: it may only be available in Italy under a different name.

ID

You are legally obliged to carry photo-ID with you at all times. Hotels will ask for a document when you check in. They should take your details and return it to you immediately.

INSURANCE

For information on car insurance, *see p297* **Driving**. For health insurance, *see p299* **Health**.

INTERNET

For useful websites, *see p309*.

A number of Italian service providers offer free internet access, including **Libero** (www.libero.it), **Tiscali** (www.tiscalinet.it), **Kataweb** (www.kataweb.com) and **Fastweb** (www.fastweb.it).

From mid 2009, Venice will be served by some 170 free Wi-Fi hotspots around the city (see the www.comune.venezia.it website or www.venis.it for information). That's in addition to the many cafés and the like that already allow their bandwidth to be used.

If you choose to go to an internet café, you will be asked to present ID to conform with anti-terrorism laws.

Access Gallery & Bookshop
San Marco 2970, calle delle Botteghe (041 241 3019/www. teleradiofuga.com). Vaporetto

Accademia or San Samuele. **Open** 10am-8pm daily. **No credit cards. Map** p323 F7.
Venetian Navigator Internet & Calling Point *Castello 5300, calle Casselleria (041 277 1056/ www.venetiannavigator.com). Vaporetto San Zaccaria.* **Open** *Apr-Oct* 10am-10pm daily. *Nov-Mar* 10am-8.30pm daily. **No credit cards. Map** p324 J6.

LANGUAGE

See p303 for language classes. For general vocabulary, *see p308*; for food terms, *see p169* **The Menu**.

LEFT LUGGAGE

Most hotels will look after your luggage for a reasonable amount of time after you have checked out.

Marco Polo airport *Arrivals hall, near the Post Office (041 260 5043).* **Open** 5am-9pm daily. **Rates** €4.50 per item per day. **No credit cards.**
Piazzale Roma bus terminus *041 523 1107.* **Open** 6am-9pm daily. **Rates** €4 per item per day. **No credit cards. Map** p320 B5.
Santa Lucia railway station *041 785 531.* **Open** 6am-11.50pm daily. **Rates** €4 per item per 5hrs; 60¢ every additional hour. **No credit cards. Map** p320 C4.

LEGAL HELP

If you are in need of legal advice, your first stop should always be your consulate or embassy (*see p299*). For diplomatic missions not listed here, look for *Ambasciate* in the phone book.

LIBRARIES

Most of the libraries listed below have online catalogues. For assistance with in-depth research at the national level consult the **Servizio bibliotecario nazionale** website (www.sbn.it). In most cases you will need ID and/or a letter of presentation to use these libraries; they do not lend books to non-members.

Archivio di Stato *San Polo 3002, campo dei Frari (041 522 2281/ www.archiviodistatovenezia.it). Vaporetto San Tomà.* **Open** 8.20am-6pm Mon-Thur; 8.30am-2pm Fri, Sat. **Map** p320 D6. The state archives house all official documents relating to the administration of the Venetian Republic, and a host of other

DIRECTORY

historic manuscripts. Material must be requested between the hours of 11am and 1pm.

Archivio Storico delle Arti Contemporanee (ASAC) *Vega-Lybra, via delle Industrie 17A, Porto Marghera (041 521 8790/www.labiennale.org/it/asac).* Open (by appointment) 9.30am-5pm Tue, Wed. The archive of the Venice Biennale contemporary art festival (*see p47*) is due to be moved to the Giardini della Biennale shortly (*see p84*).

Biblioteca Centrale IUAV *Santa Croce 191, fondamenta Tolentini (041 257 1106/iuavbc.iuav.it/sbda).* Vaporetto Piazzale Roma. Open 9am-midnight Mon-Fri (from 2pm 1st Mon of mth). Map p322 C6. The library of one of Italy's top architecture faculties has a vast collection of works on the history of architecture, town planning, art, engineering and social sciences.

Biblioteca Fondazione Giorgio Cini *Isola di San Giorgio Maggiore (041 271 0255/www.cini.it).* Vaporetto San Giorgio. Open (see website for variations; closed until Dec 2009) 9am-4.30pm Mon-Fri. Map p329 K10. The Giorgio Cini Foundation houses libraries that are dedicated to art history, Venetian history, literature, theatre and music.

Biblioteca Fondazione Scientifica Querini Stampalia *Castello 5252, campo Santa Maria Formosa (041 271 1411/www.querinistampalia.it).* Vaporetto Rialto or San Zaccaria. Open 10am-midnight Tue-Sat; 10am-7pm Sun. Map p324 J6. A collection with an emphasis on all things Venetian.

Biblioteca Generale dell'Università di Ca' Foscari *Dorsoduro 1392, Zattere (041 234 5811/www.biblio.unive.it).* Vaporetto Zattere. Open 9am-11pm Mon-Fri; 9am-2pm Sat. Map p322 D9. The university library is strong on the humanities and economics.

Biblioteca Museo Correr *San Marco 52, piazza San Marco (041 240 5211/www.comune.venezia.it/museicivici).* Vaporetto San Marco Vallaresso. Open 8.30am-1.30pm Mon, Wed, Fri; 8.30am-5pm Tue, Thur. Map p324 H8. This small library contains prints, manuscripts and books about Venetian history and art history.

Biblioteca Nazionale Marciana *San Marco 7, piazzetta San Marco (041 240 7211/www.museicivici veneziani.it).* Vaporetto San Marco Vallaresso. Open 8.10am-7pm Mon-Fri; 8.10am-1.30pm Sat. Map p324 J8.

The city's main public library has medieval manuscripts and editions of the classics dating back to the 15th century.

LOST PROPERTY

Your mislaid belongings may end up at one of the *uffici oggetti smarriti* listed below. You could also try the police (*see p302*), or get in touch with VESTA, the city's rubbish collection department (041 729 1111).

ACTV *Santa Croce, piazzale Roma (041 272 2179).* Vaporetto Piazzale Roma. Open 7am-7.30pm daily. Map p320 B5. For items found on *vaporetti* or buses.

Comune (City Council) *San Marco 4136, riva del Carbon (041 274 8225).* Vaporetto Rialto. Open 8.30am-12.30pm Mon-Fri; 2.30-4.30pm Mon, Thur. Map p321 G6.

FS/Stazione Santa Lucia *Santa Lucia railway station, next to track 14 (no phone).* Vaporetto Ferrovia. Open 6am-midnight daily. Map p320 C4. All items found on trains in the Venice area and in the station itself are brought to this deposit.

Marco Polo Airport *Arrivals Hall (lost bags 041 260 9222/lost objects 041 260 9260).* Bus 5 to Aeroporto. Open *Lost bags* 9am-8pm daily. *Lost objects* 24hrs daily.

MEDIA

Daily newspapers (national)

Sometimes lengthy, turgid and featuring indigestible political stories, Italian newspapers can be a frustrating read. On the plus side, papers are delightfully unpretentious and happily blend serious news, leaders by globally known commentators, and well-written, often surreal, crime and human-interest stories.

Sports coverage in the dailies is extensive and thorough, but if you're not sated, there are the mass-circulation sports papers *Corriere dello Sport*, *La Gazzetta dello Sport* and *Tuttosport*.

Corriere della Sera *www.corriere.it.* To the centre of centre-left, this solid, serious but often dull Milan-based daily is good on crime and foreign news. Online there is an English section called 'Italian Life', which has international news and Italocentric editorials.

Il Manifesto *www.ilmanifesto.it.* Although the Cold War may be a distant memory, there is still some corner of central Rome where hearts beat Red.

La Repubblica *www.repubblica.it.* Centre-ish, left-ish *La Repubblica* is good on the Mafia and the Vatican, and comes up with the occasional scoop on its business pages.

Il Sole-24 Ore *www.ilsole24ore.com.* This business, finance and economics daily has a great arts supplement on Sunday.

Daily newspapers (local)

Il Gazzettino *www.gazzettino.it.* *Il Gazzettino* is one of Italy's most successful local papers. It provides national and international news on the front pages and local news inside, with different editions for towns around the Veneto region.

Il Venezia *www.ilvenezia.it.* New kid on the block (from 2006), this stylish daily covers local and international news with a centre-left-ish outlook and costs 50¢, although it is available free in bars and cafés. Also contains TV and local listings and a page of useful phone numbers and contacts.

La Nuova Venezia *www.nuovavenezia.quotidianiespresso.it.* This popular, small-circulation daily – known to Venetians as *La Nuova* – contains lively editorials, crime stories, local news and event listings.

Foreign press

The *Financial Times*, *Wall Street Journal*, *USA Today*, *International Herald Tribune* and most European and (usually) UK dailies can be found on the day of issue at news-stands around town – especially those at the station, within striking distance of St Mark's and the Rialto, and at the large *edicole* at the Lido and Accademia vaporetto stops. US publications sometimes take a day or two to appear.

Magazines

News weeklies *Panorama* (roughly centre right) and *L'Espresso* (centre left-ish) provide a general round-up of the week's events, while *Sette* and *Venerdì* – respectively the colour supplements of *Corriere della Sera* (Thursday) and *La Repubblica* (Friday) – have nice photos, though the quality of the journalism often leaves much to be desired.

DIRECTORY

For *Hello!*-style scandal, try *Gente* and *Oggi* with their weird mix of sex, glamour and religion, or the generally execrable scandal sheets *Eva 3000*, *Novella 2000* and *Cronaca Vera*. *Internazionale* (www.internazionale.it) provides an excellent digest of interesting bits and pieces gleaned from around the world the previous week. *Diario della Settimana* (www.diario.it) is informed and urbane and has a flair for investigative journalism.

But the biggest-selling magazine of them all is *Famiglia Cristiana*, which alternates Vatican line-toeing with Vatican baiting, depending on the state of relations between the Holy See and the idiosyncratic Paoline monks who produce it. It is available from news-stands or in most churches.

Other publications

Aladino *www.aladinoannunci.com.* Weekly classified ads for everything from flats for rent to *gondole* for sale, available in *edicole*, their website offers free ads and has an English version.
Boom
A weekly small-ads paper that's delivered free through letterboxes or available at street dispensers. *Boom* is the place to look for flats, jobs and lonely hearts.
Gente Veneta
This weekly broadsheet, produced by the local branch of the Catholic church, blends cultural and religious listings with reports on Venetian social problems.
2night magazine *www.2night.it.* Trendy pocket-sized magazine, which comes out each month, containing art and nightlife listings for the whole Veneto, in Italian.
Venews *www.venezianews.it.* This information-packed magazine, which comes out on the first of each month, encompasses music, film, theatre, art and sports listings, plus interviews and features, in both Italian and English.

Radio

Radio Venezia FM 92.4
Pop music, pop music, pop music. Did we mention pop music?
Radio Capital FM 98.5
Heavy on advertising, but generous with information on events and news in the city. You'll hear 1980s and '90s classics with a sprinkling of current hits.
Radio Padova FM 103.9 & 88.4
Popular chart music and concert information for the Veneto area.

Television

Italy has six major networks (three are owned by the state broadcaster **RAI**, the other three belong to Silvio Berlusconi's **Mediaset** group). Dancing girls, variety shows, music and beauty competitions predominate. The standard of news and current affairs programmes varies a fair bit; most, though, offer reasonable international news coverage. Ubiquitous **MTV** is a terrestrial channel in Italy.

MONEY

Italy's currency is the euro (€). There are euro banknotes of €5, €10, €20, €100, €200 and €500, and coins worth €1 and €2 as well as 1¢ (*centesimo*), 2¢, 5¢, 10¢, 20¢ and 50¢. Notes and coins from any euro-zone country are valid.

Banks & ATMs

Most banks have cash dispensers and the vast majority of these accept cards with the Maestro, Cirrus and Visa Electron symbols. Most cashpoint machines dispense cash to a daily limit of €250.

Most banks are open 8.20am-1.20pm and 2.45-3.45pm Mon-Fri. All banks are closed on public holidays and work reduced hours the day before a holiday, usually closing at 11am. Banks are listed under *Banche ed istituti di credito* in the yellow pages.

Bureaux de change

Banks usually offer more generous exchange rates than bureaux de change (*cambio*). Commission rates in banks vary considerably. Note that 'No commission' signs in exchange offices usually mean that the exchange rate is dire. At the time of writing, there was no **American Express** office in Venice. Call the Mestre branch (041 504 0344) for information.

You will need your passport, or other valid photo ID if you want to change travellers' cheques or draw money on your credit card.

Travelex *San Marco 5126, riva del Ferro (041 528 7358/www. travelex.it).* Vaporetto Rialto.
Open 9am-7pm Mon-Fri; 9am-5.50pm Sat; 9am-4.30pm Sun.
Credit MC, V. **Map** p321 H6.
Cash and travellers' cheques exchanged with no commission. MasterCard and Visa cardholders can also withdraw cash.

Other locations San Marco 142, piazza San Marco (041 277 5057); Marco Polo Airport, arrivals (041 541 6833).

Lost or stolen credit cards

Most hotels of two stars and over will take most major credit cards. Report lost credit or charge cards to the appropriate emergency number listed below. All of the lines listed are toll-free, operate 24 hours a day and have English-speaking operators.

American Express *800 864 046/ travellers' cheques 800 872 000.*
Diners' Club 800 864 064.
MasterCard 800 870 866.
Visa 800 819 014.

Tax

For information on reclaiming IVA (VAT or sales tax), *see p193*.

OPENING HOURS

Banks *see above.*
Pharmacies *see p300.*
Post offices *see p303.*
Public transport *see p296.*
Shops *see p193.*

For advice on when to eat and drink, *see p165* **Inside Track** and *p182.* See also *p305* **Public holidays**.

The opening times given in the Sights chapters in this guide are the venues' winter hours; they may be open slightly later or longer in summer (we have noted where there is a significant difference). Ticket offices often shut an hour (or even more) before closing time.

POLICE

For emergencies, *see p299*.

Both the (nominally military) **Carabinieri** and the **Polizia di Stato** deal with crimes and emergencies of any kind. If you have your bag or wallet stolen, or are otherwise made a victim of crime, go as soon as possible to either force to report a *scippo* ('bagsnatching'). A *denuncia* (written statement) of the incident will be made for you.

Give police as much information as possible, including your passport number, holiday address and flight numbers. The *denuncia* will be signed, dated and stamped with an official police seal. It is unlikely that your things will be found, but you will need the *denuncia* for making an insurance claim.

Carabinieri *Castello 4693A,
campo San Zaccaria (041 27411).
Vaporetto San Zaccaria.*
Map p324 K7.
Polizia di Stato Questura
*Santa Croce 500, piazzale Roma
(041 271 5511/www.poliziadi
stato.it). Vaporetto Piazzale Roma.*
Map p320 B5.

POSTAL SERVICES

Italy's postal service (www.poste.it)
is generally reliable. Postage
supplies – such as large mailing
boxes and packing tape – are
available at most post offices.

Italy's standard postal service,
posta prioritaria, gets letters to
their destination within 48 hours
in Italy, three days for EU countries
and four or five for the rest of the
world. A letter of 20g or less in Italy
is 60¢, within the EU 65¢, and
to the rest of the world 85¢ or €1
(Oceania); stamps can be bought at
post offices and *tabacchi (see below)*.

Express and parcel post are also
available; for other couriers and
shippers, *see p298*.

Letterboxes are red and have two
slots: *Per la città* (for Venezia, Mestre
and Marghera), and *Tutte le altre
destinazioni* (all other destinations).

Each district has its own sub-post
office, open 8.30am-2pm Mon-Fri,
8.30am-1pm Sat. There is also a
branch at Marco Polo Airport open
the same hours (041 541 5900).

**Posta Centrale (Central Post
Office)** *San Marco 5554, salizada
del Fontego dei Tedeschi (041 271
7111). Vaporetto Rialto.* **Open**
8.30am-6pm Mon-Sat. **Map** p324 H6.
The main post office is housed in
the Fondaco dei Tedeschi (*see p55*).
You can purchase stamps, and send
packages, MoneyGrams or faxes.
It also serves stamp collectors and
has a *fermo posta* (poste restante)
service. Expect long queues,
especially in the afternoon.
Posta Piazzale Roma *Santa Croce
510, fondamenta Santa Chiara
(041 522 1976). Vaporetto Piazzale
Roma.* **Open** 8.30am-6pm Mon-Fri;
8.30am-1pm Sat. **Map** p320 B5.
Another main post office, offering
the same services, often has shorter
queues for posting.

RELIGION

Mass (*messa*) times vary from
church to church and are posted
by front doors: services are usually
held between 9am and 11am and
again at 6.30pm on Sundays
(6.45pm in **St Mark's basilica;**

see p61); most churches have Mass
on Saturdays at 6pm. *Un'ospite di
Venezia*, a free brochure, has mass
times. The church of **San Zulian**
(041 523 5383; map p324 J7) has
Mass in English at 11.30am on
Sundays throughout the year.
Listed below are the non-Catholic
denominations in the city.

Anglican

St George's *Dorsoduro 870,
campo San Vio (041 520 0571).
Vaporetto Accademia.* **Services**
Holy Eucharist 10.30am Sun.
Map p323 E9.

Greek Orthodox

San Giorgio dei Greci *Castello
3419, fondamenta dei Greci (041
523 9569). Vaporetto San Zaccaria.*
Services 9.30am, 10.30am Sun.
Map p324 L7.

Jewish

Sinagoga *Cannaregio 1146,
campo del Ghetto Vecchio (041 715
012/www.moked.it/veneziaebraica).
Vaporetto Guglie.* **Services** after
sunset Fri; Sat am. **Map** p321 E2.
For security reasons, those wishing
to attend services at the Synagogue
must present themselves, with ID,
to the main office of the Jewish
Community (as above) or call them
on 041 715 012.

Lutheran

Chiesa Evangelica Luterana
*Cannaregio 4448, campo Santi
Apostoli (041 522 7149). Vaporetto
Ca' D'Oro.* **Services** *Dec-Jan*
10am on 2nd & 4th Sun of mth;
Mar-Nov 5pm 2nd & 4th Sun of
mth. **Map** p321 H5.

Methodist & Waldensian

Chiesa Valdese *Castello 5171,
fondamenta Cavagnis (041 522
7549/www.chiesavaldese.org).
Vaporetto Rialto or San Zaccaria.*
Services 11am Sun. **Map** p324 K6.

SAFETY & SECURITY

Venice is, on the whole, an
exceptionally safe place at any time
of day or night, and violent crime
is almost unknown. Lone women
would be advised to steer clear of
dark alleyways (as far as is possible
in labyrinthine Venice) late at night,
though even there they are more
likely to be harassed than attacked
(*see also p306* **Women**).

Bag-snatchers are a rarity, mostly
because of the logistical difficulties
Venice presents for making a quick
getaway. However, pickpockets
operate in crowded thoroughfares,
especially around San Marco and
the Rialto, and on public transport,
so make sure you leave passports,
plane/train tickets and at least one
means of getting hold of money
in your hotel room safe.

If you are the victim of theft
or other serious crime, contact
the police (*see p302*).

SMOKING

Smoking is banned anywhere
with public access – including bars,
restaurants, stations and offices
and on all public transport – except
clearly designated smoking rooms.

Tabacchi

Tabacchi or *tabaccherie* (identified
by a white T on a black or blue
background) are the only places
in Italy where you can legally buy
tobacco products.

They also sell stamps, telephone
cards, individual or season tickets
for public transport, lottery tickets
and the stationery required when
dealing with bureaucracy.

Most of Venice's *tabacchi* pull
their shutters down by 7.30pm.
If you're gasping for nicotine
late in the evening or on Sunday,
you will have to try one of the
automatic cigarette vending
machines in campo Santa
Margherita, piazzale Roma, next
to the train station, on strada
Nuova near Ponte della Guglie
and near Santi Apostoli,
fondamenta della Misericordia,
Scuola di San Giorgio degli
Schiavoni and via XXII Marzo,
although these only 'open' at 9pm
to prevent sales to minors.

STUDY

Studying at either of Venice's
two main universities is likely
to involve lectures and exams in
Italian, making a good knowledge
of the Italian language a
prerequisite; however, there are
some exceptions, especially at the
more international IUAV. To find
out about entrance requirements,
consult the faculty websites
of the **Istituto Universitario
di Architettura di Venezia**
(IUAV; www.iuav.it) or the
**Università degli Studi
di Venezia Ca' Foscari**
(www.unive.it), both in English.

DIRECTORY

EU citizens have the same right to study at Italian universities as Italian nationals. You'll need to have your school diplomas translated and authenticated at the Italian consulate in your own country before presenting them to the *ufficio studenti stranieri* (foreign students' department) of any university.

Both universities run exchange programmes and participate in the EU's Erasmus scheme. The **Venice International University** (041 271 9511, www.univiu.org) is a consortium of ten universities and agencies. Students registered at one of the Venice International member universities (see their website for a list) are eligible to apply for VIU undergraduate activities. There are also Master's and PhD programmes available for foreign students.

Language classes

ASCI-Onlus – Associazione Socio-Culturale Internazionale
Corso del Popolo 117, Mestre (041 504 0433/www.ascionlus.com). Bus 4 to Mestre. **Open** 5.30-8.30pm Mon-Fri. **No credit cards.**
This association offers courses in languages including Italian, French, German, Spanish, Arabic, Hindi and Chinese. Also available are lessons in art, photography, belly dancing and much more.

Centro Linguistico d'Ateneo
Dorsoduro 1686, campo San Sebastiano (041 234 9711/www. unive.it/cli). Vaporetto San Basilio. **Open** (office hours) 9.30am-12.30pm Mon, Tue, Thur; 2.30-4.30pm Wed. **No credit cards.** **Map** p322 B8.
This school, affiliated with the University of Ca' Foscari, offers good short courses in Italian, French, Spanish and German, plus access to audiovisual equipment.

TELEPHONES

Italy's telephone company (**Telecom Italia**) is still costly despite tough competition. The minimum charge for a local call from a private phone is about 8¢ (10¢ from a public phone). Calling a mobile from a fixed line is almost triple and phoning abroad remains dear. Keep costs down by:
● phoning off-peak (6.30pm-8am Mon-Fri, 1pm Sat-8am Mon).
● not using phones in hotels, which usually carry extortionate surcharges.
● using international phone cards, available at *tabacchi* (*see p303*).
● not calling mobile phones from landlines and vice versa.

Dialling & codes

Italian landline numbers must be dialled *with* their prefixes, even if you are phoning within the local area.

Numbers in Venice and its province begin **041**; numbers in Padua province begin **049**; in Vicenza they begin **0444**; in Verona **045**.

Numbers generally have seven or eight digits after the prefix; some older ones have six, and some switchboards five. If you try a number and can't get through, it may have been changed to an eight-digit number. Check the directory (*elenco telefonico*) or ring directory enquiries (*see below*).

Numeri verdi ('green numbers') are free and start 800 or 147. Numbers beginning 840 and 848 are charged at a nominal rate. These numbers can be called from within Italy only, and some are available only within certain regions. Mobile phone numbers always begin with a 3.

When calling an Italian landline from abroad, the whole prefix, including the 0, must be dialled, so dial 00 39 041... for Venice from the UK. To make an **international call** from Venice dial 00, then the country code (*see below*), then the area code (usually without the initial 0) and the number.

Australia 61
Canada 1
Ireland 353
New Zealand 64
South Africa 27
UK 44
USA 1

Mobile phones

Standard European handsets will work in Italy, but your service provider may need to activate international roaming before you leave; beware of extortionate roaming charges. Tri-band US handsets should also work; check with the manufacturer. If your phone is not locked to your home SIM card/service provider, you can buy an Italian pay-as-go SIM card, (they may ask you for your *codice fiscale; see p306*) available from mobile phone shops for around €10, allowing you to make cheaper calls within Italy.

Vodafone Gestioni SpA
San Marco 5171, campo San Bartolomeo (041 523 9016/www. vodafone.it). Vaporetto Rialto.

Open 10am-7.30pm Mon-Sat; 10am-1pm, 2-7pm Sun. **Credit** AmEx, DC, MC, V. **Map** p324 H6.

Operator services

Directory enquiries is a jungle, and charges for information given over the phone are steep. The major services are: **1254** (Italian and international numbers); **892 412** (international numbers, in English and Italian, from mobile phones); Italian directory information can be had for free on **www.info412.it** or **www.paginebianche.it**.

For operator-assisted calls abroad or reverse-charge calls (collect) dial **170**. International directory enquiries are also on 170.

Other services include: **4114** alarm call; **186** telegrams; **4161** speaking clock; **4197** interrupts a conversation on an engaged line.

Public phones

There are some public phones in Venice along the tourist routes but many are out of service. Most public phones operate only with phone cards (*schede telefoniche*). Newer models take major credit cards, while the few remaining old-style ones take 10¢, 20¢ and 50¢ coins. Phonecards costing €2.50, €5 and €7.50 can be bought at post offices, *tabacchi* (*see p303*) and some news-stands.

To use your card, tear off one corner as marked, insert it into the appropriate slot and dial. Your credit balance will be displayed on the phone. Note that your phonecard expires on a date written in small print on the card, after which you have lost your outstanding credit.

TIME

Italy is one hour ahead of London, six ahead of New York, eight behind Sydney and 12 hours behind Wellington.

TIPPING

There are no hard and fast rules on tipping in Italy, though Venetians know that foreigners tip generously back home, and expect them to be liberal. Some upmarket restaurants (and a growing number of cheaper ones) will add a service charge to your bill: ask *il servizio è incluso?* If not, leave whatever you think the service merited (Italians leave 5%-10%). Bear in mind that all restaurants charge a cover charge (*coperto*) – a quasi-tip in itself.

TOILETS

Public toilets (*servizi igienici pubblici*) are numerous and relatively clean in Venice but you have to pay (€1) to use them, unless you have invested in the appropriate Venice Card (*see p6* **Package Deals**). Follow blue and green signs marked WC. By law, all cafés and bars should allow anyone to use their facilities; however, many Venetian bar owners don't.

TOURIST INFORMATION

Several free publications provide comprehensive tourist information in Venice, available at **APT** (*see below*) and **Hellovenezia** (*see p296*) offices, and some bars. Most hotels will provide you with a copy of the biweekly (monthly in winter) *Un'ospite di Venezia/A Guest in Venice*, a bilingual booklet compiled by hoteliers, which contains useful addresses, night pharmacies, Mass times and transport timetables.

The local press is another source of useful information on events (*see p301* **Media**), as are posters plastered on walls all over the city. *Leo*, available at the APT, has well-written features and a tear-out listing booklet of events by day.

Note that Hellovenezia (*see p296*) offices, in addition to dispensing tourist information, sell tickets for transport, concerts and events.

See the chapters in 'The Veneto' section of this guide for information offices outside Venice.

The Palazzina Santi branch (*see below*) has a selection of books and sells concert tickets. In high season, supplementary kiosks are set up around the city.

Azienda di Promozione Turistica (APT) *San Marco 71F, piazza San Marco (041 529 8740/ www.turismovenezia.it). Vaporetto San Marco Vallaresso.* **Open** 9am-3.30pm daily. **Map** p324 H8.
The APT website is worth looking at before you arrive in Venice. The offices provide information on sights and events, a list of hotels, and walking itineraries with maps for sale. They'll also put you in touch with registered guides and give details of official fees for guided tours (also available on their website).

Other APT locations
Palazzina Santi, San Marco 2, Giardinetti Reali (041 522 5150). **Open** 10am-6pm daily. **Map** p324 H8.

Venice-Santa Lucia railway station (041 529 8727). **Open** 8am-6.30pm daily. **Map** p320 C4.
Marco Polo Airport arrivals hall (041 541 5887). **Open** 9.30am-7.30pm daily.
Autorimessa Comunale, Santa Croce 465B, piazzale Roma (041 529 8711). **Open** 9.30am-1pm, 1.30-4.30pm daily. **Map** p320 B5.
Viale Santa Maria Elisabetta 6A, Lido (041 526 5721). **Open** *June-Sept* 9am-noon, 3-6pm daily. **Map** p327 BB3.

VISAS & IMMIGRATION

For EU citizens, a passport or a national identity card valid for travel abroad is sufficient. Non-EU citizens must have full passports. Citizens of the US, Canada, Australia and New Zealand do not need visas for stays of up to three months. In theory, visitors are required to declare their presence to the local police within a few days of arrival, unless they are staying in a hotel, where this will be done for them. In practice, you will not need to report to the police station unless you decide to extend your stay and you apply for a *permesso di soggiorno* (permit to stay; *see p306*).

WATER

Forget *Death in Venice*-style cholera scares: tap water here is regularly checked, safe to drink and tastes good. Fountains throughout the city provide a constant source of free tap water. For information, visit www.vestaspa.net.

WEIGHTS & MEASURES

Italy uses the metric system; remember that all speed limits are in kilometres per hour. One kilometre is equivalent to 0.62 miles (1 mile = 1.6km). Beverages are commonly measured in centilitres, so a canned soft drink may be 25cl (rather than 250ml, which equals around 8.5 fluid ounces). For groceries, it's common to order by the *etto* (plural *etti*), which equals 100 grams (3.5 ounces).

WHEN TO GO

Climate

Venice's unique position gives the city a bizarre mix of weather conditions. During the winter, high levels of humidity often make winter days seem colder than their average few degrees above zero,

and summer days become humid as soon as the thermometer rises above 25°C (77°F).

Strong north-easterlies in winter, coming off the snow-covered Alps (snow in the city is rare) have bone-chilling effects but make the weather crisp and clear, with blue skies and great views. In the still summer months, high humidity can make it stiflingly hot; a warm southerly wind called the *scirocco* makes the heat more intense.

Autumn and spring are generally mild with occasional pea-soup fog; November and March are the rainiest months, while *acqua alta* (*see p72* **Wet & Dry**) is mainly an autumn and winter event.

Public holidays

For annual events, *see pp214-217*.

On official public holidays (*giorni festivi*), public offices, banks and post offices are closed. So, in theory, are shops – but in tourism-oriented Venice, this rule is often waived. Some bars and restaurants may observe holidays: if in doubt, call ahead. You won't find much open on Christmas Day and New Year's Day.

Public transport is reduced to a skeleton service on 1 May, Christmas Day and New Year's Day, and may be rerouted or curtailed for local festivities, especially those including regattas (*see pp214-217*); details are posted at vaporetto stops and at the bus terminus in piazzale Roma.

Holidays falling on a Saturday or Sunday are not celebrated on the following Monday. By popular tradition, if a public holiday falls on a Tuesday or Thursday, many people will also take the Monday or Friday off as well, a practice known as *fare il ponte* (doing a bridge).

The public holidays are:
New Year's Day (Capodanno) 1 Jan
Epiphany (Befana) 6 Jan
Easter Monday (Pasquetta)
Liberation Day (Festa della Liberazione) and patron saint's day (San Marco) 25 Apr
Labour Day (Festa del Lavoro) 1 May
Assumption (Ferragosto) 15 Aug
All Saints' Day (Ognissanti) 1 Nov
Festa della Salute (Venice only) 21 Nov
Immaculate Conception (L'Immacolata) 8 Dec
Christmas Day (Natale) 25 Dec
Boxing Day (Santo Stefano) 26 Dec

WOMEN

Although Venice is relatively a very safe place for women travellers, it is always best to apply common sense while travelling alone.

At night, keep away from quieter, more outlying areas and from the Tronchetto car park. Stick to main through-routes to avoid getting lost in dark alleyways; if in doubt, cut walking to a minimum by taking the vaporetto to as near to your destination as possible.

Tampons (*assorbenti interni*) and sanitary towels (*assorbenti esterni*) are expensive in Italy, although it may be cheaper buying them in supermarkets than in pharmacies.

Women who experience gynaecological emergencies should make for the *pronto soccorso* (emergency ward) at the Ospedale Civile (*see p300*).

For information about family planning, *see p300* **Contraception & abortion**.

WORKING & LIVING IN VENICE

Falling in love with Venice is easy; living in the city without independent means of support is difficult. Openings for casual employment in Venice are few, though language schools (*scuole di lingua*) sometimes seek native English speakers, especially those with TEFL experience. Women *di bella apparenza* (as the ads put it) – and with some knowledge of Italian – might try contacting conference organisers (*see p298*), or the smart boutiques in the Frezzerie area around San Marco, which sometimes advertise for *commesse* (sales assistants). Some of the more exclusive hotels may have openings for experienced babysitters.

The main Ca' Foscari university building at Dorsoduro 3246, calle Foscari (vaporetto San Tomà) often has employment opportunities posted on the notice boards.

Accommodation

Student-type shares are abundant in Venice and can be found on paper announcements around the city, through the notice boards at Ca' Foscari and IUAV universities (*see p303*) or through local listings magazines (*see p302*).

For short-term rentals expect to pay upwards of €600 a week for a very basic apartment in Venice. Online, you can try www.venice apartment.com, www.venice-rentals.com or www.interflats.it.

For longer stays, an agency is your best bet; most agencies will take the equivalent of one month's rent as their commission. Most landlords will demand at least one month's (it can sometimes be as much as three months') rent as a deposit.

Giaretta *San Marco 514, campo della Guerra (041 520 9747/www.giaretta.com). Vaporetto Rialto.* **Open** 9am-1pm, 3-7pm Mon-Fri. **Map** p324 J7.
Well organised and pleasant, Giaretta offer pricey, long-term rentals and sales.

Immobil Veneta *San Polo 3132, campiello San Rocco (041 524 0088/www.immobilvenetasnc.com). Vaporetto San Tomà.* **Open** 9am-noon, 3.30-7pm Mon-Fri. **Map** p322 D6.

A reliable agency with short-term apartment rentals, monthly rentals and apartments for sale.

Bureaucracy

You may need any or all of the following documents if you plan to work or study in Venice. Be prepared for multiple office visits, long, unruly queues and irritable people who have been waiting longer than you.

Permesso di soggiorno (permit to stay)
The *permesso di soggiorno* can be obtained from the Questura in Marghera (*see below*). Get there by 7am. For details of what you will need, see www.poliziadistato.it (in English). EU citizens are given their *permesso* directly; as this guide went to press, the waiting period for renewal for non-EU citizens was 12 months.
Questura *Via Nicolodi 21, Marghera (ufficio stranieri 041 271 57671/switchboard 041 271 5511). Bus 6 from piazzale Roma.* **Open** 8.30-9.30am Tue-Fri.

Carta d'Identità (identity card)
This official Italian ID card is not really necessary for foreigners but can be obtained from the *Ufficio anagrafe* of the town hall. Take ID, your *permesso di soggiorno* and three passport photographs.
Ufficio anagrafe *San Marco 4061, calle del Carbon (041 274 8221). Vaporetto Rialto.* **Open** 8.45am-1pm Mon, Wed, Fri; 8.45am-5pm Tue, Thur. **Map** p323 G6.

Codice fiscale & partito IVA (tax code & VAT number)
Go to the Agenzia della Entrate for a *codice fiscale* (required to work legally, open a business, open a bank account or get a phone line) and/or a *Partita IVA* (VAT number).
Agenzia delle Entrate *Ufficio locale Venezia 1, San Marco 3538, campo Sant'Angelo (041 271 8111). Vaporetto Sant'Angelo.* **Open** 8.45am-12.45pm Mon, Wed, Fri; 8.45am-12.45pm, 2.45-4.45pm Tue, Thur. **Map** p323 F7.

Permesso di lavoro (work permit)
Non-EU citizens must have a work permit to be legally employed in Italy. Getting one is a minefield. For information, contact the **Uffico Provinciale del Lavoro**, via Ca' Venier 8, Mestre (041 504 2085).

THE LOCAL CLIMATE

Average temperatures and monthly rainfall in Venice.

	High (°C/°F)	Low (°C/°F)	Rainfall (mm/in)
Jan	6 / 42	-1 / 30	58 / 2.3
Feb	8 / 47	1 / 33	54 / 2.1
Mar	12 / 54	4 / 39	57 / 2.2
Apr	16 / 61	8 / 46	64 / 2.5
May	21 / 70	12 / 54	69 / 2.7
June	25 / 77	16 / 61	76 / 3.0
July	28 / 82	18 / 64	63 / 2.5
Aug	27 / 81	17 / 63	83 / 3.3
Sept	24 / 75	14 / 58	66 / 2.6
Oct	18 / 65	9 / 49	69 / 2.7
Nov	12 / 53	4 / 40	87 / 3.4
Dec	7 / 44	0 / 32	54 / 2.1

DIRECTORY

Glossary

A

amphitheatre (*ancient*) an oval open-air theatre.
apse large recess at the high-altar end of a church.

B

baldachin canopy supported by columns.
barrel vault a ceiling with arches shaped like half-barrels.
Baroque artistic period from the 17th-18th centuries, in which the decorative element became increasingly florid, culminating in the rococo (*qv*).
basilica ancient Roman rectangular public building; rectangular Christian church.
Byzantine Christian artistic and architectural style drawing on ancient models developed in the fourth century in the Eastern empire and through the Middle Ages.

C

campanile bell tower.
campo Venetian for piazza or square.
capital head of a column, generally decorated according to classical orders (*qv*).
caryatid column carved in the shape of a female.
chiaroscuro from Italian *chiaro* (light) and *scuro* (dark); juxtaposition of light and shade to bring out relief and volume.
cloister courtyard surrounded on all sides by a covered walkway.
coffered ceiling decorated with sunken square or polygonal panels.
cupola dome-shaped roof or ceiling.

E

ex-voto an offering given to fulfil a vow; often a small model in silver of the limb/organ/loved one cured as a result of prayer.

F

fan vault vault formed of concave semi-cones, meeting at the apex; it has the appearance of four backwards-leaning fans meeting.
festoon painted or carved swag or swathe decorated with fruit and/or flowers.

fresco painting technique in which pigment is applied to wet plaster.

G

Gothic architectural and artistic style of the late Middle Ages (from the 12th century), of soaring, pointed arches.
Greek cross (church) in the shape of a cross with arms of equal length.
grisailles painting in shades of grey to mimic sculpture.

I

iconostasis rood screen; screen in Eastern-rite churches separating nave from the sanctuary.
intarsia form of mosaic made from pieces of different-coloured wood; also know as **intaglio**.

L

Latin cross (church) in the shape of a cross with one arm longer than the other.
loggia gallery open on one side.
lunette semi-circular surface, usually above window or door.

M

Mannerism post-High Renaissance style of the later 16th century; characterised in painting by elongated, contorted human figures.
monoforate with one opening (cf biforate, triforate, polyforate *qv*), usually used of windows.

N

narthex enclosed porch in front of a church.
nave main body of a church; the longest section of a Latin cross church (*qv*).

O

ogival (arches, windows etc) curving in to a point at the top.
opus sectile pavement made of (usually) geometrically shaped marble slabs.
orders classical rules governing the proportions of columns, their entablatures and their capitals (*qv*), the most common being the less ornate Doric, the curlicue Ionic

and the Corinthian order, in which capitals are decorated with stylised acanthus leaves.

P

palazzo large and/or important building (not necessarily a palace).
pendentives four concave triangular sections on top of piers supporting a dome.
piano nobile showiest floor of a palazzo (*qv*), containing mainly reception rooms with very high ceilings.
pilaster column-shaped projection from a wall.
polyforate with more than one opening (cf monoforate).
polyptych painting composed of several panels (cf dyptych with two panels, triptych with three).
porphyry hard igneous rock ranging from dark green to dark purple; this latter was most commonly used, and known as *rosso antico*.
presbytery the part of a church containing the high altar.

R

reredos decorated wall or screen behind an altar.
rococo highly decorative style fashionable in the 18th century.
Romanesque architectural style of the early Middle Ages (c500 to 1200), drawing on Roman and Byzantine (*qv*) influences.
rusticated large masonry blocks with deep joints between them used to face buildings or monuments.

S

sarcophagus (*ancient*) stone or marble coffin.
stele upright slab of stone with decorative relief sculpture and/or commemorative inscription.

T

transept shorter arms of a Latin cross church (*qv*).
trilobate with three arches.
triumphal arch arch in front of an apse (*qv*), usually over the high altar.
trompe l'œil decorative painting effect to make surface appear three-dimensional.

Vocabulary

Italian is pronounced as spelled. Stresses usually fall on the second-last syllable; a stress on the final syllable is indicated by an accent.

There are three 'you' forms: the formal singular *lei*, the informal singular *tu*, and the plural *voi*. Masculine nouns and accompanying adjectives generally end in 'o' (plural 'i'), female nouns and their adjectives end in 'a' (plural 'e').

VENETIAN

The distinctive nasal Venetian drawl is more than just an accent: locals have their own vocabulary too. Venetians tend to ignore consonants, running vowels together in long diphthongs (explaining how *vostro schiavo* – 'your servant' – became *ciao*.) *Xè* is pronounced 'zay'; *gò* sounds like 'go' in 'got.' For more, visit www.veneto.org/language.

PRONUNCIATION

Vowels
a – as in ask
e – like a in age (closed e) or e in sell (open e)
i – like ea in east
o – as in hotel (closed o) or in hot (open o)
u – as in boot
Consonants
c before a, o or u – like c in cat
c before an e or an i – like the ch in check (sh as in ship in Venetian)
ch – like c in cat
g before a, o or u – like g in get
g before an e or an i – like the j in jig
gh – like the g in get
gl followed by an i – like lli in million
gn – like ny in canyon
qu – as in quick
r – always rolled
s – two sounds, as in soap or rose
sc before an e or an i – like the sh in shame
sch – like the sc in scout
z – two different sounds, like ts or dz

USEFUL PHRASES

(**English** – Italian/*Venetian*)

● **hello and goodbye** – ciao (used informally in other parts of Italy; in all social situations in Venice); **good morning, hello** – buongiorno; **good afternoon, good evening** – buonasera

● **please** – per favore, per piacere; **thank you** – grazie; **you're welcome** – prego; **excuse me** – mi scusi (polite), scusami (informal) *scusime/me scusa*
● **I'm sorry** – mi dispiace/*me dispiaxe*; **I don't understand** – non capisco, non ho capito/*no gò capìo*; **do you speak English?** – parla inglese?
● **open** – aperto/*verto*; **closed** – chiuso; **when does it open?** – quando apre?; **it's closed** – è chiuso/*xè serà*; **what's the time?** – che ore sono?
● **do you have a light?** – hai d'accendere?/*ti gà da accender, ti gà fógo?*

TRANSPORT

● **car** – macchina; **bus** – autobus; **taxi** – tassi, taxi; **train** – treno; **plane** – aereo; **stop** (bus/vaporetto) – fermata; **station** – stazione; **platform** – binario
● **ticket/s** – biglietto, biglietti; **one way** – solo andata; **return** – andata e ritorno; **I'd like a ticket to…** – Vorrei un biglietto per…

COMMUNICATIONS

phone – telefono; **mobile phone** – cellulare; **postcard** – cartolina; **stamp** – francobollo; **email** – (messaggio di) posta elettronica

DIRECTIONS

entrance – entrata; **exit** – uscita; **where is…?** – dov'è…?/*dove xè?*; **(turn) left** – (gira a) sinistra; **(it's on the) right** – (è sulla/a) destra; **straight on** – sempre dritto; **could you tell me the way to…?** – mi può indicare la strada per…?; **is it near/far?** – è vicino/lontano?

EATING & DRINKING

See also p169 The Menu.
● **I'd like to book a table for four at eight** – vorrei prenotare una tavola per quattro alle otto; **that was poor/good/delicious** – era mediocre/buono/ottimo
● **the bill** – il conto; **I think there's a mistake in this bill** – credo che il conto sia sbagliato; **is service included?** – è incluso il servizio?

ACCOMMODATION

I'd like to book a single/twin/double bedroom – vorrei prenotare una camera singola/doppia/matrimoniale; **I'd prefer a room with a bath/shower/window over the courtyard/canal** – preferirei una camera con vasca da bagno/doccia/finestra sul cortile/canale

SHOPPING

● **shop** – negozio/*botega*; **how much does it cost/is it?** – quanto costa?, quant'è?/*quanto xè?* **do you accept credit cards?** – si accettano le carte di credito? **do you have small change?** – ha delle monete?
● **I'd like to try on the blue sandals/black shoes/brown boots** – vorrei provare i sandali blu/le scarpe nere/gli stivali marroni; **I take (shoe) size** – porto il numero…; **I take (dress) size** – porto la taglia…; **it's too loose/too tight/just right** – mi sta largo/stretto/bene
● **a litre** – un litro; **100 grams of** – un etto di; **200 grams of** – due etti di; **one kilo of** – un kilo di

DAYS & TIMES

● **Monday** – lunedì; **Tuesday** – martedì; **Wednesday** – mercoledì; **Thursday** – giovedì; **Friday** – venerdì; **Saturday** – sabato; **Sunday** – domenica
● **yesterday** – ieri; **today** – oggi/*ancùo*; **tomorrow** – domani; **morning** – mattina; **afternoon** – pomeriggio; **evening** – sera; **this evening** – stasera; **night** – notte; **tonight** – stanotte

NUMBERS

0 zero; 1 uno; 2 due; 3 tre; 4 quattro; 5 cinque; 6 sei; 7 sette; 8 otto; 9 nove; 10 dieci; 11 undici; 12 dodici; 13 tredici; 14 quattordici; 15 quindici; 16 sedici; 17 diciassette; 18 diciotto; 19 diciannove; 20 venti; 21 ventuno; 22 ventidue; 30 trenta; 40 quaranta; 50 cinquanta; 60 sessanta; 70 settanta; 80 ottanta; 90 novanta; 100 cento; 1,000 mille; 2,000 duemila

Further Reference

BOOKS

Non-fiction

Paolo Barbaro *Venice Revealed: an Intimate Portrait*
Fascinating facts on the city's physical structure.
Robert Davis & Garry Marvin *Venice: the Tourist Maze*
A well-documented study of Venice's role as a tourist mecca.
Deborah Howard
The Architecture of Venice
Howard's *Architecture* is the definitive account.
WD Howells *Venetian Life*
US consul's (1861-65) account of Venetian life before mass tourism.
Peter Humfrey
Painting in Renaissance Venice
Informative and compact enough to carry with you.
Frederick C Lane
Venice: a Maritime Republic
The best single-volume scholarly history of Venice.
Mary Laven *Virgins of Venice: Broken Vows and Cloistered Lives in the Renaissance Convent*
The title says it all.
Michelle Lovric
Venice: Tales of the City
Compendium of writers on Venice.
Mary McCarthy
Venice Observed
Witty account of Venetian art.
Damiano Martin
The Da Fiore Cookbook
How to cook like they do at Da Fiore (*see p175*).
Francesco Da Mosto
Francesco's Venice
Coffee-table guide by a scion of an aristocratic Venetian family.
Jan Morris *Venice*
Impressionistic history.
John Julius Norwich *A History of Venice; Paradise of Cities*
Engagingly rambling.
John Pemble
Venice Rediscovered
On the 19th-century obsession with things Venetian.
David Rosand
Painting in 16th-Century Venice
Read before your trip.
John Ruskin
The Stones of Venice
Ruskin's hymn to the Gothic.
Gary Wills *Venice: Lion City*
Fascinating blend of history and art criticism.

Fiction & literature

See also p108 **Literary Venice**.

Lord Byron
Childe Harold's Pilgrimage; Beppo
Venice as a dream (*Harold*) and at Carnevale (*Beppo*).
Giacomo Casanova *My Life*
The great seducer's escapades in mid 18th-century Venice.
Michael Dibdin *Dead Lagoon*
Aurelio Zen returns to Venice.
Ernest Hemingway
Across the River and into the Trees
Could have been titled 'Across the Canal and into the Bar'.
Henry James
The Wings of the Dove
Melodrama concealed behind a wall of elegant prose.
Donna Leon
Acqua Alta (and many others)
Series featuring detective *commissario* Guido Brunetti.
Thomas Mann
Death in Venice
Disease, decadence, indecision, voyeurism.
Ezra Pound *The Cantos*
Full of abstruse Venetian details.
William Rivière
A Venetian Theory of Heaven
Novel set among the English community in Venice.
William Shakespeare
The Merchant of Venice; Othello
The bard's Venetian offerings.
Sally Vickers
Miss Garnett's Angel
Elderly English lady's staid life is overturned by angelic encounters.

FILM

Casanova (Lasse Halstrom, 2005)
Heath Ledger plays a sugary no-sex-please version of the legendary lover.
The Comfort of Strangers
(Paul Schrader, 1990)
Based on an Ian McEwan novel.
Death in Venice
(Luchino Visconti, 1971)
Dirk Bogarde chases boy around cholera-plagued Venice.
Don't Look Now
(Nicholas Roeg, 1973)
Chilling tale of a couple in Venice after the death of their daughter.
Eve (Joseph Losey, 1962)
Budding novelist is ensnared by a temptress.

The Merchant of Venice
(Michael Radford, 2004)
Al Pacino is Shylock in this star-studded adaptation.
Senso
(Luchino Visconti, 1954)
Tale of sadism and passion.

MUSIC

See also p68 **City of Music**.

Lorenzo Da Ponte (1749-1838)
Penned *libretti* for Mozart's *Marriage of Figaro, Don Giovanni* and *Cosi fan tutte*.
Andrea Gabrieli (c1510-1586)
Organist of St Mark's basilica, Gabrieli senior's madrigals were Venetian favourites.
Giovanni Gabrieli (c1556-1612)
composed sacred and choral music, particularly motets; *In ecclesiis* is perhaps his masterpiece.
Antonio Vivaldi (1678-1741)
There's no escaping his *Four Seasons* in Venice.

WEBSITES

www.veniceconnected.com
Essential site for pre-booking transport and services (English; *see also p6*).
www.venezia.net Apartment rentals to information on hiring a carnevale costume (English).
www.venetia.it History, useful phone numbers and good links (English).
http://english.comune.venezia. it City council's site with useful practical information (English).
www.regione.veneto.it/cultura Cultural offerings around the Veneto. Museum info in English.
www.meetingvenice.it
Hotel booking service in the city and surrounding areas, plus news on events and tourist attractions (English).
www.veniceword.com
News magazine with current events and entertainment (English).
www.venetianlegends.it
A great collection (in English) of ghost stories and grisly legends.
www.insula.it Exhaustive information on keeping Venice above water (English).
www.veneto.org Idiosyncratic site on the history and language of the Veneto region; excellent links.

DIRECTORY

Index A-Z

Note: Page numbers
in **bold** indicate
section(s) giving key
information on a topic;
italics indicate photos.

40xVenezia 31

A

abortion 300
Accademia *see* Gallerie
dell'Accademia
**accommodation
144-163**, 306
B&Bs 149
budget 151, 153, 157,
159-160, 162-163
deluxe 145-147, 151,
153-155, 157, 163
expensive 147,
151-152, 155, 158,
160-161, 163
moderate 147-149,
152-153, 155-157,
158-159, 161-162
gay & lesbian
229-230
see also p315
Accommodation
index
addresses 298
age restrictions 298
airlines & airports
295
Ala Napoleonica 44
Albergo del Selvadego
41
Albinoni, Tomaso 69
Anafesto, Paoluccio 16
Angelo Raffaele 113
antiques shops 208-209
architecture 39-46
Biennale 48
palladian villas 283
Arena di Campo
San Polo 215
Aretino 65
Arsenale **83**, **84**

art 32-38
Biennale **47-49**
galleries 224-228
supplies shops
193-194
see also museums
& galleries
Ateneo San Basso 240
ATMs 302
attitude & etiquette
298

B

B&Bs 149
bag shops 201
banks 302
Baratta, Paolo 49
Barbaria delle Tole 78
barbers 207
bars 182-192
Basilica dei Frari 240
Basilica di San Marco
41, **60**, **61**, *64*
Bassano, Jacopo 36
Battle of Lepanto 25
beaches 220
Befana, La 216
Bellini, Gentile 34, 66
Bellini, Giovanni 33,
66, 80, 92, 110, 134
Benedizione del Fuoco
214
Biblioteca Marciana
43, **60**, **66**
bicycles *see* cycling
Biennale di Venezia,
La **47-49**
Arte Contemporanea
& Architettura, d'
215
Danza-Musica-
Teatro 243
Biennale gardens 46
boating 244-246
boats 52
see also gondolas;
public transport;
traghetti

books & literature 309
for children 220
literary Venice 108
bookshops 194-197
Brenta Canal 261
bridges
Bridge of Sighs
(ponte dei Sospiri)
61, 71
ponte dei Baretteri 73
ponte dei Pugni 116
ponte degli Scalzi 54
ponte del Paradiso 81
ponte dell'Accademia
58
ponte della
Costituzione 45, 54
ponte delle Guglie 88
ponte delle Tette 102
ponte di Rialto 44, 56
Tre Ponti 107
Burano *132*, 135-139
bureaux de change 302
bus services 295, **296**
business services 298
Byron, Lord 108, 141

C

Ca' Barzizza 56
Ca' d'Oro 41, 55, 86,
90, **91**
Ca' da Mosto 55
Ca' Dario 43, **58**
Ca' del Duca 58
Ca' Foscari 57
Ca' Giustinian 59
Ca' Pesaro 44, 55
Galleria
Internazionale
d'Arte Moderna
102, **103**
Museo Orientale
102, **103**
Ca' Rampana 102
Ca' Rezzonico (Museo
del Settecento
Veneziano) 57,
116, **117**

**cafés, bars &
gelaterie 182-192**
see also p316
Cafés, Bars &
Gelaterie index
Calatrava, Santiago 45
Campanile **60**, **65**, 139
campo Angelo Raffaele
86
campo dei Frari 86
campo del Ghetto
Nuovo 93
campo della
Maddalena 86
campo San Giovanni
Crisostomo 86
campo San Marcuola 86
campo San Polo 86
campo San Zaccaria 86
campo Santa
Margherita **116**, *116*
campo Santi Giovanni
e Paolo 86
Canale delle
Fondamenta Nuove
97
Canaletto 38
canals
Cannaregio Canal 88
Grand Canal 52-59
Cannaregio 88-97
accommodation
153-157
cafés & bars 188
enoteche & *bacari*
188-189
gelaterie 189
nightlife 233-234
pasticcerie 189
restaurants 168-173
Cannaregio canal 88
Carnevale **214**, **217**
costume rental shops
199
mask shops 207
Carpaccio, Vittore 34
Carriera, Rosalba 38
cars & driving
295-296, **297**

Casa di Carlo Goldoni 107
Casa di Reclusione Femminile 128, *128*
Casanova, Giacomo 26, 101
Casinò degli Spiriti 95
Castello 77-87
  accommodation 151-153
  cafés & bars 185-187
  galleries 228
  gelaterie 187
  nightlife 233
  pasticcerie 187-188
  restaurants 165-168
Cavalli, Francesco 68
Centro Culturale Candiani 240
Certosa, La 140
children 218-220
Chioggia 252
chocolate shops 202
Christmas, New Year & Epiphany (La Befana) 216
churches 41
  as venues 240-242
  see also Angelo Raffaele; Gli Scalzi; Madonna dell'Orto; Redentore; and churches listed under saints' names, eg San Cassiano; San Giorgio dei Greci.
cinemas 221-222
classical music 238-243
climate 305, 306
clothes shops 198-199
Codussi, Mauro 43
coffee 192
Colleoni, Bartolomeo 77, 78
Commedia dell'arte 237
Conegliano, Cima da 34
conference centres 298
consulates 299
contraception 300
convention centres 298
Convento di San Francesco del Deserto 139

Corte Correr 86
Corte del Remer 86
Corte Veniera 86
Coryat, Thomas 108
costume rental shops 199
couriers 298
customs 298
cycling 247, **297**

D

d'Alemagna, Giovanni 33
dance 238-243
Dandolo, Enrico 19
Death in Venice 89
dentists 300
dialling codes 304
Dickens, Charles 108
disabled access 298-299
Diziani, Gaspare 38
Dogana di Mare 59
Doge's Palace 86
Dolomites 292
Don't Look Now 115
Dorsoduro 113-126
  accommodation 160-162
  cafés & bars 191-192
  enoteche & *bacari* 192
  galleries 228
  gelaterie 192
  nightlife 235
  pasticcerie 192
  restaurants 177-180
driving *see* cars & driving
drugs 299

E

eating *see* restaurants
electricity 299
embassies 299
emergency services 299
Epiphany 216
Esposizione Internazionale d'Arte 48

etiquette 298
Excelsior 46

F

Fabbriche Nuove 55
fabric shops 209-210
fashion shops 197-201
Fenice, La 44, 69, 76, **239, 242**
Ferragosto – Festa dell'Assunta 216
Festa del Redentore 216
Festa della Madonna della Salute 216
Festa di San Giacomo dell'Orio 215
Festa di San Marco 214
Festa di San Martino 216
Festa di San Pietro 215
Festa e Regata della Sensa 215
Festival Galuppi 243
festivals & events 214-217
  film **49, 216, 222-223**
  music 232
  performing arts 243
film 221-223
  festivals **49, 216, 222-223**
  set in Venice 309
fishing 245
florists 205
Fondaco dei Tedeschi 55
Fondazione Giorgio Cini & Benedictine Monastery 129
Fondazione Vedova 126
food *see* restaurants
food & drink shops 201-204
football 244
Forte Massimiliano 140
Fourth Crusade 19
Franco, Veronica 17
Frari, I 41, 86, **107, 109**

G

Gabrieli, Andrea 68
Gabrieli, Giovanni 68
Galleria Cini **120, 123**
Galleria Internazionale d'Arte Moderna **102, 103**
Gallerie dell'Accademia **117, 122**
galleries 224-228
Galuppi, Baldassarre **135**, 138, 243
gay & lesbian 229-230
gelaterie 182-192
Gesuati, I **125, 126**
Gesuiti, I 44, 96
Ghetto, Il 93
giardini pubblici (public gardens) 44, 48
Gibbon, Edward 108
gift shops 204
Giorgione 35
Giornate Wagneriane, Le 243
Giovane, Palma il 36
Giudecca, La & San Giorgio 127-130
  accommodation 162-163
  cafés & bars 192
  galleries 228
  nightlife 235
  restaurants 180-181
glassware
  Murano glass 136-137
  shops 205-207
Gli Scalzi 44, 54, **92**
Goldoni, Carlo 237
golf 246
gondolas 297
  see also traghetti
Grand Canal 52-59
Guardi 38
Guggenheim, Peggy 121
gyms 247

H

hairdressers 207
Harry's Bar 61
hat shops 199

INDEX

health & beauty shops
207-208
health services 299-300
history 14-26
homeware shops
208-212
hotels *see*
accommodation

I

ice-cream *see* cafés,
bars & *gelaterie*
ID 300
immigration 305
insurance 300
internet
access 300
useful websites 309
interpreters 298
Isola di San Giorgio
129, *130*
Istituto Universitario
di Architettura di
Venezia 113

J

James, Henry 91
jewellery shops 194,
199-201
Jewish population 93
Justinian I, Emperor 15

L

lace-making 138
language 308
language classes 304
Last Supper, The 92
Lazzaretto Nuovo 141
League of Cambrai 25
left luggage 300
legal advice 300
lesbian *see* gay
& lesbian
libraries 300-301
Lido & lagoon
131-141
accommodation 163
nightlife 235-236
restaurants 181
Loggetta 43
Lombardo, Pietro 43

Longhena, Baldassare
44
Longhi, Pietro 38
lost property 301
Lotto, Lorenzo 35

M

Maddalena, La 90
Madonna dell'Orto 95
magazines 301-302
Manin, Daniele 74
Mare Maggio 215
markets 202
mask shops 207
Mazzorbo 134
media 301
Mekhitar 141
mobile phones 304
Molino Stucky 46, **127**
Monastero
Mechitarista 141
money 302
Monteverdi, Claudio 68
Monument to
Bartolomeo Colleoni
77, **78**, *79*
Morosini, Francesco 26
Mostra Internazionale
d'Arte
Cinematografica
(Venice International
Film Festival) **49**,
216, **222**
motonave 52
motoscafo 52
Mueller, Marco 49
Murano 133
Murano glass 136-137
murazzi 131
Museo Archeologico
66
Museo Correr **60**, **66**
Museo del Manicomio
di San Servolo 141
Museo del Settecento
Veneziano **116**, **117**
Museo dell'Arte
Vetrario 134
Museo dell'Istituto
Ellenico **83**, **84**
Museo della
Fondazione Querini
Stampalia **77**, **78**

Museo della Musica 76
Museo di Storia
Naturale **102**, **104**
Museo di Torcello 139
Museo Diocesano di
Arte Sacra **77**, **78**
Museo Ebraico 94
Museo Orientale
102, **103**
Museo Storico Navale
83, *84*, **85**
museum passes 6
museums & galleries
archeology: Museo
Archeologico 66
art: Ca' d'Oro 41,
55, 86, **90**, **91**;
Galleria Cini **120**,
123; Galleria
Internazionale
d'Arte Moderna
102, **103**; Gallerie
dell'Accademia
117, **122**; Museo
del Settecento
Veneziano **116**,
117; Museo della
Fondazione
Querini Stampalia
77, **78**; Museo di
Torcello 139;
Peggy
Guggenheim
Collection 58, **120**,
121, **123**
fashion: Palazzo
Mocenigo **102**,
104
glass: Museo
dell'Arte Vetrario
134
history: Museo Correr
60, **66**
*Japanese art &
weaponry*: Museo
Orientale **102**,
103
Jewish: Museo
Ebraico 94
lace: Scuola di
Merletti **135**, **138**
medicine: Museo del
Manicomio di San
Servolo 141

music: Museo della
Musica 76; Piccolo
Museo della Pietà
'Antonio Vivaldi'
81, **83**, **85**
natural history:
Museo di Storia
Naturale **102**, **104**
naval history: Museo
Storico Navale
83, *84*, **85**
religious art: Museo
dell'Istituto
Ellenico **83**, **84**;
Museo Diocesano
di Arte Sacra
77, **78**
theatre: Casa di Carlo
Goldoni 107
music 231-236
festivals 232
history 68
shops 212
venues 240-243

N

Napoleon 26, 66
New Year 216
newspapers 301
nightlife 231-236
Northern Veneto
287-292

O

Olivetti showroom 46
opening hours 302
opera 239-243
opticians 207-208
Oratorio dei Crociferi
97
Orso, Ipato 16
Ospedale Civile 43,
77, *80*, **82**, 105
Ottico Fabbricatore
206
Ottoman Empire 25

P

Padua 255-264
gay & lesbian 230
painting 32-38

Palazzetto Dandolo 56
Palazzi Barbaro 58
Palazzi Giustinian 57
Palazzi Mocenigo 57
Palazzo Balbi 57
Palazzo Barbarigo
    Minotto 241
Palazzo Benzon 56
Palazzo Cappello
    Layard 56
Palazzo Contarini
    Fasan 59
Palazzo Corner della
    Ca' Grande 43
Palazzo Corner della
    Ca' Grande 58
Palazzo Corner della
    Regina 55
Palazzo Corner
    Mocenigo 43
Palazzo dei
    Camerlenghi 43, 55
Palazzo del Cinema 49
Palazzo delle
    Esposizioni 49
Palazzo delle Prigioni
    241
Palazzo Ducale 41,
    60, **67**, *67*
Palazzo Farsetti 56
Palazzo Flangini 54
Palazzo Fortuny 74
Palazzo Franchetti
    46
Palazzo Grassi 44, 46,
    57, **74**, **75**, 124
Palazzo Grimani di
    San Luca 43, 56,
    77, *78*, **79**, 115
Palazzo Labia 54
Palazzo Loredan 56
Palazzo Mangilli
    Valmarana 55
Palazzo Manin Dolfin
    56
Palazzo Mastelli 95
Palazzo Mocenigo
    102, **104**
Palazzo Nani 88
Palazzo Priuli-Manfrin
    88
Palazzo Savorgan 88
Palazzo Surian-Bellotto
    88

Palazzo Vendramin
    Calergi 55
Palazzo Venier dei
    Leoni 44, 58, **121**,
    123
Palazzo Zenobio **113**,
    115
Palio delle Antiche
    Repubbliche
    Marinare 215
palladian villas 283
Palladio, Andrea 44,
    280-281
Parco di San Giuliano
    46, 220
Parco Savorgnan 88
parks 220
Partecipazio, Angelo
    16
Partecipazio, Giovanni
    18
Partecipazio,
    Giustiniano 18
passes 6, 296
pasticcerie see cafés,
    bars & *gelaterie*
    182-192
Peggy Guggenheim
    Collection 58, **120**,
    121, **123**
Pepin 16
performing arts
    237-243
Pescaria 55
pharmacies 300
photography shops
    197
Piave, Francesco Maria
    135
piazza San Marco 60,
    61
Piazzetta, Giambattista
    38
Piccolo Museo della
    Pietà 'Antonio
    Vivaldi' 81, **83**, **85**
Pietà, La (Santa Maria
    della Visitazione) 44,
    81, *81*, **83**, **85**, *85*
Piombo, Sebastiano del
    35, 37
pizzerie see restaurants
police 302-303
Polo, Marco 90

Ponte Calatrava
    see Ponte della
    Costituzione
Ponte degli Scalzi 54
Ponte dei Baretteri 73
Ponte dei Pugni 116
Ponte dei Sospiri 61, 71
Ponte dei Tre Archi 88
Ponte del Paradiso 81
Ponte dell'Accademia
    58
Ponte della
    Costituzione 45,
    45, 54
Ponte della Donna
    Onesta 112
Ponte delle Guglie 88
Ponte delle Tette 102
Ponte di Rialto 56, 98
Pordenone 35
postal services 303
Procuratie Nuove 44
Procuratie Vecchie 43
Proust, Marcel 183
public gardens *see*
    giardini pubblici
public holidays 305
public transport
    296-297
    see also vaporetti
Punta della Dogana
    46, **120**, **123**, **124**,
    124

Q

Querini-Benzon,
    Countess Marina 56

R

radio 302
rail *see* train services
Redentore 44
Redentore, Il 129
Regata Storica 216
religion 303
restaurants
    164-181
    gay & lesbian 230
    vocabulary 169
    wine 178
    see also p315
    Restaurants index

Rialto 44, 98
    market 56, 98, *99*
    nightlife 190
Robusti, Jacopo *see*
    Tintoretto
rowing races 244
Ruga Giuffa 77
running 247
Ruskin, John 108

S

safety & security 303
Sagra del Mosto 216
Sagra del Pesce 216
sailing 245
St Mark's Basilica
    see Basilica di
    San Marco
St Mark's square *see*
    piazza San Marco
San Barnaba 119
San Cassiano **102**,
    104
San Francesco del
    Deserto 139
San Francesco della
    Vigna 43, **79**
San Giacomo dell'Orio
    41, **103**, **104**
San Giacomo di Rialto
    41, **98**, **99**, 241
San Giobbe 89
San Giorgio (island)
    129, *130*
San Giorgio 127-130
San Giorgio dei Greci
    83, **87**
San Giorgio Maggiore
    44, **129**, **130**
San Giovanni
    Crisostomo **90**, **91**
San Giovanni
    Elemosinario **99**,
    101
San Giovanni in
    Bragora **83**, **87**
San Giuliano *see*
    San Zulian
San Lazzaro degli
    Armeni 141
San Marco 60-76
    accommodation
    145-151

INDEX

INDEX

cafés & bars 183-185
galleries 225-228
gelaterie 185
nightlife 232-233
pasticcerie 185
restaurants 165
San Marcuola **90**, **92**
San Marziale **90**, **92**
San Michele (cemetery) 133
San Michele 43, 46, **77**
San Michele in Isola 133
San Moisè 44, *75*, **76**
San Nicolò 132
San Nicolò da Tolentino 111
San Nicolò dei Mendicoli 41, **113**, **115**
San Pantalon **107**, **111**
San Pietro in Castello 87
San Pietro Martire 134
San Polo & Santa Croce 98-112
accommodation 157-160
cafés & bars 189-190
enoteche & *bacari* 190-191
gelaterie 191
nightlife 234
pasticcerie 191
restaurants 173-176
San Polo 101
San Rocco 111
San Salvador 73
San Sebastiano **113**, **115**
San Servolo 141
San Silvestro **99**, **101**
San Simeone Piccolo 54
San Simeone Profeta **102**, **106**
San Stae 44, **102**, **106**
San Trovaso **117**, **119**, *120*
San Vidal **74**, **75**, 242
San Zaccaria 43, **77**, **82**, 85

San Zan Degolà (San Giovanni Decollato) **102**, **105**
San Zulian **73**, **74**
Sansovino, Jacopo 43
Sant'Alvise 96
Sant'Antonin 83
Sant'Elena **84**, **87**
Sant'Erasmov 140
Santa Caterina 135
Santa Croce *see* San Polo & Santa Croce
Santa Eufemia 129
Santa Fosca 41, 90, *138*, **139**
Santa Lucia (station) 296
Santa Margherita 116
Santa Maria Assunta 41, **139**, **140**
Santa Maria dei Carmini **116**, **119**
Santa Maria dei Derelitti **77**, **82**
Santa Maria dei Miracoli 43, *95*, **97**
Santa Maria del Giglio 44, **76**
Santa Maria della Fava **73**, **74**
Santa Maria della Salute 44, 59, **120**, *122*, **123**, 241
Santa Maria della Visitazione **125**, **126**
Santa Maria delle Penitenti 88
Santa Maria Formosa **77**, **82**, 241
Santa Maria Gloriosa dei Frari *see* Frari, I
Santa Maria Mater Domini **102**, **106**
Santi Apostoli **90**, **92**
Santi Giovanni e Paolo (San Zanipolo) 41, 77, **80**
Santi Maria e Donato 134
Santo Stefano 41, **74**, **75**
Scala Contarini del Bòvolo 76

Scaligera empire 23
Scalzi *see* Gli Scalzi
Scarpa, Carlo 46
Scola Canton 93
Scola Tedesca 93
Scuola dei Carmini 38, **116**, **119**
Scuola della Misericordia 41, 95
Scuola di Merletti **135**, **138**
Scuola di San Giorgio degli Schiavoni **83**, **85**, **87**, 105
Scuola Grande di San Giovanni Evangelista 105, **107**, **111**, 242
Scuola Grande di San Marco (Ospedale Civile) 43, **77**, *80*, **82**, 105
Scuola Grande di San Rocco 36, 105, *105*, **107**, *110*, **112**
Scuola Grande di San Teodoro 243
scuole grandi 105
Seconda del Milion 90
Serrata del Maggior Consiglio 19
Shakespeare, William 108
shiatsu 247
shipping services 298
shoe shops 201
shops & services 193-212
art supplies 193-194
books & magazines 194-197
electronics & photography 197
fashion 197-201
food & drink 201-204
gifts & souvenirs 204-207
health & beauty 207-208
house & home 208-212
music & entertainment 212
sunglasses 206
travellers' needs 212

sightseeing 51-141
for children 218-220
smoking 303
souvenir shops 204
sport & fitness 244-247
students 303-304
Su e Zo per i Ponti 214
sunglasses shops 206
swimming pools 247

T

tax 193
taxis 295
Teatro in Campo 243
Teatro La Fenice 44, 69, 76, **239**, **242**
Teatro Malibran 237, **239**
Telecom Italia Future Centre 74
telephones 304
television 302
tennis 247
theatre 237-243
tickets 212
Tiepolo, Baiamonte 19
Tiepolo, Giambattista 38
Tiepolo, Giandomenico 38
time 304
Tintoretto **36**, **37**, 96
tipping 304
Titian **35**, **37**
toilets 305
Tommaseo, Nicolò 74
Torcello 139
Torre dell'Orologio 43, **60**, *70*, **71**
tourist information 305
tours 297
traghetti 296
train services 295, **296**
translator services 298
transport *see* public transport
travel advice 298
Tre Ponti 107
Treviso 286-287
Treviso Sant'Angelo Airport 295

V

vaporetti (water buses)
52, **296**
Vecellio, Tiziano *see*
Titian
Veneto Jazz 215
Venezia Suona 215
Veneziano, Paolo 33
Venice Baroque
Orchestra 238
Venice Gateway 46
Venice International
Film Festival **49**,
216, **222**
Venice Marathon 216
Venice Marco Polo
Airport 295
Venier, Domenico 17
Verona 265-274
Veronese, Paolo 36
Via Garibaldi 44, *83*
Vicenza 275-285
Vignole 141
vintage clothes shops
198-199
visas 305
Vivaldi, Antonio 68,
81
Vivarini, Antonio 33
Vivarini, Bartolomeo
33
vocabulary 308
Vogalonga 215

W

Wagner 57
walking 297
water 305
water taxis 296-297
weather 305, 306
weights & measures
305
well-heads 86
Willaert, Adrian 68
wine 178
shops 202
women 306
working in Venice
306

Y

yoga 247

Z

Zattere, Le 125, *126*
Zecca, La 43, **67**, **72**
Zitelle, Le 129

ACCOMMODATION INDEX

Accademia – Villa
Maravege 160
Agli Alboretti 161
Ai Due Fanali 158
Al Ponte Antico 156
Al Ponte Mocenigo
157, 158
American 160
Antica Locanda
Montin 162
B&B San Marco 153
Bauer Hotels 145
Ca' dei Conti 151
Ca' del Dose 153
Ca' del Nobile *145*,
147
Ca' Dogaressa 156
Ca' Foscari 162
Ca' Maria Adele 160
Ca' Nigra Lagoon
Resort *152*, 158
Ca' Pisani 161
Ca' Sagredo *146*, 153
Ca' Zose 161
Calcina, La 161, *163*
Casa per Ferie 153
Casa Peron 159
Casa Querini 152
Casa Verardo 153
Charming House iQs,
The 151
Cipriani 162
Danieli 151
DD 724 161
Des Bains 163
Do Pozzi 147
Falier 159
Flora 149
Giorgione 156
Gritti Palace 145
Hotel Monaco &
Grand Canal 147
Hotel Rio 153
Locanda ai Santi
Apostoli 156
Locanda Art Deco 149

Locanda Cipriani 163
Locanda del Ghetto
156
Locanda La Corte 153
Locanda Marinella 159
Locanda Novecento
149
Locanda Orseolo 149
Locanda San Barnaba
162
Locanda Sturion 159
Locanda Vivaldi 152
Londra Palace 151
Luna Hotel Baglioni
147
Messner 162
Metropole 151
Oltre il Giardino 159
Ostello di Venezia
(Youth Hostel) 162
Ostello Santa Fosca
157
Palazzo Abadessa 156
Palazzo Sant'Angelo
sul Canal Grande 147
Palazzo Stern 161
Papadopoli - Sofitel
157
Residenza, La 153
Rossi 157
Salieri 160
San Cassiano – Ca'
Favretto 158
San Clemente Palace
163
San Samuele 151
Saturnia &
International 147
Savoia & Jolanda 152
Villeggiatura, La *158*,
159

RESTAURANTS INDEX

Ai Gondolieri 177
Al Covo 165
Al Diporto 165
Al Fontego dei
Pescaori 168
Al Garanghelo 173
Al Mercà 181
Al Nono Risorto 175
Al Portego 167
Algiubagiò *167*, 168

Alla Fontana 168
Alla Frasca 169
Alla Maddalena 181
Alla Madonna 173
Alla Palanca 180
Alla Zucca 173
Alle Testiere 167
Anice Stellato 169
Antica Adelaide 171
Antiche Carampane
175
Avogaria, L' 177
Bancogiro 175
Bea Vita 171
Birraria La Corte 175
Bitta, La 177
Boccadoro 171, *171*
Bottega ai Promessi
Sposi, La 171, *172*
Busa alla Torre 181
Ca' D'Oro (Alla
Vedova) 172
Casin dei Nobili 177
Cavatappi 165
Corte Sconta 167
Da Alberto 172
Da Fiore 175
Da Ignazio 175
Da Rioba 172
Dai Tosi 167
Dalla Marisa 172
Favorita, La 181
Fiaschetteria Toscana
172
Figli delle Stelle, I 180,
180
Frary's 176
Harry's Dolci 180
Locanda Cipriani 181
Met *165*, 168
Mirai 172
Mistrà 181
Naranzaria *173*, 176
Oniga 177
Osteria di Santa
Marina 168
Osteria San Marco 165
Pane, Vino e San
Daniele 180
Refolo, Il 176
Ridotto, Il 168
Vecio Fritolin 176, *176*
Vini da Gigio 173

INDEX

Advertisers' Index

Please refer to the relevant pages for contact details

HelloVenezia — **IFC**

Sights

San Marco
HelloVenezia — **62**

San Polo & Santa Croce
Hibuscus — **100**

Dorsoduro
Fondazione Vedova — **114**

Consume

Hotels
Agli Alboretti — **154**
Al Ponte Mocenigo — **154**
Locanda Marinella — **156**
La Villegiatura — **156**

Restaurants
Hard Rock Cafe — **166**

Cafés & Bars
Rosa Salva — **184**

Shops & Services
Alessi — **196**
Attombri — **200**

Arts & Entertainment

Galleries
Bugno Gallery — **226**

Directory

Terminal Fusina — **294**

Maps

NY & Co. — **318**

INDEX

Maps

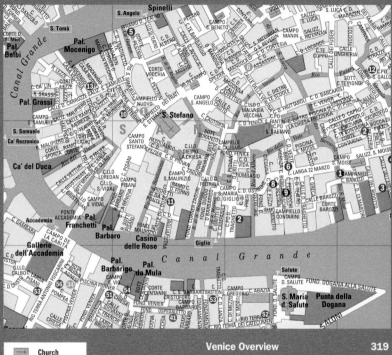

Church

✈ **Airport**

H **Hospital**

S. Angelo **Vaporetto stop**

Palazzo

Venice Overview   319

Street Maps   320
    Central Venice   320
    Lido   327
    La Giudecca   328
    Murano   328
    Burano   329
    Street Index   330

Vaporetto Map   336

Ask New York City about New York City glamour
nycgo.com

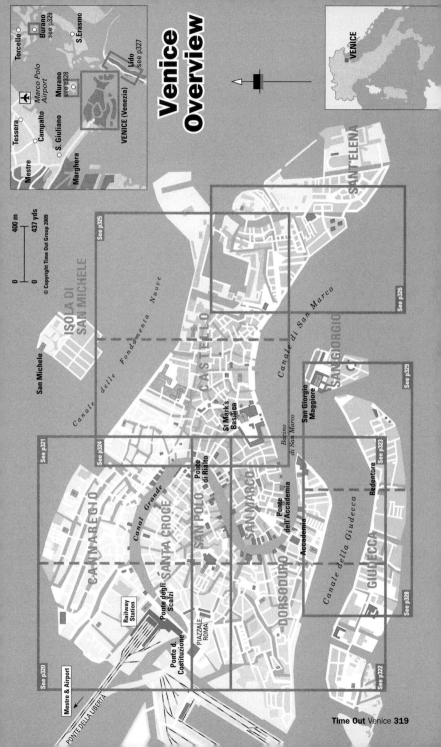

Venice Overview

VENICE

Mestre & Airport

PONTE DELLA LIBERTÀ

Railway Station

Ponte degli Scalzi

Ponte d. Costituzione

PIAZZALE ROMA

CANNAREGIO

SANTA CROCE

SAN POLO

Canal Grande

Ponte di Rialto

St Mark's Basilica

CASTELLO

Canale delle Fondamenta Nuove

ISOLA DI SAN MICHELE

San Michele

DORSODURO

Ponte dell'Accademia

Accademia

SAN MARCO

Bacino di San Marco

Canale di San Marco

SANT'ELENA

GIUDECCA

Canale della Giudecca

Redentore

San Giorgio Maggiore

SAN GIORGIO

See p320
See p321
See p324
See p325
See p326
See p322
See p323
See p328
See p329

0   400 m
0   437 yds
© Copyright Time Out Group 2009

Tessera
Mestre
Campalto
S. Giuliano
Marghera
Marco Polo Airport
Murano see p328
VENICE (Venezia)
S.Erasmo
Torcello
Burano see p329
Lido see p327

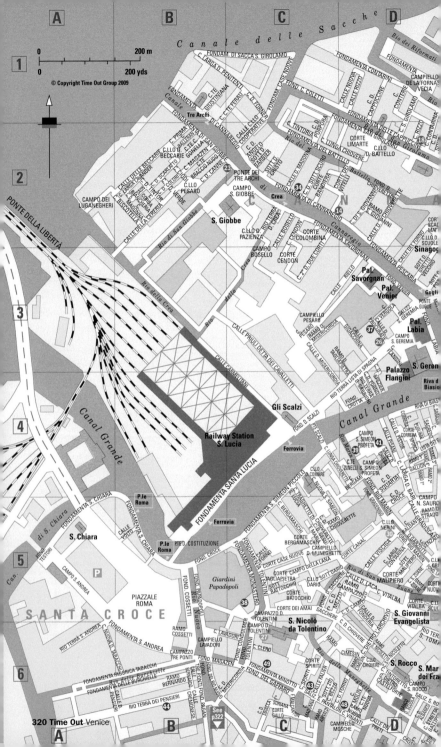

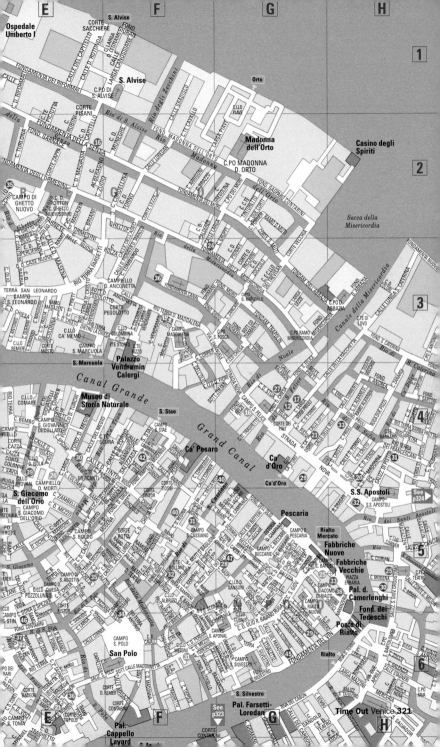

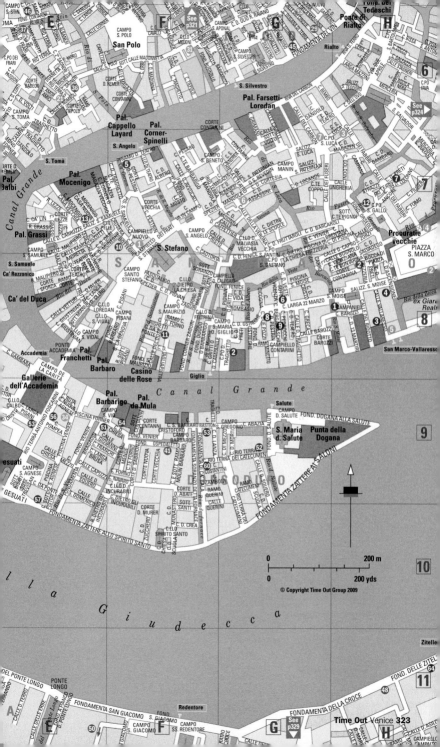

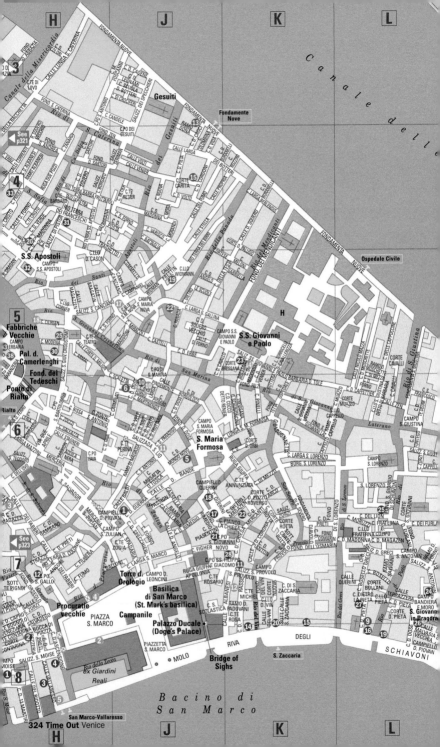

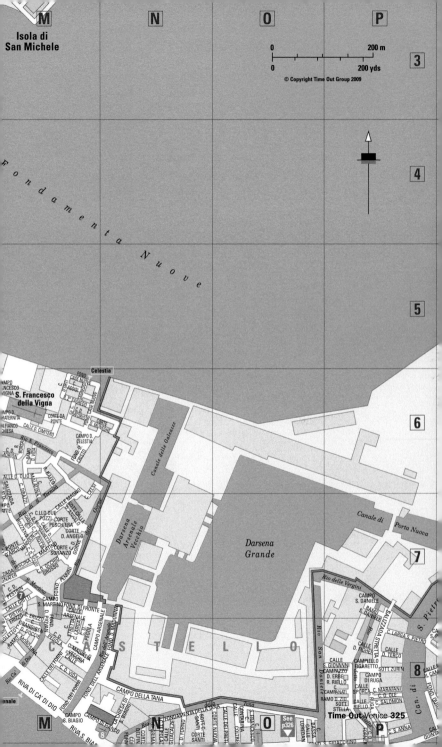

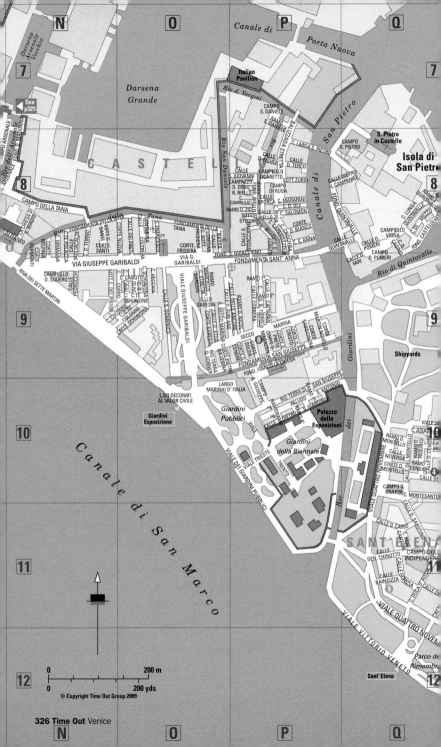

Lido

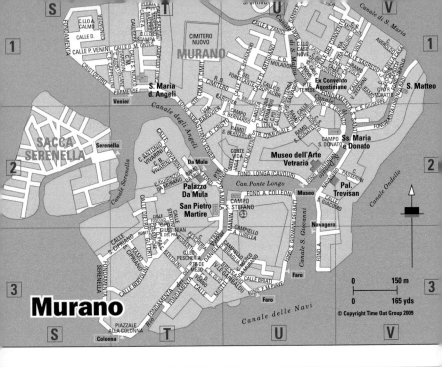

Murano

La Giudecca

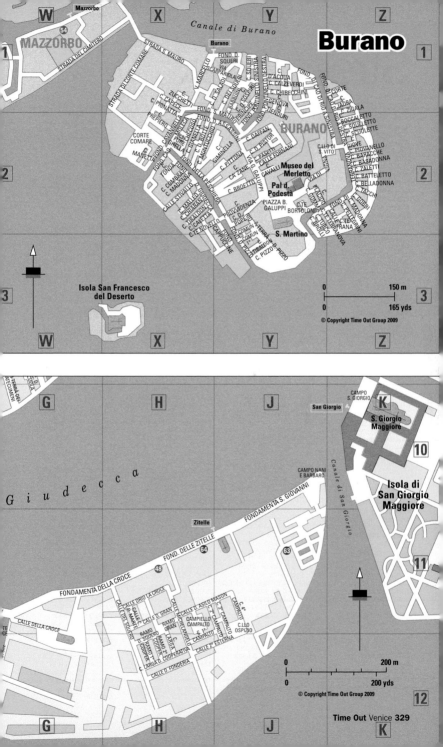

Street Index

C. Calle
C.llo Campiello
C.po Campo
C.te Corte
C.zzo Campiazzo
Fond. Fondamenta
P.zle Piazzale
P.za Piazza
Salizz. Salizzada
Sott. Sottoportego
V.le Viale

SAN MARCO
ACCADEMIA Ponte d. E8 323
ACQUILA NERA C. H6 324
ALBANESI C. d. G7 323
ALBERO C. F7 323
ALBERO Fond. d. F7 323
ANCORE C. H7 323
ANGELO C. d. J7 324
ASCENSIONE C. d. H8 323
ASSASSINI C. d. G7 323
AVVOCATI C. d. F7 323
BALBI C. H6/7 324
BALLONI C. HJ7 324
BARBARIGO C.te F7 323
BARBARO Fond. F8 323
BARCAROLI C. G7 323
BAROZZI C. H8 323
BAROZZI C.te G8 323
BEMBO C. G6 323
BERGAMASCHI C. G8 323
BISSA C. H6 324
BOCCA DI P.za H7/8 323
BOGNOLO C. H7/8 323
BOMBASERI C. H6 323
BOTTEGHE C. d. F7 323
BRENTANA C. GH7 323
CA GENOVA C. F8 323
CA' LIN C. E7 323
CAFFETTIER C. d. FG7 323
CALEGARI C.llo d. FG8 323
CAMPANA C. H7 323
CAMPANIEI C. H8 323
CAMPO C. va in F7 323
CAOTORTA C. F7/8 323
CAPRO C. d. GH7/8 323
CARBON C. d. G6/7 323
CARBON Riva d. G6 323
CARRO C. G8 323
CARROZZE C. d. E7 323
CAVALLI C. G6/7 323
CERIA C. H6 323
CHIESA E TEATRO Salizz.
  G7 323
CICOGNA C. G8 323
CLERO C. Larga d. E8 323
COLONNE Rio terà H7 323
CONTARINA C.te H8 323
CONTARINI C. G7 323
CONTARINI C.llo G8 323
CONTARINI C.te FG6 323
COPPO C.te G7 323
CORNER O MAGAZEN
  VECCHIO EF7 323
CORNER ZAGURI Fond. F8 323
CORTESIA C. d. G7 323
CRISTO C. d. FG7 323
CRISTO C. d. G8 323
CROSERA C. F7 323
DA Ponte DOGE C. F8 323
DANDOLO C. G6 323
dietro LA CHIESA C. G7/8 323
dietro LA CHIESA C.llo F8 323

dietro LE SCUOLE C. G7 323
DUE APRILE Via H6 323
DUE POZZI C. G8 323
DUODO O BARBARIGO Fond.
  F8 323
FABBRI C. d. H7 323
FELTRINA C.llo d. F8 323
FENICE C. d. G8 323
FENICE Fond. G8 323
FERRO Riva d. H6 323
FIUBERA C. H7 324
FORNO C. F8 323
FORNO C. J7 324
FORNO Ramo C. d. F8 323
FRATI C. d. F7 323
FREZZERIA H8 323
FREZZERIA Piscina d. G7 323
FRUTTAROL C. E8 323
FRUTTAROLI C. G7 323
FUMO C. H7 323
FUSERI C. d. G7 323
GALEAZZA C. H6 324
GAMBARO C. d. H7 323
GIUSTINIAN C. E8 323
GIUSTINIAN C.llo E8 323
GOLDONI C. H7 323
GRASSI C. E7 323
GRASSI Ramo E7 323
GRECA C. G8 323
GRIMANI C. G6/7 323
GRITTI O CAMPANILE C. F8 323
GUERRA C. d. J7 324
LEONCINI C.po J7 324
LEZZE C. E7 323
LEZZE C.te E7 323
LEZZE Ramo E7 323
LOCANDE C. d. H7 323
LOREDAN C.llo EF8 321
MADONNA C. d. FG7 323
MAGAZEN C. d. H7 323
MAGAZEN C. FG7 323
MAGAZEN C.te F3 323
MALATIN Sott. F8 323
MALIPIERO C. E8 323
MALIPIERO Ramo E8 323
MALIPIERO Salizz. E8 323
MALVASIA Fond. F8 323
MALVASIA VECCHIA C.llo d.
  G7 323
MANDOLA C. d. G7 323
MANDOLA Rio terà d. F7 323
MANIN C.po G7 323
MAZZINI Larga H6 323
MIANI Sott. E8 323
MINOTTO Ramo G8 323
MOCENIGO CASA NUOVA C.
  E7 323
MOCENIGO CASA VECCHIA C.
  E7 323
MORETTA C. Ramo E7/8 323
MOSTO C. E7 323
MUNEGHE C. EF7 323
MUNEGHE Ramo E7/8 323
NANI C.te E8 323
NUOVO C.llo F7 323
ORBI C. d. EF7 323
ORSEOLO Fond. H7 323
OSTREGHE C. d. G8 323
OSTREGHE Fond. G8 323
OVO C. d. H8 323
PASQUALIGO C. F8 323
PEDROCCHI C. G8 323
PELLE C.te EF7 323
PESARO C. F7 323

PESTRIN C. d. G8 323
PESTRIN C. F7 323
PESTRIN C.te d. F7 323
PIGNOI Sott. C.te H7 323
PIOVAN C. d. F8 323
PIOVAN C.llo d. HJ7 324
PIOVAN O GRITTI C. d. G8 323
PISANI C. F8 323
PISANI C.po F8 323
PISANI Ramo Sott. F8 323
PISCINA C. d. GH7 323
PRETI C. d. G8 323
PRETI C. d. H7 323
PRETI C. d. H8 323
RIALTO Ponte d. H6 323
RIDOTTO C. d. H8 323
RIGHETTI C. F8 323
ROMBASIO C. G8 323
S. BARTOLOMEO C.po H6 324
S. BENETO C.po F7 323
S. FANTIN C.po G7/8 323
S. GAETANO C.po G8 323
S. GALLO C.po H7 323
S. LUCA C. GH6/7 323
S. LUCA C.po G7 323
S. LUCA Salizz. G7 323
S. MARCO C. Larga J7 324
S. MARCO P.za H7/8 324
S. MARCO P.tta J8 324
S. MARIA D. GIGLIO C.po
  FG8 323
S. MAURIZIO C.po F8 323
S. MAURIZIO Fond. F8 323
S. MOISE C.po H8 323
S. MOISE Piscina G8 323
S. MOISE Salizz. H8 323
S. PATERNIAN Salizz. H7 323
S. PATERNIAN O S. REVEDIN
  C. G7 323
S. SALVADOR Merceria H6 324
S. SAMUELE C.po E7/8 323
S. SAMUELE Piscina F7 323
S. SAMUELE Salizz EF7 323
S. TEODORO Salizz. H6 323
S. VIDAL C.llo E8 323
S. VIDAL C.po E8 323
S. ZORZI C. H7 323
S. ZULIAN C.po HJ7 324
S. ZULIAN Merceria H7 324
S.TO STEFANO C.llo F7/8 323
S.TO STEFANO C.po F8 323
SABBION C. H6 324
SALVADEGO C. H7 323
SANT'ANDREA C. G7 323
SANT'ANGELO C.po F7 323
SFORZA C.te E8 323
SORANZO Sott. F8 323
SPADARIA C. J7 324
SPECCHIERI C. d. J7 324
SPEZIER C. F7 323
SPEZIER C. d. F8 323
STAGNERI C. H6 324
STRAZZE C. d. H7 324
TAGLIAPIETRA C. d. F8 323
TEATRO C. d. G8 323
TEATRO C. d. E8 323
TEATRO C. d. G6 323
TEATRO C.llo H7 323
TEATRO C.te E8 323
TEATRO Ramo d. E8 323
TEDESCHI C. d. E7 323
TETRO Ramo d. F7 323
TRAGHETTO C. d. F7 323
TRAGHETTO C. d. G8 323

TRAGHETTO C.po d. G8 323
TREDICI MARTIRI C. d. H8 323
UNGHERIA C. H7 323
VALLARESSO C. H8 323
VECCHIA C.te F7 323
VENEZIANA C. H7/8 323
VENIER C. G7 323
VENTIDUE MARZO C. Larga
  G8 323
VERONA C. d. G7 323
VESTE C. d. G8 323
VETTURI O FALIER C. E8 323
VICENZA Sott. G8 323
VIDA C. d. G8 323
VOLTO C. Sott. G7 323
ZAGURI C. F8 323
ZOCCO C. H6 324
ZOGIA C.te J7 324
ZOTTI C. d. E7 323

CASTELLO
ALBANESI C. JK7 324
ANCORE C. d. OP9 326
ANGELO C. M7 325
ANGELO C.te d. M7 325
ANGELO Sott. d. M7 325
ANNUNZIATA C.te K6 324
ARCO C. d. L7 324
ARCO C. d. K6 324
ARSENALE C. d. M7 325
ARSENALE C.po d. MN8 325
ARSENALE Fond. d. MN8 325
ASSISI C. M6 325
BAFFO Ramo M6 325
BANDE C. d. J6 324
BANDIERA E MORO C.po
  L7 324
BASSA C. O8 326
BIANCO C.te d. P8 326
BOLLANI C.te L7 324
BORGOLOCO C. d. J6 324
BORSA Ramo M6 325
BOSELLO C. L7 324
BOTTERA C. K6 324
BRESSANA C. K5 324
BRESSANA C.te K5 324
CA' DI DIO Riva. M8 325
CABOTTO C. O9 326
CAFFETTIER C. d. L6 324
CAGNOLETTO C. M8 325
CAMPANATI C. P8 326
CAPAROZZOLO C. P8 326
CAPELLERA C. L6 324
CAPPELLO C. K6 324
CAPPELLO C.llo K6 324
CAPPELLO Ramo K6 324
CAPPUCCINE C. d. L5 324
CARMINATI C. J6 324
CASE NUOVE Fond. M6 325
CASSELARIA C. J6/7 324
CASSELARIA Ramo J7 324
CATTAPAN C. P9 326
CAVALLI C. L6 324
CAVALLI C. O9 326
CAVALLI C.te L5 324
CAVALLO C. d. JK5 324
CELESTIA C.po d. M6 325
CELSI C. M6/7 325
CENERE C.te d. P9 326
CHIESA C. d. R7 324
CHIESA C. Fianco la JK7 324
CHIESA C.po Fianco la M6 325
CHIESA Fond. Fianco la P9 326
CIMITERO C. d. M6 325

COCCO DETTO RENIER C. JK6 324
COLONNE C. O9 326
COLONNE C.te O9 326
COLTRERA C. O8 326
CONFRATERNITA C.po d. M6 325
CONTARINA C. O8 326
COPPO C. NO9 326
COPPO C. L7 324
CORAZZIERI C. M7 325
CORAZZIERI Sott. M7 325
CORONA C. d. K7 324
CORRERA C. P9 326
CORRERA Ramo 1 P9 326
CORRERA Ramo 2 P9 326
CRISTO C.te d. P9 326
CRISTO Fond. d. M6 325
CROCIERA C. P8 326
CROSER C. M7/8 325
DA Ponte C.te M6 325
DECORATI AL VALOR CIVILE L.go O10 326
DELFINA C.te N8/9 326
DIAVOLO C. d. K7 324
DOCCIE C. d. M8 325
DOSE C. d. J6 324
DOSE C. d. L8 324
DOSE Fond. d. J6 324
DRAZZI C. M6/7 325
DUE POZZI C.llo M7 325
ERBE CAMPAZZO C. P8 326
ERIZZO C. dietro M7/8 324
ERIZZO C. M7/8 325
FAVA C. d. H6 324
FAVA C.po H6 324
FELZI Fond. K6 324
FIGARETTO C.llo P8 326
FIGHER C. d. P8 326
FIGHER C. J7 324
FONTEGO C. L6 324
FORMENTI C.te N8/9 324
FORNER C.D. P8 326
FORNER Fond.D. P8 326
FORNER Rio terà D. O9 326
FORNI Fond. d. M8 325
FORNO C. d. J6 324
FORNO C. d. L6 324
FORNO C. d. L8 324
FORNO C. d. M7 325
FORNO C. d. M8 325
FORNO C.D. N8/9 326
FORNO Ramo L7 324
FRATERNA C.llo L7 324
FRATERNA C. L7 324
FRISIERA C. Sott. O8 326
FRISIERA C.te O8 326
FRONTE Fond. d. M7 325
FRUTTAROL C. d. J6 324
FURLANE C. d. OP9 326
FURLANI C. L7 324
FURLANI Fond. d. L7 324
GARIBALDI GIUSEPPE V.le O9 326
GARIBALDI GIUSEPPE Via NO9 326
GATTE C.po d. M7 325
GATTE Salizz. D. M6/7 325
GIARDINI PUBBLICO V.le OP10 326
GIARDINO C. dietro il P10 326
GIUFFA APOLLONIA Ruga J7 324
GIUFFA Ruga K6 324
GORNE C. d. M7 325
GRANDIBEN C. M8 325
GRECI C. d. L7 324
GRECI Salizz. d. L7 324
GRIMANA C.te N8/9 326
GRITTI C. M7 325
LARGA C. J6 324

LARGA C. M8 325
LION C. d. L7 324
LOREDAN C. O8 326
MADONNA C. d. K5/6 324
MADONNA C. d. L7 324
MADONNETA C. d. K6 324
MAGAZEN C. d. L7 324
MAGAZEN C. dietro il K7 324
MAGAZEN C.te d. P9 326
MAGNO C. M7 325
MALATINA C. M6 325
MALVASIA Ramo d. J6 324
MALVASIA VECCHIA C. L8 324
MALVASIA VECCHIA C. M8 325
MANDOLIN C. M7 325
MARAFANI C. P8 326
MARCELLO Ramo O9 326
MARINAI D'ITALIA L.go OP10 324
MARTIN NOVELLO C.te P9 326
MARTINENGO C. d. J6 324
MAZZA NICOLO' C. L5 324
MENDICANTI Fond. d. K4/5 324
MERCANTI C. d. K7 324
MEZZO C. d. K6 324
MEZZO C. d. L6 324
MICHIEL C.te K7 324
MONDO NOVO C. d. J6 324
MORION C. d. M6 325
MOROSINA C. M8 325
MOROSINA Ramo M8 325
MORUZZI C. L7 324
MOSCHETTE C. d. L5 324
MOSCHETTE Ramo d. L5 324
MUAZZO C. L6 324
MUAZZO C.te L6 324
MUNEGHE C.te d. MN6 325
MUNEGHETTE C. d. M7 325
MUSATTA O TOSCA C. J6 324
NAVE C. d. J6 324
NICOL Ramo d. P9 326
NUOVA C.te C7 324
NUOVA C.te O8 326
NUOVE Fond. KL4/5 324
OCCHIO GROSSO C. d. M7 325
OLE C. d. P8 326
OLIO C. d. M6 325
OLIVI C. d. O9 326
OLIVI C. d. M6 325
ORATORIO C. d. M6 325
ORBI C. d. K6 324
ORBI C.te d. K6 324
ORTI C. d. M6 325
OSMARIN Fond. d. K7 324
OSPEDALE C. d. K6 324
PADOVANI Ramo d. K7 324
PARADISO C. d. J6 324
PASSION C. J6/7 324
PEDROCCHI C. N9 326
PEGOLA C. d. M8 325
PEGOLA Ramo 1 M8 325
PENNINI Fond. M7 325
PERINA C.te d. M7 325
PESCARIA Ramo M8 325
PESCHIERA C.te M7 325
PESTRIN C. d. M7 325
PIANTON C. d. K7 324
PIASENTINI C. J7 324
PIETA' C.llo L7 324
PIETA' C. d. L7 324
PIETA' C. dietro la L7 324
PIETA' C.te d. L7 324
PIETRO D. LESINA C.te O9 326
PIGNATER Salizz. d. M7 325
PINDEMONTE C. J6 324
PINELLI C. K6 324
PIOMBO C. J6 324
PIOVAN C.llo d. L8 324
PIOVAN Fond. d. M7/8 324

PISTOR Sott. C. N9 326
POLACCA C.te N8/9 326
Ponte d.ARCO C. M7 325
Ponte S. ANTONIO C. H6 324
POZZENO C. M7 325
POZZO ROVERSO C.te d. K6/7 324
PRETE C.te d. P9 326
PRETI C. d. KL7 324
PRETI C. d O8 326
QUERINI C.llo J6 324
QUERINI C. J6/7 324
QUERINI C. L7 324
RAMO 1 P10 326
RAMO 2 P10 326
RAMO 3 P10 326
RAMO 4 P10 326
RASSE C. d. K7 324
RIELLO C. M7 325
RIELLO C. P8 326
RIELLO Fond. P8 326
RIELLO Ramo P8 326
RIMEDIO C. d. J7 324
RIMEDIO Fond. J7 324
ROSA C.te K7 324
ROSARIO C.te J7 324
ROTTA C. C.te K7 324
ROTTA C.te K7 324
ROTTA C.te M7 325
ROTTA Sott. C.te K7 324
RUGA C. P8 326
RUGA C.po d. P8 326
S. BIAGIO C.po d. Fianco la chiesa MN8 325
S. BIAGIO C.po d. M8 325
S. BIAGIO Riva M8 325
S. DANIELE C.po P7 326
S. DANIELE Ramo P7 326
S. DOMENICO C. O9 326
S. FRANCESCO C. L6 324
S. FRANCESCO D. VIGNA C.po M6 325
S. FRANCESCO DA PAOLA C. O8 326
S. FRANCESCO Salizz. M6 325
S. GIACCHINO C. P8 326
S. GIACCHINO Fond. P8 326
S. GIORGIO D. SCHIAVONI Fond. L6/7 324
S. GIOVANNI C. P8 326
S. GIOVANNI C.te L7 324
S. GIOVANNI LATERANO C. K6 324
S. GIOVANNI LATERANO Fond. K6 324
S. GIOVANNI NUOVO C.po JK7 324
S. GIUSEPPE C.po P10 326
S. GIUSEPPE Fond. P9 326
S. GIUSEPPE Rio terà P10 326
S. LIO Salizz. J6 324
S. LORENZO BORGOLOCO K6 324
S. LORENZO C. Larga K6 324
S. LORENZO C. L6 324
S. LORENZO C.po L6 324
S. LORENZO Fond. d. K7 324
S. MARTINO C.po M7 325
S. MARTINO Piscina M7 325
S. PIETRO C. Larga P8 326
S. PROVOLO C. K7 324
S. PROVOLO C.po K7 324
S. PROVOLO Salizz. K7 324
S. SEVERO Fond. d. K7 324
S. ZACCARIA C. K7 324
S. ZACCARIA C.po d. K7 324
S. ZACCARIA Sott. K7 324
S.TA GIUSTINA C.po L6 324
S.TA GIUSTINA d. BARBARIA C.llo L6 324

S.TA GIUSTINA Fond. L5/6 324
S.TA GIUSTINA Salizz. L6 324
S.TA MARIA FORMOSA C. Lunga K6 324
S.TA MARIA FORMOSA C.po J6 324
S.TA MARINA C.po d. J5/6 324
S.TA SCOLASTICA C. J7 324
SABBIONERA C.te P9 326
SAGREDO C. M6 325
SAGREDO Ramo 2 M6 325
SALOMON C. P8 326
SALVIANI Ramo L7 324
SANT'ANNA C. P8 326
SANT'ANNA Fond. P9 326
SANT'ANTONIN C.po L7 324
SANT'ANTONIN Salizz. L7 324
SANT'ANTONIO C. J6 324
SANT'ANTONIO Paludo P10 326
SANTI ALLA TANA Sott. N8 326
SANTI C.te N8 326
SANTI Sott. C. N8 326
SARESIN C. stretta O9 326
SARESIN C.llo O9 326
SARESIN C.te O9 326
SCALETTA C. J6 324
SCHIAVONA C. O9 326
SCHIAVONA C.te O9 326
SCHIAVONCINA C. K6 324
SCHIAVONI Riva. d. KL8 324
SCUDI C. d. M7 325
SECCO MARINA P9 326
SECCO MARINA C. O9 326
SETTE MARTIRI Riva N9 326
SOLDA C.te P9 326
SORANZO C.te M7 325
SPORCA C. P8 326
SQUERO C.llo d. N9 326
SS. FILIPPO E GIACOMO C.po JK7 324
SS. GIOVANNI E PAOLO C.po K5 324
SS. GIOVANNI E PAOLO Salizz. K5 324
STELLA Sott. P8 326
STRETTA C. M8 325
STRETTA Salizz. P7/8 326
STUA C. d. O9 326
TAGLIACALZE C. N8/9 326
TANA C.po d. N8 325
TANA Fond. d. NO8 325
TEDEUM C. d. L6 324
TERCO C. P8 326
TERRAZZERA C. L7 324
TETTA Fond. K6 324
TIEPOLO GB C. P9 326
TOLE BARBARIA D. K6 324
TORELLI D. CAVALLERIZZA. C. K5 324
TRENTO V.le P10 326
TREVISANA C. K6 324
TRIESTE V.le P10 326
VECCHIA C. O9 326
VELE C. d. J6 324
VENIER C. d. K5/6 324
VIDA C. d. M8 325
VIDA Ramo d. M6 325
VIN C. d. K7 324
VIN C.llo d. K7 324
VIN Fond. d. K7 324
VOLTO C. d. J6 324
ZEN C. L6 324
ZIO Ramo d. P8 326
ZORZI C. L6 324
ZORZI Salizz. K7 324
ZURIN Sott. P8 326

SANT'ELENA
ARCO C. 1 d. Q10 326
ARCO C. 2 d. Q10 326

ASIAGO C. Q10 326
ASILO C. d. Q10 326
BAINSIZZA C. Q11 326
CANTORE GENERALE C.
 Q11 326
CARNARO C. d. Q11 326
CARSO C. d. Q11 326
CASINO C. d. Q8 326
CASTELOLIVOLO Fond. Q8 326
CENGIO C. d. Q10 326
CENGIO Ramo Q10 326
CHINOTTO GENERALE C.
 Q11 326
DIETRO IL CAMPANILE C.
 PQ8 326
DUCA D'AOSTA C. Q11 326
FARI C. d. Q9 326
FORNER C. d. Q10 326
GORIZIA C. Q11 326
INDIPENDENZA C.po d.
 Q11 326
MEZZO C. d. Q8 326
MONTELLO C. d. Q10 326
MONTELLO C.te d. Q10 326
MONTELLO Ramo d. Q10 326
MONTESANO C. Q10 326
NEVERSA C. Q10 326
OSLAVIA C. Q10/11 326
PASUBIO C. d. Q10 326
PASUBIO Ramo d. Q10 326
PODGORA C. Q11 326
POMERI C. d. Q8 326
POMERI C.po d. Q8/9 326
POZZO C. d. Q10 326
QUATTRO NOVEMBRE V.le
 Q10 326
QUINTAVALLE C. PQ8 326
QUINTAVALLE Fond. PQ8 326
QUINTAVALLE Ramo 2 Q8 326
QUINTAVALLE C. Lunga Q8 326
ROVERETO C. Q11 326
S. PIETRO C.po Q8 326
SABOTINO C. d. Q11 326
STORTA C. Sott. Q10 326
VENTIQUATTRO MAGGIO V.le
 Q10 326
VIGNA C.llo Q8 326
VITTORIO VENETO V.le
 Q11/12 326
ZUGNA C. Q11 326
ZUGNA Ramo Q11 326

CANNAREGIO
ABBAZIA C.po d. GH3 321
ABBAZIA Fond. d. GH3 321
ALBANESI C. d. H4 321
ALBANESI Ramo H4 321
ALBERANO C. E2 321
ANCONETTA C. F3 321
ANCONETTA C.llo d. F3 321
ANGELO C. d. C2 320
ANGELO C. d. J5 324
ARMAI C. H5 324
ARRIGONI C. F2 321
ASEO C. d. F2/3 321
BALLERAN C. B2 320
BANDIERA C.te C2 320
BARBA FRUTTAROLI Rio terà
 H4 324
BARBARO C.te H4 324
BARBIER Sott. d. C2 320
BATTAGLIA C. J4 324
BATTELLO C.llo d. D2 320
BATTELLO Fond. d. CD2 320
BECCARIE C. d. B2 320
BECCARIE C.llo d. B2 320
BIRRI Rio terà d. J4/5 324
BISCOTELLA C. B2 320
BOLZA C. F3 321
BORGATO Salizz. L. H4 324
BOSELLO C. C2 320

BOSELLO C.po C3 320
BOTTERI C. Larga D. JK4 324
BRACCIO NUDO C. B2 320
BRAGATIN C. H5 324
BRAZZO C. F2 321
BRIANI C. E2 321
BURANELLI C. JK4 324
BURANELLI C. K4 324
CA D'ORO Ramo G4 321
CA' D'ORO C. d G4 321
CA' MEMO C.llo E3 321
CADENE C. d. J3 324
CALDERER C. F2 321
CAMPANIEL C. J5 324
CANAL Fond. F3 321
CANDELE C. J3 324
CANNAREGIO Fond.
 BC1/2 320
CANNE C. d. B2 320
CANOSSIANE C. Larga F1 321
CAPITELLO C. d. E1/2 321
CAPPUCCINE C. d. D1 320
CAPPUCCINE Fond. D1/2 320
CARITA' C.te J4 324
CARMELITANI C. BC3/4 320
CASE NUOVE C. d. E3 321
CASE NUOVE Fond. C1 320
CASON C.llo H5 324
CASTELLI C. J5 324
CAVALLO C.te F1/2 321
CENDON C. C2 320
CENDON C.te C3 320
CERERIA C. d. B2 320
CHIESA C. d. E3 321
CHIESA C.llo G3 321
CHIESA Fond. d. G4 321
CHIOVERE C. Lunga CD2 320
CHIOVERETTE C. d. D2 320
CHIOVERETTE Fond. d. D2 320
CIODI C. B2 320
CIURIAN C. H5 324
COLETTI Fond.C. C1 320
COLOMBINA C. J4 324
COLOMBINA C.llo F3 321
COLOMBINA C.te d. C2 320
COLOMBINA C.te F3 321
COLONNA C. E3 321
COLONNE C. F3 321
COLORI C. d. B2 320
COLORI C. d. H3 321
COMMELLO C. J5 324
CONTARINI C. D1/2 320
CONTARINI Fond. D1 320
CONTARINI GASPARRO Fond.
 G2 321
CONTERIE C. D1 320
CONTIERE C. d. E3 321
COOPERATIVE C.llo C1/2 320
CORDA BIANCHERIA C. B2 320
CORDELLINA C. F2 321
CORDONI C. d. J4 324
CORNER C.llo H5 324
CORRENTE C. H4 321
CORRER C. E3 321
CORRER C. F3 321
CORTESE C. JK4/5 324
CREA Rio terà C2 320
CRISTO C. d. EF3 321
CRISTO C. d. H4 321
CRISTO C.te H4 321
CRISTO Rio terà d. E3 321
CRISTO Sott. d. C2 320
CROCI C. d. J4 324
CROCIFERI C. d. J3 324
CROTTA Fond. D4 320
DIAMANTE Sott. d. G3 321
DIEDO Fond. FG3 321
DIETRO LA CHIESA Rio terà
 E3 321
DIETRO LE SCUOLE C. J5 324
DOGE PRIULI C. Larga G4 321

DONA Ramo J3/4 324
DRAGAN Ramo H5 324
DUCA C. d. H4 324
DUE CORTI C. 2 d. C3 320
DUE CORTI C. G2 321
DUE POZZI Ruga H4 321
EMO C. E3 321
ERBE C. d. J5 324
ERBE C. H4 321
FACCHINI C.te d. G3 321
FARNESE C. E2 321
FARSETTI Rio terà E3 321
FELZI Fond. G4 321
FERAU C.te d. C1 320
FIORI C.llo d. FG4 321
FLANGINI C. D3 320
FORNASA VECIA C. de la
 E1 321
FORNASA VECIA C.llo de la
 D1 320
FORNASA VECIA Fond. de la
 D1 320
FORNER C. d. C1 320
FORNER C. G2 321
FORNER Fond. d. G3 321
FORNO C. d. F2/3 321
FORNO C. d. GH4 321
FORNO C. d. HJ5 324
FORNO C. d. J4/5 324
FORNO C. d. D2/3 320
FORNO C. d. D4 320
FOSCANNI C. M. J3 324
FRANCESCANI Rio terà H4 321
FUMO C. d. J4 324
GABRIELLA C. K5 324
GALLINA G C. Larga J5 324
GARNACE Fond. E2 321
GESUITI C.po d. J4 324
GHELTOF C. F2 321
GHETTO NUOVISSIMO C.
 E2 321
GHETTO NUOVO C.po d.
 E2 321
GHETTO NUOVO Fond. E2 321
GHETTO VECCHIO Sott. d.
 D3 320
GHETTO VECCHIO E2 321
GIOACCHINA C. D3 320
GIURATI Fond. F1 321
GIUSTINIANA C.te B1 320
GONELLA C.te C. B2 320
GRADISCO C. F1/2 321
GREGOLINA C. G2 321
GRIMANI Fond. F3 321
GRUPPI C. G2/3 321
GUGLIE Ponte D3 320
LABIA FOND D3 320
LARGA C. FG2/3 321
LAVANDER C. Larga B2 320
LEGNAME C. Larga D. F1 321
LEGNAMI C. d. J3 324
LEZZE C. Larga G3 321
LEZZE C.te F2 321
LIMARTE C.te D2 320
LISTA DI SPAGNA Rio terà
 CD3/4 320
LOMBARDO C. F3 321
LOREDAN C. F2 321
LOVO C.te d. H3 321
LUGANEGHERI C.po d. A2 320
MADDALENA C.po F3 321
MADDALENA Rio terà d.
 F3 321
MADONNA C. d. C2 320
MADONNA C. d. H4 324
MADONNA C. d. J4 324
MADONNA C. B2 320
MADONNA DELL'ORTO C.po
 G2 321
MADONNA DELL'ORTO Fond.
 F2 321

MAGAZEN C. B2 320
MAGAZEN C. E2 321
MAGAZEN C. H5 321
MAGAZEN Ramo E3 321
MAGGIONI C. J5 324
MAGGIORE C. E3 321
MALVASIA C. d. EF2 321
MASENA C. d. E2/3 321
MASENA Ramo E2/3 321
MELONI C. K5 324
MILION C.te d. H5 324
MIRACOLI C. J5 324
MISERICORDIA C. d. C3/4 320
MISERICORDIA C.po Ramo
 G3 321
MISERICORDIA Fond. d.
 FG3 321
MISERICORDIA Ramo d.
 C3 320
MODENA C. H5 324
MORA C. J4 324
MORANDI C. J4 324
MORI C.po d. G2 321
MORI Fond. d. FG2 321
MORO Fond. G3 321
MOSTO BALBI C. d. D3 320
MOSTO C.te E3 321
MUNEGHE C. d. F2 321
MUTI C.te d. G2/3 321
MUTI Ramo D. G2 321
NOVA Strada G4 321
NUOVA C. D1 320
NUOVA C. E3 321
NUOVA C. J4 321
NUOVE Fond. HJ3 324
OCA C. d. H4 324
OLIO C. d. F4 321
OLIO C. E3 321
ORMESINI Fond. d. E2 321
ORMESINI C. d. E2 321
ORTO C. E2 321
PAGLIA C. d. E3 321
PALI C.te d. G4 321
PALUDO C.te d. K4/5 324
PANADA C. J5 324
PAZIENZA C.llo C2 320
PEGOLOTTO C.te F3 321
PEGOLOTTO Sott. d. EF3 321
PENITENTI C. Larga d.
 BC1 320
PERLIERI C. d. E3 321
PESARO C. C3 320
PESARO C.llo B2 320
PESARO C.llo C3 320
PESCARIA Fond. D2/3 320
PIAVE C. Larga G2 321
PIAVE C.llo G1 321
PICIUTTA C.te E1/2 321
PIETA' C. d. J4 324
PIGNATE C. G3 321
PIGNATER D. TABACCO C.
 F2/3 321
PISANI C.te E1/2 321
PISTOR C. d. G4 321
PISTOR Salizz. d. H4 324
PONTE STORTO C.llo F3 321
PORPORA C. C1/2 320
PORTON C. d. E2 321
POSTA C. HJ4 324
POZZO Sott. C.llo D3 320
PRESTIN C. J5 324
PRETI C. d. E3 321
PRETI Sott. G4 321
PRIMA C. B2 320
PRIULI C. H4 321
PRIULI detta D. CAVALLETTI
 C. C3/4 320
PRIULI Fond. H4 321
PROCURATIE C. d. D3 320
PROPRIA C. JK4 324
QUERINI C. E3 321

RABBIA C. d. E3 321
RACCHETTA C. d. H3/4 321
REMIER C.llo E3 321
RETIER C. J4 324
RETIER C.te J4 324
RIELLO C. CD3 320
RIFORMATI C. d. E1 321
RIFORMATI Fond. d.. E1 321
RIZZO C. D1/2 320
RIZZO C.te F3 321
ROTONDA C. d. E1 321
ROZZINI C. K4 324
RUBINI C. E2 321
S. CANCIANO C.po HJ5 324
S. CANCIANO Salizz. HJ5 324
S. FELICE C. G4 321
S. FELICE C.po G4 321
S. FELICE Fond. G3/4 321
S. FOSCA C.po G3 321
S. GEREMIA C.po D3 320
S. GEREMIA Salizz. D3 320
S. GIOBBE C.po C2 320
S. GIOBBE Fond. d. B1/2 320
S. GIOVANNI C. d. D2 320
S. GIOVANNI CRISOSTOMO
Salizz. H5 324
S. GIOVANNI Ramo D. D2 320
S. GIROLAMO C. D1/2 320
S. GIROLAMO FOND D1/2
320
S. LEONARDO C.po E3 321
S. LEONARDO Rio terà E3
321
S. MARCUOLA C.po E3 321
S. MARZIALE C.po G3 321
S.TA CATERINA C.Lunga
H3 321
S.TA CATERINA Fond. H3 321
S.TA LUCIA Fond. BC4/5 320
S.TA MARIA NOVA C.llo
J5 324
S.TA MARIA NOVA C.po
J5 324
SABBIONI Rio terà D. D4 320
SACCA S. GIROLAMO Fond. d.
BC1 320
SACCHIERE C.te EF1 321
SALAMON C. d. E4 321
SANT'ANDREA Fond. H4 321
SANT'ALVISE C.po d. EF1 321
SANT'ANTONIO C. E3 321
SANT'ANTONIO C.po H3 324
SAON C. d. B2 320
SARTORI C. d. H4 324
SARTORI Fond. d. H4 324
SAVORGNAN Fond.
CD2/3 320
SCALA MATTA C.te D2 320
SCALZI Fond. d. C4 320
SCALZI Ponte C4 320
SCARLATTO C. d. B2 320
SCUOLA D. BOTTERI C.
J3 324
SCUOLE C.llo d. D2 320
SCURO C. d. Sott. C2 320
SELLE C. E2/3 321
SENSA Fond. d. E2 321
SERIMAN Salizz. J4 324
SORANZO C. E3 321
SPECCHIERI Salizz. D. J3 324
SPEZIER C. d. D4 320
SQUERO C. d. H4 324
SQUERO C. d. K4 324
SQUERO C. D2 320
SQUERO VECCHIO C. d.
J5 324
SQUERO VECCHIO Ramo
H4 321
SS. APOSTOLI C.po H5 324
SS. APOSTOLI Rio terà
H4 324

STELLA C. J4 324
STUA C. d. G4 321
TAGLIAPIETRA C. d. H4 324
TAGLIAPIETRE Ramo D.
CD3/4 320
TEATRO C.te H5 324
TESTA C. d. JK5 324
TINTOR C. d. B2 320
TINTORETTO C. C.te G2 321
TINTORIA C. C2 320
TIRACANNA C. d. E2/3 321
TRAGHETTO C. d. HJ4/5 324
TRAGHETTO C. d. G4 321
TRAPOLIN Fond. G3 321
TRE ARCHI Ponte d. C2 320
TREVISAN C. d. G3 321
TREVISAN C.llo d. G3 321
TURLONA C. E2 321
VALBARANA C. H4 324
VARISCO C. J4 324
VECCHIA C.te G2/3 321
VELE C. d. GH4 321
VENDRAMIN C. Larga F3 321
VENDRAMIN C. F3 321
VENDRAMIN Fond. G3 321
VENIER C. J4 324
VENIER Fond. D3 320
VERDE C. d. B2 320
VERDE C. d. H4 321
VERGOLA C. D3 320
VERLENDIS C. Larga K4 324
VIDA C. J4 324
VITELLI C.te d. CD2 320
VITTORIO EMANUELE Via
FG3 321
VOLTI C. J4 324
VOLTO C. d. J4 324
WIDMAN C. J5 324
WIDMAN C.llo J5 324
ZANARDI C. H4 321
ZANCANI C. G3 321
ZAPPA C.te E2 321
ZEN Fond. HJ4 324
ZOCCOLO C. G3 321
ZOLFO C. E2/3 321
ZOLFO Ramo d. E2/3 321
ZOTTI C. G4 321
ZUDIO C. E2 321
ZULIAN Sott. G4 321

SAN POLO
ALBANESI C. d. D6 320
ALBANESI C. d. E6 321
ALBRIZZI C. F5 321
ALBRIZZI C.llo F5 321
AMOR DEGLI AMICI C.
E6 321
ANGELO C. G5 321
ARCO C. d. G5 321
BADEOR C.te E6 321
BANCO SALVIATI C. F5 321
BARBARIZZA C. FG6 321
BATTISTI C C. G5 321
BECCARIE C. G5 321
BECCARIE C.po d. G5 321
BERNARDO C. F5 321
BERNARDO Ramo F5 321
BIANCA CAPPELLO C. F6 321
BO C. d. G5 321
BOLLANI C.te F5 321
BOTTA C. F5 321
BOTTERI C. d. FG5 321
BUSINELLO C. F6 321
BUSINELLO Fond. F6 321
CAFFETTIER C. E6 321
CALDERER C.te E5 321
CALICE C. d. E5 321
CAMPANEL C. E2 323
CAMPANILE C. d. G5 321
CAMPANILE C. d. G5/6 321
CAMPAZZO C. d. D5 320

CAMPAZZO Ramo D5 320
CAPPELLER C. d. G5 321
CAPPELLER Sott. G5 321
CASSETTI Ramo E6 321
CAVALLI C. d. F6 321
CHIESA C. d. E5 321
CHIESA C.po d. E5 321
CHIOVERE C.llo D6 320
CHIVERE C. d. D6 320
CIMESIN Ramo CD6 320
CINQUE C. d. G6 321
COLLALTO C. E5 321
CONTARIN C.te F6 321
CONTARINI Fond. E6 321
CORNER C. E6 321
CORTI C. d. E6 321
CRISTI C. d. E5 321
CRISTO C. d. E1 323
CRISTO C. d. EF5 321
CURNIS C.llo G6 321
DANDOLO C. E2 323
DIETRO CASTELFORTE C.
D6 320
DIETRO L'ARCHIVIO C.
D5/6 320
DOANETTA C. E6 321
DOGANA DI TERRA C. G6 321
DOLERA C. FG6 321
DONA O SPEZIER C.
E5/6 321
DONZELLA C. 1 d. G5 321
DONZELLA C. d. G5 321
ERBARIA H5 321
ERBE C. F6 321
FIGHER C. d. G5 321
FONDERIA C. D5/6 320
FORNER C.llo d. E5 321
FORNER Fond. d. E2 323
FORNER Ramo d. EF5 321
FORNO C. d. E6 321
FORNO C. d. F6 321
FRARI C.po d. E6 321
FRARI Fond. E6 321
FRUTTAROLA C. d. F5/6 321
FRUTTAROLA Fond. F5/6 321
GALEZZA C. G5 321
GALIZZI C. G6 321
GALLIPOLI C. Stretta D6 320
GAMBERO C. d. GH6 321
GOZZI G C. D6 322
LACA C. d. D5 320
LARGA C. E1 323
LARGA C. D6 321
LATE Fond. D5 320
LUGANEGHER C. F6 321
MADONNA C. d. F6 321
MADONNA C. d. G5/6 321
MADONNA C. F6 321
MADONNETTA Sott. C.
F6 321
MAGAZEN C. D6 320
MAGAZEN C. F6 321
MALVASIA C. E6 321
MELONI C.llo F6 321
MEZZO C. d. CD5 320
MEZZO C. d. F6 321
MIANI C. G5 321
MICHIEL C.te G5 321
MORO C. E6 321
MUTI C. d. F5 321
MUTI O BAGLIONI C. F5 321
NARANZERIA H5/6 321
NOMBOLI C. d. E6 321
NUOVA C.te D5 320
OLIO C. d. D5 320
OLIO C. d. G6 321
OLIO Fond. d. G6 321
OREFICI Ruga d. GH5 321
OSTERIA DI CAMPANA
G5 321
PARADISO C. d. G6 321

PARRUCCHETTA Rio terà d.
E5 321
PASSION C. d. E6 321
PERDON C. F6 321
PESCARIA C.po d. G5 321
PEZZANA O TASSO C.
EF5/6 321
PINO C. E5 321
PISANI Ramo E6 321
PISTOR C. d. E5 321
PISTOR C.te E5 321
POSTE VECCHIE C. G5 321
POZZETTO Sott. C. G5 321
POZZOLUNGO C.llo E5 321
RAFFINERIA C. F5 321
RAMPANI C. F5 321
RAMPANI Rio terà F5 321
RASPI C. G5 321
RAVANO Rughetta d. G6 321
REMER C.te d. F6 321
RIALTO Ponte d. H6 321
RIALTO NUOVO C.po G5 321
RIO TERA' C. E6 321
RIVETTA C. G5 321
RIZZO C. F5 321
RIZZO Ramo F5 321
S. BOLDO C.po E5 321
S. CASSIANO C.po F5 321
S. GIACOMO C.po GH5 321
S. GIOVANNI Ruga vecchia
G5 321
S. NICOLETTO C. D6 320
S. NICOLETTO Ramo D6 320
S. POLO C.po F6 321
S. POLO Salizz. EF6 321
S. ROCCO C.po D6 320
S. ROCCO Salizz. D6 320
S. SILVESTRO C.po G6 321
S. SILVESTRO Fond. G6 321
S. SILVESTRO Rio terà
G6 321
S. STIN C.po E6 321
S. TOMA C.po E6 321
S. TOMA Rio terà D6 320
SACCHERE C. d. C5 320
SACCHERE Fond. d. C5 320
SALE C.llo G5 321
SALE C. G5 321
SANSONI C.llo d. G5 321
SANT'AGOSTIN C.po E5 321
SANT'ANTONIO Rio terà
F6 321
SANT'APONAL C.po FG6 321
SANUDO C. E6 321
SAONERI C. 2 E6 321
SAONERI C. E6 321
SBIANCHESINI C. d. G6 321
SCALETER C. d. EF5 321
SCIMMIA C. d. dietro la
G5 321
SCIMMIA C. d. G5 321
SCOAZZERA Rio terà d.
FG5 321
SCRIMIA C. G5 321
SCUOLA C.llo D5 320
SCUOLA C. fianco D6 320
SECONDO Rio terà E5 321
SORANZO C. E5/6 321
SORANZO Ramo E5/6 321
SPADE Sott. G5 321
SPEZIALI Ruga d. G5 321
STIVALETTO C. G6 321
STORIONE C. d. G6 321
STRETTA C. F6 321
TABACCO C. E5 321
TEATRO VECCHIO C. G5 321
TIEPOLO C. EF5/6 321
TIEPOLO C.te E5 321
TINTORETTO C. G6 321
TODESCHINI C. F6 321
TOSCANA C. G5/6 321

STREET INDEX

Street Index

TRAGHETTO C. d. F6 321
TRAGHETTO C. E7 323
TRAGHETTO Fond. E6/7 323
UGANEGHER C. d. G6 321
VIDA C. d. E5 321
VIN Fond. d. GH6 321
VITALBA C. D5 320
VITALBA C.te D5 320
VOLTI C. d. E6 321
VOLTO Ruga vecchia G5 321
ZANE C. E5 321
ZEN C. E6 321

SANTA CROCE
AGNELLO C. d. F5 321
AGNELLO Fond. d. F5 321
AGNELLO Ramo d. F5 321
ALBANESI C. F4 321
AMAI C.te d. C5 320
ANATOMIA C.te E5 321
ARNALDI Ramo C6 320
BALDAN C. D5 320
BARBO Ramo CD6/7 322
BARI C. Larga d. D4 320
BARI Lista d. D4 320
BATTOCCHIO C.te C5 320
BATTOCCHIO Sott. C5 320
BEMBO C. E4 321
BERGAMASCHI C. C5 320
BERGAMASCHI C.te C5 320
BERGAMI C. D4 320
BERNARDO C. B6 320
BERNARDO Ramo B6 320
BEZZO C. C6 320
BIASIO Riva d. D4 320
BRAGADIN C. F5 321
BURCHIELLE FOND d. AB6 320
CAMPANILE O DEI PRETI C.
F4 321
CANAL C.te D5 320
CAPPELLO C. E5 321
CARMINATI Salizz. EF4/5 321
CASE NUOVE C. C5 320
CAZZA C. E4 321
CAZZA C.te E4 321
CHIESA C. d. F5 321
CHIESA Salizz. d. D4 320
CHIOVERETTE C. d. C5 320
CHIOVERETTE C. Lunga
  CD4 320
CHIOVERETTE Ramo CD5 320
CLERO C. C6 320
COLOMBO Ramo d. E4 321
COLONNE C.te E4 321
COMARE C.llo C4 320
COMARE C.llo E4 321
CONDULMER Fond. C6 320
CONTARINA C. Larga D5 320
CORNER C. F4 321
CORREGGIO C. po E4 321
CORRER C. E4 321
CORRERA C. D4 320
CORRERA C.te D4 320
COSSETTI Fond. B5 320
COSSETTI Ramo B6 320
CREMONESE C. B6 320
CRISTO C. d. D5 320
CRISTO C.llo D5 320
CROCE C. d. D4/5 320
CROCE Fond. D5 320
DARIO C.llo C5 320
DARIO Sott. C5 320
FABBRICA TABACCHI Fond.
AB6 320
FABBRO Ramo d. F5 321
FALIER C. C6 320
FILOSI C. F5 321
FORNER C. F4 321
FORNO C. d. CD6 320
FORNO C. d. F4 321
FORNO C. C5 320

GALLION C. D4 320
GALLION Ramo 1 D4 320
GALLION Ramo 2 D4 320
GALLION Ramo 3 D4 320
GALLION Ramo 4 D4 320
GALLION Ramo 5 D4 320
GESU E MARIA C. d. C5 320
GIOVANELLI C.te E4 321
GRADENIGO Fond. D4/5 320
GRADISCA C. D5 320
GRUE Fond. d. F5 321
ISOLA C. d E4 321
ISOLA C.llo d. E4 321
LANA C.po d. C5 320
LARGA C. E4 321
LAVADORI C. BC6 320
LAVADORI C.llo B6 320
LUNGA C. F5 321
MADONNA C. C6 320
MAGAZEN Sott. C. F5 321
MALIPIERO C.te D5 320
MALIPIERO Sott. D5 320
MARIONI C. Sott. E5 321
MEGIO C. d. E4 321
MEGIO Fond. d. E4 321
MERCANTI C.te E4 321
MEZZO C. d. E5 321
MINOTTO Fond. C6 320
MODENA C. d. EF5 321
MOLIN C. D6 320
MONASTERO Fond. d. C5 320
MORTI C. d. F5 321
MORTI C.llo d. E4 321
MOSCHE C.llo CD6 320
MUNEGHETTE C.llo d. C5 320
NERINI C.llo D5 320
NONZOLO C. F5 321
NUOVA C.te D6 320
NUOVA Ramo D6 320
OCHE C. d. E5 321
OCHE Ramo E5 321
ORSETTI C. D4 320
PAGAN Fond. B6 320
PAPADOPOLI Fond. B5 320
PARRUCCHETTA Fond.
  E5 321
PENSIERI C. d. AB6 320
PENSIERI Rio terà d. B6 320
PESARO C. F4 321
PESARO Fond. F4 321
PIOVAN C.llo E4 321
PISANI C. D4 320
PISTOR C. d. D4 320
PRETI C. d. E4 321
PRiva.TA C. EF4 321
PUGLIESE C. d. E4 321
RAVANO C. d. F4 321
REGINA C. d. F5 321
REGINA Ramo F5 321
RIELLO C.po E4 321
RIMPETTO MOCENIGO Fond.
  F4 321
RIO MARIN Fond. D5 320
RIO MARIN O GARZOTTI Fond.
  D4/5 320
RIO TERA' E4 321
RIODA Ramo F4 321
RIZZI Fond. B7 322
ROMA P.le B5 320
ROSA C. d. F4/5 321
ROSA Ramo d. F5 321
ROTTA C.te E4 321
RUGA BELLA E5 321
RUGA VECCHIA C.te E4 321
S. GIACOMO DELL'ORIO C.po
E5 321
S. GIOVANNI DECOLLATO
  C.po E4 321
S. PANTALON Salizz. C6 320
S. SIMEON C. Nuova
  C4/5 320

S. SIMEON PICCOLO Fond.
  C4/5 320
S. SIMEON PROFETA C.po
  D4 320
S. STAE C.po F4 321
S. STAE Salizz. F4 321
S. ZUANE C. D5 320
S. ZUANE Ramo D5 320
S.TA CHIARA Fond. AB5 320
S.TA MARIA MAGGIORE Fond.
  d. AB7 322
SAGREDO C. D4 320
SANT'ANDREA C.po A5 320
SANT'ANDREA Fond. B6 320
SANT'ANDREA Rio terà
  A6 320
SARASIN C. D4 320
SAURO N C.po D5 320
SAVIA C. d. E4 321
SCURA C.te EF4 321
SPEZIER C. E4 321
SPIRITI C. D4 320
SPIRITI C.te C6 320
SPORCA C. D4 320
SQUARTAI D4 320
STORTO C.po E5 321
STRADON Ramo d. D5 320
STROPE C.po d. E5 321
TABACCHI C. Nuova d.
AB6 320
TAGLIAPIETRA C.te C5 320
TEATRO C. d. F5 321
TEATRO Ramo d. F5 321
TESTORI Fond. A5 320
TETTE Fond. d. F5 321
TINTO C. d. EF4 321
TINTOR C. E5 321
TINTOR C.te F5 321
TIOSSI C. F5 321
TIOSSI C.te F4 321
TOLENTINI C.po C6 320
TOLENTINI C.zzo d. C5 320
TOLENTINI Fond. C5/6 320
TRAGHETTO DI SAN LUCA C.
  C4/5 320
TRE PONTI C.zzo B6 320
TRE PONTI Fond. B6 320
TRON C. F4 321
TURCHI Fond. d. E4 321
VENZATO C. D5 320
VINANTI C. D6 320
VISCIGA C. D5 320
VOLTO C. B5 320
ZAMBELLI C. E5 321
ZEN C. D4 320
ZEN Ramo D4 320
ZINELLI C.te D4 320
ZIO Sott. C6 320
ZUSTO Salizz. E4 321

DORSODURO
ABATE C.te d. F9 323
ABBAZIA C. G9 323
ALBERTI Fond. D8 322
AMBASCIATORI Ramo D8 322
ANGART C.llo D7 322
ANGELO RAFFAELE C.po
  B8 322
ARZERE Fond. d. A7 322
AVOGARIA C. d. BC8 322
AVOGARIA C.llo d. BC8 322
BALASTRO C. BC8 322
BALASTRO C.llo C8 322
BALBI C. E7 323
BARBARIGO Fond. AB8 322
BARBARO C. F9 323
BARBARO C.po F9 323
BARI Fond. d. A8 322
BASTION C. F9 323
BERNARDO C. D7 322
BEVILACQUA C. AB8 322

BEVILACQUA C.te AB8 322
BISATI Sott. E9 323
BOLDU C. D6/7 322
BOLLANI Fond. D8 322
BONAZZO C.te B7 322
BONFADINA C.te CD8 322
BONTINI C. D9 322
BONTINI Fond. D9 322
BORGO Fond. d. D8 322
BOTTEGHE C. D7/8 322
BRAGADIN Fond. E9 323
BRIANI C. B7/8 322
BRIATI Fond. B7/8 322
BROCCHETTA C. C7 322
BRUSA C. Larga E9 323
CA' BALA Fond. d. F9 323
CAFFETTIER C. C7 322
CALBO C.llo E9 323
CAMERINI C. A7 322
CANAL C. C9 322
CANAL Rio terà D7/8 322
CAPPELLER C. D7 322
CAPPELLO C. B7 322
CAPPELLO C. D7 322
CAPRERA Fossa A8 322
CAPUZZI C. E9 323
CARITA' C.po d. E8/9 323
CARMINI C.po d. C7 322
CARROZZE Sott. C7 322
CARTELLOTTI C. D9 322
CASIN C. d. D8 322
CATECUMENI Ramo
  G9/10 323
CATECUMENI Rio terà d.
  G9 323
CENTANNI C.te F9 323
CENTANNI Sott. F9 323
CENTOPIETRE C.llo D8 322
CERCHIERI C. d. D8 322
CERCHIERI Ramo D8 322
CERERI Fond. d. B7 322
CHIESA C. d. BC8 322
CHIESA C. d. D7 322
CHIESA C. d. D9 322
CHIESA C. d. EF9/10 323
CIMITERO C.po dietro il
  B8 322
COLONNELLO C. B8 322
COLORI C.te d. D8 322
CONTARINI C.te C7 322
COSTANTINI C. FG9 323
CREA C. d. F10 323
CRISTO C. d. A7 322
CRISTO C. d. E9 323
CRISTO C.te C7 322
CRISTO Sott. C7/8 322
CROSERA Ramo D8 322
CROSERA D6/7 322
DA PONTE C. E9 323
DOGANA della SALUTE Fond.
  GH9 323
DOGOLIN C. C8 322
DOLFIN C. D7 322
DONNA C. D6/7 322
EREMITE Fond. d. D8 322
EREMITE Sott. d. D8 322
FALCONA C.te C7/8 322
FONTEGO C.te d. D7 322
FORNAGHER C. C7 322
FORNER Piscina E9 323
FORNO C. C7 322
FORNO C. F9 323
FORNO C.te CD7 322
FORNO C.te F9 323
FOSCARI C. Larga D7 322
FOSCARIN Fond. C7 322
FOSCARIN ANTONIO Rio terà
  E9 323
FRANCHI C. EF9 323
FRATI C. d. B8 323
FRATI C. d. CD8 322

FRATI C. d. D9 322
GAFFARO Fond. d. C6 322
GALLO C.te C6 322
GAMBARA C. E8 323
GHERARDINI Fond. CD8 322
GUARDIANI C. d. B7 322
INCURABILI C. dietro gli
EF9/10 323
INCURABILI C.llo d.
EF9/10 323
INDORADOR C. C8 322
LANZA C. d. F9 323
LARDONA C.te AB8 322
LIZZA FUSINA Fond. A8 322
LOMBARDO Fond. D8 322
LOTTO C. D8 322
MADDALENA C. B8 322
MADONNA C. d. A7 322
MADONNA C. d. D7 322
MADONNA C.te d. D7 322
MADONNA Fond. A7 322
MAGAZEN C. d. D7 322
MAGAZEN C. d. D9 322
MAGGIORE C.te A8 322
MAGGIORE Fond. C.te A8 322
MAGGIORE Fond. C.te
BC6 322
MALCANTON Fond. C6/7 322
MALIPIERO C.te D8 322
MALPAGA C. D8 322
MALVASIA C. d. D7 322
MARCONI C. D7 322
MARCONI C.te D7 322
MASENA C. D8 322
MASENA C.llo d. D8 322
MENDE C.te d. F9 323
MERAVIGLIE Fond. D9 322
MEZZO C. d. G9 323
MEZZO C. E9 323
MEZZO DI VIDA C. D7 322
MISERICORDIA C. d. BC6 322
MOLIN BARBARO C. E Sott.
Ramo F9 323
MONASTERO C.D. F9/10 323
MOROSINI C.te C8 322
MORTI C. d. C8 322
MORTI C. d. G9 323
MORTI C.te d. C9 322
MURER C.te d. F10 323
NANI C. Larga D9 322
NANI Fond. D9 322
NAVARO C. F9 323
NAVE C. B8 322
NICOLOSI C. C8 322
NONZOLO C. C7 322
NUOVA C. B8 322
NUOVA C.te A7 322
NUOVA C.te A7 322
OCCHIALERA C. D8/9 322
OGNISSANTI C.po C9 322
OGNISSANTI Fond. C8 322
OGNISSANTI Rio terà C8 322
OLIO C. d. A7 322
ORATORIO C.llo A8 322
OSPEDALETTO Fond. F9 323
PAZIENZA C. d. C8 322
PEDROCCHI C. D7/8 322
PESCHIERA Fond. d. A8 322
PISANI C. Larga E9 323
PISTOR C. d. E9 323
PISTOR C. Sott. E9 323
POMELI C. CD8/9 322
POMPEA C. E9 323
PORTO COMMERCIALE
Banchina d. A8 322
PRETI C. d. D6 322
PRIULI Fond. D8/9 322
PROCURATIE C. d. B7 322
PROCURATIE Fond. d. B7 322
PUTI C. d. C8 322
QUERINI C. FG9 323

QUERINI Ramo FG9 323
RAGUSEI C. Larga
BC6/7 322
RAGUSEI C. C7 322
REMER C.te d. E7 323
RENIER C. C7 322
REZZONICO Fond. D8 322
RIELLO Fond. A8 322
RIELLO A8 322
RIO NUO Fond. d. B6 322
ROSA C.te B8 322
ROSSA Fond. B7 322
ROSSI C. B8 322
ROTA C. E9 323
RUGHETTA Fond. A7 322
S. BARNABA C. Lunga
CD8 322
S. BARNABA C.po D8 322
S. BASEGIO Banchina d.
B8/9 322
S. BASEGIO C.po B8/9 322
S. BASEGIO Salizz. B8 322
S. BASILIO Fond. B8 322
S. CRISTOFORO C. F9 323
S. DOMENICO C. E9 323
S. GIOVANNI C. EF9 323
S. GREGORIO C.po G9 323
S. LORENZO C.llo A8 322
S. MARCO Fond. B7 322
S. NICOLO' dei MENDICOLI
C.po A8 322
S. PANTALON C.po D7 322
S. SEBASTIANO C.po B8 322
S. SEBASTIANO C.zzo B8 322
S. SEBASTIANO Fond. B8 322
S. TROVASO C.po D9 322
S. VIO C.po EF9 323
S.TA MARGHERITA C.po
CD7 322
S.TA MARGHERITA C.te
C7/8 322
SABBION C.te d. F9 323
SALUTE C.po d. G9 323
SALUTE Fond. d. G9 323
SANT'AGNESE C. Nuova
E9 323
SANT'AGNESE C.po E9 323
SANT'AGNESE Piscina
E9 323
SANTI Sott. F10 323
SAONERI C. d. D7 322
SAONERI C.te D7 322
SAONERIA C. d. D7 322
SBIACCA C. d. C6 322
SCALETER C. d. D7 322
SCOAZZERA Rio terà d.
C7 322
SCUOLA C. d. C7 322
SCUOLA C. d. F10 323
SCUOLA C. d. G9/10 323
SECCHI C.llo d. A7 322
SECCHI Rio terà A7 322
SOCCORSO Fond. d.
BC7/8 322
SORANZO DETTA FORNACE
Fond. F9/10 323
SORIANA C. C6 322
SPEZIER C. D8 322
SPIRITO SANTO C.llo F10 323
SPORCA C. D7 322
SPORCA PAZIENZA C. C8 322
SQUELLINI C.llo D7 322
SQUERO C. d. E9 323
SQUERO C. d. G9 323
SQUERO Fond. d. CD8 322
STRETTA C. A7 322
TAGLIAPIETRA Fond. D7 322
TERESE C. Nuova A7/8 322
TERESE Fond. d. A7/8 322
TERREN C.llo A7 322
TOFFETTI Fond. D8/9 322

TOLETTA C. d. D8 322
TOLETTA C. D8 322
TRAGHETTO C. d. D8 322
TRAGHETTO C. d. F9 323
TRAGHETTO Fond. d. D8 322
TREVISAN C. D9 322
TREVISAN Sott. E9 323
TRON C.llo A8 322
TRON Fond. A8 322
TURCHETTE C. d. D8 322
UVA Sott. d. C7 322
VECCHI C. d. B8 322
VECCHIA C.te F9 323
VENIER Fond. E9 323
VENIER Fond. F9 323
VENIER Piscina E9 323
VENTO C. d. B9 322
VIDA C. d. D7 322
VIOTTI C. B7 322
ZAMBONI C. FG9 323
ZAPPA C.te C8 322
ZATTERE AI GESUATI Fond.
DE9 322/323
ZATTERE AI SALONI Fond.
G9/10 323
ZATTERE ALLO SPIRITO
SANTO Fond. EF10 323
ZATTERE P.TE LUNGO Fond.
C9 322
ZUCCHERO C. d. C8 322
ZUCCHERO C.te d. F10 323

GIUDECCA
ACCADEMIA DEI NOBILI C.
Lunga d. CD11 328
ALBERO C. d. F12 328
ASILO MASON C. d.
HJ11 329
BARI C. CITTA DI A10 322
BEATA GIULIANA D. COLLALTO
Fond. A9/10 322
BERLOMONI Fond. CD12 328
BRUNETTI M. C. Larga
A10 322
BRUNETTI M. Ramo A10 322
CAMPALTO C. 1 H11/12 329
CAMPALTO C. 2 HJ11/12 329
CAMPALTO C. 3 J11 329
CAMPALTO C. 4 J11 329
CAMPALTO C.llo H11 329
CANTIERE C. d. C11 322
CAPE C. d. F12 328
CITTA' DI BRINDISI C.llo
A9 322
CONVERTITE C. d. BC11 322
CONVERTITE Fond. d.
BC11 322
COOPERATIVA C. Larga d.
H12 329
COOPERATIVA Ramo 1
H12 329
COOPERATIVA Ramo 2
H12 329
CORDAMI C.te d. D11 328
CROCE C. d. D11 328
CROCE C. Drio la H11 329
CROCE C.llo d. F12 328
CROCE C.te G11 329
CROCE Fond. d. GH11 329
CROCE Fond. Rio d.
FG12 328/329
CROCE Ramo G11 329
DENTRO C.te d. C12 328
DO CORTE F12 328
ERBE C. d. E11 328
ESTERNA C. 2 HJ12 329
FERRANDO C. Larga
DE11 328
FERRANDO C. Stretta
DE11 328
FERRO C. d. E11 328

FISOLA C. A10 322
FISOLA C.llo A10 322
FONDERIA C. d. H12 329
FORNO C. d. D11 328
FORNO C.llo d. D11 328
FORNO Ramo d. D11 328
FRATI C. d. F12 328
GRAN C. d. H11 329
GRAN Ramo H11 329
GRANDE C.te D11 328
GRANDE Ramo 1 C.te
D11/12 328
GRANDE Ramo C.te
CD11 328
LARGA C. H12 329
LAVRANERI C.po d. A10 322
LAVRANERI Ponte d. A10 322
LONGO Ponte E11 328
LORENZETTI G Ramo
A10 322
LORENZETTI G C. A10 322
MADONNA C. d. D11 328
MANLIO DAZZI C. A10 322
MARTE C. d. H11 329
MEZZO C. BC11 322
MICHELANGELO C.
H11/12 329
MONFALCONE C. A10 322
MONFALCONE C.llo A10 322
MONFALCONE Ramo A10 322
MONTORIO C. C11 328
MONTORIO C.llo C11 328
NANI E BARBARO C.po
J10 329
NICOLI C. d. D11 328
NUOVA C.te C11 328
OLIO C. d. D11 328
ORTI C. d. F12 328
OSPIZIO C.llo J11 329
PALLADA C.po d. D11 328
PALLADA Fond. d.
DE11/12 328
PESCE C. d. F12 328
PICCOLO Ponte D11 328
PISTOR C. d. CD11 328
PONTE LONGO Fond. a fianco
d. E11/12 328
PONTE LONGO Fond. d.
E11 328
PONTE PICCOLO Fond. d.
D11 328
PRINCIPE C. d. F12 328
PRIULI C.llo B10 322
ROTONDA C.po C11 322
ROTONDA Fond. d. C11 322
S. BIAGIO Fond. C10 328
S. COSMO C. C11 328
S. COSMO C.po C11 328
S. COSMO C.zzo C11 328
S. GIACOMO C. F11 328
S. GIACOMO C.po F11 328
S. GIACOMO Fond. EF 11 328
S. GIACOMO Fond. F 11 328
S. GIORGIO C.po K10 329
S. GIOVANNI Fond.
J10/11 329
SANT'ANGELO Fond. E12 328
SANT'EUFEMIA C.llo C10 328
SANT'EUFEMIA Fond. d. rio d.
C10/11 328
SCUOLE C. d. DE12 328
SCUOLE Fond. d. D12 328
SPINI C. d. D11 328
SPONZA C.po d. E12 328
SQUERO C. d. H11/12 329
SQUERO Ramo d.
H11/12 329
SS. REDENTORE C.po F11 328
VALERI Ramo d. A10 322
VECCHIA C. d. C11 322
ZITELLE Fond. d. H11 329

STREET INDEX

Vaporetto Map

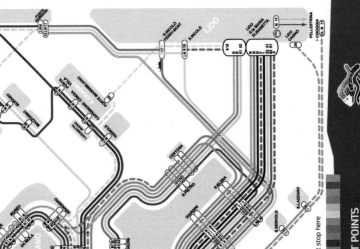

WATERBORNE ROUTES

Actv Network

imprenta e territorio, e visione del fatti.

Remember to read the timetables shown

-- Seasonal route   ✂ Helovenezia

▲ Ticket points – **Helovenezia**   The waterbus does stop here

✂ The waterbus does not stop here

41 **42** **51** **52** **61** **62** **DM** **LN** **T**

1 **2** **5** **8** **11** **13** **15** **17** **18** **20**

NIGHT SERVICE **N**

TERMINAL ROUTES

A = ALLAGUNA ARANCIO
B = ALLAGUNA BLU
O = ALLAGUNA ORO
R = ALLAGUNA ROSSA
C = CLODIA
F = FUSINA ZATTERE

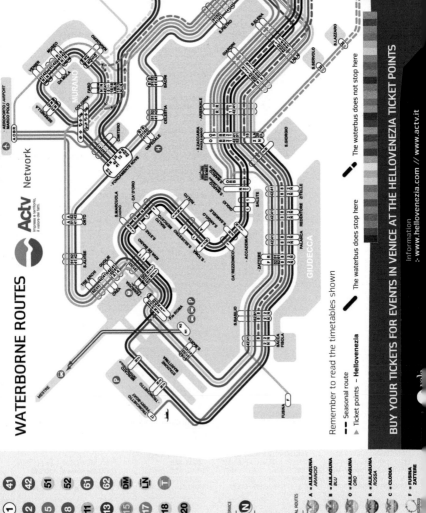